America's Founding Charters

America's Founding Charters

*Primary Documents of Colonial and
Revolutionary Era Governance*

VOLUME 2

Edited by Jon L. Wakelyn

GREENWOOD PRESS
Westport, Connecticut • London

Library of Congress Cataloging-in-Publication Data

America's founding charters : primary documents of Colonial and Revolutionary era governance /
edited by Jon L. Wakelyn.
    v. cm.
    ISBN 0–313–33155–3 (v. 1 : alk. paper)—ISBN 0–313–33156–1 (v. 2 : alk. paper)—
    ISBN 0–313–33157–X (v. 3 : alk. paper)—ISBN 0–313–33154–5 (set : alk. paper)
1. United States—Politics and government—To 1775—Sources.   2. United States—Politics
and government—1775–1783—Sources.   3. United States—Politics and government—
1783–1809—Sources.   I. Wakelyn, Jon L.
    JK54.A64   2006
    342.73009′03—dc22   2006026954

British Library Cataloguing in Publication Data is available.

Library of Congress Catalog Card Number: 2006026954
ISBN: 0–313–33154–5 (set)
        0–313–33155–3 (vol. 1)
        0–313–33156–1 (vol. 2)
        0–313–33157–X (vol. 3)

First published in 2006

Greenwood Press, 88 Post Road West, Westport, CT 06881
An imprint of Greenwood Publishing Group, Inc.
www.greenwood.com

Printed in the United States of America

Contents

PART III: CONSOLIDATION OF COLONIES AND RESISTANCE: DOMINION STATUS, 1685–1689

VOLUME 2

PART IV: GOVERNMENTAL DEVELOPMENTS DURING
THE EIGHTEENTH CENTURY

PART V: ESSAYS ON GOVERNANCE AND DEFENSE OF COLONIAL GOVERNMENT

PART VI: PLANS FOR UNITY, DIVIDED COLONIES, AND UNITED INDEPENDENCE

VOLUME 3

PART VII: THE FIRST STATE CONSTITUTIONS: DEBATES, ADOPTIONS, AND AMENDMENTS

PART VIII: THE ARTICLES OF CONFEDERATION: PROPOSED, DEBATED, AND RATIFIED

Introduction: The Colonial and Provincial Growth of American Governance: Developments and Defense, 1689–1776

Volume II, the center collection of these three books, includes documents on governance developments from the conclusion of the Glorious Revolution in 1689, with some overlap from Volume I, to the Declaration of Independence of July 4, 1776, which declared a separate nation. By necessity, because the Continental Congress began meeting in 1775, some events concerned with early state making from Volume III are included in Volume II. For example, in November 1775 the Congress authorized some colonies to write constitutions even before independence was declared. Also, key issues from the Albany Congress of 1756 controversy continued to influence events in Volume III and are referred to when the new states resisted uniting with one another. Nonetheless, this volume primarily adheres to the 1689–1776 dates.

The first part of Volume II continues to cover colonial governance developments and adds two new colonies, Delaware and Georgia, to make a total of 13. Included here are new charters, crown authority and instructions to governors, the growing duties of the assemblies (legislatures), further developments in local governance, and the suffrage issue that excluded certain peoples yet acknowledged the rise of popular sovereignty. The second part includes two general works on eighteenth-century colonial governance and defenses of colonial governance that were published during the crucial pre-Revolutionary years of 1765–1776. Support for colonial governance prerogatives poured out as many leaders in the legislatures spoke, wrote, and published their understanding of grievances with Britain. Only a few key writings have been selected for inclusion in this volume. Volume II concludes with a third part on issues of governance from the Albany Congress of 1756 to the Declaration of Independence. The third part contains documents that reveal both internal discord over governance and call for a unified movement for independence. Clearly, the colonies had grown independent of each other and had become testy over cooperation. This volume, then, tells us much about what evolved in the structure of governance over the century, as well as the problems of bringing these disparate, individualistic, and proud governing entities together in mutual commitments.

Part IV

Governmental Developments during the Eighteenth Century

The first part of Volume II carries colonial governance developments from 1689 after the Glorious Revolution down to nearly the American Revolution. Two additional colonies are added: Delaware, first discussed as part of New Jersey and Pennsylvania, received its charter in 1701 and Georgia, founded in 1733. Included are all post-1689 crown charters, revised or new. The focus in this first part is on two key instruments of governance. As England took more interest in colonial governance, the crown issued even more direct instructions to the royal colonies. In those documents, England desired to make the executive branch independent of the legislative. The legislatures in turn wanted ever more authority, as is illustrated by the increased number of statutes and other laws of governance. Through these documents it becomes clear that while claiming loyalty to the British crown authority, the legislatures wrote statutes that continued to separate their governing systems from overseas rule.

Each of the 13 colonies struggled to make changes in the structure of governance. Some of those efforts, such as in Massachusetts, New York, Pennsylvania, and Virginia, because of their size and importance, are given special attention. The best of many documents available have been selected to illustrate the evolving structure of colonial governance. In them one sees the legislatures clarifying their own duties, as they wrote laws to enhance their powers. Specifically, these documents give instructions on who could serve in office, the demands of office, and when and where to hold colony-wide elections. The legislatures as well as county and town councils showed much concern with who could vote. Although scholars have pointed out that freemen did not vote in large numbers, they have also written about how eligibility to vote continued to expand. Of course, in their efforts to obtain universal White male suffrage, the colonies also defined who could not vote. Native Americans, slaves, women, the poorest laborers and farmers, and recent immigrants were specifically prohibited from voting.

Finally, local town and county governments continued to grow apace, and they became increasingly aware of their roles in the individual colonies' scheme of governance. Acts that set the duties of township and county governance reveal a growth from the seventeenth-century emphasis on local authority. Also, as the colonials became increasingly litigious, their court systems grew in importance. Individual legislatures, aware of the powers of the governor to appoint the judiciary, attempted to give themselves the right to appoint local justices and to specify more and more duties to those magistrates. Individual and local rights also concerned the legislatures. Those developments, some say, inform the structure of governance to the present.

In his fine study of governance in Massachusetts, *King and People in Provincial Massachusetts*, Richard L. Bushman offers advice to the reader of this first part. "There was never any doubt in Massachusetts or in the other colonies about the form of the new governments. . . . It was to be republican." Bushman concludes, "It was experience, not books, that made republican government inevitable in 1776, experience that went back nearly a century" (p. 226).

15

Virginia

As Virginia grew in population and wealth, and the people continued to move westward, the early tobacco culture evolved into a mixed agricultural and exporting enterprise. Increasingly dependent on African slavery on the coast, but less so in the Piedmont, Virginians differed in their interests, if not in their support for their governing system. The colony's legislative leaders wanted to control its western growth and to vie with England for local control. The Burgesses, increasingly powerful because of their right to control taxes, set the salary for the royal governor and also trained a cadre of leaders who drafted statutes and directed the growth of governance. Some of these leaders emerged as rebels against British authority.

The year 1705 appears to have been difficult for colonial self-governance. The 1705 statutes gave the Burgesses power to set colony elections, pay delegates' expenses, define who could vote, and declared fines for illegal voting. In 1705 the Burgesses declared slaves, women, and Native Americans ineligible to vote. Affirming the power of the governor to appoint members to the general court ("Act Establishing the General Court, October 1705"), the Burgesses in turn exercised control over when the court could meet and defined its duties. Finally in 1705, the Burgesses exercised its power to found new towns, tax town settlers, and set town elections.

In 1752 the governor showed his royal powers and disallowed various Burgesses acts. Subsequent tensions over authority and governance prerogatives caused much concern among the electorate and leadership, especially during the period from 1763 to 1776. But the Burgesses continued to insist on their powers. In 1762, the Burgesses again passed laws regulating elections and adjusting payments for those who served in colonial governance. Proclaiming its moderate stance on governance issues, the Burgesses declared that crown officials had the power to enforce statutes, but this gesture became a mere formality as the years wore on.

ACT TO REGULATE ELECTIONS OF BURGESSES, OCTOBER 1705

An act for regulating the Elections of Burgesses; for settling their Privileges; and for ascertaining their allowances.

I. *BE it enacted and declared, by the governor, council and burgesses of this present generall assembly and it is hereby enacted and declared by the authority of the same,* That the Freeholders of every county that now is, or hereafter shall be in this dominion, now have, and hereafter shall have the privilege and liberty of electing and choosing two of the most fit and able men of such county respectively, to be present, and to act and vote in all General Assemblies, which, from time to time, and at any time hereafter, shall be held within this dominion; and also, that the freeholders of

James City shall have the liberty of electing and choosing one Burgess, to be present, act, and vote in the General Assembly, as aforesaid.

II. And for the more regular and legal electing of the said Burgesses in all time coming, *Be it enacted, by the authority aforesaid*, That the following rules and methods shall be observed, (to wit,) That the writs for electing the said Burgesses shall be signed by the Governor, or Commander in Chief of this dominion for the time being, with the seal of the Colony affixed to them, and shall be delivered to the Secretary, at least forty days before the day appointed for the General Assembly to begin, to be by him transmitted to the sheriffs of the respective counties: That the Secretary shall cause the said writs to be safely conveyed and delivered to the several sheriffs of each respective county, within ten days after the date of such writs: That every sheriff in three days after he receives any such writ, shall cause one copy thereof to be delivered to every minister and reader of the several parishes in his county; upon every one of which said copies, shall be indorsed by the sheriff, the time and place by him appointed for the election of Burgesses, which shall always be made at the place where the county court is accustomed to be held, at least twenty days after the sheriff shall have received the writ: That after the receipt of such copy and indorsement, the minister or reader as aforesaid, shall publish the same after Divine Service, in the Church or Chapel where they, or either of them officiate, upon every *Sunday* that shall be between the receipt of such copy, and the day appointed for the Election of Burgesses; and after such publication, the minister or reader shall return the said copy to the sheriff, with a certificate of the publication thereof, and of the time and place of the election. And if at any time hereafter, the secretary of this dominion for the time being, shall fail to cause the writs for electing of Burgesses, to be safely conveyed and delivered to the several sheriffs as aforesaid, he shall forfeit and pay the sum of forty pounds current money; one moiety thereof to our sovereign Lady the Queen, her heirs and successors, for and towards the better support of the government of this her majesty's dominion, and the contingent

charges thereof; and the other moiety thereof to such person or persons as will inform and sue for the same: To be recovered, with costs, in any court of record within this dominion, by information, bill, plaint, or action of debt, wherein no essoin, protection, or wager of law, privilege, or any more than one imparlance shall be allowed. And if at any time hereafter, the sheriff of any county within this dominion, shall fail to cause to be delivered one fair copy of any writ for election of Burgesses, with an indorsement thereupon as aforesaid, unto every minister and reader as aforesaid, within his county respectively, in such time as is before directed, such sheriff shall forfeit and pay the sum of two thousand pounds of tobacco; one moiety thereof to our sovereign lady the Queen, her heirs and successors, for and towards the better support of the government of this her majesty's dominion, and the contingent charges thereof; and the other moiety thereof to such person or persons as will inform and sue for the same: To be recovered, with costs, in any court of record within this dominion, by information, bill, plaint, or action of debt, wherein no essoin, protection, or wager of law, privilege, or any more than one imparlance shall be allowed. And if any minister or reader, who shall hereafter receive from the sheriff of his county, the copy of a writ for election of burgesses in the said county, shall, after the receipt thereof, fail to make publication and return, according to the directions of this act, such minister or reader shall forfeit and pay the sum of one thousand pounds of tobacco; one moiety thereof to our sovereign lady the Queen, her heirs and successors, for and towards the better support of the government of this her majesty's dominion, and the contingent charges thereof; and the other moiety thereof to such person or persons as will inform and sue for the same: To be recovered, with costs, in any court of record within this dominion, by information, bill, plaint, or action of debt, wherein no essoin, protection, or wager of law, privilege, or any more than one imparlance shall be allowed.

III. *And be it further enacted*, That after publication of writs, and time and place for election of burgesses as aforesaid, every freeholder, actually resident within the county where the election is to be made, respectively shall appear accordingly, and give his vote at such election, upon penalty of forfeiting two hundred pounds of tobacco to such person or persons as will inform and sue for the same: To be recovered, with costs, in any court of record within this dominion, by information, bill, plaint or action of debt, wherein no essoin, protection, or wager of law, privilege, or any more than one imparlance shall be allowed.

IV. *Provided always,* That no freeholder being a feme-sole, or feme-covert, infant, under age, or recusant convict, shall be obliged to appear, and give his or her vote in any of the said elections; neither, if they do appear, shall they have liberty to vote, but shall be excluded therefrom, as though they were not freeholders. And if any person shall presume to give his vote for election of any burgess or burgesses, not being a freeholder in the county or town respectively where he shall give his vote, such person shall forfeit and pay five hundred pounds of tobacco; one moiety thereof to our sovereign lady the Queen, her heirs and successors, for and towards the better support of the government of this her majesty's dominion, and the contingent charges thereof; and the other moiety thereof to such person or persons as will inform and sue for the same: To be recovered, with costs, in any court of record within this dominion, by information, bill, plaint, or action of debt, wherein no essoin, protection, or wager of law, privilege, or any more than one imparlance shall be allowed. And if, upon any suit brought, the question shall arise, whether any person be a freeholder, or not? In such case, the *Onus Probandi* shall lie upon the defendant. And if the election of any burgess or burgesses cannot be determined, upon the view, by consent of the freeholders, the sheriff, or, in his absence, the under-sheriff shall proceed to take the poll in manner following; *to wit,* he shall appoint such and so many person or persons, as to him shall seem fit, to take in writing, the name of every freeholder who gives his vote, and the person or persons he votes for; which person or persons so appointed, shall first take an oath for his true and impartial taking the poll; which oath the sheriff,

or, in his absence, the under-sheriff, is hereby impowered and required to administer; and then (the sheriff, or under-sheriff, as aforesaid, having provided one or more book or books for that purpose, as occasion shall require) in the court-house of the county, in presence of the several candidates nominated, if they will be present, or such other persons, as (if they think fit) they may appoint to see the poll fairly taken, the person or persons so appointed and sworn as aforesaid, shall take the poll as followeth; *to wit,* first he or they shall write down the names of all the candidates, every one in a several page of the book, or in a particular column; and then the name of every freeholder coming to give his vote, shall be fairly written in the several pages or columns respectively, under the name or names of such person or persons as he shall vote for: Provided, that no freeholder, who, at such election, shall have given his vote for two persons, shall be permitted to vote or poll for any more. And when every freeholder present, shall have given his vote in manner as aforesaid, (or upon proclamation three times made at the court-house door, if no more freeholders will give their votes) the sheriff, or under-sheriff as aforesaid, shall conclude the poll; and afterwards, upon examination thereof whatsoever person or persons of the candidates shall appear to have the most votes, the sheriff, or under-sheriff as aforesaid, shall return him or them burgess or burgesses; and if two or more candidates shall have an equal number of votes, the sheriff, or under-sheriff as aforesaid, being a freeholder, shall and may return which of them he thinks fit: And every freeholder, before he is admitted to a poll at any election, if it be required by the candidates, or any of them, or any other freeholder in their behalf, shall take the following oath; which oath the sheriff, or under-sheriff as aforesaid, is hereby impowered and required to administer; *to wit,*

YOU shall swear, that you are a freeholder of the county of and that you have not been before polled at this election.

And in case any freeholder, or other person, taking the said oath, shall thereby commit wilful and corrupt perjury, and be thereof convicted;

or if any person do unlawfully and corruptly procure or suborn any freeholder, or other person, to take the said oath, in order to be polled, whereby he shall commit such wilful and corrupt perjury, and shall be thereof convicted, he or they, for every such offence, shall forfeit and pay the sum of ten pounds current money; one moiety thereof to our sovereign lady the Queen, her heirs and successors; for and towards the better support of the government of this her majesty's dominion, and the contingent charges thereof; and the other moiety thereof to him or them that will inform or sue for the same: To be recovered, with costs, in any court of record within this dominion, by action of debt, bill, plaint, or information, in which no essoin, protection, or wager of law, shall be allowed.

V. And for prevention of disputes which may hereafter arise in elections of burgesses, who shall be accounted and pass for freeholders,

VI. *Be it enacted, by the authority aforesaid, and it is hereby enacted and declared,* That every person who hath an estate real for his own life, or the life of another, or any estate of any greater dignity, shall be accounted a freeholder, within the meaning of this act.

VII. And after the election shall be made, in manner as herein is before directed, the sheriff, or under-sheriff as aforesaid, shall make return thereof in manner following; *to wit,* upon the writ shall be indorsed thus;

The execution of this writ appears in a certain schedule hereto annexed.

And in the Schedule to the writ annexed, the execution thereof shall be certified as followeth, *mutatis mutandis,* viz.

BY virtue of this writ to me directed, in my full county, held at the court-house for my said county, upon the day of in the year of the reign of by the grace of God, of England, Scotland, France, and Ireland, Queen, defender of the faith, &c. by the assent of my said county, I have caused to be chosen (two Burgesses) of my said county, to wit, A.B. and C.D. to act and do, as in the said writ is directed and required.

And for the College of William and Mary, or for any town, the form of the return shall be thus;

BY virtue of this writ to me directed, I did make lawful publication thereof; and afterwards, to wit, upon the day of in the year of the reign of by the grace of God, of England, Scotland, France, and Ireland, Queen, defender of the faith, (at the said town of) or (at the said College) by the assent of the (freeholders) or (President and Masters, or Professors) thereof, I have caused to be chosen one Burgess for the said (town) or (College) to wit, A.B. of to act and do, as in the said writ is directed and required.

And if at any time, any candidate, or other person, in his behalf, shall desire a copy of the poll, the sheriff, or under-sheriff, who manages the election, as soon as may be, shall cause a fair copy thereof to be made, and shall deliver it, attested with his own hand, unto such candidate, or other person, as shall require the same as aforesaid.

VIII. And if, upon the death or incapacity of any member or members of the house of burgesses, the sheriff of any county shall receive a writ for the election of one or more burgess or burgesses, during the session of the general assembly; in such case, he is hereby required to appoint such and so many persons as to him shall seem fit, to give notice thereof, and of the time and place of election, unto every particular

XI. *Provided always,* That no sheriff, or other officer shall make return upon any writ or precept, that the person against whom the same issued, is not to be found, until he shall actually have been at the dwellinghouse, or place of residence of such person, and not finding him, shall have there left an attested copy of the same writ or precept.

XII. *Provided also,* That if any writ or precept shall be delivered to any sheriff, or other officer, to attach the body of any person being a known inhabitant of another county, and not of the county where the said sheriff, or officer resides; in such case, the sheriff, or officer shall make return, according to the truth of the case; and not that the person is not to be found in his county, and thereupon the process shall abate and be dismissed.

XIII. *And be it further enacted,* That all and every other act and acts, and every clause and article thereof heretofore made, for so much thereof as relates to prescribing the method of appointing sheriffs, or limiting the time of their continuance in office, or directing them in the execution thereof, in or concerning any matters or things within the purview of this act, is, and are hereby repealed and made void, to all intents and purposes, as if the same had never been made.

Reference: W.W. Hening (ed.), *The Statutes at Large of Virginia*, Vol. III (Philadephia: Thomas Neuber, 1823).

ACT DECLARING WHO SHALL NOT HOLD OFFICE, OCTOBER 1705

An act declaring who shall not bear office in this country.

BE *it enacted by the governor, council and burgesses, of this present general assembly, and it is hereby enacted by the authority of the same,* That no person whatsoever, already convicted, or which hereafter shall be convicted in her majestys kingdom of England in this or in any other her majestys dominion, colonies, islands, territorys or plantations, or in any other kingdom, dominion or place, belonging to any foreign prince or state whatsoever, of treason, murther, fellony, blasphemy, perjury, forgery or any other crime whatsoever, punishable by the laws of England, this country, or other place wherein he was convicted with the loss of life or member, nor any negro, mulatto or Indian, shall, from and after the publication of this act, bear any office, ecclesiasticall, civill or military, or be in any place of public trust or power, within this her majestys colony and dominion of Virginia, and that if any person convicted as aforesaid, or negro, mulatto or Indian shall presume to take upon him, act in, or exercise any office, ecclesiasticall, civill or military, or any place of publick trust or power, within this colony and dominion, notwithstanding he be thereunto in any manner whatsoever commissionated, appointed, chosen or impowered, and have a pardon for his crime, he shall for such his offence, forfeit and pay five hundred pounds current money, and twenty pounds of like money for every month he continues to act in or exercise such office or place after a recovery made of the said five hundred pounds, one moiety thereof to our sovereign lady the queen, her heirs and successors for and towards the better support of this government and the contingent charges thereof, and the other moiety to him or them that will inform or sue for the same, in any court of record within this her majestys colony and dominion, by action of debt, bill, plaint or information, wherein no essoin, protection, or wager of law, shall be allowed.

Provided nevertheless, and it is hereby meant and intended, That nothing in this act contained, shall extend to disable any person who before the making of this act hath been convicted as aforesaid in this her majestys colony and dominion, and hath obtained the king's or queen's pardon, from taking and bearing any office, ecclesiasticall, civill or military, or from accepting and exercising any place of public trust or power, whereunto he hath been heretofore, or shall be hereafter comissionated, appointed, chosen or impowered, but that it shall be lawfull for every such person to take and bear any such office, and accept and exercise any such place without being lyable to any fine or penalty for the same, as if this act had never been made.

And be it further enacted, by the authority aforesaid, and it is hereby enacted, That no person whatsoever, shall, from and after the publication of this act, bear any office, civill or military, or be in any place of publick trust or power, within this her majestys colony and dominion of Virginia, untill he hath been a personal resident in the same the full term of three years, and that if any person whatsoever do presume contrary to this act to take upon him, act in, or exercise any office, civill or military, or any place of trust or power within this colony and dominion, notwithstanding he be thereunto in any manner whatsoever comisionated, appointed or chosen before he hath personally resided therein three years as aforesaid, he shall for such his offence, forfeit and pay five hundred pounds current money, and twenty pounds of like money for every month he continues to act in, or exercise such office or place after a recovery made of the said five hundred pounds, untill he hath been three years in this country according to the tenor of this act, to be recovered and divided as aforesaid.

Provided always, and it is the true intent and meaning of this act, That all natives of this her majestys colony and dominion, and such persons as have comissions from her majesty, her heirs or successors, be excepted, and that it be lawfull for every such native and person to bear any office, civill or military, or to be in any place of trust or power before hath resided three years according to the directions of this act, without being lyable to any fine or penalty for it, any thing in this act before contained, to the contrary notwithstanding.

And for clearing all manner of doubts which hereafter may happen to arise upon the construction of this act, or any other act, who shall be accounted a mulatto,

Be it enacted and declared, and it is hereby enacted and declared, That the child of an Indian and the child, grand child, or great grand child, of a negro shall be deemed, accounted, held and taken to be a mulatto.

And be it further enacted, That all and every other act and acts, and every clause and article heretofore made for so much thereof as relates to declaring who shall not bear office in this country, is, and are hereby repealed and made void, to all intents and purposes as if the same had never been made.

Reference: W. W. Hening (ed.), *The Statutes at Large of Virginia,* Vol. III (Philadephia: Thomas Neuber, 1823).

ACT ESTABLISHING THE GENERAL COURT, OCTOBER 1705

An act for establishing the General Court, and for regulating and settling the proceedings therein.

I. FOR a speedy and regular determination of all controversies and differences between any persons; and for continuing, constituting, and erecting such courts as shall be competent and necessary, to hear and adjudge all such causes as shall be brought before them,

II. *Be it enacted, by the governor, council, and burgesses of this present general assembly, and it is hereby enacted, by the authority of the same,* That at some one certain place, to be lawfully appointed, and at such times as herein after directed, there shall be held one principal court of judicature, for this her majesty's colony and dominion of Virginia; which court shall be, and is hereby established, by the name of the general court of Virginia; and shall consist of her majesty's governor, or commander in chief, and the council, for the time being, any five of them to be a quorum; and they are hereby declared and appointed judges or justices, to hear and determine all suits and controversies which shall be depending in the said court.

III. *And be it enacted,* That every person, which shall, from time to time, or at any time hereafter, enjoy the office of a judge or justice of the said general court, at and before his entring into and upon the said office, shall take the oaths appointed by act of parliament to be taken, instead of the oaths of allegiance and supremacy; and shall make and subscribe the declaration appointed by one act of parliament, made in the twenty-fifth year of the reign of the late King Charles the second, intituled, An act preventing dangers which may happen from Popish recusants, and the oath mentioned in an act of parliament, intituled, An act to declare the alteration in the oath appointed to be taken by the act, intituled, An act for the further security of her majesty's person, and the succession of the crown in the protestant line; and for extinguishing the hopes of the pretended prince of Wales, and all other pretenders, and their open and secret abettors; and for declarin the association to be determined. And if any person whatsoever shall presume to sit, judge, decree, direct, act, or do, any manner of act or acts, thing or things whatsoever, appertaining and properly belonging to the office of a judge or justise of the said general court, before he hath taken the said oaths, and every of them; every person so presuming to sit, judge, decree, direct, act, or do, as aforesaid, without taking the oaths, and making and subscribing the declaration afore-mentioned, and every of them, shall, for every such offence, be fined five hundred pounds sterling; one moiety thereof to her majesty, her heirs and successors, for and towards the better support of this government, and the contingent charges thereof; and the other moiety thereof to him or them that shall inform, or sue for the same.

IV. *Provided always*, That if the said oaths, declaration, or any of them, shall be abrogated by authority of the parliament of England, or become otherwise void, the same shall also be adjudged, deemed, and taken to be abrogated, and to become void in this colony and dominion also.

V. *And be it further enacted*, That the said general court shall take cognizance of, and are hereby declared to have full power and lawful authority and jurisdiction, to hear and determine, all causes, matters, and things whatsoever, relating to or concerning any person or persons, ecclesiastic or civil, or to any other persons or things, of what nature soever the same shall be, whether the same be brought before them by original process, or appeal from any other court, or by any other ways or means whatsoever.

VI. *Provided always*, That no person shall take original process, for the trial of any thing in the general court, of less value than ten pounds sterling, or two thousand pounds of tobacco, on penalty of having such suit dismissed, and the plaintiff being non-suited, and paying costs of suit.

VII. *Provided always*, That if the justices of any county court, or the vestry of any parish, shall become liable to prosecution for the breach of any penal law, relating to their office; in such case, it shall and may be lawful for her majesty's attorney-general, or any other person or persons thereunto permitted or impowered by law, to inform or sue in the general court, for the penalty due on the breach of such penal law, although it be of less value than ten pounds sterling, or two thousand pounds of tobacco; any thing herein contained to the contrary, notwithstanding.

VIII. *And be it further enacted*, That the said general court shall be held two times every year; to wit, one court shall begin upon the fifteenth day of April, if not on a Sunday, and then on the Monday thereafter, and shall continue to be held eighteen natural days, Sundays exclusive; and one other court shall begin on the fifteenth day of October, if not on a Sunday, and then on Monday thereafter, and shall continue to be held eighteen natural days, Sundays exclusive.

Reference: W.W. Hening (ed.), *The Statutes at Large of Virginia*, Vol. III (Philadephia: Thomas Neuber, 1823).

ACT OF NATURALIZATION, OCTOBER 1705

An act for Naturalization.

I. WHEREAS nothing can contribute more to the speedy settling and peopling of this her majesty's colony and dominion, than that all possible encouragement should be given to persons of different nations to transport themselves hither, with their families and stock, for to settle, plant, or reside, by investing them with all the rights and privileges of any of her majesty's natural free-born subjects within this colony:

II. *Be it therefore enacted, by the governor, council, and burgesses, of this present general assembly, and it is hereby enacted, by the authority of the same,* That it shall and may be lawful for the governor, or commander in chief of this colony and dominion, for the time being, by a public instrument, or letters patents, under the broad seal thereof, to declare any alien or aliens, foreigner or foreigners, being already settled, or inhabitants in this colony, or which shall hereafter come to settle, plant, or reside therein, upon his, her or their taking, before him, the oaths appointed by act of parliament to be taken, instead of the oaths of allegiance and supremacy, the oath mentioned in an act, intituled, *An act to declare the alterations in the oath appointed to be taken by the act,* intituled, *An act for the further security of his majesty's person, and the succession of the crown in the protestant line, and for extinguishing the hopes of the pretended prince of* Wales, *and all other pretenders, and their open and secret abettors, and for declaring the association to be determined, and subscribing the test,* to be, to all intents and purposes, fully and completely naturalized; and that all persons having such public instrument, or letters patents, shall, by virtue of this act, have and enjoy to them, and their heirs, the same immunities and rights, of and unto the laws and privileges of this colony and dominion, as fully and amply as any of her majesty's natural-born subjects have or enjoy within the same, and as if they themselves had been born within any of her majesty's realms or dominions; and former act, law, ordinance, usage, or custom, to the contrary, notwithstanding.

III. And to the intent, the said public instrument, or letters patents, under the broad seal of this colony, as aforesaid, may be obtained, without any great difficulty or charge,

IV. *Be it further enacted,* That the governor, or commander in chief of this colony and dominion, granting such public instrument or letters patents, shall have and receive for the same, forty shillings, and his clerk, for writing of it, ten shillings, and no more.

V. And whereas several aliens and foreigners, that have formerly transported themselves to this her majesty's colony and dominion, and have taken up and patented, in their own name, several parcels of land, or otherwise made purchase of lands, houses, tenements, or other real interest, and have afterwards sold the same to some of her majesty's liege people, or inhabitants of this colony and dominion,

VI. *It is hereby further enacted,* That all persons which have purchased and held, under any such alien or aliens, any lands, houses, or tenements, be secured, and by virtue of this present act, for ever, be confirmed in the quiet and peaceable possession of the said purchases, unto them and their heirs for ever; any former law, usage, or custom, to the contrary, in anywise, notwithstanding.

VII. *Provided,* That nothing in this act contained, shall be construed to enable or give power or privilege to any foreigner, to do or execute any matter or thing, which by any of the acts made in England, concerning her majesty's plantations, he is disabled to do or execute.

Reference: W. W. Hening (ed.), *The Statutes at Large of Virginia,* Vol. III (Philadephia: Thomas Neuber, 1823).

ACTS ESTABLISHING PORTS AND TOWNS, OCTOBER 1705

Whereas her most sacred Majesty, Queen Anne, out of her princely care of this her colony and dominion of Virginia, by instructions to his Excellency Edward Nott, Esquire, her Majesty's Lieutenant and Governor-General here, has been pleased to take notice that the building of towns, warehouses, wharfs, and keys for the more expeditious lading and unlading of ships at proper places in this colony, exclusive of others, will be particularly useful and serviceable to her Majesty in bringing our people to a more regular settlement and of great advantage to trade, and has, therefore, caused it to be recommended by her said Governor to this General Assembly to pass an act for that purpose suitable to the interests and conveniences of this colony,

Be it, therefore, enacted, by the Governor, Council, and Burgesses of this Present General Assembly, and it is hereby enacted by the authority of the same, that from and after the twenty-fifth day of December, which shall be in the year of our Lord 1708, all goods, wares, and merchandises which shall be imported into this colony by water, servants, slaves, and salt, excepted, shall be entered, allowed, and landed at some one or other of the ports, wharfs, keys, or places hereafter mentioned and appointed in this act, and at none other place whatsoever, until they shall have been first landed at one of the ports or wharfs aforesaid and a certificate thereof obtained from the officer of the port appointed or to be appointed by his Excellency the Governor or the governor and commander-in-chief of this colony for the time being, by advice of the council of state here, for collection of the Virginia duties, upon pain of forfeiture and loss of all such goods, wares, and merchandises.

And be it also enacted that, from and after the said twenty-fifth day of December, 1708, all servants, slaves, and salt which shall be imported into this colony by water shall be reported and entered at some one or other of the ports, wharfs, keys, or places by this act appointed, as aforesaid and a certificate thereof obtained, as aforesaid, before they shall be landed, bought, or sold, upon pain of forfeiture and loss of every such servant and slave so landed, sold, or put to sale.

And be it also enacted that, from and after the said twenty-fifth day of December, 1708, all goods, wares, and merchandises of what nature of kind soever to be exported out of this colony by water, coal, corn and timber excepted, shall, before they be put on board any ship or vessel for exportation, be landed or cleared at some one or other of the ports, wharfs, keys, or places, as aforesaid, upon pain of forfeiture and loss of all such goods, wares and merchandises.

And because there will be an absolute necessity of warehouses and other convenient buildings for reception of all sorts of goods and persons at these ports.

Be it, therefore, enacted that a township or burgh be established at each of the places hereinafter appointed by this act for ports and that, from and after the said twenty-fifth day of December, 1708, all goods, wares, and merchandises whatsoever which shall be imported for sale into this colony, servants, slaves, and salt, excepted, shall

be bought and sold in one or other of these towns hereinafter appointed, or not within five miles of any of them waterborne or on the same side the great river the town shall stand upon, except such persons as are already inhabited, and their heirs, and such other persons as having been for the space of three years inhabitants of this colony, shall reside, at the time of claiming such privilege, within the said five miles, on pain of forfeiting and paying by the vendor the full value of the goods, wares, and merchandises so sold, with costs of suit, and on pain of forfeiture and loss by the purchaser of all goods, wares, and merchandises bought contrary to the tenor hereof. Neither shall any ordinary keeping be licensed or allowed without the limits of these towns, unless above ten miles from every of them or at a public ferry or court house.

And whereas a smuggling trade, if any such be used here, may most privately be carried on by avaricious and ill-minded persons keeping store on board their sea vessels, for prevention thereof for the future;

Be it enacted that, from and after the said twenty-fifth day of December, 1708, no goods, wares, nor merchandises whatsoever which shall be imported into this colony, servants, slaves, and salt excepted, shall be bought or sold while they are waterborne in the sea vessels they were imported in, upon pain of forfeiting and paying by the vendor the full value of all such goods, wares, and merchandises so sold, with costs of suit, and on pain of forfeiture and loss by the purchaser of all such goods, wares, and merchandises bought contrary to the tenor hereof. All which fines, forfeitures, and penalties before in the act mentioned, shall be one-third part thereof to the governor or commander-in-chief of this her Majesty's colony and dominion for the time being, one other third to the port and town whose officer shall first make claim, and the other third to the informer.

And be it also enacted that, in all duties hereafter to be laid on the trade of this colony in any sort, the town inhabitants here shall be acquit for three-fourths of the duties that all other persons shall be obliged to, unless it shall be otherwise directed by act imposing the said duties.

And be it also enacted that all persons whatsoever coming to live and reside in any of the ports and towns by this act to be constituted, or that at any time hereafter shall come to live and reside in any of them, shall be thereafter free and acquit from all levies that shall be laid on the poll in tobacco for the space of fifteen years next after the five and twentieth day of December, 1708, except for their slaves only, and also except for the payment of parish levies where the church already stands or shall hereafter be built within any of the said ports or towns respectively.

And for a further invitation of persons to cohabit in towns;

Be it enacted that no person whatsoever inhabiting, or that shall inhabit any of the ports or towns to be constituted by virtue of this act, during his being such an inhabitant, shall be obliged to muster without the town land whereof he shall be an inhabitant, nor forced to march therefrom except when the exigency shall be such that the country shall be actually engaged in war, neither then shall the inhabitant of any port or town to be constituted by virtue of this act be forced to march or be removed more than fifty miles from the burgh whereof he shall be inhabitant, nor impressed to go to war upon any other occasion.

And be it also enacted that as soon as and whenever a court of hustings shall be established in any of the burghs to be constituted by virtue of this act, no inhabitant of such burghs shall thereafter be held to plead or go to court for any summons or law business without the burgh, except in local actions where the cause shall arise without the jurisdiction of such town, or where the value of the thing in demand shall exceed thirty pounds sterling, or in the general court, or to bear evidence in some court as the laws of this country direct, neither shall they be forced to serve on a jury in any court without such burgh, except in the general court.

And be it also enacted that all fines and mulcts that shall hereafter be laid upon an inhabitant of any of the ports or towns appointed by this act shall be paid to the director of such towns whereto he shall belong, for the use and benefit of the town, and to no other use or purpose whatsoever.

And for explanation of what shall be counted an inhabitant of a town;

Be it enacted that any person keeping a family in town, or whose common residence shall have been in town for six months past next before the time of claiming such privilege, shall be counted an inhabitant of such town to all intents and purposes and within the meaning of this act.

And because such a number of people as may be hoped will in process of time become inhabitants of these ports and towns cannot expect to be supported without such regulations are made and methods put in practice as are used in the towns of other countries;

Be it enacted that each town to be erected by virtue of this act be constituted and every of them, singly and apart, is hereby constituted and established a free burgh, shall have a market at least twice a week and a fair once a year at such times as hereafter is appointed, shall have a merchant guild and community with all customs and liberties belonging to a free burgh. And when there shall be thirty families, besides ordinary keepers, resident in any of the burghs to be constituted by virtue of this act, and so on as fast as any of the said burghs shall come to have thirty families besides ordinary keepers resident in them, such burghs shall have eight of the principal inhabitants who shall be called benchers of the guild hall for the better rule and governance of the town and for managing the public affairs thereof. These benchers shall be chosen by the freeholders and inhabitants of the town of twenty-one years of age and upwards, not being servants or apprentices, to be at first called together by writ from the governor or commander-in-chief of this colony for the time being, upon application to him made by the town, and being once chosen shall continue so long as they well behave or till death or removal from such town, which shall first happen. And if any bencher shall happen to be suspended, die, or remove out of such town, then, upon proclamation made three market days in open market between the hours of eleven and one by direction of the hustings, and day and place set by them, the freeholders and inhabitants of the town shall assemble on such day and place and choose another bencher in the room of him so incapacitated, and so on from time to time as there shall be occasion. Which elections shall be determined by the major part of the votes that shall be given, according to day and place aforesaid, and all disputes therein shall be determined by the hustings. These five benchers shall annually choose one of themselves to preside, by the name of director, and if any director shall happen to die or remove within his year, the benchers or the major part of them, on the next or some convenient court day afterwards, shall meet and choose another in his room, and so on as occasion shall happen to supply the year out. And in the interval of a directors dying and another's being elected, the eldest of the benchers of such burgh then actually resident shall preside and perform what should have been incumbent on the director of such town to perform.

And for the encouragement and bettering of the markets in the said towns;

Be it enacted that no dead provision, either of flesh or fish, shall be sold within five miles of any of the ports or towns appointed by this act, on the same side the great river the town shall stand upon, but within the limits of the town, on pain of forfeiture and loss of all such provision by the purchaser and the purchase money of such provision sold by the vendor, congnizable by any justice of the county, the director, or one of the benchers of the next adjacent burgh, or any one of them, be the same of what value soever, saving an appeal to the county court or court of hustings upon security given.

And be it enacted that the director for the time being of each of the burghs appointed by this act, or his substitute, and any three or more of the benchers of his burghs, shall be and hereby are appointed a quorum to hold court, every which court shall be held, deemed, and taken to be a court of record within this colony, shall make to themselves one common seal with liberty at any time to break or change it, shall have jurisdiction on all causes of *meum* and *tuum*, bargain, traffic, and trade within their town and the road

and harbor thereto belonging, or wherein any inhabitant of the town is or shall be concerned, not exceeding the value of thirty pounds sterling, and all penal statutes of this country as also of everything relating to the town lands, saving and reserving always a liberty to any party not content with their judgment to have an appeal to the general court upon security given within four and twenty hours after such judgment, to abide the award of the said court. And if any one shall take advantage of his liberty and shall depart the town without satisfying such judgment or appealing, a copy thereof, certified by the town clerk to the clerk of any county court, shall be sufficient for him to issue execution thereon according to the tenor thereof, and he is hereby required to do the same accordingly.

Provided always, and be it enacted, that all causes of greater value than thirty pounds sterling arising within the precincts or jurisdiction of any burgh may be tried, heard, and determined by the respective county courts wherein the said burghs lie in the same manner as might have been done before the making of this act.

Moreover, they, the said director and benchers, shall take cognizance of all petty larcenies happening within the precincts of their burgh and the road and harbor thereto belonging, and all other crimes of immorality cognizable by a justice of the peace or county court as cursing, swearing, sabbath breaking, drunkenness, fornication, bastardy, and the like, when such shall happen within the precincts of their burghs respectively or the road and harbor thereof, with power likewise to impose mulcts and fines on refractory persons, not exceeding five pounds sterling, to imprison for any time not exceeding or passing by a general court, and to bind criminals in a greater degree over to the general court and take recognizances that shall be necessary on such occasions; with power, likewise, to hold court once a week called hustings, and from time to time to make choice of and swear a town clerk, bailiff, cryer, and constable, for recording, arresting, bringing before and regular proceedings in the said courts and all other inferior officers necessary for the same, and for keeping the peace and good order within their several and respective burghs. Which officers shall have full power in the execution of their several offices throughout their towns respectively, and the road and harbor thereto belonging; with power to the said court of hustings to administer and take oaths *de fedeli*, and for clearing the truth in all cases happening before them, and to turn out, change, and supply such officers as there shall be occasion upon misdemeanor, death, or removal.

And be it further enacted that the director and benchers which shall be elected by virtue of this act, and every of them, singly and apart, shall take cognizance of all breaches of the peace, swearing, cursing, sabbath breaking, drunkenness, and immorality as justices of the peace usually have or ought to have within this colony, and to cause the punishments and forfeitures to be inflicted and levied upon such offenders, their goods and chattels accordingly, within their several and respective burghs and the precincts thereof, respectively.

And be it further enacted that the benchers aforementioned, and every of them, at the time of his entering into and upon his said office, shall take such oaths of fidelity to her Majesty, her heirs and successors, as shall be from time to time appointed by law for the other people of this colony to take, and also shall take the following oath.

The Oath of a Bencher

"You shall swear that truly and faithfully you will serve our sovereign lady the Queen and the burgh of A. in the office of bencher, and that you will do equal right to all manner of people, rich and poor, and to the said burgh without favor, affection, or partiality, and that you will not directly or indirectly take any gift or reward for anything relating to your said office. So help you God."

And be it further enacted that the director and benchers of every burgh respectively to be chosen by virtue of this act shall be and they are hereby erected and constituted to be a body corporate and politic and to have a continual succession forever, by the name of the director and benchers, with power to implead, sue and be sued, to purchase and enjoy lands, tenements, and other estate, real and personal, of whatsoever nature and quality, and to dispose of and alienate the same or any part thereof at their pleasure; with power, likewise, by subscription and other voluntary gifts and bequests, to raise a joint stock or capital fund for the use and benefit of their burgh and the public necessary charges thereof, and to build and keep a place or tenement within their burgh, where they shall think most decent and honorable, to erect a guild hall and such other useful and necessary buildings as they, with the advice of the common council, shall think fit.

And when the director and benchers shall be thus constituted in any of the burghs appointed by this act, the feoffs of such burgh or town shall transfer all their right to such director and benchers and their successors, forever, who shall, thereafter, parcel out the land and lots in town in such manner and under such rules and limitations as is appointed by law to the feoffs, and that by transfer and assignments made and entered in their own books and records, without any other formality of law, reserving to themselves and their successors, forever, to the use of the town, one ounce of flax seed and two ounces of hemp seed for every lot or piece of land to be parcelled out.

And be it enacted that thereafter the director and benchers of every such burgh, as aforesaid, shall hold the lands within the precincts of their said burgh to them and their successors forever, in free and common soccage, yielding and paying to her Majesty, her heirs and successors, the annual quitrent of twelve pence for every fifty acres. And if any person, having a lot in town upon the water side, will build out into the water before his own lot for the better conveniency of landing shipping off goods, such persons shall have the whole benefit of such building and the land so built upon shall be reckoned as part of his own lot and it shall entirely be his as the lot itself, without any further duty or acknowledgment.

And be it also enacted that when there shall be resident in any burgh appointed by this act sixty families, then such burgh shall have fifteen persons who shall be called brethren assistants of the guild hall, who shall be of common council to the burgh in the making and declaring statutes and ordinances touching or concerning the good regiment, state, and governance of the burgh, and from time to time shall be assistant to the director and benchers of such burgh for the time being, that then the constitution shall be held perfect; that thereafter the director and benchers, or the major part of them, with the advice and consent of the common council, or the major part of them, shall have power to raise a levy on their own inhabitants by such ways and means as they shall think fit for the necessities and benefit of the burgh, and shall make, ordain, and institute, and under their common seal publish and declare statutes and ordinances for the better rule and governance of the burgh and of all things happening therein or within the precincts, road, and harbor thereof, and again the same to revoke and alter as, with the advice and consent aforesaid, shall be found convenient and necessary.

Provided, always, that no statute or ordinance thus to be made shall be contradictory to act of Assembly nor shall be binding upon anyone until it shall have been published three market days in open market between the hours of nine and eleven in the forenoon, and that the town clerk have it in keeping to give a copy thereof to anyone that shall demand it for the charge of fifteen pence fee for every such statute or ordinance.

And be it further enacted that the election of the common council or brethren assistants of the guild hall, aforesaid, shall be made by the freeholders and inhabitants of each burgh, respectively, being men of twenty-one years of age and upwards and not servants, who shall be called together by proclamation from the court of hustings, made three market days successively in open market, between the hours of nine and eleven in the forenoon, and every member of the common council, being once chosen so,

shall continue so long as he well-behaves or till death or removal from such town; and as one dies, removes, or happens to be suspended, another in like manner shall be chosen in his stead.

And be it further enacted that the brethren assistants aforementioned, and every of them, at the time of his entering into and upon his said office, shall take such oaths of fidelity to her Majesty, her heirs and successors, as shall be from time to time appointed by law for the other people of this colony to take and also shall take the following oath.

The Oath of an Assistant

"You shall swear as an assistant of the guild hall of the burgh of A. that to all things proposed you shall deliver your opinion faithfully, justly, and honestly for the general good and prosperity of this burgh and every member thereof, and to do your endeavor to prosecute; that without mingling therewith any particular interest of any person or persons wheresoever. So help you God.

And be it further enacted that when the constitution of any of the burghs appointed by this act shall become perfect, as aforesaid, then such burgh shall have one burgess to represent them in the General Assembly of this dominion with the like powers and authorities to vote and act in the said assembly as fully and amply as any other burgess has or ought to have. Which burgess shall be returned by the director for the time being of such burgh upon writ to him directed from the governor or commander-in-chief of this colony for the time being, in the form of the other writs, *mutatis mutandis,* and shall be chosen by the freeholders and housekeepers of the town, being men of twenty-one years of age and upwards.

And for prevention of exactions in the charge of warehouse room, which will most likely happen in the beginning, while there shall be but few houses built;

Be it enacted that the warehouses rent for any cask containing sixty gallons or upwards, or any bail or parcel of the like or greater bulk, shall be twelve pence for the first day or for the first three months, and six pence for every month afterwards; and for any cask under sixty gallons and every bail or parcel of less bulk than a sixty gallon cask, six pence and three pence in form aforesaid; that these rates shall continue in each burgh, respectively, until the director, benchers, and common council shall have been constituted one year and afterwards to be in their power to set and regulate the rates for wharfage, lighteridge, and warehouse room, cartage and the like, from time to time as they shall see occasion.

And if any shall exact greater prices for warehouse room than is in this act set down or, after the constitution shall be perfect, shall exact greater prices for wharfage, lighteridge, warehouse room, cartage, or other labor than shall be appointed and allowed by the director, benchers, and common council of such burgh, respectively, he shall be liable to pay to the party injured ten pence for every penny so exacted over and above the rates aforesaid admitted and allowed, or to be admitted and allowed with cost, cognizable by a justice of the peace of the county until the director and benchers shall be chosen for such town and thereafter only by the director or any of the benchers of the burgh, saving appeal to the court of hustings upon security given. . . .

And be it further enacted that where any port is by this act appointed to be at a place that has land already purchased and laid out for a town, such land so laid out is hereby declared to be the land where the ports and towns appointed by this act shall be settled and built. And where a port or town is appointed by this act at any place not having land purchased for that purpose, the county court is hereby empowered and required to purchase fifty acres of land for the uses in this act mentioned. And if the proprietor of any land designed by this act for a town shall not be willing to make sale of his land or shall demand too great a consideration for it, or shall be a *feme covert* under the age of twenty-one years or out of the country, in all these cases it shall be lawful for the county court that is to purchase the land to issue their precept to the

sheriff of one of the adjacent counties at their discretion, requiring the said sheriff to summon five justices of the peace of his county to appear at such time and place as in the said precept shall be directed to value the land as aforesaid and, accordingly, the valuation of the said five justices of the peace, or of any three of them, upon their oaths, and which oath any justice of the peace of the county whereof the land lies is hereby empowered to administer, returned under their hands and seals to the next county court and entered upon record there, shall be taken as the true value of the land, and thereupon the said county court shall cause the land to be surveyed and laid out into lots of half acres, which shall also be recorded, and upon demand made by the person that has a lawful right to have and receive the value of the said land, shall raise the same in tobacco by a levy upon the poll in their county. And the conveyance of any proprietor that is willing to make sale of his land or the valuation thereof recorded, as aforesaid, shall be sufficient in law to vest a firm, absolute, and indefeasible estate in fee simple in such feoffs as shall be from time to time appointed by the county court to sell and dispose of the same for the uses aforesaid, and the feoffs, until the director and benchers shall be elected for such burgh respectively, shall convey and make over unto any person requesting the same and paying the first cost and fifty per cent advance, for the reimbursement of the county, one half acre or lot of land in the said town, reserving the annual rent of one ounce of flax seed and two ounces of hemp seed to be paid the tenth of October in every year to the director and benchers of such town, when they shall be elected; and with this limitation, that the said grantee, his heirs or assigns, shall, within twelve months next ensuing such grant, begin and without delay proceed to build and finish on the said lot one good house to contain twenty feet square at the least, otherwise such grant to be void and the said lot liable to the choice and purchase of any other person in manner as aforesaid.

Reference: W. W. Hening (ed.), *The Statutes at Large of Virginia*, Vol. III (Philadephia: Thomas Neuber, 1823).

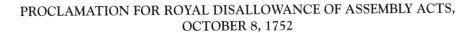

PROCLAMATION FOR ROYAL DISALLOWANCE OF ASSEMBLY ACTS, OCTOBER 8, 1752

Whereas all laws, statutes, and ordinances made and passed in the general assembly of this dominion are, according to the constitution of this government by his Majesty's letters patent under the great seal of Great Britain, to be transmitted to his Majesty for his royal approbation or disallowance, and such of the said laws, statutes, and ordinances as shall be thereupon disallowed or disapproved, and so signified by his Majesty under his sign manual and signet or by order in privy council, are from thenceforth to cease, determine and become utterly void. And whereas his Majesty in council has been pleased to signify his disapprobation and disallowance of several acts passed in the years 1748 and 1749, to wit,

An Act for Allowing Fairs to be Kept in the Town of Suffolk, and Preventing Hogs and Goats Going at Large Therein, and for Altering the Time of Holding Fairs in the Town of Newcastle.

Also, an act entitled, An Act for Establishing a Town in Augusta County, and Allowing Fairs to be Kept There.

Also, an act entitled, An Act Declaring Slaves to be Personal Estate, and For Other Purposes Therein Mentioned.

Also, an act entitled, An Act For the Distribution of Intestates Estates.

Also, an act entitled, An Act For Establishing the General Court and For Regulating and Settling the Proceedings Therein.

Also, an act entitled, An Act For Limitation of Actions and Avoiding of Suits.

Also, an act entitled, An Act Concerning Servants and Slaves.

Also, an act entitled, An Act to Prevent Tending Seconds.

Also, an act entitled, An Act For the Better Support of the College of William and Mary.

And, an act entitled, An Act to Prevent the Building Wooden Chimneys in the Town of Walkerston and Also to Prevent the Inhabitants Thereof From Raising and Keeping Hogs.

I do, therefore, in pursuance thereof, by this proclamation, publish and declare that the said acts of assembly are repealed and utterly void and of none effect. And for the more solemn signification thereof I do appoint the proclamation to be read and published at the court house of the several counties within this dominion and the sheriffs are to take care the same be done accordingly. Given at the council chamber, this eighth day of April, one thousand seven hundred and fifty two, in the XXV year of his Majesty's reign.

Robert Dinwiddie.

GOD SAVE THE KING.

Reference: W. W. Hening (ed.), *The Statutes at Large of Virginia*, Vol. III (Philadephia: Thomas Neuber, 1823).

ACT FOR DIRECTING AND REGULATING THE ELECTIONS OF BURGESSES

At a General Assembly, begun and held at the Capitol, in the City of Williamsburg, on Tuesday the 26th of May in the first year of the reign of our sovereign lord George III. by the grace of God of Great-Britain, France and Ireland, king, defender of the faith, &c. and in the year of our Lord, 1761, and from thence continued by several prorogations to Tuesday the 2d of November 1762, in the third year of his majesty's reign; and then held at the Capitol, in the City of Williamsburg; being the fourth session of this General-Assembly.

CHAP. I.

An Act for directing and better regulating the elections of Burgesses, for settling their privileges, and for ascertaining their Allowances.

I. WHEREAS the laws now in being for regulating the election of burgesses, and declaring the qualifications of voters at such elections, have proved defective; and it hath been found, by long experience, that frequent new assemblies tend greatly to the happiness and good government of this colony; we your majesty's most loyal and obedient subjects, the lieutenant-governour, council and burgesses, of this present general assembly, do humbly beseech your most excellent majesty that it may be declared and enacted, and *Be it enacted, by the Lieutenant Governour, Council, and Burgesses of this present General-Assembly; and it is hereby enacted by the authority of the same,* That from henceforth a general assembly shall be holden once in three years at the least.

II. *And be it further enacted,* That within three years at the furthest from and after the dissolution of this present general-assembly, and so from time to time forever hereafter, within three years at the furthest from and after the determination of every other general-assembly, legal writs under the seal of the colony shall be issued by direction of the governour or commander in chief for the time being, in manner herein after directed, for calling, assembling and holding, a new general-assembly.

III. *And be it further enacted, by the authority aforesaid,* That the freeholders of every county which now is, or hereafter shall be, within this dominion, qualified as is by this act hereafter directed and declared, have, and shall have, the privilege and liberty of electing two of the most able and fit men, being freeholders, qualified to vote in such county respectively; to be present, and to act and vote, as representatives of such county, in all general-assemblies to be sommoned and held as aforesaid: and that the freeholders of James City shall have the liberty of electing one burgess, to be present, act and vote, in all such general assemblies.

IV. And for settling what freeholders shall have a right to vote, *Be it further enacted, by the authority aforesaid,* That every person shall have a right to vote at any election of Burgesses for any county who hath an estate of freehold for his own life, or the life of another, or other greater estate, in at least fifty acres of land, if no settlement be made upon it, or twenty five acres, with a plantation and house thereon, at least twelve feet square, in his possession, or in the possession

of his tenent or tenants, for term of years, at will or sufferance, in the same county where he gives such vote; and any person having such estate, in fifty acres of land, in one tract, uninhabited, lying in two or more counties, shall have a right to vote in that county only wherein the greater quantity of the said land lies, although the same shall not amout to fifty acres, in either county; and every person possessed of twenty-five acres, with a plantation and house thereon, as aforesaid, lying in two or more counties, shall have a right to vote in that county only where the house shall be, and every person possessed of a lot, or part of a lot, in any city or town established by act of assembly, with a house thereon; at least twelve feet square, shall have a right to vote at such election.

V. *Provided always,* That where lands are held by several joint tenants, or tenants in common, or the interest of any such house and lot, or part of a lot, is or shall be divided among several persons, no more than one single vote shall be admitted in right of such lands, or house and lot, or part of a lot, and that only in case all the parties interested can agree; otherwise no vote shall be allowed to be given for such freehold, unless the quantity of such lands shall be sufficient to allot to such tenant fifty acres at least, if the same be uninhabited, or twenty five acres, with a house and plantation, as aforesaid.

VI. *Provided also,* That no person shall vote for the electing any burgess in right of any lands or tenements whereof he has not been in possession, or hath had a legal title, for one whole year, next before the teste of the writ for such election, unless such lands or tenements came to such person within that time by descent, marriage, marriage settlement, or devise.

VII. *And be it further enacted,* That no feme, sole or covert, infant under the age of twenty-one, recusant, convict, or any person convicted in Great Britain or Ireland, during the time for which he is transported, nor any free negro, mulatto or Indian, although such persons be freeholders, shall have a vote, or be permitted to poll, at any election of burgesses, or capable of being elected; and if any person, not being a freeholder, qualified as by this act is directed and required, shall presume to vote or poll at any such election, he shall forfeit and pay five hundred pounds of tobacco; one moiety to the king, his heirs and successours, for the better support of this government, and the contingent charges thereof; the other moiety to the informer, to be recovered with costs, by action of debt or information, in any county court of this dominion: And if in such suit a question shall arise whether such person be a freeholder as aforesaid or not, the *onus probandi* shall lie on the defendant.

VIII. And for the more regular and legal electing such burgesses, *Be it further enacted, by the authority aforesaid,* That the following rules and methods shall be observed to wit: the writs for the election of burgesses shall be signed by the governour or commander in chief of this dominion for the time being, with the seal of the colony affixed to them, and shall be delivered to the secretary of this colony, for the time being, forty days at least before the day appointed for the general-assembly to meet and be held; the secretary shall cause such writs to be conveyed and safely delivered to the sheriff of each county respectively, within ten days after the date thereof; every sheriff within three days after his receipt of such writ shall cause a copy thereof to be delivered to the minister and reader of every parish in his county, and shall upon the back of every such copy endorse the time and place by him appointed for the election, which shall always be at the court-house of his county, twenty days at least after his receiving such writ; every minister and reader receiving such copy and endorsement shall publish the same in his church or chapel, where they, or either of them, officiate, immediately after divine service, every Sunday, between the receipt of such copy and the day of election, and shall return the same copy to the sheriff, together with a certificate of the due publication thereof; and if at any time the secretary shall fail to cause the writs for electing burgesses to be safely conveyed and delivered to the several sheriffs as aforesaid, he shall forfeit and pay the sum of one hundred pounds current money for every writ he shall fail to deliver as aforesaid; and if the sheriff of any county shall fail to cause a fair copy of such writ and such endorsement thereon

to be delivered to every parish minister and reader within his county as aforesaid, within the time before directed, such sheriff shall forfeit and pay fifty pounds current money; and if any minister or reader, receiving such copy, shall fail to make publication and return thereof as aforesaid, he shall forfeit and pay twenty-five pounds current money; which said several forfeitures shall be recoverable with costs, by action of debt or information, in any court of record in this dominion, wherein the same shall be cognizable; and one moiety thereof shall be to our sovereign lord the king, his heirs and successours, for and towards the better support of this government, and the contingent charges thereof; and the other moiety to the person or persons who shall inform, or sue for the same.

IX. *And be it further enacted, by the authority aforesaid,* That after publication of such writs, and at the day and place of election, every freeholder actually resident within his county shall personally appear and give his vote, upon penalty of forfeiting two hundred pounds of tobacco, to any person or persons, who will inform or sue for the same; recoverable with costs, by action of debt or information, in any county-court of this dominion.

X. *And be it further enacted,* That when the election of any burgess or burgesses cannot be determined upon the view, by consent of the freeholders and candidates, the sheriff, or in his absence the under-sheriff, shall proceed to take the poll in manner following, that is to say: he shall appoint such persons as he shall think fit, who shall take an oath to be administered by such sheriff or under-sheriff, for their true and impartial taking the poll; and thereupon, having books or lists prepared for that purpose, they shall in the courthouse, and before the candidates, or their agents the present, enter the names of every candidate in a distinct list or column, and the name of every freeholder giving his vote, under the name or names of the person or persons he votes for, but no freeholder who has voted once shall be admitted to poll any more at that election. And that every person having a right to vote for two burgesses at such election shall name the two persons he votes for when he first offers to be polled, and if he refuses to name more than one at such time he shall not afterwards at that election be allowed to vote for another; and when no more freeholders appear to vote after proclamation thrice made at the courthouse door, the sheriff shall, within one hour at the most, conclude the poll.

XI. *Provided always,* That where more freeholders appear at such election than can be so polled before sunsetting on the day of election, the sheriff or under-sheriff shall be empowered and required, at the request of any of the candidates, or their agents, to adjourn the concluding the poll until the next day, of which notice shall be published at the courthouse door; and the same sheriff or under-sheriff shall, on such next day, proceed in taking and concluding the poll, in manner aforesaid: and when the poll shall be concluded as aforesaid, the person or persons appearing upon examination to have most votes shall be delivered and returned burgess or burgesses; and if two or more candidates shall have an equal number of votes, the sheriff, or in his absence the under-sheriff, being a freeholder, shall and may return which of them he thinks fit.

XII. *And be it further enacted,* That if upon a scrutiny of the poll before the house of burgesses it shall appear that the petitioner and sitting member have an equal number of legal votes, and the sheriff or under-sheriff, being a freeholder, who took the poll at such election, shall declare upon oath that if the votes had been equal at the election he would have returned the petitioner, such petitioner shall be declared duly elected, and his name inserted in the return in the room of the sitting member.

XIII. *And be it further enacted,* That every person before he is admitted to poll at such election, shall, if required by any candidate, or person appointed by any candidate, first declare whether he votes in right of fifty acres of unsettled land, twenty-five acres with a house and plantation thereon, or a house and lot, or part of a lot, in a town, and shall take one of the following oaths, as adapted to such freehold, or being one of the people called Quakers, shall declare to the same effect, that is to say: If for fifty acres of land in

the same county, unseated, "You shall swear that you are a freeholder in the county of and have at least fifty acres of freehold land unseated, lying and being in the said county, in your sole possession, or in the possession of your tenant or tenants, for years, at will or sufferance; that you or such tenant have been so possessed, or that you have had the legal estate thereof, for at least one year last past, and that you have not been before polled at this election." If for fifty acres of land in two counties, unseated, "You shall swear that you have fifty acres of land unseated, lying and being in the counties of and in your sole possession, or in the possession of your tenant or tenants, for years, at will or sufference; that you or such tenant have been so possessed, or that you have had the legal estate thereof, for at least one year last past, and that the greatest part of the said land doth lie in the county of and that you have not been before polled at this election." If for twenty-five acres of land, with a house and plantation, in the same county, "You shall swear that you are a freeholder, and sole owner of twenty-five acres of land, with a house and plantation upon it, lying and being in the county of and in your sole possession, or in the possession of your tenant or tenants, for years, at will or sufferance; that you or such tenant have been so possessed, or that you have had the legal estate thereof, for at least one year last past, and that you have not been before polled at this election." If for twenty-five acres of land, with a house and plantation, in two counties, "You shall swear that you are a freeholder, and sole owner of twenty-five acres of land, with a house and plantation upon it, lying in the counties of and in your sole possession, or in the possession of your tenant or tenants, for years, at will or sufferance; that you or such tenant have been so possessed, or that you have had the legal estate thereof, for at least one year last past; that the house is in the county of and that you have not been before polled at this election."—If for a house and lot, or part of a lot, in a town, "You shall swear that you are a freeholder of a house and lot, or a house and part of a lot, lying and being in the city or town of in your sole possession, or in the possession of your tenant or tenants, for years, at will or sufferance; that you or such tenant have been so possessed, or that you have had the legal estate thereof, for at least one year last past, and that you have not been before polled at this election." Which oath or affirmation the sheriff, or under-sheriff, taking such poll, is hereby empowered and required to administer, and cause the clerk attending to take the poll to enter, sworn or affirmed against the name of every voter who shall take such oath or affirmation, as aforesaid; and in case any freeholder, or other person taking the said oath or affirmation, shall thereby commit wilful and corrupt perjury, and be thereof convicted, or if any person do suborn any freeholder or other person to take a false oath or affirmation, in order to his being polled, every such offender being thereof convicted shall suffer as for wilful perjury committed in a court of record.

XIV. And whereas some persons, being real freeholders, for want of being proper judges of their freeholds, may scruple to take the said oath, and be thereby deprived of their votes, *Be it further enacted*, that where any freeholders, qualified as is hereinbefore directed, shall offer to give his vote at any election, but being required to take the oath or affirmation aforesaid shall refuse so to do, such vote shall not be added to the poll; but the sheriff, or under-sheriff, shall cause the name of every such person, and who he votes for, to be entered in a separate list; and if there be any scrutiny of such poll before the house of burgesses, every such vote shall be allowed in the same manner as if it had been entered on the poll at the election.

XV. *And be it further enacted, by the authority aforesaid*, That within twenty days next after every such election, the sheriff or under-sheriff, taking such poll, shall, upon oath to be administered by any justice of the peace, deliver to the clerk of his county-court, attested copies of the original poll of such election, and the list taken of such as offer to vote, but refuse to take the oath or affirmation as aforesaid, to be by such clerk recorded.

XVI. *And be it further enacted*, That after the election shall be concluded as aforesaid, the sheriff or under-sheriff taking the poll shall make return of such election, in manner following: upon the writ shall be endorsed "the execution of this writ appears in a certain schedule hereunto annexed." And in the schedule to the writ annexed, the execution thereof shall be certified as follows: "By virtue of this writ to me directed, in my full county, held at the courthouse for my said county, upon the day of in the year of the reign of by the grace of God of Great-Britain, France and Ireland, king defender of the faith, &c. by the assent of my said county, I have caused to be chosen two burgesses of my said county, to wit, A.B. and C.D. to act and do as in the said writ is directed and required;" and for the College of William and Mary, or for any city or town, the return shall be thus: "By virtue of this writ to me directed, I did make publication thereof, and afterwards, to wit upon the day of in the year of the reign of by the grace of God of Great-Britain, France and Ireland king, defender of the faith, &c. at the said city (or town) of (or at the said college) by assent of the freeholders and other legal electors (or the president, masters or professors) I have caused to be chosen one burgess for the said city (or town, or college) to wit, A.B. of to act and do as in the said writ is directed and required. And if at any time any candidate, or other person on his behalf, shall desire a copy of the poll, the sheriff or under-sheriff shall cause a fair attested copy thereof to be delivered to such candidate or person requiring the same.

XVII. *And be it further enacted by the authority aforesaid*, That when upon the death or disability of any member of the house of burgesses the sheriff shall receive a writ for the election of one or more burgesses, during the session of any general assembly, such sheriff is hereby required to appoint such and so many persons as he shall think fit to give notice thereof, and of the day and place of election, unto every freeholder residing within the county, city or town, for which such election is to be; and the same shall be thereupon made as soon as possible, in the manner herein before directed, and the person or persons so elected returned in form aforesaid. And if any sheriff, or in his absence the under sheriff, shall refuse to take the poll, when required by any candidate or freeholder, before the return is made, or shall take it in other manner than by this act is directed, or shall refuse to give a copy of the poll when required as aforesaid, or shall make a false return, or fail to make return, and cause the same to be delivered to the clerk of the secretary's office for the time being, or to such other person as shall attend in the said office to receive the same, one day at least before the day in such writ limited for the return thereof, every sheriff or under sheriff so offending or failing shall forfeit and pay one hundred pounds current money; one moiety thereof to our sovereign lord the king, his heirs and successours, for the better support of this government, and the contingent charges thereof; the other moiety to the informer, or person who shall sue for the same; to be recovered with costs, by action of debt or information, in any court of record in this colony.

XVIII. *And be it further enacted,* That the writs for electing burgesses at the college of William and Mary and for James town shall be delivered to the sheriff of James-City, who is hereby declared to be the proper officer for returning the said writs.

XIX. *And be it further enacted, by the authority aforesaid,* That no person hereafter to be elected a member of the general assembly for any county, city, town or corporation, within this dominion, shall, after the dissolution of any general assembly, or after any vacancy happening in this or any succeeding general-assembly, & before his election either himself, or by any other person or persons on his behalf, and at his charge, directly or indirectly, give, present or allow, to any person or persons, having voice or vote in such elections, any money, meat, drink, entertainment or provision, or make any present, gift, reward or entertainment, or any promise, agreement, obligation or engagement, to or for any person or persons, or to or for any county, city, town or corporation, or to or for the use, benefit, employment or preferment, of any person or persons, county, city, town or corporation, in order to be elected, or for being elected, a burgess for such county, city, town or corporation; & every person so giving, promising or engaging, shall be, and is hereby declared to be disabled and rendered incapable to sit or vote as

a member of the house of Burgesses; but shall be, to all intents and purposes, incapacitated, as if he had never been elected.

XX. *And be it further enacted and declared,* That all and every member of the general-assembly is and ought to be, and forever hereafter shall be, in his and their persons, servants and estates, real and personal, free, exempted and privileged, from all arrests attachments executions, and all other process whatsoever, save only for treason, felony, or breach of the peace, during his or their attendance in general-assembly, and for the space of ten days before, and ten days after, every session; and if any civil process shall be depending against such member or members, before his or their election, such process shall be stayed for ten days before and after every session as aforesaid; but may then be prosecuted, as it might otherwise have been, without discontinuance or abatement. And when any general-assembly shall be adjourned or prorogued longer than twenty days, process may be commenced and presented against any member or members thereof; but shall be stayed ten days before and after every session or meeting, by prorogation or adjournment, as aforesaid.

XXI. *And be it further enacted, by the authority aforesaid,* That every burgess shall be allowed and paid by his county fifteen shillings a day for coming to, attending at, and returning from, every session of assembly; and, over and above the said daily allowances, there shall be paid and allowed for going to and returning from the general-assembly as followeth, to wit: To every burgess for the counties of James City, York, Warwick, Elizabeth city, New Kent, Gloucester, Charles City, Surry and Isle of Wight, one day for coming, and one day for returning; to every burgess for the counties of Henrico, Chesterfield, Nansemond, Sussex, Southampton, Norfolk, Prince-Anne, King-William, Prince-George, King and Queen, Middlesex and Essex, and to the burgesses of the borough of Norfolk, two days for coming, and two days for returning; to every burgess for the counties of Lancaster, Amelia, Richmond, Caroline, Goochland, Hanover, King-George, Cumberland, Dinwiddie and Brunswick, three days for coming, and three days for returning; to every burgess for the counties of Accomack, Northampton, Northumberland, Westmoreland, Stafford, Spotsylvania, Louisa and Prince-Edward, four days for coming, and four days for returning; to every burgess for the counties of Prince-William, Fauquier, Culpeper, Orange, Albemarle, Buckingham, Bedford, Lunenburg, Fairfax and Loudoun, five days for coming, and five days for returning; and every burgess for the counties of Augusta, Amherst, Frederick, Halifax & Hampshire, six days for coming, and six days for returning; but no burgess shall demand or receive any salary or wages for any day or days he shall fail to attend his service in the house of burgesses, Sundays excepted; and if any burgess shall be taken sick or lame, during his attendance on any session, or in his journey thereto, so as to be unable to attend, such burgess shall be allowed and paid for every day of the session, in the same manner as if he had attended the service of the house.

XXII. *And be it further enacted, by the authority aforesaid,* That when any session of assembly shall be held, and upon examination of the treasurer's accounts it shall appear that there are monies sufficient in his hands to discharge all the money debts due from the publick, together with the burgesses wages, and the salaries and allowances to the respective officers of the general-assembly, that then the burgesses wages, for such session, according to the regulations before-mentioned, and the wages for the attendance of every burgess for any city, town or corporation, at fifteen shillings per day each, shall be paid by John Robinson, Esquire, treasurer, or the treasurer for the time being, appointed by or pursuant to act of assembly, out of the public money in his hands.

XXIII. *Provided always,* That where the assembly shall be adjourned for more than twenty days, in that case the burgesses attending such assembly shall be paid their wages to the time of such adjournment, either by their counties, or the treasurer, according to the rules and regulations aforesaid, in the same manner as if such assembly was prorogued.

XXIV. *And be it further enacted, by the authority aforesaid,* That at the time and place of election

of burgesses; for any county, the sheriff, or in his absence the under sheriff, of such county, respectively, at the door of the courthouse, by proclamation to be there three times made, between the hours of one and three of the clock in the afternoon, shall give public notice of the time appointed for a court to be held for receiving the propositions and grievances, and the publick claims, of all and every person and persons within his county; which propositions and grievances shall be signed by the person or persons presenting the same to the court, and thereupon the clerk, by the direction of the court, shall certify the same to the general assembly, and shall deliver the same to the burgesses of the county, to be by them presented accordingly: And in like manner a court for receiving and certifying propositions and grievances, and publick claims, as aforesaid, shall be appointed and held in each county respectively, before every session of the general assembly; and the sheriff of the county is hereby required to cause publick notice to be given of the time appointed for the holding such court, at every respective church and chapel within his county.

XXV. And whereas it hath been found inconvenient, and may prove of evil consequence, if any member of the house of burgesses should except of the office of sheriff, or of any place of profit, in this government, or if any sheriff, under-sheriff, or inspector of tobacco, should be elected and allowed to sit and vote as a member of the house of burgesses: *Be it further enacted, by the authority aforesaid,* That any person who now is, or hereafter shall be, sheriff or under sheriff of any county, or inspector of tobacco at any of the publick warehouses, during the time he shall be inspector, and for two years next after he shall be out of office, shall not be capable of sitting and voting as a member of the house of burgesses; and a writ shall issue for electing a new member in his stead, in the same manner as if such person was naturally dead: Nor shall any such inspector of tobacco, during the time aforesaid, presume to intermeddle or concern himself with any election of a burgess or burgesses, otherwise than by giving his vote, or endeavour to influence any person or persons to give his or their vote, under the penalty of fifty pounds; one half to our sovereign lord the king, his heirs and successours, for and towards defraying the contingent charges of this government, and the other moiety to the informer; to be recovered with costs, by action of debt or information, in any court of record within this dominion.

XXVI. And every member of this present, or any future house of burgesses, during the time of his being so, shall be exempted from being made or appointed sheriff; and if any member of the house of burgesses shall accept any office of profit whatsoever in this government, or hold the same in his own name, or in the name of any other person in trust for him, or for his use and benefit or shall execute by himself or his deputy any such office or place, such person shall be incapable of sitting or voting as a member of the house of burgesses, and a writ shall issue for electing a new member in his stead, in the same manner as if he was naturally dead; but such person shall be capable of being re-elected, and thereupon admitted to his place in the house of burgesses.

XXVII. *Provided always,* That nothing in this act shall be construed to hinder the legal electors of the city of Williamsburg, the borough of Norfolk, and the college of William and Mary, from choosing a representative in general assembly for the said city, town or college; but they, and each of them, shall and may continue so to do, according to their charters of incorporation, and the laws now in being, in the same manner as if this act had never been made.

XXVIII. *And be it further enacted, by the authority aforesaid,* That from hence-forth no general assembly whatsoever that shall at any time hereafter be called, assembled or held, shall have any continuance longer than for seven years at the furthest; to be accounted from the day on which, by the writs of summons, the said general-assembly shall be appointed to meet: And that this present general assembly shall cease and determine on the twenty-sixth day of May, 1768, unless the governour or commander in chief of this dominion for the time being shall think fit to dissolve it sooner.

XXIX. *And be it further enacted,* That all and every other act and acts, clause and clauses, heretofore made, as to so much thereof as is contrary to any thing within the purview of this act, be, and the same is hereby repealed.

XXX. *Provided always,* That the execution of this act shall be, and is hereby suspended, until his majesty's approbation thereof shall be obtained.

Reference: W. W. Hening (ed.), *The Statutes at Large of Virginia,* Vol. III (Philadephia: Thomas Neuber, 1823).

16

Massachusetts Bay

Massachusetts Bay received a new charter in 1691. The colony's freemen considered a written charter very important because it set the prerogatives of who governed in the colony. The relevance of the towns in the political system, especially Boston, was highlighted in this new charter. Towns continued to grow, making local governance increasingly important to the citizens. The colony's General Court (legislature) continued to struggle for power with the royal governor and the governor-appointed council, although many governors were natives of Massachusetts. These tensions inflamed Massachusetts' politics until the Revolution (See James Otis's pamphlet, "A Vindication of the British Colonies." in this volume.)

Of the many Massachusetts documents on local, legislative, and executive prerogatives, five documents have been selected for this Chapter. Queen Anne's 1702 instructions to Governor Joseph Dudley shows the degree to which Britain wanted to control governance in Massachusetts. Dudley's powers to decide on military defense sent chills through the citizenry who believed guns could be turned on them. But the explanatory charter of 1725, a document much desired by the General Court, made an effort to clarify crown prerogatives as well as define the rights of the colonists. Understanding that town governance was crucial for order and stability in the colony, the General Court wrote a number of statutes asserting town prerogatives. The final document in this Chapter, on the selectmen of Lexington, removes a selectman for abusing taxing powers. However, the General Court also affirmed Lexington selectmen's right to choose their own constable, thus making a statement on local controls

NEW CHARTER OF MASSACHUSETTS BAY, 1691

WILLIAM & MARY by the grace of God King and Queene of England Scotland France and Ireland Defenders of the Faith &c *To all* to whome these presents shall come Greeting *Whereas* his late Majesty King James the First Our Royall Predecessor by his Letters Patents vnder the Greate Seale of England bearing date at Westminster the Third Day of November in the Eighteenth yeare of his Reigne did Give and Grant vnto the Councill established at Plymouth in the County of Devon for the Planting Ruleing Ordering and Governing of New England in America and to their Successors and Assignes all that part of America lying and being in Breadth from Forty Degrees of Northerly Latitude from the Equinoctiall Line to the Forty Eighth Degree of the said Northerly Latitude Inclusively, and in length of and within all the Breadth aforesaid throughout all the Main Lands from Sea to Sea together alsoe with all the firme Lands Soiles Grounds Havens Ports Rivers Waters Fishings Mines and Mineralls as well Royall Mines of Gold and Silver as other Mines and Mineralls Pretious Stones Quarries and all and singular other Comodities Jurisdiccõns Royalties Privileges Franchises and Preheminences both within the said Tract of Land vpon the Main and alsoe within the Islands and Seas adjoyning *Provided* always that the said Lands Islands or any the premises by the said Letters Patents intended or meant to be Granted were not then actually possessed or Inhabited by any other Christian Prince or State or within the bounds Limitts or Territories of the Southern Collony then before granted by the said late King James the First [to be plantedc] by divers of his Subjects in the South parts *To Have* and to hold possesse and enjoy all and singular the aforesaid Continent Lands Territories Islands Hereditaments and Precincts Seas Waters Fishings with all and all manner of their Comodities Royalties Liberties Preheminences and Profitts that should from thenceforth arise from thence with all and singular their appurtenances and every part and parcell thereof vnto the said Councill and their Successors and Assignes for ever to the sole and proper vse and benefitt of the said Councill and their Successors and Assignes for ever *To* be holden of his said late Majestie King James the First his Heires and Successors as of his Mannor of East Greenwich in the County of Kent in free and Comon Soccage and not in Capite or by Knights Service *Yielding* and paying therefore to the said late King his Heires and Successors the Fifth part of the Oar of Gold and Silver which should from time to time and at all times then after happen to be found gotten had and obteyned in att or within any of the said Lands Limitts Territories or Precincts or in or within any part or parcell thereof for or in respect of all and all manner of duties demands and services whatsoever to be done made or paid to the said late King James the first his Heires and Successors (as in and by the said Letters Patents

amongst sundry other Clauses Powers Priviledges and Grants therein conteyned more at large appeareth *And Whereas* the said Councill established at Plymouth in the County of Devon for the Planting Ruleing Ordering and Governing of New England in America Did by their Deed Indented vnder their Comon Seale bearing Date the Nineteenth Day of March in the Third yeare of the Reigne of Our Royall Grandfather King Charles the First of ever Blessed Memory Give Grant Bargaine Sell Enffeoffe Alien and Confirme to Sir Henry Roswell Sir John Young Knights Thomas Southcott John Humphreys John Endicot and Simond Whetcomb their Heires and Assines and their Associats for ever All that part of New England in America aforesd which lyes and extends betweene a great River there comonly called Monomack ats Merrimack and a certaine other River there called Charles River being in a Bottom of a certaine Bay there comonly called Massachusetts ats Massatusetts Bay And alsoe all and singular those Lands and Hereditaments whatsoever lying within the space of Three English Miles on the South part of the said Charles River or of any and every part thereof And alsoe all and singular the Lands and Hereditaments whatsoever lying and being within the space of three English Miles to the Southward of the Southermost part of the said Bay called the Massachusetts ats Mattachusetts ats Massatusetts Bay And alsoe all those Lands and Hereditaments whatsoever which lye and be within the space of three English Miles to the Northward of the said River called Monomack ats Merrimack or to the Northward of any and every part thereof And all Lands and Hereditaments whatsoever lying within the Limitts aforesaid North and South in Latitude and in Breadth and in length and longitude of and within all the Breadth aforesaid throughout the Main Lands there from the Atlantick and Western Sea and Ocean on the East parte to the South Sea on the West part and all Lands and Grounds Place and Places Soile Woods and Wood Grounds Havens Ports Rivers Waters Fishings and Hereditaments whatsoever lying within the said Bounds and Limitts and every parte and parcell thereof and alsoe all Islands lying in America aforesaid in the said Seas or either of them on the Western or Eastern Coasts or Parts of the said Tracts of Land by the said Indenture mencõned to be Given and Granted Bargained Sold Enffeoffed Aliened and Confirmed or any of them. And alsoe all Mines and Mineralls aswell Royall Mines of Gold and Silver as other Mines and Mineralls whatsoever in the said Lands and Premisses or any parte thereof and all Jurisdiccõns Rights Royalties Liberties Freedoms Imunities Priviledges Franchises Preheminences and Comõdities whatsoever which they the said Council established at Plymouth in the County of Devon for the planting Ruleing Ordering and Governing of New England in America then had or might vse exercise or enjoy in or within the said Lands and Premisses by the same Indenture mencõned to be given granted bargained sold enffeoffed and confirmed in or within any part or parcell thereof To Have and to hold the said parte of New England in America which lyes and extends and is abutted as aforesaid and every parte and parcell thereof And all the said Islands Rivers Ports Havens Waters Fishings Mines Mineralls Jurisdiccõns Franchises Royalties Liberties Priviledges Comõdities Hereditaments and premises whatsoever with the appurtenances vnto the said Sir Henry Roswell Sir John Young Thomas Southcott John Humphreys John Endicott and Simond Whetcomb their Heires and appointed and Commissionated by Vs Our Heires and Successors and Eight and Twenty Assistants or Councillors to be advising and assisting to the Governour of Our said Province or Territory for the time being as by these presents is hereafter directed and appointed which said Councillors or Assistants are to be Constituted Elected and Chosen in such forme and manner as hereafter in these presents is expressed And for the better Execucõn of Our Royall Pleasure and Grant in this behalfe Wee doe by these presents for Vs Our Heires and Successors Ncminate Ordeyne make and Constitute Our Trusty and Welbeloved Simon

Broadstreet John Richards Nathaniel Saltenstall Wait Winthrop John Phillipps James Russell Samuell Sewall Samuel Appleton Barthilomew Gedney John Hawthorn Elisha Hutchinson Robert Pike Jonathan Curwin John Jolliffe Adam Winthrop Richard Middlecot John Foster Peter Serjeant Joseph Lynd Samuell Hayman Stephen Mason Thomas Hinckley William Bradford John Walley Barnabas Lothrop Job Alcott Samuell Daniell and Silvanus Davis Esquires the first and present Councillors or Assistants of Our said Province to continue in their said respective Offices or Trusts of Councillors or Assistants vntill the last Wednesday in May which shall be in the yeare of Our Lord One Thousand Six Hundred Ninety and Three and vntill other Councillors or Assistants shall be chosen and appointed in their stead in such manner as in these presents is expressed And Wee doe further by these presents Constitute and appoint Our Trusty and welbeloved Isaac Addington Esquier to be Our first and present Secretary of Our said Province during Our Pleasure And Our Will and Pleasure is that the Governour of Our said Province from the time being shall have Authority from time to time at his discretion to assemble and call together the Councillors or Assistants of Our said Province for the time being and that the said Governour with the said Assistants or Councillors or Seaven of them at the least shall and may from time to time hold and keep a Councill for the ordering and directing the Affaires of Our said Province And further Wee Will and by these presents for Vs Our Heires and Successors doe ordeyne and Grant that there shall and may be convened held and kept by the Governour for the time being vpon every last Wednesday in the Moneth of May every yeare for ever and at all such other times as the Governour of Our said Province shall think fitt and appoint a great and Generall Court of Assembly Which said Great and Generall Court of Assembly shall consist of the Governour and Councill or Assistants for the time being and of such Freeholders of Our said Province or Territory as shall be from time to time elected or deputed by the Major parte of the Freeholders and other

Inhabitants of the respective Townes or Places who shall be present at such Eleccõns Each of the said Townes and Places being hereby impowered to Elect and Depute Two Persons and noe more to serve for and represent them respectively in the said Great and Generall Court or Assembly To which Great and Generall Court or Assembly to be held as aforesaid Wee doe hereby for Vs Our Heires and Successors give and grant full power and authority from time to time to direct appoint and declare what Number each County Towne and Place shall Elect and Depute to serve for and represent them respectively in the said Great and Generall Court or Assembly *Provided* alwayes that noe Freeholder or other Person shall have a Vote in the Eleccõn of Members to serve in any Greate and Generall Court or Assembly to be held as aforesaid who at the time of such Eleccõn shall not have an estate of Freehold in Land within Our said Province or Territory to the value of Forty Shillings per Annũ at the least or other estate to the value of Forty pounds Sterl' And that every Person who shall be soe elected shall before he sitt or Act in the said Great and Generall Court or Assembly take the Oaths mencõned in an Act of Parliament made in the first yeare of Our Reigne Entituled an Act for abrogateing of the Oaths of Allegiance and Supremacy and appointing other Oaths and thereby appointed to be taken instead of the Oaths of Allegiance and Supremacy and shall make Repeat and Subscribe the Declaracõn mencõned in the said Act before the Governour and Lievtent. or Deputy Governour or any two of the Assistants for the time being who shall be therevnto authorized and Appointed by Our said Governour and that the Governour for the time being shall have full power and Authority from time to time as he shall Judge necessary to adjourne Prorogue and dissolve all Great and Generall Courts or Assemblyes met and convened as aforesaid And Our Will and Pleasure is and Wee doe hereby for Vs Our Heires and Successors Grant Establish and Ordeyne that yearly once in every yeare for ever hereafter the aforesaid Number of Eight and Twenty Councillors or Assistants shall be by the Generall

Court or Assembly newly chosen that is to say Eighteen at least of the Inhabitants of or Proprietors of Lands within the Territory formerly called the Collony of the Massachusetts Bay and four at the least of the Inhabitants of or Proprietors of Lands within the Territory formerly called New Plymouth and three at the least of the Inhabitants of or Proprietors of Land within the Territory formerly called the Province of Main and one at the least of the Inhabitants of or Proprietors of Land within the Territory lying between the River of Sagadahoc and Nova Scotia And that the said Councillors or Assistants or any of them shall or may at any time hereafter be removed or displaced from their respective Places or Trust of Councillors or Assistants by any Great or Generall Court or Assembly And that if any of the said Councillors or Assistants shall happen to dye or be removed as aforesaid before the Generall day of Eleccõn That then and in every such Case the Great and Generall Court or Assembly at their first sitting may proceed to a New Eleccõn of one or more Councillors or Assistants in the roome or place of such Councillors or Assistants soe dying or removed And Wee doe further Grant and Ordeyne that it shall and may be lawfull for the said Governour with the advice and consent of the Councill or Assistants from time to time to nominate and appoint Judges Commissioners of Oyer and Terminer Sheriffs Provosts Marshalls Justices of the Peace and other Officers to Our Councill and Courts of Justice belonging *Provided* always that noe such Nominacõn or Appointment of Officers be made without notice first given or sumõns yssued out seaven dayes before such Nominacõn or Appointment vnto such of the said Councillors or Assistants as shall be at that time resideing within Our said Province *And Our* Will and Pleasure is that the Governour and Leivtent. or Deputy Governour and Councillors or Assistants for the time being and all other Officers to be appointed or Chosen as aforesaid shall before the Vndertaking the Execucõn of their Offices and Places respectively take their severall and respective Oaths for the due and faithfull performance of their duties in their severall and respective

Offices and Places and alsoe the Oaths appointed by the said Act of Parliament made in the first yeare of Our Reigne to be taken instead of the Oaths of Allegiance and Supremacy and shall make repeate and subscribe the Declaracõn menc̃oned in the said Act before such Person or Persons as are by these presents herein after appointed (that is to say) The Governour of Our said Province or Territory for the time being shall take the said Oaths and make repeate and sub-scribe the said Declaracõn before the Leivtent. or Deputy Governour or in his absence before any two or more of the said Persons hereby Nominated and appointed the present Councillors or Assistants of Our said Province or Territory to whom Wee doe by these presents give full power and Authority to give and admin-ister the same to Our said Governour accordingly and after Our said Governour shall be sworn and shall have subscribed the said Declaracõn that then Our Leivtent. or Deputy Governour for the time being and the Councillors or Assistants before by these presents Nominated and appointed shall take the said Oaths and make repeat and subscribe the said Declaracõn before Our said Governour and that every such person or persons as shall (at any time of the Annuall Eleccõns or otherwise vpon death or removeall) be appointed to be the New Councillors or Assistants and all other Officers to bee hereafter chosen from time to time shall take the Oaths to their respective Offices and places belonging and alsoe the said Oaths appointed by the said Act of Parliament to be taken instead of the Oaths of Allegiance and Supremacy and shall make repe-ate and subscribe the declaracõn menc̃oned in the said Act before the Governour or Leivtent. or Deputy Governour or any two or more Councillors or Assistants or such other Person or Persons as shall be appointed thereunto by the Governour for the time being to whom Wee doe therefore by these presents give full power and authority from time to time to give and adminis-ter the same respectively according to Our true meaning herein before declared without any Com̃ission or further Warrant to bee had and obteyned from vs Our Heires and Successors in

that behalfe *And* Our Will and Pleasure is and Wee doe hereby require and Com̃and that all and every person and persons hereafter by Vs Our Heires and Successors nominated and appointed to the respective Offices of Governour or Leivt. or Deputy Governour and Secretary of Our said Province or Territory (which said Governour or Leivt. or Deputy Governour and Secretary of Our said Province or Territory for the time being Wee doe hereby reserve full power and Authority to Vs Our Heires and Successors to Nominate and appoint accordingly, shall before he or they be admitted to the Execuc̃on of their respective Offices take as well the Oath for the due and faithfull performance of the said Offices respec-tively as alsoe the Oaths appointed by the said Act of Parliament made in the said First yeare of Our Reigne to be taken instead of the said Oaths of Allegiance and Supremacy and shall alsoe make repeate and subscribe the Declaracõn appointed by the said Act in such manner and before such persons as aforesaid *And further* Our Will and Pleasure is and Wee doe hereby for Vs Our Heires and Successors Grant Establish and Ordaine That all and every of the Subjects of Vs Our Heires and Successors which shall goe to and Inhabit within Our said Province and Territory and every of their Children which shall happen to be born there or on the Seas in goeing thither or returning from thence shall have and enjoy all Libertyes and Immunities of Free and naturall Subjects within any of the Dominions of Vs Our Heires and Successors to all Intents Construccõns and purposes whatsoever as if they and every of them were borne within this Our *Realme* of England and for the greater Ease and Encouragement of Our Loveing Subjects Inhabiting our said Province or Territory of the Massachusetts Bay and of such as shall come to Inhabit there Wee doe by these presents for vs Our heires and Successors Grant Establish and Ordaine that for ever hereafter there shall be a liberty of Conscience allowed in the Worshipp of God to all Christians (Except Papists) Inhabiting or which shall Inhabit or be Resident within our said Province or Territory *And* Wee doe hereby Grant and Ordaine that the Gouernor or leivetent or Deputy Gouernor of our said Province or Territory for the time being or either of them or any two or more of the Councill or Assistants for the time being as shall be thereunto appointed by the said Gouernor shall and may at all times and from time to time hereafter have full Power and Authority to Administer and give the Oathes appointed by the said Act of Parliament made in the first yeare of Our Reigne to be taken instead of the Oathes of Allegiance and Supremacy to all and every pesrson and persons which are now Inhabiting or resideing within our said Province or Territory or which shall at any time or times hereafter goe or passe thither And wee doe of our further Grace certaine knowledge and meer mocõn Grant Establish and Ordaine for Vs our heires and Successors that the great and Generall Court or Assembly of our said Province or Territory for the time being Convened as aforesaid shall for ever have full Power and Authority to Erect and Constitute Judicatories and Courts of Record or other Courts to be held in the name of Vs Our heires and successors for the Hearing Trying and Determining of all manner of Crimes Offences Pleas Processes Plaints Accõns Matters Causes and things whatsoever ariseing or happening within Our said Province or Territory or between persons Inhabiting or resideing there whether the same be Criminall or Civill and whether the said Crimes be Capitall or not Capitall and whether the said Pleas be Reall personall or mixt and for the awarding and makeing out of Execution thereupon To which Courts and Judicatories wee doe hereby for vs our heirs and Successors Give and Grant full power and Authority from time to time to Administer oathes for the better Discovery of Truth in any matter in Controversy or depending before them And wee doe for vs Our Heires and Successors Grant Establish and Ordaine that the Gouernor of our said Province or Territory for the time being with the Councill or Assistants may doe execute or performe all that is necessary for the Probate of Wills and Granting of Administracõns for touching or concerning any Interest or Estate which any person or persons shall have within our said

Province or Territory *And whereas* Wee judge it necessary that all our Subjects should have liberty to Appeale to vs our heires and Successors in Cases that may deserve the same Wee doe by these presents Ordaine that incase either party shall not rest satisfied with the Judgement or Sentence of any Judicatories or Courts within our said Province or Territory in any Personall Accõn wherein the matter in difference doth exceed the value of three hundred Pounds Sterling that then he or they may appeale to vs Our heires and Successors in our or their Privy Councill Provided such Appeale be made within Fourteen dayes after ye Sentence or Judgement given and that before such Appeale be allowed Security be given by the party or parties appealing in the value of the matter in Difference to pay or Answer the Debt or Damages for the which Judgement or Sentence is given With such Costs and Damages as shall be Awarded by vs Our Heires or Successors incase the Judgement or Sentence be affirmed *And Provided* alsoe that no Execution shall be stayd or suspended by reason of such Appeale vnto vs our Heires and Successors in our or their Privy Council soe as the party Sueing or takeing out Execution doe in the like manner give Security to the value of the matter in difference to make Restitucion in Case the said Judgement or Sentence be reversed or annul'd upon the said Appeale *And* we doe further for vs our Heires and Successors Give and Grant to the said Governor and the great and Generall Court or Assembly of our said Province or Territory for the time being full power and Authority from time to time to make ordaine and establish all manner of wholsome and reasonable Orders Laws Statutes and Ordinances Directions and Instructions either with penalties or without (soe as the same be not repugnant or contrary to the Lawes of this our Realme of England) as they shall Judge to be for the good and welfare of our said Province or Territory And for the Gouernment and Ordering thereof and of the People Inhabiting or who shall Inhabit the same and for the necessary support and Defence of the Government thereof *And* wee doe for vs our Heires and Successors Giue and grant that the said Generall Court or Assembly shall have full power and Authority to name and settle annually all Civill Officers within the said Province such Officers Excepted the Election and Constitution of whome wee have by these presents reserved to vs Our Heires and Successors or to the Governor of our said Province for the time being and to Settforth the severall Duties Powers and Lymitts of every such Officer to be appointed by the said Generall Court or Assembly and the formes of such Oathes not repugnant to the Lawes and Statutes of this our Realme of England as shall be respectiuely Administered vnto them for the Execution of their severall Offices and places And alsoe to impose Fines mulcts Imprisonments and other Punishments And to impose and leavy proportionable and reasonable Assessments Rates and Taxes vpon the Estates and Persons of all and every the Proprietors and Inhabitants of our said Province or Territory to be Issued and disposed of by Warrant vnder the hand of the Governor of our said Province for the time being with the advice and Consent of the Councill for Our service in the necessary defence and support of our Government of our said Province or Territory and the Protection and Preservation of the Inhabitants there according to such Acts as are or shall be in force within our said Province and to dispose of matters and things whereby our Subjects inhabitants of our said Province may be Religiously peaceably and Civilly Governed Protected and Defended soe as their good life and orderly Conversation may win the Indians Natives of the Country to the knowledge and obedience of the onely true God and Saviour of Mankinde and the Christian Faith which his Royall Majestie our Royall Grandfather king Charles the first in his said Letters Patents declared was his Royall Intentions And the Adventurers free Possession to be the Princepall end of the said Plantation And for the better secureing and maintaining Liberty of Conscience hereby granted to all persons at any time being and resideing within our said Province or Territory as aforesaid *Willing* Comanding and Requireing and by these presents for vs Our heires and Successors Ordaining and appointing that all such Orders Lawes Statutes and Ordinances Instructions and Directions as

shall be soe made and published vnder our Seale of our said Province or Territory shall be Carefully and duely observed kept and performed and put in Execution according to the true intent and meaning of these presents *Provided* alwaies and Wee doe by these presents for vs Our Heires and Successors Establish and Ordaine that in the frameing and passing of all such Orders Laws Statutes and Ordinances and in all Elections and Acts of Government whatsoever to be passed made or done by the said Generall Court or Assembly or in Councill the Governor of our said Province or Territory of the Massachusetts Bay in New England for the time being shall have the Negative voice and that without his consent or Approbation signified and declared in Writeing no such Orders Laws Statutes Ordinances Elections or other Acts of Government whatsoever soe to be made passed or done by the said Generall Assembly or in Councill shall be of any Force effect or validity anything herein contained to the contrary in anywise notwithstanding *And* wee doe for vs Our Heires and Successors Establish and Ordaine that the said Orders Laws Statutes and Ordinances be by the first opportunity after the makeing thereof sent or Transmitted vnto vs Our Heires and Successors vnder the Publique Seale to be appointed by vs for Our or their approbation or Disallowance And that incase all or any of them shall at any time within the space of three years next after the same shall have presented to vs our Heires and Successors in Our or their Privy Councill be disallowed and reiected and soe signified by vs Our Heires and Successors vnder our or their Signe Manuall and Signett or by or in our or their Privy Councill vnto the Governor for the time being then such and soe many of them as shall be soe disallowed and riected shall thenceforth cease and determine and become vtterly void and of none effect *Provided* alwais that incase Wee our Heires or Successors shall not within the Terme of Three Yeares after the presenting of such Orders Lawes Statutes or Ordinances as aforesaid signifie our or their Disallowance of the same Then the said orders Lawes Statutes or Ordinances shall be and continue in full force and effect according to the true Intent and meaneing of the same vntill the Expiracon thereof or that the same shall be Repealed by the Generall Assembly of our said Province for the time being *Provided* alsoe that it shall and may be Lawfull for the said Governor and Generall Assembly to make or passe any Grant of Lands lying within the Bounds of the Colonys formerly called the Collonys of the Massachusetts Bay and New Plymouth and province of Main in such manner as heretofore they might have done by vertue of any former Charter or Letters Patents which grants of lands within the Bounds aforesaid Wee doe hereby Will and ordaine to be and continue for ever of full force and effect without our further Approbation or Consent *And* soe as Neverthelesse and it is Our Royall Will and Pleasure That noe Grant or Grants of any Lands lying or extending from the River of Sagadehock to the Gulph of St: Lawrence and Canada Rivers and to the Main Sea Northward and Eastward to be made or past by the Governor and Generall Assembly of our said Province be of any force validity or Effect vntill Wee Our Heires and Successors shall have Signified Our or their Approbacõn of the same *And* Wee doe by these presents for vs Our Heires and Successors Grant Establish and Ordaine that the Governor of our said Province or Territory for the time being shall have full Power by himselfe or by any Cheif Comãnder or other Officer or Officers to be appointed by him from time to time to traine instruct Exercise and Governe the Militia there and for the speciall Denfence and Safety of Our said Province or Territory to assemble in Martiall Array and put in Warlike posture the Inhabitants of Our said Province or Territory and to lead and Conduct them and with them to Encounter Expulse Repell Resist and pursue by force of Armes aswell by Sea as by Land within or without the limitts of Our said Province or Territory and alsoe to kill slay destroy and Conquer by all fitting wayes Enterprises and meanes whatsoever all and every such Person and Persons as shall at any time hereafter Attempt or Enterprize the destruccõn Invasion Detriment or Annoyance of Our said Province or Territory

and to vse and exercise the Law Martiall in time of actuall Warr Invasion or Rebellion as occasion shall necessarily require and alsoe from time to time to Erect Forts and to fortifie any place or Places within Our said Province or Territory and the same to furnish with all necessary Amũnicõn Provisions and Stores of Warr for Offence or Defence and to comitt from time to time the Custody and Government of the same to such Person or Persons as to him shall seem meet And the said Forts and Fortificacõns to demolish at his Pleasure and to take and surprise by all waies and meanes whatsoever all and every such Person or Persons with their Shipps Arms Ammuncõn and other goods as shall in a hostile manner Invade or attempt the Invading Conquering or Annoying of Our said Province or Territory *Provided* alwayes and Wee doe by these presents for Vs Our Heires and Successors Grant Establish and Ordeyne That the said Governour shall not at any time hereafter by vertue of any power hereby granted or hereafter to be granted to him Transport any of the Inhabitants of Our said Province or Territory or oblige them to march out of the Limitts of the same without their Free and voluntary consent or the Consent of the Great and Generall Court or Assembly or Our said Province or Territory nor grant Comĩssions for exerciseing the Law Martiall vpon any the Inhabitants of Our said Province or Territory without the Advice and Consent of the Councill or Assistants of the same *Provided* in like manner and Wee doe by these presents for Vs Our Heires and Successors Constitute and Ordeyne that when and as often as the Governour of Our said Province for the time being shall happen to dye or be displaced by Vs Our Heires or Successors or be absent from his Government That then and in any of the said Cases the Leivtenant or Deputy Governour of Our said Province for the time being shall have full power and authority to doe and execute all and every such Acts Matters and things which Our Governour of Our said Province for the time being might or could by vertue of these Our Letter Patents lawfully doe or execute if he were personally present vntill the returne of the Governour soe absent or Arrivall or Constitucõn of such other Governour as shall or may be appointed by Vs Our Heires or Successors in his stead and that when and as often as the Governour and Leivtenant or Deputy Governour of Our said Province or Territory for the time being shall happen to dye or be displaced by Vs Our Heires or Successors or be absent from Our said Province and that there shall be no person within the said Province Comissionated by Vs Our Heires or Successors to be Governour within the same Then and in every of the said cases the Councill or Assistants of Our said Province shall have full power and Authority and Wee doe hereby give and grant vnto the said Councill or Assistants of Our said Province for the time being or the Major parte of them full power and Authority to doe and execute all and every such Acts matters and things which the said Governour or Leivtenant of Deputy Governour of Our said Province or Territory for the time being might or could lawfully doe or exercise if they or either of them were personally present vntill the returne of the Governour Leivtenant or Deputy Governour soe absent or Arrivall or Constitucõn of such other Governour or Leivtenant or Deputy Governour as shall or may be appointed by Vs Our Heires or Successors from time to time *Provided* alwaies and it is hereby declared that nothing herein shall extend or be taken to Erect or grant or allow the Exercise of any Admirall Court Jurisdicõn Power or Authority but that the same shall be and is hereby reserved to Vs and Our Successors and shall from time to time be Erected Granted and exercised by vertue of Comissions to be yssued vnder the Great Seale of England or vnder the Seale of the High Admirall or the Comissioners for executing the Office of High Admirall of England *And further* Our expresse Will and Pleasure is And Wee doe by these present for Vs Our Heires and Successors Ordaine and appoint that these Our Letters Patents shall not in any manner Enure or be taken to abridge bar or hinder any of Our loveing Subjects whatsoever to vse and exercise the Trade of Fishing vpon the Coasts of New England but that they and every of them shall have full and free power and Libertie to continue and vse their said Trade of Fishing vpon the said Coasts in any of the seas therevnto adjoyning or any Arms of the said Seas or Salt Water Rivers where they have been wont to fish and to build and set vpon the Lands within Our said Province or Collony lying wast and not then possesst by perticuler Proprietors such Wharfes Stages and Workhouses as shall be necessary for the salting drying keeping and packing of their Fish to be taken or gotten vpon that Coast And to Cutt down and take such Trees and other Materialls there growing or being or growing vpon any parts or places lying wast and not then in possession of particular proprietors as shall be needfull for that purpose and for all other necessary easments helps and advantages concerning the Trade of Fishing there in such manner and forme as they have been heretofore at any time accustomed to doe without makeing any Wilfull Wast or Spoile any thing in these presents conteyned to the contrary notwithstanding

Reference: The Charters and General Laws of the Colony and Province of Massachusetts Bay (Boston: T. B. Walt and Co., 1814), 18–37.

QUEEN'S INSTRUCTIONS TO GOVERNOR DUDLEY, APRIL 6, 1702

Anne R.. Instructions for our trusty and well-beloved Joseph Dudley, Esquire, our Captain-General and Governor-in-Chief in and over our province and territory of the Massachusetts Bay in New England. Given at our court at St. James, the sixth day of April 1702, in the first year of our reign.

With these our instructions you will receive our commission, under the great seal of England, constituting you our Captain-General and Commander-in-Chief of the militia and of all the forces by sea and land within our colonies of Rhode Island, Providence Plantation, and the

Narraganset Country or Kings Province in New England, and of all our forts and places of strength within the same.

You are therefore to fit yourself with all convenient speed, and to repair to our said Province of the Massachusetts Bay, and, being arrived there, you are to take upon you the execution of the place and trust we have reposed in you, and forthwith to call together the members of our council in that province.

You are, with all due and usual solemnity, to cause our said commission to be published at the said meeting, and notification to be also given to our colonies of Rhode Island, Providence Plantation, and the Narraganset Country, of the power wherewith you are entrusted concerning the militia forces and forts within our said colonies and country as aforesaid.

You shall yourself take, and also administer to each of the members of our said council, as well the oaths appointed by act of Parliament to be taken instead of the Oaths of Allegiance and Supremacy, as also the test together with an oath for the due execution of your and their places and trusts, as well with regard to the equal and impartial administration of justice in all causes that shall come before you as otherwise, and likewise the oath required to be taken by governors of plantations to do their utmost that the laws relating to the plantations be observed. And both you and they shall also subscribe the association mentioned in a late act of Parliament entitled. *An Act for the Better Security of his Majesty's Royal Person and Government.*

You are to communicate forthwith to our said council such and so many of these our instructions, wherein their advice and consent are mentioned to be requisite, as likewise all such others, from time to time, as you shall find convenient for our service to be imparted to them.

You are to permit the members of our said council of Massachusetts Bay to have and enjoy freedom of debate and vote in all affairs of public concern that may be debated in council.

You are, from time to time, to send to us by one of our principal secretaries of state, and to our commissioners for trade and plantations, the names and qualities of the members appointed to be of our said council, by the first conveniency after such appointment.

And in the choice and appointment of the members of our said council, as also of the principal officers, judges, justices, sheriffs and others, you are always to take care that they be men of good life and well affected to our government and of good estates and abilities, and not necessitous people, or much in debt.

You are hereby authorized to use the public seal appointed or to be appointed by us for the sealing of all things whatsoever that shall pass the seal of our said province under your government.

You are to take care that all writs be issued in our royal name throughout our said province.

You are to observe in the passing of laws that the style of enacting the same be by the governor, council, and assembly and no other.

You are also, as much as possible, to observe the passing of all laws that whatever may be requisite upon each different matter be accordingly provided for by a different law, without intermixing in one and the same act such things as have no relation to each other. And you are more especially to take care that no clause or clauses be inserted in or be annexed to any act which shall be foreign to what the title of such respective act imports.

You are to transmit authentic copies, under the public seal, of all laws, statutes, and ordinances that are now made in force, which have not yet been sent, or which at any time hereafter shall be made and enacted within our said province under your government and command, each of them separately under the public seal, to us, and to our said commissioners for trade and plantations, within three months, or by the first opportunity after their being enacted, together with duplicates thereof by the next conveyance upon pain of our highest displeasure, and of the forfeiture of that year's salary wherein you shall at any time or upon any pretense whatsoever omit to send over the said laws, statutes, and ordinances as aforesaid, within the time above limited, as also of such other penalty as we shall please to inflict. But if it shall happen that, during time of war, no shipping shall come from our said province within three months after the making such laws, statutes, and ordinances, whereby the same may be transmitted as aforesaid, then the said laws, statutes, and ordinances are to be transmitted as aforesaid by the next conveyance after the making thereof, whenever it may happen for our approbation or dissallowance of the same.

And forasmuch as great prejudice may happen to our service and the security of our said province by your absence from those parts without a sufficient cause and especial leave from us, for the prevention thereof, you are not, upon any pretence whatsoever, to come to Europe from your government without having first obtained leave for so doing from us under our sign manual and signet, or by order in our privy council.

You are to take care that in all acts or orders to be passed within that our province in any case for levying money or imposing fines and penalties express mention be made, that the same is granted or reserved to us, our heirs and successors, for the public use of that our province, and the support of the government thereof, as by the said act or order shall be directed.

Whereas it is necessary that due provision be made for the support of the government of our said province by setting apart sufficient allowances to you our captain-general and governor-in-chief and to our lieutenant-governor or commander-in-chief for the time being residing within the same, and whereas our said province of Massachusetts Bay has not hitherto taken any manner of care in that matter, though the like provision generally made in our other plantations in America which are under immediate government, notwithstanding that divers of them are much less able to do it, you are, therefore, to propose to the general assembly of our said province, and accordingly to use your utmost endeavors with them, that an act be passed for settling and establishing fixed salaries upon yourself and others our captains-general that may succeed you in that government, as likewise upon our lieutenant-governor or commanders-in-chief for the time being, suitable to the dignity of those respective offices.

And you are also earnestly to recommend to the assembly in our name that care be taken by them for the building of a fit and convenient house to receive you, and the governor for the time being, which may be appropriated to that use.

You are not to permit any clause whatsoever to be inserted in any law for levying money or the value of money whereby the same shall not be made liable to be accounted for to us here in England, and to our commissioners of our treasury for our high treasurer for the time being.

You are to take care that fair books of accounts of all receipts and payments of all such money be duly kept, and the truth thereof attested upon oath, and that the said books be transmitted every half year or oftener to our commissioners of our treasury, or high treasurer for the time being, and to our commissioners for trade and plantations, and duplicates thereof by the next conveyance. In which books shall be specified every particular sum raised or disposed of, together with the names of the persons to whom any payment shall be made; to the end we may be satisfied of the right and due application of the revenue of our said province.

You are not to suffer any public money whatsoever to be issued or disposed of otherwise than by warrant under your hand, by and with the advise and consent of our said council, but the assembly may be, nevertheless, permitted, from time to time, to view and examine the accounts of money or value of money disposed of by virtue of laws made by them, which you are to signify to them as there shall be occasion.

And it is our express will and pleasure that no law for raising any imposition on wines and other strong liquors be made to continue for less than one whole year, as also that all other laws whatsoever for the good government and support of our said province be made indefinite and without limitation of time, except the same be for a temporary end, and which shall expire and have its full effect within a certain time.

And, therefore, you shall not re-enact any law which has or shall have been once enacted there, except upon very urgent occasions; but in no case more than once without our express consent.

You shall not permit any act or order to pass in our said province whereby the price or value of the current money within your government, whether it be foreign or belonging to our dominions, may be altered without our particular leave or direction for the same.

And you are particularly not to pass any law, or do any act by grant, settlement, or otherwise, whereby our revenue may be lessened or impaired, without our especial commands therein.

You are to take all possible care in the granting of lands within our province under your government, not already disposed of, that such limitations and methods be observed as may best tend to the safety and due improvement of our said province.

And whereas we have been informed that great spoils are daily committed in our woods in the province of Maine and other parts within your government of the Massachusets Bay, by cutting down and converting to private uses such trees as are or may be proper for the service of our royal navy; and it being necessary that all practices which tend so evidently to deprive us of those supplies be effectually restrained; our will and pleasure is that, upon consideration of the occasion of such abuses, the methods by which they are carried on, and the inconveniences that attend them, you use your endeavours with our council and the assembly of the Massachusets Bay to dispose them to pass acts for the better preventing the further spoil of those woods, and for preserving a nursery of such trees as may be useful for our service; and in case you cannot prevail with them to pass acts proper and sufficient for those purposes, that you send over hither the heads of such a bill as may be effectual for those ends and fit to be enacted here.

You shall not remit any fines or forfeitures whatsoever above the sum of ten pounds, nor dispose of any escheats, fines, or forfeitures whatsoever, until upon signifying to our commissioners of our treasury, or our high treasurer for the time being, and to our commissioners for trade and plantations, the nature of the offense and the occasion of such fines, forfeitures, or escheats,

with the particular sums or values thereof, which you are to do with all speed you shall have received our direction therein. But you may, in the meantime, suspend the payment of the said fines and forfeitures.

In case any goods, money, or other estate of pirates or piratically taken, shall be brought in or found within our said province of the Massachusetts Bay, or taken on board any ships or vessels, you are to cause the same to be seized and secured until you shall have given us an account thereof and received our pleasure concerning the disposal thereof. But in case such goods or any part of them are perishable, the same shall be publicly sold and disposed of, and the produce thereof in like manner secured until our further order.

And whereas we have been pleased to grant commissions to several persons in our respective plantations in America for the trying of pirates in those parts, pursuant to the act for the more effectual suppression of piracy; and by a commission already sent to our province of the Massachusets Bay, you, as captain-general and governor-in-chief of our said province, are empowered, together with others therein mentioned, to proceed accordingly in reference to our said province, our will and pleasure is that in all matters relating to pirates, you govern yourself according to the intent of the act and commission aforementioned. But, whereas accessories in cases of piracy beyond the seas are by the said act left to be tried in England, according to the statute of the 28th of King Henry VIII, we do hereby further direct and require you to send all such accessories in cases of piracy in our foresaid province, with the proper evidences that you may have against them, into England in order to their being tried here.

You are to require the secretary of our said province for the time being to furnish you with transcripts of all such acts and public orders as shall be made from time to time, together with copies of the journals of the council and asembly, to the end the same may be transmitted to us and to our commissioners for trade and plantations, as above directed, which he is duly to perform upon pain of incurring the forfeiture of his place.

You shall transmit to us and to our commissioners for trade and plantations by the first opportunity a map with the exact description of the whole territory under your government, with the several plantations upon it, and of the fortifications. And you are likewise to use your best endeavours to produce a good map to be drawn of all the Indian country in the neighborhood of our plantations in those parts, marking the names of the several nations, as they call themselves and are called by the English and French, and the places where they inhabit, and to transmit the same in like manner.

You are likewise to send a list of all officers employed under your government, together with all public charges and an account of the present revenue with the probability of the increase or diminution thereof under every head or article.

You are to transmit to us and to our commissioners for trade and plantations, with all convenient speed, a particular account of all establishments of jurisdictions, courts, offices, and officers, powers, authorities, fees, and privileges granted or settled within our said province, to the end you may receive our further directions therein.

You shall likewise take especial care with the advice and consent of our said council to regulate all salaries and fees belonging to places, or paid upon emergencies, that they be within the bounds of moderation, and that no exaction be made upon any occasion whatsoever, as also that tables of all fees be publicly hung up in all places where such fees are to be paid. And you are to transmit copies of all such tables of fees to us and to our commissioners for trade and plantations, as aforesaid.

Whereas it is very necessary for our service that there be an attorney general appointed and settled who may, at any time, take care of our rights and interest within our said province, you are, with all convenient speed, to nominate a fit person for that trust.

You are to permit a liberty of conscience to all persons, except Papists, so they be contented with a quiet and peaceable enjoyment of the same, not giving offense or scandal to the government.

You are to take care that drunkeness and debauchery, swearing and blasphemy be discountenanced and punished, and that none be admitted to public trusts and employments in our said province under your government whose ill fame and conversation may occasion scandal.

You shall administer or cause to be administered the oaths appointed by act of parliament to be taken instead of the oaths of allegiance and supremacy, as also the test, to the members and officers of our council and assembly and to all judges, justices, and all other persons that hold any office or place of trust or profit in our said province, whether by virtue of any patent under our great seal of England or our seal of the Massachusets Bay, or otherwise; and likewise require them to subscribe the forementioned association; without which you are not to admit any person whatsoever into any public office, nor suffer those that have been admitted formerly to continue therein.

You shall send an account to us and to our commissioners for trade and plantations of the present number of planters and inhabitants, men, women and children, as well masters as servants, free and unfree, and of the slaves in our said province, as also a yearly account of the increase or decrease of them, and how many of them are fit to bear arms in the militia of our said province.

You shall also cause an exact account to be kept of all persons born, christened, and buried, and you shall yearly send fair abstracts thereof to us and to our commissioners for trade and plantations, as aforesaid.

You are to take care that no mans life, member, freehold, or goods be taken away or harmed in our said province under your government, otherwise than by established and known laws, not repugnant to, but as much as may be agreeable to, the laws of England.

You shall take care that all planters and christian servants be well and fitly provided with arms and that they be listed under good officers, and when and as often as shall be thought fit, mustered and trained, whereby they may be in a better readiness for the defence of our province under your government. And you are to use your utmost endeavors that such planters do each of them keep such a number of white servants, as by law is directed, and that they appear in arms at all such times as they shall be required.

You are to take special care that neither the frequency nor unreasonableness of remote marches, musters, and trainings be an unnecessary impediment to the affairs of the inhabitants.

You shall not upon any occasion whatsoever establish or put in execution any articles of war, or other law martial, upon any of our subjects, inhabitants of our said province, without the advice and consent of our council there.

And whereas there is no power given you by your commission to execute martial law in time of peace upon soldiers in pay, and that nevertheless it may be necessary that some care be taken for the keeping of good discipline amongst those that we may at any time think fit to send into our said province, which may properly be provided for by the legislative power of the same, you are, therefore, to recommend to the general assembly of our said province that, if not already done, they prepare such act or law for the punishing of mutiny, desertion, and false musters and for the better preserving of good discipline among the said soldiers, as may best answer those ends.

And whereas upon complaints that have been made to us of the irregular proceedings of the captains of some of our ships of war in the pressing of seamen in several of our plantations; we have thought fit to order, and have given direction to our lord high admiral accordingly, that when any captain or commander of any of our ships of war in any of our said plantations shall have occasion for seamen to serve on board our ships under their command, they do make their application to the governors and commanders-in-chief of our plantations respectively, to whom, as vice admirals, we are pleased to commit the sole power of impressing seamen in any of our plantations in America, or in sight of any of them. You are, therefore, hereby required, upon such application made to you by any of the commanders of our said ships of war within our foresaid province under your government, to take care that our said ships of war be furnished with the number of seamen that may be necessary for our service on board them, from time to time.

You are to demand an account from all persons concerned, of the arms, ammunition, and stores sent to our said province under your government from our office of ordinance here, as likewise what other arms, ammunition and stores have been bought with the public money for the service of our said province, and how the same have been employed, and if any, how many of them have been sold, spent, lost, decayed, or disposed of, and to whom, and to what uses.

You shall take an inventory of all arms, ammunition, and stores remaining in any of our magazines or garrisons within our said province and territory, and transmit an account of them forthwith after your arrival, and the like account yearly to us and to our commissioners for trade and plantations.

You are to take especial care that fit store houses be settled throughout our said province for receiving and keeping of arms, ammunition, and other public stores.

Whereas it is absolutely necessary that we be exactly informed of the state of defense of all our plantations in every respect, and more especially with relation to the forts and fortifications that are in each plantation, and what more may be necessary to be built for the defense and security of the same, you are, so soon as possible after your arrival in your government, to prepare an account of the state of defense thereof in the most particular manner, and to transmit the same to us and to our commissioners for trade and plantations, and the like accounts afterwards yearly, in order to our exact information therein from time to time.

And whereas we have been constantly at great charge in sending thither and maintaining ships of war to cruise upon the coasts of that province, in order to their protection against enemies by sea, and have also lately been graciously pleased upon the desire of our council and the general assembly to assist them in this conjuncture with stores of war from our office of ordinance here, you are, therefore, the more earnestly to require and press our said council and the assembly vigorously to exert themselves in fortifying all places necessary for the security of our said province by land; more especially in rebuilding that important fort at Pemaquid, which they too easily suffered to be taken and demolished by the French during the late war; and in providing what else may be necessary in all respects for their further defense. In order whereunto you are also to cause a survey to be made of all the considerable landing places and harbors within our said province and, with the advice of our said council, to erect in any of them such fortifications as shall be necessary for their security and advantage.

In case of any distress of any other of our plantations, you shall, upon application of the respective governors thereof to you, assist them with what aid the condition and safety of your government can permit. And more especially, in case our province of New York be at any time invaded by an enemy, you are to call upon our council and the general assembly of the Massachusetts Bay to make good in men, or money in lieu thereof, their quota of assistance according to the repartition formerly sent thither; assuring them that in case of the like invasion of the province of Massachusets Bay they will be mutually assisted from New York.

You are, from time to time, to give an account, as before directed, what strength your neighbors have, be they Indians or others, by sea and land, and of the condition of their plantations and what correspondence you do keep with them.

And whereas, by our commission for the government of our said province of the Massachusets Bay, we have given you all the powers and authorities of any captain-general over our colonies of Rhode Island, Providence Plantation, and the Narraganset Country or Kings Province, our royal pleasure and intention is that in time of peace the militia within each of the said colonies be left to the government and disposition of the respective governors of the same. But so as that, nevertheless, in case of apparent danger, or other exigency, you do at all times take upon yourself the superior command of those forces, as in the said commission is directed.

And that we may be better informed of the trade of our said province, you are to take especial care that due entries be made in all ports of our said province of all goods and commodities, their species and quantities, imported and exported from thence, with the names, burden, and guns of all ships importing and exporting the same, also the names of their commanders, and likewise expressing from and to what places the said ships do come and go, a copy whereof the naval officer is to furnish you with; and you are to transmit the same to us, as before directed, to the commissioners of our treasury or our high treasurer for the time being, and to our commissioners for trade and plantations, quarterly, and duplicates thereof by the next conveyance.

And whereas we have been pleased to give orders for the commissionating of fit persons to be vice-admirals and officers of our admiralty and customs in our several plantations in America, and it is of great importance to the trade of this kingdom and to the welfare of our plantations that illegal trade be everywhere discouraged; you are to give all due countenance and encouragement to the said officers of our admiralty and customs in the execution of their respective offices and trusts.

You are to encourage the Indians upon all occasions, so that they may apply themselves to the English trade and nation rather than to any other.

You are to suppress the engrossing of commodities, as tending to the prejudice of that freedom which commerce and trade ought to have, and to settle such orders and regulations therein, with the advice of our said council, as may be most acceptable to the generality of the inhabitants.

You are to give all due encouragement and invitation to merchants and others who shall bring trade to our said province, or any way contribute to the advantage thereof, and in particular to the Royal African Company of England.

And you are to take care that there be no trading from our said province to any place in Africa within the charter of the Royal African Company otherwise then prescribed by the late act of Parliament, entitled, *An Act to Settle the Trade to Africa.*

You are not to grant commissions of marque or reprisals against any prince or state or their subjects in amity with us to any person whatsoever without our especial command.

You are, for the better administration of justice, to endeavour to get a law passed in the Assembly, if not already done, wherein shall be set the value of men's estates, either in goods or lands, under which they shall not be capable of serving as jurors.

You shall endeavour to get a law passed, if not already done, for the restraining of any inhumane severity, which by ill masters or overseers may be used towards their Christian servants and their slaves, and that provision be made therein that the willful killing of Indians and Negroes may be punished with death, and that a fit penalty be imposed for the maiming of them.

You are, with the assistance of the council and assembly, to find out and settle the best means to facilitate and encourage the conversion of Negroes and Indians to the Christian religion.

You are to recommend to the council and assembly the raising of stocks and building public workhouses in convenient places for the employing of poor and indigent people.

You are to propose an act to be passed in the assembly whereby the creditors of persons becoming bankrupts in England, and having estates in the Massachusets Bay, may be relieved and satisfied for the debts owing to them.

You are to take care, by and with the advice and assistance of our said council, that the prison there, if it want reparation, be forthwith repaired and put into and kept in such a condition as may sufficiently secure the prisoners that are or shall be there in custody of the provost marshal.

And for as much as great inconveniences may arise by the liberty of printing within our said province, you are to provide by all necessary orders that no person keep any press for printing, nor that any book, pamphlet, or other matters whatsoever be printed without your especial leave and license first obtained.

You are, upon all occasions, to send to us by one of our principal secretaries of state and to our commissioners for trade and plantations a particular account of all your proceedings and of the condition of affairs within your government.

You are, from time to time, to give to us and to our commissioners for trade and plantations, as aforesaid, an account of the wants and defects of our said province, what are the chief products thereof, what new improvements are made therein by the industry of the inhabitants or planters, and what further improvements you conceive may be made or advantages gained by trade, and which we may contribute thereunto.

If anything shall happen which may be of advantage or security of our said province under your government, which is not herein or by your commission provided for, we do hereby allow to you, with the advice and consent of our said province under your government, which is not herein or by your commission provided for, we do hereby allow to you, with the advice and consent of our said council, to take order for the present therein, giving to us by one of our principal secretaries of state and to our foresaid commissioners for trade and plantations speedy notice thereof, that so you may receive our confirmation, if we shall approve the same.

Provided always, and our will and pleasure is, that you do not, by color of any power or authority hereby given you, commence or declare war without our knowledge and particular commands therein, except it be against Indians upon emergencies, wherein the consent of our council shall be had and speedy notice thereof given to us.

Whereas we have been pleased by our commission to direct that in case of your death or absence from our said province, and in case there be at that time no person upon the place commissionated or appointed by us to be our lieutenant-governor or commander-in-chief, the then present council of our foresaid province of the Massachusets Bay shall take upon them the administration of the government and execute our said commission and the several powers and authorities therein contained, in the manner therein directed. It is, nevertheless, our express will and pleasure that in such case the said council shall forbear to pass any acts but what are immediately necessary for the peace and welfare of our said province, without our particular order for that purpose.

And whereas the lords spiritual and temporal in Parliament upon consideration of the great abuses practiced in the plantation trade, have by a humble address represented to the late king of glorious memory the great importance it is of, both to this our kingdom and to our plantations in America, that the many good laws which have been made for the government of the said plantations and particularly the act passed in the seventh and eighth years of the late king's reign entitled, *An Act for Preventing Frauds and Regulating Abuses in the Plantation Trade*, be strictly observed, you are, therefore, to take notice that, notwithstanding the many good laws made from time to time for preventing of frauds in the plantation trade, it is nevertheless manifest that great abuses have been and continue still to be practised to the prejudice of the same, which abuses must needs arise either from the insolvency of the persons who are accepted for security or from the remissness or connivance of such as have been or are governors in the several plantations, who ought to take care that those persons who give bond should be duly prosecuted in case of non performance, we take the good of our plantations and the improve-

ment of the trade thereof, by a strict and puctual observance of the several laws in force concerning the same, to be of so great importance to the benefit of this our kingdom and to the advancing of the duties of our customs here that if we shall be hereafter informed that at any time there shall be any failure in the due observance of those laws within our foresaid province of the Massachusetts bay, by any willful fault or neglect on your part, we shall look upon it as a breach of the trust reposed in you by us, which we shall punish with the loss of your place in that government, and such further marks of our displeasure as we shall judge reasonable to be inflicted upon you for your offense against us, in a matter of this consequence that we now so particularly charge you with.

By her Majesty's Command
Manchester.

Reference: Collections, Massachusetts Historical Society, 3rd Ser., Vol. IX (Boston: Charles C. Little and James Brown, 1801), 102–116.

EXPLANATORY CHARTER FOR MASSACHUSETTS BAY, AUGUST 26, 1725

George, by the grace of God, of Great Britain, France, and Ireland, king, Defender of the Faith, etc. To all to whom these presents shall come greeting.

Whereas our late royal predecessors, William and Mary, King and Queen of England, etc., did, by their letters patents under their Great Seal of England bearing date at Westminster the seventh day of October in the third year of their reign, for themselves, their heirs and successors, unite, erect, and incorporate the territories and colonies commonly called or known by the names of the colony of the Massachusetts Bay and colony of New Plymouth, the Province of Maine, the territory called Acadia or Nova Scotia, and all that tract of land lying between the said territories of Nova Scotia and the said Province of Maine into one real province by the name of Our province of the Massachusetts Bay in New England. And whereas their said late majesties, King William and Queen Mary, did, by the said recited letters

patents, amongst other things therein contained, for themselves, their heirs and successors, ordain and grant that there should and might be convened, held, and kept by the governor for the time being, upon every last Wednesday in the month of May every year forever and at all such other times as the governor of their said province should think fit and appoint, a great and general court or assembly, which said great and general court or assembly should consist of the governor and council or assistants for the time being and of such freeholders of their said province or territory as should be from time to time elected or deputed by the major part of the freeholders and other inhabitants of the respective towns or places who should be present at such elections each of the said towns and places, being, thereby, empowered to elect and depute two persons and no more to serve for and represent them respectively in the said great and general court or assembly; and that the governor for the time being should have full power and authority from time to time as he should judge necessary to adjourn, prorogue, and dissolve all great and general courts or assemblies met and convened, as aforesaid; and did, thereby, also, for themselves, their heirs and successors, provide, establish, and ordain that in the framing and passing of all orders, laws, statutes and ordinances and in all elections and acts of government whatsoever to be passed, made, or done by the said general court or assembly or in council the governor of the said province or territory of the Massachusets Bay in New England for the time being should have the negative voice, and that without his consent or approbation signified and declared in writing no such orders, laws, statutes, ordinances, elections, or other acts of government whatsoever so to be made, passed, or done by the said general assembly or in council should be of any force effect or validity, anything therein contained to the contrary in any wise notwithstanding, as in and by the said letters patents, relation being thereunto had, may more fully and at large appear. And whereas no provision is made by the said recited letters patents touching the nomination and election of a speaker of the representatives assembled in any great and general court of our said province, nor any particular reservation made of the right of us, our heirs and successors, to approve or disapprove of such speaker by the governor of the said province appointed, or to be appointed by us or them, for the time being; and no power is granted by the said recited letters patents to the said House of Representatives to adjourn themselves for any time whatsoever, by means whereof, divers doubts and controversies have arisen within our said province to the interruption of the public business thereof and the obstruction of our service. Know you, therefore, that for removing the said doubts and controversies and preventing the like mischiefs for the future, and also for the further explanation of the said recited letters patents, we, of our especial grace, certain knowledge, and mere

motion, have granted, ordained, and appointed, and by these presents, for us, our heirs and successors, do will, grant, ordain, and appoint that for ever hereafter the representatives assembled in any great or general court of our said province to be hereafter summoned shall, upon the first day of their assembling, elect a fit person out of the said representatives to be speaker of the House of Representatives in such general court; and that the person so elected shall, from time to time, be presented to the governor of our said province for the time being or in his absence to the lieutenant-governor or commander-in-chief respectively. We do hereby for us, our heirs and successors give full power and authority to approve or disapprove of the person so elected and presented, which approbation or disapprobation shall be signified by him by message in writing under his hand to the said House of Representatives. And in case such governor, lieutenant-governor, or commander-in-chief shall disapprove of the person so elected, and presented, being approved, as aforesaid, shall happen to die or by sickness or otherwise be disabled from officiating, in every such case the said representatives so assembled shall forthwith elect another person to be speaker of the House of Representatives, to be presented and approved or disapproved in manner as aforesaid, and so from time to time as often as the person so elected and presented shall be disapproved of or happen to die or become disabled, as aforesaid. And our further will and pleasure is, and we do by these presents of our more abundant grace, for us, our heirs and successors, grant, ordain, and appoint that it shall and may be lawfull to and for the representatives assembled in any great court or general court of our said province for the time being, forever hereafter, to adjourn themselves from day to day, and if occasion shall require, for the space of two days without leave from the governor, or, in his absence, from the lieutenant-governor or commander-in-chief of our said province for the time being first had and obtained in that behalf, anything in the said recited letters patents contained to the contrary thereof in any wise notwithstanding. Provided always, that nothing in these presents contained shall extend or be construed to extend, to revoke, alter, or prejudice the power and authority by the said recited letters patents granted to the governor of the said province for the time being to adjourn, prorogue, and dissolve all great and general courts or assemblies of our said province. And lastly we do, by these presents, for us, our heirs and successors, grant that these our letters patents, or the enrollment or exemplification thereof, shall be in and by all things good, firm, valid, and effectual in the law, according to the true intent and meaning thereof; notwithstanding the not rightly or fully reciting, mentioning, or describing the said recited letters patents or the date thereof, or any other omission, imperfection, defect, matter cause, or thing whatsoever to the contrary thereof in any wise notwithstanding. In witness whereof, we have caused these our letters to be made patents. Witness, William, Archbishop of Canterbury, and the rest of the guardians and justices of the kingdom at Westminster, the six and twentieth day of August in the twelfth year of our reign.

References: Francis Newton Thorpe (ed.), *The Federal and State Constitutions, Colonial Charters, and Other Organic Laws of the States,* Vol. III (Washington: GPO, 1909), 1886–1888.

ACT FOR REGULATING TOWNSHIPS AND CHOICE OF TOWN OFFICERS, JANUARY 15, 1742

Whereas in and by an act made in the fourth year of the reign of King William and Queen Mary, [e][i]ntitled "An Act for regulating of townships, choice of town officers, and setting forth their power," the freeholders and inhabitants of each town who are rateable at twenty pounds estate to one single rate besides the poll, are impow[e]red to assemble and to give their votes in choice of town officers in the month of March annually, but no rule of valuation is therein prescribed, whereby such estate, qualifying to vote as aforesaid, shall be estimated, nor is it declared whether the like estate shall qualify a voter in other town affairs; and there being no law of this province expresly setting forth and ascertaining the qualification of voters in precincts and parishes, by reason of which many doubts and controversies have arisen; for preventing whereof for the future,—

Be it enacted by the Governo[u]r, Council and House of Represent-[ati]ves,

[SECT. 1.] That henceforward no person shall be deemed duly qualified or be admitted to vote in the choice of officers, or in the other affairs to be transacted at any meeting of the town, precinct or parish where he dwells, but such only who are personally present at such meeting, and have a rateable estate in such town or district, besides the poll, amounting to the value of twenty pounds, by the following method of estimation; viz[t]., real estate to be set at so much only as the rents or income thereof for the space of six years would amount to were it let at a reasonable rate; and personal estate and faculty to be estimated according to the rule of valuation prescribed in the act from time to time made for apportioning and assessing publick taxes.

And be it further enacted,

[SECT. 2.] That when any dispute shall arise respecting the qualifications of any person offering his vote in any such publick meeting, the same shall be determined by the moderator of such meeting according to the list and valuation of estates and faculties of persons, in such town or district, last made by assessors under oath; and if it thereby appear that such person is not qualified as by this act is provided, his vote shall not be received: *provided,* that the value of lands leased shall not be reckoned to qualify the ter-tenant, but to qualify the lessor if he be an inhabitant in such town, precinct or parish.

Provided also,—

[SECT. 3.] That when such dispute shall happen to arise in any town, precinct or parish meeting, before a moderator shall be chosen, in such case the major part of the selectmen then present, or of the precinct or parish committee, shall, respectively, determine the same in manner as aforesaid; and the assessors of each town and district are hereby required to lodge with the clerk of their respective towns and districts an attested copy of such their list and valuation from year to year, which he shall produce for the purpose afores[ai]d as there shall be occasion; and every assessor, belonging to such town or precinct where the inhabitants are not usually doomed, neglecting his duty herein, shall forfeit and pay the sum of forty shillings, to be recovered before any of his majesty's justices of the peace of the same county.

And be it further enacted,

[SECT. 4.] That if the moderator of any such meeting shall countenance and permit any person not qualified as aforesaid, whose qualification for voting has been called in question, to give his voice in any such meeting, he shall forfeit and pay the sum of five pounds; and whosoever shall presume to put in more than one vote at a time shall forfeit and pay the sum of five pounds; one moiety of the said forfeitures to be for the use of the poor of the town where the offence shall be committed, and the other moiety to him or them that shall inform or sue for the same in any of his majesty's courts of record.

And whereas several towns of the province do not give in an exact account of their rateable estate, and so the assessors are obliged to doom the inhabitants according to the best of their skill and judgment, whereby the qualification of voters in such places may be more difficult to come at; wherefore,—

Be it enacted,

[SECT. 5.] That where a full invoice and valuation of the rateable estates in any town or district is not taken, and the assessors, on oath, do doom the inhabitants, those persons only shall be allowed to vote who are rated two-third parts so much for their estates and faculties as for one single poll, in the last tax of such town or district, respectively.

Provided always,—

[SECT. 6.] That nothing in this act shall be interpreted to exclude any person[s] from the privilege of voting in the choice of representatives, who are duly qualified therefor according to the royal charter.

[SECT. 7.] This act to continue for the space of four years, and no longer. [*Passed January* 15; *published January* 17, 1742–43.]

Reference: *The Acts and Resolves, Public and Private, of the Province of Massachusetts Bay*, Vol. III (Boston: Albert J. Wright, 1878).

ACT EMPOWERING SELECTMEN OF LEXINGTON TO CALL TOWN MEETINGS, APRIL 27, 1757

A PETITION of John Clapham of Lexington, setting forth That he was chosen Constable for said Town in the year, 1757, and has Collected part of the Rates, That he is now engaged in his Majesty's Service, being Adjutant to Col Nichols's Regiment, and hath inlisted fifteen Men; And praying that the Selectmen of Lexington may be impowered to appoint some other person in his stead to Collect the remainder of the Taxes.

Read and

Ordered That the prayer of this petition be so far granted, as that the Selectmen of Lexington be and they hereby are impowered forthwith to call a Meeting of said Town of Lexington (if they see

cause) to choose a Constable in the room of the petitioner to finish the Collecting of the Assessments committed to him; The Petitioner first returning the Assessments and Warrants for Collecting said Taxes to the said Selectmen with an Account of what part of the Taxes he has gathered and paying in the same to the several Treasurers to whom said Assessments are payable, And the Constable so chosen shall receive said Assessments with proper Warrants for Collecting and paying the same. [*Passed April 27.*]

Reference: *The Acts and Resolves, Public and Private, of the Province of Massachusetts Bay*, Vol. XVI (Boston: Albert J. Wright, 1909), 490.

17

Maryland

In July 1689, the colonial militia took control of the Maryland government, ousted the proprietary governor, and for a time dispensed with proprietary government. The crown seemed to support the end of Roman Catholic proprietary governance. In 1691, the crown's Governor Lionel Copley received specific instructions as to his duties but the lower house of the assembly set the governor's salary, thus making him beholden to the colonials. Around 1715 the Calvert proprietor became a Protestant, and a reduced proprietary government was restored to Maryland. The proprietor now selected the governor, but the assembly continued to set the governor's salary and controlled the colony's taxing system. Maryland, then, did not quite have the same struggles between governor and the legislature as did the royal colonies, but tensions over the division of powers continued until the Revolution. Roman Catholics still were denied the vote and participation in governance but they nonetheless prepared to enter government affairs once their restrictions were lifted.

Maryland continued to develop its governance system throughout the eighteenth century. In 1751 the Assembly passed an act that expanded the Protestant freeholder franchise, set expenses for Assembly members, and affirmed the duties of the growing judicial system. In 1753, questions arose about having a colonial agent in England to vie with the governor's voice there. These questions resulted in a letter from the Assembly to English authorities demanding the privilege of selecting local judges. The lower house strenuously resisted yet deferred to the powers of the upper house (Governor's Council). In an act of 1753 the Assembly defended its rights over local governance. Most important for governance in the future, in 1753 the Assembly passed a law providing for immediate publication of colonial statutes. Henceforth, the freeholders right to know the laws and to react to legislative activities was made easier. Open proceedings in governance heralded the voters' rights to information concerning their interests

ROYAL SEIZURE OF MARYLAND GOVERNMENT, JULY 25, 1689

The Declaration of the Reason and Motive for the Present Appearing in Arms of his Majesties' Protestant Subjects in the Province of Maryland.

Although the nature and state of affairs relating to the government of this province is so well and notoriously known to all persons anyway concerned in the same, as to the people inhabitants here who are more immediately interested, as might excuse any declaration or apology for this present inevitable appearance; yet forasmuch as, by the plot, contrivances, insinuations, remonstrances, and subscriptions carried on, suggested, extorted, and obtained by the Lord Baltimore, his deputies, representatives, and officers here, the injustice and tyranny under which we groan is palliated and most if not all the particulars of our grievances shrouded from the eyes of observation and the hand of redress, we thought fit, for general satisfaction and particularly to undeceive those that may have a sinister account of our proceedings, to publish this declaration of the reasons and motives inducing us thereunto. His Lordship's right and title to the government is, by virtue of a charter to his father Cecilius from King Charles the First of blessed memory, how his present Lordship has managed the power and authority given and granted in the same we could mourn and lament only in silence, would our duty to God, our allegiance to his vice regent, and the care and welfare of ourselves and posterity permit us.

In the first place, in the said charter is a reservation of the faith and allegiance due to the Crown of England, the province and inhabitants being immediately subject thereunto, but how little that is manifested is too obvious to all unbiased persons that ever had anything to do here; the very name and owning of that sovereign power is some times crime enough to incur the frown of our superiors and to render our persons obnoxious and suspected to be ill-affected to the government; the ill usage of and affronts to the King's officers belonging to the customs here were a sufficient argument of this. We need but instance the business of Mr. Badcock and Mr. Rousby, of whom the former was terribly detained by his Lordship from going home to make his just complaints in England, upon which he was soon taken sick and 'twas more then probably conjectured that the conceit of his confinement was the chief cause of his death which soon after happened. The latter was barbariously murdered upon the execution of his office by one that was an Irish papist and our chief governor.

Allegiance here by those persons under whom we suffer is little talked of, other than what they would have done and sworn to to his Lordship the Lord Proprietary, for it was very lately owned by the President himself, openly enough in the Upper House of Assembly, that fidelity to his Lordship was allegiance and that the denying of the one was the same thing with the refusal or denial of the other. In that very oath of fidelity that was then imposed under the penalty of banishment there is not so much as the least word or intimation of any duty, faith, or allegiance to be reserved to our sovereign lord the King of England.

How the *jus regale* is improved here and made the prerogative of his Lordship is so sensibly felt by us all in that absolute authority exercised over us, and by the greatest part of the inhabitants in the service of their persons, forfeiture and loss of their goods, chattels, freeholds, and inheritances.

In the next place, churches and chapels, which by the said charter should be built and consecrated according to the ecclesiastical laws of the kingdom of England, to our great regret and discouragement of our religion are erected and converted to the use of popish idolatry and superstition. Jesuits and seminary priests are the only incumbents; for which there is a supply provided by sending our popish youth to be educated at St. Omers, as also the chief advisers and councilers in affairs of government, and the richest and most fertile land set apart for their use and maintenance, while other lands that are piously intended and given for the maintenance of the protestant ministry become escheats and not taken as forfeit, the ministers themselves discouraged, and no care taken for their subsistence.

The power to enact laws is another branch of his Lordship's authority, but how well that has been executed and circumstances is too notorious. His present Lordship, upon the death of his father, in order thereunto sent out writs for four, as was over the usage, for each county to serve as representatives of the people. But when elected there were two of each respective four picked out and summoned to that convention, whereby many laws were made and the greatest levy yet known laid upon the inhabitants. The next session the house was filled up with the remaining two that was left out of the former in which there were many and the best of our laws enacted to the great benefit and satisfaction of the people. But his Lordship soon after dissolved and declared the best of these laws, such as he thought fit, null and void by proclamation. Notwithstanding, they were assented to in his Lordship's name by the Governor in his absence, and he himself some time personally acted and governed by the same, so that the question in our courts of judicature, in any point that relates to many of our laws, is not so much the relation it has to the said laws, but whether the laws themselves be agreeable to the pleasure and approbation of his Lordship. Whereby our liberty and property is become uncertain and under the arbitrary disposition of the judge and commissioners of our courts of justice.

The said assembly being some time after dissolved by proclamation, another was elected and met consisting only of two members for each county, directly opposite to an act of Assembly for four, in which several laws with his Lordship's personal assent were enacted, among the which, one for the encouragement of trade and erecting of towns. But the execution of that act was soon after, by proclamation from his Lordship out of England, suspended the last year, and all officers, military and civil, severely prohibited executing and inflicting the penalties of the same. Notwithstanding which suspension being in effect a dissolution and abrogating of the whole act, the income of three pence per hogshead to the government, by the said act payable for every hogshead of tobacco exported, is carefully exacted and collected. How fatal and of what pernicious consequence that unlimited and arbitrary pretended authority may be to the inhabitants is too apparent, but by considering that by the same reason all the use of the laws, whereby our liberties and properties subsist, are subject to the same arbitrary disposition, and if timely remedy be not had must stand or fall according to his Lordship's good will and pleasure.

Nor is this nullifying and suspending power the only grievance that does perplex and burthen us in relation to laws, but these laws that are of a certain and unquestioned acceptation are executed and countenanced as they are more or less agreeable to the good liking of our Governor in particular. One very good law provides that orphan children should be disposed of to persons of the same religion with that of their dead parents. In direct opposition to which, several children of Protestants have been committed to the tutelage of papists and brought up in the Romish superstition. We could instance in a young woman that has been lately forced by order of council from her husband, committed to the custody of a papist and brought up in his religion.

'Tis endless to enumerate the particulars of this nature, while on the contrary those laws that enhance the grandeur and income of his said Lordship are severely imposed and executed, especially one that is against all sense, equity, reason, and law punishes all speeches, practices, and attempts relating to his Lordship and government that shall be thought mutinous and seditious by the judge of the provincial court, with either whipping, branding, boring through the tongue, fines, imprisonments, banishment, or death, all or either of the said punishments at the discretion of the said judges, who have given a very recent and remarkable proof of their authority in each particular punishment aforesaid, upon several the good people of this province, while the rest are in the same danger to have their words and actions liable to the construction and punishment of the said judges, and their lives and fortunes to the mercy of their arbitrary fancies, opinions, and sentences.

To these grievances are added excessive officers' fees, and that too under execution directly against the law made and provided to redress the same, wherein there is no probability of a legal remedy, the officers themselves that are parties and culpable being judges. The like fee being imposed upon and extorted from masters and owners of vessels trading into this province, without any law to justify the same and directly against the plain words of the said charter that say there shall be no imposition or assessment without the consent of the freemen in the assembly, to the great obstruction of trade and prejudice of the inhabitants.

The like excessive fees imposed upon and extorted from the owners of vessels that are built here or do really belong to the inhabitants, contrary to an act of Assembly made and provided for the same wherein moderate and reasonable fees are ascertained for the promoting and encouragement of shipping and navigation amongst ourselves.

The frequent pressing of men, horses, boats, provisions, and other necessaries in time of peace and often to gratify private designs and occasions, to the great burthen and regret of the inhabitants, contrary to law and several acts of Assembly in that case made and provided.

The service and apprehending of protestants in their houses with armed force consisting of papists, and that in time of peace, thence hurrying them away to prisons without warrant or cause of committment; these kept and confined with popish guards a long time without trial.

Not only private but public outrages and murders committed and done by papists upon protestants without redress, but rather connived at and tolerated by the chief in authority, and indeed it were in vain to desire or expect any help or other measures from them, being papists, and guided by the councils and instigation of the Jesuits, either in these or any other grievances or oppresions. And yet these are the men that are our chief judges at the common law, in chancery, of the probate of wills, and the affairs of administration in the Upper House of Assembly, and chief military officers and commanders of our forces being still the same individual persons in all these particular qualifications and places.

These and many more even infinite pressures and calamities, we have hitherto lain with patience under and submitted to, hoping that the same hand of providence that has sustained us under them would at length in due time release us. And now at length, forasmuch as it has pleased almighty God, by means of the great prudence and conduct of the best of princes, our most gracious King William, to put a check to that great inundation of slavery and popery that had like to overwhelm their Majesties' protestant subjects in all their territories and dominions, of which none have suffered more or are in greater danger than ourselves, we hoped and expected in our particular stations and qualifications a proportionable show in so great a blessing.

But our greatest grief and consternation, upon the first news of the great overture and happy change in England, we found ourselves surrounded with strong and violent endeavors from our governors here, being the Lord Baltimore's deputies and representatives, to defeat us of the same.

We still find all the means used by these very persons and their agents, Jesuits, priests, and lay papists, that are of malice, can suggest to devise the obedience and loyalty of the inhabitants from their most sacred Majesties' to that height of impudence, solemn masses and prayers are used, as we have very good information, in their chapels and oratories for the prosperous success of the popish forces in Ireland and the French designs against England, whereby they would involve us in the same crime of disloyalty with themselves and render us obnoxious to the insupportable displeasure of their Majesties.

We, everywhere, have not only public protestations against their Majesties' rights and possessions of the Crown of England, but their most illustrious persons vilified and aspected with the worst and most traitorous expressions of obloquy and detraction.

We are every day threatened with the loss of our lives, liberties, and estates, of which we have great reason to think ourselves in eminent danger by the practices and machinations that are on foot to betray us to the French, northern and other Indians, of which some have been dealt withal and others invited to assist in our destruction, well-remembering the incursion and invade of the said northern Indians in the year 1681, who were conducted into the heart of this province by French Jesuits and lay sore upon us while the representatives of the country, then in the Assembly, were severely pressed upon by our superiors to yield them an unlimited and tyrannical power in the affairs of the militia. As so great a piece of villany cannot be the result but of the worst of principles, so we should, with the greatest difficulty, believe it to be true if undeniable evidence and circumstances did not convince us.

Together with the promises we have, with all due thinking and deliberation, considered the endeavors that are making to disunite us among ourselves, to make and inflame differences in our neighbor colony of Virginia, from whose friendship, vicinity, great loyalty, and sameness of religion we may expect assistance in our greatest necessity. We have considered that all the other branches of their Majesties' dominions in this part of the world, as well as we could be informed, have done their duty in proclaiming and asserting their undoubted right in these and all other their Majesties' territories and counties.

But above all, with due and mature deliberation, we have reflected upon that vast gratitude and duty, incumbent likewise upon us, to our sovereign lord and lady the King and Queen's most Excellent Majesties, in which as it would not be safe for us so it will not suffer us to be silent in so great and general a jubilee, withal considering and looking upon ourselves discharged, dissolved, and free from all manner of duty, obligation, or fidelity to the Deputy Governor or Chief Magistrate here as such, they having departed from their allegiance, upon which alone our said duty and fidelity to them depends, and by their complices and agents, aforesaid, endeavored the destruction of our religion, lives, liberties, and properties, all which they are bound to protect.

These are the reasons, motives, and considerations which we do declare have induced us to take up arms to preserve, vindicate, and assert the sovereign dominion and right of King William and Queen Mary to this province, to defend the Protestant religion among us, and to protect and shelter the inhabitants from all manner of violence, oppression, and destruction that is plotted and designed against them; the which we do solemnly declare and protest we have no designs or intentions whatsoever.

For the more effectual accomplishment of which, we will take due care that a full and free assembly be called and convened with all possible expedition, by whom we may likewise have our condition, circumstances, and our most dutiful addresses represented and tendered to their Majesties, from whose great wisdom, justice, and special care of the Protestant religion we may reasonably and comfortably hope to be delivered from our present calamity and for the future be secured under a just and legal administration from being ever more subjected to the yoke of arbitrary government of tyranny and popery.

we will take care and do promise that no person now in arms with us, or that shall come to assist us, shall commit any outrage or do any violence to any person whatsoever that shall be found peaceable and quiet and not oppose us in our said just and necessary designs, and that there shall be a just and due satisfaction made for provisions and other necessaries had and received from the inhabitants, and the soldiers punctually and duly paid in such ways and methods as have been formerly accustomed or by law ought to be.

And we do, lastly, invite and require all manner of persons whatsoever, residing or inhabiting in this province, as they tender their allegiance, the Protestant religion, their lives, fortunes, and families, to aid and assist us in this our undertaking.

Given under our hands, Maryland, the 25th day of July in the first year of their Majesties reign, *anno.domini* 1689.

Reference: W.H. Browne, et al. (eds.), *Archives of Maryland*, Vol. VIII (Baltimore: Maryland Historical Society, 1883–1912), 101–110.

INSTRUCTIONS TO GOVERNOR OF MARYLAND, AUGUST 26, 1691

Instructions for our trusty and well-beloved Lionel Copley, Esquire, our Captain-General and Governor-in-Chief in and over our province and territory of Maryland in America, and in his absence to the governor or commander-in-chief of our said province for the time being.

26th August, 1691.

With these our instructions you will receive our commission under our great seal of England constituting you our Captain-General and Governor-in-Chief in and over our province and territory of Maryland in America, where being arrived you are forthwith to call together the members of our Council for that our province and territory, by name, Sir Thomas Lawrence, Knight and Baronet, Henry Jowles, Nehemiah Blakiston, Nicholas Greenbury, Charles Hutchins, Charles Robotham, David Browne, Thomas Tench, John Addison, John Coates, James Frizby, and Thomas Brooks, Esquire. At which meeting, after having published in usual manner our said commission constituting you our Captain-General and Governor-in-Chief of our said province and territory, you shall take yourself and also administer unto each of the members of our said council as well the oaths appointed by act of Parliament to be taken instead of the oaths of allegiance and supremacy and the test, as the oath for the due execution of their places and trust.

You are to communicate unto our said Council from time to time such and so many of our instructions as you shall find convenient for our service to be imparted unto them.

Our will and pleasure is that the members of our Council shall and may have and enjoy freedom of debate and votes in all things to be debated of in council.

And although by our commission aforesaid we have thought fit to direct that any three of our councilors make a quorum, it is, nevertheless, our will and pleasure that you do not act with a quorum of less than five members unless upon extraordinary emergencies.

And that we may be always informed of the names and characters of persons fit to supply the vacancies of our said council, you are to transmit unto us, by one of our principal secretaries of state and to the Lords of our Privy Council appointed a Committee of Trade and Plantations, with all convenient speed, the names and characters of twelve persons, inhabitants of our said province, whom you shall esteem the best qualified to succeed in that trust and so from time to time when any of them shall die, depart out of our said province, or become otherwise unfit, you are to nominate so many other persons to us in their stead. And in the choice and nomination of the

members of our said council as also of the principal officers, judges, assistants, justices, and sheriffs, you are always to take care that they be men of estate and ability and not necessitous people or much in debt and that they be persons well-affected to our government.

You are not to suspend the members of our Council without good and sufficient cause; and in case of suspension of any of them, you are forthwith to transmit unto us, as aforesaid, and to our Committee for Trade and Plantations your reasons for so doing, together with the charges and proofs against the said persons and their answers thereunto.

You are, from time to time, to send unto us and to our said committee the names and qualities of any members by you put into our said Council by the first conveniency after your so doing.

You are to transmit authentic copies under the public seal of all laws, statutes, and ordinances now in force or which at any time shall be made and enacted within our said province unto us and our Committee for Trade and Foreign Plantations within three months or sooner after their being enacted, together with duplicates thereof, by the next conveyance, upon pain of our highest displeasure and the forfeiture of that year's wherein you shall, at any time or upon any pretense whatsoever, omit to send over the said laws and ordinances, as aforesaid, within the time above limited.

And that it may be better understood what acts and laws are in force in our province of Maryland, you are, with the assistance of our Council, to take care that all laws now in force be revised and considered and if there be anything either in the matter or style of them which may be fit to be retrenched or altered, you are to represent the same unto us with your opinion touching the said laws now in force, whereof you are to send a complete body to us, with such alterations as you shall think requisite, to the end our approbation or disallowance may be signified thereupon.

You shall take care that the members of the Assembly be elected only by freeholders as being most agreeable to the custom of England, to which you are as near as may be to conform yourself.

And you shall reduce the salary of the members of the Assembly to such a moderate proportion as may be no grievance to the country, wherein, nevertheless, you are to use your discretion so as no inconvenience may arise thereby.

You are to take care that no man's life, member, freehold, or goods be taken away or harmed in our said province, but by established and known laws not repugnant to, but as much as may be agreeable to, the laws of our kingdom of England.

You shall administer or cause to be administered the oaths appointed by act of Parliament to be taken instead of the oaths of allegiance and supremacy and the test unto the members and officers of our Council and Assembly, all judges and justices, and all other persons that hold any office in our said province by virtue of any patent under our great seal of England or the public seal of Maryland. And you are to permit a liberty of conscience to all persons so they be contented with a quiet and peaceable enjoyment of it, not giving offense or scandal to the government.

You are not to pass any act or order within that our province, in any case, for levying money and inflicting fines and penalties whereby the same shall not be reserved to us for the public uses, as by the said act or order shall be directed. And we do particularly require and command that no money or value of money whatsoever be given or granted by any act or order of Assembly to any governor, lieutenant-governor, or commander-in-chief of our said province which shall not, according to the style of acts of Parliament in England, be mentioned to be given and granted unto us with the humble desire of such assemblies that the same be applied to the use and behoof of such governor, lieutenant-governor, or commander-in-chief, if we shall so think fit, or, if we shall not approve of such gift or application, that the said money or value of money be then disposed of and appropriated to such other uses as in the said act or order shall be mentioned and that from the time the same shall be raised it remain in the hands of the receiver or receivers of that our province until our royal pleasure shall be known therein.

And whereas we are willing, in the best manner, to provide for the support of our government in Maryland by setting apart sufficient allowance to such as shall be our lieutenant-governor or commander-in-chief for the time being within the same, our will and pleasure, therefore, is that when it shall happen that you shall be absent from our said province, one full moiety of your salary and of all perquisites and emoluments whatsoever, which should otherwise become due unto you during the time of your absence, shall be paid and satisfied unto such lieutenant-governor or commander-in-chief who shall be resident upon the place for the time being, which we do hereby order and allot to him for the better maintenance and for the support of the dignity of that our government. Our will and pleasure is that all public monies raised or to be raised within our said province and territory of Maryland for the use and support of the government there by issued out by warrant from you by and with the advice and consent of the Council and not otherwise.

And whereas by an act passed in the Assembly in Maryland the thirtieth day of April, 1679, an impost of two shillings per hogshead is laid upon all tobacco exported out of our said province, one moiety of which impost is by the said act appropriated for the use and support of the government, our will and pleasure is that towards the maintenance in the government of our said province you take to your own use three-fourth parts of the said moiety of the impost of two shillings per hogshead of tobacco, appropriated as aforementioned by the said act, and you are to take especial care that, according to the intention of the said act, the remaining fourth part of the moiety of the said impost be duly applied towards the maintaining a constant magazine with arms and ammunition for the defense of our said province.

And that an exact account be made up of what has been received of the said impost since the meeting of the late convention in Maryland until the time of your arrival in our said province, and that the same be transmitted into our Committee of Trade and Plantations and commissioners of our Treasury for our information.

And you are further to recommend to the Assembly, in our name, the raising of such other supplies from time to time as may be sufficient for the better support of you our Governor, or our governor-in-chief for the time being, and for defraying the necessary charges of the government.

You are to permit the Lord Baltimore, by his agents or officers appointed by him, to collect and receive the other moiety of the said impost of two shillings per hogshead, together with the duty of 14 pence per ton upon shipping trading to Maryland, for his own use as proprietary of our said province. And you are not in anywise yourself, or any other by your order, to intermeddle with the said moiety of the said impost of two shillings per hogshead or the said duty of fourteen pence per ton, but to permit the same to be collected and received by the Lord Baltimore or his agents, as aforesaid, without any hindrance or molestation whatsoever.

You are, from time to time, to permit the Assembly to view and examine the account of money or value of money disposed of by virtue of such laws as are now in force or shall be passed by them, which you to signify unto them as occasion shall serve. Our express will and pleasure is that all laws whatsoever for the good government and support of your said province be made indefinite and without limitation of time, except the same be for a temporary end which shall expire and have its full effect within a certain time. And, therefore, you shall not enact any law which shall be once enacted by you except upon very urgent occasions, but in no case more than once without our express consent.

You shall not remit any fines or forfeitures whatsoever above the sum of ten pounds before or after sentence given, nor dispose of any escheats, fines, or forfeitures until you upon signifying unto our Committee of Trade and Plantations and to the commissioners of our Treasury for the time being the nature of the offense or occasion of such fines, forfeitures, or escheats with the particular sums you shall have received our directions

therein. But you may, in the meantime, suspend the payment of the said fines and forfeitures.

You shall not permit any act or order to pass within our said province whereby the price or value of current money within your government may be altered, without our particular leave or direction therein. And you are particularly not to pass any law or do any act by grant, settlement, or otherwise, whereby our revenue may be lessened or impaired without our especial leave or commands therein. You are to require the secretary of our province, or his deputy for the time being, to provide transcripts of all such acts and public orders as shall be made from time to time, together with a copy of the journal of the Council, to the end the same may be transmitted unto us as above directed, which he is duly to perform upon pain of incurring the forfeiture of his place.

You shall not displace any of the judges, justices, sheriffs, or other officers or ministers within our said province without good and sufficient cause, to be signified to us and our Committee of Plantations; nor shall you execute yourself or by deputy any of the said offices nor suffer any person to execute more offices than one by deputy.

You shall not erect any court or office of judicature not before erected and established without our especial order, and you are to transmit unto us, with all convenient speed, a particular account of all establishments of jurisdictions, courts, offices, and officers, powers, authorities, fees, and privileges granted or settled within our said province, to the end you may receive our especial direction therein. You shall likewise take especial care, with the advice and consent of our said Council, to regulate all salaries and fees belonging to places or paid upon emergencies, that they be within the bounds of moderation and that no exaction be made upon any occasion whatsoever.

And that God Almighty may be more inclined to bestow his blessing upon us and you in the welfare and improvement of that our province, you shall take especial care that he be devoutly and duly served within your government, the Book of Common Prayer, as it is now established, read each Sunday and holiday, and the blessed sacrament administered according to the rites of the Church of England. You shall take care that the churches already built there shall be well and orderly kept and more built as the colony shall, by God's blessing, be improved, and that besides a competent maintenance to be assigned to the minister of each church, a convenient house be built at the common charge for each minister. You are not to prefer any minister to any ecclesiastical benefice in that our province without a certificate from the Right Reverend the Bishop of London of his being conformable to the doctrine and discipline of the Church of England and of a good life and conversation, and if any person already preferred shall appear to you to give scandal either by his doctrine or manners you are to use the best means for the removal of him and to supply the vacancy in such manner as we have directed. And you are to give order forthwith, if the same be not already done, that every orthodox minister within your government be one of the vestry in his respective parish and that no vestry be held without him, except in case of sickness or that after notice of a vestry summoned he absent himself. And you are to inquire whether there be any minister within your government who preaches and administers the sacrament in any orthodox church or chapel without being in due orders, whereof you are to give an account to the said Bishop of London.

And to the end the ecclesiastical jurisdiction of the said Bishop of London may take place in that our province as far as conveniently may be, we do think fit that you give all countenance and encouragement in the exercise of the same, excepting only the collating to benefices, granting licenses for marriage, and probate of wills, which we have reserved to you our Governor or the commander-in-chief for the time being. You are to take care that a table of marriages established by the Church of England be hung up in every orthodox church and duly observed and to endeavor to get a law, if the same be not already passed in the Assembly, for the strict observation of the said table.

You are to take care that drunkenness and debauchery, swearing and blasphemy be severely punished and that none be admitted to public trust and employment whose ill-fame and conversation

may bring scandal thereupon. You shall take care that all planters and christian servants be well and fitly provided with arms and that they be listed under officers and when and as often as you shall think fit, mustered and trained, whereby they may be in a better readiness for the defense of our said colony and dominion under your government. You are to take especial care that neither the frequency nor unreasonableness of remote marches, musters, and trainings be an unnecessary impediment to the affairs of the planters.

And for the greater security of that our province, you are to appoint fit officers and commanders in the several parts of the country bordering upon the Indians, who, upon any invasion, may raise men and arms to oppose them until they shall receive your directions therein. In case of distress of any our plantations, you shall, upon application of the respective governors to you, assist them with what aid the condition and safety of your government will permit.

You shall cause a survey to be taken of all the considerable landing places and harbors in our said province and, with the advice of our Council, erect in any of them such fortifications as shall be necessary for the security and advantage of our province, which shall be done at the public charge of the country, not doubting of the cheerful concurrence of the inhabitants thereunto from the common security and benefit they will receive thereby.

You shall take an inventory of all arms, ammunition, and stores remaining in any of our magazines or garrisons in our said province and send an account of them yearly to us, by one of our principal secretaries of state and to our Committee for Trade and Plantations. You are to take especial care that fit storehouses be settled throughout our province for receiving and keeping of arms, ammunition, and other public stores. That we may be better informed of the trade of our said province, you are to take care that due entries be made in all ports of all goods and commodities imported or exported from thence and from and to what places they come and go, and that a yearly account thereof be transmitted by you unto us by one of our principal secretaries of state and to our Committee for Trade and Plantations. You are to take especial care that all tobaccos shipped in Maryland, from what part soever they come, do pay Maryland duties. And that all possible means may be used for the security of merchants ships in their return home, you are hereby directed to take care that in time of war no ship do come from Maryland but in fleets and at such time as shall be notified from hence for their meeting of convoys; and in case of imminent danger, you are to expect directions from hence what precautions shall be necessary for their security.

You are to suppress the engrossing of commodities and to settle such orders and regulations therein with the advice of our council as may be most acceptable to the inhabitants.

You are to give all encouragement and invitation to merchants and others who shall bring trade unto our said colony or any ways contribute to their advantage and in particular to the Royal African Company. And you are to take care that there be no trading from Maryland to any place in Africa within the charter of the Royal African Company and you are not to suffer any ships to be sent thither without their leave or authority.

You are carefully to observe all the articles contained in the treaty for the composing of differences and the establishing of peace in America concluded at Madrid the 8/18 day of July, 1670, with the Crown of Spain. And in case any private injury or damage shall be offered or done to any of our subjects in those parts by any of the subjects of the King of Spain or of any other prince or state in amity with us, you shall take care to give us an account with all convenient speed, by one of our principal secretaries of state and to our Committee for Trade and Plantations and not to permit or encourage reparations to be sought in other way than what is directed and agreed in the said *Article of Madrid* and other treaties, and you are particularly not to grant commissions of war or reprisals against any prince or state or their subjects in amity with us to any person whatsoever without our especial command and to transmit the same to us.

You are not to permit or allow of any appeals whatsoever to be made from the Governor and Council unto the Assembly. But whereas we judge it absolutely necessary that all our subjects may have liberty to appeal unto us, in cases that may deserve the same, our will and pleasure is that if either party shall not rest satisfied with the judgement or sentence of our Governor or the Commander-in-Chief and Council, they may then appeal unto us in our Privy Council; provided the matter in difference exceed the real value or sum of three hundred pounds sterling and that such appeal be made within one fortnight after sentence and security first given by the appellant to answer such charges as shall be awarded in case the sentence of our Governor or Commander-in-Chief and Council in Maryland be confirmed; provided, also, that execution be not suspended by reason of any such appeal unto us. And in as much as it may not be fit that appeals be too frequently and for too small a value brought unto our governor and council, you shall, therefore, with the advice of the Council propose a law to be passed wherein the method and limitation of appeals unto our Governor and Council may be settled and restrained in such manner as shall be found most convenient and easy to our subjects in Maryland.

You shall endeavor to get a law passed for the restraining of inhuman severities, which by ill masters or overseers may be used toward their christian servants or slaves and that provision be made therein that the willful killing of Indians and Negroes may be punished with death and that a fit penalty be imposed for the maiming of them.

You are also, with the assistance of our Council and Assembly, to find out the best means to facilitate and encourage the conversion of Negroes and Indians to the christian religion.

You are to recommend to our Council and Assembly the raising of a stock and building public workhouses in convenient places for the employing of poor and indigent people.

And forasmuch as great inconveniences may arise by the liberty of printing without our province of Maryland, you are to provide by all necessary orders that no person use any press for printing, upon any occasion whatsoever, without your special license first obtained.

Lastly, if anything shall happen that may be of advantage or security to our said province which is not herein or by our commission provided for, we do hereby authorize and direct you, with the advice and consent of our Council, to take order for the present therein, giving us, by one of our principal secretaries of state and the Lords of our Privy Council appointed a Committee for Trade and Foreign Plantations speedy notice thereof and of all your proceedings and the condition of affairs within your government for our information and direction. Provided, always, that you do not, by color of any power or authority hereby given you, commence or declare war without our knowledge and command therein, except it be against Indians upon emergencies, wherein the consent of our council shall be had and speedy notice thereof given unto us.

Given at our court at Whitehall, the 26th day of August, 1691, in the third year of our reign.

By her Majesty's command.

Nottingham.

Reference: W.H. Browne, et al. (eds.), *Archives of Maryland*, Vol. VIII (Baltimore: Maryland Historical Society, 1883–1912), 271–280.

MANNER OF SUMMONING AND ELECTING DELEGATES TO THE ASSEMBLIES, 1715

Forasmuch as the chief and only foundation and support of any kingdom, state, or commonwealth is the providing, establishing, and enacting good and wholesome laws for the good rule and government thereof, and also, upon any necessary and emergent occasion, to raise and levy money for the defraying the charges of the said government and the defense thereof, neither of which according to the constitution of this province can be made, ordained, established, or raised but by and with the consent of the freemen of this province by their several delegates and representatives by them freely nominated, chosen, and elected to serve for their several cities and counties in a general assembly. Forasmuch as the safest and best rule for this province to follow in electing such delegates and representatives is the precedents of the proceedings in Parliaments in England, as near as the constitution of this province will admit, the Governor, Council, and delegates of this present General Assembly do humbly pray that it may be enacted.

And be it enacted by the King's most excellent Majesty, by and with the advice and consent of his Majesty's Governor, Council, and Assembly of this province, and the authority of the same, that for the future when and as often as his Excellency the Governor of this province for the time being shall, upon any accident or urgent affair of this province, think fit to call and convene in assembly, and to send out writs for electing of burgesses and delegates to serve in such Assembly, writs shall issue forth forty days at least before the meeting of such assembly. The form of which writ for election of delegates and representatives shall be as follows.

George, by the grace of God, of Great Britain, France, and Ireland, King, Defender of the Faith, etc. To the sheriff of [. . .] county, greeting.

These are to command and authorize and empower you immediately upon receipt hereof to call together three or more justices of your county, whereof one to be of the quorum, with the clerk of the County Court, who are hereby required to sit as a court and during their sitting, by virtue of your office, to make or cause to be made public proclamation thereby giving notice to all the freemen of your said county who have within the said county a freehold of fifty acres of land, who shall be residents or have a visible estate of forty pounds sterling at the least therein, requiring them to appear at your county court house at a certain time, not less than ten days after such proclamation made, for electing and choosing deputies and delegates to serve for your said county in a General Assembly to be holden at the day of, to which time you shall adjourn your said court. And during the courts sitting the said freemen so required to appear, or the major part of such of them as shall then appear, shall and may and are hereby authorized and required to elect and choose four several and sufficient freemen of your county each of them having a freehold of fifty acres of land or who shall be a resident and have a visible estate of forty pounds sterling at the least within your county, whether the party so elected be present or absent. The said election to be made in such manner and form as the laws of England and this province do direct and provide. And you are to insert the names of the said persons elected in certain indentures to be then made between you, the said sheriff, and the electors, that is to say, two indentures for each delegate, each indenture having thereto your hand and seal and the hands and seals of the several electors by them subscribed, that the said deputies and delegates, for themselves and the county aforesaid, may have severally full and sufficient power to do and consent to those things which then and there by the favor of God shall happen to be ordained by the advice and consent of the great council of this province concerning such occasion and affairs as shall relate to the government, state, and defense thereof. But we will not [?] in anywise that you or any other sheriff in our said province be elected, and that upon such election you, the said sheriff, so soon as conveniently may be, give notice to the parties elected, if absent, and certify and transmit to the chancellor of this province for the time being one of the two several and respective indentures affixed to these presents, close, sealed up, and directed to the chancellor of the said province for the time being, and the other part of the said indentures you are to keep for your justification. Witness, etc.

And be it further enacted, by the authority aforesaid, by and with the advice and consent aforesaid, that the aforesaid four delegates to be elected in the respective counties within this province be and are hereby bound and obliged to attend at the time and place of the meeting of such assembly without any further writ or summons to be to them sent, under the penalty of such fines as shall be by the house of delegates imposed upon them, unless upon sufficient excuse to be admitted by the house of delegates their absence be dispensed with, any law, usage or custom to the contrary notwithstanding.

Provided, also, that no ordinary keeper within this province, during the time of his ordinary keeping, or any other person disabled by any laws of England from sitting in Parliament, shall be elected, chosen, or serve as a deputy or representative in the said General Assembly so to be hereafter called, convened, and appointed as aforesaid.

And be it further enacted, by the authority aforesaid, that any sheriff within this province who shall not give speedy notice to the inhabitants of his county of the time and place where such election shall be made, as well by proclamation as aforesaid, and by causing the same to be read in all churches, chapels, and all other public places within his said county, as also by notes thereof set up at all places, thereby the better to inform the inhabitants of the county requiring them, under the penalty of one hundred pounds of tobacco, to appear at such time and place appointed for election; and if any sheriff, as aforesaid, who shall make or cause to be made any undue or illegal election or returns thereof, or neglect to make returns of the delegates so to be elected by indenture before the day of sitting of such assembly pursuant to the directions of the said writ, shall for every such fault be fined two hundred pounds sterling; one-half to his Majesty, his heirs and successors, for the support of government and the other half to the informer or him or them that shall sue for the same, to be recovered in any court of record within this province that may have jurisdiction of the same, by action of debt, bill, plaint, or information, wherein no essoin, protection, or wager of law to be allowed.

And be it further enacted, by the authority aforesaid, by and with the advice and consent aforesaid, that all freeholders, freemen, and other persons qualified to give votes in the election of delegates shall and are hereby obliged to be and appear at the time and place appointed for elections to be hereafter had and made of any delegates, burgesses, and citizens to serve in any assembly for this province, under the penalty of one hundred pounds of tobacco for every person, so qualified as aforesaid, neglecting to appear; one-half thereof to the King's Majesty, his heirs and successors, for and towards the county charge, and the other half to the informer that shall complain to any one or more justices or magistrates of such absence, which justice or justices or other magistrates are hereby empowered to determine such complaints and award execution for the said penalty unless such person or persons shall, at the next county court after such election, show sufficient cause for his or their absence to be allowed and approved of by the justices of the several county courts in this province.

Provided, nevertheless, that this act or anything herein contained shall not extend to be construed to exclude county or counties, city or cities, borough or boroughs hereafter to be erected and made within this province from the liberty of such elections of delegates and representatives as is before expressed, but that such writ as aforesaid shall, upon calling every General Assembly of this province for the future, be directed to the sheriff of every such county when the same shall be erected and made into county, as aforesaid, and to the mayor or recorder and aldermen of every such city or borough, commanding such sheriff or mayor, recorder, or aldermen to cause four freemen of the said county and two freemen of the said city or borough, qualified as in the aforesaid writ as expressed, to serve as delegates and representatives of the same county, city, or borough in the general assembly next ensuing. Which said four delegates for every such county and two for the city or borough shall, from thenceforth, be reputed and deemed to be members of the house of the General Assembly of this province, anything in this act in any wise to the contrary notwithstanding.

And for the ascertaining and limiting and allowing unto the several and respective councilors, deputies, and delegates that serve or shall serve in the General Assembly of this province, and of the several and respective commissioners of the provincial and county courts of this province, such sum and sums of tobacco as is hereby thought necessary and sufficient for their defraying their charges in attending such assemblies and courts.

Be it enacted, by the authority aforesaid, by and with the advice and consent aforesaid, that all such councilors be allowed the sum of one hundred and fifty pounds of tobacco per day and the delegates and burgesses of assembly shall be allowed the sum of one hundred and forty pounds of tobacco per day during the time they shall attend such assemblies and no more, besides their itinerant charges, to be paid and allowed them out of the public levy of this province; and the several and respective commissioners of the provincial court for their defraying their charges and expenses during the time they shall sit in and attend such courts the sum of one hundred and forty pounds of tobacco per day and no more, besides their itinerant charges, to be paid them likewise out of the public levy of this province, as aforesaid; and the several commissioners of the county courts shall be allowed for the defraying their expenses during the time they shall sit and attend such court, as aforesaid, the sum of eighty pounds of tobacco per day and no more; which sum of eighty pounds of tobacco, as aforesaid, the commissioners of the county courts are hereby empowered to assess and levy on the taxable persons of the several counties where such commissioners shall serve as aforesaid for the defraying the expenses aforesaid and no more.

Reference: W.H. Browne, et al. (eds.), *Archives of Maryland,* Vol. XXX (Baltimore: Maryland Historical Society, 1883–1912), 270–274.

ACT TO RAISE FUNDS TO PAY COLONIAL AGENT, TOGETHER WITH LETTER TO THE GOVERNOR, MAY 1, 1739

Whereas it is both necessary and convenient that there should be An Agent at the Imperial Seat of Our mother country Great Britain in Order there to transact the emergent and necessary Business of this Province and inasmuch as many Occasions do and may require a Sollicitation from his Majestys dutiful liege Subjects the Inhabitants of this province to his most sacred Royal and Gracious person who is the Protector and Father of his People and likewise to their noble Lord Proprietary residing there And Whereas such Agent cannot be supported but at the publick Charge nor such Sollicitations made or necessary Business transacted without a Fund to that purpose And for that this General Assembly are willing and desirous to charge themselves in the Staple Commodity of this province with Reasonable Tax to so good and desirable an end it is humbly prayed that it may be enacted And be it Enacted by the Right Honourable the Lord Proprietary by and with the Advice and Consent of his Lordships Governor, and the Upper and Lower Houses of Assembly and the Authority of the same that immediately from and after the expiration of this Session of Assembly every Master or Commander of any Ship or Vessel trading into this province before the Clearing such Ship or Vessel shall pay unto the several and respective Naval Officers clearing such Ship or Vessel the sum of Six Pence Sterling money of Great Britain for every Hogshead or Quantity of an Hogshead of Tobacco taken on Board such Ship or Vessel in Order to be transported out of this province and for every hundred weight of Tobacco taken on Board such Ship or Vessel in order to be Transported as aforesaid either in Bundles Chests Case or other Package one Penny Sterling for every hundred weight and so pro Rato for a greater or lesser quantity And be it further Enacted by the Authority Advice and Consent aforesaid that the said several and respective Naval Officers within this province shall be and Are hereby Obliged yearly and every year during the Continuance of this Act to Collect the money arising by this Act in Sterling money in Specie or good Bills of Exchange made payable in Great Britain unto such respective naval Officer collecting the same and [said] Naval Officer shall be and he is hereby Obliged to pay the same so by him received to such Person or Persons as shall from time to time (by Warrant or Authority from

the House of Delegates in Assembly convened under the hand of the Speaker of the same House for the time being) be appointed Trustees to receive the same deducting for the Trouble and care of such Naval Officer in such Collection and Payment aforesaid five pounds ℗ Cent out of such money so to be received and paid and no more

And be it further Enacted by the Authority Advice and Consent aforesaid that such Person or persons so to be appointed Trustees as aforesaid shall Yearly and every year during the Continuance of this Act with all Convenient speed transmit such money or bill or Bills of Exchange by them to be received from the several and respective Naval Officers aforesaid unto Mr Samuel Hyde Merchant in London who is hereby Authorized and Impowered to receive & Collect the money in such Bill or Bills mentioned and that such Money when so by him received shall remain in his hands and be as a fund for the Purposes aforesaid and paid by him to such Person or Persons as the Trustees so to be appointed as aforesaid or the Survivor or Survivors of them shall by Writing under their hands Order and direct the same and not otherwise And be it further Enacted by the Authority Advice and Consent aforesaid that such Person or Persons as shall from time to time be appointed as aforesaid to receive the Money arising by this Act from the Naval Officers aforesaid shall be and are hereby obliged to render and lay an Account thereof before the House of Delegates of this province when and so often as the same shall be by them required And be it further Enacted by the Authority aforesaid that the money arising by the duty aforesaid shall be applied towards the Payment of An Agent to be employed for this province to reside at London in Great Britain and to such other uses and purposes as shall from time to time be thought necessary by the Trustees aforesaid or the Survivors of them and not otherwise this Act to Continue until the twenty ninth day of September which shall be in the year of our Lord God One Thousand seven hundred and forty two and the following Indorsements thereon viz.

And the following message
The following address to his Excellency viz.

To his Excellency Samuel Ogle Esqr Governor and Commander in Chief in and over the province of Maryland.

The humble Address of the House of Delegates.
May it please your Excellency.

We his Majestys liege Subjects the Delegates of the Freemen of the Province of Maryland in General Assembly convened being divested of all partial or self interested Views and prompted only by our Zeal for the publick Good, according to the duty of our Station have maturely considered the several particulars hereafter mentioned, concerning which we have received the loud Complaints of those we represent, and encouraged by your Excellencys kind Declaration at the opening of this Session that no man is come to this Assembly more sincerely desirous of the Welfare of the province than yourself or more willing to give a helping hand to the removal of every Obstacle to its Happiness and Prosperity beg leave to lay them before you as Grievances under which we and our constituents labour and whereof the evil consequences daily grow upon us not doubting, that when they are set in their proper light, we shall have your Excellencys helping hand to the removal of them as real Obstacles to Our Happiness and prosperity, that the people of this Province are Subjects of Great Britain and entituled to all the Rights Priviledges and Liberties of that their Mother country, is a truth we hope none will attempt to deny; and that the Basis on which their priviledges are principally founded is the right they have, of not being subject to any payments whether they be Taxes, Dutys Imposts fees or under any other denomination whatsoever but what shall be raised settled and appointed by laws to which by themselves or their Substitutes they give their Assent is a matter we conceive can admit of no Contradiction

We therefore acknowledge ourselves at a loss to know by what right or law fourteen Pence Sterling for every Tun of Burthen has for a considerable time past been levied on Vessels trading here and not properly belonging to this province We very well know that an act was made in 1661 for raising half A Pound of Powder and three Pound of Shot by the Tun on such Vessels and we as well know that by that law the same was not appropriated to the proprietarys for their own use, although they have ever since exacted the fourteen pence in lieu thereof and applied the same to their private [use]

We are not insensible of the Kings order in Council concerning that money in 1692 but beg leave nevertheless to say that whatever Obedience was paid to that Royal Order (which only did or indeed could regard the Application) yet the Act whereby it was pretended to be taken being repealed by another made in 1704 that Order must necessarily cease, and altho we dont immediately pay that money, yet as Merchants generally reckon Port and other dutys as Part of the cost of what they sell or Transact and account it as part of the price of what they purchase, we cannot but think it becomes a charge on the Province at last.

We are sorry to find the Avenues to Justice in great measure shut up to the people by their being denied Access to some of the greatest Offices belonging to the Courts of Justice and refused their necessary Business there, without the severe Terms of entering into Bonds with Judgments some for fees before they become due, and others with conditions in large Sums on purpose to have recoveries in the Courts where the fees will arise to ten or more times the Value of the Principal debt which by the laws of this province might be recovered at the expence of half A Crown, and those Bonds yearly sent to the Sheriffs with discretionary powers to put them in Suit who by experience we find have in many Instances made the worst use of those powers in order to create fees for themselves as well as to the party who take such Bonds

The Power of late Assumed by his Lordship of setling and ascertaining the fees of the officers in the Courts of Justice by way of Proclamation, is what we cannot submit to, without prostituting the rights of his Majestys Subjects within this Province.

We do not know that ever the Kings of Great Britain exercised their prerogative in such Case, especially since the happy Revolution and on this Occasion we entreat your Excellency to consider that part of the Royal Charter which directs that no Ordinances made by the Proprietary or his Heirs their Magistrates or officers without consent of the Freemen or their Delegates shall affect the right or Interest of any Person or Persons of or in their Life Member Freehold Goods or Chattels which Clause is consonant to the great Charter to the Benefit whereof we hope we shall not be denied a right, however to avoid all Disputes on this Head we had with great pains and application prepared A Bill for setling those fees and made them considerably Higher than those of our neighbouring colonies yet we cannot obtain the Assent of his Lordships Council to the same without such conditions as would in our Apprehension prove destructive, to the People, for Reasons your Excellency cannot be a Stranger to viz: that of making it a perpetual law: and how Reasonable it is that the Gentlemen of that Board, who without any Warrant from the Royal Charter assume a Negative on the proceedings of the Delegates of this Province, and whose Seats at that Board are only at the Will of the Right Honourable the Lord Proprietary and who (with a single Exception only) are composed of such as hold the chief Offices and Posts of Profit in the Government during pleasure, the Exorbitancy of whose fees, illegally charged and the oppressive manner of extorting them from the People, was what was endeavoured by that Bill to be remedied, how far we say they ought to be Judges and have a negative in an affair wherein they are so deeply interested we leave to our Superiors and the world to judge, whilst we are upon this Article of fees we cannot omit mentioning to your Excellency another practice lately crept in amongst us, that of Buying and selling the Offices of the County Clerks

and the very persons who receive the Profits of the Offices of Clerks & Registers Practising as Attorneys in the Courts to which these Offices belong that such Sales are unlawful is too obvious to be denied, and whether the same Person Acting in the different Capacities of Clerk and Attorney having the Custody of the Papers and Evidences of the Person against whom he is concerned and the entring up of the Judgment in the cause may not be Introductive of Corruption Injustice and Oppression we submit to your Excellency or any other Unprejudiced Person. The Exacting Alienation fines on Devises is we conceive a thing contrary to the Tenor and Conditions of our Grants, a Project Introduced to drain Money from the People within these three or four years last past from a forced construction of the Words of our pattents.

We are far from desiring to wrong his Lordship of what properly belongs to him, but cannot help complaining of that prerogative and authority he has lately taken upon himself to Vacate his own Grants of land to the people of this Province on Account of Surplus or any other matter, as Invasive of our propertys, & a thing not to be done by any Subject

The Naval Officers of this province we think are or ought to be Subject, to the laws of it yet notwithstanding the express clause in the paper currency Act that all contracts to be made from and after, the publication of that Act should be paid and satisfied in Bills of Credit, they to this time have Obliged Masters of all Ships or Vessels entering or Clearing with them to pay their fees in Gold or Silver. Strange! that the holding an Office (the fees and perquisites whereof arise from the labour and Industry of a People) should set persons above the law and Invest them with A Power to oppress that People

The last thing we shall trouble your Excellency with in this Address is a Priviledge lately invented and claimed by the members of his Lordships council. It is well known that the greater number of the Gentlemen of that Board are possessed of Offices of the greatest profit and trust in the Province some being Treasurers, some Trustees of the Paper Currency and others Naval Officers; yet those Gentlemen being called upon to give an Account of the Countrys Money refuse to answer in Person alledging it below the dignity of their House as they term it to appear before the House of Delegates much less any Committee of it We think it the Countrys undoubted right to call all those who have the collecting keeping or disposing of the publick Money to Account for it nor can we foresee any other consequence from this Usurped dignity, than that the possessors of those Offices may with Impunity commit what frauds Extortions or Embezzlements they shall think fit by being adopted into his Lordships Council

These Sir amongst many others too numerous at this time to Recite are Grievances which the people whom we represent daily suffer, which call aloud for Redress and which we without a manifest Violation of the Trust reposed in us cannot forbear in the most humble manner to lay before your Excellency.

We have taken the liberty to annex hereunto several Reports of Our Committee of Aggrievances concerning many of the Facts herein Complained of, and do flatter our selves that after mature Consideration we shall not fail of your Excellencys Assistance towards our Relief, was read Approved and Ordered to be ingrossed

To which aforegoing Address were annexed the following reports viz. The Report of the Committee of Aggrievances dated in May 1739 about 14 Tunnage

Reference: Bernard Christian Steiner (ed.), *Archives of Maryland*, Vol. XL: *Proceedings and Acts of the General Assembly 1737–1740* (Baltimore: Maryland Historical Society, 1921).

ACT FOR ADVANCEMENT OF JUSTICE, NOVEMBER 9, 1753

Whereas, notwithstanding the several Laws heretofore made for the Advancement of Justice, Amendment of the Law, and aiding and supplying several Defects in Judicial Proceedings, great Delay, Trouble, and Expences have been, and still are occasioned by Demurrers, arresting and reversing of Judgments, and staying Executions by Writs of Error and Appeal; there being yet no sufficient Provision made for the aiding such Omissions, Errors, and Imperfections as are usually taken Advantage of by Special Demurrers; and also for aiding such Defects in the Entries of Clerks, as are frequently taken Advantage of, on the Prosecuting Writs of Error or Appeals, as well as divers other Advantages of other Defects, or pretended Defects or Errors, which only serve to prevent or divert the Examination of, and giving Judgment on the very Right of the Cause: For Remedy whereof,

Be it Enacted, by the Right Honourable the Lord Proprietary, by and with the Advice and Consent of his Lordship's Governor, and the Upper and Lower Houses of Assembly, and the Authority of the same, That in all Actions to be commenced after the End of this Session of Assembly, the Justices of the several Courts of Law within this Province, shall proceed and give Judgment according as the very Right of the Cause and Matter in Law shall appear to them, without regarding any such Omission, Defects, Advantages, or Pretences as aforesaid, so as sufficient Matter shall appear in the Proceedings, upon which the Court may proceed to give Judgment according to the very Right of the Cause and Matter in Law, and that it shall appear that the Action shall be commenced after the Cause thereof shall accrue; and that no such Judgment shall be reversed or set aside, or Execution thereon delayed, for or by Reason of any such Imperfection, Omission, or Defect; any Law, Usage, or Custom, to the contrary notwithstanding.

Provided always, and be it Enacted, by the Authority aforesaid, That nothing in this Act shall extend, or be construed to extend, to any Writ, Declaration, or Suit of Appeal of Felony or Murder, or to any Indictment or Presentment of Treason, Felony, or Murder, or other Matter, or to any Process upon any of them, or to any Writ, Bill, Action, or Information, upon any Penal Statute.

And be it further Enacted. That in all Actions in the County Courts, where the Matter or Thing in Dispute shall not exceed the Sum of Twenty Pounds Sterling Money, or Five Thousand Pounds of Tobacco, the Justices of the County Court, where such Action shall be brought, may and shall (at the Prayer of either Plaintiff or Defendant, either before or after Judgment, or Verdict of a Jury, at Common Law), hear and determine the same, according to the Rules of Equity and good Conscience, as fully and amply as the Chancellor, or Keeper of the Great Seal might do in any Case within the Jurisdiction of the Chancery Court; any Law, Usage, Verdict of a Jury, or Custom, to the contrary notwithstanding.

And be it Enacted, That where any Person or Persons is or are bound in any Bond, or other Obligation, for the Payment of Money, Tobacco, or other Goods, or indorse any Bill of Exchange that shall be Protested, and the Money, Tobacco, or other Goods, or such Part thereof as shall be unpaid by the principal Debtor, shall be paid or tendered by the Surety or Indorser, that the Obligee or Indorsee shall be obliged to assign such Bond, Obligation, or protested Bill, to the Surety paying or tendering the Money, Tobacco, or other Goods, due as aforesaid; and that the Assignee shall and may by Virtue of such Assignment and this Act, have an Action in his or her own Name, against the principal Debtor; any Law, Usage, or Custom, to the contrary notwithstanding.

And be it Enacted, That where any Person or Persons hath recovered, or shall recover, any Judgment against the principal Debtor and Surety, and such Judgment hath been, or shall be, satisfied by Sureties, that the Creditor shall be obliged to assign such Judgment to the Surety satisfying the same, and that the Assignee shall be entitled unto, and have the same Execution against the principal Debtor, by Virtue of such Assignment

and this Act, as the Creditor might or ought to have had; and that where any Judgment hath been, or shall be, rendered against several Sureties, and one of them hath satisfied, or shall satisfy the whole, the Plaintiff, or Creditor shall be obliged to assign such Judgment to the Surety satisfying the same, and that the Assignee shall have, and be entitled to an Execution against the other Sureties, against whom Judgment hath been, or shall be, obtained by the principal Creditor, for a proportionable Part of the Debt or Damage paid by such Assignee; any Law, Usage, or Custom, to the contrary notwithstanding. Provided always, That no Defendant, or Defendants, shall be precluded or debarred of his or their Remedy against the Plaintiff, by Audita querela, or other Proceeding whatsoever; any Thing in this Act to the contrary notwithstanding.

And be it Enacted by the Authority aforesaid, That upon all Bonds, or other Obligations, under Seal, that have or shall be assigned under Hand and Seal, the Assignee shall and may, by Virtue of such Assignment, maintain an Action or Actions in his or her Name, against the Obligor or Obligors therein named; and if it shall happen that such Obligor or Obligors shall be unable to pay the Debt mentioned in such Obligation, or cannot be found in the Place or County of his usual Abode, or any other Thing or Casualty should happen, whereby the Assignee should not be able to receive or recover his Debt from such Obligor or Obligors, that then, and in every such Case, the like Action shall and may be maintainable, by such Assignee, against the Obligee or Obligees in such Obligation mentioned; any Law, Usage, or Custom, to the contrary notwithstanding. Provided, That where any Debt shall be lost by the Negligence or Default of the Assignee or Assignees, that the Assignor or Assignors shall not be liable, any such Assignment notwithstanding.

Provided also, That no Action or Actions shall be maintained in the Name or Names of any Assignee or Assignees, unless the Assignor or Assignors have made or shall make Oath (or Affirmation, if a Quaker) before some Magistrate, that he, she, or they, hath or have received no

Part of the Sum mentioned in such Obligation, or but such Part thereof as shall be mentioned in such Oath or Affirmation, at the Time of making any such Assignment, to be indorsed on such Bond or Obligation.

And be it likewise Enacted, That any Person knowingly swearing or affirming falsely in the Premises, and being thereof convict by due Course of Law, shall suffer as in the Case of wilful and corrupt Perjury.

And be it further Enacted, by the Authority aforesaid, That an Attorney being concerned for either Plaintiff or Defendant, in any Cause of Equity to be heard before the County Courts as aforesaid, shall have and receive One Hundred Pounds of Tobacco, where the Debt doth not exceed Ten Pounds Sterling, or Two Thousand Five Hundred Pounds of Tobacco; and where the Debt doth exceed Ten Pounds Sterling, or Two Thousand Five Hundred Pounds of Tobacco, in any such Case, the Quantity of Two Hundred Pounds of Tobacco, and no more.

This Act to continue for Three Years, and unto the End of the next Session of Assembly which shall happen after the End of the said Three Years.

9th Novemr 1753 Read and Assented to by the Lower House of Assembly

On behalf of the Right Honourable the Lord Proprietary of this Province I will this be a Law

9 Novemr 1753 Read and Assented to by the Upper House of Assembly

Reference: J. Hall Pleasants (ed.), *Archives of Maryland,* Vol. L: *Proceedings and Acts of the General Assembly 1752–1754* (Baltimore: Maryland Historical Society, 1933).

ACT FOR SPEEDY PUBLICATION OF THE LAWS OF THIS PROVINCE, NOVEMBER 17, 1753

Be it Enacted, by the Right Honourable the Lord Proprietary, by and with the Advice and Consent of his Lordship's Governor, and the Upper and Lower Houses of Assembly, and the Authority of the same, That the Justices of the several and respective County Courts within this Province shall, and they are hereby impowered and directed, to make an Allowance of Twenty Pounds, Current Money of this Province, to the said Jonas Green, in the Levy to be laid for each respective County after this present Session of Assembly; and that the said Twenty Pounds (with the Sheriff's Commission for collecting the same) so to be allowed and assessed as aforesaid, shall be collected by the Sheriff of each respective County, and yearly paid by them respectively, free from all Charges of Collection, to the said Jonas Green, or his Order, for Printing, Stitching, Covering with Marble, Blue Paper, Vellum, or Parchment, and Delivering a Copy of the Public Laws, made this present Session of Assembly, by the First Day of March next, and the Votes and Proceedings of the Lower House of Assembly of this present Session, by the First Day of April next, and also a Copy of the Laws of any future Session, within Three Months, and of the Votes and Proceedings of the Lower House of Assembly, within Four Months respectively, after the End of every such Session yearly, during the Continuance of this Act, to the Governor and each Member of the Upper and Lower Houses of Assembly, and One Book of the Votes and Proceedings to the Clerk of each House, and Three Books of the Votes and Proceedings aforesaid, to the Clerks of the several and respective County Courts, for the Perusal of the Inhabitants of the several and respective Counties, and a Copy of the Public Laws, during the Continuance of this Act, to every Provincial and County Magistrate; and a Copy of each Law bound up in Leather to each House of Assembly, the high Court of Appeals, the Provincial Court, and to each County Court within this Province.

And be it likewise Enacted, That if it should so happen, that in any Year during the Continuance of this Act, there should not be any Session of Assembly held within this Province, whereby the said Jonas Green may be enabled to print Laws, and deliver them within such Year, that then and in such Case, the said Justices of each respective County shall nevertheless, and they are hereby directed and required to levy the Sum of Fifteen Pounds Current Money, free from Deduction, in each respective County, to be paid by the Sheriffs of the several Counties respectively, to the said Jonas Green, or his Order, for his better Support and Encouragement in serving this Province, and residing within the same: For the Collection and Payment of which, or any other Sum or Sums herein before mentioned, there shall be allowed to the said Sheriffs respectively a Commission of Five Pounds Per Centum, and no more.

Provided always, That the said Jonas Green shall actually reside at Annapolis during the Continuance of this Act, and comply with the Terms thereof; and that upon the Death of the said Jonas Green, or his Removal from Annapolis, or ceasing to comply with the Terms of this Act on his Part, the Payment of the Sums of Money directed by this Act to be paid to him shall cease; any Thing contained in this Act to the contrary notwithstanding.

And be it likewise Enacted, That the Copy of the Public Laws made this present Session of Assembly, as well as those made at any future Session during the Continuance of this Act, shall have marginal Notes made and printed thereto, as also the Date of the Year, wherein such Laws were respectively made, inserted in each Page; and a List of such Laws made at the End of each Session, with the Page where they are printed: All which the said Jonas Green is hereby required and obliged to do, as well as all other Services herein before mentioned, for the yearly Salary aforesaid.

Provided always, and be it hereby Enacted, That it shall and may be lawful for the taxable Inhabitants of this Province, upon whom the above Sums of Money shall be assessed, to discharge and pay the same in Gold and Silver, at the same Rates as by the Act entituled, An Act for amending the Staple of Tobacco, for preventing Frauds in his Majesty's Customs, and for the Limitation of Officers Fees, made at this present Session of Assembly, Gold and Silver is directed to be received in all Payments made in Virtue of that Act.

Provided also, That it shall and may be lawful for the Sheriffs of the several Counties respectively, and they are hereby required not to pay to the said Jonas Green the said Sum of Money mentioned in this Act or any Part thereof, to be assessed and levied for his Use, unless it shall be made appear to them by a Certificate from the Clerk of the respective County, (which Certificate shall be given by the Clerk without Fee or Reward,) that the Public Laws, and the Votes and Proceedings of this present Session, and every future Session during the Continuance of this Act, were printed and delivered in Manner and Form, and within the Time by this Act respectively directed; any Thing herein before contained to the contrary in any wise notwithstanding.

And whereas it is thought expedient that each Inspection Office, and Vestry, within this Province, be furnished with Laws relating to the Inspection of Tobacco, the better to enable them to know and perform the Duty thereby required: Be it further Enacted, That for the annual Allowance by this Act made and provided for the said Jonas Green, he be hereby further obliged, and it be deemed Part of his Duty, to print, stitch, and deliver to the Clerks of the respective Counties, by the First Day of April next, to be by them delivered to each Vestry, and to the Inspector of Inspectors of each Inspecting Office within their Counties respectively, as well the Law made this present Session of Assembly entituled, An Act for amending the Staple of Tobacco, for preventing Frauds in his Majesty's Customs, and for the Limitation of Officers Fees, as all and every Law and Laws relating to the Inspection of Tobacco, which shall be made at any future Assembly during the Continuance of this Act.

And be it likewise Enacted, That the several and respective Sheriffs within this Province shall, and they are hereby directed and required to receive and forward the said Laws, with the Votes and Proceedings aforesaid, to the Clerks of the several County Courts, and the Members of each House of Assembly, as other Public Letters are by the Laws of this Province directed to be forwarded.

Reference: J. Hall Pleasants (ed.), *Archives of Maryland,* Vol. L: *Proceedings and Acts of the General Assembly 1752–1754* (Baltimore: Maryland Historical Society, 1933).

18

Connecticut

Connecticut freemen, although living in a royal colony, had a strong voice in the selection of their governor. The colony, now completely freed from Dominion status and subservience to Massachusetts Bay, experienced large agricultural growth in the Connecticut River Valley and along Long Island sound. Trade in agricultural goods created an urban landscape, with much emphasis placed on town government. The colonial assembly, similarly to many others, gained power and sought repeal of the hostile British restrictions to its growth.

Shortly after the rebellion of 1689, the Connecticut lower house passed statutes that determined the method of selecting its membership. All town freemen had the right to elect members of the legislature, the deputy governor, and governor. In 1698, the assembly defined carefully the powers of the governor and set restrictions on the governor's prerogative to decide when to come to the aid of other colonies. The year 1698 also saw the division of the assembly into two houses. In 1707 the assembly decided again to declare the freemen's right to select their governor. Although suffrage restrictions meant that only freeholders could vote, in actuality most White males voted for town officers. Ever fearful of corruption in elections and among officials, an act was passed to keep prospective officials from buying votes. The careful control of its prerogatives and its reputation for honesty gave the lower house of the Assembly much power, so much so that in 1764 it took solace in congratulating itself on successfully directing the governor to argue against the Stamp Act.

METHOD OF ELECTING ASSISTANTS, OCTOBER 10, 1689

It is ordered by this court that for the future the freemen in the several plantations shall meet in their several towns upon the third Tuesday in March yearly at their meeting house about nine of the clock in the morning and there each freeman shall give in the names of twenty persons, fairly written upon a piece of paper to the constable and commissioner or townsmen of their town, who they choose for to be nominated at the election for assistants, who shall receive them and seal them up in a piece of paper. And the constables shall, the next Friday after the said meeting, carry their said votes to the county town and the constable of the county town shall, by himself or one appointed by the constables met at the county town, carry the votes of the several towns to Hartford, there to meet on the last Tuesday in March yearly in the court chamber and the assistants present, or secretary, shall administer an oath to those that shall come from the said county towns faithfully to sort the said votes. And the names of those twenty they shall find to have most votes shall by the secretary be sent back to the several county towns by the said persons that shall bring up their votes. And from thence, the several towns shall have notice of those twenty that are by the freemen appointed to stand for the nomination at the court of election. And upon the last Tuesday in April the freemen in each town in this colony are to meet as aforesaid, about nine of the clock in their meeting house and out of that number of twenty chosen for the nomination they are to give in their votes for the governor, with his name fairly written upon a piece of paper. In like manner, they are to give in their votes for the deputy-governor, with his name fairly written upon a piece of paper. All which are to be sealed up and written upon, "These are the votes for the Governor," and so for the deputy-governor. They are also to go over the whole nomination person

by person according as they are set down in the nomination [and] every freeman is to bring in his vote to the constable for every one which shall be in the nomination, which votes shall be a white paper for a blank and a paper with some writing upon it for election. And each man's vote shall be sealed up and the name of the person that is voted for shall be written on the outside of the paper. And so they are to pass through the nomination and to give in their votes for treasurer and secretary, which in like manner are to be sealed up and written upon. And the votes put into the hands of the deputies of their town, who are to bring them up to the election and deliver them at the time of the election as they are called for, any former order to the contrary notwithstanding. And those twelve men that have most votes when the whole number is gone over shall be declared assistants for the year ensuing.

Reference: J.H. Trumbull and C.J. Hoadly (eds.), *The Public Records of the Colony of Connecticut, 1636–1776*, Vol. II (15 vols.; Hartford: Lockwood & Brainard, 1850–1890), 11–12.

POWERS OF GOVERNOR AND COUNCIL, MAY 12, 1698

Ordered by this court that it shall be in the power of the governor, and in his absence of the deputy-governor, with the advice of the council, and in the want of a sufficient number of assistants to make a council, with the advice of such assistants as shall be present, with so many of the deputies as the governor or deputy-governor shall think fit to call to council, upon any sudden exigent to raise men and to send them forth for the succor and relief of the neighbor provinces of Massachusetts and New York, if invaded, and

also to act in all affairs that concern the preservation of the rights and privileges of his Majesty's subjects in this corporation, particularly respecting the differences with Rhode Island about the dividing line, [and] the composing any matters depending concerning the towns of Rye and Bedford.

Reference: J.H. Trumbull and C.J. Hoadly (eds.), *The Public Records of the Colony of Connecticut, 1636–1776*, Vol. IV (15 vols.; Hartford: Lockwood & Brainard, 1850–1890), 262–263.

DIVISION OF ASSEMBLY INTO TWO HOUSES, OCTOBER 13, 1698

It is ordered by this court, and the authority thereof, that for the future this general assembly shall consist of two houses. The first shall

consist of the governor, or, in his absence of the deputy-governor, and assistants, which shall be known by the name of the Upper House. The other shall consist of such deputies as shall be legally returned from the several towns within this colony to serve as members of this general assembly, which shall be known by the name of the Lower House, wherein a speaker chosen by themselves shall preside. Which houses so formed shall have a distinct power to appoint all needful officers and to make such rules as they shall severally judge necessary for the regulat-

ing of themselves. And it is further ordered that no act shall be passed into a law of this colony, nor any law already enacted be repealed, nor any other act proper to this general assembly, but by the consent of both houses.

Reference: J. H. Trumbull and C. J. Hoadly (eds.), *The Public Records of the Colony of Connecticut, 1636– 1776,* Vol. IV (15 vols.; Hartford: Lockwood & Brainard, 1850–1890), 267.

CONNECTICUT FREEMEN ELECT GOVERNOR, DECEMBER 1707

Whereas in the printed law, title *Election,* it is said, "Out of which number the governor and deputy-governor shall be chosen," this assembly does now see cause to repeal that part of the said law, and it is hereby repealed; and do now order and enact that for the future the several freemen in the respective have liberty to choose for the

governor and deputy-governor, where they see cause, of all or any of the freemen within this colony.

Reference: J. H. Trumbull and C. J. Hoadly (eds.), *The Public Records of the Colony of Connecticut, 1636– 1776,* Vol. V (15 vols.; Hartford: Lockwood & Brainard, 1850–1890), 39.

ASSEMBLY REPORT ON THE PLAN OF UNION, OCTOBER 1754

Report of A Committee, chosen by The General Assembly of Connecticut, respecting The Foregoing Plan of Union.

To the Honourable General Assembly, sitting at New-Haven, October, 1754.

WE, your Honours' committee, appointed to take into consideration the proposed plan for an union of his Majesty's governments in North-America, to give our opinion thereon, and the reasons of such our opinion, &c. humbly report on the premises, viz.

Having duly and maturely considered said plan, we are of opinion, that the same has a tendency greatly to weaken and injure his majesty's interest, and that it is subversive of the just rights and privileges of his good and faithful subjects inhabiting his dominions on this continent; and for such our opinion, we with much submission, offer the following reasons.

1. We find his Majesty's territories, from the south-west part of Georgia to Menis, is more than seventeen hundred miles; of which, from the

head of St. John's (which we suppose to be the north-east extent of the Massachusetts province) to the Apilachi mountains, (which we suppose to be the south-west extent of the colony of South-Carolina,) is, on the frontiers by land, about fifteen hundred miles; which last extent is all within the limits of the proposed plan of union, so that the president-general and council have to provide for this large extent of frontiers; and should Georgia and Nova-Scotia, when able to assist, be added, it makes the same yet greater. The sea-coast, we find, varies very little from the extent by land; and we think it impracticable that his Majesty's interest, and the good of his people, inhabiting so great a country, can, in any advantageous or tolerable manner, be considered and condu-cted by the proposed president-general and council.

2. The president-general and council having authority to nominate and commissionate all military commission officers, we apprehend, will be highly disadvantageous to his Majesty's interest. Under this head we consider that our officers generally are chosen out of the best yeomen of this colony, who live on their own lands, in peace and plenty; but have ever been ready to serve their country in the field, when called: their commissions have always been prepared and delivered into their hands gratis. Under these officers, thus chosen and commisionated, freeholders' sons, the youth of this colony, have on all occasions, with great cheerfulness and alacrity, generally enlisted; and their country's good (not necessity) has led them to arms. Now, should officers be sent from abroad, we are fully satisfied, such youth would not enlist; and to press these generous young men into service will be not only hard and grievous, but in all probability will greatly dishearten and dispirit them, and this, we conclude, is very much the case in other his Majesty's provinces and colonies on the continent.

3. His Majesty's subjects, now inhabiting this country, are a very great body; and in every twenty-five years the increase of inhabitants is so great, they are supposed to become double. This power and strength being brought into one point, all to move under the direction of said president-general and council, we fear, may in time be of dangerous consequence to his Majesty's interest, and the good of his loyal subjects here.

4. Further, we apprehend his Majesty's interest is in great danger from the president-general's having a negative voice; for if it ever be, that that officer should not well understand or pursue proper methods for the country's good, all may be ruined before relief can be had from the throne; and it seems to us, that the Grand Council are most likely to understand the true interest and weal of this people.

5. We think the proposal, in said plan contained, for the President-General and Council to lay and levy taxes, &c. as they please, throughout this territory, is a very extraordinary thing, and against the rights and privileges of Englishmen in general; *and such an innovation or breach on charter privileges, we fear, will greatly discourage and dishearten his Majesty's good subjects.* All which, with a draught for a union, delivered in herewith, is humbly submitted, by

Your Honours' committee

The reasons considered and offered, by the Assembly of the Colony of Connecticut, concerning the plan of Union the Commissioners of the Several Colonies in North-America, who met at Albany on the 14th june, 1754, have proposed for Uniting the said Colonies into one General Government, for the purposes therein expressed, are as follows.

1. THE limits of the proposed plan of union are of too large extent; from Nova-Scotia on the north, to Georgia on the south, is fifteen hundred miles; so that the President-General and Grand Council must have to provide for this large extent of frontiers; and this plan seems calculated only to render this general government, therein proposed, capable to defend against the French, and to proclaim war, and make peace with the Indians. Now it seems plain, that it is impracticable that his Majesty's interest, and the good of his people inhabiting so great a country, with frontiers of so great length, can be advantageously defended, or in any good manner considered and conducted, by the proposed President-General and council: and it may be justly observed here, that a defensive war, on the part of this government, with so large a frontier, will prove detrimental and ruinous to it; while the French have it in their power, at any time, as well in a time of peace, as of a war, to send out small parties of their Indians, to skulk about in the woods, and fall upon, and surprise any part of the frontiers; and with but little hazard to themselves, and small expense, keep this proposed government in a continued alarm, in one or other part thereof, and put them to

vast expense to defend themselves, and thereby weaken, impoverish, and greatly dishearten the King's subjects in every part of this large extent of frontiers; while the enemy will be encouraged, and grow strong and wealthy. This, indeed, cannot be remedied, but by carrying the war into the enemy's country, for which this plan makes no provision.

2. The President-General and Council to have authority to nominate and commission all military officers, will be highly detrimental to his Majesty's interest; as it cannot be apprehended that they can be well acquainted, in the various parts of so large a government, with the persons who will best serve to encourage soldiers to enlist, and who may conduct them with prudence, and encourage their hearts. It hath hitherto been practised in the New-England governments to appoint officers out of their best yeomen, who live in good circumstances on their own property in lands; and when chosen freely, and without any application of their own for such offices, and receive their commissions gratis, they look on themselves obliged, and are always ready, to serve their country in the field, when thus called thereto; and under such officers, well known and esteemed among the people, freeholders' sons, not moved by necessity, but their country's good, generally have enlisted with cheerfulness and alacrity. Now, should officers be sent among them from abroad, and to whom they are strangers, it is plain such youth will not enlist; and to press such generous young men into service, must be not only hard and grievous, but very much dishearten and dispirit them: and this, no doubt, will prove the case in other of the American colonies, as well as of those in New-England.

3. His Majesty's subjects, now inhabiting this large and extensive country, take them collectively, are become a very great number; and, through the smiles of divine Providence hitherto, are greatly increased, and it is supposed to become double in every twenty-five years: now this growing power and strength to be brought into one point, all to move under the direction of such President-General and Council, may in time be of dangerous consequence to his Majesty's interest, and the good of his loyal subjects here.

4. The President-General to have a negative voice on the Council, may bring his Majesty's interest into danger: That officer, in so extensive a territory, not well understanding, or carefully pursuing proper methods for the country's good, all may be ruined before relief can be had from the throne; and in a country, where the greatest encouragement to go through the hardship and fatigue of a new settlement is the hope of enjoying liberty, and securing a small property in land to themselves, every thing that doth make any encroachment thereon will discourage the people, and thereby injure his Majesty's interest: And it seems the Council, from the respective colonies, are most likely to understand the true interest and weal of the people.

5. The proposal, in said plan contained, for the President-General and Council to lay and levy taxes, &c. as they please, throughout this extensive government, is a very extraordinary thing, and against the rights and privileges of Englishmen, which is esteemed, and highly prized by the people of these colonies, who have now a due sense of their dependence on their mother country, and delight in obedience to, and admire the protection and privileges of, the laws of England; which, with the special favours and charter privileges to them granted, and hitherto kept sacred and inviolate, have encouraged the people inhabiting here, at their own great expense, industry, and hazard of their lives as well as fortunes, to settle, plant, and cultivate these remote places; and it is not to be doubted, that any great innovations, or breach of their original charters and constitutions, will greatly discourage the industry of the inhabitants, who are jealous of their privileges; and, while they are secured, are zealous to secure his Majesty's dominions here and pursue the enlargement thereof.

At this place, it may be worthy observation, that heavy taxes on the inhabitants, of the northern colonies especially, must be attended with grievous complaints from the main body of the people, who are not well furnished with money, and not able to carry on any considerable trade abroad, thereby to bring home *money*, more than is absolutely necessary to carry on their ordinary affairs; being principally employed in clearing, fencing, and cultivating their lands, and fitting them for future more profitable improvements; and from their first settlement have had the barbarous natives of the country frequently making war upon them, and their restless French neighbours setting on the Indians, in a barbarous manner, to kill or captivate the people, and that even in times of peace; which hath occasioned a very great expense, and loaded these colonies with a heavy debt, and brought on the necessity of creating and issuing bills of public credit; which, through their weakness and poverty, they were not able seasonably to sink and discharge, and thereby lessened credit in these parts; from which disadvantages, these colonies are not quite freed to this day; and although they are well spirited to secure and defend all his Majesty's territories in North-America, and therein to lay themselves out to their utmost ability; yet, to bring on themselves large and heavy taxes, more than they are well able to pay, must occasion grievous complaints, and prove very discouraging.

For these reasons, more largely insisted on, and discoursed at the congress of the commissioners in Albany, in June last—The gentlemen, who went commissioners from the colony of Connecticut, objected to the proposed plan; and thought they were never answered or obviated, and therefore never came into, or gave any consent to the same.

And in addition hereunto, it is further to be considered and alleged, that the people of this colony, from their first settlement to this day, in their general assemblies, by their acts and resolutions therein made and passed, have shewn true loyalty, and sincere disposition to promote his Majesty's interest; and have always yielded cheerful obedience to his Majesty's commands; and have readily given assistance and aid to any of his Majesty's colonies, when the same hath been requested; and still remain in the same good disposition, and readily to conform to his Majesty's will and pleasure, signified to this colony by the Right Honourable the Earl of Holderness. The last paragraph of his letter to this colony, dated August 28, 1753, is in the following words, viz.

"And whereas it may be greatly conducive to his Majesty's service, that all his provinces in America should be aiding and assisting each other, in case of any invasion, I have it particularly in charge from his Majesty, to acquaint you, that it is his royal will and pleasure, that you should keep up an exact correspondence with all his Majesty's Governors on the continent; and in case you shall be informed, by any of them, of any hostile attempt, you are immediately to assemble the general assembly within your government, and lay before them the necessity of a mutual assistance, and engage them to grant such supplies as the exigency of affairs may require."

It may justly be alleged and considered, that the securing the five nations or cantons of Indians, subject to his Majesty's dominions, and maintaining a peaceable and friendly disposition in them towards the people inhabiting these colonies, is of very great importance, and the principal good end that may be served by said proposed plan, by regulating the Indian trade, and bringing it under due management; which may be better served by commissioners of his Majesty's appointment, with powers and authorities to regulate and manage the trade with said Indians, and the other natives who are in friendship with them, and to make such rules and orders, with pains and penalties annexed thereto, as they shall judge necessary, and to see the same duly executed; and to hear, consider, and find means and ways to redress the grievances and complaints of said Indians; the necessity of which appears by the representation made at Albany, when the commissioners were present: And also to build forts needful for the defence of such Indians, and security of the trade with them, and keep them sufficiently garrisoned; the charge whereof may be principally defrayed by the profits of such trade, when well regulated and managed.

And if his Majesty should be graciously pleased to encourage his subjects to settle and plant a government or colony on such lands, in their country, as the Indians will readily sell, to be formed and conducted as the New-England colonies have been, nothing would tend more to secure those Indians to his Majesty's interest, and attach their friendship to the English, and prevent the encroachments of the French; and so the great ends proposed effectually answered, without any discouragement to the people of these colonies, and without the least prejudice or injury to their privileges.

General Assembly at New-Haven, Thursday, Oct. 2d, 1754.

In the Upper House. The foregoing reasons, concerning the Plan of Union, &c. were read, considered, and approved, and ordered to lie on file in the Secretary's office. Test. GEORGE WYLLYS, Sec'ry.

In the Lower House, concurred. Test. E. CHAUNCY, Clerk.

Reference: Collections, Massachusetts Historical Society, 1st Ser., Vol. VII (Boston: Charles C. Little and James Brown, 1801).

ACT TO PREVENT BRIBERY AND CORRUPTION IN ELECTION OF MEMBERS OF GENERAL ASSEMBLY, MAY 1756

Whereas bribery and corruption is destructive of civil communities and of dangerous tendency in any state,

Be it enacted by the Governor, Council and Representatives, in General Court assembled, and by the authority of the same, That no person or persons do or shall give, offer, accept or receive, any sum or sums, or any other matter or thing by way of gift, fee or reward, for giving or refusing to give any vote or suffrage for electing any member of the General Assembly of this Colony, nor promise, procure or any ways confer any gratuity, reward or preferment, for or on account of any vote or suffrage given or to be given in any such election; and every person so giving, offering, accepting or receiving as aforesaid, shall in every such case forfeit and pay the sum of five pounds, one half to him or them that shall sue for and prosecute the same to effect and the other half to the treasury of the town where the offence is committed.

And be it further enacted by the authority aforesaid, That every person who shall be elected by means of such evil and illegal practice as aforesaid, shall be and hereby is declared to be uncapable to serve as a member in such Assembly, unless such person shall be able to satisfy said Assembly that the same was done altogether without his privity, and that he was not directly or indirectly concern'd therein.

And be it further enacted by the authority aforesaid, That it shall be the duty of every constable and grandjury-man to enquire after and make presentment of all breaches of this act, and that the constables in the several towns in this Colony shall at the opening of the freeman's meeting publicly read this act, or cause the same to be read in said meeting.

Reference: Charles J. Hoadly (ed.), *The Public Records of the Colony of Connecticut, 1751–1757,* Vol. X (Hartford: Case, Lockwood, Brainard Co., 1852).

ASSEMBLY ASKS GOVERNOR TO WRITE TO KING ON STAMP ACT REPEAL, MAY 1766

This Assembly desire his Honour the Governor to consider of and prepare an humble, dutiful and loyal Address to his Majesty, expressive of the filial duty, gratitude and satisfaction, of the Governor and Company of this Colony on the happy occasion of the beneficial repeal of & par

the late American Stamp Act, so soon as he shall be possessed of all the materials and intelligence which are expedient and necessary in order to preparing and finishing such address in a decent and proper manner. And his Honour the Deputy Governor, Hezh Huntington, Mathew Griswold,

Eliphalet Dyer, William Pitkin junr, Roger Sherman, Robert Walker, Wm. Samuel Johnson, George Wyllys, Zebulon West, John Ledyard, Alexander Wolcott, Jedidiah Elderkin, and William Williams, Esqrs, are hereby appointed a committee fully authorized and directed, to assist and advise his Honour the Governor in preparing and compleating, as soon as it may conveniently be done, such address, and any other addresses as they shall judge expedient and proper on this joyful and happy event; the same to be signed and forwarded by his Honour the Governor in the name and on behalf of this Corporation; and also desire his Honour the Governor to return the most ardent and grateful thanks of this Assembly to all those who have distinguished themselves as the friends and advocates of the British

Colonies in America on this important occasion, whether as Members of the British Parliament, or otherways.

Resolved by this Assembly, That his Honour the Governor be and he is hereby desired to issue his Proclamation appointing a day for public Thanksgiving, to be religiously observed throughout this Colony, on the happy occasion of the beneficial repeal of the late Stamp Act, as soon as conveniently may be done after he shall be possessed of all the materials and intelligence of the late interesting and important occurrences in the British Parliament relative to and shewing all circumstances attending this joyful and happy event.

Reference: Charles J. Hoadly (ed.), *The Public Records of the Colony of Connecticut, 1751–1757*, Vol. X (Hartford: Case, Lockwood, Brainard Co., 1852).

19

Rhode Island

Like Connecticut, Rhode Island emerged from the Revolution of 1689 free of dominion status and able to choose its own governor. Although a royal colony, Rhode Island's legislature held much power over its governor. In January 1690, the Council of Rhode Island asked the crown to restore its government to the form it took under the first charter. That charter became sacred in Rhode Island, as its citizens believed it had given them popular governance. Only a few today claim that early Rhode Island was a democracy. Still, its citizens believed in popular representation, in selection of government officials, and in the people's role in government decision making, certainly setting it apart from other colonies. The importance of the charter to the people was confirmed in 1776, when the citizens refused to make a state constitution and expected the Assembly to continue to govern as it had in the colonial period (See Volume III, Part I).

The records and proceedings of the Rhode Island Assembly reveal a colony that was directed largely by its town governments. In 1715 the Assembly set a precedent for elections that eventually influenced other colonies. Heretofore, all citizens had signed their ballots at election time, and many freemen believed that elected officials for whom they had not voted would use their signatures against them. The Assembly repealed the signature act and provided for a secret ballot, which gave the voters privacy. The same statute made it a crime to offer or receive a bribe for a vote. Also, the Assembly, seeking to respond further to popular demands, added to that statute a provision to publish immediately all acts of the assembly. Statute Law had entered a period of openness. In 1760, the Assembly again passed an act to regulate the general election in the colony. Although the Assembly clarified just who was able to vote, in that statute it also made voting easier by giving towns control over elections. Clearly the Assembly of Rhode Island recognized that voters gave their elected officials a mandate for governing.

PETITION TO THE KING, JANUARY 30, 1689

Most dread Sovereign: We your Majesties' most humble subjects and supplicants of your Collony of Rhode Island and Providence Plantations, in New England, having received the joyful tidings of both your Majesties' safe arrival in England, after your your so great and hazardous undertaking, for the good of the nation, to relieve them from Popery and arbitrary power; as also concerning your accessions to the Crown.

The Governor of this your Majesties' Collony, by the advice of his Councill, gave order for the proclaiming both your Majesties in each respective town in this your Collony; which accordingly was done in most solemn manner, with all alacrity, beseeching the God of heaven to continue your Majesties with a long and prosperous reign, not at all doubting but your Majesties will take care of all your subjects in this your dominion of New England, as opportunity shall present, that they may be not only freed from arbitrary power, but also may enjoy their lands and other ancient rights and privileges; and therefore we humbly petition your Most Excellent Majesties' grace and favor towards us your most humble subjects and supplicants, that you would please, being Pater Patrio nostro, to extend your fatherly care in the granting a confirmation to our Charter, which although it was submitted to his late Majesty, nevertheless it was not condemned nor taken from us; and therefore since the late Revolution, concerning Sir Edmund Andros, his being deposed from the government, we your Majesties' subjects, being destitute of government, saw cause under grace and favor, to re-assume the government according to our Charter, the 1st of May last past, being the Election day appointed by our said Charter, in which Assembly it was ordered, that the former Governor, Deputy Governor, and Assistants that were in place in the year of our Lord 1686, before the coming over of Sir Edmund Andros, our late Governor, should be established in their respective places for the year ensuing, or further order

from England; since which time Sir Edmund Andros made his escape from his confinement in your Majesties' Collony of the Massachusetts, unto Rhode Island, where he was speedily seized and secured until the Governor and Council of the Massachusetts Collony demanded him, by Commissioners sent for that purpose. And accordingly we, the Deputy Governor, and some of the Assistants, gave special order for his return, taking care that all moderation should be used in the conveyance of him; and we humbly conceive it hath been a great providence of God, in this Revolution, to prevent New England from partaking in Ireland's miseries.

May it please your Excellent Majesties, your transcendent love and favor extended towards us, hath so radicated itself in our hearts never to be forgotten, that it obliges us to offer up ourselves, lives and fortunes to be at your Majesties' service beyond the power of any command. And we beg the God of Heaven to give both your Majesties a long and prosperous reign over us, and we humbly desire that your Majesties will be pleased to cause us to be enrolled amongst your loving subjects.

Dated at Newport, on Rhode Island, your Majesty's Collony of Rhode Island, and Providence Plantations, in New England, January the 30th, 1689–90. Subscribed by us, your loyal subjects, and most humble supplicants.

Reference: J.R. Bartlett (ed.), *Records of the Colony of Rhode Island and Providence Plantations in New England*, Vol. III (10 vols.; Providence: A.C. Greene, 1856–1865).

CALL TO THE PEOPLE OF RHODE ISLAND TO ASSUME THEIR FORMER GOVERNMENT, APRIL 23, 1689

Whereas, we have seen a printed paper, dated from Boston, the 18th of April last, which signifieth that Sir Edmund Andros, our late Governor, with several others, are seized and confined, so that many of the free people of this place are bent to lay hold of their former privileges:

Neighbors and Friends, we therefore, cannot omit to recommend unto you, our present griev-

ance, to wit, that we are sufficiently informed, that our late government under which we were subservient, is now silenced and eclipsed, we, under a sense of our deplorable and unsettled condition, do offer to you, whether it may not be expedient for the several towns of this late Colony, the several principal persons therein, to make their personal appearance at Newport, before the day of usual Election by Charter, which will be the 1st day of May next, there to consult and agree of some suitable way in this present juncture, and whether our ancient privileges and former methods may not be best to insist upon, which we leave to your judicious consideration, and that you may not say, you were ignorant, but had the most timeliest notice that could be given at so little warning, is all at present from your real friends and neighbors.

W.C.

Newport, this 23d April, 1689.

J.C.

Reference: J.R. Bartlett (ed.), *Records of the Colony of Rhode Island and Providence Plantations in New England,* Vol. III (10 vols.; Providence: A.C. Greene, 1856–1865).

VOTING FOR TOWN OFFICERS, JUNE 19, 1715

Whereas, the method and way prescribed by an act of this colony, that all freemen of towns and of the colony, upon their voting for town and general officers, shall write their names upon the back of their votes, hath given great dissatisfaction and uneasiness to many of the good people of this colony, who deem it a very great hardship to have their names exposed upon such occasions, to the creating of animosity and heart-burning of their particular friends, &c.;—

This Assembly, taking the matter into consideration, do see cause to repeal that act, which obliges the freemen to subscribe their names upon the back of their votes; and the said act is hereby repealed.

And for the orderly voting for the future, for general or town officers, &c., be it enacted by this Assembly and authority thereof, that the Assembly that annually meets the day before the election, to make preparations for the election, shall order and appoint the way and manner of voting for general officers in the best and most regular method they shall judge most proper, to prevent frauds, so as not oblige any to subscribe their names to their votes.

And it is further enacted by the authority aforesaid, that at any quarter or town meeting, appointed to elect deputies or town officers, in any town in this colony, the moderator, with the advice of the freemen present, shall prescribe and settle such orderly way of voting, as shall then be thought most expedient, to prevent frauds, as aforesaid.

And be it further enacted, that if in case any person at the general elections shall be convicted by two witnesses, or by confession, of putting or delivering into the hat, or to the receivers of votes for that end, more than one vote for one officer, he shall be fined by the Governor and council for his contempt, in any sum not exceeding £5, or punished by whipping, not exceeding forty stripes, or imprisoned or set in the stocks, at the discretion of the Governor and council.

And in case any person shall be convicted of the like crime in any quarter or town meeting, as aforesaid, he shall, by order of the assistants, justices or wardens, where such crime shall be committed, be fined not exceeding forty shillings, or punished by whipping, not exceeding twenty-one stripes, or set in the stocks, at the discretion of the assistants, &c.; any act or acts, clause or clauses of any act or acts, to the contrary hereof, notwithstanding.

It is further to be understood, that this act has no reference to proxy votes, which are to be signed according to former custom, &c, viz.:

To be delivered to the town clerk in a public town meeting, with their names written upon the back of their votes; and the votes being received by the town clerk, he is forthwith to deliver them to the head officer of the town, to be sealed up in a packet, in order for the said officer to deliver them to the Governor, or in his absence, to the next superior officer in the Assembly, upon the day of election.

Voted by this Assembly, that the Honorable Jos. Jencks, Esq., the present deputy governor of this colony, be allowed out of the general treasury £20 for his salary for this year's service.

Whereas, Capt. John Eldredge and Major Frye, by a former act of Assembly, were improved by this colony to build a bridge over Reynolds's, alias Hunt's river, in the Narragansett country, within this colony, and £60 ordered for the same out of the impost office on slaves, and the said Capt. Eldredge and Major Frye having informed this Assembly that there is not money sufficient in the impost office, to answer the work aforesaid;—

Therefore, it is ordered by this Assembly, that the said Capt. Eldredge, &c., be paid £20 out of the general treasury, to complete the said sum of £60, and to be paid into the general treasury by the naval officer as soon as he receives it.

It is ordered by this Assembly, that Mr. Nicholas Lang, Mr. Nathaniel Nudigate and Richard Ward, be a committee to transcribe the laws of this colony in a regular form, fit for the press, and to take the Governor's advice in all points of difficulty; and upon completing thereof, to be rewarded for their service out of the general treasury, to their content, as the Governor and council shall think reasonable.

It is ordered by this Assembly, that the acts of this Assembly be compiled in a body, and published in the town of Newport, by beat of drum, under the colony seal, on the 10th day of this instant May.

And this Assembly is adjourned to the 19th day of June next ensuing.

God save the King.

Reference: J.R. Bartlett (ed.), *Records of the Colony of Rhode Island and Providence Plantations in New England,* Vol. IV (10 vols.; Providence: A.C. Greene, 1856–1865).

ACT TO REGULATE GENERAL ELECTIONS, FEBRUARY 1760

Whereas, it is found, by long experience, that the freemen going to Newport, to put in their votes for general officers, at the election, is very injurious to the interest and public weal of the colony, and occasions a very great loss of peoples' time, at a season of the year when their labor is abundantly necessary for preparing the ground, and planting the seed; on which the produce of the whole summer must depend; and as all the ends of voting for general officers may be as fully attained, by the freemens' putting in their proxy votes at the town meeting in their own towns, appointed by law for that purpose, agreeably to the ancient and laudable custom of most of the prudent freemen,—

Therefore, be it enacted by this General Assembly, and by the authority thereof it is enacted, that for the future, every freeman, who is disposed to give his suffrage for the election of general officers in this colony, shall do it by putting in a proxy vote, in the town meeting in the town to which he belongs, on the third Wednesday in April next preceding the general election, agreeably to the law, and well known custom of proxing; and no freeman shall be permitted to vote for general officers, at the general election, held at Newport, on the first Wednesday in May, but only such as be members of the Assembly.

And be it further enacted by the authority aforesaid, that no person in this colony, for the future, shall vote and act as a freeman, in any case, whatsoever, but such only, who at the time of voting, shall be truly and really possessed of land or real estate, to be valued and determined agreeably to the former laws, of the full value of £40, lawful money, or that will rent yearly for forty shillings, lawful money, or the eldest son of such a freeman; that every person newly admitted free of any town, shall be admitted to put in his proxy vote for general officers, at the town meeting at his own town; and such of them as shall be admitted freemen of the colony, by the General Assembly, their proxies shall be received and numbered at the general election; and such as shall not be so admitted free by the Assembly, shall be rejected and thrown out.

Reference: J.R. Bartlett (ed.), *Records of the Colony of Rhode Island and Providence Plantations in New England,* Vol. VI (10 vols.; Providence: A.C. Greene, 1856–1865).

20

New York

New York also emerged from the Glorious Revolution of 1689 with its government in tact. Heretofore, that royal colony had been under the control of James II who named the governor and resisted legislative powers. In 1691 the Assembly expressed gratitude to the new monarch for acknowledging its authority and placing the crown-appointed governor as a part of the colony's governing system. The Rights and Privileges of 1691 became a guide to assembly prerogatives. Likewise, the duties the crown set for the executive in 1692 restricted the powers of Governor Benjamin Fletcher. In 1699 the General Assembly took on the task of regulating its own elections and claimed increased duties in the colony's governance.

In that statute of 1699, the Assembly also acknowledged just how significant the towns and cities were in the colony's governance. Continued immigration and growth in income of the port towns had given them much power in the colony's governance structure. Towns henceforth directed the time and place of voting and conducted elections. For example, the charter of the city of New York of 1730 opened the city to full governance prerogatives. In 1734, the Assembly again showed the importance of town governance in competition with manorial power by severely restricting old manorial prerogatives while giving more authority to the towns in counties such as Westchester. Although New Yorkers squabbled over power throughout the eighteenth century and after, and formed political factions much like modern parties, there was much support for the growing powers of the Assembly members as representatives of the towns.

RIGHTS AND PRIVILEGES OF SUBJECTS, MAY 13, 1691

Forasmuch as the representatives of this their Majesties' province of New York now convened in General Assembly are deeply sensible of their Majesties' most gracious favor in restoring to them the undoubted rights and privileges of Englishmen by declaring their royal will and pleasure in their letters patents to his Excellency, who they have appointed their Captain-General and Governor-in-Chief over this their province, that he should, with the advice and consent of their council, from time to time, as need shall require, to summon and call general assemblies of the inhabitants, being freeholders, according to the usage of their Majesties' other plantations in America. And that this most excellent constitution so necessary and so much esteemed by our ancestors may ever continue unto their Majesties' subjects within this province of New York, the representatives of this their Majesties' province convened in General Assembly do, with all duty and submission, humbly pray that the rights, privileges, liberties, and franchises according to the laws and statutes of their Majesties' realm of England may be confirmed unto their Majesties' most dutiful and loyal subjects inhabiting within this their province of New York by authority of this General Assembly. Be it, therefore, enacted by the Governor and Council and the representatives met in General Assembly, and it is hereby enacted and declared by the authority of the same, that the supreme legislative power and authority under their Majesties, William and Mary, King and Queen of England etc. shall forever be and reside in a governor-in-chief and council appointed by their Majesties, their heirs and successors, and the people by their representatives met and convened in General Assembly; that the exercise and administration of the government over the said province shall, persuant to their Majesties' letters patents, be in the said governor-in-chief, and council with whose advice and consent, or with at least five of them, he is to rule and govern the same according to the laws thereof, and for any defect therein according to the laws of England and not otherwise. That in case the governor-in-chief shall die or be absent out of the province and that there be no person within the said province commissionated by their Majesties, their heirs or successors, to be governor or commander-in-chief, that then the council for the time being, or so many of them as are in the said province, do take upon them the administration of the government and the execution of the laws thereof and powers and authorities belonging to the governor-in-chief and council, the first in nomination in which council is to preside until the said governor shall return and arrive in the said province again, or the pleasure of their Majesties, their heirs or successors, be further known. That for the good government and rule of their Majesties' subjects, a session of a General Assembly be held in this province once in every year. That every freeholder within this province

and freeman in any corporation shall have his free choice and vote in the electing, of the representatives without any manner of constraint or imposition; and that in all elections the majority of votes shall carry it; and by freeholders is to be understood every one who shall have forty shillings *per annum* in freehold. That the persons to be elected to sit as representatives in the General Assembly from time to time for the several cities, towns, counties, shires, divisions, or manors of this province and all places within the same shall be according to the proportion and number hereafter expressed, that is to say, for the city and county of New York, four; for Suffolk County, two; for Queens County, two; for Kings County, two; for the County of Richmond, two; for the County of Westchester, two; for the County of Ulster, two; for the city and county of Albany, two; for the colony of Renslaerswick, one; Dukes County, two; and as many more as their Majesties, their heirs and successors, shall think fit to establish. That all persons chosen and assembled in manner aforesaid, or the major part of them, shall be deemed and accounted the representatives of this province in General Assembly; that the representatives convened in General Assembly may appoint their own times of meeting during their sessions and may adjourn their house from time to time as to them shall seem meet and convenient. That the said representatives, as aforesaid, convened are the sole judges of the qualifications of their own members and likewise of all undue elections and may from time to time purge the house as they shall see occasion. That no member of the General Assembly or their servants, during the time of their sessions and whilst they shall be going to and returning from the said Assembly, shall be arrested, sued, imprisoned, or any ways molested or troubled or be compelled to make answer to any suit, bill, plaint, declaration or otherwise, cases of high treason and felony only excepted. That all bills agreed upon by the representatives, or the major part of them, shall be presented unto the Governor and the Council for their approbation and consent; all and every which said bills so approved of and consented to by the Governor and the Council shall be esteemed and accounted the laws of this province; which said laws shall continue and remain in force until they be disallowed by their Majesties, their heirs and successors, or expire by their own limitation. That in all cases of death or absence of any of the said representatives, the governor for the time being shall issue out a writ of summons to the respective cities, towns, counties, division, or manors for which he or they so deceased or absent were chosen, willing and requiring the freeholders of the same to elect others in their places and stead. That no freeman shall be taken and imprisoned or be deseized of his freehold or liberty or free customs or outlawed or exiled or any other ways destroyed, nor shall be passed upon, adjudged, or condemned but by the lawful judgement of his peers and by the law of this province. Justice nor right shall be neither sold, denied, or delayed to any person within this province. That no aid, tax, tollage, assessment, custom, loan, benevolence, gift, excise, duty, or imposition whatsoever shall be laid, assessed, imposed, levied, or required of or on any of their Majesties' subjects within this province, etc., or their estates, upon any manner of color or pretense whatsoever but by the act and consent of the Governor and Council and representatives of the people in General Assembly met and convened. That no man of what estate or condition soever shall be put out of his lands, tenements, nor taken nor imprisoned nor disinherited nor banished nor anyways destroyed or molested without first being brought to answer by due course of law. That a freeman shall not be amerced for a small fault but after the manner of his fault and for a great fault after the greatness thereof, saving to him his freehold and a husbandman saving to him his wainage; and a merchant saving to him his merchandise; and none of the said amercements shall be assessed but by the oath of twelve honest and lawful men of the vicinage, provided the faults and misdemeanors be not in contempt of courts or judicature. All trials shall be by the verdict of twelve men and as near as may be peers or equals of the neighborhood of the place where the fact shall arise or grow, whether the same be by indictment, declaration, or information or otherwise against the person or defendant. That in all cases capital or criminal there shall be a grand inquest who shall first present the offense; and then twelve good men of the neighborhood to try the offender, who, after his plea to the indictment, shall be allowed his reasonable challenges. That in all cases whatsoever bail by sufficient sureties shall be allowed and taken, unless for treason or felony plainly and specially expressed and mentioned in the warrant of committment, and that the felony be such as is restrained from bail by the law of England. That no freeman shall be compelled to receive any soldiers or mariners; except innholders and other houses of public entertainment who are to quarter for ready money, into his house and there suffer them to sojourn against their wills, provided it be not in time of actual war within this province. That no commission for proceeding by martial law against any of his Majesty's subjects within this province, etc., shall issue forth to any person or persons whatsoever lest by color of them any of his Majestys' subjects be destroyed or put to death, except all such officers and soldiers that are in garrison and pay during the time of actual war. That all the lands within this province shall be esteemed and accounted to the tenure of East Greenwich in their Majesties' realm of England. That no estate of a *feme covert* shall be sold or conveyed but by deed acknowledged by her in some court of record; the woman being secretly examined if she does it freely without threats or compulsion of her husband. That all wills in writing, attested by three or more credible witnesses, shall be of the same force to convey lands as other conveyances, being proved and registered in the proper offices in each county within [...] days after the testators death. That all lands and heritages within this province and dependencies shall be free from all fines, licenses upon alienations, and from all heriots, wardships, liveries, primer seisins, year, day, and waste, escheat, and forfeitures upon the death of parents and ancestors, natural, unnatural, casual, or judicial, and that forever, cases of high treason only excepted. That no person of what degree or condition soever throughout this province chosen, appointed, commissionated to officiate or execute any office or place civil or military within this province, etc., shall be capable in the law to take upon him the charge of such places before he has first taken the oaths appointed by act of Parliament to be taken in lieu of the oaths of supremacy and allegiance and subscribes the test. That no person which profess faith in God by Jesus Christ his only son shall at any time be anyways molested, punished, disturbed, disquieted, or called in question for any difference in opinion or matter of conscience in religious concernment who do not, under that pretense, disturb the civil peace of the province; and that all and every such person or persons may from time to time and at all times hereafter freely and fully enjoy his or their opinion, persuasions,

judgments in matters of conscience and religion throughout all this province and freely meet at convenient places within this province and there worship according to their respective persuasions without being hindered or molested, they behaving themselves peaceably, quietly, modestly, and religiously and not using this liberty to licentiousness nor to the civil injury or outward disturbance of others. Always provided that nothing herein mentioned or contained shall extend to give liberty for any persons of the romish religion to exercise their manner of worship contrary to the laws and statutes of their Majesties' kingdom of England.

Reference: The Colonial Laws of New York from the Year 1664 to the Revolution, Vol. I (5 vols.; New York: J. B. Lyon, 1894), 244–248.

COMMISSION OF GOVERNOR BENJAMIN FLETCHER, MARCH 18, 1692

William and Mary, by the grace of God, King and Queen of England, Scotland, France, and Ireland, Defender of the Faith, etc. To our trusty and well-beloved Benjamin Fletcher, Esquire, greeting.

We, reposing especial trust and confidence in the prudence, courage, and loyalty of you, the said Benjamin Fletcher, out of our special grace, certain knowledge, and mere motion, have thought fit to constitute and appoint, and we do by these presents constitute and appoint you, the said Benjamin Fletcher, to be our Captain-General and Governor-in-Chief in and over our province of New York and the territories thereon depending in America. And we do hereby require and command you to do and execute all things in due manner that shall belong unto your said command and the trust we have reposed in you, according to the several powers and directions granted or appointed you by this present commission and the instructions herewith given you, or by such further powers, instructions, and authorities as shall at any time hereafter be granted or appointed you under our signet and sign manual or by our order in our Privy Council, and according to such

reasonable laws and statutes as now are in force or hereafter shall be made and agreed upon by you with the advice and consent of the Council and Assembly of our said province under your government, in such manner and form as is hereafter expressed.

And we do hereby give and grant full power unto you, the said Benjamin Fletcher, after you shall first have taken an oath for the due execution of the office and trust of our Captain General and Governor-in-Chief in and over our said province of New York and the territories depending thereon, which our said Council or any five of them have hereby full power and authority and are required to administer unto you, to give and administer unto each of the members of our said council as well the oaths appointed by act of Parliament to be taken instead of the oath of allegiance and supremacy as the test and the oath for the due execution of their places and trust.

And we do hereby give and grant unto you full power and authority to suspend any of the members of our said Council from sitting, voting, and assisting therein if you shall find just cause for so doing.

And if it shall at any time happen that by the death, departure out of our said province, suspension of any of our said councilors, there shall be a vacancy in our said Council, any three whereof we do hereby appoint be a quorum, our will and pleasure is that you signify the same unto us by the first opportunity, that we may, under our signet and sign manual, constitute and appoint other in their stead. But that our affairs at that distance may not suffer for want of a due number of councilors, if ever it shall happen that there be less than seven of them residing in our said province, we do hereby give and grant unto you full powers and authority to choose as many persons out of the principal freeholders, inhabitants thereof, as will make up the full number of our said Council to be seven and no more. Which persons, by virtue of such choice, shall be, to all intents and purposes, councilors in our said province until they shall be confirmed by us or that by the nomination of others by us under our sign manual and signet the said Council shall have seven persons in it.

We do hereby give and grant unto you full power and authority, with the advice and consent of our said Council from time to time as need shall require, to summon and call General Assemblies of the inhabitants, being freeholders within your government, according to the usage of our colony of New York.

And our will and pleasure is that the persons thereupon duly elected by the major part of the freeholders of the respective counties and places and so returned and having, before their sitting, taken the oaths appointed by act of Parliament to be taken instead of the oaths of allegiance and supremacy and subscribed the test, which you shall commissionate fit persons under our seal of New York to administer, and without taking and subscribing whereof none shall be capable of sitting though elected, shall be called and held the General Assembly of that our province and territories depending thereon.

And that you, the said Benjamin Fletcher, by and with the consent of our said Council and Assembly, or the major part of them respectively, shall have full power and authority to make, constitute, and ordain laws, statutes, and ordinances for the public peace, welfare, and good government of our said province and of the people and inhabitants thereof and such others as shall resort thereto and for the benefit of us, our heirs, and successors.

Which said laws, statutes, and ordinances are to be, as near as may be, agreeable to the laws and statutes of this our kingdom of England.

Provided that all such laws, statutes, and ordinances, of what nature or duration soever, be, within three months or sooner after the making thereof, transmitted unto us under our seal of New York for our approbation or disallowance of the same, as also duplicates thereof by the next conveyance.

And in case any or all of them, being not before confirmed by us, shall at anytime be disallowed and not approved and so signified by us, our heirs, and successors under our or their sign manual and signet, or by order of our or their privy council, unto you, the said Benjamin Fletcher, or to the commander-in-chief of our said province for the time being, then such and so many of them as shall be so disallowed and not approved shall from thenceforth cease, determine, and become utterly void and of none effect, anything to the contrary thereof notwithstanding.

And to the end nothing may be passed or done by our said Council or [and] Assembly to the prejudice of us, our heirs, and successors, we will and ordain that you, the said Benjamin Fletcher, shall have and enjoy a negative voice in the making and passing of all laws, statutes, and ordinances, as aforesaid.

And that you shall and may likewise, from time to time as you shall judge it necessary, adjourn, prorogue, and dissolve all General Assemblies as aforesaid.

Our will and pleasure is that you shall and may keep and use the public seal appointed or to be appointed by us for our province of New York.

We do further give and grant unto you, the said Benjamin Fletcher, full power and authority, from time to time and at any time hereafter, by yourself, or by any other to be authorized by you in that behalf, to administer and give the oaths appointed by act of Parliament to be taken instead of the oaths of allegiance and supremacy to all and every such person or persons as you shall think fit who shall, at any time or times, pass into our said province or shall be resident or abiding there.

And we do, by these presents, give and grant unto you full power and authority, with the advice and consent of our said Council, to erect, constitute, and establish such and so many courts of judicature and public justice within our said province and the territories under your government as you and they shall think fit and necessary for the hearing and determining of all causes as well criminal as civil, according to law and equity, and for awarding of execution thereupon with all reasonable and necessary powers, authorities, fees, and privileges belonging unto them, as also to appoint and commissionate fit persons in the several parts of government to administer the oaths appointed by act of Parliament to be taken instead of the oaths of allegiance and supremacy and the test unto such as shall be obliged to [take] the same.

And we do hereby authorize and empower you to constitute and appoint judges, justices of the peace, and other necessary officers and ministers in our said province for the better administration of justice and putting the laws in execution, and to administer or cause to be administered such oath or oaths as are usually given for the due execution and performance of offices and places and for the clearing of truth in judicial causes.

We do further, by these presents, will and require that appeals be permitted to be made in cases of error from our courts in New York unto you, our Governor, and to our Council in civil causes; provided the value appealed for do exceed the sum of one hundred pounds sterling and that security be first given by the appellant to answer such charges as shall be awarded in case the first sentence shall be affirmed.

And whereas we do judge it necessary that all our subjects may have liberty to appeal to our royal person in cases that may deserve the same, our will and pleasure is that if either party shall not rest satisfied with the judgment or sentence of our Governor and Council, they may then appeal unto us in our Privy Council; provided the matter in difference exceed the real value and sum of three hundred pounds sterling and that such appeal be made within one fortnight after sentence and security be likewise duly given by the appellant to answer such charges as shall be awarded in case the sentence of the Governor and Council be confirmed; and provided, also, that execution be not suspended by reason of any such appeal unto us.

And we do hereby give and grant unto you full power and authority, where you shall judge any [offender or] offenders, in criminal matters or for any fines or forfeitures, fit objects of our mercy, to pardon and remit such offenders, fines, and foreitures before or after sentence given, treason and willful murder only excepted. In which cases you shall likewise have power, upon extraordinary occasions, to grant reprieves to the offenders until our royal pleasure may be known therein.

We do, by these presents, authorize and empower you to collate any person or persons in any churches, chapels, or other ecclesiastical benefices within our said province and territories aforesaid as often as any of them shall happen to be void.

We do hereby give and grant unto you, the said Benjamin Fletcher, by yourself, your captains, and commanders by you to be authorized, full power and authority to levy, arm, muster, command, and employ all persons whatsoever [residing] within our said province of New York and other the territories under your government, and, as occasion shall serve, them to transfer from one place to another for the resisting and withstanding of all enemies, pirates, and rebels, both at sea and at land, and to transport such forces to any of our plantations in America as occasion shall require for the defense of the same against the invasion or attempts of any of our enemies; and them, if occasion shall require, to prosecute in or out of the limits of our said province and plantations or any of them; and, if it shall please God, them to vanquish, apprehend, and take and, being taken, either, according to the laws of arms, to put to death or keep and preserve alive at your discretion.

And to execute martial law in time of invasion, insurrection or war and during the continuance of the same, as also upon soldiers in pay, and to do and execute all and every other thing or things which to a captain-general does or ought of right to belong, as fully and amply as any our captain general does or has usually done.

And we do hereby give and grant unto you full power and authority to erect, raise, and build in our said province and territories depending thereon such and so many forts and platforms, castles, cities, boroughs, towns, and fortifications as you, by the advice aforesaid, shall judge necessary; and the same or any of them to fortify and furnish with ordnance, ammunition, and all sorts of arms fit and necessary for the security and defense of our said province.

And we do hereby give and grant unto you, the said Benjamin Fletcher, full power and authority to erect one or more court or courts admiral within our said province and territories for the hearing and determining of all marine and other causes and matters proper therein to be heard, with all reasonable and necessary powers, authorities, fees, and privileges.

As also to exercise all powers belonging to the place and office of Vice Admiral of and in all the seas and coasts within your government, according to such commission, authorities, and instructions as you shall receive from ourself under the seal of our Admiralty or from our High Admiral or commissioners for executing the office of High Admiral of our foreign plantations for the time being.

And forasmuch as diverse mutinies and disorders do happen by persons shipped and employed at sea, and to the end that such as shall be shipped or employed at sea may be the better governed and ordered, we do hereby give and grant unto you, the said Benjamin Fletcher, our Captain-General and Governor-in-Chief, full power and authority to constitute and appoint captains, masters of ships, and other commanders, and to grant to such captains, masters of ships, and other commanders commissions to execute the law martial and to use such proceedings, authority, punishment, correc-

tion, and execution upon any offender or offenders which shall be mutinous, seditious, disorderly, or any way unruly, either at sea or during the time of [their] abode or residence in any of the ports, harbors, or bays of our said province or territories, as the cause shall be found to require, according to martial law; provided that nothing herein contained shall be construed to the enabling you or any by your authority to hold plea or have jurisdiction of any offense, cause, matter, or thing committed or done upon the high sea, or within any of the havens, rivers, or creeks of our said province and territories under your government by any captain, commander, lieutenant, master, or other officer, seaman, soldier, or person whatsoever who shall be in actual service and pay in and on board any of our ships of war or other vessels acting by immediate commission or warrant from our commissioners for executing the office of our High Admiral of England for the time being, but that such captain, commander, lieutenant, master, officer, seaman, soldier, or other person so offending shall be left to be proceeded against and tried as the merits of their offense shall require, either by commission under our great seal of England, as the statute of the 28th of Henry the 8th directs, or by commission from our said High Admiral according to the act of Parliament passed in the 13th year of the reign of the late King Charles the Second, entitled, *An Act for the Establishing Articles and Orders for the Regulating and Better Government of His Majesty's Navies, Ships of War and Forces by Sea,* and not otherwise; saving only that it shall and may be lawful for you, upon any such captain or commander refusing or neglecting to execute or upon his negligent or undue execution of any of the written orders he shall receive from you for our service and the service of our said province, to suspend him the said captain or commander from the exercise of his said office of commander and commit him into safe custody either on board his own ship or elsewhere, at the discretion [of you], in order to his being brought to answer for the same by commission under our great seal of England or from our said High Admiral as is before expressed. In which case, our will and pleasure is that the captain or commander so by you suspended shall, during such his suspension and commitment, be succeeded in his said office by such commission or warrant officer of our said ship, appointed by our commissioners for executing the office of our High Admiral of England or by our High Admiral of England for the time being, as by the known practice and discipline of our navy does and ought next to succeed him as in case of death, sickness, or other ordinary disability happening to the commander of any of our ships of war and not otherwise, you standing also accountable to us for the truth and importance of the crime and misdemeanor for which you shall so proceed to the suspending of such our captain or commander.

Provided, also, that all such disorders or misdemeanors committed on shore by any captain, commander, lieutenant, master, or other officer, soldier, seaman, or person whatsoever belonging to our ship of war, or other vessel acting by immediate commission or warrant from our commissioners for executing the office of our High Admiral of England under the seal of our Admiralty or from our High Admiral of England for the time being, may be tried and punished according to the laws of the place where any such disorders, offenses, and misdemeanors shall be so committed on shore, notwithstanding such offender be in our actual service and borne in our pay on board any such our ships of war or other vessels acting by immediate commission or warrant from our commissioners for executing the office of our High Admiral or from our High Admiral, as aforesaid, so as he shall not receive any protection for the avoiding of justice for such offenses committed on shore from any pretense of his being employed in our service at sea.

Our will and pleasure is that all public monies raised or to be raised within our said province and other the territories under your government be issued out by warrant from you and with the advice and consent of the Council and disposed of by you for the support of the government and not otherwise.

And we do hereby likewise give and grant unto you full power and authority, by and with the advice of our said Council, to agree with the inhabitants of our province and territories aforesaid for such lands, tenements, and hereditaments

as now are or hereafter shall be in our power to dispose; and them to grant to any person or persons for such term and under such moderate quit-rents, services, and acknowledgement, to be thereupon reserved unto us, as you, by and with the advice aforesaid, shall think fit.

Which said grants are to pass and to be sealed by our seal of New York, and being entered upon record by such officer or officers as you shall appoint thereunto, shall be good and effectual in law against us, our heirs, and successors.

And we do hereby give you full power to order and appoint fairs, marts, and markets, as also such and so many ports, harbors, bays, havens, and other places for the convenience and security of shipping and for the better loading and unloading of goods and merchandises as by you, with the advice and consent of the said Council, shall be thought fit and necessary; and in them or any of them to erect, nominate, and appoint custom houses, warehouses, and officers relating thereunto and them to alter, change, place, or displace from time to time as with the advice aforesaid shall be thought fit.

And we do, by these presents, will, require, and command you to take all possible care for the discountenance of vice and encouragement of virtue and good living, that by such example the infidels may be invited and desire to partake of the christian [religion].

And our further will and pleasure is that you shall not, at any time hereafter, by color of any power or authority hereby granted or mentioned to be granted, take upon you to give, grant, or dispose of any office or place within our said province and territories which now are or shall be granted under the great seal of England, any further than that you may, upon the vacancy of any such office or suspension of any officer by you, put in any person to officiate in the interval until the said place be disposed of by us under the great seal of England or that our directions be otherwise given therein.

And we do hereby require and command all officers and ministers, civil and military, and all other inhabitants of our said province and the territories depending thereon to be obedient, aiding, and assisting unto you, the said Benjamin Fletcher, in the execution of this our commission and of the powers and authorities hereto contained, and, in case of your death or absence out of our said province or territories under your government, unto such person as shall be appointed by us to be commander-in-chief of our said province, to whom we do, by these presents, give and grant all and singular the powers and authorities aforesaid, to be executed and enjoyed by him during our pleasure or until your arrival within our said province and territories. And if upon such death or absence there be no person upon the place commissionated or appointed by us to be commander-in-chief, our will and pleasure is that the then present council of our said province do take upon them the administration of the government and execute this commission and the several powers and authorities herein contained relating to our said province, and that the first councilor who shall be at the time of your death or absence residing within the same do preside in our said Council with such powers and

preheminences as any former president has used and enjoyed within our said province or any other our plantations in America, until our pleasure be further known or your arrival as aforesaid.

And lastly, we do hereby declare, ordain, and appoint that you, the said Benjamin Fletcher, shall and may hold, execute, and enjoy the office and place of Captain-General and Governor-in-Chief in and over our province of New York and the territories depending thereon, together with all and singular the powers and authorities hereby granted unto you for and during our will and pleasure. In witness whereof, we have caused these our letters to be made patents. Witness ourselves at Westminster, the eighteenth day of March in the fourth year of our reign.

Reference: John R. Brodhead, *Documents Relative to the Colonial History of the State of New York*, Vol. III (15 vols.; Albany: Weed, Person, and Co., 1853–1887), 827–833.

REGULATING ELECTIONS OF REPRESENTATIVES TO THE GENERAL ASSEMBLY, MAY 16, 1699

Whereas of late the election of the representatives to serve in Assembly in the respective cities and counties of this province have been managed with great outrage, tumult, and deceit to the grievious oppression and depriving of the subject of his chiefest birthright in choosing of his representatives in Assembly; for remedy whereof for the time to come and that the subject may freely enjoy his undoubted right of electing his representatives without disturbance or molestation. Be it enacted by his Excellency the Governor, Council, and Representatives convened in General Assembly, and it is hereby enacted by the authority of the same, that the Representatives of the cities and counties to be chosen within this province to come to the Assembly of our lord the King in this province hereafter to be holden shall be chosen, in every city and county and manor of this province who have right to choose, by people dwelling and resident in the same cities, counties, and manors

whereof everyone of them shall have land or tenements improved to the value of forty pounds in free hold, free from all incumbrances, and have possessed the same three months before the test of the said writ; and they which shall be chosen shall be dwelling and resident within the same cities, counties, and manors, and such as have the greatest number of them who shall have land or tenements improved to the value of forty pounds in freehold, free from incumbrances as aforesaid, shall be returned by the sheriffs of every city, counties, and manors representatives for the Assembly by indenture sealed betwixt the said sheriffs and the said choosers so to be made. And every sheriff of this province shall be hereby empowered and have authority to examine upon oath every such chooser whether he be qualified by having such an estate, as aforesaid, to choose, and if any sheriff shall return representatives to come to the Assembly contrary to the intent of this act, and thereof be convict in the Supreme Court of this province, shall incur the pain and forfeiture of fifty pounds to the use of our lord the King, his heirs and successors, and the representatives returned contrary to this act shall not be qualified to sit in Assembly and shall lose their wages. And whereas the freeholders and others in their right of election, as also the persons by them elected to be their representatives, have heretofore been greatly injured and abused. Now for remedying of the same and preventing the like for the future, be it further enacted, by the authority aforesaid, that when any new Assembly shall at anytime hereafter be summoned or called, there shall be forty days between the test and returns of the writs of summons, and that the secretary or clerk of the Crown of this province shall issue out the writs for the election of representatives to serve in the same Assembly with as much expedition as the same may be done. And the writs shall be sealed and delivered to the respective sheriffs of the cities and counties, aforesaid; and that every such sheriff, upon the receipt of the same writ, shall upon the back thereof endorse the day he received the same and, within six days after he has received the said writ of election, shall cause public notice to be given of the time and place of election and give six days notice at least of the day appointed to the constable of each town within his bailiwick, to be by the said constables affixed to the most public place of each town, as aforesaid, for the election. And be it further enacted, by the authority aforesaid, that neither the sheriff or under sheriff in any city or county within this province shall give, pay, receive, or take any free reward or gratuity whatsoever for the making out receipt, delivery return, or execution of any such writ or precept. And be it further enacted, by the authority aforesaid, that upon every election to be made of any representative to serve in this or any future Assembly, the sheriff of the city or county where such election shall be made shall hold his court for the same election at the most public and usual place of election within the said city or county where the same has most usually been made. And in case the said election be not determined upon the view with the consent of the electors there present, but that a poll shall be required for the determination thereof, then the said sheriff, or, in his absence, his under sheriff, with such others as shall be deputed by him, shall forthwith there proceed to take the said poll in some open or public place or places by the same sheriff or his under sheriff, as aforesaid, in his absence, or others appointed for the taking thereof as aforesaid. And for the more due and orderly proceeding in the said poll, said sheriff, or, in his absence, his under sheriff or such as he shall depute, shall appoint such number of clerks as to him shall seem meet and convenient for taking thereof, which clerks shall all take the said poll in the presence of the said sheriff or his under sheriff or such as he shall depute. And before they begin to take the said poll, every clerk so appointed shall, by the said sheriff or his under sheriff, as aforesaid, be sworn truely and indifferently to take the same poll and to set down the names of each elector and the place of his freehold and for whom he shall poll and to poll no elector who is not sworn if so required by the candidates or any of them then and there present. Which oath of the said clerks the said sheriff or his under sheriff, or such as he shall depute, are hereby empowered to administer. And the sheriff, or, in his absence, the undersheriff, as aforesaid, shall appoint for each candidate such one person as shall be nominated to him by each candidate then and there present to be inspectors of every clerk who shall be appointed for taking of the poll. And every elector before he is admitted to poll at the same election shall, if required by the candidates or any of them, first take the oath hereinafter mentioned. Which oath the said sheriff, by himself or his under sheriff or such sworn clerk by him appointed for taking of the said poll as aforesaid, are hereby authorized to administer, viz., "You shall swear that you are a freeholder for the country of and have improved land or tenement to the value of forty pounds lying at within the said county of freehold, and that you have not been before polled at this election nor have you procured this freehold to gain your voice in this election, so help you God." And in case any freeholder or any other person taking the said oath shall thereby commit willful corrupt perjury and be thereof convicted, or if any person does unlawfully or corruptly procure or suborn any freeholder as aforesaid or other person and shall be thereof convicted, he and they, for every such offense, shall incur the like pains and penalties as are in and by one act of Parliament made in the fifth year of the reign of the late Queen Elizabeth, entitled, *An Act for Punishment of Such*

Persons As Shall Procure or Commit Any Willful Perjury, enacted against all such who shall commit willful perjury or suborn or procure any person to commit any unlawful and corrupt perjury contrary to the said act. And be it further enacted, by the authority aforesaid, that the said sheriff, or, in his absence, his under sheriff or such as he shall depute, as aforesaid, shall at the same place of election proceed to the polling all the elections then and there present and shall not adjourn the poll then and there held to any other town or place within the same county without the consent of the candidates then and there present, nor shall, by any unnecessary adjournment in the same place of election, protract or delay the election, but shall duly and orderly proceed in the taking of the said poll from time to time from day to day without any further or other adjournment without the consent of the candidates then and there present until all the electors then and there present shall be polled and no longer. And be it further enacted, by the authority aforesaid, that every sheriff, under sheriff, or other deputed by him, to whom the election shall belong for the electing of representatives to serve in Assembly, shall forthwith deliver to such person or persons as shall desire the same a copy of the poll taken at such election, paying only a reasonable charge for writing the same. And every sheriff, under sheriff, or other person deputed by him, to whom the execution of any writ or precept for electing representatives to serve in Assembly do belong, for every willful offense contrary to this act shall forfeit to every party so grieved the sum of thirty pounds; to be received by him or them his or their executors or administrators, together with full costs of suit, and for which he or they may sue by

action of debt, bill, plaint, or information in any court of record in this province where no essoin, protection, wager of law, privilege, or imparlance shall be admitted or allowed. And be it further enacted, by the authority aforesaid, that no person whatsoever being under the age of twenty-one years shall at any time hereafter be admitted to give his vote for election of any representative or representatives to serve in this or any future Assembly, and that no person hereafter shall be capable of being elected a representative to serve in this or any future Assembly who is not of the age of twenty-one years. And every election return of any person under that age is hereby declared to be null and void; and if any such minor hereafter chosen shall presume to sit or vote in Assembly he shall incur such penalties and forfeitures as if he had presumed to sit and vote in Assembly without being chosen and returned. Always provided that the freemen in the corporations of the cities of New York and Albany have liberty to vote in their respective corporations, provided that they have been freemen of the said corporations and have actually dwelt there three months before the last of any such writ of election in manner aforesaid shall be issued out, any usage, custom, or law to the contrary hereof in anywise notwithstanding; and always provided that nothing herein contained shall be construed to have any representative of this Assembly of his right of sitting therein so long as the same shall continue, anything to the contrary hereof in any ways notwithstanding.

Reference: *The Colonial Laws of New York from the Year 1664 to the Revolution,* Vol. I (5 vols.; New York: J. B. Lyon, 1894), 405–408.

CHARTER OF THE CITY OF NEW YORK, JANUARY 5, 1730

George the Second, by the grace of God, of Great Britain, France, and Ireland, King, Defender of the Faith, etc. To all whom these present letters shall come, greeting.

Whereas on the twenty-second day of April in the year of our Lord one thousand six hundred eighty and six, Thomas Dongan, then Lieutenant-Governor and Vice-Admiral of New York and its dependencies under our predecessor James the Second then King

of England, etc., did make and execute a certain grant or instrument in writing under the seal of the province of New York in these words following.

Thomas Dongan, Lieutenant-Governor and Vice-Admiral of New York and its dependencies under his Majesty James the Second, by the grace of God, of England, Scotland, France, and Ireland, King, Defender of the Faith, supreme lord and proprietor of the colony and province of New York and its dependencies in America, etc. To all to whom this shall come sends greeting. Whereas the city of New York is an ancient city within the said province and the citizens of the said city have anciently been a body politic and corporate and the citizens of the said city have held, used, and enjoyed, as well within the same as elsewhere in the said province, diverse and sundry rights, liberties, privileges, franchises, free customs, pre-eminences, advantages, jurisdictions, emoluments, and immunities as well by prescription as by charter, letters patents, grants, and confirmations, not only of diverse governors and commanders-in-chief in the said province but also of several governors, directors-general, and commanders-in-chief of the Nether Dutch nation whilst the same was or has been under their power and subjection. And whereas diverse lands, tenements, and here-ditaments, jurisdictions, liberties, immunities, and privileges have heretofore been given and granted or mentioned to be given and granted to the citizens and inhabitants of the said city, sometimes by the name of schout, burghermasters, and schepens of the city of New Amsterdam and sometimes by the name of the mayor and aldermen, and by diverse other names as by their several letters, patents, charters, grants, writings, records, and immunities amongst other things may more fully appear. And whereas the citizens and inhabitants of the said city have erected, built, and appropriated at their own proper costs and charges several public buildings, accomodations, and conveniences for the said city, that is to say, the City Hall or Stathouse with the ground thereunto belonging, two market houses, the bridge into the dock, the wharves or dock with their appurtenances, and the new burial place without the gate of the city, and have established and settled one ferry from the said city of New York to Long Island for the accomodation and conveniency of passengers the said citizens and travellers. And whereas several the inhabitants of the said city and of Manhattan Island do hold from and under his most sacred

Majesty respectively, as well by several and respective letters patent, grants, charters, and conveyances made and granted by the late lieutenants-governors or commanders-in-chief of the said province as otherwise several and respective messuages, lands, tenements, and hereditaments upon Manhattan Island and in the city of New York, aforesaid, and their heirs and assigns respectively may hold exercise and enjoy not only such and the same liberties, privileges, and franchises, rights, royalties, free customs, jurisdictions, and immunities as they have anciently had, used, held, and enjoyed, but also such public buildings, accomodations, conveniences, messuages, tenements, lands, and hereditaments in the said city of New York and upon Manhattan Island, aforesaid, which, as aforesaid, have been by the citizens and inhabitants erected and built or which have, as aforesaid, been held, enjoyed, granted, and conveyed unto them or any of them respectively. Know ye, therefore, that I, the said Thomas Dongan, by virtue of the commission and authority unto me given and power in me residing, at the humble petition of the now mayor, aldermen, and commonalty of the said city of New York, and for diverse other good causes and considerations me thereunto moving, have given, granted, ratified, and confirmed and by these presents, for and on the behalf of his most sacred Majesty, aforesaid, his heirs, successors, and assigns, do give, grant, ratify, and confirm unto the said mayor, aldermen, and commonalty of the said city all and every such and the same liberties, privileges, franchises, rights, royalties, free customs, jurisdictions, and immunities which they, by the name of the Mayor, Aldermen, and Commonalty or otherwise, have anciently had, held, used, or enjoyed; provided, always, that none of the said liberties, privileges, franchises, rights, free customs, jurisdictions, or immunities be inconsistent with or repugnant to the laws of his Majesty's kingdom of England or any other the laws of the General Assembly of this province, and the aforesaid public buildings, accomodations, and conveniences in the said city, that is to say, the aforesaid City Hall or Stathouse, with the ground thereunto belonging, two market houses, the bridge into the dock, the wharves or dock, the said new burial place, and the aforementioned ferry, with their and every of their rights, members, and appurtenances, together with all the profits, benefits, and advantages which shall or may accrue and arise at all times hereafter for dockage or wharfage within the said dock, with all and singular the rents, issues, profits, gains, and advantages which shall or may arise, grow, or accrue by the said City Hall or Stathouse and ground thereunto belonging, market, houses, bridge, dock, burying place, ferry, and other the above mentioned premises or any of them, and also all and every the streets, lanes, highways, and alleys within the said city of New York and Manhattan Island, aforesaid, for the public use and service of the inhabitants of Manhattan Island, aforesaid, and travellers there; together with full power, license, and authority to the said mayor, aldermen, and commonalty and their successors forever to establish, appoint, order, and direct the establishing, making, laying out, ordering, amending, and repairing of all streets, lanes, alleys, highways, water courses, ferry, and bridges in and throughout the said city of New York and Manhattan Island, aforesaid, necessary, needful, and convenient for the inhabitants of the said city and Manhattan Island, aforesaid, and for all travellers and passengers there; provided, always, that this said license so as above granted for the establishing, making, and laying out of streets, lanes, alleys, highways, ferry, and bridges be not extended or be construed to extend to the taking away of any person or persons right or property without his, her, or their consent or by some known law of the said province. And for the considerations aforesaid, I do likewise give, grant, ratify, and confirm unto all and every the respective inhabitants of the said city of New York and of Manhattan Island, aforesaid, and their several and respective heirs and assigns, all and every the several and respective messuages, tenements, lands, and hereditaments situate, lying, and being in the said city and Manhattan Island, aforesaid, to them severally and respectively granted, conveyed, and confirmed by any of the late governors, lieutenants, or commanders-in-chief of the said province, or by any of the former mayors or deputy mayors and

aldermen of the said city of New York, by deed, grant, conveyance, or otherwise howsoever, to hold to their several and respective heirs and assigns forever. And I do, by these presents, give and grant unto the said mayors, aldermen, and commonalty of the said city of New York all the waste, vacant, unpatented, and unappropriated lands lying and being within the said city of New York and on Manhattan Island, aforesaid, extending and reaching to the low water mark in, by, and through all parts of the said city of New York and Manhattan Island, aforesaid, together with all rivers, rivulets, coves, creeks, ponds, waters, and water-courses in the said city and island, or either of them, not heretofore given or granted by any of the former governors, lieutenants, or commanders-in-chief under their or some of their hands and seals or seal of the province, or by any of the former mayors or deputy mayors and aldermen of the said city of New York, to some respective person or persons late inhabitants of the said city of New York or Manhattan Island or of other parts of the said province. And I do, by these presents, give, grant, and confirm unto the said mayor, aldermen, and commonalty of the said city of New York and their successors, forever, the royalties of fishing, fowling, hunting, hawking, minerals, and other royalties and privileges belonging or appertaining to the city of New York and Manhattan Island, aforesaid, gold and silver mines only excepted, to have, hold, and enjoy all and singular the premises to the said mayor, aldermen, and commonalty of the said city of New York and their successors, forever, rendering and paying, therefore, unto his most sacred Majesty, his heirs, successors, or assigns, or to such officer or officers as shall be appointed to receive the same, yearly, forever hereafter, the annual quit-rent or acknowledgement of one beaver skin, or the value thereof in current money of this province, in the said city of New York on the five and twentieth day of March yearly, forever. And, moreover, I will and by these presents do grant, appoint, and declare that the said city of New York and the compass, precincts, and limits thereof and the jurisdiction of the same shall from henceforth extend and reach itself and may and shall be able to reach forth and extend itself, as well in length and in breadth as in circuit, to the furthest extent of and in and throughout all the said Island Manhattan and in and upon all the rivers, rivulets, coves, creeks, waters, and water courses belonging to the same island as far as low water mark. And I do also, for and on behalf of his most sacred Majesty aforesaid, his heirs and successors, firmly enjoin and command that the aforesaid mayor, aldermen, and commonalty of the city, aforesaid, and their successors, shall and may freely and quietly have, hold, use, and enjoy the aforesaid liberties, authorities, jurisdictions, franchises, rights, royalties, privileges, exemptions, lands, tenements, hereditaments, and premises aforesaid, in manner and form aforesaid, according to the tenor and effect of the aforesaid grants, patents, customs, and letters patents of grant and confirmation without the let, hinderance, or impediment of me or any of my successors, governors, lieutenants, or other officers whatsoever. And also I do, for and on behalf of his most sacred Majesty aforesaid, his heirs and successors, grant to the mayor, aldermen, and commonalty of the said city of New York and their successors, by these presents, that for the better governing of the said city, liberties, and precincts thereof there shall be, forever hereafter, within the said city a mayor and recorder, town clerk, and six aldermen and six assistants to be appointed, nominated, elected, chosen, and sworn as hereinafter is particularly and respectively mentioned, who shall be forever hereafter called the Mayor, Aldermen, and Commonalty of the City of New York, and that there shall be forever one chamberlain, treasurer, one sheriff, one coroner, one clerk of the market, one high constable, seven subconstables, and one marshal or sergeant-at-mace to be appointed, chosen, and sworn in manner hereinafter mentioned. And I do, by these presents, for and on the behalf of his most sacred Majesty aforesaid his heirs, successors, and assigns, declare, constitute, grant, and appoint that the mayor, recorder, aldermen, and assistants of the said city of New York for the time being, and they which hereafter shall be the mayor, recorder, and aldermen and assistants of the said city of New York for the time being, and their successors, forever hereafter, be and shall be

by force of these presents one body corporate and politic in deed, fact, and name. I do really and fully create, ordain, make, constitute, and confirm, by these presents, and that by the name of the mayor, aldermen, and commonalty of the city of New York they may have perpetual succession and that they and their successors, forever, by the name of the mayor, aldermen, and commonalty of the city of New York, be and shall be, forever hereafter, persons able and in law capable to have, get, receive, and possess lands, tenements, rents, liberties, jurisdictions, franchises, and hereditaments to them and their successors in fee simple or for term of life, lives, or years or otherwise, and also goods and chattels, and also other things of what nature, kind, or quality soever, and also to give, grant, let, set, and assign the same lands, tenements, hereditaments, goods, and chattels, and to do and execute all other things about the same by the name aforesaid; and also that they be and forever shall be hereafter persons able in law capable to plead and be impleaded, answer and be answered unto, defend and be defended in all or any of the courts of his said Majesty and other places whatsoever and before any judges, justices, and other person or persons whatsoever in all and all manner of actions, suits, complaints, demands, pleas, causes, and matters whatsoever of what nature, kind, or quality soever, in the name and in like manner and form as other people of the said province being persons able and in law capable may plead and be impleaded, answer and be answered unto, defend and be defended by any lawful ways and means whatsoever; and that the said mayor, aldermen, and commonalty of the said city of New York and their successors shall and may, forever hereafter, have one common seal to serve for the sealing of all and singular their affairs and business touching or concerning the said corporation, and it shall and may be lawful to and for the said mayor, aldermen, and commonalty of the said city of New York and their successors, as they shall see cause, to break, change, alter, and new make their said common seal when and as often as to them shall seem convenient. And further know ye that I have assigned, named, ordained, and constituted and by these presents do assign, name, ordain, and constitute Nicholas Bayard now mayor of the said city of New York to be present mayor of the said city and that the said Nicholas Bayard shall remain and continue in the office of mayor there until another fit person shall be appointed and sworn in the said office according to the usage and custom of the said city and as in and by these presents is hereafter mentioned and directed. And I have assigned, named, ordained, and constituted and by these presents do assign, name, ordain, and constitute, create, and declare James Graham, Esquire, to be the present recorder of the said city, to do and execute all things which unto the office of recorder of the said city does or may in anywise appertain or belong. And I have assigned, named, ordained, and constituted and by these presents do assign, name, ordain, constitute, create, and declare John West, Esquire, town clerk of the said city to do and execute all things which unto the office of town clerk may anywise appertain or belong. And I have named, assigned, constituted, and made and by these presents do assign, name, constitute, and make Andrew Bown, John Robinson, William Beekman, John Delavall, Abraham Depeyster, and Johannes Kip, citizens and inhabitants of the said city of New York, to be the present aldermen of the said city. And also I have made, assigned, named, and constituted and by these presents do assign, name, constitute, and make Nicholas Dernyer, Johannes Van Brugh, John De Bruyne, Theunis Dekey, Abraham Corbit, and Wolfert Weber, citizens of the said city, to be the present assistants of the said city. And also I have assigned, chosen, named, and constituted and by these presents do assign, choose, name, and constitute Peter Delancy, citizen and inhabitant of the said city, to be the present chamberlain or treasurer of the city aforesaid. And I have assigned, named, constituted, and appointed and by these presents do assign, name, constitute, and appoint John Knight, Esquire, one other of the said citizens there, to be present sheriff of the said city; and have assigned, named, constituted, and appointed and by these presents do assign, name, constitute, and appoint Jarvis Marshall, one other of the said citizens there, to be the present marshal of the said city. And I do, by these presents, grant

to the said mayor, aldermen, and commonalty of the said city of New York and their successors that the mayor, recorder, aldermen, and assistants of the said city for the time being, or the mayor, recorder, and any three or more of the aldermen and any three or more of the assistants for the time being, be and shall be called the Common Council of the said city and that they or the greater part of them shall or may have full power and authority, by virtue of these presents, from time to time, to call and hold common council within the Common Council House or City Hall of the said city and there, as occasion shall be, to make laws, orders, ordinances, and constitutions in writing and to add, alter, diminish, or reform them from time to time as to them shall seem necessary and convenient, not repugnant to the prerogative of his most sacred Majesty, aforesaid, his heirs and successors, or to any of the laws of the kingdom of England or other the laws of the General Assembly of the province of New York, for the good rule, oversight, correction, and government of the said city and liberties of the same and of all the officers thereof and for the several tradesmen, victuallers, artificers, and of all other people and inhabitants of the said city, liberties, and precincts, aforesaid, and for the better preservation of government and disposal of all lands, tenements, and hereditaments, goods, and chattels of the said corporation. Which laws, orders, ordinances, and constitutions shall be binding to all the inhabitants of the said city, liberties, and precincts, aforesaid, and which laws, orders, ordinances, and constitutions, so by them made as aforesaid, shall be and remain in force for the space of three months and no longer unless they shall be allowed of and confirmed by the governor and council for the time being. And I do further, on the behalf of his sacred Majesty aforesaid, his heirs and successors, appoint and grant that the said common council of the said city for the time being, as often as they make, ordain, and establish such laws, orders, ordinances, and constitutions as aforesaid, shall or may make, ordain, limit, provide, set, impose, and tax reasonable fines and amerciaments against and upon all persons offending against such laws, orders, ordinances, and constitutions as aforesaid, or any of them to be made, ordained, and established as aforesaid, and the same fines and amerciaments shall and may require, demand, levy, take, and receive by warrants under the common seal to and for the use and behalf of the mayor, aldermen, and commonalty of the said city and their successors, either by distress and sale of the goods and chattels of the offender therein, if such goods and chattels may be found within the said city, liberties, and precincts thereof, rendering to such offender and offenders any overplus, or by any other lawful ways or means whatsoever. And I do, by these presents, appoint and ordain the assigning, naming, and appointment of the mayor and sheriff of the said city that it shall be as follows, namely: upon the feast day of St. Michael the Arch Angel, yearly, the lieutenant-governor or commander-in-chief for the time being, by and with the advice of his council, shall nominate and appoint such person as he shall think fit to be mayor of the said city for the year next ensuing and one other person of sufficient ability and estate and of good capacity in understanding to be sheriff of the said city of New York for the year next ensuing, and that such person as shall be named, assigned, and appointed mayor and such person as shall be named, assigned, and appointed sheriff of the said city, as aforesaid, shall, on the fourteenth day of October then next following, take their several and respective corporal oaths before the governor and council for the time being for the due execution of their respective offices, as aforesaid, and that the said mayor and sheriff, so to be nominated, assigned, and appointed as aforesaid, shall remain and continue in their said respective offices until another fit person shall be nominated and sworn in the place of mayor and one other person shall be nominated and appointed in the place of sheriff of the said city in manner aforesaid; and further that, according to the now usage and custom of the said city, the recorder, town clerk, and clerk of the market of the said city shall be persons of good capacity and understanding and such persons as his most sacred Majesty, aforesaid, his heirs and successors, shall in the said respective offices of recorder, town clerk, and clerk of the market appoint and commissionate; and

for defect of such appointments and commissionating by his most sacred Majesty, aforesaid, his heirs and successors, to be such persons as the lieutenant-governor or commander-in-chief of the said province for the time being shall appoint and commissionate. Which persons so commissionated to the said offices of recorder, town clerk, and clerk of the market shall have, hold, and enjoy the said offices according to the tenor and effect of their said commissions and not otherwise; and further that the recorder, town clerk, and clerk of the market, aldermen, assistants, chamberlain, high constable, petty constables, and all other officers of the said city, before they or any of them shall be admitted to enter upon and execute their respective offices, shall be sworn faithfully to execute the same before the mayor or any three or more of the aldermen for the time being. And I do, by these presents, for and on the behalf of his most sacred Majesty, his heirs and successors, grant and give power and authority to the mayor and recorder of the said city for the time being to administer the same respective oaths to them accordingly. And further I do, by these presents, grant for and on the behalf of his most sacred Majesty, aforesaid, his heirs and successors, that the mayor and recorder of the said city for the time being and three or more of the aldermen of the said city, not exceeding five, shall be justices and keepers of the peace of his most sacred Majesty, his heirs and successors, and justices to hear and determine matters and causes within the said city and liberties and precincts thereof and that they or any three or more of them, whereof the mayor and recorder or one of them for the time being to be there, shall and may, forever hereafter, have power and authority, by virtue of these presents, to hear and determine all and all manner of petty larcenies, riots, routs, oppressions, extortions, and other trespasses and offenses whatsoever within the said city of New York and the liberties and precincts, aforesaid, from time to time arising and happening and which arise or happen and anyways belong to the offices of justices of the peace and the correction and punishment of the offenses, aforesaid, and every of them according to the laws of England and the laws of the said province; and to do and execute all other things in the said city, liberties, and precincts, aforesaid, so fully and in ample manner as to the commissioners assigned and to be assigned for the keeping of the peace in the said county of New York does or may belong. And moreover I do, by these presents, for and on the behalf of his most sacred Majesty, aforesaid, his heirs and successors, appoint that the aldermen, assistants, high constables, and petty constables within the said city be yearly chosen on the feast day of Saint Michael the Arch Angel, forever, namely: one alderman, one assistant, and one constable for each respective ward and one constable for each division in the outward, in such public place in the said respective wards as the aldermen for the time being for each ward shall direct and appoint, and that the aldermen, assistants, and petty constables be chosen by a majority of voices of the inhabitants of each ward and that the high constable be appointed by the mayor of the said city for the time being and that the chamberlain shall be yearly chosen on the said feast day in the said city hall of the said city by the mayor and aldermen and assistants, or by the mayor or three or more of the aldermen and three or more of the assistants of the said city for the time being. And I do, by these presents, constitute and appoint the said John West to be the present town clerk of the peace and clerk of the court of pleas to be holden before the mayor, recorder, and aldermen, within the said city and the liberties and precincts thereof. And further I do, by these presents, for and on behalf of his most sacred Majesty, aforesaid, his heirs and successors, require and strictly charge and command that the sheriff, town clerk, clerk of the peace, high constable, petty constables, and all other subordinate officers in the said city for the time being, and every of them, respectively, jointly, and severally, as cause shall require, shall attend upon the said mayor, recorder, and aldermen of the said city for the time being and every or any of them, according to the duty of their respective places, in and about the executing of such the commands, precepts, warrants, and processes of them and every of them as belongs and appertains to be done or executed; and that the aforesaid

mayor, recorder, and aldermen and every of them as justices of the peace for the time being by their or any of their warrants all and every person and persons for high treason or petty treason, or for suspicion thereof, or for other felonies whatsoever, and all malefactors and disturbers of the peace and other offenders for other misdemeanors who shall be apprehended within the said city or liberties thereof, shall and may send and commit or cause to be sent and committed to the common gaol of the said city, there to remain and be kept in safe custody by the keeper of the said gaol or his deputy for the time being until such offender and offenders shall be lawfully delivered thence. And I do, by these presents, for and on the behalf of his most sacred Majesty, aforesaid, his heirs and successors, charge and require the keeper and keepers of the said gaol for the time being and his and their deputy and deputies to receive, take, and in safe custody to keep all and singular such person and persons so apprehended or to be apprehended, sent, and committed to the said gaol by warrant of the said justices or any of them, as aforesaid, until he and they so sent and committed to the said gaol shall from thence be delivered by due course of law. And further I do grant and confirm, for and on the behalf of his most sacred Majesty aforesaid, his heirs and successors that the said mayor of the said city for the time being and no other, according to the usage and custom practiced in the said city of New York in the times of my predecessors the several lieutenant-governors and commanders-in-chief of the province, shall have power and authority to give and grant licenses annually under the public seal of the said city to all tavern keepers, innkeepers, ordinary keepers, victuallers, and all public sellers of wine, strong waters, cider, beer, or any other sort of liquors by retail within the city, aforesaid, Manhattan Island, or the liberties and precincts thereof; and that it shall and may be lawful to and for the said mayor of the said city for the time being to ask, demand, and receive, for such license by him to be given and granted as aforesaid, such sum or sums of money as he and the person to whom such license shall be given or granted shall agree for, not exceeding the sum of thirty shillings for each license. All which money, as by the said mayor shall be so received, shall be used and applied to the public use of the said mayor, aldermen, and commonalty of the said city of New York and their successors without any account thereof to be rendered, made, or done to any of the lieutenants or governors of this province for the time being or any of their deputies. And know you that, for the better government of the said city and for the welfare of the said citizens, tradesmen, and inhabitants thereof, I do, by these presents, for and on the behalf of his most sacred Majesty, his heirs and successors, give and grant to the said mayor, aldermen, and commonalty of the said city and their successors that the mayor, recorder, and aldermen, or the mayor and any three or more of the aldermen for the time being, shall, from time to time and all times hereafter, have full power and authority under the common seal to make free citizens of the said city and liberties thereof and no person or persons whatsoever other than such free citizens shall hereafter use any art, trade, mystery, or manual occupation within the said city, liberties, and precincts thereof, saving in the times of fairs there to be kept during the continuance of such fairs only. And in case any person or persons whatsoever, not being free citizens of the said city, as aforesaid, shall, at any time hereafter, use or exercise any art, trade, mystery, or manual occupation, or shall, by himself, themselves, or others, sell or expose to sale any manner of merchandise or wares whatsoever by retail in any house, shop, or place or standing within the said city or the liberties or precincts thereof, no fair being then kept in the said city, and shall persist therein after warning to him or them given or left by the appointment of the mayor of the said city for the time being at the place or places where such person or persons shall so use or exercise any art, trade, mystery, or manual occupation or shall sell or expose to sale any wares or merchandises as aforesaid by retail, then it shall be lawful for the mayor of the said city for the time being to cause such shop windows to be shut up and also to impose such reasonable fine for such offense, not exceeding five pounds for every respective offense, and the same fine and fines so imposed to levy and take by warrant under the

common seal of the said city for the time being by distress and sale of the goods and chattels of the person or persons so offending in the premises found within the liberties or precincts of the said city, rendering to the party or parties the overplus, or by any other lawful ways or means whatsoever, to the only use of the said mayor, aldermen, and commonalty of the said city of New York and their successors, without any account to be rendered, made, or done to the lieutenants, governors, or commanders-in-chief of this province for the same; provided that no person or persons shall be made free as aforesaid but such as are his Majesty's natural born subjects or such as shall first be naturalized by act of General Assembly or shall have obtained letters of denization under the hand of the lieutenant-governor or commander-in-chief for the time being and seal of the province, and that all persons to be made free, as aforesaid, shall and do pay for the public use of the said mayor, aldermen, and commonalty of the said city such sum and sums of money as heretofore have been used and accustomed to be paid and received on their being admitted freemen, as aforesaid, provided it is not exceeding the sum of five pounds. And further I do, by these presents, for and on the behalf of his most sacred Majesty aforesaid, his heirs and successors, grant to the mayor, aldermen, and commonalty of the said city that they and their successors be forever persons able and capable and shall have power to purchase, have, take, and possess in fee simple lands, tenements, rents, and other possessions within or without the same city to them and their successors forever, so as the same exceed not the yearly value of one thousand pounds *per annum*, the Statute of Mortmain or any other law to the contrary notwithstanding, and the same lands, tenements, hereditaments, and premises or any part thereof to demise, grant, lease, set over, sign, and dispose at their own will and pleasure and to make, seal, and accomplish any deed or deeds, lease or leases, evidences or writings for or concerning the same or any part thereof which shall happen to be made and granted by the said mayor, aldermen, and commonalty of the said city for the time being. And further I do, by these presents, for and on the behalf of his most sacred Majesty, aforesaid, his heirs and successors, grant to the said mayor, aldermen, and commonalty that they and their successors shall and may forever hereafter hold and keep within the said city in every week of the year three market days, the one upon Tuesday and the other upon Thursday and other upon Saturday, weekly, forever. And also I do, by these presents, for and on the behalf of his most sacred Majesty, aforesaid, his heirs and successors, grant to the mayor, aldermen, and commonalty of the said city that they and their successors and assigns shall and may, at any time or times hereafter when it to them shall seem fit and convenient, to take in, fill up, and make up, and lay out all and singular the lands and grounds in and about the said city and Island Manhattan, and the same to build upon or make use of in any other manner or way as to them shall seem fit, as far into the rivers thereof and that encompass the same at low water mark, aforesaid. And I do, by these presents, for and on the behalf of his most sacred Majesty, aforesaid, his heirs and successors, give and grant unto the aforesaid mayor, aldermen, and commonalty of the said city of New York and their successors that they and their successors shall and may have, hold, and keep, within the said city and liberties and precincts thereof, in every week in every year, forever, upon Tuesday, one court of common pleas for all actions of debt, trespass, trespass upon the case, detinue, ejectment, and other personal actions, and the same to be held before the mayor, recorder, and aldermen, or any three of them whereof the mayor or recorder to be one, who shall have power to hear and determine the same pleas and actions according to the rules of the common law acts of the General Assembly of the said province. And I do, by these presents, for and on behalf of his most sacred Majesty, aforesaid, his heirs and successors, grant to the said mayor, aldermen, and commonalty of the said city of New York and their successors that the said mayor, aldermen, and commonalty of the said city and their successors shall have and enjoy all the privileges, franchises, and powers that they have and use or that any of their predecessors at any time within the space of twenty years last past had, took, or enjoyed

or ought have had by reason or under any pretence of any former charter, grant, prescription, or any other right, custom, or usage although the same have been forfeited, lost, or have been ill-used or not used or abused or discontinued, albeit they be not particularly mentioned, and that no officer shall disturb them therein under any pretence whatsoever, not only for their future but their present enjoyment thereof; provided, always, that the said privileges, franchises, and powers be not inconsistent with or repugnant to the laws of his Majesty's kingdom of England or other the laws of the General Assembly of this province, as aforesaid, and saving to his most sacred Majesty, aforesaid, his heirs, successors, and assigns, and the lieutenants, governors, and commanders-in-chief and other officers under him and them in Fort James, in or by the city of New York, and in all the liberties, boundaries, extents, privileges thereof, for the maintenance of the said fort and garrison there, all the right, use, title, and authority which they or any of them have, had, used, or exercised there, and also one messuage or tenement next the City Hall and one messuage by the fort now in the possession of Thomas Coker, gentleman, the piece of ground by the gate called the Governor's Garden, and the land without the gate called the King's Farm, with the swamp next to the same land by the fresh water, and saving the several rents and quit-rents reserved, due, and payable from several persons inhabiting within the said city and island of Manhattan by virtue of former grants to them made and given, and saving to all other bodies politic and corporate, their heirs, successors, and assigns all such right, title, and claim, possessions, rents, services, commons, emoluments, interest in and to anything which is theirs, save only the franchises aforesaid, in as ample manner as if this charter had not been made. And further I do appoint and declare that the incorporation to be founded by this charter shall not at any time hereafter do or suffer to be done anything by means whereof the lands, tenements, or hereditaments, stock, goods, or chattels thereof, or in the hands, custody, possession of any of the citizens of the said city such as have been set, let, given, granted, or collected to and for the pious and charitable uses shall be wasted or misemployed contrary to the trust or intent of the founder or giver thereof, and that such and no other construction shall be made thereof than that which may tend most to advantage religion, justice, and the public good and to suppress all acts and contrivances to be invented or put in use contrary thereunto. In witness whereof, I have caused these presents to be entered in the secretary's office and the seal of the said province to be hereunto affixed this seven and twentieth day of April in the second year of the reign of his most sacred Majesty, aforesaid, and in the year of our lord God one thousand six hundred and eighty-six. Thomas Dongan.

By virtue or under pretext whereof the said citizens and inhabitants, from the date thereof, hitherto have held or claim to hold and still do hold or claim to hold and enjoy all and singular the rights, privileges, franchises, preeminences, advantages, jurisdictions, courts, powers, profits, immunities, lands, tenements, hereditaments, and other the premises therein particularly mentioned and thereby intended to be granted. And whereas the citizens and inhabitants of the said city of New York, besides the several public buildings, accomodations, conveniences, and other things in the before recited grant or writing mentioned to have been by them erected, built, and appropriated, have, since the making thereof, built and appropriated at their own proper costs and charges several public buildings, accomodations, and conveniences for the said city, that is to say, the present city hall, gaols, rooms, and places for the sitting of courts of justice and chambers adjoining, with the ground and appurtenances thereunto belonging, five market houses, the present crane, and bridge with the common shore, leading through the great dock, and a magazine or powder house near the fresh water, and several other public buildings and conveniences in the said city, and have built the new ferry houses on the island of Nassau for the reception of travellers, with a barn, stables, and pen or pound for cattle. And whereas our late royal predecessor Queen Anne, by her letters patent under the broad seal of the province of New York made, bearing date the nineteenth day of April in the seventh year of her reign, did grant, ratify, and confirm unto the then mayor, aldermen, and commonalty of the city of New York and to their successors and assigns in these words following, to wit.

Reference: The Colonial Laws of New York from the Year 1664 to the Revolution, Vol. II (5 vols.; New York: J. B. Lyon, 1894), 575–639.

CHOICE OF REPRESENTATION IN WESTCHESTER COUNTY, JUNE 22, 1734

Whereas his late Majesty, King William the Third, of glorious memory, by his letters patent under the great seal of the colony of New York, bearing date the seventeenth day of June in the ninth year of his reign, did, among other things, grant unto Collo Stephanis Van Cortlandt, since deceased, and to his heirs and assigns, forever, the right, liberty, and privilege of returning and sending a discreet inhabitant in and of the said manor in every assembly, after the expiration of the term of twenty years from the date thereof, to be summoned and held within this province. Which representative so returned and sent should be received into the House of Representatives of Assembly as a member of the said House, to have and enjoy such privileges as the other representatives returned and sent from any of the other counties and manors of the said province have had and enjoyed in any former assembly held within the said province as in and by the said in part recited letters patent may more fully appear. And whereas, pursuant to a writ lately issued to the freeholders of and in the said manor to elect and choose such fit person to represent them in the present General Assembly, Philip Verplank of the said manor, esquire, has been elected and returned as such, but inasmuchas the heirs of the said Stephanus Van Cortlandt, by reason of the said manors remaining undivided among them and otherwise and not until very lately asserted and claimed their said privilege, and there not being sufficient provision made in the said grant for the regulating and orderly choosing of such representatives, some debates and controversies did arise in the House of Representatives upon the return made to them of the choice of the said Philip Verplank as aforesaid. And thereupon, for the more regular admission of the said Philip, it was ordered he should have leave to bring in a bill for that purpose wherefore and to the end such representative may be the more orderly and duly elected for the future. Be it enacted by his Excellency the Governor, the Council, and the General Assembly of the said colony, and it is hereby enacted by the authority of the same, that the election and return of the said Philip Verplank, as aforesaid, shall and is hereby approved of and confirmed and the said Philip Verplank is accordingly hereby admitted and declared to be a representative of the said Manor of Cortlandt and as such to serve in the present House of Representatives and invested with the same and like powers and privileges as any other member of the said House has or ought to have; provided he, the said Philip Verplank, do first qualify himself by taking the oaths appointed by law as the other members of this House have done before he be admitted to act as such. And be it further enacted, by the authority aforesaid, that, from henceforth and forever hereafter, it shall and may be lawful to and for the freeholders of the said Manor of Cortlandt, when and as often as need shall be and required, to assemble and meet together in the said Manor at such time and place as the constable or other returning officer or officers of the said manor, for that purpose, shall direct and appoint, and then

and there by plurality of voices of the freeholders to elect, choose, and send a fit and discreet inhabitant and freeholder of and in the said Manor to be a representative of the said Manor in every general assembly hereafter to be summoned and held within this colony. Which inhabitant and freeholder, to be so chosen from time to time to represent the said Manor, is hereby declared to be a member of the General Assembly of this colony and to be received into the House as such. And be it further enacted, by the authority aforesaid, that the returning officer or officers of the said Manor, for the time being, shall and is hereby fully empowered and authorized to take the votes of the freeholders of the said Manor upon every election hereafter to be made and to proceed in all disputes and controversies which may happen to arise thereupon and administer such proper oaths as by law are appointed or shall be appointed for that purpose in the same and like manner as the sheriffs of any county within this colony is or shall be empowered to do. Provided, and be it enacted by the authority aforesaid, that the freeholders and inhabitants of the said Manor of Cortlandt shall at all times pay the wages of their own representative, and that nothing herein contained shall exempt them from paying their due and equal proportion of the wages of the deputies or the representatives for the county of Westchester and of all other the annual public and necessary charges of the same county.

Reference: The Colonial Laws of New York from the Year 1664 to the Revolution, Vol. II (5 vols.; New York: J. B. Lyon, 1894), 835–837.

FREQUENT ELECTIONS OF REPRESENTATIVES TO THE GENERAL ASSEMBLY, DECEMBER 16, 1737

Whereas the frequent electing of the members that constitute the General Assembly of this colony and meeting of the same in General Assembly not only tends very much to preserve the liberty and safety of the inhabitants of this colony, but also tends to create a good and lasting harmony and agreement, necessary for the honor and inter-

est of his Majesty and the safety and well-being of his subjects, here to subsist between the governor for the time being and the inhabitants of this colony, and to establish and preserve the same upon the most solid firm and lasting foundation. Be it, therefore, enacted by his honor the lieutenant-governor, the Council, and the General Assembly, and it is hereby enacted by the authority of the same, that the General Assembly of this colony for the time being shall meet and be held once in every year at least at the city of New York, unless the governor or commander-in-chief for the time being, by and with the advice and consent of a majority of his Majesty's Council for this colony, which majority shall consist at least of five, shall think fit, under the seal of the province, to name and appoint some other place within this colony. And be it enacted, by the authority aforesaid, that within six months at the farthest from and after the dissolution of this present General Assembly and so from time to time, forever hereafter, within six months at farthest from and after the determination of every general assembly of this colony, legal writs under the great seal of the province shall be issued for calling, choosing, assembling, and holding a new General Assembly which said new General Assembly shall be held at least once

in every year during its continuance, as aforesaid. And be it further enacted, by the authority aforesaid, that from henceforth no General Assembly whatsoever that shall hereafter be elected, chosen, called, held, or assembled shall have any longer continuance than for three years only at the farthest, to be accounted from the day on which, by the writs for election or summons, the said General Assembly shall be appointed to meet. And be it enacted, by the authority aforesaid, that this present General Assembly shall cease and determine on the fifteenth day of June, which shall be in the year of our Lord one thousand seven hundred and thirty-nine, unless the Governor or commander-in-chief of this colony shall think fit to dissolve the same sooner.

Reference: The Colonial Laws of New York from the Year 1664 to the Revolution, Vol. II (5 vols.; New York: J. B. Lyon, 1894), 951–952.

21

New Jersey

Freed from the Stuart monarchy, the two Jerseys returned to proprietary status in 1689. In 1702 Queen Anne took away proprietary rights, turned the colony into a royal one, and united the two Jerseys into one colony. The assembly members had previously fought with the proprietors over rights, and many of them were pleased to come under the protection of the crown. Queen Anne placed Lord Edward Cornbury, later the Third Earl of Clarendon, as governor in 1702, and his instructions gave him immense authority. For the next 20 years a weak Assembly fought to gain power from the royal authority.

In 1735, the New Jersey assembly petitioned the crown to give it a governor separate from the one in New York. Once a separate governor was named the Assembly began to ask for more authority in governing the colony. For example, in 1758, after George III named Francis Bernard governor, the Assembly took charge of his compensation. The Assembly forced the governor to share appointment powers, and the Assembly took over the colony's taxing system. New Jersey now joined the other colonies in the rise of Assembly authority and in the power struggles with royal governors.

REMONSTRANCE OF EAST JERSEY, 1700

To the King's most Excellent Majesty. The remonstrance and humble petition of your Majesty's loyal subjects inhabiting in your Majesty's province of East New Jersey in America.

Humbly sheweth: that whereas your Majesty's humble petitioners did remove and settle themselves into the said province of East New Jersey and, by virtue of a license from the honorable Colonel Richard Nicholls, Governor of the said province under his then Royal Highness the Duke of York to purchase lands of the native pagans, did, according to the said license, purchase lands of the said natives at their own proper costs and charges. And whereas since his said Royal Highness did sell and transfer all his right and interest to the said province of East New Jersey to certain proprietors, by whose license several other your Majesty's loyal subjects have also since purchased lands at their own proper costs and charges of the native pagans of the same place, whereby they humbly conceive they have acquired and gained a right and property to the said lands so purchased. Yet, notwithstanding, your Majesty's loyal subjects are molested, disturbed, and dispossessed of their said lands by the said proprietors or their agents, who, under pretense and color of having bought the government with the soil, have distrained from and ejected several persons for and under pretense of quit-rent and lord's rent, whereby your Majesty's liege subjects have been sued and put to great trouble and charges and have been compelled to answer to vexatious actions and after they have defended their own rights and obtained judgement in their favor could not have their charges as according to law they ought to have, but have been forced to sit down under the loss of several hundreds of pounds sustained by their unjust molestations.

And further, notwithstanding, your Majesty's liege subjects have purchased their lands at their own proper costs and charges, by virtue of the aforesaid licenses. Yet the said proprietors, gover-nors, or agents, without any pretended process of law, have given and granted great part of the said lands by patent to several of the said proprietors and others as to them seemed fit.

And notwithstanding their pretense to gov-ernment, yet they left us from the latter end of June, 1689, till about the latter end of August, 1692, without any government, and that too in time of actual war. So that had the enemy made a descent upon us, we were without any military officers to command or give directions in order to our defense or magistrates to put the laws in execu-tion. And during the whole time the said propri-etors have governed this your Majesty's province they have never taken care to preserve or defend us from the native pagans or other enemies by sending or providing any arms, ammunition, or stores, but rather have provoked and incensed the said natives to make war upon us by surveying and patenting their lands contrary to their liking without purchasing the same from them, or mak-ing any satisfaction in consideration thereof, and sometimes, when the said natives have sold and disposed their lands as to them seemed meet, they the said proprietors have disposed of the same to others or else forced them who had the property in it to purchase it of them upon their own terms, which the said natives have highly resented and often complained of and may justly be feared, wait only for an opportunity to revenge it upon the inhabitants of this your Majesty's province.

And further to manifest the illegal and arbi-trary proceedings of the said proprietors in con-tempt of your Majesty's laws and against their own knowledge signified in a letter by them to the council here in East New Jersey, wherein they say as follows: We have been obliged against our inclinations to dismiss Colonel Hamilton from the government, because of a late act of Parliament disabling all Scotch men to serve in places of public trust or profit and obliging all proprietors of colonies to present their respective governors to the King for his approbation. So we have appointed our friend Jeremiah Basse to suc-ceed Colonel Hamilton in government, whom we have also presented to the King and he is by him owned and approved of.

Notwithstanding which letter they have super-seded the said Jeremiah Basse, whom they wrote was approved by your Majesty, and have commis-sionated the said Colonel Hamilton again with-out your Majesty's royal approbation, although removed before by them as a person disabled by law, who now by virtue of their the said propri-etors commission only would impose himself upon us as governor. And when in government before superseded by the aforesaid Basse was by them continued about a year after the twenty-fifth of March, 1697, without taking the oath enjoined by law, and does now presume to exercise gov-ernment not having legally taken the said oath or having your Majesty's royal approbation, the said proprietors of East New Jersey have also, in contempt of your Majesty's known laws, commis-sionated a native of Scotland to be Secretary and Attorney-General of this your Majesty's province, being both places of the greatest trust next the Governor, and one of the same nation to be Clerk of the Supreme Court of this your Majesty's prov-ince, which may be of ill-consequence in relation to the *Act of Trade and Navigation* and to the great hindrance of your Majesty's loyal subjects, the power of government being chiefly in the hands of natives of Scotland, from informing against any illegal or fraudulent trading by Scotchmen or others in this province.

We, your Majesty's loyal subjects, labor-ing under these and many other grievances and oppressions by the proprietors of this your Majesty's province of East New Jersey, do in most humble manner lay ourselves before your Majesty (the fountain of justice), humbly imploring your Majesty will be graciously pleased, according to your princely wisdom, to take into consideration our evil circumstances under the present proprietors, if the right of government is invested in them, and that your Majesty will be graciously pleased to give your royal orders to the said proprietors that, with your Majesty's royal approbation, they commissionate for governor a fit person qualified according to law, who, as an indifferent judge, may decide the controversies arising between the proprietors and the inhabitants of this your Majesty's province and settle all the differences which at present they labor under.

And your Majesty's petitioners, as in duty bound, shall ever pray, etc.

Reference: W. A. Whitehead, et al. (eds.), *Archives of the State of New Jersey,* Vol. II (33 vols.; Newark: State Historical Society, 1888–1928), 322–325, 344–352.

INSTRUCTIONS TO GOVERNOR LORD CORNBURY, NOVEMBER 16, 1702

Instructions for our right trusty and well-beloved Edward Lord Cornbury, our Captain-General and Governor in Chief in and over our province of Nova Cesaria, or New Jersey, in America. Given at our Court at St. James, the sixteenth day of November, 1702, in the first year of our reign.

1. With these our instructions you will receive our commission under our great seal of England constituting you our Captain-General and Governor-in-Chief of our province of New Jersey.

2. You are, with all convenient speed, to repair to our said province and, being there arrived, you are to take upon you the execution of the place and trust we have reposed in you and forthwith to call together the following persons, whom we do by these presents appoint and constitute members of our Council in and for that province, viz., Edward Hunloke, Lewis Morris, Andrew Bowne, Samuel Jenings, Thomas Revell, Francis Davenport, William Pinhorne, Samuel Leonard, George Deacon, Samuel Walker, Daniel Leeds, William Sandford, and Robert Quarry, Esquires.

3. And you are, with all due solemnity, to cause our said commission under our great seal of England, constituting you our Captain-General and Governor-in-Chief as aforesaid, to be read and published at the said meeting of our Council and to cause proclamation to be made in the several most public places of our said province of your being constituted by us our Captain-General and Governor-in-Chief, as aforesaid.

4. Which being done, you shall yourself take and also administer to each of the members of our said council so appointed by us the oaths appointed by act of Parliament to be taken instead of the oaths of allegiance and supremacy, and the oath mentioned in an act, entitled, *An Act to Declare the Alteration in the Oath Appointed to be Taken by the Act, entitled, An Act for the Further Security of His Majesty's Person and the Succession of the Crown in the Protestant Line and for Extinguishing the Hopes of the Pretended Prince of Wales and all Other Pretenders and Their Open and Secret Abettors and for Declaring the Association to be Determined;* as also the test mentioned in an act of Parliament made in the twenty-fifth year of the reign of King Charles the Second, entitled, *An Act for Preventing Dangers Which May Happen From Popish Recusants;* together with an oath for the due execution of your and their places and trusts, as well with regard to the equal and impartial administration of justice in all causes that shall come before you as otherwise, and likewise the oath required to be taken by governors of plantations to do their utmost that the laws relating to the plantations be observed.

5. You are forthwith to communicate unto our said council such and so many of these our instructions, wherein their advice and consent

are mentioned to be requisite, as likewise all such others from time to time as you shall find convenient for our service to be imparted to them.

6. And whereas the inhabitants of our said province have of late years been unhappily divided and, by their enmity to each other, our service and their own welfare has been very much obstructed; you are, therefore, in the execution of our commission, to avoid the engaging yourself in the parties which have been formed amongst them and to use such impartiality and moderation to all as may best conduce to our service and the good of the colony.

7. You are to permit the members of our said council to have and enjoy freedom of debate and vote in all affairs of public concern that may be debated in council.

8. And although, by our commission aforesaid, we have thought fit to direct that any three of our councilors make a quorum, it is, nevertheless, our will and pleasure that you do not act with a quorum of less than five members, except in case of necessity.

9. And that we may be always informed of the names and characters of persons fit to supply the vacancies which shall happen in our said council, you are to transmit unto us, by one of our principal secretaries of state, and to our commissioners for trade and plantations, with all convenient speed, the names and characters of six persons, inhabitants of the eastern division, and six other persons, inhabitants of the western division, of our said province, whom you shall esteem the best qualified for that trust; and so from time to time when any of them shall die, depart out of our said province, or become otherwise unfit, you are to nominate unto us so many other persons in their stead, that the list of twelve persons fit to supply the said vacancies, viz., six out of the east and six out of the west division, as aforesaid, may be always complete.

10. You are from time to time to send to us, as aforesaid, and to our commissioners for trade and plantations, the names and qualities of any members by you put into our said council, by the first conveniency after you so doing.

11. And in the choice and nomination of the members of our said council, as also of the principal officers, judges, assistants, justices, and sheriffs, you are always to take care that they be men of good life and well-affected to our government, of good estates and abilities, and not necessitous people or much in debt.

12. You are neither to augment nor diminish the number of our said council as it is hereby established nor to suspend any of the present members thereof without good and sufficient cause. And in case of suspension of any of them, you are to cause your reasons for so doing, together with the charges and proofs against the said persons and their answers thereunto, unless you have some extraordinary reason to the contrary, to be duly entered upon the council books; and you are, forthwith, to transmit the same, together with your reasons for not entering them upon the council books, in case you do not enter them, unto us and to our commissioners for trade and plantations, as aforesaid.

13. You are to signify our pleasure unto the members of our said council that if any of them shall, at any time hereafter, absent themselves and continue absent above the space of two months together from our said province without leave from you, or from our governor or commander-in-chief of our said province for the time being, first obtained, or shall remain absent for the space of two years, or the greater part thereof successively, without our leave given them under our royal sign manual; their place or places in our said council shall immediately thereupon become void and that we will forthwith appoint others in their stead.

14. And in order to the better consolidating and incorporating the two divisions of East and West New Jersey into and under one government, our will and pleasure is that, with all convenient speed, you call together one General Assembly for the enacting of laws for the joint and mutual good of the whole; and that the said General Assembly do sit in the first place at Perth Amboy in East New Jersey and afterwards the same, or other the next General Assembly, at Burlington in West New Jersey; and that all future general

assemblies do set at one or the other of those places alternately, or, in cases of extraordinary necessity, according as you, with the advice of our foresaid council, shall think fit to appoint them.

15. And our further will and pleasure is that the General Assembly so to be called do consist of four and twenty representatives, who are to be chosen in the manner following, viz., two by the inhabitants householders of the city or town of Perth Amboy in East New Jersey, two by the inhabitants householders of the city and town of Burlington in West New Jersey, ten by the freeholders of East New Jersey and ten by the freeholders of West New Jersey; and that no person shall be capable of being elected a representative by the freeholders of either division, or afterwards of sitting in general assemblies, who shall not have one thousand acres of land of an estate of freehold in his own right within the division for which he shall be chosen; and that no freeholder shall be capable of voting in the election of such representative who shall not have one hundred acres of land of an estate of freehold in his own right within the division for which he shall so vote; and that this number of representatives shall not be enlarged or diminished, or the manner of electing them altered, otherwise than by an act or acts of the General Assembly there, and confirmed by the approbation of us, our heirs, and successors.

16. You are, with all convenient speed, to cause a collection to be made of all the laws, orders, rules, or such as have hitherto served or been reputed as laws amongst the inhabitants of our said province of Nova Cesaria, or New Jersey, and, together with our aforesaid Council and Assembly, you are to revise, correct, and amend the same as may be necessary; and, accordingly, to enact such and so many of them as by you, with the advice of our said Council and Assembly, shall be judged proper and conducive to our service and the welfare of our said province, that they may be transmitted unto us in authentic form for our approbation or disallowance.

17. You are to observe in the passing of the said laws and of all other laws that the style enacting the same be by the Governor, Council and Assembly, and no other.

18. You are also, as much as possible, to observe, in the passing of all laws, that whatever may be requisite upon each different matter be accordingly provided for by a different law, without intermixing in one and the same act such things as have no proper relation to each other; and you are especially to take care that no clause or clauses be inserted in or annexed to any act which shall be foreign to what the title of such respective act imports.

19. You are to transmit authentic copies of the forementioned laws that shall be enacted, and of all laws, statutes, and ordinances which shall at any time hereafter be made or enacted within our said province, each of them separately, under the public seal, unto us and to our said commissioners for trade and plantations, within three months or by the first opportunity after their being enacted, together with duplicates thereof by the next conveyance, upon pain of our high displeasure and of the forfeiture of that year's salary wherein you shall at any time, or upon any pretense whatsoever, omit to send over the said laws, statutes, and ordinances, as aforesaid, within the time above limited, as also of such other penalty as we shall please to inflict. But if it shall happen that, during time of war, no shipping shall come from our said province or other our adjacent or neighboring plantations within three months after the making such laws, statutes, and ordinances, whereby the same may be transmitted, as aforesaid, then the said laws, statutes, and ordinances are to be so transmitted, as aforesaid, by the next conveyance after the making thereof, whenever it may happen, for our approbation or disallowance of the same.

20. You are to take care that in all acts or orders to be passed within that our province in any case for levying money or imposing fines and penalties, express mention be made that the same is granted or reserved to us, our heirs, or successors, for the public uses of that our province, and the support of the government thereof, as by the said act or orders shall be directed.

21. And we do particularly require and command that no money, or value of money whatsoever, be given or granted by an act or order of Assembly to any governor, lieutenant-governor, or commander-in-chief of our said province, which shall not, according to the style of acts of Parliament in England, be mentioned to be given and granted unto us, with the humble desire of such assembly that the same be applied to the use and behoof of such governor, lieutenant-governor, or commander-in-chief, if we shall so think fit; or if we shall not approve of such gift or application, that the said money, or value of money, be then disposed of and appropriated to such other uses as in the said act or order shall be mentioned; and that from the time the same shall be raised, it remain in the hands of the receiver of our said province until our royal pleasure shall be known therein.

22. You shall also propose with the said General Assembly, and use your utmost endeavors with them that an act be passed for raising and settling a public revenue for defraying the necessary charge of the government of our said province; in which, provision be particularly made for a competent salary to yourself as Captain-General and Governor-in-Chief of our said province, and to other our succeeding captain-generals, for supporting the dignity of the said office, as likewise due provision for the salaries of the respective members of our Council and Assembly and of all other officers necessary for the administration of that government.

23. Whereas it is not reasonable that any of our colonies or plantations should, by virtue of any exemptions or other privileges whatsoever, be allowed to seek and pursue their own particular advantages by methods tending to undermine and prejudice our other colonies and plantations which have equal title to our royal care. And whereas the trade and welfare of our province of New York would be greatly prejudiced, if not entirely ruined, by allowing unto the inhabitants of Nova Cesaria, or New Jersey, any exemption from those charges which the inhabitants of New York are liable to. You are, therefore, in the settling of a public revenue as before directed, to propose to the Assembly that such customs, duties, and other impositions be laid upon all commodities imported or exported in or out of our said province of Nova Cesaria, or New Jersey, as may equal the charge that is or shall be laid upon the like commodities in our province of New York.

24. And whereas we are willing in the best manner to provide for the support of the government of our said province by setting apart sufficient allowances to such as shall be our governor or commander-in-chief, residing for the time being within the same. Our will and pleasure, therefore, is that when it shall happen that you shall be absent from the territories of New Jersey and New York, of which we have appointed you Governor, one full moiety of the salary and of all perquisites and emoluments whatsoever, which would otherwise become due unto you, shall, during the time of your absence from the said territories, be paid and satisfied unto such governor or commander-in-chief who shall be resident upon the place for the time being, which we do hereby order and allot unto him towards his maintenance and for the better support of the dignity of that our government.

25. Whereas great prejudice may happen to our service and the security of our said province under your government by your absence from those parts, without a sufficient cause and especial leave from us. For prevention thereof, you are not, upon any pretense whatsoever, to come to Europe from your government without first having obtained leave for so doing under our signet and sign manual or by our order in our Privy Council.

26. You are not to permit any clause whatsoever to be inserted in any law for the levying money, or the value of money, whereby the same shall not be made liable to be accounted for unto us here in England and to our High Treasurer, or to our commissioners of our Treasury for the time being.

27. You are to take care that fair books of accounts of all receipts and payments of all such money be duly kept and the truth thereof attested upon oath, and that the said books be transmitted every half year or oftner to our High Treasurer

or to our commissioners of our Treasury for the time being, and to our commissioners for trade and plantations, and duplicates thereof by the next conveyance. In which books shall be specified every particular sum raised or disposed of, together with the names of the persons to whom any payment shall be made, to the end we may be satisfied of the right and due application of the revenue of our said province.

28. You are not to suffer any public money whatsoever to be issued or disposed of otherwise than by warrant under your hand, by and with the advice and consent of our said Council. But the assembly may be, nevertheless, permitted, from time to time, to view and examine the accounts of money, or value of money, disposed of by virtue of laws made by them, which you are to signify unto them as there shall be occasion.

29. And it is our express wish and pleasure that no law for raising any imposition on wines or other strong liquors be made to continue for less than one whole year; as also that all laws whatsoever for the good government and support of our said province be made indefinite and without limitation of time, except the same be for a temporary end, which shall expire and have its full effect within a certain time.

30. And, therefore, you shall not reenact any law which shall have been once enacted there by you except upon very urgent occasions, but in no case more than once without our express consent.

31. You shall not permit any act or order to pass in our said province whereby the price or value of the current coin within your government, whether it be foreign or belonging to our dominions, may be altered, without our particular leave or direction for the same.

32. And you are particularly not to pass any law or do any act, settlement, or otherwise whereby our revenue, after it shall be settled, may be lessened or impaired, without our especial leave or commands therein.

33. You shall not remit any fines or forfeitures whatsoever above the sum of ten pounds, nor dispose of any escheats, fines, or forfeitures whatsoever, until upon signifying unto our High

Treasurer or to our commissioners of our Treasury for the time being, and to our commissioners for trade and plantations, the nature of the offense and the occasion of such fines, forfeitures, or escheats, with the particular sums or value thereof, which you are to do with all speed you shall have received our directions therein. But you may, in the meantime, suspend the payment of the said fines and forfeitures.

34. You are to require the secretary of our said province, or his deputy for the time being, to furnish you with transcripts of all such acts and public orders as shall be made from time to time, together with a copy of the journals of the Council, to the end the same may be transmitted unto us and to our commissioners for trade and plantations as above directed; which he is duly to perform, upon pain of incurring the forfeiture of his place.

35. You are also to require from the clerk of the Assembly, or other proper officer, transcripts of all the journals and other proceedings of the said Assembly, to the end the same may in like manner be transmitted, as aforesaid.

36. Our will and pleasure is that for the better quieting the minds of our good subjects, inhabitants of our said province, and for settling the properties and possessions of all persons concerned therein, either as general proprietors of the soil under the first original grant of the said province made by the late King Charles the Second to the late Duke of York, or as particular purchasers of any parcels of land from the said general proprietors, you shall propose to the General Assembly of our said province the passing of such act or acts whereby the right and property of the said general proprietors to the soil of our said province may be confirmed to them according to their respective rights and title; together with all such quit-rents as have been reserved or are or shall become due to the said general proprietors from the inhabitants of our said province, and all such privileges as are expressed in the conveyances made by the said Duke of York, excepting only the right of government which remains in us. And you are further to take care that, by the said act or acts so to be

passed, the particular titles and estates of all the inhabitants of that province and other purchasers claiming under the said general proprietors be confirmed and settled as of right does appertain, under such obligations as shall tend to the best and speediest improvement or cultivation of the same; provided, always, that you do not consent to any act or acts to lay any tax upon lands that lie unprofitable.

37. You shall not permit any other person or persons besides the said general proprietors, or their agents, to purchase any land whatsoever from the Indians within the limits of their grant.

38. You are to permit the surveyors and other persons appointed by the forementioned general proprietors of the soil of that province for surveying and recording the surveys of land granted by and held of them to execute accordingly their respective trusts. And you are, likewise, to permit, and, if need be, aid and assist, such other agent or agents as shall be appointed by the said proprietors for that end to collect and receive the quit-rents which are or shall be due unto them from the particular possessors of any parcels or tracts of land from time to time; provided, always, that such surveyors, agents, or other officers appointed by the said general proprietors do not only take proper oaths for the due execution and performance of their respective offices or employments and give good and sufficient security for their so doing, but that they likewise take the oaths appointed by act of Parliament to be taken instead of the oaths of allegiance and supremacy and the oath mentioned in the aforesaid act, entitled, *An Act to Declare the Alteration in the Oath Appointed to be Taken by the Act, entitled, An Act for the Further Security of His Majesty's Person and the Succession of the Crown in the Protestant Line and for Extinguishing the Hopes of the Pretended Prince of Wales and all Other Pretenders and Their Open and Secret Abettors and for Declaring the Association to be Determined,* as also the forementioned test. And you are more particularly to take care that all lands purchased from the said proprietors be cultivated and improved by the possessors thereof.

39. You shall transmit unto us and to our commissioners for trade and plantations, by the first opportunity, a map with the exact description of our whole territory under your government and of the several plantations that are upon it.

40. You are, likewise, to send a list of officers employed under your government, together with all public charges.

41. You shall not displace any of the judges, justices, sheriffs, or other officers or ministers within our said province without good and sufficient cause to be signified unto us and to our said commissioners for trade and plantations. And to prevent arbitrary removal of judges and justices of the peace, you shall not express any limitation of time in the commissions which you are to grant, with the advice and consent of the Council of our said province, to persons fit for those employments, nor shall you execute yourself, or by deputy, any of the said offices nor suffer any persons to execute more offices than one by deputy.

42. Whereas we are given to understand that there are several offices within our said province granted under the great seal of England and that our service may be very much prejudiced by reason of the absence of the patentees and by their appointing deputies not fit to officiate in their stead. You are, therefore, to inspect the said offices and to inquire into the capacity and behavior of the persons now exercising them and to report thereupon to us and to our commissioners for trade and plantations what you think fit to be done or altered in relation thereunto. And you are, upon the misbehavior of any of the said patentees, or their deputies, to suspend them from the execution of their places till you shall have represented the whole matter and received our directions therein. But you shall not, by color of any power or authority hereby or otherwise granted or mentioned to be granted unto you, take upon you to give, grant, or dispose of any office or place within our said province which now is or shall be granted under the great seal of England, any further than that you may, upon the vacancy of any such office or place or suspension of any such officer by you as aforesaid, put in any fit person to officiate in the interval till you

shall have represented the matter unto us and to our commissioners for trade and plantations, as aforesaid, which you are to by the first opportunity, and till the said office or place be disposed of by us, our heirs or successors, under the great seal of England, or that our further directions be given therein.

43. In case any goods, money, or other estate of pirates, or piratically taken, shall be brought in or found within our said province of Nova Cesaria, or New Jersey, or taken on board any ships or vessels, you are to cause the same to be seized and secured until you shall have given us an account thereof and received our pleasure concerning the disposal of the same. But in case such goods or any part of them are perishable, the same shall be publicly sold and disposed of and the produce thereof in like manner secured until our further order.

44. And whereas commissions have been granted unto several persons in our respective plantations in America for the trying of pirates in those parts, pursuant to the act for the more effectual suppression of piracy and by a commission already sent to our province of New York, you, as Captain-General and Governor-in-Chief of our said province of New York, are empowered, together with others therein mentioned, to proceed accordingly in reference to our provinces of New York, New Jersey, and Connecticut. Our will and pleasure is that in all matters relating to pirates you govern yourself according to the intent of the act and commission aforementioned. But whereas accessories in cases of piracy beyond the seas are by the same act left to be tried in England, according to the statute of the second of King Henry the Eighth, we do hereby further direct and require you to send all such accessories in cases of piracy in our aforesaid province of Nova Cesaria, or New Jersey, with the proper evidences that you may have against them, into England, in order to their being tried here.

45. You shall not erect any court or office of judicature, not before erected or established, without our especial order.

46. You are to transmit unto us and to our commissioners for trade and plantation, with all convenient speed, a particular account of all establishment of jurisdictions, courts, offices, and officers, powers, authorities, fees, and privileges which shall be granted or settled within the said province by virtue and in pursuance of our commission and instructions to you our Captain-General and Governor-in-Chief of the same, to the end you may receive our further direction therein.

47. And you are, with the advice and consent of our said Council, to take especial care to regulate all salaries and fees belonging to places or paid upon emergencies, that they be within the bounds of moderation and that no exaction be made on any occasion whatsoever; as also, that tables of all fees be publicly hung up in all places where such fees are to be paid; and you are to transmit copies of all such tables of fees to us and to our commissioners for trade and plantations, as aforesaid.

48. Whereas it is necessary that our rights and dues be preserved and recovered and that speedy and effectual justice be administered in all cases relating to our revenue; you are to take care that a court of exchequer be called and do meet at all such times as shall be needful, and you are to inform us and our commissioners for trade and plantations whether our service may require that a constant court of exchequer be settled and established there.

49. You are to take care that no man's life, member, freehold, or goods be taken away or harmed in our said province otherwise than by established and known laws, nor repugnant to, but as much as may be, agreeable to the laws of England.

50. You shall administer, or cause to be administered, the oaths appointed by act of Parliament to be taken instead of the oaths of allegiance and supremacy and the oath mentioned in the aforesaid act, entitled, *An Act to Declare the Alteration in the Oath Appointed to be Taken by the Act, entitled, An Act for the Further Security of His Majesty's Person, and the Succession of the Crown in the Protestant Line and for Extinguishing the Hopes of the Pretended Prince of Wales and All Other Pretenders and Their Open and Secret Abettors and for Declaring the Association to be Determined,*

as also the forementioned test, to the members and officers of the Council and Assembly, and to all judges, justices, and all other persons that hold any office or place of trust or profit in the said province, whether by virtue of any patent under our great seal of England or otherwise; without which you are not to admit any person whatsoever into any public office nor suffer those who have been admitted formerly to continue therein.

51. You are to permit a liberty of conscience to all persons, except papists, so they may be contented with a quiet and peaceable enjoyment of the same, not giving offense or scandal to the government.

52. And whereas we have been informed that diverse of our good subjects inhabiting those parts do make a religious scruple of swearing and, by reason of their refusing to take an oath in courts of justice and other places, are or may be liable to many inconveniences. Our will and pleasure is that in order to their ease in what they conceive to be matter of conscience, so far as may be consistent with good order and government, you take care that an act be passed in the General Assembly of our said province to the like effect as that passed here in the seventh and eighth years of his Majesty's reign, entitled, *An Act That the Solemn Affirmation and Declaration of the People Called Quakers Shall be Accepted Instead of an Oath in the Usual Form*, and that the same be transmitted to us and to our commissioners for trade and plantations, as before directed.

53. And whereas we have been further informed that in the first settlement of the government of our said province it may so happen that the number of inhabitants fitly qualified to serve in our council in the General Assembly and in other places of trust or profit there will be but small. It is, therefore, our will and pleasure that such of the said people called Quakers as shall be found capable of any of those places or employments, and accordingly be elected or appointed to serve therein, may, upon their taking and signing the declaration of allegiance to us in the form used by the same people here in England, together with a solemn declaration for true discharge of

their respective trusts, be admitted by you into any of the said places or employments.

54. You shall send an account unto us and to our commissioners for trade and plantations of the present number of planters and inhabitants, men, women, and children, as well masters as servants, free and unfree, and of the slaves in our said province, as also a yearly account of the increase or decrease of them, and how many of them are fit to bear arms in the militia of our said province.

55. You shall cause an account to be kept of all persons born, christened, and buried, and you shall yearly send fair abstracts thereof to us and to our commissioners for trade and plantations, as aforesaid.

56. You shall take care that all planters and christian servants be well and fitly provided with arms and that they be listed under good officers, and when and as often as shall be thought fit, mustered and trained, whereby they may be in a better readiness for the defense of our said province under your government. And you are to endeavor to get an act passed, if not already done, for apportioning the number of white servants to be kept by every planter.

57. You are to take especial care that neither the frequency nor unreasonableness of their marches, musters, and trainings be an unnecessary impediment to the affairs of the inhabitants.

58. You shall not, upon any occasion whatsoever, establish or put in execution any articles of war or other law martial upon any of our subjects, inhabitants of our said province, without the advice and consent of our Council there.

59. And whereas there is no power given you by your commission to execute martial law in time of peace upon soldiers in pay, and that, nevertheless, it may be necessary that some care be taken for the keeping of good discipline amongst those that we may at any time think fit to send into our said province, which may properly be provided for by the legislative power of the same. You are, therefore, to recommend to the General Assembly of our said province that they prepare such act or law for the punishing of mutiny, desertion, and false musters, and for the better preserving of good

discipline amongst the said soldiers, as may best answer those ends.

60. And whereas, upon complaints that have been made of the irregular proceedings of the captains of some of our ships of war in the pressing of seamen in several of our plantations, we have thought fit to order, and having given directions to our High Admiral accordingly, that when any captain or commander of any of our ships of war in any of our said plantations shall have occasion for seaman to serve on board our ships under their command, they do make their application to the governors and commanders-in-chief of plantations, respectively, to whom, as vice admirals, we are pleased to commit the sole power of impressing seamen in any of our plantations in America, or in sight of any of them. You are, therefore, hereby required, upon such application made to you by any of the commanders of our said ships of war within our province of Nova-Cesaria, or New Jersey, to take care that our said ships of war be furnished with a number of seamen that may be necessary for our service on board them from time to time.

61. And whereas together with other powers of Vice Admiralty you will receive authority from our dearest husband Prince George of Denmark, our High Admiral of England and of our plantations, upon the refusal or neglect of any captain or commander of any of our ships of war to execute the written orders he shall receive from you for our service of our province under your government, or upon his negligent or undue execution thereof, to suspend him, such captain or commander, from the exercise of his said office of captain or commander and to commit him into safe custody either on board his own ship or elsewhere, at your discretion, in order to his being brought to answer for such refusal or neglect by commission either under our great seal of England, or from our High Admiral or our commissioners for executing the office of our High Admiral of England for the time being.

62. And whereas you will likewise receive directions from our said dearest husband, as our High Admiral of England and of our plantations, that the captain or commander, so by you

suspended, shall, during such his suspension and commitment, be succeeded in his said office by such commission or warrant officer of our said ship, appointed by our said High Admiral of England or by our commissioners for executing the office of our High Admiral of England for the time being, as by the known practice and discipline of our navy does and ought to succeed him next as in case of death, sickness, or other ordinary disability happening to the commander of any of our ships of war and not otherwise, you standing also accountable for the truth and importance of the crime and misdemeanor for which you shall so proceed to the suspending of such our captain or commander. You are not to exercise the said power of suspending any such captains or commanders of our ships of war otherwise than by virtue of such commission or authority from our said High Admiral, any former custom or usage to the contrary notwithstanding.

63. Whereas it is absolutely necessary that we be exactly informed of the state of defense of all of our plantations in America, as well in relation to the stores of war that are in each plantation as to the forts and fortifications there, and what more may be necessary to be built for the defense and security of the same. You are, so soon as possible, to prepare an account thereof, with relation to our said province of Nova Cesaria, or New Jersey, in the most particular manner, as you are therein to express the present state of the arms, ammunition, and other stores of war, either in any public magazines or in the hands of private persons, together with the state of all places either already fortified or that you judge necessary to be fortified, for the security of our said province; and you are to transmit the said account to us and to our commissioners for trade and plantations by the first opportunity and other like accounts yearly in the same manner.

64. And that we may be the better informed of the trade of our said province, you are to take especial care that due entries be made in all ports in our said province of all goods and commodities, their species or quantities imported or exported from thence, with the names, burden, and guns of all ships importing and exporting the same,

also the names of their commanders, and likewise expressing from and to what places the said ships do come and go, a copy whereof the naval officer is to furnish you with, and you are to transmit the same unto us, or our high treasurer or our commissioners of our Treasury for the time being and to our commissioners for trade and plantations, quarterly, and duplicates thereof by the next conveyance.

65. And whereas great losses have been sustained by our subjects trading to our plantations in America by ships sailing from those parts without convoy, or without the company of other ships which might protect them from our enemies, by which means many of them have been taken by the French in their return to England. To the end, therefore, the ships of our subjects may be the better secured in their return home, you are to take care that, during this time of war, no ships trading to our province of Nova Cesaria, or New Jersey, be permitted to come from thence to England but in fleets or under the convoy or protection of some of our ships of war, or at such a time as you shall receive notice from hence of their meeting such convoys as may be appointed for the bringing them safe to some of our ports in this kingdom; and in case of any danger, you are to expect directions from hence what precautions shall be further necessary for their security.

66. You are, likewise, to examine what rates and duties are charged and payable upon any goods imported or exported within our province of Nova Cesaria, or New Jersey, whether of the growth or manufacture of the said province or otherwise, and to use your best endeavors for the improvement of the trade in those parts.

67. And whereas orders have been given for the commissionating of fit persons to be officers of our admiralty and customs in our several plantations in America; and it is of great importance to the trade of this kingdom and to the welfare of all our plantations that illegal trade be every where discouraged. You are, therefore, to take especial care that the acts of trade and navigation be duly put in execution. And in order thereunto, you are to give constant protection and all encouragement to the said officers of our admiralty

and customs in the execution of their respective offices and trusts within our territories under your government.

68. You are, from time to time, to give an account as before directed what strength your bordering neighbors have, be they Indians or others, by sea and land, and of the condition of their plantations and what correspondence you do keep with them.

69. You shall take especial care that God Almighty be devoutly and duly served throughout your government, the Book of Common Prayer, as by law established, read each Sunday and holy day, and the blessed sacrament administered according to the rites of the Church of England.

70. You shall be careful that the churches already built there be well and orderly kept and that more be built as the colony shall, by God's blessing, be improved; and that, besides, a competent maintenance to be assigned to the minister of each orthodox church, a convenient house be built at the common charge for each minister, and a competent proportion of land assigned to him for a glebe and exercise of his industry.

71. And you are to take care that the parishes be so limited and settled as you shall find most convenient for the accomplishing this good work.

72. You are not to prefer any minister to any ecclesiastical benefice in that our province without a certificate from the Right Reverend Father in God the Lord Bishop of London, of his being conformable to the doctrine and discipline of the Church of England and of a good life and conversation. And if any person already preferred to a benefice shall appear to you to give scandal either by his doctrine or manners, you are to use the best means for the removal of him and to supply the vacancy in such manner as we have directed.

73. You are to give order that every orthodox minister within your government be one of the vestry in his respective parish and that no vestry be held without him, except in case of sickness or that after the notice of a vestry summoned he omit to come.

74. You are to inquire whether there be any minister within your government who preaches and administers the sacrament in any orthodox church or chapel without being in due orders, and to give account thereof to the said Lord Bishop of London.

75. And to the end the ecclesiastical jurisdiction of the said Lord Bishop of London may take place in our said province so far as conveniently may be, we do think fit that you give all countenance and encouragement to the exercise of the same, excepting only the collating to benefices, granting licenses for marriages, and probate of wills, which we have reserved to you our Governor and the Commander-in-Chief of our said province for the time being.

76. And you are to take especial care that a table of marriages established by the cannons of the Church of England be hung up in every orthodox church and duly observed. And you are to endeavor to get a law passed in the Assembly of our said province, if not already done, for the strict observation of the said table.

77. You are to take care drunkenness and debauchery, swearing and blasphemy, be discountenanced and punished. And for the further discountenance of vice and encouragement of virtue and good living, that by such example the infidels may be invited and desire to partake of the Christian religion, you are not to admit any person to public trusts and employments in our said province under your government whose ill-fame and conversation may occasion scandal.

78. You are to suppress the engrossing of commodities as tending to the prejudice of that freedom which commerce and trade ought to have, and to settle such orders and regulations therein, with the advice of the Council, as may be most conduce to the benefit and improvement of that colony.

79. You are to give all due encouragement and invitation to merchants and others who shall bring trade unto our said province or any way contribute to the advantage thereof, and in particular the Royal African Company of England.

80. And whereas we are willing to recommend unto the said company that the said province may

have a constant sufficient supply of merchantable Negroes at moderate rates, in money or commodities; so you are to take especial care that payment be duly made and within a competent time according to their agreements.

81. And you are to take care that there be no trading from our said province to any place in Africa within the charter of the Royal African Company, otherwise than prescribed by an act of Parliament, entitled, *An Act to Settle the Trade of Africa.*

82. And you are, yearly, to give unto us and to our commissioners for trade and plantations an account of what number of Negroes our said province is yearly supplied with and at what rates.

83. You are, likewise, from time to time, to give unto us and to our commissioners for trade and plantations, as aforesaid, an account of the wants and defects of our said province, what are the chief products thereof, what new improvements are made therein by the industry of the inhabitants or planters, and what further improvements you conceive may be made or advantages gained by trade, and in what manner we may best advance the same.

84. You are not to grant commissions of marque or reprisals, against any prince or state, or their subjects in amity with us, to any person whatsoever without our especial command.

85. Our will and pleasure, that appeals be made in cases of error from the courts in our said province of Nova Cesaria, or New Jersey, unto you and the council there, and in your absence from our said province to our commander-in-chief for the time being and our said Council, in civil causes, wherein such of our said Council as shall be at that time judges of the court from whence such appeal shall be made to you our Governor, and Council, or to the commander-in-chief for the time being and council, as aforesaid, shall not be admitted to vote upon the said appeal. But they may, nevertheless, be present at the hearing thereof to give the reasons of the judgment given by them in the cause wherein such appeal shall be made. Provided, nevertheless, that in all such appeals, the sum or value appealed for exceed one hundred pounds sterling and that security be first duly given by the appellant to answer such

charges as shall be awarded in case the first sentence be affirmed.

86. And if either party shall not rest satisfied with the judgment of you, or the commander-in-chief for the time being, and Council as aforesaid, our will and pleasure is that they may then appeal unto us in our Privy Council; provided the sum or value so appealed for unto us do exceed two hundred pounds sterling and that such appeal be made within fourteen days after sentence, and that good security be given by the appellant that he will effectually prosecute the same and answer the condemnation, as also pay such costs and damages as shall be awarded by us in case the sentence of you, or the commander-in-chief for the time being, and Council, be affirmed; and provided, also, that execution be not suspended by reason of any such appeal to us.

87. You are also to permit appeals to us in council in all cases of fines imposed for misdemeanors; provided the fines so imposed amount to or exceed the value of two hundred pounds, the appellant first giving good security that he will effectually prosecute the same and answer the condemnation if the sentence by which such fine was imposed in our said province of Nova Cesaria, or New Jersey, shall be confirmed.

88. You are, for the better administration of justice, to endeavor to get a law passed, if not already done, wherein shall be set the value of the men's estates, either in goods or lands, under which they shall not be capable of serving as jurors.

89. You shall endeavor to get a law passed for the restraining of any inhuman severity which by ill masters or overseers may be used towards their Christian servants and their slaves, and that provision be made therein that the willful killing of Indians and Negroes may be punished with death and that a fit penalty be imposed for the maiming of them.

90. You are also, with the assistance of the Council and Assembly, to find out the best means to facilitate and encourage the conversion of Negroes and Indians to the Christian religion.

91. You are to endeavor, with the assistance of the Council to provide for the raising of stocks and building of public work houses in convenient places for the employing of poor and indigent people.

92. You are to propose an act to be passed in the assembly whereby the creditors of persons becoming bankrupts in England and having estates in our aforesaid province of New Jersey, may be relieved and satisfied for the debts owing to them.

93. You are to encourage the Indians upon all occasions so as they may apply themselves to the English trade and nation rather than to any other of Europe.

94. And whereas the preservation of the northern frontiers of our province of New York against the attempts of any enemy by land is of great importance to the security of our northern plantations on the continent of America, and more especially of our said province of New Jersey, which lies so near adjoining to our province of New York, and the charge of erecting and repairing the fortifications and of maintaining the soldiers necessary for the defense of the same is too great to be borne by the single province of New York without contributions from others concerned therein. For which reason, we have, upon several occasions, required such contributions to be made and accordingly settled a quota to regulate the proportions thereof. You are, therefore, to take further care to dispose the General Assembly of our said province of New Jersey to the raising of such other supplies as are or may be necessary for the defense of our province of New York, according to the signification of our will and pleasure therein, which has already been made to the inhabitants of New Jersey or which shall at any time hereafter be made to you our Governor, or to the commander-in-chief of our said province for the time being.

95. And in case of any distress of any of our plantations, you shall, upon application of the respective governors to you, assist them with what aid the condition and safety of your government will permit; and more particularly in case our province of New York be at any time attacked by an enemy, the assistance you are to contribute towards the defense thereof, whether in men or money, is according to the forementioned quota

or repartition, which has already been signified to the inhabitants of our foresaid province under your government, or according to such other regulations as we shall hereafter make in that behalf and signify to you or the commander-in-chief of our said province for the time being.

96. And for the greater security of our province of New Jersey, you are to appoint fit officers and commanders in the several parts of the country bordering upon the Indians, who, upon any invasion, may raise men and arms to oppose them until they shall receive your directions therein.

97. And whereas we have been pleased by our commission to direct that in case of your death or absence from our said province, and in case there be at that time no person upon the place commissionated or appointed by us to be our lieutenant-governor or commander-in-chief, the then present council of our said province shall take upon them the administration of the government and execute our said commission and the several powers and authorities therein contained in the manner therein directed. It is, nevertheless, our express will and pleasure that in such case the said council shall forbear to pass any acts but what are immediately necessary for the peace and welfare of our said province, without our particular order for that purpose.

98. You are to take care that all writs be issued in our name throughout our said province.

99. Forasmuch as great inconveniences may arise by the liberty of printing in our said province, you are to provide by all necessary orders that no person keep any press for printing, nor that any book, pamphlet, or other matters whatsoever be printed without your especial leave and license first obtained.

100. And if anything shall happen that may be of advantage and security to our said province which is not herein or by our commission to you provided for, we do hereby allow unto you, with the advice and consent of our Council of our said province, to take order for the present therein, giving unto us by one of our principal secretaries of state, and to our commissioners for trade and plantations, speedy notice thereof, that so you

may receive our ratification if we shall approve of the same.

101. Provided, always, that you do not, by any color of any power or authority hereby given you, commence or declare war without our knowledge and particular commands therein, except it be against Indians upon emergencies, wherein the consent of our Council shall be had and speedy notice given thereof unto us as aforesaid.

102. And you are, upon all occasions, to send unto us by one of our principal secretaries of state, and to our commissioners for trade and plantations, a particular account of all your proceedings and of the condition of affairs within your government.

103. And whereas the Lords Spiritual and Temporal in Parliament, upon consideration of the great abuses practiced in the plantation trade, did, by an humble address, represent to his late Majesty the great importance it is of both to this our kingdom and to our plantations in America that the many good laws which have been made for the government of the said plantations, and particularly the act passed in the seventh and eighth years of his said Majesty's reign, *An Act for Preventing Frauds and Regulating Abuses in the Plantation Trade*, be strictly observed. You are, therefore, to take notice that whereas notwithstanding the many good laws made from time to time for preventing frauds in the plantation trade, it is, nevertheless, manifest that very great abuses have been and continue still to be practised to the prejudice of the same, which abuses must needs arise either from the insolvency of the persons who are accepted for the security or from the remissness or connivance of such as have been or are governors in the several plantations, who ought to take care that those persons who give bond should be duly prosecuted in case of nonperformance. We take the good of our plantations and the improvement of the trade thereof by a strict and punctual observance of the several laws in force concerning the same, to be of so great importance to the benefit of this our kingdom and to the advancing of the duties of our customs here that if we shall be hereafter informed that at any time there shall be any failure in the

due observance of those laws within our foresaid province of Nova Cesaria, or New Jersey, by any willful fault or neglect on your part, we shall look upon it as a breach of trust reposed in you by us, which we shall punish with the loss of your place in that government and such further marks of our displeasure as we shall judge reasonable to be inflicted upon you for your offense against us in a matter of this consequence that we now so particularly charge you with.

Reference: W. A. Whitehead, et al. (eds.), *Archives of the State of New Jersey*, Vol. II (33 vols.; Newark: State Historical Society, 1888–1928), 506–536.

PETITION TO REQUEST A SEPARATE GOVERNOR, MARCH 18, 1735

To the Kings most Excellent Majesty.

The humble petition of your Majesty's President and Council of your province of New Jersey, the Speaker and diverse of the members of their General Assembly on behalf of themselves and others the inhabitants of the said colony.

Shows

That upon the surrender of the government of this province to your Majesty's royal predecessor Queen Anne the proprietors and inhabitants of this colony had great reason to hope the governor then appointed over this province would have been distinct from the person that was to be governor of New York. But, to the great disappointment of this colony, the person then governor of New York was also appointed governor of this province and the several persons who have since been appointed governors of New York have also at the same time been appointed governors of this province.

That the great value of the government of New York beyond that of New Jersey, your petitioners humbly conceive, has always induced the governor of both for the time being not only to prefer New York to this province for his almost continual residence, but often to prefer the interests of that colony to the great prejudice of this. And should it be your Majesty's pleasure to continue us under the same governor with the province of New York, we have too great reason to fear the like inconveniences will insure to the great detriment of this colony.

That the absence of the governor for the time being from this province, sometimes for a whole year together, has too often occasioned almost an entire neglect of the affairs of this government and great delays in the administration of justice both in causes depending before the governor in chancery and those before the governor and council on writs of error and otherways, to the great impoverishing of the parties who there seek right and to the great discouragement of your Majesty's loyal subjects of this province.

That although the application heretofore made on the behalf of this province for relief in the premises have proved ineffectual, yet, as we are sensible your Majesty is the common parent of all your subjects that they are equally the objects of your royal care and indentures, your petitioners flatter themselves that when your Majesty shall be informed how inconvenient and detrimental it is to this your province and how prejudicial to your Majesty's service to have the same person governor of New Jersey that is governor of New York and that the inhabitants of this your Majesty's province are equally willing and able to support a distinct governor with diverse of the neighboring colonies who enjoy that benefit under your Majesty, that you, in your royal goodness, will be induced at this juncture on the occasion of the death of his Excellency William Cosby, Esquire, late our governor, to grant us our humble prayer.

May it, therefore, please your Majesty, in your great clemency and goodness, to relieve your dutiful and loyal subjects, the inhabitants of this your province, in the premises by commissionating some person to be their governor different and distinct from the person that is to be governor of your province of New York.

And your petitioners, as in duty bound, shall ever pray, etc.

Reference: W. A. Whitehead, et al. (eds.), *Archives of the State of New Jersey*, Vol. V (33 vols.; Newark: State Historical Society, 1888–1928), 441–443.

COMMISSION TO GOVERNOR FRANCIS BERNARD, 1758

George the Second, by the grace of God, of Great Britain, France, and Ireland, King, Defender of the Faith, etc. To our trusty and well-beloved Francis Bernard, Esquire, greeting.

We, reposing especial trust and confidence in the prudence, courage, and loyalty of you, the said Francis Bernard, of our especial grace, certain knowledge, and mere motion, have thought fit to constitute and appoint and, by these presents, do constitute and appoint you, the said Francis Bernard, to be our Captain-General and Governor-in-Chief in and over our province of Nova Caesarea or New Jersey, viz. the division of East and West New Jersey in America, which we have thought fit to reunite into one province and settle under one entire government.

And we do hereby require and command you to do and execute all things in due manner that shall belong unto your said command and the trust we have reposed in you, according to the several powers and directions granted or appointed you by this present commission and the instructions and authorities herewith given you, or by such further powers, instructions, and authorities as shall at any time hereafter be granted or appointed you under our signet and sign manual, or by our order in our Privy Council, and according to such reasonable laws and statutes as now are in force or hereafter shall be made and agreed upon by you, with the advice and consent of our Council and the Assembly of our said province under your government, in such manner and form as is hereafter expressed.

And our will and pleasure is that you, the said Francis Bernard, after the publication of these our letters patents, do, in the first place, take the oaths appointed to be taken by an act passed in the first year of our late Royal Father's reign,

entitled, *An Act for the Further Security of His Majesty's Person and Government and the Succession of the Crown in the Heirs of the Late Princess Sophia, Being Protestants, and for Extinguishing the Hopes of the Pretended Prince of Wales and His Open and Secret Abettors.* As also that you make and subscribe the declaration mentioned in an act of Parliament made in the 25th year of the reign of King Charles the Second, entitled, *An Act for Preventing Dangers Which may Happen From Popish Recusants,* and likewise that you take the usual oath for the due execution of the office and trust of our Captain-General and Governor-in-Chief in and over our said province of Nova Caesarea or New Jersey, as well with regard to the due and impartial administration of justice as otherwise. And further that you take the oath required to be taken by governors of plantations to do their utmost that the several laws relating to trade and the plantation be observed. Which said oaths and declaration our Council in our said province, or any three of the members thereof, have hereby full power and authority and are required to tender and administer unto you, and in your absence to our Lieutenant Governor, if there be any upon the place. All which being duly performed, you shall administer to each of the members of our said Council, as also to our Lieutenant Governor, if there be any upon the place, the oaths mentioned in the said act, entitled, *An Act For the Further Security of His Majesty's Person and Government and the Succession of the Crown in the Heirs of the Late Princess Sophia, Being Protestants, and for Extinguishing the Hopes of the Pretended Prince of*

Wales and His Open and Secret Abettors. You shall also cause them to make and subscribe the afore-mentioned declaration and administer to them the oath for the due execution of their places and trusts.

And we do hereby give and grant unto you full power and authority to suspend any of the members of our said Council, from sitting, voting, and assisting therein if you shall find just cause for so doing.

And if it shall at any time happen that by the death, departure out of our said province, or suspension of any of our said councilors or otherwise, there shall be a vacancy in our said council, any three whereof we do hereby appoint to be a quorum, our will and pleasure is that you signify the same unto us by the first opportunity, that we may, under our signet and sign manual, constitute and appoint others in their stead.

But that our affairs may not suffer at that distance for want of a due number of councilors, if ever it shall happen that there be less than seven of them residing in our said province, we do hereby give and grant unto you, the said Francis Bernard, full power and authority to choose as many persons out of the principal freeholders, inhabitants thereof, as will make up the full number of our said council to be seven, and no more. Which persons so chosen and appointed by you shall be, to all intents and purposes, councilors in our said province until either they shall be confirmed by us or that by the nomination of others by us under our sign manual and signet our said council shall have seven or more persons in it.

And we do hereby give and grant unto you full power and authority, with the advice and consent of our said Council, from time to time as need shall require, to summon and call General Assemblies of the said freeholders and planters within your government, in manner and form as shall be directed in our instructions, which shall be given you together with this our commission.

And our will and pleasure is that the persons thereupon duly elected by the major part of the freeholders of the respective counties and places and so returned shall, before their sitting, take the oaths mentioned in the said act, entitled, *An Act*

for the Further Security of His Majesty's Person and Government and the Succession of the Crown in the Heirs of the Late Princess Sophia, Being Protestants, and for Extinguishing the Hopes of the Pretended Prince of Wales and His Open and Secret Abettors; as also make and subscribe the aforementioned declaration, or, being of the people called Quakers, shall take the affirmation and make and subscribe the declaration appointed to be taken and made instead of the oaths of allegiance, supremacy, and abjuration, by an act passed within our said province of Nova Caesarea or New Jersey, in the first year of our reign, entitled, *An Act Prescribing the Forms of Declaration of Fidelity, the Effect of the Abjuration, Oath, and Affirmation Instead of the Forms Heretofore Required in Such Cases; and for Repealing the Former Acts in the like Cases Made and Provided.* Which oaths, affirmation, and declaration you shall commissionate fit persons, under our seal of Nova Caesarea or New Jersey, to tender and administer unto them; and until the same shall be so taken, made, and subscribed, no person shall be capable of sitting though elected. And we do hereby declare that the persons so elected and qualified shall be called and deemed the General Assembly of that our province.

Oaths, affirmation, and declaration you shall commissionate fit persons, under our seal of Nova Caesarea or New Jersey, to tender and administer unto them; and until the same shall be so taken, made, and subscribed, no person shall be capable of sitting though elected. And we do hereby declare that the persons so elected and qualified shall be called and deemed the General Assembly of that our province.

And you, the said Francis Bernard, with the consent of our said Council and Assembly, or the major part of them respectively, shall have full power and authority to make, constitute, and ordain laws, statutes, and ordinances for the public peace, welfare, and good government of our said province and of the people and inhabitants thereof, and such others as shall resort thereto, and for the benefit of us, our heirs and successors. Which said laws, statutes, and ordinances are not to be repugnant, but as near as may be agreeable unto the laws and statutes of this our kingdom of

Great Britain; provided that all such laws, statutes, and ordinances, of what nature or duration
soever, be, within three months or sooner after
the making thereof, transmitted unto us, under
our seal of Nova Caesarea or New Jersey, for our
approbation or disallowance of the same, as also
duplicates thereof by the next conveyance.

And in case any or all of the said laws, statutes,
and ordinances, being not before confirmed by us,
shall at any time be disallowed and not approved
and so signified by us, our heirs or successors,
under our or their sign manual and signet, or by
order of our or their Privy Council, unto you,
the said Francis Bernard, or to the commander-
in-chief of our said province for the time being,
then such and so many of the said laws, statutes,
and ordinances as shall be so disallowed and not
approved shall from henceforth cease, determine,
and become utterly void and of none effect, anything to the contrary thereof notwithstanding.

And to the end that nothing may be passed or
done by our said Council or Assembly to the prejudice of us, our heirs and successors, we will and
ordain that you, the said Francis Bernard, shall
have and enjoy a negative voice in the making
and passing of all laws, statutes, and ordinances,
as aforesaid.

And you shall and may likewise, from time
to time, as you shall judge it necessary, adjourn,
prorogue, and dissolve all General Assemblies, as
aforesaid.

And our further will and pleasure is that you
shall and may use and keep the public seal of our
province of Nova Caesarea or New Jersey for sealing all things whatsoever that pass the great seal
of our said province under your government.

And we do further give and grant unto you,
the said Francis Bernard, full power and authority, from time to time and at any time hereafter,
by yourself or by any other to be authorized by you
in that behalf, to administer and give the above-
mentioned oaths and affirmations to all and every
such person and persons as you shall think fit who
shall, at any time or times, pass into our said province or shall be resident or abiding there.

And we do further, by these presents, give
and grant unto you, the said Francis Bernard, full

power and authority, with the advice and consent of our said Council, to erect, constitute, and
appoint such and so many courts of judicature
and public justice within our said province under
your government as you and they shall think fit
and necessary for the hearing and determining
all causes, as well criminal as civil, according to
law and equity, and for awarding of execution
thereupon, with all reasonable and necessary
powers, authorities, fees, and privileges belonging
thereto; as also to appoint and commissionate fit
persons in the several parts of your government
to administer the oaths mentioned in the aforesaid act, entitled, *An Act for the Further Security of
Our Person and Government and the Succession of
the Crown in the Heirs of the Late Princess Sophia,
Being Protestants, and for Extinguishing the Hopes
of the Pretended Prince of Wales and His Open and
Secret Abettors;* as also to tender and administer
the aforesaid declarations and affirmations unto
such persons belonging to the said courts as shall
be obliged to take the same.

And we do hereby authorize and empower you
to constitute and appoint judges, and in cases
requisite commissioners of oyer and terminer,
justices of the peace, and other necessary officers
and ministers in our said province for the better
administration of justice and putting the laws
in execution, and to administer or cause to be
administered unto them such oath or oaths as are
usually given for the due execution and performance of offices and places and for the clearing of
truth in judicial causes.

And we do hereby give and grant unto you full
power and authority, where you shall see cause or
shall judge any offender or offenders in criminal
matters or for any fines or forfeitures due unto us,
fit objects of our mercy, to pardon all such offenders and to remit all such offenses, fines, and forfeitures, treason and willful murder only excepted,
in which cases you shall likewise have power
upon extraordinary occasions to grant reprieves
to the offenders until and to the intent our royal
pleasure may be known therein.

And we do, by these presents, authorize and
empower you to collate any person or persons
to any churches, chapels, or other ecclesiastical

benefices within our said province as often as any of them shall happen to be void.

And we do hereby give and grant unto you, the said Francis Bernard, by yourself or by your captains and commanders by you to be authorized, full power and authority to levy, arm, muster, command, and employ all persons whatsoever residing within our said province of Nova Caesarea or New Jersey under your government, and, as occasion shall serve, to march from one place to another or to embark them for the resisting and withstanding of all enemies, pirates, and rebels, both at sea and land, and to transport such forces to any of our plantations in America, if necessity shall require, for the defense of the same against the invasion or attempts of any of our enemies, and such enemies, pirates, and rebels, if there shall be occasion, to pursue and prosecute in or out of the limits of our said province and plantations or any of them; and, if it shall so please God, them to vanquish, apprehend, and take, and, being taken, either according to law to put to death or keep and preserve alive at your discretion, and to execute martial law in time of invasion or other times when by law it may be executed, and to do and execute all and every other thing and things which to our captain-general and governor-in-chief does or ought of right to belong.

And we do hereby give and grant unto you full power and authority, by and with the advice and consent of our said Council, to erect, raise, and build in our said province of Nova Caesarea or New Jersey such and so many forts and platforms, castles, cities, boroughs, towns, and fortifications as you, by the advice aforesaid, shall judge necessary; and the same or any of them to fortify and furnish with ordnance, ammunition, and all sorts of arms fit and necessary for the security and defense of our said province, and, by the advice aforesaid, the same again or any of them to demolish or dismantle as may be most convenient.

And forasmuch as diverse mutinies and disorders may happen by persons shipped and employed at sea during the time of war, and to the end that such as shall be shipped and employed at sea during the time of war may be better governed and

ordered; we do hereby give and grant unto you, the said Francis Bernard, full power and authority to constitute and appoint captains, lieutenants, masters of ships, and other commanders and officers, and to grant unto such captains, lieutenants, masters of ships, and other commanders and officers commissions to execute the law martial during the time of war, according to the directions of an act passed in the 22nd year of our reign, entitled, *An Act for Amending, Explaining, and Reducing into One Act of Parliament the Laws Relating to the Government of His Majesty's Ships, Vessels, and Forces by Sea*; and to use such proceedings, authorities, punishments, corrections, and executions upon any offenders who shall be mutinous, seditious, disorderly, or any way unruly, either at sea or during the time of their abode or residence in any of the ports, harbors, or bays of our said province, as the cause shall be found to require, according to martial law and the said directions, during the time of war, as aforesaid; provided, that nothing herein contained shall be construed to the enabling you, or any by your authority, to hold plea or have any jurisdiction of any offense, cause, matter, or thing committed or done upon the high sea, or within any of the havens, rivers, or creeks of our said province under your government, by any captain, commander, lieutenant, master, officer, seaman, soldier, or other person whatsoever who shall be in actual service and pay in or on board any of our ships of war or other vessels acting by immediate commission or warrant from our commissioners for executing the office of our High Admiral, or from our High Admiral of Great Britain for the time being under the seal of our admiralty; but that such captain, commander, lieutenant, master, officer, seaman, soldier, or other person so offending shall be left to be proceeded against and tried as their offenses shall require, either by commission under our great seal of Great Britain, as the statute of the 28th of Henry the Eight directs, or by commission from our said commissioners for executing the office of our High Admiral, or from our High Admiral of Great Britain for the time being, according to the aforementioned *Act for Amending, Explaining, and Reducing into One Act of Parliament the Laws Relating to the Government of His Majesty's Ships, Vessels, and Forces by Sea,* and not otherwise.

Provided, nevertheless, that all disorders and misdemeanors committed on shore by any captain, commander, lieutenant, master, officer, seaman, soldier, or other person whatsoever, belonging to any of our ships of war or other vessels acting by immediate commission or warrant from our said commissioners for executing the office of our High Admiral or from our High Admiral of Great Britain for the time being under the seal of our admiralty, may be tried and punished according to the law of the place where any such disorders, offenses, and misdemeanors shall be committed on shore, notwithstanding such offender be in our actual service and borne in our pay on board any such our ships of war or other vessels acting by immediate commission or warrant from our said commissioners for executing the office of our High Admiral or from our High Admiral of Great Britain for the time being as aforesaid, so as he shall not receive any protection for the avoiding justice for such offenses committed on shore from any pretense of his being employed in our service at sea.

Our further will and pleasure is that all public money raised or which shall be raised by any act hereafter to be made within our said province be issued out by warrant from you, by and with the advice and consent of our Council, and disposed of by you for the support of the government, and not otherwise.

And we do hereby give you, the said Francis Bernard, full power and authority to order and appoint fairs, marts, and markets, as also such and so many ports, harbors, bays, havens, and other places for the convenience and security of shipping and for the better loading and unloading of goods and merchandise as by you, with the advice and consent of our said Council, shall be thought fit and necessary.

And we do hereby require and command all officers and ministers, civil and military, and all other inhabitants of our said province, to be obedient, aiding, and assisting unto you, the said Francis Bernard, in the execution of this our commission and of the powers and authorities herein contained; and in case of your death or absence out of our said province, to be obedient, aiding, and assisting unto such person as shall be appointed by us to be our lieutenant governor or commander-in-chief of our said province, to whom we do, therefore, by these presents, give and grant all and singular the powers and authorities herein granted to be by him executed and enjoyed during our pleasure, or until your arrival within our said province.

And if upon your death or absence out of our said province there be no person upon the place commissionated or appointed by us to be our lieutenant governor or commander-in-chief of our said province, our will and pleasure is that the eldest councilor whose name is first placed in our said instructions to you, and who shall be at the time of your death or absence residing within our said province of New Jersey, shall take upon him the administration of the government and execute our said commission and instructions and the several powers and authorities therein contained, in the same manner and to all intents and purposes as other our governor or commander-in-chief of our said province should or ought to do, in case of your absence until you return, or in all cases until our further pleasure be known therein.

And we do hereby declare, ordain, and appoint that you, the said Francis Bernard, shall and may hold, execute, and enjoy the office and place of our Captain-General and Governor-in-Chief in and over our province of Nova Caesarea or New Jersey, together with all and singular the powers and authorities hereby granted unto you for and during our will and pleasure. In witness whereof, we have cause these our letters to be made patents. Witness ourself at Westminster the day of 1758, in the thirty-first year of our reign. And for so doing this shall be your warrant. Given at our court at St. James, the day of 1758, in the thirty-first year of our reign.

Reference: W. A. Whitehead, et al. (eds.), *Archives of the State of New Jersey,* Vol. IX (33 vols.; Newark: State Historical Society, 1888–1928), 23–34.

22

South Carolina

The Carolinas long had separate Assemblies (legislatures), but the same proprietor controlled both of them until 1720 when they became separate crown colonies. From at least 1700 both Carolinas' legislatures experienced a protracted struggle with the proprietary governor, who ruled under the revised Fundamental Constitutions. South Carolina's legislature, more powerful than town governments, struggled with the governor over the construction of a local court system. North Carolina's legislature, under the influence of Virginia, struggled with a deputy governor appointed by the governor of South Carolina. The North Carolina legislature, growing under a powerful county-dominated set of freeholders, developed a different focus of governance than that of South Carolina. The growth of each colony's governance in the eighteenth century will be taken up in turn in this part.

South Carolina's act of 1694, which determined the general assembly's activities, reveals the struggles between the legislature and the proprietary governor. The South Carolina revolt against the proprietor in 1719 is shown in the "Narrative Proceedings of the People of South Carolina, May 1719." The crown instructions to royal governor Francis Nicholson in 1720 described the exact duties for the executive and gave the legislature a strong role in governance. The legislature took control of the county court system in 1721. In 1759 the Assembly passed a law that determined who could serve in the legislature and who could elect its members. By 1759, then, the powerful merchants and planter members of the Assembly competed for authority with the governor. South Carolinians shared the worries with other more egalitarian colonies about the tensions between the legislature and the royal governor.

ACT FOR DETERMINATION OF THE GENERAL ASSEMBLY, JUNE 20, 1694

Be it enacted by his Excellency, William Earl of Craven, Palatine, and the rest of the true and absolute lords and proprietors of this province, by and with the advice and consent of the rest of the members of the General Assembly now met at Charlestown for the southwest part of this province, and by the authority of the same, that this present General Assembly shall determine and be dissolved at the expiration of three years next after the date of the writs issued out for calling the same. And that every General Assembly hereafter called by virtue of any writs by the right honorable the Palatine and the rest of the true and absolute lords and proprietors of this province, or their deputies, shall determine and be dissolved every two years next after the date of the respective writs by which they are called.

And be it further enacted that the sitting and holding of General Assemblies shall not be discontinued or intermitted above one year at the most, but that within one year at the most from and after the determination of this or any other General Assembly, or, if occasion be oftener, new writs be issued out by the Palatine and lords proprietors, or their deputies, for calling, assembling, and holding of another General Assembly.

And be it further enacted, by the authority aforesaid, and it is enacted by the authority of the same, that all and every member of this General Assembly or of any and every General Assembly hereafter called, held, and assembled shall forfeit the sum of ten shillings current money of this province for every day they or he shall be absent from the house or depart without leave first obtained from the governor or speaker, by and with the consent of the major part of the members then present, or unless sickness, or some other weighty and important business, of which the major part of that respective house to which that member so absent does belong, shall be judge, be offered and allowed for excuse, and that the governor or speaker shall sign a warrant directed to the messenger or sergeant of their respective house to levy upon the goods and chattels of the person forfeiting and which refuse to pay for every day they shall be adjudged to have absented themselves causelessly; and upon the messenger's and sergeant's return of no goods or chattels to be found, the governor and speaker shall sign warrants directed to the sergeant or messenger of their respective house against their respective members which have been absent, as aforesaid, to apprehend their or his body and in safe custody to keep until they shall pay their respective forfeitures or be discharged by any order of their respective house. And all the money paid or levied by virtue of this act shall be disposed of by the major part of that house to which that member so absent does belong in defraying the charges and expenses of the members which attend the service of the house.

Provided that this act, nor anything therein contained, shall be construed to take away the power and prerogative that the lords proprietors have from the Crown to adjourn, prorogue, or dissolve any General Assembly of this part of this province when and as often as they shall think fit and expedient so to do.

Read three times and ratified in open Assembly, June 20, 1694.

Reference: Thomas Cooper (ed.), *Statutes at Large of South Carolina*, Vol. II (10 vols.; Columbia, SC: A.S. Johnston, 1836–1841), 79–80.

NARRATIVE PROCEEDINGS OF THE PEOPLE OF SOUTH CAROLINA, MAY 1719

THE *Lords Proprietors of Carolina* being at this Time soliciting His Majesty for the Restitution of their Government of *South-Carolina*, from whose Authority the Inhabitants revolted in the Year 1719, and humbly besought His Majesty to take them under his own immediate Government and Protection; I could not help thinking this a proper Juncture to acquaint the World how those People came to take such extraordinary Measures, as those they did, has the Appearance of to them who are not acquainted with the Springs and Motives which agitated and push'd them on to such violent Proceedings.

And being furnish'd with proper Materials, the *Original Papers*, and an Eye-Witness to most that then pas'd in that Province, I can answer for the Truth of the Facts hereafter related: and as the Continuance of the Government of that Province under the Crown is of the greatest Consequence, not only to the Province itself, but to all the Settlements in *North-America*, to which it is a Frontier; I hope it will not be thought an impertinent Work to acquaint the Publick with an Affair, which altho' so remote, is of so great Importance.

But before I proceed to Particulars, it will be necessary to give the Reader a short View of the Nature of the Settlement and Government of that Province, and of the Accidents and Contingencies that first gave the people a Dislike to the *Lords Proprietors*; and which, by degrees, so far irritated them, that they at last resolv'd to be no longer subject to their Government.

This Province was first settled at the Charge and Expence of several Persons of Quality, to whom King *Charles* II. granted it by Charter, soon after his Restoration; and a Scheme was then by them drawn, for the forming and settling the Legislature, and for encouraging Settlers to go over: It will be sufficient only to mention here, that by their Charter, they had Power given them to call an Assembly of the Freemen of the Province, or their Delegates, and with them, *either by themselves or their lawful Deputies*, to enact and make Laws, *not repugnant to the Laws of* England; and it had been usual with them, to appoint a Governor and seven Deputies, called the Council, the first of which (the Governor) represented the Palatine, and the others the rest of the *Lords Proprietors*, respectively, and were called the Upper House of Assembly: Thus the Laws were pass'd, and the Country govern'd for upwards of Fifty Years; when, after some Years Intercourse and Dealing between the Inhabitants and several Nations of the *Indians*, with whom they Traded, as they now do for several Thousand Pounds a Year, the said *Indians* unanimously agreed to destroy the whole Settlement, by murdering and cutting to pieces all the Inhabitants, on a Day they had agreed on; and altho' some private Intimations were given the People of this their Design, it was totally disbeliev'd; so that on that certain Day, in the Year 1715, they killed all, or most of the Traders that were with them in their Towns; and going among the Plantations murder'd all who could not fly from their cruelty, and burned their Houses. The Occasion of this Conspiracy, which was so universal, that all the *Indians* were concerned in it, except a small Clan or two that lived amongst the Settlements, insomuch that they amounted to between Eight and Ten Thousand Men, was attributed to some ill Usage they had receiv'd from the Traders, who are not (generally) Men of the best Morals; and that, no doubt of it, might give some Cause to their Discontents; to which may be added the great Debts they owed the Inhabitants, which it

is said amounted to near 10,000 *l*. Sterling, with the Goods then amongst them; all which they seiz'd and made their own, and never paid their Debts, but cancell'd them, by murdering their Creditors.

In this War near 400 of the Inhabitants were destroy'd, with many Houses and Slaves, and great numbers of Cattle, especially to the Southward near *Port-Royal*, from whence the Inhabitants were entirely drove, and forced into the Settlements near *Charles Town*.

This Town being fortified, they there had Time to think what to do; and not mustering above 1200 Men, they sent to *Virginia* and the neighbouring Colonies for Assistance; and for want of Money, of which they have very little in the Country, they formed *Bills of Credit*, to pass Current in all Payments, of which we shall have Occasion to speak hereafter. This their necessary Defence brought the Publick in Debt near 80,000 *l*. and intail'd great Annual Charges upon them, to maintain Garrisons, which they were forced to keep at great Expences.

In this very great Extremity, they sent Agents to *England* with an Account of their deplorable State, and to beg Assistance from their Proprietors: But not having very great Expectations from them, as very rightly imagining they would not be brought to expend their *English* Estates, to support much more precarious ones in *America*, their Agents were directed to lay a State of their Circumstances before her then Majesty Queen *Anne*, and to beg the Assistance of the Crown.

Their Agents soon sent them an Account, that they found a Disposition in Her Majesty to send them Relief, and to protect them; but that the Objection was, they were a *Proprietory Government*; and it was the Opinion of the then Lords Commissioners of Trade and Plantations, that if the Queen was at the Expence of Protecting and Relieving the Province, the Government thereof should be in the Crown.

This first contracted in the Inhabitants in general, an Opinion of their being very unhappy in living under a Government that could not protect them; the Effects of which were also worse, since it hinder'd the Crown from doing what they (the *Proprietors*) could not do themselves.

The Publick Emergencies had occasion'd the Stamping the aforesaid Sum of 80,000*l*. in Bills of Credit, to pay their Soldiers, and other Charges the Country was forced to be at; and it was Enacted by the Assembly, They should be Current in all Payments between Man and Man. But the precarious State the Province was in by the *Indian* War, and the Danger it was exposed to, by being a Frontier, to the *French and Spaniards*, gave the Merchants in *England* who Traded thither, and to whom the Inhabitants were considerably Indebted, so great an Alarm, that they writ to their Correspondents, to make them Returns at any Rate, for fear of losing the Whole.

The great Demand for the *Commodities* of the Country that this necessarily occasion'd, together with the Scarcity of *them* by the Peoples being taken from their Labour to defend themselves, and there being no other way of paying their Debts to the Merchants in *England* but by the Produce of the Country, the Money being National, having no Intrinsick Value in it; all these things concurr'd to raise the Price of the Rice, Pitch and Tar, and other Productions, to such a height, that the Bill that was made for Twenty Shillings, would not purchase what was worth intrinsically more than a Half a Crown. From whence it follow'd, that those who had Money owing them on Bond or otherwise before the War, and who must have been paid in Gold or Silver, or its Value, if those Bills had not been made Current in all Payments, by their being so, lost Seven Eighths of their Money: These Losses fell chiefly on the Merchants and such of the Inhabitants of *Charles Town* as were Money'd Men; and, on the contrary, the Planters, who were their Debtors, were the Gainers.

This so very great a Loss falling upon the *Merchants* (tho' I do truly believe it was not foreseen by the People) made very great Clamours in *England*, from *them*, who applied to the *Lords Proprietors* for Redress, and desired that a Stop might be put to the Increase of that sort of Currency, and that some Way might be found for the calling-in, and sinking what was then Current of them. In this Condition and thus

Circumstanced, Mr. *Johnson* found the People on his Arrival, who was appointed Governor by the *Lords Proprietors* Commission dated 30th of *April* 1717; and agreeable to an Act of Parliament in that Case provided, he was Approv'd of by His MAJESTY, under his Sign Manual.

At his first coming, he applied himself to the Assembly, to call-in those Bills, which had brought so great Inconveniencies upon themselves, as well as on the Traders; and in Justice and Honour, (he told them) they ought to make good; and so far prevail'd on them, that altho' there were great Contentions in the Assembly, between the Planting and the Mercantile Interest; altho' the Annual Expences of the Country were then very great, the *Indian* War with some Nations still continuing, Coast very much infested with Pyrates, who had several times block'd up the Harbour for several Weeks together, and taken all the Ships coming in or going out, which had put the Country to great Expences; they having fitted out Vessels twice, and taken two of them, one commanded by Major *Steed Bounett*, in *Cape-Fear* River, and the other by *Worley*, off the Bar of *Charles Town*; in which last Expedition Mr. *Johnson* went himself in Person: I say, notwithstanding they then labour'd under these Difficulties, they passed an Act for Sinking and Paying off all their Paper Credit in three Years, by a Tax on Lands and Negroes, which gave a general Satisfaction.

It will be necessary here to make a Digression, to inform the Reader, that at the first Settling the Country, before it was divided into Parishes, the whole Lower House of Assembly were chosen at *Charles Town*, and were Representatives of the whole Province; which Custom had continued after the Country was laid out in Parishes, until about a Year before Mr. *Johnson* arriv'd: When in the Government of Mr. *Daniel*, who was left Deputy Governour by Mr. *Craven* when he came for *England*, they pass'd a Law for Regulating the Elections for Members of the Assembly; wherein amongst other Things it was *Enacted*, That every Parish should send a certain Number of Representatives, 36 in all, and that they should be Balloted for at their respective Parish-Churches, or some other Place convenient, on a Day to be mention'd in the Writs, which were to be directed to the Church-Wardens, and they to make Return of the Elected Members: and of this *Act*, the People were very fond; finding it gave them a greater Freedom of Election, and was more easy to them than going out of their respective Countries to *Charles Town*; at which Elections, there had been very often great Tumults; and besides, that it came nearer the Methods used in *England*.

On the other hand, as it pleased the Generality of the People, because of the Freedom it gave them in their Choice, it was sure to displease two of the *Lords Proprietors* Principal Officers; their Chief Justice and Receiver General Mr. *Trott*, and Mr. *Rhett* his Brother in Law; who by the former Method of Electing at *Charles Town*, had used to have a great Sway in the Elections, which they thought would be lessen'd by this new method; and therefore they did what they could to obstruct the Passing the Bill, which they failed in; but so represented it to the *Lords Proprietors* with whom they had always too much interest, either for their Lordships or the Peoples Good, that just at the Juncture when they had been at the aforesaid great Expence to drive the Pyrates off their Coast, that they were mightily pleas'd with Mr. *Johnson* for exposing his own Person in that Expedition against them, had pass'd the Law for sinking their paper Currency, and were contriving to pay for their Expeditions against the Pyrates, and their other contingent Debts, and they were never observ'd to be in so good a Disposition towards the *Proprietors*, but were doing every Thing that could be ask'd of them. At this Juncture arriv'd an Order to the Governor to Dissolve the Assembly forthwith, and to call a New one to be Elected according to the Ancient Custom, they not acknowledging the New Election Law, because not approv'd and ratified by them in *London*, as the former was and therefore they insisted; the Legislature of *Carolina* could not Repeal it, and substitute a New one in the Place, without their Consent, they being (notwithstanding their Impowering their Deputies in *Carolina*) the Head of the Legislative Body of the Province, and had a Right to put a Negative on such Laws as they did not approve of; at the same time they also Repeal'd an Act of the Assembly for laying a Duty on *Negroes*, Liquors, &c. imported into the said Province, for raising a Sum of Money to defray the Contingent Charges of the Province, and for other Services therein mention'd.

Mr. *Johnson* and his Council, (that is, the major part of them for Mr. *Trott* was of that body) were very much surpris'd at the receipt of these Orders; and after having duly consider'd the Consequences they might produce, resolv'd to suspend the Execution of them, especially that part which directed the Dissolution of the Assembly; but on the contrary, thought it best they should sit until they accomplish'd the Business then before them. But as the Repeal of the Duty-Law was by Order of the King in Council, because of a part of it that laid a Duty on Goods manufactur'd in *Great-Britain*, the Council therefore resolv'd to acquaint the Assembly with the King's Dislike to that part of the Law, and require them to make a New Act, in which to leave out the part complained of. These Orders and Repeals, altho' all Endeavours were used that they should be kept secret, came to the Knowledge of the Assembly, and begat prodigious Heats and Debates about the *Proprietors* Right of Repeal, or of their Authority to allow of, or disallow any of the Laws pass'd in that Province; which the Assembly alledg'd being assented to by their Deputies who acted for them; and at that time, by a sort of Deputation, every *Proprietor* gave in the Nature of a Power of Attorney, to act for him, and in his stead; they insisted, bound them, according to the Tenor of their Charter, as much as if they themselves had been present, and had ratified and confirm'd those Acts.

Just before the arrival of these unhappy Orders, there had been presented to the Assembly, Articles of Complaint against the Chief Justice *Trott*, being Thirty one in Number, which in the Whole set forth, "That he had been guilty of many Partial Judgments; that he had contriv'd many Ways to multiply and increase his Fees, contrary to Acts of Assembly, and to the great Grievance of the Subjects; and that amongst others, he Contriv'd a Fee for Continuing Causes from one Court (or Term) unto another, and then had Put off the Hearing for several Years together; that he took upon him to give Advice in Causes depending in his Courts, and did not only act as a Councellor in that Particular, but also had and did draw Deeds and other Writings between Party and Party, some of which had been contested before him as Chief Justice; in the determining of which, he had shewn great Partialities, with many other Particulars; and lastly, complaining that the whole Judicial Power of the Province was lodg'd in his Hands alone; of which it was evident he had made a very ill Use, he being at that time sole Judge of the *Pleas* and *King's-Bench*, and Judge of the Court of *Vice-Admiralty*; so that no Prohibition could be lodg'd against the Proceedings of that Court, he being in that Case to grant a Prohibition against himself; he was also, at the same time, one of the *Council*, and of consequence, of the Court of *Chancery*."

These Complaints took their Rise from the Attornies who practis'd in the Courts, and were fully made appear to be Facts to the Commons House of Assembly; but the Judges Commission from the *Proprietors* being *Quam diu se bene gesserit*, and he insisting his Actions were not to be tried but before the *Proprietors* themselves, they were constrained to apply to the *Proprietors* for Redress; and therefore sent a Message to the Governor and Council, desiring they would join with them in representing his Male-Administration to the

Lords, and in supplicating them, that if they did not think fit to remove him entirely from presiding in their Courts of Justice, (which they desired,) then that they would at least leave him only one single Jurisdiction, that they might have the Liberty of Appealing from his *sole,* and too often, Partial Judgment.

The Governor and a Majority of his Council agreed with them, to represent the Grievances they complain'd of, to the *Proprietors;* and thinking it might be better done by one of their own Members, who had been present in all their Debates, than by Letters, they agreed on Mr. *Yonge* to go to *Great-Britain,* to give their *Lordships* a true State of this, as well as of their other Affairs, who was accordingly properly instructed, and in the Month of *May,* 1719, arrived in *London.*

The Lord CARTERET the *Palatine* was then just going on his Embassy to the Court of *Sweden,* who therefore was pleased to refer him to the rest of the *Proprietors;* and after having waited on them two or three times, he presented them with the following *Memorial.*

Reference: Peter Force (comp.), *Tracts and Other Papers, Relating Principally to the Origin, Settlement, and Progress of the Colonies in North America,* Vol. II (Washington: W. Q., 1836).

INSTRUCTIONS FOR GOVERNOR FRANCIS NICHOLSON, AUGUST 30, 1720

Instructions for Francis Nicholson, Esw., his Majesty's Captain-General and Commander-in-Chief in and over his Majesty's province and territory of Carolina in America. Given at Whitehall the [. . .].

1. With these instructions you will receive his Majesty's commission under the great seal of Great Britain constituting you Captain-General and Governor-in-Chief in and over his Majesty's province and territory of Carolina in America.

2. And for the better administration of justice and management of the public affairs of his Majesty's said province, you are required to choose and appoint such fitting and discreet persons, either planters or inhabitants there, not exceeding the number of twelve, as you shall judge most proper to be his Majesty's Council in his said

province, until his Majesty's further pleasure be known. And you are forwith to transmit to his Majesty and to his Commissioners for Trade and Plantations a list of the names and qualifications of all the said persons so by you appointed to be his Majesty's Council there.

3. And you are, with all due and usual solemnity, to cause his Majesty's said commission under the great seal of Great Britain constituting you his Majesty's Captain-General and Governor-in-Chief, as aforesaid, to be read and published at the said meeting.

4. Which being done, you shall administer to each of the members of his Majesty's said Council as well the oaths appointed to be taken by an act passed in the first year of his Majesty's reign, entitled, *An Act for the Further Security of His Majesty's Person and Government and the Succession of the Crown in the Heirs of the Late Princess Sophia, Being Protestants, and for Extinguishing the Hopes of the Pretended Prince of Wales and His Open and Secret Abettors*, as also cause the members of his Majesty's said Council to make and subscribe the declaration mentioned in an act of Parliament made in the 25th year of the reign of King Charles II, entitled, *An Act for Preventing Dangers Which May Happen from Popish Recusants*. And every of them are likewise to take an oath for the due execution of their offices to their equal and impartial administration of justice.

5. You are forthwith to communicate unto his Majesty's said Council such and so many of these instructions wherein their advice and consent are mentioned to be requisite, as likewise all such others from time to time as you shall find convenient for his Majesty's service to be imparted unto them.

6. You are to permit the members of his Majesty's said Council to have and enjoy freedom of debate and vote in all affairs of public concern that may be debated in Council.

7. And that his Majesty may be always informed of the names and characters of persons fit to supply the vacancies which shall happen in his said Council, you are to transmit unto his Majesty, by one of his principal secretaries of state, and to his Commissions for Trade and Plantations, with all convenient speed, the names and characters of twelve persons, inhabitants of this said province, whom you shall esteem the best qualified for that trust; and so from time to time when any of them shall die, depart out of the said province, or become otherwise unfit, you are to nominate so many other persons to his Majesty in their stead, that the list of twelve persons fit to supply the said vacancies may be always complete.

8. You are, from time to time, to send to his Majesty, as aforesaid, and to his Commissioners for Trade and Plantations the names and qualities of any members by you put into the said Council by the first conveniency after your so doing.

9. And in the choice and nomination of the members of his Majesty's said Council, as also of the chief officers, judges, assistants, justices, and sheriffs, you are always to take care that they be men of good life and well-affected to his Majesty's government and of good estates and abilities and not necessitous persons or much in debt.

10. You are neither to augment nor diminish the number of his Majesty's said Council, nor to suspend any of the members thereof, without good and sufficient cause, nor without the consent of the majority of the said Council. And in case of suspension of any of them, you are to cause your reasons for so doing, together with the charges and proofs against the said persons and their answers thereunto, to be duly entered upon the Council books and forthwith to transmit copies thereof to his Majesty, as aforesaid, and to his Commissioners for Trade and Plantations. Nevertheless, if it should happen that you should have reasons for suspending of any councillor not fit to be communicated to the Council, you may in that case suspend such person without their consent; but you are thereupon immediately to send to his Majesty, by one of his principal secretaries of state, and to his Commissioners for Trade and Plantations, an account thereof with your reasons for such suspension, as also for not communicating the same to the Council, and duplicates thereof by the next occasion.

11. And you are likewise to signify his Majesty's pleasure unto the members of his said Council that if any of them shall hereafter absent themselves from the said province and continue absent above the space of twelve months together, without leave from you or from the commander-in-chief of the said province for the time being first had and obtained under your or his hand and seal, or shall remain absent for the space of two years successively without his Majesty's leave given him or them under his royal signature, their place or places in the said Council shall immediately thereupon become void, and that his Majesty will forthwith appoint others in their stead.

12. And although, by your commission aforesaid, his Majesty has thought fit to direct, that any three of the councillors make a quorum, it is, nevertheless, his Majesty's will and pleasure that you do not act with a quorum of less than five members, unless upon extraordinary emergencies when a greater number than three cannot conveniently be had.

13. And whereas his Majesty is sensible that effectual care ought to be taken to oblige the members of his Council to a due attendance therein, in order to prevent the many inconveniences that may happen for want of a quorum of the Council to transact business as occasion may require. It is his Majesty's will and pleasure that if any of the members of the said Council then residing in the province shall hereafter wilfully absent themselves when duly summoned, without a just and lawful cause, and shall persist therein after admonition, you suspend the said councillors so absenting themselves till his Majesty's further pleasure be known, giving his Majesty timely notice thereof. And you are to signify this his Majesty's pleasure to the several members of the said Council aforesaid, and that it be entered in the Council books of the said province as a standing rule.

14. You shall take care that the members of the Assembly be elected only by freeholders, as being more agreeable to the custom of this kingdom, to which you are as near as may be to conform yourself in this particular.

15. You are to observe in the passing of laws that the style of enacting the same be by the Governor, Council, and Assembly, and no other. You are also, as much as possible, to observe in the passing of all laws that whatever may be requisite upon each different matter be accordingly provided for by a different law, without intermising in one and the same act such things as have no proper relation to each other. And you are more especially to take care that no clause or clauses be inserted in or annexed to any act which shall be foreign to what the title of such respective act imports; and that no perpetual clause be part of any temporary law, and that no act whatever be suspended, altered, revised, confirmed, or repealed by general

words, but that the title and date of such act so suspended, altered, revised, confirmed, or repealed be particularly mentioned and expressed.

16. You are also to take care that no private act he passed in which there is not a saving of the right of his Majesty, his heirs and successors, all bodies politic or corporate, and of all other persons, except such as are mentioned in the said act.

17. And whereas great mischiefs may arise by passing bills of an unusual and extraordinary nature and importance in the plantations, all bills remaining in force there from the time of enacting, until his Majesty's pleasure be signified to the contrary. You are hereby required not to pass or give your consent hereafter to any bill or bills in the Assembly of the said province of unusual and extraordinary nature and importance, wherein his Majesty's prerogative or the property of his subjects may be prejudiced or the trade or shipping of this kingdom in anyways affected, until you shall have first transmitted unto his Majesty the draught of such a bill or bills and shall have received his Majesty's pleasure thereupon; unless you take care in the passing of any bill of such nature as before mentioned that there be a clause inserted therein suspending and deferring the execution thereof until his Majesty's pleasure shall be known concerning the same, which you are likewise to observe in the passing of all acts that shall repeal any act or acts that have had the royal assent.

18. And that it may be the better understood what acts and laws are in force in the said province of Carolina, you are, with the assistance of the Council, to take care that all laws now in force be revised and considered; and if there be anything either in the matter or style of them which may be fit to be retrenched or altered, you are to represent the same unto his Majesty with your opinion touching the said laws now in force. Whereof you are to send a complete body unto his Majesty and to his Commissioners for Trade and Plantations, with such alterations as you shall think requisite, to the end his Majesty's approbation or disallowance may be signified thereupon.

19. You are to transmit authentic copies of all laws, statutes, and ordinances that are now made and in force which have not yet been sent,

or which at any time hereafter shall be made or enacted within the said province, each of them separately under the public seal, unto his Majesty and to his said Commissioners for Trade and Plantations, within three months or sooner after their being enacted, together with duplicates thereof by the next conveyance. Both which copies and duplicates are to be fairly abstracted in the margin, upon pain of his Majesty's high displeasure, and of the forfeiture of that year's salary wherein you shall, at any time or upon any pretence whatsoever, omit to send over the said laws, statutes, and ordinances, aforesaid, within the time above limited, as also of such other penalty as his Majesty shall please to inflict. But if it shall happen that during the time of war no shipping shall come from the said province within three months after the making such laws, statutes, and ordinances, whereby the same may be transmitted as aforesaid, then the said laws, statutes, and ordinances are to be transmitted by the next conveyance after the making thereof, whenever it may happen, for his Majesty's approbation or disallowance of the same.

20. And his Majesty's further will and pleasure is that upon every act which shall be transmitted there be the several dates, or respective times, when the same passed the Assembly, the Council, and received your assent. And you are to be as particular as may be in your observations to be sent to his Majesty's Commissioners for Trade and Plantations upon every act, that is to say, whether the same is introductive of a new law, declaratory of a former law, or for the repeal of any law in being; and you are likewise to send to the said commissioners the reasons for the passing of such law, unless the same do fully appear in the preamble of the said act.

21. You are, for the better administration of justice, to endeavor to get a law passed wherein shall be set the value of men's estates either in goods or lands, under which they shall not be capable of serving as jurors.

22. You shall administer or cause to be administered the oaths appointed to be taken by the aforesaid *Act for the Further Security of His Majesty's Person and Government and the Succession of the Crown in the Heirs of the Late Princess Sophia, Being Protestants, and for Extinguishing the Hopes of the Pretended Prince of Wales and His Open and Secret Abettors*, unto all members and officers of the Council and Assembly, all judges and justices, and all other persons that hold any office or peace of trust or profit in the said province, and you shall also cause them to make and subscribe the foresaid declaration, without the doing of all which you are not to admit any person whatsoever into any public office nor suffer those that have been admitted formerly to continue therein.

23. You are to take care that in all acts or orders to be passed within that province in any case for levying money or imposing fines and penalties, express mention be made that the same is granted or reserved to his Majesty, his heirs and successors, for the public uses of that province and the support of the government thereof as by the said act or order shall be directed.

24. And his Majesty does particularly require and command that no money or value of money whatsoever be given or granted by any act or order of Assembly to you the Governor, Lieutenant-Governor, or Commander-in-Chief of the said province which shall not, according to the style of acts or Parliament of Great Britain, be mentioned to be given and granted unto his Majesty, with the humble desire of such Assembly that the same be applied to the use and behoof of such governor, lieutenant-governor, or commander-in-chief if his Majesty shall think fit; or if he shall not approve of such gift or application, that the said money or value of money be then disposed of and appropriated to such other uses as in the act or order shall be mentioned; and that from the time the same shall be raised, it remain in the hand of the receiver-general of the said province until his Majesty's pleasure shall be known therein.

25. And whereas several inconveniences have arisen to his Majesty's governments in the plantations by gifts and presents made to the governors by the general assemblies. You are, therefore, to propose unto the said General Assembly, and use your utmost endeavors with them, that an act be passed for raising and settling a public revenue for defraying the necessary charge of the government

of the said province and that therein provision be particularly made for a competent salary to yourself as Captain-General and Governor-in-Chief of the said province, and to any other succeeding captain-general for supporting the dignity of the said office, as likewise due provision for the contingent charges of due Council and Assembly and for the salaries of the respective clerks and other officers thereunto belonging, as likewise of all other officers necessary for the administration of that government. And when such revenue shall so have been settled and provision made as aforesaid, then his Majesty's express will and pleasure is that neither you the Governor nor any governor, lieutenant-governor, commander-in-chief, or president of the Council of the said province of Carolina for the time being, do give your or their consent to the passing any law or act for any gift or present to be made to you or them by the Assembly, and that neither you nor they do receive any gift or present from the Assembly or others on any account or in any manner whatsoever, upon pain of his Majesty's highest displeasure and of being recalled from that government.

26. And his Majesty does further direct and require that this declaration of his royal will and pleasure be communicated to the Assembly at their first meeting after your arrival in that province and entered into the journals of the Council and Assembly, that all persons whom it may concern may govern themselves accordingly.

27. And whereas his Majesty is willing in the best manner to provide for the support of the government of the said province by setting apart sufficient allowances to such as shall be governors or commander-in-chief residing for the time being within the same. His Majesty's will and pleasure, therefore, is that when it shall happen that you shall be absent from that province, one moiety of the salary and of all perquisites and emoluments whatsoever, which would otherwise become due unto you, shall, during the time of your absence, be paid and satisfied unto such governor or commander-in-chief who shall be resident within the said province for the time being, which his Majesty does order and allot unto him for his maintenance, and for the better support of the dignity of that government.

28. And whereas great prejudice may happen to his Majesty's service and the security of that province by your absence from those parts. You are not, upon any pretence whatsoever, to come into Great Britain without having first obtained leave for so doing from his Majesty under his royal signet and sign manual, or by his Majesty's order in his Privy Council. But in case of your being seized by any dangerous sickness, which may make it necessary for you to change the air by removing to some other climate in order to the recovery of your health, his Majesty does permit you to repair to New York or such other northern plantations on the continent of America as you judge most convenient; provided you do not remain absent from your government any longer than shall be absolutely necessary for your recovery from such dangerous sickness.

29. And whereas his Majesty has thought fit by his commission to direct that in case of your death or absence from the said province, and in case there be at that time no person upon the place commissionated or appointed by his Majesty to be lieutenant-governor or commander-in-chief, the eldest councillor who shall be, at that time of your death or absence, residing within the province of Carolina shall take upon him the administration of the government and execute his Majesty's said commission and instructions and the several powers and authorities therein contained in the manner therein directed. It is, nevertheless, his Majesty's express will and pleasure that in such case the said president shall forbear to pass any acts but what are immediately necessary for the peace and welfare of the said province, without his Majesty's particular order for that purpose.

30. You are not to permit any clause whatsoever to be inserted in any law for levying money or the value of money whereby the same shall not be made liable to be accounted for unto his Majesty in this kingdom and to the commissioners of his Majesty's Treasury, or to his High Treasurer of Great Britain for the time being.

31. And his Majesty does particularly require and enjoin you, upon pain of his highest displeasure, to take care that fair books of accounts of all receipts and payments of all such money be duly kept and the truth thereof attested upon

oath, and that the said books be transmitted every half year or oftener to the commissioners of his Majesty's Treasury, or to his High Treasurer for the time being, and to his Commissioners for Trade and Plantations, and duplicates thereof by the next conveyances. In which books shall be specified every particular sum raised or disposed of, together with the names of the persons two whom any payment shall be made, to the end his Majesty may be satisfied of the right and due application of the revenue of the said province.

32. You are not to suffer any public money whatsoever to be issued to disposed of otherwise than by warrant under your hand, by and with the advice and consent of the Council. But the Assembly may, nevertheless, be permitted, from time to time, to view and examine the accounts of money or value of money disposed of by virtue of laws made by them, which you are to signify to them as there shall be occasion.

33. It is his Majesty's express will and pleasure that no law for raising any imposition on wines or other strong liquors be made to continue for less than one whole year; and that all other laws made for the supply and support of the government shall be indefinite and without limitation, except the same be for a temporary service, and which shall expire and have their full effect within the time therein prefixed.

34. And whereas several other laws have formerly been enacted in the plantations for so short a time that his Majesty's assent or refusal thereof could not be had thereupon before the time for which such laws were enacted did expire. You shall not for the future give your assent for any law that shall be enacted for less time than two years, except in the cases mentioned in the foregoing article, and you shall not reenact any law to which his Majesty's assent has once been refused, without express leave for that purpose first obtained from his Majesty, upon a full representation by you to be made of the reasons and necessity of raising such laws.

35. And whereas the members of several assemblies in the plantations have of late years assumed to themselves privileges no ways belonging to them, especially of being protected from suits at law during the term the remain of the

assemblies, to the great prejudice of their creditors and the obstructing of justice. And some others have presumed to adjourn themselves at pleasure without leave from his Majesty's governor first obtained. And others have taken upon them the sole framing of money bills, refusing to let the Council alter or amend the same. All which are very detrimental to his Majesty's prerogative. If, upon your calling an Assembly in Carolina, you find them insist upon any of the abovesaid privileges, you are to signify to them that it is his Majesty's express will and pleasure that you do not allow any protection to any member of the Council or Assembly further than in their persons and that only during the sitting of the Assembly, and that you are not to allow them to adjourn themselves otherwise than *de die in diem*, except Sundays and holdays, without leave from you or the commander-in-chief for the time being first obtained, and that the Council have the like power of framing, amending, or altering money bills as the Assembly. And you are hereby expressly enjoined not to allow the members of Assembly in Carolina any power or privilege whatsoever which is not allowed by his Majesty to members of the House of Commons in Great Britain.

36. You shall take care than an act passed here in the sixth year of the reign of her late Majesty Queen Ann, entitled, *An Act for Ascertaining the Rates of Foreign Coins in the Plantations in America*, be duly observed and put in execution.

37. And you are particularly not to pass any law, or do any act by grant, settlement, or otherwise, whereby the public revenues may be lessened or impaired, without his Majesty's especial leave or command therein.

38. You shall not remit any fines or forfeitures whatsoever above the sum of £10, nor dispose of any escheats, fines, or forfeitures whatsoever until upon signifying to the commissioners of his Majesty's Treasury or his High Treasurer for the time being, and to his Commissioners for Trade and Plantations the nature of the offense and the occasion of such fines, forfeitures, or escheats, with the particular sums or value thereof, which you are to do with all speed, you shall have received his Majesty's directions therein: but you may in

the meantime suspend the payment of such fines and forfeitures.

39. You are to require the secretary of the said province to furnish you with transcripts of all such acts and public orders as shall be made from time to time, together with a copy of the journals of the Council, and that such transcripts and copies be fairly abstracted in the margins, to the end the same may be transmitted unto his Majesty and to his Commissioners for Trade and Plantations, as above directed, which he is duly to perform upon pain of incurring the forfeiture of his office.

40. You are to require from the clerk of the Assembly, or other proper officer, transcripts of all journals and other proceedings of the said Assembly, and that all such transcripts be fairly abstracted in the margins, to the end the same may be in like manner transmitted to his Majesty and to his Commissioners for Trade and Plantations, as aforesaid.

41. You shall transmit to his Majesty and to his Commissioners for Trade and Plantations, by the first opportunity, a map with the exact description of the whole province under your government with the several plantations upon it and of the fortifications.

42. You are to transmit unto his Majesty and to his Commissioners for Trade and Plantations, with all convenient speed, a particular account of all establishments of jurisdictions, courts, offices and officers, powers, authorities, fees, and privileges which shall be granted or settled within the said province by virtue and in pursuance of his Majesty's commission and instructions to you, the said Captain-General and Governor-in-Chief of the same, to the end you may receive his Majesty's further directions therein.

43. You shall send a list of all the officers employed under your government, together with an account of both the ordinary and extraordinary or contingent charges thereof and of such funds as are or shall be settled and appropriated to discharge the same.

44. You shall send an account to his Majesty and to his Commissioners for Trade and Plantations of the present number of planters and inhabitants, men, women and children, as well masters as servants, free and unfree, and of the slaves in the said province, as also a yearly account of the increase or decrease of them and how many of them are fit to bear arms in the militia of the said province.

45. You shall also cause an exact account to be kept of all persons born, christened, and buried and send yearly fair abstracts thereof to his Majesty and his Commissioners for Trade and Plantations, as aforesaid.

46. You shall not displace any of the judges, justices, sheriffs or other officers or ministers within the said province without good and sufficient cause, to be signified unto his Majesty and to his Commissioners for Trade and Plantations. And to prevent arbitrary removals of judges and justices of the peace, you shall not express any limitation of time in the commissions which you are to grant with the advice and consent of the Council of the said province to persons fit for those employments, nor shall you execute yourself or by deputy any of the said offices nor suffer any person to execute more offices than one by deputy.

47. You shall not erect any court or office of judicature not before erected or established nor dissolve any court or office already erected or established, without his Majesty's especial order.

48. And you are, with the advice and consent of his Majesty's said Council, to take care to regulate all salaries and fees belonging to places or paid upon emergencies, that they be within the bounds of moderation, and that no exaction be made on any occasion whatsoever; as also that tables of all fees be publicly hung up in all places where such fees are to be paid: and you are to transmit copies of all such tables of fees to his Majesty and to his Commissioners for Trade and Plantations, as aforesaid.

49. Whereas it is necessary that his Majesty's rights and dues be preserved and recovered, and that speedy and effectual justice be administered in all cases relating to the revenue, you are to take care that a court of exchequer be called and do meet at all such times as shall be needful. And you are, upon your arrival, to inform his Majesty and his Commissioners for Trade and Plantations

whether his Majesty's service may require that a constant court of exchequer be settled and established there.

50. You are to take care than no man's life, member, freehold, or goods be taken away or harmed in the said province otherwise than by established and known laws, not repugnant to, but as near as may be agreeable to, the laws of this kingdom.

51. You are to take care that all writs within the said province be issued in his Majesty's name.

52. And whereas frequent complaints have been made to his Majesty of great delays and undue proceedings in the courts of justice in several of the plantations, whereby many of his Majesty's subjects have very much suffered, and it being of the greatest importance to his Majesty's service and to the welfare of the plantations that justice be everywhere speedily and duly administered and that all disorders, delays, and other undue practices in the administration thereof be effectually prevented. His Majesty does particularly require you to take especial care that, in all courts where you are authorized to provide, justice be impartially administered and that in all other courts established within the said province all judges and other persons therein concerned do likewise perform their several duties without any delay or partiality.

53. His Majesty does further, by these presents, will and require you to permit appeals to be made in cases of errors from the courts in Carolina unto you the Governor and Council in civil causes, provided the value appealed for do exceed the sum of £100 sterling and security be first duly given by the appellant to answer such charges as shall be awarded in case the first sentence shall be affirmed; provided, also, that if any of the said Council shall at that time be judges of the court from whence such appeal shall be made to you, his Majesty's Governor, and Council, or to the commander-in-chief for the time being and Council, such Council or councillors shall not be admitted to vote upon the said appeal, but he or they may, nevertheless, be present at the hearing thereof to give the reasons of the judgment given by him or them in the cause wherein such appeal shall be made.

54. And whereas his Majesty judges it necessary that all his subjects may have liberty to appeal unto himself in cases that may require the same. His Majesty's will and pleasure, therefore, is that if either party shall not rest satisfied with the judgment or sentence of his Governor and Council, they may then appeal unto his Majesty in his Privy Council; provided the matter in difference exceed the real value and sum of £300 sterling, and that such appeal be made within fourteen days after sentence, and that security be likewise duly given by the appellant to answer such charges as shall be awarded in case the sentence of the Governor and Council be affirmed; and provided, also, that execution be not suspended by reason of any such appeal unto his Majesty.

55. In case any goods, money, or other estate of pirates or piratically taken shall be brought in or found within his Majesty's said province of Carolina, or taken on board any ships or vessels, you are to cause the same to be seized and secured until you shall have given his Majesty an account thereof and received his pleasure concerning the disposal of the same. But in case such goods or any part of them are perishable, the same shall be publicly sold and disposed of and the produce thereof in like manner secured until his Majesty's further order.

56. Whereas commissions have been granted unto several persons in the respective plantations in America for the trying of pirates in those parts, pursuant to the *Act for the More Effectual Suppression of Piracy*, you will, likewise, herewith receive a commission to the same purpose and his Majesty's will and pleasure is that in all matters relating to pirates you govern yourself according to the intent of the said act and commission. But whereas accessories in cases of piracy beyond the seas are by the said act left to be tried in England, according to the statute of the 28th of King Henry VIII, you are hereby further directed and required to send all such accessories in cases of piracy in the aforesaid province of Carolina, with the proper evidences that you may have against them, into Great Britain in order to their being tried here. It is his Majesty's further will and pleasure that no

persons for the future be sent as prisoners to this kingdom from the said province of Carolina without sufficient proof of their crimes, and that proof transmitted along with the said prisoners.

57. You are to permit a liberty of conscience to all persons, except papists, so they be contented with a quiet and peaceable enjoyment of the same, not giving offense or scandal to the government.

58. You shall take care that all planters, inhabitants, and christian servants be well and fitly provided with arms and that they be listed under good officers and, when and as often as shall be thought fit, mustered and trained whereby they may be in a better readiness for the defense of the said province. And for the greater security thereof, you are to appoint fit officers and commanders in the several parts of that country bordering upon the Indians, who, upon any invasion, may raise men and arms to oppose them until they shall receive your directions therein.

59. You are to take especial care that neither the frequency nor unreasonableness of remote marches, musters, or trainings be an unnecessary impediment to the affairs of the inhabitants.

60. You shall not, upon any occasion whatsoever, establish or put in execution any articles of war or other law martial upon any of his Majesty's subjects, inhabitants of the said province, without the advice and consent of his Majesty's Council there.

61. And whereas you will receive from his Majesty's commissioners for executing the office of High Admiral of Great Britain and of the plantations a commission of Vice Admiral of the said province of Carolina, you are hereby required and directed carefully to put in execution the several powers thereby granted you.

62. You shall take an inventory of all such arms, ammunition, and stores as are remaining in any magazines or garrisons in the said province and transmit the said account and inventory to his Majesty and to his Commissioners for Trade and Plantations with all speed, and the like inventory afterwards, half yearly, as also duplicate thereof, to the master-general or principal officers of the ordinance. Which accounts are to express

the particulars of ordinance, carriages, ball, powder, and all other sorts of arms and ammunition in the public stores, and so from time to time of what shall be sent you or bought with the public money, and to specify the time of the disposal and the occasion thereof; it being his Majesty's pleasure, that such accounts be transmitted, as aforesaid, every six months, or oftener as opportunity shall offer, for his Majesty's better information, and duplicates thereof by the next conveyance.

63. You are to take especial care that fit store houses be settled in the said province for receiving and keeping of arms, ammunition, and other public stores.

64. And whereas it is absolutely necessary that his Majesty be exactly informed of the state of defense of all his plantations in America in every respect and more especially with relation to the forts and fortifications that are in each plantation and what more may be necessary to be built for the defence and security of the same. You are, so soon as possible after your arrival at Carolina, to prepare an account thereof with relation to the said province in the most particular manner and to transmit the same to his Majesty and to his Commissioners for Trade and Plantations and the like accounts afterwards yearly.

65. You shall cause a survey to be made of all the considerable landing places and harbors in the said province and, with the advice of his Majesty's Council there, erect in any of them such fortifications as shall be necessary for the security and advantage of the said province, which shall be done at the public charges; and you are accordingly to move the General Assembly to the passing of such acts as may be requisite for the carrying on of that work, in which his Majesty does not doubt of their cheerful concurrence from the common security and benefit they will receive thereby.

66. And that his Majesty may be the better informed of the trade of the said province, you are to take especial care that due entries be made in all ports thereof of all goods and commodities, their species and quantities, imported or exported from thence, with the names, burden, and guns of all ships importing and exporting the same, as

also the names of their commanders, and further expressing from and to what places the said ships do come and go, a copy whereof the naval officer is to furnish you with, and you are to transmit the same unto his Majesty and to his commissioners of the increase of, or the High Treasurer of Great Britain for the time being, and to his Commissioners for Trade and Plantations quarterly, and duplicates thereby by the next conveyance.

67. Whereas his Majesty has been informed that during the late war intelligence has frequently been had in France of the state of the plantations by letters from private persons to their correspondents in Great Britain, taken on board ships coming from the plantations and carried into France, which may be of dangerous consequence. His Majesty's will and pleasure, therefore, is that you signify to all merchants, planters, and others that they be very cautious in time of war in giving any account by letters of the public state and condition of the said province of Carolina; and you are further to give directions to all masters of ships or other persons to whom you may intrust your letters that they put such letters into a bag with a sufficient weight to sink the same immediately in case of imminent danger from the enemy; and you are also to let the merchants and planters know how greatly it is for their interest that their letters should not fall into the hands of the enemy, and, therefore, that they should give the like orders to the masters of ships in relation to their letters. And you are further to advise all masters of ships that they do sink all letters in case of danger in the manner before mentioned.

68. And whereas in the late wars the merchants and planters in the West Indies did correspond and trade with the French and carry intelligence to them to the great prejudice and hazard of the British plantations. You are, therefore, by all possible methods to endeavor to hinder all such trade and correspondence with the French whose strength in the West Indies gives very just apprehensions of the mischiefs that may ensue if the utmost care be not taken to prevent them.

69. Whereas by the fifth and sixth articles of the treaty of peace and neutrality in America concluded between England and France November 16, 1686, the subjects, inhabitants etc. of each kingdom are prohibited to trade and fish in all places possessed or which shall be possessed by the other in America, and that if any ships shall be found trading contrary to the said treaty, upon due proof, the said ships shall be confiscated. But in case the subjects of either King shall be forced by stress of weather, enemies, or other necessity into the ports of the other in America, they shall be treated with humanity and kindness and may provide themselves with victuals and other things necessary for their sustenance and repairation of their ships at reasonable rates; provided, they do not break bulk nor carry any goods out of their ships exposing them to sale, nor receive any merchandise on board under penalty of confiscation of ships and goods. Notwithstanding which treaty, his Majesty is given to understand that an illegal trade has been carried on between the British plantations and the French settlements in America on pretence that there is no law in force against such trade. It is, therefore, his Majesty's will and pleasure that you signify to all his subjects under your government the purport and intent of the abovesaid two articles, and that you take particular care that the same be punctually observed and put in execution, and that no illegal trade be carried on between his Majesty's subjects in Carolina and the French settlements by any of his Majesty's ships of war attending that province or by any other British ships, as likewise that none of the French subjects be allowed to trade from their said settlements to Carolina.

70. You are from time to time to give an account, as before directed, what strength your bordering neighbors have, be they Indians or others, by sea and land, and of the condition of their plantations and what correspondence you do keep with them.

71. And whereas there is great reason to believe that the Indians on the frontiers of Carolina, who have of late years fallen off from the British interest there, have been in some measure provoked thereunto by the injustice or ill usage received from his Majesty's subjects in your government; and it being highly necessary for the welfare of Carolina that a good understanding should be maintained with the said Indian

nations, as well for the promoting of trade as for the security of the frontiers of your government. You are hereby particularly enjoined to use all possible ways and means for regaining the affections of the said Indians and to preserve a good correspondence with such of them as remain faithful to his Majesty's interest, but especially with the Cherokee Indians inhabiting the mountains on the northwest side of the said province of South Carolina. And you are likewise hereby directed to recommend in the strongest terms to the Indian traders to be just and reasonable in their dealing with the native Indians, and likewise to propose to the Assembly, if you and his Majesty's Council shall judge it necessary, to pass one or more laws for the better regulation of the said Indian trade and for the encouragement and protection of such Indians as shall adhere to his Majesty's interest.

72. You shall take especial care that God Almighty be devoutly and duly served throughout your government, the *Book of Common Prayer*, as by law established, read each Sunday and holiday, and the blessed sacrament administered according to the rites of the Church of England.

73. You shall take care that the churches already built there be well and orderly kept, and that more be built as the province shall, by God's blessing, be improved, and that, besides a competent maintenance to be assigned to the minister of each orthodox church, a convenient house be built at the common charge for each minister and a competent proportion of glebe assigned him.

74. And you are to take care that the parishes be so bounded and settled as you shall find most convenient for accomplishing this good work.

75. You are not to prefer any minister to any ecclesiastical benefice in that province without a certificate from the right reverend father in God the Lord Bishop of London, or some other bishop, of his being conformable to the doctrine and discipline of the Church of England and of a good life and conversation; and if any person preferred already to a benefice shall appear to you to give scandal, either by his doctrine or manners, you are to use the proper and usual means for the removal of him and to supply the vacancy in such manner as his Majesty has directed.

76. You are to give orders forthwith, if the same be not already done, that every orthodox minister within your government be one of the vestry in his respective parish and that no vestry be held without him, except in case of sickness, or that after notice of a vestry summoned he omit to come.

77. You are to inquire whether there be any minister within your government who preaches and administers the sacrament in any orthodox church or chapel without being due orders, and to give an account thereof to the said Lord Bishop of London.

78. And to the end the ecclesiastical jurisdiction of the Lord Bishop of London may take place in that province so far as conveniently may be, his Majesty thinks fit that you give all countenance and encouragement to the exercise of the same, excepting only the collating to benefices, granting licenses for marriages, and probates of wills, which his Majesty has reserved to you and to the commander-in-chief of the said province for the time being, as far as by law he may.

79. And his Majesty does further direct that no schoolmaster be hence forward permitted to come from this kingdom and to keep school in that province without the license of the said Lord Bishop of London. But when such persons so qualified as above shall be wanted for the promotion of learning and good education, you may yourself license such other persons as you shall think qualified for such employments and that no other person now there or that shall come from other parts shall be admitted to keep school in Carolina without your license first obtained.

80. And you are to take especial care that a table of marriages established by the commons of the Church of England be hung up in every orthodox church and duly observed, and you are to endeavor to get a law passed in the Assembly of that province, if not already done, for the strict observation of the said table.

81. You are to take care that drunkenness and debauchery, swearing and blasphemy be discountenanced and punished; and for the further discountenance of vice and encouragement of virtue and good living, that by such example the infidels may be invited and desire to embrace the

christian religion, you are not to admit person to public trusts and employments in the province under your government whose ill fame and conversation may occasion scandal.

82. You are to suppress the engrossing of commodities as tending to the prejudice of that freedom which commerce and trade ought to have, and to settle such orders and regulations therein, with the advice of the Council, as may be most acceptable to the generality of the inhabitants.

83. You are to give all due encouragement and invitation to merchants and others who shall bring trade unto the said province or any way contribute to the advantage thereof, and in particular to the Royal African Company.

84. And his Majesty is willing to recommend unto the said company that the said province may have a constant and sufficient supply of merchantable Negroes at moderate rates in money or commodities, so you are to take especial care that payment be duly made and within a competent time according to their agreement.

85. And whereas the said company have frequently great sums of money owing to them in the plantations in America, they have been much hindered in the recovery of their just debts there and discouraged in their trade by their too frequent adjournment of courts; and it being absolutely necessary that all obstructions in the course of justice be effectually removed. You are to take care that courts of justice be duly to be frequently held in the said province of Carolina under your government so that all his Majesty's subjects in the said province, and particularly the Royal African Company and others trading to Africa, may enjoy the benefit thereof and not to receive any undue hindrance in the recovery of their just debts.

86. And you are further expressly commanded and required to give unto his Majesty and to the Commissioners for Trade and Plantations an account every half year of what number of Negroes the said province is supplied with, that is, what number by the African Company and what by separate traders, and at what rates sold.

87. You are likewise, from time to time, to give unto his Majesty and to the Commissioners for Trade and Plantations, as aforesaid, an account

of the wants and defects of the said province, what are the chief products thereof, what new improvements are made therein by the industry of the inhabitants or planters, and what further improvements you conceive may be made or advantages gained by trade and which way his Majesty may contribute thereunto.

88. You are not to grant commissions of marque or reprisals against any prince of state or their subjects in amity with his Majesty to any person whatsoever, without his Majesty's especial command.

89. Whereas great inconveniences do happen by merchant ships and other vessels in the plantations wearing the colors born by his Majesty's ships of war under pretence of commissions granted to them by the governors of the said plantations and that by trading under those colors not only among his Majesty's subjects, but also those of other princes and states, and committing diverse irregularities, they do very much dishonor his Majesty's service. For prevention whereof, you are to oblige the commanders of all ships to which you shall grant commissions to wear no other jack than according to the sample here described, that is to say, such as is worn by his Majesty's ships of war, with the distinction of a white excutcheon in the middle thereof, and that the mark of distinction may extend itself to one half of the depth of the jack and one third of the fly thereof.

90. And whereas there has been great irregularities in the manner of granting commissions in the plantations to private ships of war; you are to govern yourself according to the commissions and instructions granted in this kingdom. Copies whereof will be herewith delivered you.

91. In case of any distress of any other of his Majesty's plantations, you shall, upon application of the respective governors thereof to you, assist them with what aid the condition and safety of the province under your government can spare.

92. You are to endeavor to get a law passed, if not already done, for the restraining of any inhuman severity which by ill masters or overseers may be used towards their christian servants or their slaves, and that provisions be made therein that the willful killing of Indians and Negroes may be punished with death and that a fit penalty

be imposed for the maiming of them. And you are also, with the assistance of the Council and Assembly, to find out the best means to facilitate and encourage the conversion of Negroes and Indians to the christian religion.

93. You are to endeavor to get an act passed, if not already done, whereby the creditors of persons becoming bankrupts in this kingdom and having estates in Carolina may be relieved and satisfied for the debts owing to them.

94. If his Majesty shall judge it necessary for his service to appropriate a lieutenant-governor of North Carolina, you are hereby required to give him an authentic copy of your instructions whereby he will conduct himself in the government of that province, and he will be directed by his commission to obey such orders as he shall from time to time receive from you for his Majesty's service.

95. If anything shall happen that may be of advantage and security to his Majesty's said province which is not herein or by your commission provided for his Majesty does hereby allow unto

you, with the advice and consent of the Council, to take order for the present therein, giving to his Majesty, by one of his principal secretaries of state and to his aforesaid Commissioners for Trade and Plantations, speedy notice thereof, that so you may receive his Majesty's ratification if he shall approve of the same. Provided always, that you do not, by color of any power or authority hereby given you, commence or declare war without his Majesty's knowledge and particular commands therein, except it be against Indians upon emergencies, wherein the consent of his Majesty's Council shall be had and speedy notice given thereof unto his Majesty as aforesaid.

96. And you are upon all occasions, to send unto his Majesty and to his Commissioners for Trade and Plantations a particular account of all your proceedings and of the condition of affairs within your government.

Reference: A. A. Salley (ed.), *Records in the British Public Records Office Relating to South Carolina*, Vol. III (5 vols.; Atlanta: Foote and Davies, 1928–1947), 101–138.

ACTS TO ASCERTAIN MANNER OF ELECTING MEMBERS OF THE GENERAL ASSEMBLY, SEPTEMBER 1721

Whereas the choosing members of the Commons House of Assembly for this province by parishes or precincts has been found by experience to be the most just and least expensive method that can be devised, and approaches nearest to the form and method of choosing or electing members in other his Majesty's dominions and plantations, and not liable to the inconveniencies that attend any other method heretofore used or practiced in this province; therefore, for preserving the same inviolable, we humbly pray your most sacred Majesty that it may be enacted,

I. And be it enacted by his Excellency Francis Nicholson, Esq., Governor, etc., by and with the advice and consent of his Majesty's honorable Council and the Assembly of this province, and by the authority of the same, that the persons who

shall be chosen to serve as members of Assembly after the ratification of this act shall be elected and chosen after the manner and at the places appointed by this act.

II. And be it further enacted, by the authority aforesaid, that all writs for the future elections of members of Assembly shall be issued out by the Governor and Council for the time being, and shall bear date forty days before the day appointed for the meeting of the said members, and shall be directed to the church warden or church wardens of the several parishes hereafter named, or in case there should be wanting church wardens in any parish then to such other proper persons as the Governor and Council shall think fit to nominate in the said writs to manage such elections, every one of whom are hereby empowered and required to execute the said writs faithfully according to the true intent and meaning of this act, to which every person shall be sworn by any one justice of the peace for the county, who is hereby required to administer such oath without fee or reward and shall give public notice in writing of all and every such writs two Sundays before the appointed time of election at the door of each parish church, or at some other public place as shall be appointed in the said writs in such parishes as have yet no churches erected, to the intent the time and place of election may be better and more fully made known; which writs shall be executed upon the same days at all places where elections are appointed.

III. And be it further enacted, by the authority aforesaid, that every free white man, and no other person, professing the christian religion, who has attained to the age of one and twenty years and has been a resident and an inhabitant in this province for the space of one whole year before the date of the writs for the election he offers to give his vote at, and has a freehold of at least 50 acres of land, or has been taxed in the precedent year twenty shillings, or is taxed twenty shillings the year present to the support of this government, shall be deemed a person qualified to vote for and may be capable of electing a representative or representatives to serve as a member or members of the Commons House of Assembly for the parish or precinct wherein he actually is a resident, or in any other parish or precincts wherein he has the like qualification.

IV. And for the preventing of frauds in all elections as much as possible, it is hereby enacted, by the authority aforesaid, that the names of the electors for members of the Commons House of Assembly shall be fairly entered in a book or roll, for that purpose provided by the churchwardens or other persons appointed for managing elections, to prevent any person's voting twice at the same election; and the manner of their voting shall be as herein after is directed, that is to say, each person qualified to vote, as is above directed, shall put into a box, glass, or sheet of paper, prepared for that purpose by the said church wardens or other persons, as is above directed, a piece of paper rolled up, wherein is written the names of

the representatives he votes for, and to which paper the elector shall not be obliged to subscribe his name; and if upon the scrutiny two or more papers with persons written thereon for members of Assembly be found rolled up together, or more person's names be found written in any paper than ought to be voted for, all and every such paper or papers shall be invalid and of no effect; and that those persons who, after all the papers and votes are delivered in and entered as aforesaid, shall be found, upon the scrutiny made, to have the majority of votes, are and shall be deemed and declared to be members of the succeeding Commons House of Assembly, so as they be qualified as is hereinafter directed.

V. And be it further enacted, by the authority aforesaid, that the said election shall not continue longer than two days and that the said elections shall begin at nine in the morning and end at four in the evening, and that at adjourning of the poll at convenient hours, in the time of the aforesaid election the church wardens, or other persons, as aforesaid, empowered to manage the said elections, shall seal up the said box, glass, or paper wherein are put all the votes then delivered in and rolled up by the electors, as aforesaid, with their own seals and the seals of any two or more of the electors that are there present, and upon opening the poll shall unseal the said box, glass, or paper in the presence of the said electors, in order to proceed in the said elections.

VI. And be it further enacted, by the authority aforesaid, that the said church wardens, or other persons appointed in each parish to manage the elections aforesaid, shall, within seven days after the scrutiny is made, give public notice in writing at the church door, or at such other public places in the parishes that have no churches where the election was made, to the person or persons so elected that the inhabitants of the said parish have made choice of him or them to serve as their representative or representatives in the next succeeding Commons House of Assembly, under the penalty of one hundred pounds current money of this province for his default or neglect therein, to be recovered and disposed of in such manner and form as is hereafter in this act directed.

VII. And be it further enacted, by the authority aforesaid, that the inhabitants of the several parishes in this province qualified to vote for members of Assembly, as is before in this act directed, shall, upon the days of election, according to the Governor's and Council's precept for the time being, meet at their respective parish churches, or at some other public place in such parishes as have not yet any churches erected in them, as shall be appointed by the said precept, and there proceed to choose their representatives according to the number following; that is to say, the parish of St. Philip's Charlestown, five members; for the parish of Christ church, two members; for the parish of St. John's, three members; for the parish of St. Andrew's, three members; for the parish of St. George's, two members; for the parish of St. James Goose Creek, four members; for the parish of St. Thomas and St. Dennis, three members, the election to be made at the parish church of St. Thomas; for the parish of St. Paul's, four members; for the parish of St. Bartholomew's, at such place in the said parish as shall be appointed by the governor and Council's precept, until the parish church is erected, four members; for the parish of St. Helena, four members, the election to be made at Beauford in the said parish; and for the parish of St. James Santee, with Winyaw, two members. And the said several members who, upon a scrutiny, are found to have the majority of votes, so as they are qualified as is hereinafter directed, shall be and they are hereby declared and adjudged to be the true representatives for the said parish.

VIII. And be it further enacted, by the authority aforesaid, that every person who shall be elected and returned, as is before directed by this act, to serve as a member of the Commons House of Assembly, shall be qualified as follows; viz., he shall be a free born subject of the kingdom of Great Britain, or of the dominion thereunto belonging, or a foreign person naturalized by act of Parliament in Great Britain or Ireland, that has attained to the age of twenty-one years, and has been resident in this province for twelve months before the date of the said writs; and having in this province a settled plantation or freehold, in his own right, of at leave 500 acres of land, and ten slaves, or has in his own proper person and in his own right, to the value of £1,000 in houses, buildings, town lots, or other lands in any part of this province.

IX. And be it further enacted, by the authority aforesaid, that any of his Majesty's justices of the peace returned to serve as a member of the said Commons House of Assembly shall read over to the rest of the members returned to serve in the said house, before they be admitted to sit as such, the last mentioned qualifying clause, and then each member, before he be admitted to sit as such in the said house, shall take the following oath on the holy evangelists. I, A B, do sincerely swear that I am duly qualified to be chosen and serve as a member of the Commons House of Assembly of this province for the parish of . . . . , according to the true intent and meaning of this act. So help me God.

X. And be it further enacted, by the authority aforesaid, that if any member or members hereafter chosen to serve in any Commons House of Assembly should die or depart this province, or refuse to qualify him of themselves as in this act directed, or be expelled by the said House of Commons, then and in such cases the said House shall by message to the Governor and Council for the time being desire them to issue out a new writ or writs, and the said Governor and Council shall, on such a message to them presented, issue out a new writ or writs, directed as before in this act is appointed, for choosing another person or persons to serve in the place or places of such member or members so dead or departed this province, or who shall refuse to qualify him or themselves, or be expelled as aforesaid. Which person or persons, so chosen and summoned as before directed, shall attend the Commons House of Assembly, as by the precept is directed, under the same fines and penalties the several church wardens or other persons appointed to manage elections according to the directions of this act are liable to the said act.

XI. And be it further enacted, by the authority aforesaid, that all and every member and members of the Commons House of Assembly of this province, chosen by virtue of this act, shall have as much power and privilege to all intents and purposes as any member or members of the Commons House of Assembly of this province heretofore of right had, might, could, or ought to have in the said province; provided the same are such as are according to his Majesty's thirty-fifth instruction.

XII. And be it further enacted, by the authority aforesaid, that if any person or persons appointed by this act to manage any election for a member or members of the Commons House of Assembly, as aforesaid, shall willingly or knowingly admit of or take the vote of any person not qualified according to the purport of this act, or, after any vote delivered in at such election, shall open or suffer any person whatsoever to open any such vote before the scrutiny is begun to be made, or shall make an undue return of any person for a member of the Commons House of Assembly, each person so offending, shall forfeit for each such vote taken and admitted of, opened, or suffered to be opened, as aforesaid, and for each such return, the sum of one hundred pounds current money of this province, to be recovered and disposed of in such manner and form as hereafter in this act is directed.

XIII. And be it further enacted, by the authority aforesaid, that all and every person and persons appointed to take votes, or to manage elections of members to serve in the Commons House of Assembly, as aforesaid, shall for that purpose attend at the time and place of election according as he or they are directed by the said writs and attend likewise on the said Commons House of Assembly the two first days of their sitting, unless he or they have leave sooner to depart, to inform them of all such matters and disputes that did arise or may have arisen about the election of any member or members to serve as aforesaid, or at any place or places where the same was or were appointed to be managed, and shall show to said House the list of the votes of every person returned to be a representative to serve as aforesaid, or which otherwise ought to have been returned as such, if any complaint of a false return has been made to the Commons House of Assembly; and every person appointed to take votes, as aforesaid, who shall omit or

refuse to attend at either of the times and places, as aforesaid, shall forfeit the sum of ten pounds current money of this province, to be recovered and disposed of in such manner and form as is hereafter directed by this act.

XIV. And be it further enacted, by the authority aforesaid, that if any person or persons whatsoever shall, on any day appointed for the election of a member or members of the Commons House of Assembly as aforesaid, presume to violate the freedom of the said election by any arrest, menaces, or threats, or endeavor or attempt to overawe, fright, or force any person qualified to vote against his inclination or conscience, or otherwise by bribery obtain any vote, or who shall, after the said election is over, menace, despitefully use, or abuse any person because he has not voted as he or they would have had him, every such person so offending, upon due and sufficient proof made of such his violence or abuse, menacing or threatening, before any two justices of the peace, shall be bound over to the next general sessions of the peace, himself in fifty pounds current money of this province, and two sureties, each in twenty-five pounds of like money, and to be of good behavior, and abide the sentence of the said court, where, if the offender or offenders are convicted and found guilty of such offense or offenses, as aforesaid, then he or they shall each of them forfeit the sum of fifty pounds current money of this province, and be committed to jail without bail or mainprize till the same be paid; which fine so imposed shall be paid unto one of the church wardens of the parish where the offense was committed for the use of the poor thereof; and if any person offending as aforesaid shall be chosen a member of the Commons House of Assembly, after conviction of illegal practices proved before the said House, shall by a vote of the said House be rendered uncapable to sit or vote as a member of that Commons House of Assembly.

XV. And be it further enacted, by the authority aforesaid, that no civil officer whatsoever shall execute any writs or other civil process whatsoever upon the body of any person qualified to vote for members of the Commons House of Assembly, as before in this act is directed, either in his journey to or in his return from the place of such election, or during his stay there on that account, or within forty-eight hours after the scrutiny for such elections is finished, under the penalty of twenty pounds current money of this province, to be recovered of and from the officer which shall arrest or serve any process, as aforesaid, after such manner and form and to be disposed of as hereinafter is directed; and all such writs or warrants executed on the body of any person either going to or being at, within the time limited by this clause, or returning from the place of such election is appointed to be managed, he being qualified to give in his vote thereat, are hereby declared void and null.

XVI. And be it further enacted, by the authority aforesaid, that every justice of the peace who shall refuse or neglect to do his duty in and by this act enjoined and required shall, for every default, forfeit the sum of one hundred pounds current money of this province, to be recovered and disposed of as is hereinafter directed by this act.

XVII. And be it further enacted, by the authority aforesaid, that in any succeeding Commons House of Assembly, no less than nineteen members duly met shall make an House to transact the business of the same; and for passing any law therein, there shall not be less than ten affirmatives; nor shall a less number than seven members of the said House met together have power to adjourn, which number are hereby declared to have power, in the absence of the speaker, to choose a chairman to adjourn the members from day to day and to summons by their messenger any absenting member or members to appear and give their attendance in the said House.

XVIII. But forasmuch as, by the great distance of the habitation of several of the members of Charlestown, through bad weather and other accidents it may often happen that such a number may not meet to make an adjournment, be it, therefore, enacted, by the authority aforesaid, that in case none of the members of the Commons House of Assembly, or a less number than seven of them, should appear in the said House according to the directions of the writs appointing their first meeting, or to their last prorogation or adjournment, that then and

in such case it shall be and it is hereby declared lawful for the governor for the time being, with the advice and consent of his council, to name a further day for the meeting of the said Commons House of Assembly, and that the said House shall not be dissolved by their not meeting as aforesaid, any law, custom, or usage to the contrary thereof in anyway notwithstanding.

XIX. And be it further enacted, by the authority aforesaid, that whosoever for the future shall be elected a member to serve in the Commons House of Assembly, before he be permitted to sit and vote in the said house, shall further qualify himself for the same by taking the usual oaths and make and sign the declaration appointed by several acts of Parliament of Great Britain.

XX. And be it further enacted, by the authority aforesaid, that all the fines and forfeitures mentioned in this act and not before particularly disposed of, the one-half thereof shall be to his Majesty for the use of the poor of the parish of St. Philip's Charlestown, to be paid to the church wardens of the said parish, and the other half to him or them that will sue for the same by action of debt, suit, bill, plaint, or information in any court of record in this province, wherein no essoign, protection, privilege, or wager of law, or stay of protection shall be admitted or allowed of.

XXI. And be it further enacted, by the authority aforesaid, that this present General Assembly shall determine and be dissolved at the expiration of three years next after the date of the writs issued out for calling the same, and that every General Assembly hereafter called by virtue of any writs, as aforesaid, shall determine and be dissolved every three years next after the date of the respective writs by which they were called, except sooner dissolved by the Governor.

XXII. And be it further enacted, by the authority aforesaid, that the sitting and holding of General Assemblies shall not be discontinued or intermitted above six months, but shall within that time, from and after the determination of this or any other General Assembly, or oftener if occasion require, new writs to be issued out by the Governor for the time being for calling, assembling, and holding of another General Assembly.

XXIII. And be it further enacted and declared that this present Assembly, having been elected and called together by virtue of his Majesty's royal commissions and instructions to his Excellency Francis Nicholson, Esq., his Majesty's Governor and Commander-in-Chief of this his province of South Carolina, shall in all things whatsoever be deemed and held to be a true and lawful Assembly, and all acts and ordinances duly passed by them, by and with the consent of his Majesty's honorable Council and assented to by his Excellency, shall be deemed and accounted laws and orders of the said province, anything in any former act of this province heretofore made notwithstanding.

XXIV. And be it further enacted, by the authority aforesaid, that all former acts of Assembly of this province relating to or concerning the elections of members to serve in the Commons House of Assembly be, from and after the ratification of this act, repealed, and they are hereby declared void and repealed.

James Moore,
Speaker
Charlestown, […] 19, 1721.
Assented to by Francis Nicholson, Governor

Reference: Thomas Cooper (ed.), *Statutes at Large of South Carolina*, Vol. III (10 vols.; Columbia, SC: A.S. Johnston, 1836–1841), 135–140.

ACT TO ESTABLISH COUNTY COURTS, SEPTEMBER 20, 1721

Whereas it has been found a great charge and burden to the several inhabitants of this province to be obliged to repair from all parts of the country to one general court at Charlestown for the trial of all causes, whether civil or criminal; and, by reason of the parties and witnesses living at such great distances, diverse suits have been delayed and protracted, several persons discouraged from seeking and recovering their just rights, and his Majesty's peace less orderly kept. We therefore humbly pray your most sacred Majesty that it may be enacted.

I. And be it enacted, by his Excellency Francis Nicholson, Esquire, Governor, etc., by and with the advice and consent of his Majesty's honorable Council and the Assembly of this province, and by the authority of the same, that a court of pleas, assize, and jail delivery shall be forthwith erected and established in Berkeley county at the place commonly called Wassamsaw in the parish of St. James Goose Creek, to Turkey Creek, St. George's, and St. John's shall be annexed and attendant, and all pleas, civil and criminal, happening or arising within the same parishes be decided and determined; and also one other court of pleas, assize, and jail delivery at Echaw in the parish of St. James Santee in Craven County

in such convenient part of place thereof as the judge of the said court shall see fit; at which court, all the inhabitants of Craven County aforesaid shall be attendant and all pleas, civil and criminal, happening or arising within the same be decided and determined; and also one other court of pleas, assize, and jail delivery at Willtown in Colleton County in such convenient part or place thereof as the judges of the said court shall see fit, to which said court all the inhabitants of the said county shall be attendant, except the inhabitants of John's Island which shall be attendant at the general court at Charlestown, and all pleas, civil and criminal, happening or arising within the same be decided and determined; and also one other court of pleas, assize, and jail delivery at Beauford town in Granville County, at which court all the inhabitants of Granville County shall be attendant and all pleas, civil and criminal, happening or arising within the same be decided and determined.

II. And be it further enacted, by the authority aforesaid, that one other court of pleas, assize, and jail delivery shall be forthwith erected and established at or near the plantation of Lewis Dutarque in Berkeley County, as the justices shall agree, and shall be called Wando Precinct. At which said court the several parishes of St. Thomas's, St. Dennis's, and Christ Church shall be attendant and all pleas, civil and criminal, happening or arising within the same be decided and determined.

III. And be it further enacted, by the authority aforesaid, that any five of the magistrates of the said parishes and precincts respectively, who shall be in the commission of the peace, and shall be commissionated by his Excellency the Governor for the time being for that purpose, shall be judges and justices of the said county and precinct courts, respectively, any three whereof shall be a quorum, and shall have full power to associate and assemble themselves at the respective courts within their respective jurisdictions at such days and times as hereinafter is prescribed and, being there associated and assembled, shall have full power to hold pleas of all matters civil and criminal within their said respective jurisdictions, according to the laws, usage, and customs of the province of South Carolina, so that such laws be not repugnant to the laws of Great Britain, but as near as may be agreeable thereto.

IV. And be it further enacted, by the authority aforesaid, that the first in commission shall be president of the court, and in case he be absent by reason of sickness or other accident, the next in commission shall act as president, and so of the rest successively and in course as they shall be named in the said commission; and the president of the said court shall administer unto the other justices, before they enter on their offices, the following oath: "I, A. B., do swear that I will do equal and impartial justices in all causes that come before me in the precinct court of without favor or affection to either party, and that I will not receive myself, nor suffer any other person to receive for my use, benefit, or advantage, any present of money or money's worth, on account of any action at any time pending in the said court, excepting the fees allowed to me be law." And then shall take the same oath himself from the hand of one of the other justices.

V. And be it further enacted, by the authority aforesaid, that the said judges and justices shall meet and assemble themselves at their respective courts at such days and times as hereinafter are mentioned, that is to say, the said precinct court at Wassamsaw in Berkeley County on the second Tuesday in January, April, July, and October; the said court called Wando precinct on the second Tuesday in December, March, June and September; the said court in Echaw in Craven County on the third Tuesday in December, March, June, and September; the said court at Willtown in Colleton County on the last Tuesday in January, April, July, and October; and the said court at Beauford town in Granville County on the last Tuesday in February, May, August, and November; between the hours of nine and ten in the morning, and there sit *de die in diem*, not exceeding three days, till the business of the said court be finished; and what business cannot be finished by the time abovesaid shall be continued over until the meeting of the next court; provided, always, nevertheless, that nothing herein before contained shall extend or be construed to give power to the said county or precinct courts to hold plea of any criminal matter extending to life or limb, but that the same shall be tried and determined at the general sessions to be held at Charlestown; and the jurors shall be drawn out of the balloting box from the whole province, as heretofore has been used: provided also, that in civil causes, if the matter in difference do exceed the value of one hundred pounds sterling, the same shall be decided and determined at the general court to be held for the said province at Charlestown, as hereinafter is mentioned: and that no *habeas corpus cum causa* be allowed for removing the cause or body of the defendant out of the said county or precinct court, unless the cause there brought be for above the said sum of one hundred pounds.

VI. And be it further enacted, by the authority aforesaid, that if any person shall not rest satisfied with the judgment of the said courts hereby erected, in any cause or suit where the matter in difference does not exceed the value of twenty-five pounds sterling, that then it shall and may be lawful to and for all and every such person or persons to appeal to the general court to be held four times in every year in Charlestown, as usual;

and the said general court shall have full power to hear and determine all such appeals and confirm or reverse such judgments on hearing said appeals as may be consistent with the laws and statutes of Great Britain and according to the laws, usage, and customs of South Carolina, not repugnant thereto; provided, that such appeals be craved at the time that such judgment be given in the said county or precinct courts, or at the next sitting thereof, and that before such appeal be allowed the parties so appealing do enter into a bond or recognizance before the said court in double the value of the matter in difference to pay or answer the sum or value of the sum or thing adjudged, together with all such costs as shall be awarded by the said general court in case the said judgment be affirmed; provided, also, that no execution of such judgment in the county and precinct courts shall be stayed or suspended by reason of such appeal, so as the party taking out such execution do, in the like manner, enter into bond or recognizance before the said court, with sufficient security, to the value of the sum or other matter adjudged and recovered, to make restitution to the appellant if such judgment be reversed or annulled by the said general court in twelve months after obtaining such judgment in the said county or precinct courts.

VII. And to prevent as much as may be litigious and vexatious appeals, be it further enacted, by the authority aforesaid, that in case the judgment be affirmed and the judges of appeals shall be of opinion that such appeal was groundless and vexatious, they shall certify the same on the back of the said appeal; and that then and in such case, the party appellant shall pay and satisfy to the appellee treble the costs of suit awarded in the said county or precinct courts.

VIII. And be it further enacted, by the authority aforesaid, that no clerk of any county or precinct courts shall act as an attorney or solicitor in any cause whatsoever, either in the court where he is clerk or in any other county or precinct court, or on any appeal from the said court whereof he is clerk, under the penalty of one hundred pounds current money for every time he shall offend in the premises, to be recovered by action of debt,

bill, plaint, or information in any court of record in this province; one-half to the informer and the other half to the church wardens for the use of the poor of the parish, and the loss of his office.

IX. And be it further enacted, by the authority aforesaid, that if the defendant live in the parish of St. James, Goose Creek, in the parish of St. George's, or in the parish of St. John's, the action shall be brought and the *venire* laid in the parish where the defendant lives or is arrested and the cause tried and determined at the said precinct court to be held at Wassamsaw; and if the defendant live in Wando precinct, the action shall be brought, the *venire* laid, and the cause tried in Wando precinct; and if the defendant shall happen to live or be arrested in other part of Berkeley County, the action shall be brought, the *venire* laid, and the cause tried and determined at the general court of pleas or sessions to be held at Charlestown; and if the defendant shall happen to live in Craven County, Colleton County, or Granville County, the action shall be brought, the *venire* laid, and the cause tried in the respective counties and precincts where the defendant lives or is arrested.

X. And whereas it has been heretofore allowed for law in this province that books of accounts shall be allowed for evidence, the plaintiff swearing to the same, by reason that the merchants and shopkeepers in South Carolina have not the same opportunity of getting apprentices and servants to deliver out their goods and keep their books of accounts as the merchants and shopkeepers have in South Britain, and it may prove inconvenient to the merchants and shopkeepers to send their books to the said county courts. Be it further enacted, by the authority aforesaid, that such merchants, shopkeepers, and others shall be at liberty to draw out their accounts and compare the same before any of the justices at Charlestown and then to sign and swear to the same, which accounts so drawn out and sworn to, as aforesaid, shall be allowed to be as good evidence as if the books themselves had been produced to the said court; provided, nevertheless, that all special courts for transient persons shall be held in Charlestown as heretofore has been used.

XI. And be it further enacted, by the authority aforesaid, that the original or first process issuing out of the said courts, hereby erected respectively, shall be either *summons* or *capias,* which writ of *summons* or *capias* shall contain the declaration setting forth the cause of action, time, and other circumstances on which the plaintiff grounds his complaint, and signed by the attorney as usual and sealed by the clerk of the court in the margin thereof, a copy whereof shall be served on the defendant or left at his house or most usual place of residence and abode one calendar month at least before the sitting of the court; and the defendant shall put in his plea and file the same with the said clerk the next meeting of the court or, otherwise, judgment shall pass against him by default on oath being made of the service of the said writ or summons, and execution forthwith issue against the defendant. And if the plea be to issue, the cause shall be tried the following court of course, without any notice to be given by either party to the other of them. But if the said plea be special and require a replication, the plaintiff shall reply or demur in six weeks after the sitting of the first court, without any rule or notice for that purpose, or a non-suit be entered by the clerk of the court of course for want of such replication; and if need be, the defendant shall rejoin or join in demurrer at the second court and the cause shall be then tried or argued of course without any notice from either party to the other of them, so that every cause may be decided and determined at the second court at the farthest.

XII. And the justices of the said court, or the major part of them, shall and may establish such other rules of court for dispatch of business and the ease of the clients, not repugnant to this act, as to them shall be thought reasonable.

XIII. And be it further enacted, by the authority aforesaid, that writs of replevin and all other original writs shall and may be grantable out of the general court of Charlestown and other the county and precinct courts hereby erected, as has been allowed in the other American plantations.

XIV. And to prevent security of actions and multiplying of suits, if the plaintiff be indebted to the defendant, the defendant shall be at liberty, if he see fit, to give the same in evidence by way of discount and the same shall be noted and judgment entered up for the balance only; and if the plaintiff be indebted to the defendant more than the defendant is indebted to the plaintiff, judgment shall be entered up for the defendant for the overplus and execution go against the plaintiff for such overplus and the verdict shall be special and the judgment entered up specially; provided, nevertheless, that the defendant, intending to discount any sums of money alleged to be owing him by the plaintiff, do, in one month before the trial, make a copy of such articles and sums which he intends to insist upon at the trial to have discounted and deliver the same to the plaintiff or his attorney one calendar month before such cause comes to be tried, to the intent the plaintiff may be prepared to disprove the same if he see fit, and the articles of such discount shall be proved to the court by such vouchers and in such manner as the law requires.

XV. And be it further enacted, by the authority aforesaid, that the captains of the several companies in the several parishes of St. James Goose Creek, St. George's, St. John's, and Wando precinct shall return, at the first meeting of the court, a list of the several names of all and every person belonging to their respective companies, in order that juries may be taken from then to serve at the said courts; and the several captains of companies in Craven County, Colleton County, and Granville County shall do the like.

XVI. And be it further enacted, by the authority aforesaid, that the clerks of the courts, respectively, shall, at the precinct charge, prepare balloting boxes for putting in the names of the persons to be appointed for jurors, after the method for the balloting boxes in the court of pleas in Charlestown; and the justices of the courts, respectively, shall have full power to prepare lists of the jurors and put the same in the said balloting boxes, and shall draw out from them twenty-four names for jurors in every grand and petit juries and juries for the common pleas, and no more; and the names of the jurors shall be sealed up by the justices and delivered to the marshal; and the said justices shall observe such

other methods, as near as may be, for empanel-
ing of jurors as are prescribed in the several acts
of this province concerning juries, not repugnant
hereto. And if a sufficient number do not appear,
then a *tales de circumstantibus* being moved for,
shall be granted by the said judges, according to
the usage of South Britain and the laws in that
case made and provided. And to prevent any
abuse that may be made by the allowance of such
a *tales*, the said justices are hereby required to put
double the names that are wanting to make up
the jury into a hat and draw out their names by
balloting until they have completed the number
of the jurors wanted; and the general court of
Charlestown shall have the same power for granting a *tales de circumstantibus*, and shall observe the
like method. And the *talesmen* refusing to serve
shall be subject to the same penalties as the other
jurors. And every of the justices, jurors, coroners,
and constables not appearing at each court shall
be fined the sum of five pounds, to be levied on
their goods and chattels the next court after their
non-appearance, unless they shall then give satisfactory reasons to the court for their absence.

XVII. And be it further enacted, by the
authority aforesaid, that every witness who shall
not appear at the respective courts, being duly
served with a subpoena *testificandum* in civil
causes, or appearing shall refuse to answer the
questions proposed by the court, shall forfeit to
the plaintiff or defendant by whom he was so
subpoenaed the sum of twenty pounds current
money, to be recovered by action of debt, to be
brought in the name of the plaintiff in any of the
said county or precinct courts where such witness
resides, with costs of suit.

XVIII. And be it further enacted, by the
authority aforesaid, that if any witness in any
criminal cause, not being bound over by recognizance to appear, shall refuse or neglect to appear
on service of subpoena, or appearing shall refuse
to answer, shall be fined by the court any sum
not exceeding twenty pounds current money and
stand committed till he pay the same; and the
witnesses subpoenaed to appear at the general
court of pleas or general sessions at Charlestown
and neglecting to appear, or appearing shall

refuse to answer, shall be under the like penalties
and forfeitures; and each witness shall be allowed
for his attendance in civil causes, by the plaintiff
or defendant who subpoenaed such witness, the
sum of ten shillings *per diem* current money, to be
taxed in the bill of costs and paid to the witness
before he gives in his evidence, if he desire it; and
the jurors shall be allowed in civil causes, each
cause, fifteen shillings.

XIX. And be it further enacted, by the
authority aforesaid, that no jurors, being obliged
to serve at any of the courts respectively, shall be
obliged to serve at any other county or precinct
courts out of the counties or precincts where they
respectively live and reside, after the said courts
are there respectively erected, unless it be at the
court of general sessions in Charlestown; any
law or statutes heretofore made to the contrary
thereof in any way notwithstanding.

XX. And be it further enacted that all matters
of freehold shall be tried and determined in the
respective courts of the counties and precincts
where such lands do lie, though of never so great
a value, anything herein before contained to
the contrary notwithstanding, allowing appeals,
nevertheless, to the general court if the value be
above twenty-five pounds sterling, as in other
cases.

XXI. And whereas diverse disputes do arise
between the inhabitants about the lines of their
respective plantations. Be it further enacted, by
the authority aforesaid, that if any cause shall be
pending in the said courts where the lines shall be
brought in dispute, the justices of the said court
shall appoint surveyors, at the nomination of the
parties, to survey the same at the charge of the
said parties, and to return such survey on oath at
the next sitting of the court. And in case either
of the parties shall refuse to nominate a surveyor
duly sworn and qualified, then the court shall proceed to nominate two or more such surveyors as
they shall think fit in order for the better finding
out and discovering the truth of the said matter
in difference; and if the court shall acquiesce in
the return of the surveyors, so given in on oath
as aforesaid, the same shall be allowed as evidence. And in case any action shall be brought

for a trespass or waste committed in the plaintiff's lands or tenements, the justices of the said courts shall have power to appoint two or more sufficient persons to view the said trespass or waste, if need be, who shall return an account thereof on oath at the next court and the true value of the damages occasioned by such trespass and waste and the same shall be allowed as evidence, if the court shall see fit.

XXII. And be it further enacted, by the authority aforesaid, that the said courts hereby erected shall likewise have power to fine all persons for misbehavior in court, not exceeding the sum of twenty pounds, and to commit persons to prison till they have paid the same; and the clerks of the said courts, respectively, are hereby required to transmit an account yearly of all the fines and forfeitures imposed in the said courts and also of all recognizances forfeited into the court of exchequer, if any such there be, and if there be no such court, then to transmit such accounts and recognizances to the Governor and Council in order to be put in suit.

XXIII. And be further enacted, by the authority aforesaid, that the said courts hereby erected shall have full power to imprison obstinate and incorrigible servants who shall desert their master's service or refuse to work, and to appoint their allowance to be bread and water, for which the marshal or keeper or the prison shall be allowed two shillings and six pence current money, *per diem*, in full for all fees, and no more, and to inflict corporal punishment, if they shall continue obstinate, as often as they in their discretion shall see needful, not exceeding twenty lashes each time on the bare back. And the said courts hereby erected shall likewise have full power, within their respective jurisdictions, to license all taverns, victualling houses, ale houses, punch houses, and public inns and the same, or any of them, again to suppress if they shall be convicted of being disorderly, as entertaining of servants, negroes, common drunkards, lewd and idle and disorderly persons, selling liquors on Sundays, or times of divine service. And if any person shall keep any such tavern, victualling house, ale house, punch house, or public inn, without license first had and

obtained from the said justices and signed by the president of the said court respectively, he shall forfeit the sum of twenty pounds current money for every such offence and give security for his good behavior for the future that he shall not hereafter keep any such tavern, ale house, punch house, or public inn within the said counties or precincts without a license first had and obtained from such justices; and also to take an account of all idle and disorderly persons and to compel them to work and labor and to betake themselves to honest employments, or to find sureties for their good behavior, and to imprison them and to compel them to labor in prison or to inflict corporal punishment till they shall do so; and also to punish all common drunkards, profane cursers or swearers, Sabbath-breakers, and to suppress all vice and immorality within their respective jurisdictions.

XXIV. And be it further enacted, by the authority aforesaid, that the said courts hereby erected shall have power to take order concerning all bastards, in as full and ample manner as is given to the chief justice or judges of the court of general sessions in and by an act entitled *An act against Bastardy*, ratified the seventeenth day of September, 1703.

XXV. And be it further enacted, by the authority aforesaid, that the said courts respectively shall have full power to sue for all legacies, gifts, and donations given to free schools and other public uses within their respective counties, precincts, and jurisdictions, and to appoint one or more treasurers for collecting the same, who shall be likewise treasurer for all sums levied in the said county and in whose name or names all actions or suits for such gifts, legacies, and donations shall be brought.

XXVI. And be it further enacted, by the authority aforesaid, that the president of the several courts, aforesaid, except the chief justice for Charlestown, shall, with the advice and consent of the major part of the other judges, at the time of the sitting of the courts, have full power to determine the right of administration of the estates of persons dying intestate in their several jurisdictions and also all disputes concerning wills and executorships, in as full and ample manner as the same have or might have been heretofore determined by any governor or governor and council of this province, saving the right of appeal to the governor and council in case any party shall find himself aggrieved thereby and shall send such letters of administration or letters testamentary to be signed by his excellency the governor for the time being, who shall be allowed his usual fees, and the secretary likewise. And the said justices are hereby required to take sufficient bond, with one or more good and sufficient sureties, for the party's due administration of the intestate's estates, according to law, which shall be entered of record in the said court. And the said judges and justices, or the major part of them, whereof the president to be one, shall have full power likewise to take order concerning all orphans' estates, viz., that all orphans be duly educated and provided for out of the interest and income of his estate and stock, if the same will bear it; otherwise such orphan to be bound apprentice to some handicraft trade or other good employment whereby he may learn to get his livelihood; to appoint guardians for such orphans and to remove the same and appoint others, if there be occasion, and to change the masters to which such orphans are bound apprentice, if not taught their trade nor account of such his speaking or pleading or for any other matter relating to the said cause.

XXX. And be it further enacted, by the authority aforesaid, that all persons attending the said county and precinct courts shall be free from arrests during the sitting of the said courts and also during the time of their coming to and going from the said courts, not exceeding the space of one day before the sitting of the court and one day after the rising of the same court, unless it be in a criminal matter, breach of the peace, or other misdemeanor.

XXXI. And whereas, by reason of the credit usually given in this province, diverse careless persons spend their time in punch houses, etc., instead of betaking themselves to labor, and also run themselves in debt to county stores much beyond what they are able to pay and then make their escapes to North Carolina and other parts of America, for fear of arrests and lying in prison, whereby the persons so trusting are greatly defrauded, idleness greatly encouraged, and the country deprived of the benefit of the labor of such persons and of their service in the war against the public enemy. To the intent, therefore, that persons may be more cautious in giving such credit for the future and to prevent the desertion of such poorer sort of people, which is so great a prejudice to this province be it, therefore, enacted, by the authority aforesaid, that where any person shall be in prison on mean process or execution for any debt above forty shillings, current money, and has no visible real or personal estate or yearly salary, or any goods or chattels to the value of five pounds current money, or be not of any handicraft trade by the labor of which he may pay his just debts, and shall make oath in open court before the judges of the said county or precinct courts, or any judges of any other court in this province, that he is not worth forty shillings sterling in any worldly substance either in debts owing to him or otherwise howsoever, over and besides his wearing apparel; and if there be no person then present that can contradict or gainsay the same, then such person shall immediately be set at liberty and stand forever discharged of all his debts so sued for, and costs of such suit or suits. But in case such person shall hereafter be discovered to have sworn falsely, he shall be indicted at the respective courts for perjury and, if convicted, shall lose both his ears in the pillory and serve four years as a soldier in one of the remote garrisons. Provided, nevertheless, that nothing in this act contained shall extend, or be construed to extend, or concern any debt or debts contracted before the ratification of this act.

XXXII. And be it further enacted, by the authority aforesaid, that the judges and justices hereby appointed shall, with all convenient speed, assemble and associate themselves together in order to consult and agree for the purchase of a piece of ground for erecting and building a convenient brick courthouse and brick prison in the several places hereby appointed and shall and are hereby empowered to compute the charge thereof and to levy the same rateably and proportionably on the several inhabitants of their respective counties and precincts, by a proportionable assessment on lands and slaves, according to the precedent year's tax before such assessment, and to issue warrants against defaulters and have as full and ample power in that behalf for levying thereof as is given to any commissioners of taxes by virtue of any act of assembly of this province, giving the inhabitants three months notice of the time and place of paying in the same.

XXXIII. And be it further enacted, by the authority aforesaid, that all actions brought for any debts contracted before the ratification of this act shall and may be sued for at the general court of pleas in Charlestown, at the election of the plaintiff, so that any persons be not obliged to serve as jurors out of their respective counties and precincts, respectively, after the courts have been there respectively held.

XXXIV. And to prevent persons from escaping out of one county or precinct into another or removing their goods to avoid the payment of their just debts after judgment had against them. Be it further enacted, by the authority aforesaid, that all executions on judgments obtained either in the general court at Charlestown or in any of the said county or precinct courts, either against the body or the goods, shall run and be directed into all the counties and precincts of this province and be returnable into the same court from whence they issued; but that all mean process issuing out of the said general court at Charlestown, or out of any other the said county or precinct courts, shall be directed only to the marshal or sheriff of the said county or precinct, respectively, excepting it be for a debt, *bona fide*, of the value of one hundred pounds sterling, which shall be issued out of the said general court at Charlestown, and run into all the said counties and precincts; and except before excepted, for a debt contracted before the ratification of this act, in which case the process shall run into all the said counties as heretofore has been used.

XXXV. And be it further enacted, by the authority aforesaid, that the provost marshal for the time being shall, from time to time, at the request of the said justices respectively, appoint deputies for executing all process issuing out of the said county and precinct courts, one for each court, who shall be commorant in the prison house, unless his excellency the governor for the time being shall think fit to appoint some other proper officer for that purpose. And the provost marshal shall be answerable for all escapes of prisoners out of the said prison or out of the hands of his deputies or other misfeazances and neglect of his said deputies and shall be subject to such action or actions, penalties, and fines as any sheriff or sub-sheriff in South Britain are subject unto. Provided, nevertheless, that such suits, penalties, and fines shall be recovered and imposed on the provost marshal at the general court in Charlestown.

XXXVI. And be it further enacted, by the authority aforesaid, that the justices of the said county and precinct courts shall be allowed the same fees as are allowed to the chief justice in Charlestown, to be equally divided between all the said justices for their expenses, and the other officers of the said courts shall be allowed the same fees as the officers of the courts in Charlestown.

XXXVII. And be it further enacted, by the authority aforesaid, that the said county and precinct courts erected, and every of them, shall and are hereby deemed and declared to be courts of record and shall and may act and proceed accordingly.

XXXVIII. And be it further enacted, by the authority aforesaid, that all process of subpoena for witnesses, as well in civil as criminal causes, issuing out of the said supreme court in Charlestown, or out of any other the said county and precinct courts, shall run and be issued into all the counties and precincts of this province, and also all writs of attachment for contempt and other compulsory process forcing obedience to any interlocutory or final order, judgment, sentence, or decree had and obtained in any of the courts aforesaid.

XXXIX. And whereas it may prove inconvenient to have the original records taken out of the respective offices in order to be produced as evidence at the several courts in this province, be it further enacted, by the authority aforesaid, that an attested copy of any act or ordinance of the general assembly of this province, signed by the secretary of this province, and also attested copies of all records, signed by the keeper of such records respectively, shall be deemed and allowed for as good evidence in the said courts as the original could or might have been if produced to the said courts, and also all testimonials, probates, certificates, and other instruments under the great seal of this province or any of the other governments in America, bishop of any diocese, lord mayor of London, or mayor, or chief magistrate of any town corporate in Great Britain, Ireland, or any of the plantations or elsewhere, or under the court seal of any court of judicature, or under the sign manual and notarial seal of any notary public of any the places, aforesaid, shall be likewise deemed and allowed to be good evidence in any of the courts of judicature in this province.

James Moore,
Speaker
Charlestown, September 20, 1721
Assented to by:
Francis Nicholson,
Governor

Reference: David J. McCord (ed.), *Statues at Large of South Carolina,* Vol. VII (Columbia, SC: A. S. Johnston, 1840), 166–176.

ACT ON ELECTING MEMBERS TO THE COMMONS HOUSE OF ASSEMBLY, APRIL 7, 1759

AN *Additional* ACT TO AN ACT ENTITLED *"An Act to ascertain the manner and form of electing Members to represent the Inhabitants of this Province in the Commons House of Assembly, and to appoint who shall be deemed and adjudged capable of choosing or being chosen Members of the said House,"* PASSED THE TWENTY-FIRST DAY OF SEPTEMBER, IN THE YEAR OF OUR LORD 1721, AND FOR REPEALING SEVERAL CLAUSES IN THE SAID ACT.

WHEREAS, it may be of evil consequence that any person or persons who have lately become resident in this Province, and are not possessed of a sufficient freehold or personal estate, should have a right to vote for representatives of the inhabitants of this Province in General Assembly, and it may be of equal detriment to admit any person or persons to serve as members of Assembly who are not possessed of a competent and unencumbered estate; we therefore humbly pray your most sacred Majesty that it may be enacted,

I. *And be it enacted,* by his Excellency William Henry Lyttelton, Esq., Captain General and Governor-in-chief in and over his Majesty's Province of South Carolina, by and with the advice and consent of his Majesty's Council and the Commons House of Assembly of the said Province, and by the authority of the same, That from and after the determination of this present General Assembly, every free white man, and no other person, professing the Protestant religion, who shall have attained the age of twenty-one years, and shall have been a resident and inhabitant in this Province for the space of one year, at any time before the date of the writ to be issued for that election at which he shall offer to give his vote, and shall have a freehold estate in a settled plantation, or not less than one hundred acres of land unsettled, for which he shall have paid tax the preceding year, or shall have a freehold estate in houses, lands or town lots or parts thereof, of the value of sixty pounds proclamation money situate in Charlestown, or any other town in this Province, for which he shall have paid tax the preceding year, or shall have paid the sum of ten shillings proclamation money for his own proper tax the preceding year, shall be deemed a person qualified to vote for, and is hereby declared capable of voting at the election of, a representative or representatives, to serve as a member or members of the Assembly, for the parish or precinct where such elector shall be actually resident, or for any other parish or precinct where he shall have the like qualification.

II. *And be it enacted* by the authority aforesaid, That if any doubt or question shall arise about the qualification of any person offering to ballot at such election, that before such person shall be admitted to ballot at the said election, the said clause of qualification of electors shall be read over by the church-warden or churchwardens, or person or persons appointed to manage such election, to such person offering to give his vote as aforesaid, who shall swear or affirm (as the case may be) that he is duly qualified, according to the said clause, to give his vote at such election, and shall, if required, specify and declare what such qualification is, which oath or affirmation the said church-warden or churchwardens, or person or persons appointed to manage such election, is and are hereby authorized and obliged to administer.

III. *And be it further enacted* by the authority aforesaid, That every person who, after the determination of this present General Assembly, shall be duly elected and returned to serve as a member of the said Assembly, shall be qualified as followeth: that is to say, he shall be a free born subject of the kingdom of Great Britain, or of the dominions thereunto belonging, or a foreign person, naturalized by Act of Parliament of Great Britain, who shall have attained the age of twenty-one years, and shall profess the Protestant religion, and shall have been a resident in this Province for one year at any time before the date of the said writs, and who shall have in this Province a settled plantation or free-hold estate of at least five hundred acres of land and twenty slaves, over and above what he shall owe, or shall have in his own proper person and in his own right to the value of one thousand pounds proclamation money in houses, buildings, town lots or other lands in any part of this Province, over and above what he shall owe.

IV. *And be it further enacted* by the authority aforesaid, That every person who after the determination of the present General Assembly, shall be returned to serve as a member of the said Assembly, before he be admitted to sit as such, shall, and is hereby enjoined to, take a corporal oath in the form following: "I, A.B., do swear that I am a free-born subject of the Kingdom of Great Britain or of the dominions thereunto belonging, or a foreign person naturalized by Act of Parliament of Great Britain, (as the case may be,) and that I have attained the age of twenty-one years, do profess the protestant religion, and have been resident in this Province for one year at some time before the date of the writ in virtue whereof I am elected, and that I have in this Province, truly and bona fide, to and for my own use and benefit, a settled plantation or freehold estate of five hundred acres of land and twenty slaves, over and above what I owe, or to the value of one thousand pounds proclamation money, in houses, buildings, town lots or other lands in this Province, over and above what I owe, (as the case may be,) and that my said plantation and slaves or houses, buildings, town lots or other lands, (as the case may be,) are situate and being in the parish of———, in the county of———, in the said Province, or in the several parishes of——— and———, in the county of———, or in the several counties of———and———, within the said Province," (as the case may be.)

V. *And it is hereby enacted* by the authority aforesaid, That the said oath shall be respectively administered, from and after the determination of the present General Assembly, by any of his Majesty's justices assigned to keep the peace within the said Province, who shall be thereafter returned to serve as a member of the General Assembly.

VI. *And be it further enacted* by the authority aforesaid, That all and every church warden or church wardens, or person or persons having the execution and return of any writ of election of members to serve in the House of Assembly, shall attend for that purpose at the time and place of election by such writ directed, and shall on or before the day that any future Assembly shall be called to meet, and within ten days after any election made by virtue of any new writ, (unless prevented by sickness, and in such case by some person or persons by him or them appointed for that purpose,) make return of the same to the master in chancery, to be by him filed, and shall within the two first days of the meeting of the House of Assembly, after such return made as aforesaid, attend the said House with the master in chancery, (who is hereby directed to attend accordingly with the said return,) and shall then produce and leave with the clerk of the said House a list of the persons who voted at such election; and all and every church warden or church wardens, or person or persons appointed to execute and return any writ of election, who shall neglect or refuse to attend the execution of any such writ, or who shall wilfully and knowingly admit or take the ballot of any person not duly qualified according to this Act, or refuse to admit or take the ballot of any person who is duly qualified, or shall after any ballot has been given open, or suffer to be opened, any piece of paper containing the name of any person for whom any ballot is given, before the election is finally closed, and then only in the presence of the candidate or candidates, or of one of the electors at least who have ballotted at such election, or shall make any undue return, or shall act contrary to the directions and true intent and meaning of this Act, or of the Act intitled "An Act to ascertain the manner and form of electing members to represent the inhabitants of this Province in the Commons House of Assembly, and to appoint who shall be deemed and adjudged capable of choosing or being chosen members of the said House," passed the 21st day of September, in the year of our Lord one thousand seven hundred and twenty-one, shall for each and every such offence forfeit and incur the penalty of fifty pounds proclamation money, a moiety of which sum, as well as of all other penalties and forfeitures imposed by the said Acts, shall be to his Majesty, to be disposed of by the General Assembly of this Province, and the other moiety to him or them that shall sue for the same, to be recovered by action of debt, bill, plaint or information, in any court of record in this Province, together with full costs of suit, wherein no essoign, protection, priviledge, wager of law, or stay of prosecution, shall be allowed.

VII. *And be it further enacted* by the authority aforesaid, That the third, sixth, eighth, ninth, twelfth, thirteenth and twentieth paragraphs or clauses of the Act herein before mentioned, entitled "An Act to ascertain the manner and form of electing members to represent the inhabitants of this Province," &c.; and also an Act entitled "An Additional Act to an Act of the General Assembly of this Province entitled an Act for enlarging the qualifications of the electors as well as of the persons to be elected to serve as members of the General Assembly of this Province," passed the twelfth day of March, in the year of our Lord one thousand seven hundred and forty-seven, and every matter and thing in the said clauses or paragraphs and additional Act, and every or any of them contained—be, from and after the determination of the present General Assembly, absolutely repealed and vacated, to all intents and purposes whatsoever.

B. SMITH, *Speaker.*
In the Council Chamber, the 7th day of April, 1759.
Assented to: WILLIAM HENRY LYTTELTON.

Reference: Thomas Cooper (ed.), *Statutes at Large of South Carolina*, Vol. IV (10 vols.; Columbia, SC: A.S. Johnston, 1836–1841).

23

North Carolina

Before North Carolina became a separate colony, its legislature dissented from the authority of the deputy governor, which was imposed on it by the governor of South Carolina. By 1715, the colonial legislature sought the power to control its elections. In 1755, taking its rightful place as an aggrieved assembly, the North Carolina legislature remonstrated against a crown that had threatened to repeal colonial laws and give excessive power to the governor. North Carolinians seemed quite worried about what they perceived as threats to their rights of governance. Legislators from that rather poor colony aired their grievances against the British crown, and would have a large role in the movement toward independence.

ACT FOR ESTABLISHING A LASTING FOUNDATION OF GOVERNMENT, JULY 1711

Whereas several revolutions have heretofore happened in this colony, which were fomented and carried on by factious and seditious persons, to the great loss and damage of the inhabitants thereof and to the repeated breaches of her Majesty's peace and violation of the loyalty and obedience due from subjects to their lawful sovereigns and superiors; and what most nearly has concerned us are the late unhappy dissentions among ourselves in this colony, whereby injustice and oppression took place and overspread our colony, our trade decreased, and daily differences and animosities increased to the ruin of religion and our liberties. Since which time it has pleased God, in a great measure, to influence us with a deep concern of our calamities and put into our hands a power and resolution of removing those threatening evils and dangers and for the future to procure a happy restoration of peace and tranquility among us but mak-

ing such good and wholesome laws whereby religion and virtue may flourish, our duty to our prince and governors be put in practice and maintained, our laws, liberties, and estates preserved and kept unviolated, and justice and trade encouraged. We, therefore, the Commons assembled, do pray that it may be enacted and be it enacted by his Excellency the Palatine and Lords Proprietors, by and with the advice and consent of this present General Assembly and the authority thereof, and it is hereby enacted, that any person or persons whatsoever who shall, at any time after the date hereof, speak any seditious words or speeches or spread abroad false news, write or disperse scurrilous libels against the present government now lawfully established, disturb or obstruct any lawful officer in the executing his office, or that shall instigate others to sedition cabal or meet together to contrive, invent, suggest, or insite rebellions, conspiracies, riots, or any manner of unlawful feuds or differences, thereby to stir up against or maliciously to contrive the ruin and disturbance of the Queen's peace and of the safety and tranquility of this government, the said person or persons so offending shall and are to be reputed as utter enemies to the Queen's peace and the welfare and good of this government, and shall be punished accordingly by fine, imprisonment, pillory, or otherwise at the discretion of the justices of the general court, who are hereby empowered to hear and determine the same. And the said person or persons so offending shall be compelled to give good and sufficient security for his or their good behavior during the courts pleasure and be incapable of bearing any office or place of trust within this government for the space of three years or accordingly as the demerit of the crime shall appear before the judges thereof; and if any person or persons shall at any time hereafter know of such evil practices as aforesaid, and shall conceal the same, that then they shall be punished in the same manner as if they themselves had committed such crimes. And for the further prevention of traitorous conspiracies and rebellions against her sacred Majesty of Great Britain, her crown and dignity, and the better to distinguish and prevent any disaffected ministers or officers, either military or civil, from acting or being tolerated, commissionated, or empowered to act in, possess, or hold or remain to act by virtue of any commission, deputed commission, or any power whatsoever until the said person, whosoever he be, has first qualified himself according to the strictness of the laws of Great Britain now in force. And be it enacted, by the authority aforesaid, what person soever shall act in any place of profit or trust as aforesaid, without being so qualified, shall forfeit the sum of one hundred pounds, to be recovered by action of debt, bill, plaint, or information in any court of record within this province, one half to the governor or president for the time being for the support of the government and the other half to him or them that shall sue for the same, and shall forfeit his right to the same place or benefice; provided that all military officers may take the oaths in order to their qualification before any one member of the council or of the general court, who

are hereby empowered to administer the same and give them certificates thereof; and moreover, that person or persons who hereafter shall equivocate, alter, add to, or diminish any word or clause of the oaths appointed to be taken by law, shall be deemed and held guilty of forgery and high crimes, and shall be punished accordingly. And whereas this province is annexed to and declared to be a member of the crown of England, yet notwithstanding disputes do often arise concerning the laws of England how far they are in force in this government and it appearing by the charter that the power therein granted of making laws are limited with this expression, viz., provided such laws be consonant to reason, and as near as may be agreeable to the laws and customs of our kingdom of England, from whence it is manifest that the laws of England are the laws of this government, so far as they are compatible with our way of living and trade. Be it therefore enacted, by the authority aforesaid, and it is hereby enacted and declared, that the common law is and shall be in force in this government except such part of the practice in the issuing out and return of writs and proceedings in the court of Westminster which, for want of several officers, cannot be put in execution, which ought to be supplied by rules of the general court of this government, being first approved of by the Governor in council, which shall be good in law from time to time till it shall be altered by act of Assembly. And be it further enacted and declared, by the authority aforesaid, that all statute laws of England made for maintaining the Queen's royal prerogative and the security of her royal person and succession of the crown, and all such laws made for the establishment of the church, and the laws made for granting indulgencies to protestant dissenters, and all laws providing for the privilege of the people and security of trade, as also statute laws made for limitation of actions and for preventing of vexatious laws suits, and for preventing immorality and frauds, and confirming inheritances and titles of land, are and shall be in force here, although this province or the plantations in general are not therein named. And because that it has always happened that upon vacancy of the government seditious and evil-minded persons have taken occasion to dispute the authority of the succeeding governor or president, howsoever elected or qualified, for want of certain rules being laid down and approved of by the lords proprietors, we pray, therefore, that it may be enacted, and be it enacted, by the authority aforesaid, that in case of any such vacancy the eldest lords proprietors' deputy shall summon the rest of the deputies, with all convenient speed, to meet at the usual place for the Council's meeting and there they or the major part of them that meet shall choose a president and in case of an equality of votes the voice of the elder councillor shall have preference; and if it shall happen that the eldest councillor shall refuse to summon the rest of the deputies as aforesaid within ten days after notice of such vacancy, then the next eldest councillor shall summon as aforesaid. And be it further enacted that in case of the vacancy of any lords proprietors' deputy, the governor or president in time being, with the consent of the major part of the deputies then being, shall choose one to supply that vacancy till that proprietor shall signify his pleasure to the contrary, and if any of the lords proprietors deputy shall at any time neglect or refuse to give their attendance, being cited thereto, the act or acts of the remaining deputy shall be good and valid in the law to all intents and purposes. And be it further enacted, by the authority aforesaid, that in case of extraordinary occasion, if the governor, deputy governor, or president for the time being shall depart the government, and shall first declare the cause of his departure in council, his absence not exceeding six months shall not be deemed a vacancy, but the eldest councillor shall preside in council during his absence.

Reference: William L. Saunders (ed.), *The Colonial Records of North Carolina*, Vol. I (10 vols.; Raleigh: State Archives, 1886–1890), 787–790.

ACT REGULATING ELECTIONS TO THE ASSEMBLY, 1715

Whereas his Excellency the Palatine and the rest of the true and absolute lords proprietors of Carolina, having duly considered the privileges and immunities wherewith kingdom of Great Britain is induced and being desirous that this their province may have such as may thereby enlarge this settlement and that the frequent sitting of assemblies is a principal safeguard of their peoples privileges, have thought fit to enact.

And be it enacted by the said Palatine and Lords Proprietors, by and with the advice and consent of the present Grand Assembly now met at Little River for the northeast part of the said province, and it is hereby enacted, that for the due election and constituting of members of the biennial and other assemblies, it shall be lawful for the freemen of the respective precincts of the county of Albemarle to meet the first Tuesday in September every two years in the places hereafter mentioned, that is to say, the inhabitants of Chowan at the land laid out for a town on the fork of Queen Arms Creek, the inhabitants of Perquimons at the upper side of the mouth of Suttons Creek, the inhabitants of Pasquotank at the plantation now in possession of Mr. Joseph Glaister on New Begunn Creek, the inhabitants of Currituck at the plantation of Mr. Thomas Vandermulin, the inhabitants of Beaufort in Bath in Bath Town, the inhabitants of Hyde precinct at the plantation at Mr. Webstersons the west side of Matchapungo, a river, the inhabitants of Craven at Swift's plantation at the mouth of Handocks Creek, the inhabitants of New Bern at the town so called, and then there to choose such members as are to sit in that Assembly, which shall be five freeholders out of every precinct in Albemarle County aforesaid.

And be it further enacted that it shall and may be lawful for the inhabitants and freemen in each precinct in every other county or counties that now is or shall be hereafter erected in this government aforesaid to meet as aforesaid at such

454 Governmental Developments during the Eighteenth Century

place as shall be adjudged most convenient by the marshal of such county, unless he be otherwise ordered by the special commands of the Governor or Commander-in-Chief, to choose two freeholders out of every precinct in the county aforesaid to sit and vote in the said Assembly.

And be it further enacted that the burgesses so chosen in each precinct for the biennial Assembly shall meet and sit the first Monday in November then next following, every two years at the same place the assembly last sat, except the Palatines' Court shall, by their proclamation published twenty days before the said meeting, appoint some other place; and there, with the consent and concurrence of the Palatines' Court, shall make and ordain laws as shall be thought most necessary for the good of this government.

Provided always, and nevertheless, that the powers granted to the Lords Proprietors from the crown of calling, proroguing, and dissolving Assemblies are not hereby meant or intended to be invaded, limited, or restrained.

And it is hereby further enacted, by the authority aforesaid, that no person whatsoever, inhabitant of this government, born out of the allegiance of his Majesty and not made free, no Negro, Mulatto, or Indians shall be capable of voting for members of Assembly and that no other person or persons shall be allowed or admitted to vote for members of Assembly in the government unless he be of the age of one and twenty years and has been one full year resident in the government and has paid one year's levy preceeding the election.

And be it further enacted that all persons offering to vote for members of Assembly shall bring a list to the marshal or deputy taking the poll containing the names of the persons he votes for and shall subscribe his own name or cause the same to be done. And if any such person or persons shall be suspected either by the marshal or any other candidates not to be qualified according to the true intent and meaning of this act then the marshal, deputy marshal, or other officer that shall be appointed to take and receive such votes or lists shall have power to administer an oath or attestation to every such suspected person of his qualification and ability to choose members

of Assembly and whether he has not before given in his list at that election.

And be it further enacted that every officer or marshal which shall admit of or take the vote of any person not truly qualified according to the purport and meaning of this act, provided the objection be made by any candidate or inspector, or shall make undue return of any person for member of Assembly, shall forfeit, for such vote taken and admitted and for such returns, twenty pounds, to be employed for and towards the building of any court house, church, or chapels as the governor for the time being shall think fit; but if no such building require it, then to the lords proprietors, and twenty pounds to each person of right and by a majority of votes ought to have been returned, to be recovered by action of debt, bill, plaint, or information in any court of record in this government wherein no essoin, wager of law, or protection shall be allowed or admitted.

And be it further enacted that every marshal or officer whose business and duty it is to make return of elections of members of Assembly shall attend the Assembly the three first days of their sitting, unless he have leave of the assembly to depart, to inform the Assembly of all matters and disputes as shall arise about elections and shall show to the Assembly the list of the votes for every person returned and have made complaint of false returns to the Assembly. And every marshal or other officer, as aforesaid, which shall deny and refuse to attend as aforesaid shall forfeit the sum of twenty pounds, to be recovered and disposed of in such manner and form as the forfeitures before by this act appointed.

And be it further enacted that whatsoever representative, so elected as aforesaid, shall fail in making his personal appearance and giving his attendance at the Assembly precisely at the day limited by the writ or on the day appointed for the meeting of the biennial Assembly, when the election is for a biennial Assembly, shall be fined for every day's absence during the sitting of the Assembly, unless by disability or other impediment to be allowed by the Assembly, twenty shilling, to be seized by a warrant from the Speaker and so to be applied to such uses as the lower house of Assembly shall think fit.

And be it further enacted that every member of the Assembly that shall be elected as aforesaid after the ratifying this act shall not be qualified to sit as a member in the House of Burgesses before he shall willingly take the oath of allegiance and supremacy, the abjuration oath, and all such other oaths as shall be ordered and directed to be taken by the members of Parliament in Great Britain.

And be it further enacted that the quorum of the House of Burgesses for voting and passing up bills shall not be less than one full half of the House and that no bill shall be signed and ratified except there be present eight of the members, whereof the Speaker to be one; and in case eight members shall meet at any Assembly those eight shall have full power to adjourn from day to day till sufficient number can assemble to transact the business of the government.

> *Charles Eden*
> *N. Chevin*
> *C. Gale*
> *Francis Foster*
> *T. Knight*
> *Edward Moseley,*
> Speaker

Reference: William L. Saunders (ed.), *The Colonial Records of North Carolina*, Vol. II (10 vols.; Raleigh: State Archives, 1886–1890), 213–216.

ADDRESS OF THE ASSEMBLY CONCERNING REPEALED LAWS, MAY 7, 1755

P.M. The house met according to adjournment [January 9, 1755]

Mr. Barker, according to order, presented an address to his excellency the Governor which he and Mr. Jones had prepared, which was read and is as follows:

To his Excellency Arthur Dobbs, Esquire, Captain-General and Commander-in-Chief of the province of North Carolina.

The humble address of the Assembly of the said province.

We, his majesty's most dutiful and loyal subjects the members of the Assembly of North Carolina in full assembly, beg leave to lay before your Excellency a state of the towns and counties heretofore erected within this province and the great injury the inhabitants would sustain by the repeal of the laws whereby they are erected and established, which we have lately heard has been proposed to his Majesty by the right honorable the Lords Commissioners of Trade and Plantations and that your Excellency should confirm the rights of the several towns and counties by charter.

As we apprehend, the repealing those laws would, in many instances, be attended with great inconvenie̲.̲.̲.̲.̲s from obvious reasons not hitherto represented to their lordships. We presume, with the greatest deference, to offer our sentiments on whatsoever essentially concerns our constituents and their posterity.

In the year 1722 there were nine precincts only out of which, as the province increased in numbers and the people extended their settlements, other precincts were by acts of assembly erected by dividing and subdividing those which had before existed in the most advantageous manner for the ease of the people.

By an act of assembly passed in the year 1738 all the precincts in the province were denominated counties and since that time, by subsequent acts, have undergone many divisions and alterations and others have been erected out of them and the boundaries settled and altered from time to time as were most suitable to the circumstances of the inhabitants.

By an act passed in the year 1722 the justices of the respective precinct courts were empowered and directed to purchase an acre of land for the use of their respective precincts, and in virtue of that and several later acts have purchased lands whereon the court houses and prisons are erected in the several and respective counties.

In the year 1705 sixty acres of land on Old Town Creek in Bath County was erected into a township by the name of Bath Town and by several subsequent acts other quantities of land in different parts of the province have been erected into townships and laid out in lots which have, by commissioners therein appointed, been sold and conveyed to purchasers who, in faith of the said acts, have purchased the same and laid out and expended large sums of money in buildings and other improvement thereon.

From this state of the case, we humbly apprehend that if the said laws should be repealed it would be greatly prejudicial and give universal dissatisfaction to the inhabitants of this province. The settling the colony by the accession of people from other places renders it necessary often to divide counties and erect a part of one into another and frequently to alter the boundaries which could not be done were they established by charter, inasmuch as every county incorporated must remain entire unless the charter were forfeited or surrendered by general consent. Another great inconvenience from the repealing those laws would be that the lands whereon the public buildings are erected, although purchased and paid for, would revert to the persons or their heirs who had sold and received the consideration money for the same. The inhabitants of the towns, in case of a repeal of the laws by which they are established, would be wholly divested of their tenements, having no other title than deeds executed by commissioners authorized by such laws passed with the consent and at the request of the former owners of the land for considerations long since paid; and yet, in case of such repeals, as a charter could not take away the legal title, the estates would revert in such former owners and their heirs and the fair purchasers be dispossessed of their lots and improvements.

From the many instances and undoubted proofs that we have had of your Excellency's benevolence and endeavors to promote the welfare of this province, we hope, sir, you will permit us to request that you will be pleased to cause these matters to be properly represented to his Majesty in order to prevent the repeal of those laws which would create the greatest disorder and confusion and induce many troublesome and litigious suits in law to the impoverishment of many honest purchasers; and in case the said laws should be repealed before such representation can be made that you will endeavor to obtain his Majesty's permission to pass other acts for the re-establishing the said towns and counties and to confirm the rights and titles to the people as they now stand; and from time to time pass laws for erecting new counties and towns and for altering, dividing, and new modeling counties in such manner as at any time hereafter, from an increase of inhabitants and their extending their settlements, the same may become necessary in such manner as has been heretofore accustomed, which method, from many years experience as well in this as the neighboring governments, has been found greatly to conduce to the advantage and benefit of the inhabitants; and as after passing such acts, the power of granting charters incorporating towns, establishing fairs, and appointing places for holding the courts of justice will still remain in the crown.

We most humbly hope that this application will not be construed by his Majesty to proceed from the least desire of encroaching on his royal prerogative, which we shall always, with the greatest ardour and zeal, endeavor to the utmost of our abilities to maintain, well knowing that he is invested therewith for the honor, dignity, and support of the Crown and for the happiness and safety of his people.

Resolved that the same stand for the address of this House and be sent to his excellency the Governor.

On motion, ordered that Mr. Jones and Mr. Barker wait on his excellency the Governor and acquaint him that this House has prepared an address to him and desire to know when they shall attend him with the same.

Then the House adjourned till tomorrow morning 10 o'clock.

At the council chamber, Whitehall, the 7th day of May 1755. By the right honorable the Lords of the committee of Council for Plantation Affairs.

Whereas his Majesty was pleased to refer unto this committee a representation from the Lords Commissioners for Trade and Plantations, setting forth that they have lately received a letter from Arthur Dobbs, Esquire, Governor of his Majesty's province of North Carolina, enclosing the copy of an address presented to him by the Assembly of that province relating to the great inconveniences which the inhabitants would sustain by the repeal of several acts, whereby certain towns and counties have heretofore been erected and established within the said province, and by confirming the respective rights of such towns and counties by charter. And it appearing by the said representation that the several acts referred to in the said address are repealed by his Majesty's order-in-council dated the 8th of April 1754, and that by the sixteenth article of his Majesty's instructions to Governor Dobbs, he is directed to grant charters of incorporation to the several towns and counties erected by the said laws. The said Lords Commissioners have, therefore, proposed that an instruction may be given to the Governor of North Carolina authorizing him to give his assent to any act or acts for re-establishing the several towns and counties heretofore erected by the laws which have been so repealed by his Majesty's order-in-council of the 8th of April 1754, provided such new acts do not give power to such towns or counties to send representatives to the Assembly nor ascertain the number of representatives to be sent, and, provided also, that any other laws which may have been passed in the said order-in-council which might not, at that time, be laid before his Majesty, by which any counties or townships may have been erected and empowered to send representatives to the Assembly, be repealed and other laws passed for the said purposes not liable to that objection. The Lords of the committee this day took the said representation into consideration and are hereby pleased to order that the said Lords Commissioners for Trade and Plantation do prepare and lay before this committee the draft of an additional instruction agreeable to what is above proposed, to be sent by the Lords Justices to the Governor his Majesty's province of North Carolina.

Reference: William L. Saunders (ed.), *The Colonial Records of North Carolina*, Vol. V (10 vols.; Raleigh: State Archives, 1886–1890), 301–407.

24

New Hampshire

Small in population (containing mostly rural settlements along the Connecticut River and the Atlantic coastal town of Portsmouth), New Hampshire shared with other New England colonies its scrape with dominion status in 1689. But New Hampshire continued into the eighteenth century to worry about Massachusetts encroaching on its territory. The legislature of New Hampshire was particularily concerned in 1689 that the royal governor of Massachusetts would try to govern the colony. In 1689 the colony received a separate royal governor whose duties were set by the crown. But New Hampshire's citizens resented royal authority and in 1728 the legislature demanded the right to select its own speaker. The assembly wanted to expand its voter lists, link them to legislative prerogatives, and resist the powers of the governor.

UNSETTLED STATE OF THE PROVINCE, MARCH 15, 1689

Copy of a Letter from Nathaniel Weare, Esq., to Major Robert Pike, one of the Assistants of Massachusetts Colony.

Major PIKE.

Honoured Sir. The many revolutions and chainges that has happened abroad is very wonderfull and almost amazinge; Besides what has hapned amonge and upon ourselves is very awfull and thinges loke very darke, the consideration thereof is so oppressive that [I] cannot but seke for some ease, and I know no better way [as to man] then to communicat some things to your honour, from whose prudent direction I may receive mutch sasiffaction, and shall therefore crave the boldness to ofer a few lynes to your consideration not to medell with thinges further off. I shall, as brief as I may, ofer you what

has happned in this province of New Hampshire, and more pertiquerly in the towne of Hampton. Sir, it is no new thynge to tell you how that him [Gov. Andros] that was both governor in your colony and also in our province was seazed and the occashon thereof, whereupon, wee had only the Justices and Inferior officers left; the superior commanders being layd aside, that great questions arose whether Justices retayned theire power or any Captain, or other officer derivinge his authority from him so seased: My opinion I shall alltogether wave in that matter: But so it was that it was for the most part concluded of, that we had no governors nor authority in this province so as to answer the ends of government, and to command and doe in the defence of theire majestys subjects against the comon enemy, therefore many asayes was maid in this provance to make some government till theire Majestys should take further order, but all proved ineffectuall. At first there was in the severall Towns in the Province persons chosen to manage the affairs of government in this juncture of time, but that was for some reasons laid aside, afterward there was in the town of Hampton 3 persons chosen in the towne of Hampton to meet with the Comiss: [Commissioners] of the other towns if they see cause to apoint any to debate and conclude of what was necessary at this time to be done in relation to some orderly way of Government and to make theire returns to the severall Townes for approbation or otherwise. But the inhabitants of Portsmouth met and made choice of some persons to meet with the Commissioners of the other Towns to Debate and consider of what was to be done in order to the settlement of some Government, till their Majestys should give order in the matter.

What they did, they ingaged themselves certainly to comply with. The inhabitants of the town of Hampton began to be very jealous of their friends and neighbours that they would bring them under severall inconveniences in comanding from them their men, and mony as they pleased, and so were very hard to be brought to any thing, but after severall meetings and debates, did chose 6 persons as Comissioners, with power according to the other towns (viz) Portsmouth, Dover and Exeter, and after debats jointly and fully every man then present agreed to such a method as was then drawne up. Then the severall towns was to nominate and chose meet persons for the end aforesaid; but whereas the Inhabitance of the Towne of Hampton meet on warning for that end, the major part by far of the said towne seemed to bee ferful and suspicious of theyer neighbour townes [that] they did not intend to doe as was pretended, but to bring them under to theyer disadvantage, which I thought was very ill so

to think, yet they would give som instance of som former acts don, which notwithstanding, I seposed they were too uncharitable.

And so they made a voat they would not chose any person according to the direction of the Committee meet and so all proved inefectuall. After some time the apprehention of the necessity of some orderly way of government and therby to be in the beter method to defend themselves against the common enemy, seemed to inforse them to another asay for the obtayning thereof, and so the inhabitance of Portsmouth, drew up and signed, so many as did, a pettition, as I am informed (for I never saw it,) to the honorable the governor and councill of the Matathusetts Collony to take this province into theire care and protection, and government as formerly; and so the other townes, Dover and Exeter complyed with it how generally I know not, and so brought to Hampton on Wednesday, the 26th of February last past, when the soldiers were there warned to appeare for consernes specified in said order, but no intemation given for the end of signinge to the petition, so that severall children and servants made up the number of names, when theyer parrants and masters, its said, did know nothinge of the maters, and I doubt too true. It was quickly after by William Vaughan Esq and Capt. John Pickeringe brought into the province declareing to bee excepted [accepted] by the said governor and councell, with orders given forth to meet on such a day for chusing of selectmen and constables and other towne oficers according to former usage and custom as appears by order given to Justice Greene, bearinge date the 4th of March, 1689–90. Coppes I sepose yourselfe have. What was done on that day I need not tell. Yourselfe knows very well. But this I shall insert—that chusinge of major treasurer, and recorder was not according to former usage and custom. It was prest by some to have it voated whether they would in this towne of Hampton acquies and comply with the pettition and the returne, or words to that efect, which yourselfe was pleased to say all would bee knoct on the head at one blow. Now how comfortable it will bee for about 50 persons to prescribe the method and way of government for about 200 I shall leave to your honour to consider.

For my owne part its well knowne I am for government, and so are severall others whose names are not to the petition and hath a great esteme of and good will to, the Matathusetts government, and to those worthy persons that doth administer the same. And with very littell alteration, I doubt not but many more would have, if they might have their hands to the pettition; but to have hands in the several towns to the same petition to bee under the government of the Mattathusetts collony as formerly, when we are so differently sarcomstanced as som of us know wee have been, is hard; to draw such a pettition and when such a petition is drawn, subscribed as it is, and excepted [accepted] of, for the subscribers to act contrary to the same is very strange. Formerly, not to medell with the custom and usage of the gentlemen of Pascataway, wee at Hampton had the choice of our magistrats and publike oficers, as yourselfe knows; and how the assistance or magistrats at Portsmouth can grant any warrants or exercise the administration of government over Hampton that never chose them, I know not; so that upon the whole, the government of the Matathusetts cannot I suppose exercise nor apoint any governors over us till they have authority so to doe from the crowne of England, or wee or the major part in the severall towns doe pray for it which at present is not in Hampton as it plainly appears; So that to bee subjected to a government in the province and principally at Portsmouth, which have bin so much spoken against by so many in Hampton will be very teadious to them; and the chusinge of militery oficers as hath bin to give all due respects to those persons, I shall not say of excedentell quallefications so well knowne to yourselfe, but only say that ffranzey leaders may happen to have mad followers; so that to have a government so imposed, what will I feare follow but destractions, hart burnings, disobedience to the seposed comanders, publike diclerations, remonstrenses set forth that may reach as far as England, and so make way for a person to be deputed by the crowne of England, that may, under the collor of Commission, exercise his owne will, not to speak of declerations of userpations still continued in the collony. Some have thought forthwith publekly to declare themselves to the governors in said collony that all may be healed as quietly and as sillently as it may bee, and I doubt not your wisdome will be exersised in this matter, and that wee may have peace and unety with you, and that at length we may have a happy peaseable settlement:

And that the God of peace would by all means geve us peace and truth, is the desier and prayer of your very humble servant

NATH[ll] WEARE.
Hampton, this 15th of March. 1689–90.

Reference: Nathaniel Bouton (comp. and ed.), *Documents and Records Relating to the Province of New-Hampshire,* Vol. II (Concord: George E. Jenks, 1868).

COMMISSION OF THE EARL OF BELLOMONT, JUNE 18, 1689

WILLIAM THE THIRD, by the Grace of God, of England, Scotland, France, and Ireland, king and defender of the Faith, &c. TO our Right Trusty and Right well beloved Cousin Richard, Earle of Bellomont, Greeting:

WEE, Reposing especiall trust and Confidence in the Prudence, courage and loyalty of you the said Earle of Bellomont, of our especial grace, certain knowledge and meere motion, have thought fit to Constitute and appoint, and by these presents doe Constitute and appoint you the said Richard Earle of Bellomont, to be our Governor and Commander in Chiefe of all that parte of our Province of New Hampshire within our Dominion of New England in America, lyeing and extending itselfe from three miles Northward of Merrimack River or any part thereof, unto the Province of Main with the south part of the Isle of Shoals. AND WEE doe hereby require and command you to doe and execute all things in due manner, that shall belong unto your said Command, and the trust wee have reposed in you according to the Severall powers and directions granted or appointed you by this present Commission; and the Instructions herewith given you or by such further powers or instructions as shall at any time hereafter be granted or appointed you, under our signett or Signe manual, and according to such reasonable Lawes and Statutes as now are or hereafter shall be made and agreed upon by you, with the Advice and consent of our Council and the Assembly of our Province and Plantation, under your Government in such manner and form as is hereafter expressed: AND wee doe hereby give full power unto you the said Earle of Bellomont after you shall have first taken the Oath for the due execution of the office and trust of our Governor and Commander in Chiefe in and over our said Province of New Hampshire, which the Sd Councill or any five of them have hereby fall power and authority and are required to administer unto you, to give and administer to each of the Members of our sd Councill as well the Oaths appointed by Act of Parliament to be taken instead of the Oaths of Allegiance and Supremacye, as the Test and an Oath for the due execution of their places and trust, and likewise to require them to subscribe the late Association mentioned in an Act of Parliament made in the Seaventh and Eight years of our Reigne, Entitled, an Act for the better security of his Maj[ties] Royall person and Government. AND WEE DOE hereby give and grant unto you full power and authority to suspend any of the members of our said Council from sitting, voting, or assisting therein, if you shall finde just cause for soe doing; AND our will and pleasure is that if by the death, departure out of the Province, or suspension of any of our Councillors, there shall happen to be

a vacancy in our said Councill, any three whereof wee doe hereby appoint to be a Quorum; Wee doe hereby require you to certifie us by the first opportunity of such vacancy by the death, departure, suspension or otherwise of any of our Councillors, that wee may under our Signett & Signe Manuel Constitute and appoint others in their Roome. And if it shall at any time happen, that there are less than seaven of them residing in our said Province, wee doe hereby give and grant unto you full power & Authority to choose as many persons out of the principal free holders, Inhabitants of our said Province, as will make up the full number of the Councill to be seaven and noe more; which persons soe chosen and appointed by you shall be to all intents and purposes our Councillors in our said Province, till either they are confirmed by us, or untill by the Nomination of other Councillors by us, under our Signe Manuall and Signett, the said Councill have above seaven persons in itt. AND WEE DOE hereby give and grant unto you full power and Authority with the Advice and Consent of our said Council, from time to time, as need shall require, to summon and call Assemblyes of the freeholders within your Government in such manner and forme as by the advice of our Councill you shall finde most convenient for our service and the good of our said Province: AND OUR WILL and pleasure is that the persons thereupon duly elected by the Major part of the Freeholders and being soe returned, and having before their sitting taken the Oaths appointed by Act of Parliament to be taken, instead of the Oaths of Allegiance and Supremacy, and subscribed the Test and Association aforesaid, which Oaths you shall Commissionate fitt persons under the publike Seale to Administer, and without taking the said Oaths and Subscribing the said Test and Association none shall be capable of sitting tho' elected—shall be called and held the Assembly of our said Province: And that you, the said Earle of Bellomont, by and with the Advice and Consent of our said Councill and Assembly or the Major part of them respectively, have full power and authority to Constitute and ordaine Lawes, Statutes and Ordinances for the Publike peace, welfare and good Government, of our said Province and Plantation, and of the people & Inhabitants thereof, and such other as shall resort thereto; and for the benefitt of us our heires and successors, which said Lawes, Statutes and Ordinances, are to be as near as may be agreeable unto the Lawes and Statutes, of this our kingdome of England:—PROVIDED that all such Statutes and Ordinances, of what nature & duration soever, be within three months or sooner after the making of the same, transmitted unto us under the Publicke Seale, for our approbation or Disallowance of them, as alsoe duplicates thereof by the next conveyance; AND in case all or any of them being not before Confirmed by us, shall at any time be disallowed and not approved, and soe signified by us, our Heires and successors, under our or their Signe Manuall & Signett, or by order of our or their privy Council unto you, the said Earle of Bellomont, or to the Commander in Chiefe of our said Province for the time being: then such or soe many of them as shall be disallowed, and not approved of shall from thenceforth cease, determine, and be utterly voyd and of none effect, anything to the contrary thereof in any wise notwithstanding: AND to the end nothing may be passed or done by the said Councill and Assembly to the prejudice of us, our heires, and successors, wee will and Ordaine that you the said Earle of Bellomont shall have and enjoy a Negative voice in making and passing of all Lawes, Statutes and Ordinances, as aforesaid: AND that you shall and may likewise from time to time as you shall Judge it necessary prorouge and dissolve all General Assemblyes, as aforesaid; AND our will and pleasure is that you shall and may keep and use the publicke seale appointed or to be appointed by us for that our Province: AND WEE DOE further give and grant unto you the said Earle of Bellomont, full power and authority from time to time, and at all times, hereafter, by yourselfe or by any other to be authorized by you in that behalfe, to administer the Oaths appointed by act of Parliament to be given instead of the Oaths of Allegiance and Supremacy, to all and every such person or persons

as you shall think fitt who shall at any time or times passe into our said Province or shall be resident or abiding there: WEE doe hereby give and grant unto you full power and Authority to erect, Constitute and Establish such and soe many Courts of Judicature and Publick Justice, within our said Province, as you and they shall thinke fitt and necessary for the hearing and determining of all Causes as well Criminall as Civill according to law & equity, and for awarding of execution thereupon with all reasonable and necessary powers, Authorities, Fees, and privileges belonging unto them; as alsoe to appoint and Commissionate fitt persons in the Severall parts of your Government, to Administer the Oaths appointed by act of Parliament to be taken instead of the Oaths of Allegiance & Supremacy, and the Test unto such as shall be obliged to take the same: AND WEE DOE hereby Authorize and Impower you to Constitute and appoint Judges, Justices of the peace, Sheriffs and other Necessary Officers and Ministers in our said Province for the better administration of Justice, and putting the Lawes in Execution, and to Administer, or Cause to be administered such oath or Oaths as are usuall for the due Execution and performance of place and places of trust, and for the clearing of truth in Judiciall Causes: WEE DOE further by these presents will and require that Appeals be permitted to be made in cases of Error from our Courts in New Hampshire, unto you our Governor, and to our Councill, and in your absence from our said Councill in Civill Causes, PROVIDED the value appealed for doe exceed the sum of one hundred Pounds sterling, and that security be first given by the Appellant to answer such charges as shall be awarded in case the first sentence shall be affirmed. AND WHEREAS wee judge it necessary that all our subjects may have liberty to appeale to our Royal person in cases that may deserve the same, OUR will and pleasure is that if either partie shall not rest satisfied with the Judgement or Sentence of the Superior Court of our Said Province, they may then appeale unto us in our Privy Councill, provided the matter in difference exceed the true value and sum of Three hundred Pounds Sterling; and that such appeals be made within fourteen days after sentence, and that Security likewise be duly given by the Appellant to Answer Such Charges as shall be awarded in case the first Sentence be confirmed, and provided, alsoe, that execution be not suspended by reason of any such appeale unto us: AND WEE doe hereby give and grant unto you full power and authority, where you shall see cause, and thereupon shall Judge any Offender or Offenders in Criminall matters or for any fines or forfeitures fitt objects of our mercy, to pardon and remitt all such offences, fines and forfeitures, before or after Sentence given, (Treason and wilfull murder only excepted.) In which Cases you shall likewise have power upon extraordinary occasions to grant Reprieves to the Offenders untill, and to the intent, our pleasure may be known therein. AND WEE doe hereby give and grant unto you, the said Earle of Bellomont, by your selfe, your Captaines and Commanders by you to be authorized, full power and authority to levy, Arme, Muster, Command or imploy all persons whatsoever residing within our said Province of New Hampshire; and as occasion shall serve them to Transferre from one place to another for the Resisting and withstanding of all enemies, Pirates and Rebells, both at Land and Sea and to Transport such forces to any of our Plantations in America, as occasion shall require for defence of the same against the Invasion or Attempts of any of our Enemies; and them if occasion shall require, to prosecute in or out of the limitts of our said Province or Plantations or any of them, AND if it shall please God, them to vanquish, apprehend and take, and being taken either according to the Law of Armes to putt to death, or keep and preserve alive at your discretion, and to Execute Martiall Law in time of Invasion, Insurrection or warr, and during the Continuance of the Same; as alsoe upon Souldiers in pay, and to doe and Execute all and every other thing and things which to a Captaine Generall doth or ought of Right to belong, as fully and Amply as any our Captaine Generall doth or hath usually

done: AND WEE hereby give and grant unto you full power and authority by and with the advice and Consent of our said Councill to Erect, raise and build in our Province, such and soe many forts, Platforms, Castles, Cittyes, Burroughs, Townes, and fortifications, as by the advice aforesaid shall be judged necessary; and the same or any of them to fortify and furnish with Ordinance, Ammunition and all other sort of Armes fitt and necessary for the security and defence of our said Province, and by the advice aforesaid, the same againe or any of them to demolish or dismantle as may be most convenient.

WEE DOE HEREBY give and grant unto you, the said Earle of Bellomont, full power and Authority to Erect one or more Court or Courts Admirall, within our said Province, for the hearing and determining all Marine and other Causes and matters proper to be heard therein, with all Reasonable and necessary powers, Authorities, fees, and priviledges, as alsoe to exercise all power belonging to the place and office of Vice Admirall, of and in all the Seas and Coasts belonging to your Government, according to such Commission, Authority, and Instructions as you shall receive from our Selfe under the Seale of our Admiralty; or from our high Admirall or Commissioner for Executing the office of Lord high Admirall of our foreign Plantations, for the time being; AND FORAS-MUCH as divers mutinies and disorders doe happen by persons shipped and Imployed at Sea, to the end therefore that such persons may be the better Governed and ordered, we doe hereby give and grant unto you the said Earle of Bellomont, our Captaine Generall and Governor in Chiefe, full power and Authority t o Constitute and appoint Captaines, Masters of Shipps and other Commanders, and to grant to such Captaines, Masters of Shipps and other Commanders, Commissions to execute the Law Martiall and to use such proceedings, Authority, Punishment, Correction, and Execution, upon any Offender or Offenders which shall be mutinous, Seditious, disorderly, or any way unruly either at Sea or during the time of abode or residence in any of the ports, Harbours, or Bays of our said Province or Territories as the Cause shall be found to require, according to Martiall Law: PROVIDED that nothing herein contained shall be construed to the enabling you, or any by your Authority, to hold Plea or have jurisdiction of any Offence, cause, matter or thing committed or done upon the high Sea or within any of the havens, Rivers, or Creekes, of our said Province or Territories under your Government, by any Captains, Commanders, Lieutenants, master or other officer, Seaman, Souldier, or person whatsoever, who shall be in actuall Service and pay in and on board any of our Shipps of warr, or other vessels, acting by immediate Commission or Warrant from our Commissioners for executing the office of our High Admirall of England, under the Seale of our Admiralty or from our High Admirall of England for the time being. But that such Captains, Commander, Lieutenant, Master, officer, Seaman, Souldier, or any other person soe offending shall be left to be proceeded against and tryed, as the meritt of their offences shall require, either by Commission under our Great Seale of England, as the Statute of the Twenty-Eight of Henry the Eight directs, or by Commission from our said high Admirall, according to the Act of Parliament passed in the thirteenth year of the Reigne of the late King Charles the Second, Entitled, Act for Establishing Articles and Orders for the regulation and better Government of his Majtys Navys Shipps of warr, and forces by Sea, and not other wise; saving only, that it shall and may be lawful for you upon any such Captain or Commander refusing or neglecting to execute, or upon his negligent or undue execution of any of the written orders he shall receive from you for our service, and the service of our said Province, to suspend him the said Capt or Commander from the Exercise of his said office of Commander, & commit him into safe Custody either on board his own shipp or elsewhere, at the discretion of you in order to his being brought to answer for the same by Commission, under Our Great Seale of England or from our said High Admirall

as is before Expressed IN WHICH case, our will and pleasure is that the Capt or Commander soe by you suspended, shall, during such his suspension and Committment, be succeeded in his said office by such Commission or warrant officer of our said Shipp, appointed by our Commissioner for executing the office of our High Admirall of England or by our high Admirall of England for the time being, as by the knowne practice and discipline of our Navy does and ought next to succeed him, as in case of death, sicknesses, or other ordinary disability happening to the Commander of any our shipps of warr, and not otherwise, you standing alsoe accountable to us for the truth & Importance of the Crimes and Misdemeanors, for which you shall soe proceed to the suspending of such our Captain or Commander; PROVIDED alsoe that all such disorders & misdemeanors committed on shore by any Capt., Commander, Lieutenant, Master, or other officer, seamen, souldier, or person whatsoever belonging to any of our shipps of warr or other vessels acting by immediate Commission or warrant from our Commissioners for Executing the Office of our High Admirall of England, under the Seale of our Admiralty or from our High Admirall of England for the time being, may be tryed and punished according to the Lawes of the place where any such disorders, offences and misdemeanors shall be soe committed on shoare, notwithstanding such offender be in our actual service, and born in our pay on board any such our shipps of Warr, or other vessels acting by Imediate Commission or Warrant from our Commissioners for executing the office of our High Admirall, or from our high Admirall as aforesaid, soe he shall not receive any protection for the avoyding of justice, for such offences Committed, on shoare, from any pretence of his being Imployed in our service at Sea: OUR WILL AND pleasure [is] that all publicke moneys raised or to be raised within our said Province, and other the Territories depending thereupon, be issued out by warrant from you by and with the Advice and consent of the Councill, and disposed of by you for the support of the Government and not otherwise: AND WEE doe hereby likewise give and grant unto you full power & Authority by and with the advice of our said Councill, to agree with the Inhabitants of our Province and Territories aforesaid, for such Lands, Tenements, AND Hereditaments, as now are or hereafter shall be in our power to dispose of, and them to grant to any person or persons for such Tearmes and under such moderate Quitt rents, Services, and acknowledgements to be thereupon referred unto us, as you by and with the advice aforesaid shall think fitt, which sd grants are to pass and be sealed, by our seale of New Hampshire, and being entered upon Record by such Officer and Officers as you shall appoint thereunto, shall be good and effectuall in Law against us, our heires and Successors. AND WEE do hereby give you full power to appoint faires, Marts, & Markets within our said Province as you, with the advice of our said Councill shall think fitt, and to order & appoint such and soe many Ports, Harbours, Bays, Havens and other places, for the Convenience and Security of shipping and for the better loading and unloading of goods and merchandizes, in such and soe many places, as by you with the Advice and Consent of our said Councill, shall be thought fitt and Convenient, and in them or any of them to erect, Nominate and appoint, Custom Houses, Ware houses, and offices relating thereunto, and them to alter, Change, place or displace from time to time, as with the advice aforesaid, shall be thought fitt. AND WEE doe, by these presents Will, require and Command you to take all possible care for the discountenance of vice and encouraging of virtue and good Living, that by such examples the Infidells may be invited and desire to partake of the Christian faith: AND FURTHER our will and pleasure is, that you shall not at any time hereafter, by colour of any power or Authority hereby granted or mentioned to be granted, take upon you to give, grant or dispose of any Office or place within our said Province and Territories, which now is or shall be granted under the Great Seale of England, any further than that you may, upon the Vacancy of any

such office or Suspension of any Officer by you, putt in any person to officiate in the intervall, untill the said place be disposed of by us under the Great Seale of England, or that our directions be otherwise given therein; AND WEE doe hereby require & Command all officers and Ministers Civil and Military, and all other Inhabitants of our said Province to be obedient, Ayding and Assisting unto you the said Earle of Bellomont, in the execution of this our Commission, & of the powers and authorities therein contained; and in case of your death or absence out of our said Province, unto such person as shall be appointed by us to be our Lieutenant Governor or Commander in Chiefe of our said Province, to whom we doe therefore by these presents, give and grant all and singular the powers and Authorities aforesaid to be executed and enjoyed by him during our pleasure, or untill you returne to our sd Province: AND if upon such death or absence there be noe person upon the place Commissionated by us to be Commander in Chiefe, OUR WILL and pleasure is that then the present Councill of New Hampshire, doe take upon them the administration of the Government and Execute this Commission, and the severall powers and Authorities therein contained, and that such Counsellor who shall be at the time of your death residing within OUR Province of New Hampshire, and Nominated in our Instructions to you before any other at that time residing there, doe preside in our said Councill, with such powers and preheminences as any former President hath used and enjoyed within our said Province, untill our pleasure shall be knowen therein, or your return as aforesaid. LASTLY, wee doe hereby ordaine and appoint that you the said Earle of Bellomont shall and may hold, Execute, and enjoy the Office and place of our Governor & Commander in Chiefe, in and over our Province & Plantation of New Hampshire, together with all & singular the powers and authorities hereby granted unto you, for and during our pleasure, immediately upon your Arrivall within our said Province of

New Hampshire, and the Publication of this our Commission, from which time our Commission to our Trusty and well beloved SAMUEL ALLEN, Esq., to be Governor and Commander in Chiefe of our said Province of New Hampshire, is immediately to cease & become voyd; & IN WITNESS whereof, wee have caused these our letters to be made Patents. WITTNESSE Thomas Archbishop of Canterbury, and the rest of the Guardians and justices of the Kingdome at Westminister, the Eighteenth day of June, in the Ninth year of our Reigne.

CHUTE.

Reference: Nathaniel Bouton (comp. and ed.),*Documents and Records Relating to the Province of New-Hampshire,* Vol. II (Concord: George E. Jenks, 1868).

RIGHT TO CHOOSE A SPEAKER, APRIL 11, 1728

May it please your hon'r

With the Greatest Defference to your honrs Comissn & utter abhorence of Every thing that looks like the Least Infringmt on the Power therein Granted Wee humbly take leave to Remonstrate: that wee have Maturely Considered your honrs Disallowance of our Choice of a Speaker: and those Clauses in the Governors Commission which have been offered to Support the Same: and that the Negative voice to be Enjoyed by ye Comander in Chief: by virtue thereof Cannot in our humble oppinion by any Rational Construction Extend your honrs power: to the Negativeing Such orders & Rules of this house as only Concern the Settlement & Regulating thereof as in this Case for that the Negativeing Power Relates Wholly to Laws Statutes and Ordinances to be passed by the Govr Councill & assembly & no other: as Will most obviously appeare by Comparing one part of the Comission with the other: and besides wee have it from the famous Bishop Burnet in the history of his own times that it was a Settled Point in the house of Comons in the Dayes of King Cha the Second: that the house had an undoubted Right of Chuseing their Speaker: and that the presenting him to the King was only Matter of Course and not for approbation: which Settlemt we Cannot Learn has Ever been Questioned by any King or Queen of Great Brittn Since: Wherefore upon the whole wee do humbly Insist upon and adhere to our Choice & Earnestly pray that we may have yr honrs favor in proceeding to the other business of the Sessions

James Jeffry Clr assm

Reference: Nathaniel Bouton (comp. and ed.), *Documents and Records Relating to the Province of New-Hampshire,* Vol. IV (Concord: George E. Jenks, 1870).

25

Pennsylvania

Pennsylvania, a colony that remained proprietary until the Revolution, grew wealthy, diverse in population, and contentious over the proprietar appointed governor's powers. The colony's legislative leaders fiercely defended their local prerogatives. The legislature also squabbled with the Quaker Penn family's authority. Although the proprietors often talked of legislative privileges, the colonists wanted a legislature independent of their control. Unlike the other North American colonies, the Pennsylvania legislators continued to defend their rights to have only a single house of representatives. The eighteenth-century story of Pennsylvania governance, although unique like Maryland, nevertheless repeated the pattern of its sister colonies as tensions mounted between legislature and governor.

In 1691, the Penn's acknowledged the growth of towns by granting a charter to Germantown that announced greater freedom in local governance. When the crown, with the support of the Penn family, named Benjamin Fletcher as governor, the governor took control of the assembly. In 1696, the proprietary council wrote a "Frame of Government" for the colony that promised much more power to the popularly elected legislature. In 1701, a "Charter of Liberties" replaced the "Frame" and gave even more authority to the legislature. In 1705, the legislature set regulations for its elections, which was a sign of growing legislative powers. In 1706, the legislature created a judicial system and in 1745, the legislature stated that those early grants of power had not given it enough authority in the colony. The legislature then set further rules to control elections and subsequently put elections in the hands of local districts, encouraged popular participation in elections, and required elected representatives to take their offices.

CHARTER FOR INHABITANTS OF GERMANTOWN, MARCH 30, 1691

I, William Penn, Proprietor of the province of Pennsylvania in America under the Imperial Crown of Great Britain by virtue of letters patents under the great seal of England, do grant unto Francis Daniel Pastorius, civilian; and Jacob Telner, merchant; Dirck Isaacs Optegraff, linen maker; Herman Isaacs Optegraff, town President;

T. Abraham Isaacs Optegraaf, linen maker; Jacob Isaacs, Johanes Casselle, Heywart Hapon, Coender Herman Bon, Dirck Vankolk, all of Germantown, yeomen, that they shall be one body politic and corporate aforesaid in name and by the name of the Bailiff, Burgesses, and Commonalty of Germantown in the County of Philadelphia in the province of Pennsylvania, and them by that name one body politic and corporate by deed and in name forever, I do, for me, my heirs and successors, proclaim and declare by these presents, and that by the same name of Bailiff, Burgesses, and Commonalty of Germantown be and at all times hereafter shall be persons able and capable in law with joint stock to trade, and with the same or any part thereof to have, take, purchase, possess, and enjoy manors, messuages and lands, tenements and rents of the yearly value of fifteen hundred pounds *per annum*, liberties, privileges, jurisdictions, franchises and hereditaments of what kind, nature, or quality soever to them and their successors and assigns; and also to give, grant, demise, alien, assign, and dispose of the same; and that they and their successors by the name of the Bailiff, Burgesses, and Commonalty of Germantown shall and may be persons able and capable in law to plead and be impleaded, answer and be answered, and heard and be defended in whatsoever courts and places and before whatsoever judges and justices, officers and ministers of me, my heirs and successors, in all and singular pleas, actions, suits, causes, quarrels, and demands whatsoever and of what kind, nature, and sort soever; and that it shall and may be lawful to and for the said corporation and their successors to have and use a common seal for any business of or concerning the said corporation, and the same from time to time at their will to change or alter. And for the better government of the said corporation, I do further grant to the said corporation that there shall be, from henceforth, one of the said corporation to be elected and to be bailiff of the said corporation and four others of the said corporation to be elected and to be chosen burgesses of the said such corporation and that there shall be, from henceforth, six persons, members of the said corporation, elected and be committee men of the said corporation. Which said bailiff, burgesses, and committee men shall be called the General Court of the Corporation of Germantown; and that they or any three or more of them, whereof the bailiff with two or, in his absence, any three of the burgesses to be always some, shall be and are hereby authorized, according to such rules, orders, and directions as shall

from time to time be made and given unto them by the General Court of the said corporation; and for want of such rules, orders, and directions when desired, as they themselves shall think meet, shall manage, govern, and direct all the affairs and business of the said corporation, and all their servants and ministers whatsoever, and generally to act and do in all those matters and things whatsoever, so as they shall judge necessary and expedient for the well-governing and government of the said corporation and the improvement of their lands, tenements, and other estate in joint stock and trade; and to so enjoy, perform, and execute all the powers, authorities, privileges, acts, and things in like manner, to all intents and purposes as if the same were done at and by a General Court of the said corporation. And I do, by these presents, assign, nominate, declare, and make the said Francis Daniel Pastorius of Germantown, civilian, to be the first and present bailiff; and the aforesaid Jacob Telner, Dirck Isaacs, Optegraaf, Herman Isaacs, Optegraaf, and Tennis Coender to be the first and present burgesses; and the aforesaid Abraham Isaacs, Optegraaf, Jacob Isaacs, Johannes Casselle, Heywart Hapon, Herman Bon, and Dirck Vankolk the first and present committee men of the said corporation; the said bailiff and burgesses and committee men to continue in their respective offices and places until the first day of December next ensuing the date hereof, and from thence until there be a new choice of other persons duly to succeed them according as it is hereinafter directed, unless they or any of them shall happen to die or be removed by order to be made by a General Court of the said corporation before the expiration of that time. And in case any of them shall happen to die or be removed before the said first day of December, it shall and may be lawful to and for the persons assembled at any General Court of the said corporation, whereof the bailiff if present with two or, in his absence, with three of the burgesses to be some, to make choice of any other fit person being a member of the said corporation, in the place of such person so deceased or removed; which persons to be chosen shall continue in the said place and office during the residue of the said time. And I do, further, for me, my heirs and successors, give and grant to the said bailiff, burgesses, and committee men of Germantown and their successors that it shall and may be lawful to and for the said bailiff, burgesses and committee men, at and upon the said first day of December in every year successively, forever hereafter, unless the said first day of December happen to fall on the first day of the week and then at and upon the next day following, to assembly and meet together in some convenient place to be appointed by the bailiff, or, in his absence, by any three of the burgesses of the said corporation for the time being. Which assembly and meeting of the said corporation, at such time and place as aforesaid, shall be called a General Court of the said corporation of Germantown; and that they being so assembled, it shall and may be lawful to or for the major part of them which shall be then present, not being less than seven in number, whereof the bailiff and two of the burgesses or, in absence of the bailiff, three of the burgesses for the time being to be some, to elect and nominate one bailiff, four burgesses, and six committeemen for the purposes aforesaid, and also such other officers as they shall think necessary for the more due government of the said corporation out of the members of the said corporation, who are to continue in their respective offices and places for the ensuing year, unless within that time they shall happen to die or be removed for some reasonable cause as aforesaid. And upon the death or removal of the bailiff, any burgesses or any of the six committeemen or any other officer at any time within the year and before the said first day of December, it shall and may be lawful to and for the commonalty of them, the said bailiff, burgesses, and committee men for the time being, or the major part of them present at any General Court of the said corporation to be for that purpose assembled, whereof the bailiff and two of the burgesses or, in absence of the bailiff, three of the burgesses for the time being to be always some, to elect and nominate a bailiff, burgess, burgesses, committeeman or committeemen as there shall be vacancy in the place and room of such person or persons respectively as shall so happen to die or be removed; and likewise that it shall and may be lawful to and for the bailiff and two of the burgesses or, in absence of the bailiff,

three of the burgesses of the said corporation for the time being, from time to time, so often as they shall find cause, to summon a General Court of the said corporation of Germantown; and that no assembly or meeting of the said corporation shall be deemed and accounted a General Court of the said corporation unless the bailiff and two of the burgesses or, in absence of the bailiff, three of the burgesses and four of the committeemen at least be present. And I do for me, my heirs and successors, give and grant unto the said corporation of Germantown and their successors full and free liberty, power, and authority, from time to time, at any of their General Courts to admit such and so many persons into their corporation and society and to increase, contract, or divide their joint stock or any part thereof, when so often and in such proportions and manner as they or the greatest part of them then present, whereof the bailiff and two of the burgesses or, in his absence, three of the burgesses for the time being to be always some, shall think fit; and also that the said bailiff, burgesses, and committeemen, for the time being, from time to time, at their said General Court shall have power to make and they may make, ordain, constitute, and establish such and so many good and reasonable laws, ordinances, and constitutions as to the greatest part of them at such General Court and Courts assembled, whereof the bailiff and two of the burgesses or, in absence of the bailiff, three of the burgesses for the time being to be always some, shall deem necessary and convenient for the good government of the said corporation and their affairs, and the same laws, orders, ordinances, and constitutions so made to be put in use and execution accordingly, and at their pleasure to revoke, alter, and make anew as occasion shall require; and also to impose and set such mulcts and amerciaments upon the breakers of such laws and ordinances as to them or the greatest part of them so assembled, whereof the bailiff and two of the burgesses or, in absence of the bailiff, three of the burgesses to be always some, in their discretion shall be thought reasonable. Which said laws and ordinances shall be put in execution by such officers of the said corporation, for the time being, as shall be by the said court appointed for that purpose, the call of such appointment by the bailiff and two of the burgesses or, in absence of the bailiff, by three of the burgesses for the time being, to be chosen, and the said mulcts and amerciaments so imposed and set upon the breakers of the same laws and ordinances, as aforesaid, shall, from time to time, be levied and received by such the officers and servants of the said corporation, in that behalf to be appointed in manner as aforesaid, and for the use of the said corporation and their successors, by distress or otherwise, in such manner as the said General Court shall direct and appoint not contrary to law, without the impediment of me, my heirs and successors, or of any the officers and ministers of me, my heirs and successors, and without any account to be made, rendered, or given to me, my heirs and successors, for the same or any part thereof; or else that the said mulcts and amerciaments, or any part thereof, may, upon the offenders submission or conformity, be remitted, pardoned, or released by the said General Court of the said corporation at their will and pleasure; and that the bailiff and two oldest burgesses for the time being shall be justices of the peace and shall have full power and authority to act as justices of the peace within the said corporation and to do such act and acts, thing and things whatsoever which any other justice or justices of the peace can or may do within my said province. And further, I do hereby grant to the said bailiff, burgesses, and commonalty of Germantown that they and their successors shall and may have, hold, and keep before the bailiff and three of the oldest burgesses of the said corporation, and the recorder for the time being of the said corporation, one Court of Record to be held every six weeks in the year, yearly, for such time as they shall think fit, for the hearing and determining of all civil causes, matters, and things whatsoever arising or happening betwixt the inhabitants of the said corporation, according to the laws of the said province and of the kingdom of England, reserving the liberty of appeal according to the same; and also to have, hold, and keep one public market every sixth day in the week in such convenient place and manner as the provincial charter does direct; and further to do and act any other matter or thing whatsoever for the good government of the said corporation and the members thereof and for the managing and ordering of the estate, stock, and affairs of the said corporation, as they shall at any time or times think or judge expedient or necessary, and as any other corporation within my said province shall, may, or can do, by laws not being inconsistent to the laws of England or of my said province, hereby giving and granting that this, my present charter or grant shall in all courts of law and equity be construed and taken most favorably and beneficially for the grantees and the said corporation. Given under my hand and the lesser seal of the said province at London, this twelfth day of the month called August, in the year of our Lord one thousand six hundred eighty and nine, and under the great seal of the province of Pennsylvania, the thirtieth day of the third month, 1691.

William Penn.

Reference: Samuel Hazard, et al. (eds.), *Pennsylvania Archives*, Vol. I (12 vols.; Philadelphia: J. Severns, 1852–1870), 111–115.

COMMISSION OF GOVERNOR BENJAMIN FLETCHER, OCTOBER 21, 1692

His Excellency Benjamin Fletcher, his commission under the great seal of England, to be Captain-General and Governor-in-Chief in and over their Majesties' province of Pennsylvania and county of New Castle, etc.

William and Mary, by the grace of God, King and Queen of England, Scotland, France, and Ireland, Defenders of the Faith, etc. To our trusty and well-beloved Benjamin Fletcher, Esquire, our Captain-General and Governor-in-Chief of our province of New York and the territories depending thereon, in America, greeting.

Whereas by our commission, under our great seal of England, bearing date the eighteenth day of March in the fourth year of our reign, we have constituted and appointed you, the said Benjamin

Fletcher, to be our Captain-General and Governor-in-Chief in and over our province of New York and the dependencies thereon in America, and have thereby granted unto you full power and authority, with the advice and consent of our council, as need shall require, to summon and call general assemblies of the inhabitants, being freeholders, within our said province, according to the usage of our province of New York. And that the persons thereupon duly elected by the major part of the freeholders of the respective counties and places, and so returned and having before their sitting taken the oaths appointed by act of Parliament to be taken instead of the oaths of allegiance and supremacy, and subscribed the test, and without taking and subscribing whereof none shall be capable of sitting though elected, shall be called and held the General Assembly of that our said province. And have thereby granted unto you, the said Benjamin Fletcher, by and with the consent of our said council and assembly, or the major part of them, full power and authority to make, constitute and ordain laws, statutes, and ordinances for the public peace, welfare, and good government of our said province and of the people and inhabitants thereof; which said laws, statutes, and ordinances are to be, as near as may be, agreeable to the laws and statutes of this our kingdom of England. Provided, that all such laws, statutes, and ordinances be within three months, or sooner, after the making thereof, transmitted unto us, under our seal of New York, for our approbation or disallowance of the same; and in case any or all of them, being not before confirmed by us, shall at any time be disallowed and not approved, and so signified by us, our heirs, and successors, under our or their signet manual or signet, or by order of our or their Privy Council unto you, the said Benjamin Fletcher, or to the commander-in-chief of our province of New York for the time being, then such and so many of them as shall be so disallowed and not approved shall from thenceforth cease, determine, and become utterly void and of none effect. And to the end that nothing may be passed or done by our said council or assembly to the prejudice of us, our heirs, and successors, we

have thereby willed and ordained that you, the said Benjamin Fletcher, shall have and enjoy a negative voice in the making and passing of all laws, statutes, and ordinances, as aforesaid; and that you shall and may likewise, from time to time, as you shall judge it necessary, adjourn, prorogue, and dissolve all General Assemblies, as aforesaid; with full power and authority, from time to time, by yourself or by any other to be authorized by you in that behalf, to administer and give the oaths appointed by act of Parliament to be taken instead of the oaths of allegiance and supremacy, to all and every such person or persons, as you shall think fit, who shall at any time or times pass into our said province or shall be resident or abiding there; and, with the advice and consent of our said council, to erect, constitute, and establish courts of judicature and public justice within our said province, and for the hearing and determining of all causes, as well criminal as civil, according to law and equity, and for awarding of execution thereupon, with all reasonable and necessary powers, authorities, fees, and privileges belonging unto them; as also to appoint and commissionate fit persons in the several parts of our said province to administer the oaths appointed by act of Parliament to be taken instead of the oaths of allegiance and supremacy and the test, unto such as shall be obliged to take the same; and also to constitute and appoint judges, justices of the peace, and other necessary officers and ministers in our said province for the better administration of justice and putting the laws in execution, and to administer or cause to be administered such oath or oaths as are usually given for the due execution and performance of offices and places and for the clearing of truth in judicial causes. And whereas we judge it necessary that all our subjects may have liberty to appeal to our Royal person in civil causes that may deserve the same, we have thereby further signified our pleasure that if either party shall not rest satisfied with the judgment or sentence of the superior courts of our said province, they may then appeal unto us in our Privy Council, provided the matter in difference exceed the real value and sum of three hundred pounds sterling and that such appeal be made within one fortnight after sentence and that security be likewise duly given by the appellant to answer such charges as shall be awarded in case the first sentence shall be confirmed; and provided, also, that execution be not suspended by reason of any such appeal unto us. And where you shall judge any offender or offenders in criminal matters, or for any fines or forfeitures, fit objects of our mercy, you have full power and authority to pardon and remit such offences, fines, and forfeitures, before or after sentence given, treason and willful murder only excepted. In which cases, upon extraordinary occasions, you are to grant reprieves to the offenders until our royal pleasure may be known therein. And whereas, by our said commission, we have given and granted unto you, the said Benjamin Fletcher, by yourself, your captains and commanders by you to be authorized, full power and authority to levy, arm, muster, command, and employ all persons whatsoever residing within our said province under your government and as occasion shall serve, them to transfer from one place to another for the resisting and withstanding of all enemies, pirates, and rebels, both at sea and land, and to transport such forces to any of our plantations in America, as occasion shall require, for the defense of the same against the invasion or attempts of any of our enemies; and to execute martial law in time of invasion, insurrection, or war and during the continuance of the same, as also upon soldiers in pay; and to do and execute all and every other thing and things which to a captain-general does or ought of right to belong; and also, to erect, raise and build in our said province such forts, platforms, castles, cities, boroughs, towns, and fortifications as you, by the advice aforesaid, shall judge necessary; and the same, or any of them, to fortify and furnish with ordnance, ammunition, and all sorts of arms fit and necessary for the security and defense of our said province. And whereas we have thereby further given and granted to you, the said Benjamin Fletcher, full power and authority to erect one or more court or courts admiral within our province of New York for the hearing and determining of all marine and other causes and matters proper

therein to be heard, with all reasonable and necessary powers, authorities, fees, and privileges, and to exercise all powers belonging to the place and office of Vice Admiral of and in all the seas and coasts about our said province, according to such commission, authority, and instructions as you shall receive from ourself, under the seal of our admiralty or from our High Admiral or commissioners for executing the office of High Admiral of our foreign plantations for the time being; and to order and appoint fairs, marts, and markets; as also, such and so many ports, harbors, bays, havens, and other places for the convenience and security of shipping and for the better loading and unloading of goods and merchandises as by you, with the advice and consent of our said council, shall be thought fit and necessary; and in them, or any of them, to erect, nominate, and appoint custom houses and officers relating thereunto and them to alter, change, place, or displace, from time to time, as with the advice aforesaid, shall be thought fit, with several other powers and authorities granted and appointed you by our said commission for the good governing and for the defense and security of our said province of New York and inhabitants thereof.

And whereas, by reason of great neglects and miscarriages in the government of our province of Pennsylvania in America and the absence of the proprietor the same is fallen into disorder and confusion, by means whereof not only the public peace and administration of justice, whereby the properties of our subjects should be preserved in those parts, is broken and violated, but there is also great want of provision for the guard and defense of our said province against our enemies, whereby our said province and the adjacent colonies are much exposed and in danger of being lost from the crown of England. For the prevention whereof, as much as in us lies, and for the better defense and security of our subjects inhabiting those parts during this time of war, we find it absolutely necessary to take the government of our province of Pennsylvania into our own hands and under our immediate care and protection. We, therefore, reposing especial trust and confidence in the prudence, courage, and loyalty of you, the said

Benjamin Fletcher, have thought fit to constitute and appoint you, the said Benjamin Fletcher, to be our Captain-General and Governor-in-Chief in and over our province of Pennsylvania and country of New Castle and all the tracts of land depending thereon in America. And we do, accordingly, by these presents, command and require you to take the said province and country under your government. And for the better ordering, governing, and ruling our said province and country and the tracts and territories depending there, we do hereby give and grant unto you, the said Benjamin Fletcher, all and every the like powers and authorities as in our said commission, bearing date the eighteenth day of March in the fourth year of our reign, are given, granted, and appointed you for the ruling and governing our province of New York, to be exercised in like manner by you, the said Benjamin Fletcher, in and over our said province of Pennsylvania and country of New Castle and the territories and tracts of land depending thereon in America. And we do hereby require and command you to do and execute all things in due manner that shall belong unto your said command and the trust we have reposed in you, according to the several powers and directions granted or appointed you by this present commission, or our commission aforesaid, and such other instructions and authorities as are or at any time hereafter shall be granted or appointed you, under our signet and sign manual, or by our order in our Privy Council, and according to such reasonable laws and statutes as now are in force, or hereafter shall be made and agreed upon by you, with the advice and consent of the council and assembly of our province of Pennsylvania and country of New Castle aforesaid. And our will and pleasure is, and we do by these presents require and command you, the said Benjamin Fletcher, until our further pleasure shall be known, to nominate and appoint a lieutenant-governor of our said province of Pennsylvania and country of New Castle, unto which lieutenant-governor we do hereby give and grant full power and authority to do and execute whatsoever he shall be by you authorized and appointed to do, in pursuance and according to the powers and authorities hereby granted unto

you. And our further will and pleasure is and we do by these presents require and command you in like manner to nominate and appoint such and so many councilors as you shall think requisite for our service, not exceeding the number of twelve persons at the most, out of the principal freeholders and inhabitants of our said province and country, which said councilors, or any three of them, shall be at all times held and deemed a council to be aiding and assisting to you and to our lieutenant-governor with their advice in the administration of the public affairs of that our province and country. And we do hereby give and grant unto you full power and authority from time to time to suspend such our lieutenant-governor, or any of the members of our council, so appointed by you, from their respective places and trusts if you shall find just cause for so doing and to appoint others in their stead. And whereas we have been informed of the good affection of the inhabitants of our colonies of East and West New Jersey in America and that the militia of these colonies consist of fourteen hundred men, well armed and disciplined: and it being convenient in this time of danger that the forces of our subjects inhabiting those parts be united as much as may be upon all occasions that may require the same, we have, therefore, thought fit, and we do by these presents grant full power and authority to you, the said Benjamin Fletcher and to the governor and commander-in-chief of our province of New York for the time being, for and during this present war between us and the French King, to draw out and command any part of the militia of our colonies of East and West New Jersey in America, not exceeding seven hundred men at any one time, and to cause them to march out of our said colonies for the security or defense of New York or Albany or any other parts or places of our province of New York under your government, in case of any invasion, insurrection, or attempt of the French or Indians upon our said province or any part thereof. And we do hereby require and command all officers and ministers, civil and military, and all other the inhabitants of our province of Pennsylvania and country of New Castle and our colonies of East and West New Jersey, respectively, to be obedient, aiding and assisting unto you, the said Benjamin Fletcher, in the execution of this our commission and the powers and authorities herein contained. And in case of your death or absence out of our province of New York and Pennsylvania, our country of New Castle, and our colonies of East and West New Jersey, to be obedient, aiding and assisting to such person as shall be appointed by us to be commander-in-chief of our province of New York for the time being; to whom we do therefore, by these presents, give and grant all and singular the powers and authorities, aforesaid, to be executed and enjoyed by him for and during our pleasure or until your arrival within our province and countries aforesaid. And if upon such death or absence there be no person residing within our said provinces or countries commissionated or appointed by us to be commander-in-chief of our province of New York, our will and pleasure is that the then present council of New York do take upon them the administration of the government of our province of Pennsylvania and country of New Castle and execute this commission and the powers and authorities herein contained, in like manner as in the government of our province of New York. And lastly, we do, by these presents, declare and appoint that you, the said Benjamin Fletcher, shall and may hold, exercise, and enjoy the office and place of Captain-General and Governor-in-Chief in and over our province of Pennsylvania and country of New Castle and the territories and tracts of land depending thereon in America during our will and pleasure. In witness whereof, we have caused our letters to be made patents. Witness ourselves at Westminster, the one and twentieth day of October, in the fourth year of our reign.

Reference: Colonial Records of Pennsylvania, Vol. I (16 vols.; Philadelphia: J. Severns, 1852–1853), 312–317.

FRAME OF GOVERNMENT, NOVEMBER 7, 1696

The Frame of Government of the Province of Pennsylvania, and the territories thereunto belonging; passed by Governor Markham, November 7, 1696

WHEREAS, the late king Charles the Second, in the three and thirtieth year of his reign, by letters patent under the great seal of *England*, did, for the considerations therein mentioned, grant unto *William Penn*, his heirs and assigns, for ever, this colony, or tract of land, thereby erecting the same into a province, called *Pennsylvania*, and constituting him, the said *William Penn*, absolute Proprietary thereof, vesting him, his Deputies and Lieutenants, with divers great powers, pre-eminences, royalties, jurisdictions and authorities, necessary for the well-being and good government of the said province. And whereas the late Duke of *York* and *Albany*, &c., for valuable considerations, did grant unto the said *William Penn*, his heirs and assigns, all that tract of land which hath been cast, or divided into three counties, now called *Newcastle, Kent,* and *Sussex,* together with all royalties, franchises, duties, jurisdictions, liberties and privileges thereunto belonging; which last mentioned tract being intended as a beneficial and requisite addition to the territory of the said Proprietary, he, the said Proprietary and Governor, at the request of the freemen of the said three counties, by their deputies, in Assembly met, with the representatives of the freemen of the said province at *Chester,* alias *Upland,* on the sixth day of the tenth month, 1682, did (with the advice and consent of the Members of the said Assembly) enact, that the said three counties should be annexed to the province of *Pennsylvania,* as the proper territories thereof: and whereas king *William* and the late queen *Mary,* over *England,* &c., by their letters patent and commission, under the great seal of *England*, dated the twenty-first day of October, in the fourth year of their reign, having, (for the reasons therein mentioned) taken the government of this said province and territories into their hands, and under their care and protection, did think fit to constitute *Benjamin Fletcher*, Governor of New York, to be their Captain General, and Governor in Chief, over this province and country. And whereas, also the said king and queen afterwards, by their letters patent, under the great seal of *England*, dated the twentieth day of August, in the sixth year of their reign, have thought fit, upon the humble application of the said *William Penn*, to restore him to the administration of the government of the said province and territories; and that so much of their said commission as did constitute the said *Benjamin Fletcher*, their Captain General and Governor in Chief of the said province of *Pennsylvania*, country of *Newcastle*, and the territories and tracts of land depending thereupon, in *America*, together with all the powers and authorities thereby granted for the ruling and governing their said province and country, should, from the publication of the said last recited letters patent, cease, determine and become void; and accordingly the same are hereby declared void; whereupon the said *William Penn* did commissionate his kinsman, *William Markham*, Governor under him, with directions to act according to the known laws and usages of this government.

Now, forasmuch as the former frame of government, modelled by act of settlement, and charter of liberties, is not deemed, in all respects, suitably accommodated to our present circumstances, therefore it is unanimously desired that it may be enacted. And be it enacted by the Governor aforesaid, with the advice and consent of the representatives of the freemen of the said province and territories, in Assembly met, and by the authority of the same, that this government shall, from time to time, consist of the Governor, or his Deputy, or Deputies, and the freemen of the said province, and territories thereof, in form of a Council and Assembly; which Council and Assembly shall be men of most note for virtue, wisdom and ability; and shall, from and after the tenth day of the first month next, consist of two persons out of each of the counties of this government, to serve as the people's representatives in Council; and of four persons out of each of the said counties, to serve as their representatives in Assembly; for the electing of which representatives, it shall and may be lawful to and for all the freemen of this province and territory aforesaid, to meet together on the tenth day of the first month yearly hereafter, in the most convenient and usual place for election, within the respective counties, then and there to chuse their said representatives as aforesaid, who shall meet on the tenth day of the third month yearly, in the capital town of the said province, unless the Governor and Council shall think fit to appoint another place.

And, to the end it may be known who those are, in this province and territories, who ought to have right of, or to be deemed freemen, to chuse, or be chosen, to serve in Council and Assembly, as aforesaid, Be it enacted by the authority aforesaid, That no inhabitant of this province or territories, shall have right of electing, or being elected as aforesaid, unless they be free denizens of this government, and are of the age of twenty-one years, or upwards, and have fifty acres of land, ten acres whereof being seated and cleared, or be otherwise worth *fifty pounds*, lawful money of this government, clear estate, and have been resident within this government for the space of two years next before such election.

And whereas divers persons within this government, cannot, for conscience sake, take an oath, upon any account whatsoever, Be it therefore enacted by the authority aforesaid, That all and every such person and persons, being, at any time hereafter, required, upon any lawful occasion, to give evidence, or take an oath, in any case whatsoever, shall, instead of swearing, be permitted to make his, or their solemn affirmation, attest, or declaration, which shall be adjudged, and is hereby enacted and declared to be of the same force and effect, to all intents and purposes whatsoever, as if they had taken an oath; and in case any such person or persons shall be lawfully convicted of having wilfully and corruptly affirmed, or declared any matter or thing, upon such solemn affirmation or attest, shall incur the same penalties and forfeitures as by the laws and statutes of *England* are provided against persons convicted of wilful and corrupt perjury.

And be it further enacted by the authority aforesaid, That all persons who shall be hereafter either elected to serve in Council and Assembly, or commissioned or appointed to be Judges, Justices, Masters of the Rolls, Sheriffs, Coroners, and all other offices of State and trust, within this government, who shall conscientiously scruple to take an oath, but when lawfully required, will make and subscribe the declaration and profession of their Christian belief, according to the late act of parliament, made in the first year of king *William,* and the late queen *Mary,* entitled, An act for exempting their majesties' Protestant subjects, dissenting from the Church of *England,* from the penalty of certain laws, shall be adjudged, and are hereby declared to be qualified to act in their said respective offices and places, and thereupon the several officers herein mentioned, shall, instead of an oath make their solemn affirmation or declaration in manner and form following; that is to say,

The form of Judges' and Justices' attest shall be in these words, *viz:*

Thou shalt solemnly promise that as Judge, or Justice, according to the Governor's commission to thee directed, thou shalt do equal to the Governor's commission to thee directed, thou shalt do equal right to the poor and rich, to the best of thy knowledge and power, according to law, and after the usages and constitutions of this government; thee, but shalt well and truly do thy office in every respect, according to the best of thy understanding.

The form of the attests to be taken by the Masters of the Rolls, Secretaries, Clerks, and such like officers, shall be thus, *viz:*

Thou shalt well and faithfully execute the office of, &c., according to the best of thy skill and knowledge; taking such fees only as thou oughtest to receive by the laws of this government.

The form of the Sheriffs' and Coroners' attest, shall be in these words, *viz:*

Thou shalt solemnly promise, that thou wilt well and truly serve the King and Governor in the office of the Sheriff (or Coroner) of the county of, &c., and preserve the King and Governor's rights, as far forth as thou canst, or mayest; thou shalt truly serve, and return, all the writs and precepts to thee directed; thou shalt take no bailiff, nor deputy, but such as thou wilt answer for; thou shalt receive no writs, except from such judges and justices who, by the laws of this government, have authority to issue and direct writs unto thee; and thou shalt diligently and truly do and accomplish all things appertaining to thy office, after the best of thy wit and power, both for the King and Governor's profit, and good of the inhabitants within the said county, taking such fees only as thou oughtest to take by the laws of this government, and not otherwise.

The form of a Constable's attest shall be this, *viz:*

Thou shalt solemnly promise, well and duly, according to the best of thy understanding, to execute the office of a Constable for the town (or county) of P. for this ensuing year, or until another be attested in thy room, or thou shalt be legally discharged thereof.

The form of the Grand Inquest's attests shall be in these words, *viz:*

Thou shalt diligently enquire, and true presentment make, of all such matters and things as shall be given thee in charge, or come to thy knowledge, touching this present service; the King's counsel, thy fellows, and thy own, thou shalt keep secret, and in all things thou shalt present the truth, and nothing but the truth, to the best of thy knowledge.

This being given to the Foreman, the rest of the Inquest shall be attested thus, by three at a time, *viz:*

The same attestation that your Foreman hath taken on his part, you will well and truly keep on your parts.

The form of the attest to be given to the Traverse Jury, by four at a time, shall be thus, *viz:*

You solemnly promise that you will well and truly try the issue of traverse between the lord the King, and A. B. whom you have in charge, according to your evidence.

In civil causes, thus, *viz:*

You solemnly promise that you will well and truly try the issue between A. B. plaintiff, and C. D. defendant, according to your evidence.

Provided always, and it is hereby intended, that no person shall be, by this act, excused from swearing, who, by the acts of parliament, for trade and navigation, are, or shall be required to take an oath.

And, that elections may not be corruptly managed, on which the good of the government so much depends, Be it further enacted by the authority aforesaid, that all elections of the said representatives shall be free and voluntary, and that the electors, who shall receive any reward, or gift, for giving his vote, shall forfeit his right to elect for that year; and such person or persons, as shall give, or promise, any such reward to be elected, or that shall offer to serve for nothing, or for less wages than the law prescribes, shall be thereby rendered incapable to serve in Council, or Assembly, for that year; and the representatives so chosen, either for Council or Assembly, shall yield their attendance accordingly, and be the sole judges of the regularity, or irregularity of the elections of their respective Members; and if any person, or persons, chosen to serve in Council, or Assembly, shall be wilfully absent from the service, he or they are so chosen to attend, or be deceased, or rendered incapable, then, and in all such cases, it shall be lawful for the Governor, within ten days after knowledge of the same, to issue forth a writ to the Sheriff of the county, for which the said person, or persons, were chosen, immediately to summons the freemen of the same to elect another member in the room of such absent, deceased, or incapable person or persons; and in case any Sheriff shall misbehave himself, in the management of any of the said elections, he shall be punished accordingly, at the discretion of the Governor and Council, for the time being.

Be it further enacted by the authority aforesaid, That every member now chosen, or hereafter to be chosen, by the freemen as aforesaid, to serve in Council, and the Speaker of the Assembly, shall be allowed five shillings by the day, during his and their attendance; and every Member of Assembly shall be allowed four shillings by the day, during his attendance on the service of the Assembly; and that every Member of Council and Assembly shall be allowed towards their traveling charges after the rate of two pence each mile, both going to, and coming from, the place, where the Council and Assembly is, or shall be, held; all which sums shall be paid yearly out of the county levies, by the county receivers respectively.

And be it further enacted by the authority aforesaid, That the Governor, or his Deputy, shall always preside in the Council, and that he shall, at no time, perform any public act of state whatsoever, that shall, or may relate unto the justice, treasury or trade of the province and territories, but by and with the advice and consent of the Council thereof, or major part of them that shall be present.

And be it further enacted by the authority aforesaid, That all the Sheriffs and Clerks of the respective counties of the said province, and territories, who are, or shall be, commissionated, shall give good and sufficient security to the Governor, for answering the king and his people, in matters relating to the said offices respectively.

And be it further enacted by the authority aforesaid, That the Council, in all cases and matters of moment, as about erecting courts of justice, sitting in judgment upon persons impeached, and upon bills and other matters, that may be, from time to time, presented by the Assembly, not less than two-thirds shall make a *quorum*; and that the consent and approbation of the majority of that quorum shall be had in all such cases and matters of moment; and that in cases of less moment, not less than one-third of the whole shall make a quorum; the majority of which shall, and may, always determine in all such matters of lesser moment, as are not above specified: and in case the Governor's power shall hereafter happen to be in the Council, a President shall then be chosen out of themselves by two-thirds, or the major part of them; which President shall therein preside.

Be it further enacted by the authority aforesaid, That the Governor and Council shall take care that all the laws, statutes and ordinances, which shall at any time be made within the said province and territories, be duly and diligently executed.

Be in further enacted by the authority aforesaid, That the Governor and Council shall, at all times, have the care of the peace of this province and territories thereof, and that nothing be, by any persons, attempted to the subversion of this *frame of government*.

And be it further enacted by the authority aforesaid, That the Governor and Council for the time being, shall, at all times, settle and order the situation of all cities and market towns, modeling therein all public buildings, streets and market places; and shall appoint all public landing places of the towns of this province and territories: and if any man's property shall be judged by the Governor and Council to be commodious for such landing place in the said towns, and that the same be by them appointed as such, that the owner shall have such reasonable satisfaction given him for the same as the Governor and Council shall see meet, to be paid by the said respective towns.

Be it further enacted by the authority aforesaid, That the Governor and Council shall, at all times, have power to inspect the management of the public treasury, and punish those who shall convert any part thereof to any other use, than what hath been agreed upon by the Governor, Council and Assembly.

Be it further enacted by the authority aforesaid, That the Governor and Council shall erect and order all public houses, and encourage and reward the authors of useful sciences and laudable inventions in the said province, and territories thereof.

And be it further enacted by the authority aforesaid, That the Governor and Council shall, from time to time have the care of the management of all public affairs, relating to the peace, safety, justice, treasury, trade, and improvement of the province and territories, and to the good education of youth, and sobriety of the manners of the inhabitants therein, as aforesaid.

And be it further enacted by the authority aforesaid, That the representatives of the freemen, when met in Assembly, shall have power to prepare and propose to the Governor and Council all such bills as they or the major part of them, shall, at any time, see needful to be passed into laws, within the said province and territories.

Provided always, That nothing herein contained shall debar the Governor and Council from recommending to the Assembly all such bills as they shall think fit to be passed into laws; and that the Council and Assembly may, upon occasion, confer together in committees, when desired; all which proposed and prepared bills, or such of them, as the Governor, with the advice of the Council, shall, in open Assembly, declare his assent unto, shall be the laws of this province and territories thereof, and published accordingly, with this stile, *By the Governor, with the assent and approbation of the freemen in General Assembly met*; a true transcript, or duplicate whereof, shall be transmitted to the king's privy council, for the time being, according to the said late king's letters patent.

And be it further enacted by the authority aforesaid, That the Assembly, shall sit upon their own adjournments, and committees, and continue, in order to prepare and propose bills, redress grievances, and impeach criminals, or such persons as they shall think fit to be there impeached, until the Governor and Council, for the time being, shall dismiss them; which Assembly shall, notwithstanding such dismiss, be capable of Assembling together upon summons of the Governor and Council, at any time during that year; two-thirds of which Assembly, in all cases, shall make a quorum.

And be it enacted by the authority aforesaid, That all elections of representatives for Council and Assembly, and all questions to be determined by them, shall be by major part of votes.

Be it further enacted by the authority aforesaid, That as oft as any days of the month, mentioned in any article of this act, shall fall upon the first day of the week, commonly called the Lord's day, the business appointed for that day, shall be deferred till the next day, unless in cases of emergency.

Be it further enacted by the authority aforesaid, That if any alien, who is, or shall be a purchaser of lands, or who doth, or shall inhabit in this province, or territories thereof, shall decease at any time before he can well be denizised, his right and interest therein shall notwithstanding descend to his wife and children, or other, his relations, be he testate, or intestate, according to the laws of this province and territories thereof, in such cases provided, in as free and ample manned, to all intents and purposes, as if said alien had been denizised.

And that the people may be accommodated with such food and sustenance as God, in his providence, hath freely afforded, Be it enacted by the authority aforesaid, That the inhabitants of this province and territories thereof, shall have liberty to fish and hunt, upon the lands they hold, or all other lands therein, not inclosed, and to fish in all waters in the said lands, and in all rivers and rivulets, in and belonging to this province and territories thereof, with liberty to draw his, or their fish upon any man's land, so as it be not to the detriment or annoyance of the owner thereof, except such lands as do lie upon inland rivulets, that are not boatable, or which hereafter may be erected into manors.

Be it further enacted by the authority aforesaid, That all inhabitants of this province and territories, whether purchasers, or others, and every one of them, shall have full and quiet enjoyment of their respective lands and tenements, to which they have any lawful or equitable claim, saving only such rents and services for the same, as are, or customarily ought to be, reserved to the lord, or lords of the fee thereof, respectively.

Be it further enacted by the authority aforesaid, That no act, law, or ordinance whatsoever, shall, at any time hereafter, be made or done, by the Governor of this province, and territories thereunto belonging, or by the freemen, in Council, or Assembly, to alter, change or diminish the form and effect of this act, or any part, or clause thereof, contrary to the true intent and meaning thereof, without the consent of the Governor, for the time being, and six parts of seven of the said freemen, in Council, and Assembly met. This act to continue, and be in force, until the said Proprietary shall signify his pleasure to the contrary, by some instrument, under his hand and seal, in that behalf.

Provided always, and it is hereby enacted, That neither this act, nor any other act, or acts whatsoever, shall preclude, or debar the inhabitants of this province and territories, from claiming, having and enjoying any of the rights, privileges and immunities, which the said Proprietary, for himself, his heirs, and assigns, did formerly grant, or which of right belong unto them, the said inhabitants, by virtue of any law, charter or grants whatsoever, any thing herein contained to the contrary notwithstanding.

Reference: Francis Newton Thorpe (ed.), *The Federal and State Constitutions, Colonial Charters, and Other Organic Laws of the States*, Vol. V (Washington: GPO, 1909).

CHARTER OF PRIVILEGES, OCTOBER 28, 1701

WILLIAM PENN, Proprietary and Governor of the Province of *Pensilvania* and Territories thereunto belonging, To all to whom these Presents shall come, sendeth Greeting.

WHEREAS King CHARLES *the Second*, by His Letters Patents, under the Great Seal of *England*, bearing Date the *Fourth* Day of *March*, in the Year *One Thousand Six Hundred and Eighty-one*, was graciously pleased to give and grant unto me, and my Heirs and Assigns for ever, this Province of *Pensilvania*, with divers great Powers and Jurisdictions for the well Government thereof.

AND WHEREAS the King's dearest Brother, JAMES *Duke of* YORK *and* ALBANY, &c. by his Deeds of Feoffment, under his Hand and Seal duly perfected, bearing Date the *Twenty-Fourth* Day of *August, One Thousand Six Hundred Eighty and Two*, did grant unto me, my Heirs and Assigns, all that Tract of Land, now called the Territories of *Pensilvania,* together with Powers and Jurisdictions for the good Government thereof.

AND WHEREAS for the Encouragement of all the Freemen and Planters, that might be concerned in the said Province and Territories, and for the good Government thereof, I the said WILLIAM PENN, in the Year *One Thousand Six Hundred Eighty and Three,* for me, my Heirs and Assigns, did grant and confirm unto all the Freemen. Planters and Adventurers therein, divers Liberties, Franchises and Properties, as by the said Grant, entituled, *The* FRAME *of the Government of the Province of* Pensilvania, *and Territories thereunto belonging, in* America, may appear; which Charter or Frame being found in some Parts of it, not so suitable to the present Circumstances of the Inhabitants, was in the *Third* Month, in the Year *One Thousand Seven Hundred,* delivered up to me, by *Six* Parts of *Seven* of the Freemen of this Province and Territories, in General Assembly met, Provision being made in the said Charter, for that End and Purpose.

AND WHEREAS I was then pleased to promise, That I would restore the said Charter to them again, with necessary Alterations, or in lieu thereof, give them another, better adapted to answer the present Circumstances and Conditions of the said Inhabitants; which they have now, by their Representatives in General Assembly met at *Philadelphia,* requested me to grant.

KNOW YE THEREFORE, That for the further Well-being and good Government of the said Province, and Territories; and in Pursuance of the Rights and Powers before-mentioned, I the said *William Penn* do declare, grant and confirm, unto all the Freemen, Planters and Adventurers, and other Inhabitants of this Province and Territories, these following Liberties, Franchises and Privileges, so far as in me lieth, to be held, enjoyed and kept, by the Freemen, Planters and Adventurers, and other Inhabitants of and in the said Province and Territories thereunto annexed, for ever.

FIRST

BECAUSE no People can be truly happy, though under the greatest Enjoyment of Civil

Liberties, if abridged of the Freedom of their Consciences, as to their Religious Profession and Worship: And Almighty God being the only Lord of Conscience, Father of Lights and Spirits; and the Author as well as Object of all divine Knowledge, Faith and Worship, who only doth enlighten the Minds, and persuade and convince the Understandings of People, I do hereby grant and declare. That no Person or Persons, inhabiting in this Province or Territories, who shall confess and acknowledge *One* almighty God, the Creator, Upholder and Ruler of the World; and profess him or themselves obliged to live quietly under the Civil Government, shall be in any Case molested or prejudiced, in his or their Person or Estate, because of his or their conscientious Persuasion or Practice, nor be compelled to frequent or maintain any religious Worship, Place or Ministry, contrary to his or their Mind, or to do or suffer any other Act or Thing, contrary to their religious Persuasion.

AND that all Persons who also profess to believe in *Jesus Christ,* the Saviour of the World, shall be capable (notwithstanding their other Persuasions and Practices in Point of Conscience and Religion) to serve this Government in any Capacity, both legislatively and executively, he or they solemnly promising, when lawfully required, Allegiance to the King as Sovereign, and Fidelity to the Proprietary and Governor, and taking the Attests as now established by the Law made at *New-Castle,* in the Year *One Thousand and Seven Hundred,* entitled, *An Act directing the Attests of several Officers and Ministers,* as now amended and confirmed this present Assembly.

II

FOR the well governing of this Province and Territories, there shall be an Assembly yearly chosen, by the Freemen thereof, to consist of *Four* Persons out of each County, of most Note for Virtue, Wisdom and Ability, (or of a greater number at any Time, as the Governor and Assembly shall agree) upon the *First* Day of *October* for ever; and shall sit on the *Fourteenth* Day of the same Month, at *Philadelphia,* unless the Governor and Council for the Time being, shall see

Cause to appoint another Place within the said Province or Territories: Which Assembly shall have Power to chuse a Speaker and other their Officers; and shall be Judges of the Qualifications and Elections of their own Members; sit upon their own Adjournments; appoint Committees; prepare Bills in order to pass into Laws; impeach Criminals, and redress Grievances; and shall have all other Powers and Privileges of an Assembly, according to the Rights of the free-born Subjects of *England*, and as is usual in any of the King's Plantations in *America*.

AND if any County or Counties, shall refuse or neglect to chuse their respective Representatives as aforesaid, or if chosen, do not meet to serve in Assembly, those who are so chosen and met, shall have the full Power of an Assembly, in as ample Manner as if all the Representatives had been chosen and met, provided they are not less than *Two Thirds* of the whole Number that ought to meet.

AND that the Qualifications of Electors and Elected, and all other Matters and Things relating to Elections of Representatives to serve in Assemblies, though not herein particularly expressed, shall be and remain as by a Law of this Government, made at *New-Castle* in the Year *One Thousand Seven Hundred*, entitled, *An Act to ascertain the Number of Members of Assembly, and to regulate the Elections*.

III

THAT the Freemen in each respective County, at the Time and Place of Meeting for Electing their Representatives to serve in Assembly, may as often as there shall be Occasion, chuse a double Number of Persons to present to the Governor for Sheriffs and Coroners to serve for *Three* Years, if so long they behave themselves well; out of which respective Elections and Presentments, the Governor shall nominate and commissionate one for each of the said Offices, the *Third* Day after such Presentment, or else the *First* named in such Presentment, for each Office as aforesaid, shall stand and serve in that Office for the Time before respectively limited; and in Case of Death or Default, such Vacancies shall be supplied by the Governor, to serve to the End of the said Term.

PROVIDED ALWAYS, That if the said Freemen shall at any Time neglect or decline to chuse a Person or Persons for either or both the aforesaid Offices, then and in such Case, the Persons that are or shall be in the respective Offices of Sheriffs or Coroners, at the Time of Election, shall remain therein, until they shall be removed by another Election as aforesaid.

AND that the Justices of the respective Counties shall or may nominate and present to the Governor *Three* Persons, to serve for Clerk of the Peace for the said County, when there is a Vacancy, one of which the Governor shall commissionate within *Ten* Days after such Presentment, or else the *First* nominated shall serve in the said Office during good Behavior.

IV

THAT the Laws of this Government shall be in this Stile, viz. *By the Governor, with the Consent and Approbation of the Freemen in General Assembly met;* and shall be, after Confirmation by the Governor, forthwith recorded in the Rolls Office, and kept at *Philadelphia*, unless the Governor and Assembly shall agree to appoint another Place.

V

THAT all Criminals shall have the same Privilege of Witnesses and Council as their Prosecutors.

VI

THAT no Person or Persons shall or may, at any Time hereafter, be obliged to answer any Complaint, Matter or Thing whatsoever, relating to Property, before the Governor and Council, or in any other Place, but in ordinary Course of Justice, unless Appeals thereunto shall be hereafter by Law appointed.

VII

THAT no Person within this Government, shall be licensed by the Governor to keep an Ordinary,

Tavern or House of Publick Entertainment, but such who are first recommended to him, under the Hands of the Justices of the respective Counties, signed in open Court; which Justices are and shall be hereby impowered, to suppress and forbid any Person, keeping such Publick-House as aforesaid, upon their Misbehaviour, on such Penalties as the Law doth or shall direct; and to recommend others from time to time, as they shall see Occasion.

VIII

IF any person, through Temptation or Melancholy, shall destroy himself; his Estate, real and personal, shall notwithstanding descend to his Wife and Children, or Relations, as if he had died a natural Death; and if any Person shall be destroyed or killed by Casualty or Accident, there shall be no Forfeiture to the Governor by reason thereof.

AND no Act, Law or Ordinance whatsoever, shall at any Time hereafter, be made or done, to alter, change or diminish the Form or Effect of this Charter, or of any Part or Clause therein, contrary to the true Intent and Meaning thereof, without the Consent of the Governor for the Time being, and *Six* Parts of *Seven* of the Assembly met.

BUT because the Happiness of Mankind depends so much upon the Enjoying of Liberty of their Consciences as aforesaid, I do hereby solemnly declare, promise and grant, for me, my Heirs and Assigns, That the *First* Article of this Charter relating to Liberty of Conscience, and every Part and Clause therein, according to the true Intent and Meaning thereof, shall be kept and remain, without any Alteration, inviolably for ever.

AND LASTLY, I the said *William Penn*, Proprietary and Governor of the Province of *Pensilvania*, and Territories thereunto belonging, for myself, my Heirs and Assigns, have solemnly declared, granted and confirmed, and do hereby solemnly declare, grant and confirm, That neither I, my Heirs or Assigns, shall procure or do any Thing or Things whereby the Liberties in this Charter contained and expressed, nor any Part thereof, shall be infringed or broken: And if any

thing shall be procured or done, by any Person or Persons, contrary to these Presents, it shall be held of no Force or Effect.

IN WITNESS whereof, I the said *William Penn*, at *Philadelphia* in *Pensilvania*, have unto this present Charter of Liberties, set my Hand and broad Seal, this *Twenty-Eighth* Day of *October*, in the Year of Our Lord *One Thousand Seven Hundred and One*, being the *Thirteenth* Year of the Reign of King WILLIAM *the Third*, over *England, Scotland, France* and *Ireland*, &c. and the *Twenty-First* Year of my Government.

AND NOTWITHSTANDING the Closure and Test of this present Charter as aforesaid, I think fit to add this following Proviso thereunto, as Part of the same, *That is to say*, That notwithstanding any Clause or Clauses in the above-mentioned Charter, obliging the Province and Territories to join together in Legislation, I am content, and do hereby declare, that if the Representatives of the Province and Territories shall not hereafter agree to join together in Legislation, and that the same shall be signified unto me, or my Deputy, in open Assembly, or otherwise from under the Hands and Seals of the Representatives, for the Time being, of the Province and Territories, or the major Part of either of them, at any Time within *Three* Years from the Date hereof, that in such Case, the Inhabitants of each of the *Three* Counties of this Province, shall not have less than *Eight* Persons to represent them in Assembly, for the Province; and the Inhabitants of the Town of *Philadelphia* (when the said Town is incorporated) *Two* Persons to represent them in Assembly; and the Inhabitants of each County in the Territories, shall have as many Persons to represent them in a distinct Assembly for the Territories, as shall be by them requested as aforesaid.

NOTWITHSTANDING which Separation of the Province and Territories, in Respect of Legislation, I do hereby promise, grant and declare, That the Inhabitants of both Province and Territories, shall separately enjoy all other Liberties, Privileges and Benefits, granted jointly to them in this Charter, any Law, Usage or Custom of this Government heretofore made and practised, or any Law made and passed by this General Assembly, to the Contrary hereof, notwithstanding.

WILLIAM PENN.

This Charter of Privileges being distinctly read in Assembly; and the whole and every Part thereof, being approved of and agreed to, by us, we do thankfully receive the same from our Proprietary and Governor, at Philadelphia, this Twenty-Eighth Day of October, One Thousand Seven Hundred and One. Signed on Behalf, and by Order of the Assembly,

per JOSEPH GROWDON, *Speaker*.
EDWARD SHIPPEN, GRIFFITH OWEN,
PHINEAS PEMBERTON, CALEB PUSEY,
SAMUEL CARPENTER, THOMAS STORY,
Proprietary and Governor's Council.

Reference: Francis Newton Thorpe (ed.), *The Federal and State Constitutions, Colonial Charters, and Other Organic Laws of the States*, Vol. V (Washington: GPO, 1909).

ACT TO REGULATE THE NUMBER OF MEMBERS OF THE ASSEMBLY, 1705

Be it enacted by John Evans, Esquire, by the Queen's royal approbation, Lieutenant-Governor under William Penn, Esquire, absolute proprietary and Governor-in-Chief of the province of Pennsylvania and territories, by and with the advice and consent of the freemen of the said province in General Assembly met, and by the authority of the same, that for the well governing of this province there shall be an Assembly yearly chosen. And for that end it shall and may be lawful to and for the freemen and inhabitants of the city of Philadelphia, as also for the freemen and inhabitants of the respective counties of this province, without any writ or summons, to meet on the first day of October yearly, forever, at the most usual place of elections in the said respective counties; that is to say, for the city and county of Philadelphia at or near the market place in the said city; and for the county of Bucks, upon the courthouse ground in the town of Bristol; and for the county of Chester, at or near the courthouse in the town of Chester; and then and there choose their representatives or delegates to serve them in Assembly, which shall consist of not less than two persons for the said city of Philadelphia and eight persons for each county of this province, or a greater number as the Governor and Assembly shall at any time hereafter agree. And that the members so to be elected shall meet and sit in Assembly on the fourteenth day of October yearly, forever, at the said city of Philadelphia, unless the Governor and Council for the time being shall see cause to appoint another place within this province to sit at.

But when any of the said days of election or meeting of Assembly shall happen to fall on the first day of the week, called Sunday, then such election and meeting shall be held on the next day following.

Provided, always, that no inhabitant of this province shall have right of electing, or being elected as aforesaid, unless he or they be natural born subjects of England or be naturalized in England or in this government, and unless such person or persons be of the age of twenty-one years or upwards and be a freeholder or freeholders in this province and have fifty acres of land or more well seated, and twelve acres thereof or more cleared and improved, or be otherwise worth fifty pounds lawful money of this province, clear estate, and have been resident therein for the space of two years before such election.

And to the end that elections, upon which the good of the government so much depends, may not be corruptly managed or obtained;

Be it enacted, by the authority aforesaid, that all the elections of the said representatives shall be free and voluntary, by persons having estates and being qualified as aforesaid in the respective county or counties for which he or they shall elect or be elected.

Provided, that the electors and elected for the said city of Philadelphia shall have a freehold estate or be worth fifty pounds, clear personal estate, within the same city and be otherwise qualified, as aforesaid. And that the elector who is not so qualified, as aforesaid, or that shall receive any reward or gift for his vote, shall forfeit his right of electing for that year and shall pay the sum of five pounds, the one-half thereof to the Governor and the other half to him or them that shall sue for the same in any court of record within this province.

And that he or they who shall give, offer, or promise any reward to be elected, or shall offer to serve for nothing or less allowance than the law prescribes, shall forfeit five pounds, the one-half thereof to the Governor and the other to him or them that will sue for the same in manner aforesaid, and be incapable to serve for that year.

And be it further enacted, by the authority aforesaid, that every sheriff, or, in his absence, his undersheriff or such as he shall depute, or for want of such deputation, the coroner or such as he shall appoint, or for want of such appointment, any two of the freeholders who, by the major part of the electors then and there present, shall be nominated and appointed judges of the said elections in the absence of the sheriff or coroner, shall attend at the said election and shall appoint such a number of clerks for taking the poll or votes of the electors as the inspectors hereafter mentioned shall appoint; who shall all take the said poll or names of the electors in the presence of the said sheriff, coroner, or other judges so nominated as aforesaid, or such as any of them shall depute or appoint, and shall make as many distinct columns on fair paper as there shall be candidates voted for, as is hereinafter expressed. But before they begin every clerk so appointed shall, by the said sheriff or coroner, or by some magistrate then present, be attested or charged upon his solemn affirmation truly and indifferently to take the said poll and set down the names of each freeholder and elector and the place of his freehold or estate, and to poll no elector who is not attested, if so required by the inspectors of such clerks. Which inspectors are to be nominated by the major part of the electors as aforesaid.

And every person coming to elect members for the city of Philadelphia, as also every person coming to elect members for the said respective counties, shall deliver in writing the names of those persons for whom they vote to the sheriff, or some other of the said persons so as aforesaid appointed judges of the said elections; who shall open the paper if the elector be illiterate and read the persons names contained therein and ask such elector whether these are the persons for whom he votes. Which paper, upon his affirmative, shall be received and put with the rest of the electors papers in a box which every sheriff is hereby required to provide for that purpose.

But if the elector brings no such paper or ticket, or if the illiterate elector will not vote for the persons contained in his paper, then and in all such cases the elector shall verbally give in the names of the persons he mostly desires should be chosen; which names shall be entered down by the said clerks.

Provided, always, that every elector, before he be admitted to poll, if required by any of the said inspectors, shall upon his solemn affirmation declare that he is twenty-one years of age and a freeholder for the county of and has fifty acres of land or more well seated, and twelve acres thereof or more cleared; or, that he is otherwise worth fifty pounds money of this province, clear estate, and has been resident therein for the space of two years, and that he has not been before polled at that election.

And in case any person taking the said affirmation shall be lawfully convicted of willfully and corruptly making a false affirmation therein, or if any shall suborn any person to take such false affirmation, he and they shall incur the same penalties and forfeitures as by the laws and statutes of England are provided against persons convicted of willful and corrupt perjury and subornation of perjury respectively.

And that the said poll shall not be delayed, nor the election adjourned to another place or part of the county other than where the same begins, but shall continue from day to day till the freeholders and electors then and there present shall be polled, and no longer. And when all the electors then appearing shall have delivered in all their papers or names, the said box shall be opened by the sheriff, or some other of the persons appointed by this act to officiate as judges of the said elections, and the said papers taken out in the presence of the said inspectors and delivered, one by one, to the said clerk or clerks to enter the names therein expressed in fair columns or otherwise, so that they shall cast up how many times each person's name is repeated in the same and set it down; and shall then pronounce publicly to the people him whose name is oftenest mentioned in the said papers to be first elected, and so the next highest number successively until the whole eight persons for the county be pronounced elected by majority as aforesaid. And the same method shall be used concerning the two members to be elected for the city of Philadelphia.

But if, when the said papers are opened, there appear more names in any one of them, or more than one paper deceitfully folded together, containing more names than by this act is allowed any one elector to vote for, such papers shall be rejected and not accounted amongst the votes.

And after the said representatives are so chosen as aforesaid, their names, be they present or absent, shall be written in a pair of indentures, sealed between the said sheriff or other persons officiating as judges of the said elections, and six or more of the said choosers.

And every sheriff or other persons officiating as judges of the said elections shall, on the first day of the meeting of every assembly, in person or by deputy, present one part of the said indentures to the Governor for the time being and the other part thereof to the House of Representatives. Which said indentures shall be deemed and taken to be the sheriff's return of the representatives or delegates of the freemen of this province to serve and act in the legislative or General Assemblies of the same province from time to time. And the representatives so as aforesaid chosen shall yield their attendance accordingly.

And if any person or persons so chosen and returned to serve, as aforesaid, shall be absent from the service for which he or they shall be so elected, he or they shall forfeit any sum not exceeding ten pounds current money, the one-half thereof to the Governor and the other half to him or them that shall sue for the same in manner aforesaid; unless his or their excuse for such absence shall be allowed of by the Assembly.

And if any person so chosen and returned, as aforesaid, shall happen to die or be willfully absent, or by vote of the House be disabled to sit or serve in Assembly, then and in every such case the secretary for the time being shall, by the Speaker's order, issue out writs to the respective sheriffs of the counties where there shall be occasion for electing such new members. But in case the secretary shall delay the making of such writs for the space of two days next after he has notice of the Speaker's order in that behalf, it shall be lawful for the Speaker of the Assembly for the time being to issue forth the said writs, which shall be made in the Governor's name under the hand and seal of the Speaker. Whereupon, every sheriff or other officer to whom such writ or writs are directed shall endorse the day of his receipt thereof on the back of the writ and, with all convenient speed after he receives such writ, shall cause public notice to be given of the time and place of election and proceed to elect thereupon in manner aforesaid, within the space of five days after his receipt of the said writ, and give two days notice at least of the day appointed for election. Which notice shall be given in writing and shall be proclaimed in the most public places of the capital town or place where such election is to be, and the said sheriff or other officer shall cause copies of such notice or advertisement to be posted upon some tree or house in the way leading from every township or precinct to the town or place where the said election is to be, as also upon the courthouses and public fixed meeting houses for religious worship in the said respective counties.

And when those elections are made by virtue of the said writs in manner aforesaid, the sheriff, or other officer who shall officiate as judges of such elections, shall write the names of the persons so elected in a pair of indentures, sealed and presented [sic] one part thereof to the Governor and the other part to the Assembly, on the day of the return of such writs; which said indentures shall be deemed and taken to be the sheriff's return of such representatives.

All which said elections shall begin between the hours of ten in the morning and two in the afternoon; and that no person or persons whatsoever, by force of arms or menacing, shall disturb the freemen of this province in the free election of their said representatives, but that the same election shall be freely and indifferently made.

And be it further enacted, by the authority aforesaid, that if any sheriff shall refuse or neglect to give notice of the said elections by writs, he shall forfeit one hundred pounds, money aforesaid, one-half to the Governor and the other half to him that shall sue for the same in manner aforesaid. And upon such neglect or refusal, the coroner of the respective county where the same shall happen is hereby required, by himself or his deputy, to officiate and perform all that the said sheriff or his deputy ought to have done and performed at the said elections, according to the tenor and directions of this act; under the penalty of fifty pounds, to be recovered as aforesaid, one-half to the Governor, and the other half to him that shall sue for the same.

And every sheriff or other officer not making good and true returns of the said elections of representatives or members of Assembly according to the direction of this act, or refusing or willfully neglecting to do and perform what is hereby required to be done at and after the said elections, shall forfeit, for every such offense, the sum of one hundred pounds, money aforesaid, one-half thereof to the Governor and the other moiety to him that will sue for the same in manner aforesaid.

And be it further enacted, by the authority aforesaid, that the representatives so chosen and met according to the direction of this act shall be the Assembly of this province and shall have power to choose a Speaker and other their officers, and shall be judges of the qualifications and elections of their own members, sit upon their own adjournments, appoint committees, prepare bills in order to pass into laws, impeach criminals and redress grievances, and shall have all other powers and privileges of an Assembly according to the rights of the freeborn subjects of England and as is usual in any of the Queen's plantations in America.

And if any county or part of this province shall refuse or neglect to choose their respective representatives, as aforesaid, or, if chosen, do not meet to serve in Assembly, those who are so chosen and met shall have the full power of an Assembly in as ample manner as if all the representatives had been chosen and met, provided they are not less than two-thirds of the whole that ought to meet.

And be it further enacted, by the authority aforesaid, that no person who shall be hereafter a member of the Assembly or House of Representatives of this province shall be capable to vote in the said house or sit there during any debate after their Speaker is chosen until he shall make and subscribe the following declarations and profession of his christian belief, viz.,

I, A. B., do sincerely promise and solemnly declare, before God and the world, that I will be faithful and bear true allegiance to Queen Anne. And I do solemnly profess and declare that I do from my heart abhor, detest, and renounce as impious and heretical that damnable doctrine and position that princes excommunicated or deprived by the Pope or any authority of the See of Rome, may be deposed or murdered by their subjects or any other whatsoever. And I do declare that no foreign prince, person, prelate, state, or potentate has or ought to have any power, jurisdiction, superiority, preheminence, or authority, ecclesiastical or spiritual, within the realm of England or the dominions thereunto belonging.

And I, A. B., do solemnly and sincerely, in the presence of God, profess, testify, and declare that I do believe that in the sacrament of the Lord's Supper there is not any transubstantiation of the elements of bread and wine into the body and blood of Christ, at or after the consecration thereof, by any person whatsoever; and that the invocation or adoration of the Virgin Mary or any other saint, and the sacrifice of the Mass, as they are now used in the Church of Rome, are superstitious and idolatrous.

And I do solemnly, in the presence of God, profess, testify, and declare that I do make this declaration and every part thereof in the plain and ordinary sense of the words read unto me, as they are commonly understood by English Protestants, without any evasion, equivocation, or mental reservation whatsoever, and without any dispensation already granted me for this purpose by the Pope or any other authority or person whatsoever, or without any hope of any such dispensation from any person or authority whatsoever; or without thinking I am or may be acquitted before God or man or absolved of this declaration or any part thereof, although the Pope or any other person or persons or power whatsoever should dispense with or annul the same or declare that it was null or void from the beginning.

And I, A. B., profess faith in God the Father and in Jesus Christ his eternal son, the true God, and in the Holy Spirit, one God blessed for evermore; and do acknowledge the Holy Scriptures of the Old and New Testament to be given by divine inspiration.

Which said declarations and profession of faith shall be, in the next and every succeeding Assembly to be held in this province, solemnly and publicly made and subscribed betwixt the hours of nine in the morning and four in the afternoon by every such member of the House of Representatives is there sitting with their Speaker in his chair; and during the making and subscribing thereof, all business and debates in the said House shall cease.

And the clerk of the Assembly is hereby required to record the same in rolls or books prepared for that purpose; and every member of Assembly shall pay the clerk for recording thereof five pence, and no more. And that the manner and method of making the said declarations shall be as follows, to wit. The Speaker shall first read and subscribe the same, and after him every

member, as he is called over, shall either read and subscribe the said declarations or else subscribe them as they shall be read unto him by the clerk of the Assembly.

And be it enacted, by the authority aforesaid, that no person whatsoever who at any time shall be elected member of Assembly in this province and who shall make and be willing and offer to make and subscribe the said declarations, in manner and form aforesaid, shall be rejected or denied to sit, debate, and act in the House of Representatives or General Assembly of this province.

Provided, nevertheless, that nothing herein contained shall extend to, debar, or hinder the House of Representatives to reject such persons as are or shall be unduly elected members to serve in Assembly, or such as the Assembly or the major part of them shall see cause from time to time, by vote, to expel or disable to sit or serve there by reason of ill practice in elections or misbehavior in the House.

And be it further enacted, by the authority aforesaid, that every member chosen or to be chosen to serve in Assembly as aforesaid, shall be allowed the sum of six shillings per day, and the Speaker ten shillings per day, during his and their attendance in the service thereof; and that every member of Assembly shall be allowed towards his traveling charges after the rate of three pence a mile coming to and going from the place where the Assembly is or shall be held.

Reference: J. T. Mitchell and H. Flanders (eds.), *Statutes at Large of Pennsylvania*, Vol. II (15 vols.; Harrisburg: Carence M. Busch, 1896–1908), 212–221.

ORDINANCE FOR ESTABLISHING COURTS, FEBRUARY 22, 1706

Whereas the Queen's most excellent Majesty, by her order in council held at St. James on the seventh day of February in the year one thousand seven hundred and five, was pleased to repeal, declare to be utterly void several laws formerly enacted in this government, amongst others one

certain law entitled, *An Act for Establishing Courts of Judicature in this Province.* And upon the publication of which order all the several courts that were founded upon the said act become discontinued, and thereupon an entire failure in the administration of justice in this province has ensued. And whereas the present House of Representatives of the said province, having undertaken to provide another act for reviving and establishing the said courts, have not yet thought fit to agree to such a bill for that purpose as in the just discharge of the trust reposed in me by the Queen's Majesty and the proprietary, I could by any means assent to. By reason of which her Majesty's subjects here have been long deprived of the common benefit of a public administration of justice by courts of judicature. For remedy whereof, I have, after a long delay, found myself obliged, by virtue of the royal letters patents of King Charles the Second, granting unto the proprietary and his heirs and to his other deputies and lieutenants, in the following words, full power and authority to appoint any judges and justices, magistrates and officers whatsoever for what causes soever and to do all every other thing and things which unto the complete establishment of justice, unto courts and tribunals, forms of judicature, and manner of proceedings do belong, although in these presents express mention be not made thereof, etc. To restore the said courts of judicature and for the general benefit and advantage of her Majesty's subjects therein, to open the current of public justice again, and, accordingly, by virtue of the powers aforesaid, I have, by the advice of the Council, thought fit to appoint and establish and do by these presents ordain and declare to be appointed and established for the public administration of justice in the said province, the several courts and judicatories hereinafter following. That is to say, that there shall be holden in every county of this province, that is to say, at Philadelphia, and kept a court of record, twice in every year for the county and city of Philadelphia on the tenth day of April and the four and twentieth day of September; at Bristol for the county of Bucks, on the fourteenth day of April and the eight and twentieth day of September; and at Chester for the county of Chester the eighteenth day of April and second day of October; which said court shall be called and styled the Supreme or Provincial Court of Pennsylvania. And there shall be three persons of known integrity and ability appointed

and commissionated by the governor, or his lieutenant, from time to time, by several distinct patents or commissions, under the great seal of this province, to be judges of the said court, one of whom shall be distinguished in his commission by the name of Chief Justice. Which said judges or any one of them shall have full power to hold the said Supreme Courts and therein to hear and determine all pleas, plaints, and causes which shall be removed or brought there from the Court of General Quarter Sessions of the Peace, or County Court of Common Pleas, or from the Sessions or Court of Records held for the city of Philadelphia, or from any other court or courts of record within the said respective counties, by writs of *habeas corpus, certiorari,* writs of error, prohibitions, injunctions, *audita, querela,* or any other remedial writ or writs of what nature or kind soever. And to examine and to correct all and all manner of errors of the justices and magistrates of this province in their judgements, process, proceedings, as well in all pleas of the crown as in all pleas real, personal, and mixed, and thereupon to reverse or affirm the said judgements, as the law does or shall direct. Also to examine, correct, and punish the contempts, omissions, favors, corruptions, and defaults of all justices of the peace, sheriffs, coroners, clerks, and other officers within the said respective counties; and generally shall minister common justice to all persons, concerning all and singular the premises according to law, as fully and amply to all intents and purposes whatsoever as the justices of the Court of Queen's Bench, Common Pleas and Exchequer, at Westminster, may or can do. All which said writs and every of them shall be granted of course, and shall issue forth of the office of the clerk or prothonotary of the said Supreme Court, and shall be made in the name and style of the Queen, her heirs and successors, and bear test in the name of the said Chief Justice for the time being, and shall be sealed with the provincial seal or seal of the said province. And I do further ordain, by the authority aforesaid, that there shall be a Court of Equity held by the judges of the said respective Supreme or Provincial Courts, in every county of this province. Which said judges, or any of them, within the limits of their commissions, shall have full power and are hereby empowered and authorized to hear and decree all such matters of equity as by appeals from the respective inferior courts shall come before them, and thereupon to revoke, make void, alter, or confirm such decrees and sentences, acts or proceedings, of the said inferior courts relating thereto, and to make such decrees and take such orders therein as shall be agreeable to equity and justice, with full power by legal and due process to force obedience to their decrees of judgements. And I do further ordain, by the authority aforesaid, that there shall be a competent number of justices in every of the said counties, nominated, appointed, authorized by the governor, or lieutenant governor, for the time being, by commission under the broad seal of this province. Which said justices, or any three of them, shall and may hold the said general sessions of the peace and gaol delivery. And each of them shall keep or cause be kept the peace of our said Lady the Queen, her heirs and successors, and all acts and statutes made and to be made for the conservation of the peace and for the quiet rule and government in the respective counties for which they shall be so commissionated, according as those acts and statutes do or shall direct; and to chastise and punish all persons offending against those acts and statutes, with full power and authority to and for the said justices to award process, bind to the peace and good behavior, and to hear, try, and determine all and all manner of matters, causes, and things whatsoever, as near as conveniently may be to the laws of England, and according to the laws and usages of this province, with full powers to hold special and private sessions when and as often as occasion shall require as any justice or justices of the peace in England, in and out of their sessions, may or can do. Which said General Quarter Sessions of the Peace in the respective counties of this province shall begin on the Tuesday on the same week in which the respective County Courts of Common Pleas hereafter mentioned are appointed to be held. And I do further ordain, by the authority aforesaid, that the justices of the said Courts of General Quarter

Sessions of the Peace, in the respective counties for which they are commissionated, as aforesaid, shall hold and keep a court of record in every county, which shall be called and styled the County Court of Common Pleas and shall be holden four times in every year at the places where the said Quarter Sessions of the Peace shall be respectively kept as aforesaid. That is to say, at Philadelphia, for the county and city of Philadelphia, the first Thursday in the months of March, June, September and December; at Bristol, for the county of Bucks, the second Wednesday in every of the aforesaid months; at Chester, the last Wednesday in the months of February, May, August, and November. Which said justices, or any three of them, shall hold pleas of assize, *scire facias*, replevins, and hear and determine all and all manner of pleas, actions, suits, and causes, civil, personal, real, and mixed, as near as conveniently may be the course and practice of the Queens Court of Common Pleas in England, and according to the laws and constitutions of this province, from time to time, having due regard to the regular process and proceedings of former county courts, always keeping, as near as may be, to brevity, plainness, and verity in all declarations and pleas. And that all writs and process upon the pleas, plaints, and actions, aforesaid, shall as heretofore issue out of the office of the clerk or prothonotary of the said respective counties, under the respective county seals, into whose office all returns shall be made. And I do further ordain, by the authority aforesaid, that any one or more of the said justices in every county of this province, as they shall see occasions, may sit once in every six weeks at the place where the said Courts of Common Pleas shall be usually held, to the end only that the original writs and process may be made returnable there and rules for pleas, replications, and other pleadings may be there given and issues joined, and other preparations made for expediting the trials of causes depending in the said County Courts of Common Pleas. And I do further ordain, by the authority aforesaid, that there shall be a Court of Equity held by the justices of the said respective County Courts of Common Pleas, four times a year at the respective places and near the said times as the said Courts of Common Pleas are held in every county of this province, and that the prothonotary of the Common Pleas shall be the register of the said Court of Equity in every county. Which said justices, or any three of them, within the limits of their commissions, shall have full power and are hereby empowered and authorized to hear and decree all such matters and causes of equity do as shall come before them in the said courts, where the proceedings shall be as heretofore by bill and answer, with such other pleadings as are necessary in Chancery courts, proper in these parts, with power also, for the said justices of the respective Courts of Equity, to issue forth all manner of subpoenas and all other process do, as may be needful to oblige and force the defendants to answer suits there, as also to award commissions for taking answers and examining witnesses, and to grant injunctions for staying suits in law and stopping wastes as there may be occasion, observing as near as may be the practice and proceedings of the High Court of Chancery in England; with power also to make orders and award all manner of process and do all other things necessary for bringing causes to hearing and to force obedience to their decrees in equity, as the laws and practice in such cases does or shall direct, and admit of bills of *revior* as the case may require. And for the better execution of the powers and jurisdiction hereby erected or intended, it may be lawful to and for the said judges and justices of the said respective courts to

make and publish all and every such reasonable rules and orders as may be fit and necessary to regulate the officers and ascertain the practice of the courts they belong to. And I do further ordain that special commissions of oyer and terminer and gaol delivery may be granted unto any the respective counties of this province for the hearing, trying, and determining of all high and capital offenses where the life of any person may or shall be brought in question. And I do further ordain that if any person or persons being defendant or defendants in any suit or action, who shall, by reason of their speedy departure out of this province, require a more speedy determination in the premises than can be had in the said County Court of Common Pleas, that upon application to the justices of the said County Court of Common Pleas they may grant such defendants special courts and may proceed to hear and determine the premises, such persons having first given sufficient bail to stand to and abide their judgement, according to the course and practice of the said County Court of Common Pleas. Given under my hand and great seal of the province at Philadelphia, the two and twentieth day of February, in the fifth year of the reign of our sovereign Lady Ann, by the grace of God, of England, Scotland, France, and Ireland, Queen, Defender of the Faith, etc. *anno.domini* 1706.

John Evans.

Reference: J. T. Mitchell and H. Flanders (eds.), *Statutes at Large of Pennsylvania*, Vol. I (15 vols.; Harrisburg: Carence M. Busch, 1896–1908), 319–323.

ACT TO AMEND THE ELECTION OF MEMBERS TO THE ASSEMBLY, MARCH 4, 1745

Whereas notwithstanding the just and impartial method prescribed for electing of members of assembly by the charter of privileges granted by the Honorable William Penn, Esquire, late proprietor and governor-in-chief of the Province of Pennsylvania, and counties of Newcastle, Kent and Sussex upon Delaware, to the inhabitants

thereof, and of the several acts of assembly of the said province, made in pursuance of the said charter, for the more free, impartial and peaceable election of members to serve in the general assembly of the said province, and of sheriffs, coroners, commissioners, assessors, and of inspectors to assist in the said election, it was nevertheless found upon experience that the method formerly prescribed by the laws of this province for choosing inspectors to assist the sheriff and for receiving the poll or votes at the said elections did not answer the good purposes for which it was intended, but great numbers of disorderly persons, many of whom, not being qualified to vote for members of assembly, mixed themselves among the electors at the time of choosing inspectors and by their rude and disorderly behavior disturbed the electors and created strifes and quarrels, to the great danger and disquiet of the peaceable people there met together and in delay of the said elections.

And whereas it often happened that the said inspectors were chosen, most or all of them, out of one part of the county, and by reason thereof could not be so well acquainted with the estates and circumstances of all the electors, which was the principal end of their first appointment.

For remedying of which inconveniences an act of the general assembly of this province was passed in the twelfth year of the present reign, entitled "A supplement to the act for electing members of Assembly," and also one other act was passed in the sixteenth year of the same reign, entitled "An act for continuing and amending the act of assembly," last aforesaid; which acts, with some amendments, are thought necessary to be perpetuated:

[Section I.] Therefore be it enacted by the Honorable George Thomas, Esquire, with the King's Royal Approbation Lieutenant-Governor under the Honorable John Penn, Thomas Penn and Richard Penn, Esquires, true and absolute Proprietors of the Province of Pennsylvania and the counties of Newcastle, Kent and Sussex upon Delaware, by and with the advice and consent of the representatives of the freemen of said Province in General Assembly met, and by the authority of the same, That the eight several districts into which the several counties within this province have been divided by the justices of the said counties, in pursuance of the acts of assembly aforesaid, do and shall continue, and they are hereby declared to be and shall continue unalterable; except in such cases as are here[in]after provided, for the purposes hereinafter-mentioned.

And that if any new townships, since the passing of the acts aforesaid have been or shall be erected out of several districts within any of the said counties, that it shall and may be lawful for the justices aforesaid respectively, at their quarter-sessions of the peace next after publication of this act, and at the quarter-sessions of the peace next following the erecting such townships, and they are hereby enjoined and required, to annex such township or townships to the district or districts out of which the greater part of the said townships respectively were taken, and to deliver to the sheriff of the respective counties an account to what district the same township or townships are annexed, with the names of all the new erected townships; all which the said sheriff shall make known to the respective constables of the said township with all expedition, thereby to enable them to discharge their several trusts, in pursuance of the directions of this act.

[Section II.] And be it further enacted by the authority aforesaid, That the freeholders and others qualified to elect members of assembly in each township shall meet on the twenty-seventh day of September yearly; but if the same shall happen upon a first day of the week, then upon the day before, at some convenient place with[in] their said respective townships to be appointed by the constable of the said township, or in case of his absence, neglect or refusal, then at such convenient place within such township as the overseers of the poor shall appoint; and the said electors, being qualified to vote for members of assembly, shall, between the hours of nine in the forenoon and three in the afternoon the same day, during all which time the election shall continue, in the presence of the constable and such two freeholders as he shall call to his assistance, or, in case of his absence, neglect or refusal, the overseer of the poor, proceed to elect by balloting one able and discreet freeholder residing within the said township, who may be supposed to be best acquainted with the estates and circumstances of the inhabitants; the name of which person so nominated and chosen is to be taken down in writing by the constable or overseer of the poor, as the case shall happen, with the name of the township for which he is chosen, and shall be delivered to the sheriff of the county at the place of election or to such person or persons as shall happen to be judges of the election before the hour of nine in the forenoon of the day whereupon the election of members of assembly shall happen. And the sheriff or other judge of the election, having then and there received the names of all the persons chosen for the respective townships within his county, or so many of them as shall be delivered to him, in manner aforesaid, he shall call to his assistance at least four freeholders of the county, and in their presence shall put all the names of the persons returned for each district, wrote on several pieces of paper, to be cut and folded up after the usual manner of folding tickets, as near as may be of equal size and bigness, into a separate box, to be provided by him for that purpose, and shall likewise, in the presence of the said freeholders, call some indifferent person, who shall draw one name out of each box, and deliver the same to the sheriff or other judge of the election; which being done, the persons whose names shall happen to be drawn and being present shall for that year be the inspectors of the election, and as such shall be published by the sheriff in the presence of the electors or so many of them as shall be present.

[Section III.] And be it enacted by the authority aforesaid, That it shall and may be lawful for the inhabitants of the respective wards of the city of Philadelphia qualified to vote for members of assembly to meet together at the time hereinbefore-mentioned for the meeting of the inhabitants of the respective townships in this province, and at some convenient place within their respective wards, to be appointed by the constable of the ward to which he belongs, of which public notice shall be given in writing by affixing the same upon four of the most public places within each of the said wards of the city of Philadelphia aforesaid at least six days before the said twenty-seventh day of September, and there shall, in the presence of the constable of the ward and such two freeholders of the said ward as he shall call to his assistance, proceed to choose by balloting one substantial freeholder of ability and integrity

residing within the said ward, whose name, when so chosen shall be taken in writing and certified by the constable and freeholders aforesaid to the sheriff of the county or other judge of the said election in the manner before directed for the constables of townships; and the sheriff shall put the names of all the persons so to him returned, wrote upon several pieces of paper, to be cut and folded up after the usual manner of folding tickets, as near as may be of equal size and bigness, into a box, and shall call some indifferent person, who shall draw four of the said names out of the said box and deliver the same to the sheriff, who shall read the same publicly in the presence of the electors then present; and the four persons whose names shall so happen to be drawn shall, together with the inspectors chosen out of the several districts of the said county, be the inspectors for that year for the election, and as such shall be qualified in the manner before directed for other inspectors; and the other six persons who names shall remain in the box or any four of them shall be the inspectors for that year at the election of burgesses and assessors for the city of Philadelphia, and shall be qualified in manner aforesaid. But before they proceed to act in assisting the sheriff to receive the poll or votes of the said electors, they shall be qualified by oath or affirmation by the sheriff of the proper county or other judges of the elections, who are hereby required and empowered to administer the same, that they the said inspectors will duly attend the ensuing election during the continuance thereof, and will truly and faithfully assist the sheriff, coroners or other judges of the said election to prevent all frauds and deceits whatsoever of electors or others in carrying on the same and in causing the poll or votes at such election to be taken and cast up according to the direction of the before-recited act. And the said inspectors shall and are hereby authorized to administer to every elector or person who presents his ticket an oath or affirmation in the words directed by the aforesaid act of assembly, unless the qualification of such elector be generally well known or some one or more of the said inspectors shall and will openly declare to the rest that they know such elector to be qualified as in the aforesaid act of assembly is required; and the votes or tickets of such as offer to poll and refuse to take the said oath or affirmation shall be openly rejected, and the votes or tickets of every person who takes the said oath or affirmation shall, with the other lawful tickets or votes, be put into the box, and no ticket so received shall be suppressed.

And to the end this act may be duly executed and the peace preserved:

[Section IV.] Be it therefore enacted by the authority aforesaid, That the constables of the respective townships [within the several counties] of this province, or, in case of the death, neglect or absence of the said constables, then the overseers of the poor of such township or one of them, shall at least six days before the said twenty-seventh day of September in every year give public notice in writing by affixing the same at the most public places in the respective townships of the place where the inhabitants of the township in which they live shall meet, to elect a fit person according to the direction of this act; and that the said constable, or, in his absence, the overseer of the poor as aforesaid, shall there attend at the time appointed in this act; and such constable or overseer of the poor shall call to his assistance two substantial freeholders of the said township, being there present, who shall assist him in judging of the said election and in taking the votes, and who, together with himself, shall certify to the sheriff of the county or other judge of the election under their hands that such person was elected by a majority of lawful votes by the township to which he belongs; the name of which person so elected as aforesaid shall be delivered to the sheriff or other judge or judges of the election of the county to which they belong in the manner hereinbefore directed.

And if any sheriff or coroner, constable or overseer of the poor, being the judge of such election as aforesaid, shall neglect to do the duty hereby enjoined them respectively or shall willfully misbehave himself or themselves in the execution of his or their duty and be thereof legally convict, such person so offending, if sheriff or coroner, shall forfeit the sum of one hundred pounds, and if a constable or overseer of the poor, [shall forfeit] five pounds, to any person who will sue for the same.

And if any of the persons elected as aforesaid and returned for any township within this province or for any of the wards of the city of Philadelphia, in the manner before directed, shall neglect or refuse to give his attendance at the time and place of electing members of assembly, every such person so offending shall likewise forfeit the sum of five pounds to any person who will sue for the same, the said several forfeitures to be recovered by action of debt in any court of record within this province with costs of suit.

And if the person whose name shall happen to be drawn, being called, shall not appear, then the name of another person belonging to the same district shall be drawn, and [he] shall be qualified and proceed to officiate as an inspector in the manner before directed in this act for inspectors.

[Section V.] And be it enacted by the authority aforesaid, That an act of the general assembly of this province, entitled "A supplementary act to the act for ascertaining the number of members of assembly and to regulate elections," passed in the thirteenth year of the reign of King George the First, and every article and clause therein, shall be and is hereby repealed.

Provided always, That nothing herein contained shall be deemed or taken to alter or make void the act of general assembly, . . . but that every clause, article and sentence therein . . . shall be and remain in a full force and virtue as the same way before the making of this act . . ."

Passed March 7, 1745

Reference: J. T. Mitchell and H. Flanders (eds.), *Statutes at Large of Pennsylvania,* Vol. V (15 vols.; Philadelphia: Stanley Ray, 1898).

26

Delaware

Delaware, finally freed from Pennsylvania and New Jersey, obtained its own charter in 1701. Because Delaware was a crown colony, the British king appointed its governor and council. But provision was made in the charter for a legislature to grow and become a viable part of colonial governance. Most significant for the development of governance was the charter given to the town of New Castle in 1724, because it signaled further growth of local governance. The charter of New Castle set up a mayor and council system and linked local governance to colony-wide governance. Delaware had joined with the other colonies sensitive to its local governance prerogatives and worried about the powers the crown exercised over its legislature.

CHARTER OF DELAWARE, 1701

WILLIAM PENN, Proprietary and Governor of the Province of *Pennsylvania* and Territories thereunto belonging, To all to whom these Presents shall come, sendeth Greeting.

WHEREAS King CHARLES the Second, by his Letter Patents, under the Great Seal of *England,* bearing Date the *Fourth* Day of *March,* in the Year *One Thousand Six Hundred and Eighty,* was graciously pleased to give and grant unto me, and my Heirs and Assigns for ever, this Province of *Pennsylvania,* with divers great Powers and Jurisdictions for the well Government thereof.

AND WHEREAS the King's dearest Brother, JAMES Duke of YORK and ALBANY, &c. by his Deeds of Feoffment, under his Hand and Seal duly perfected, bearing Date the *Twenty-Fourth* Day of *August, One Thousand Six Hundred Eighty and Two,* did grant unto me, my Heirs and Assigns, all that Tract of Land, now called the Territories of *Pennsylvania,* together with Powers and Jurisdictions for the good Government thereof.

AND WHEREAS, for the Encouragement of all the Freemen and Planters, that might be concerned in the said Province and Territories, and for the good Government thereof, I the said WILLIAM PENN, in the Year *One Thousand Six Hundred Eighty and Three,* for me, my Heirs and Assigns, did grant and confirm unto all the Freemen, Planters and Adventurers therein, divers Liberties, Franchises and Properties, as by the said Grant, entitled, *The FRAME of the Government of the Province of* Pennsylvania, *and Territories thereunto belonging, in* America, may appear; which Charter or Frame being found, in some Parts of it, not so suitable to the present Circumstances of the Inhabitants, was in the *Third* Month, in the Year *One Thousand Seven Hundred,* delivered up to me, by *Six* Parts of *Seven* of the Freemen of this Province and Territories, in General Assembly met, Provision being made in the said Charter, for that End and Purpose.

AND WHEREAS I was then pleased to promise, That I would restore the said Charter to them again, with necessary Alterations, or in lieu thereof, give them another, better adapted to answer the present Circumstances and Conditions of the said Inhabitants; which they have now, by their Representatives in General Assembly met at *Philadelphia*, requested me to grant.

KNOW YE THEREFORE, That for the further Well-being and good Government of the said Province, and Territories; and in Pursuance of the Rights and Powers before-mentioned, I the said *William Penn* do declare, grant and confirm, unto all the Freemen, Planters and Adventurers, and other Inhabitants in this Province and Territories, these following Liberties, Franchises and Privileges, so far as in me lieth, to be held, enjoyed and kept, by the Freemen, Planters and Adventurers, and other Inhabitants of and in the said Province and Territories thereunto annexed, for ever.

FIRST

BECAUSE no People can be truly happy, though under the greatest Enjoyment of Civil Liberties, if abridged of the Freedom of their Consciences, as to their Religious Profession and Worship: And Almighty God being the only Lord of Conscience, Father of Lights and Spirits; and the Author as well as Object of all divine Knowledge, Faith and Worship, who only doth enlighten the Minds, and persuade and convince the Understandings of People, I do hereby grant and declare, That no Person or Persons, inhabiting in this Province or Territories, who shall confess and acknowledge *One* almighty God, the Creator, Upholder and Ruler of the World; and professes him or themselves obliged to live quietly under the Civil Government, shall be in any Case molested or prejudiced, in his or their Person or Estate, because of his or their consciencious Persuasion or Practice, nor be compelled to frequent or maintain any religious Worship, Place

or Ministry, contrary to his or their Mind, or to do or suffer any other Act or Thing, contrary to their religious Persuasion.

AND that all Persons who also profess to believe in *Jesus Christ*, the Saviour of the World, shall be capable (notwithstanding their other Persuasions and Practices in Point of Conscience and Religion) to serve this Government in any Capacity, both legislatively and executively, he or they solemnly promising, when lawfully required, Allegiance to the King as Sovereign, and Fidelity to the Proprietary and Governor, and taking the Attests as now established by the Law made at *Newcastle*, in the Year *One Thousand and Seven Hundred*, entituled, *An Act directing the Attests of several Officers and Ministers*, as now amended and confirmed this present Assembly.

II.

FOR the well governing of this Province and Territories, there shall be an Assembly yearly chosen, by the Freemen thereof, to consist of *Four* Persons out of each County, of most Note for Virtue, Wisdom and Ability, (or of a greater Number at any Time, as the Governor and Assembly shall agree) upon the *First* Day of *October* for ever; and shall sit on the *Fourteenth* Day of the same Month, at *Philadelphia*, unless the Governor and Council for the Time being, shall see Cause to appoint another Place within the said Province or Territories: Which Assembly shall have Power to chuse a Speaker and other their Officers; and shall be Judges of the Qualifications and Elections of their own Members; sit upon their own Adjournments; appoint Committees; prepare Bills in order to pass into Laws; impeach Criminals, and redress Grievances; and shall have all other Powers and Privileges of an Assembly, according to the Rights of the free-born Subjects of *England*, and as is usual in any of the King's Plantations in *America*.

AND if any County or Counties, shall refuse or neglect to chuse their respective Representatives as aforesaid, or if chosen, do not meet to serve in Assembly, those who are so chosen and met, shall have the full Power of an Assembly, in as ample Manner as if all the Representatives had been chosen and met, provided they are not less than *Two Thirds* of the whole Number that ought to meet.

AND that the Qualifications of Electors and Elected, and all other Matters and Things relating to elections of Representatives to serve in Assemblies, though not herein particularly expressed, shall be and remain as by a Law of this Government, made at *Newcastle*, in the Year *One Thousand Seven Hundred*, entituled, *An Act to ascertain the Number of Members of Assembly, and to regulate the Elections*.

III.

THAT the Freemen in each respective County, at the Time and Place of Meeting for electing their Representatives to serve in Assembly, may as often as there shall be Occasion, chuse a double Number of Persons to present to the Governor for Sheriffs and Coroners, to serve for *Three* Years, if so long they behave themselves well; out of which respective Elections and Presentments, the Governor shall nominate and commissionate one for each of the said Offices, the *Third* Day after such Presentment, or else the *First* named in such Presentment, for each Office as aforesaid, shall stand and serve in that Office for the Time before respectively limited; and in case of Death or Default, such Vacancies shall be supplied by the Governor, to serve to the End of the said Term.

PROVIDED ALWAYS, That if the said Freemen shall at any Time neglect or decline to chuse a Person or Persons for either or both the aforesaid Offices, then, and in such Case, the Persons that are or shall be in the respective Offices of Sheriffs or Coroners, at the Time of Election, shall remain therein, until they shall be removed by another Election as aforesaid.

AND that the Justices of the respective Counties shall or may nominate and present to the Governor *Three* Persons, to serve for Clerk of the Peace for the said County, when there is a Vacancy, one of which the Governor shall commissionate within *Ten* Days after such Presentment, or else the *First* nominated shall serve in the said Office during good Behaviour.

IV.

THAT the Laws of this Government shall be in this Stile, viz. *By the Governor, with the Consent and Approbation of the Freemen in General Assembly met;* and shall be, after Confirmation by the Governor, forthwith recorded in the Rolls Office, and kept at *Philadelphia*, unless the Governor and Assembly shall agree to appoint another Place.

V.

THAT all Criminals shall have the same Privileges of Witnesses and Council as their Prosecutors.

VI.

THAT no Person or Persons shall or may, at any Time hereafter, be obliged to answer any Complaint, Matter or Thing whatsoever, relating to Property, before the Governor and Council, or in any other Place, but in ordinary Course of Justice, unless Appeals thereunto shall be hereafter by Law appointed.

VII.

THAT no Person within this Government, shall be licensed by the Governor to keep an Ordinary, Tavern, or House of publick Entertainment, but such who are first recommended to him, under the Hands of the Justices of the respective Counties, signed in open Court; which Justices are and shall be hereby impowered, to suppress and forbid any Person, keeping such Publick-House as aforesaid, upon their Misbehaviour, on such Penalties as the Law doth or shall direct; and to recommend others, from time to time, as they shall see Occasion.

VIII.

IF any Person, through Temptation or Melancholy, shall destroy himself, his Estate, real and personal, shall notwithstanding descend to his Wife and Children, or Relations, as if he had died a natural Death; and if any Person shall be destroyed or killed by Casualty or Accident, there shall be no Forfeiture to the Governor by Reason thereof.

AND no Act, Law or Ordinance whatsoever, shall at any Time hereafter, be made or done, to alter, change or diminish the Form or Effect of this Charter, or of any Part or Clause therein, contrary to the true Intent and Meaning thereof, without the Consent of the Governor for the Time being, and *Six* Parts of *Seven* of the Assembly met.

BUT, because the Happiness of Mankind depends so much upon the Enjoying of Liberty of their Consciences, as aforesaid, I do hereby solemnly declare, promise and grant, for me, my Heirs and Assigns, That the *First* Article of this Charter relating to Liberty of Conscience, and every Part and Clause therein, according to the true Intent and Meaning thereof, shall be kept and remain, without any Alteration, inviolably for ever.

AND LASTLY, I the said *William Penn*, Proprietary and Governor of the Province of *Pennsylvania*, and Territories thereunto belonging, for myself, my Heirs and Assigns, have solemnly declared, granted and confirmed, and do hereby solemnly declare, grant and confirm, That neither I, my Heirs or Assigns, shall procure or do any Thing or Things whereby the Liberties in this Charter contained and expressed, nor any Part thereof, shall be infringed or broken: And if any thing shall be procured or done, by any Person or Persons, contrary to these Presents, it shall be held of no Force or Effect.

IN WITNESS whereof, I the said *William Penn*, at *Philadelphia* in *Pennsylvania*, have unto this present Charter of Liberties, set my Hand and broad Seal, this *Twenty-Eighth* Day of *October*, in the Year of Our Lord *One Thousand Seven Hundred and One*, being the *Thirteenth* Year of the Reign of King WILLIAM the Third, over *England, Scotland, France*, and *Ireland*, &c., and the *Twenty-First* Year of my Government.

AND NOTWITHSTANDING the Closure and Test of this present Charter as aforesaid, I think fit to add this following Proviso thereunto, as Part of the same, *That is to say*, That notwithstanding any Clause or Clauses in the above-mentioned Charter, obliging the Province and Territories to join together in Legislation, I am content, and do

hereby declare, that if the Representatives of the Province and Territories shall not hereafter agree to join together in Legislation, and that the same shall be signified unto me, or my Deputy, in open Assembly, or otherwise, from under the Hands and Seals of the Representatives, for the Time being, of the Province and Territories, or the major part of either of them, at any Time within *Three* Years from the Date hereof, that in such Case, the Inhabitants of each of the *Three* Counties of this Province, shall not have less than *Eight* Persons to represent them in Assembly, for the Province; and the Inhabitants of the Town of *Philadelphia* (when the said Town is incorporated) *Two* Persons to represent them in Assembly; and the Inhabitants of each County in the Territories, shall have as many Persons to represent them in a distinct Assembly for the Territories, as shall be by them requested as aforesaid.

NOTWITHSTANDING which Separation of the Province and Territories, in Respect of Legislation, I do hereby promise, grant and declare, That the Inhabitants of both Province and Territories, shall separately enjoy all other Liberties, Privileges and Benefits, granted jointly to them in this Charter, any Law, Usage or Custom of this Government, heretofore made and practised, or any Law made and passed by this General Assembly, to the Contrary hereof, notwithstanding.

WILLIAM PENN.

This Charter of Privileges being distinctly read in Assembly, and the whole and every part thereof being approved and agreed to, by us, we do thankfully receive the same from our Proprietary and Governor, at Philadelphia, this Twenty-Eighth Day of October, One Thousand Seven Hundred and One. Signed on Behalf, and by Order of the Assembly,

per JOSEPH GROWDON, *Speaker.*
EDWARD SHIPPEN GRIFFITH OWEN
PHINEAS PEMBERTON CALEB PUSEY
SAMUEL CARPENTER THOMAS STORY
Proprietary and Governor's Council.

Reference: Francis Newton Thorpe (ed.), *The Federal and State Constitutions, Colonial Charters, and Other Organic Laws of the States,* Vol. I (Washington: GPO, 1909).

CHARTER OF NEW CASTLE, MAY 28, 1724

The Constitution, or System of Government, agreed to and resolved upon by the Representatives in full Convention of the Delaware State, formerly styled "The Government of the Counties of New Castle, Kent, and Sussex, upon Delaware," the said Representatives being chosen by the Freemen of the said State for that express Purpose.

ARTICLE 1. The government of the counties of New Castle, Kent and Sussex, upon Delaware, shall hereafter in all public and other writings be called The Delaware State.

ART. 2. The Legislature shall be formed of two distinct branches; they shall meet once or oftener in every year, and shall be called, "The General Assembly of Delaware."

ART. 3. One of the branches of the Legislature shall be called, "The House of Assembly," and shall consist of seven Representatives to be chosen for each county annually of such persons as are freeholders of the same.

ART. 4. The other branch shall be called "The council," and consist of nine members; three to be chosen for each county at the time of the first election of the assembly, who shall be freeholders of the county for which they are chosen, and be upwards of twenty-five years of age. At the end of one year after the general election, the councillor who had the smallest number of votes in each county shall be displaced, and the vacancies thereby occasioned supplied by the freemen of each county choosing the same or another person at a new election in manner aforesaid. At the end of two years after the first general election, the councillor who stood second in number of votes in each county shall be displaced, and the vacancies thereby occasioned supplied by a new election in manner aforesaid. And at the end of three years from the first general election, the councillor who had the greatest number of votes in each county shall be displaced, and the vacancies thereby occasioned supplied by a new election in manner aforesaid. And this rotation of a councillor being displaced at the end of three

years in each county, and his office supplied by a new choice, shall be continued afterwards in due order annually forever, whereby, after the first general election, a councillor will remain in trust for three years from the time of his being elected, and a councillor will be displaced, and the same or another chosen in each county at every election.

ART. 5. The right of suffrage in the election of members for both houses shall remain as exercised by law at present; and each house shall choose its own speaker, appoint its own officers, judge of the qualifications and elections of its own members, settle its own rules of proceedings, and direct writs of election for supplying intermediate vacancies. They may also severally expel any of their own members for misbehavior, but not a second time in the same sessions for the same offence, if reelected; and they shall have all other powers necessary for the legislature of a free and independent State.

ART. 6. All money-bills for the support of government shall originate in the house of assembly, and may be altered, amended, or rejected by the legislative council. All other bills and ordinances may take rise in the house of assembly or legislative council, and may be altered, amended, or rejected by either.

ART. 7. A president or chief magistrate shall be chosen by joint ballot of both houses, to be taken in the house of assembly, and the box examined by the speakers of each house in the presence of the other members, and in case the numbers for the two highest in votes should be equal, then the speaker of the council shall have an additional casting voice, and the appointment of the person who has the majority of votes shall be entered at large on the minutes and journals of each house, and a copy thereof on parchment, certified and signed by the speakers respectively, and sealed with the great seal of the State, which they are hereby authorized to affix, shall be delivered to the person so chosen president, who shall continue in that office three years, and until the sitting of the next general assembly and no longer, nor be eligible until the expiration of three years after he shall have been out of that office. An adequate but moderate salary shall be settled on him during his continuance in office. He may draw for such sums of money as shall be appropriated by the general assembly, and be accountable to them for the same; he may, by and with the advice of the privy council, lay embargoes or prohibit the exportation of any commodity for any time not exceeding thirty days in the recess of the general assembly; he shall have the power of granting pardons or reprieves, except where the prosecution shall be carried on by the house of assembly, or the law shall otherwise direct, in which cases no pardon or reprieve shall be granted, but by a resolve of the house of assembly, and may exercise all the other executive powers of government, limited and restrained as by this constitution is mentioned, and according to the laws of the State. And on his death, inability, or absence from the State, the speaker of the legislative council for the time being shall be vice-president, and in case of his death, inability, or absence from the State, the speaker of the house of assembly shall have the powers of a president, until a new nomination is made by the general assembly.

Art. 8. A privy council, consisting of four members, shall be chosen by ballot, two by the legislative council and two by the house of assembly: *Provided*, That no regular officer of the army or navy in the service and pay of the continent, or of this, or of any other State, shall be eligible; and a member of the legislative council or of the house of assembly being chosen of the privy council, and accepting thereof, shall thereby lose his seat. Three members shall be a quorum, and their advice and proceedings shall be entered of record, and signed by the members present, (to any part of which any member may enter his dissent,) to be laid before the general assembly when called for by them. Two members shall be removed by ballot, one by the legislative council and one by the house of assembly, at the end of two years, and those who remain the next year after, who shall severally be ineligible for the

three next years. The vacancies, as well as those occasioned by death or incapacity, shall be supplied by new elections in the same manner; and this rotation of a privy councillor shall be continued afterwards in due order annually forever. The president may by summons convene the privy council at any time when the public exigencies may require, and at such place as he shall think most convenient, when and where they are to attend accordingly.

Art. 9. The president, with the advice and consent of the privy council, may embody the militia, and act as captain-general and commander-in-chief of them, and the other military force of this State, under the laws of the same.

Art. 10. Either house of the general assembly may adjourn themselves respectively. The president shall not prorogue, adjourn, or dissolve the general assembly, but he may, with the advice of the privy council, or on the application of a majority of either house, call them before the time they shall stand adjourned; and the two houses shall always sit at the same time and place, for which purpose immediately after every adjournment the speaker of the house of assembly shall give notice to the speaker of the other house of the time to which the house of assembly stands adjourned.

Art. 11. The Delegates for Delaware to the Congress of the United States of America shall be chosen annually, or superseded in the mean time, by joint ballot of both houses in the general assembly.

Art. 12. The president and general assembly shall by joint ballot appoint three justices of the supreme court for the State, one of whom shall be chief justice, and a judge of admiralty, and also four justices of the courts of common pleas and orphans' courts for each county, one of whom in each court shall be styled "*chief justice*," (and in case of division on the ballot the president shall have an additional casting voice,) to be commissioned by the president under the great seal, who shall continue in office during good behavior; and during the time the justices of the said supreme court and courts of common pleas remain in office, they shall hold none other except in the militia. Any one of the justices of either of said courts shall have power, in case of the noncoming of his brethren, to open and adjourn the court. An adequate fixed but moderate salary shall be settled on them during their continuance in office. The president and privy council shall appoint the secretary, the attorney-general, registers for the probate of wills and granting letters of administration, registers in chancery, clerks of the courts of common pleas and orphans' courts, and clerks of the peace, who shall be commissioned as aforesaid, and remain in office during five years, if they behave themselves well; during which time the said registers in chancery and clerks shall not be justices of either of the said courts of which they are officers, but they shall have authority to sign all writs by them issued, and take recognizances of bail. The justices of the peace shall be nominated by the house of assembly; that is to say, they shall name twenty-four persons for each county, of whom the president, with the approbation of the privy council, shall appoint twelve, who shall be commissioned as aforesaid, and continue in office during seven years, if they behave themselves well; and in case of vacancies, or if the legislature shall think proper to increase the number, they shall be nominated and appointed in like manner. The members of the legislative and privy councils shall be justices of the peace for the whole State, during their continuance in trust; and the justices of the courts of common pleas shall be conservators of the peace in their respective counties.

ART. 13. The justices of the courts of common pleas and orphans' courts shall have the power of holding inferior courts of chancery, as heretofore, unless the legislature shall otherwise direct.

ART. 14. The clerks of the supreme court shall be appointed by the chief justice thereof, and the recorders of deeds, by the justices of the courts of common pleas for each county severally, and commissioned by the president, under the great seal, and continue in office five years, if they behave themselves well.

ART. 15. The sheriffs and coroners of the respective counties shall be chosen annually, as heretofore; and any person, having served three years as sheriff, shall be ineligible for three years after; and the president and privy council shall have the appointment of such of the two candidates, returned for said offices of sheriff and coroner, as they shall think best qualified, in the same manner that the governor heretofore enjoyed this power.

ART. 16. The general assembly, by joint ballot, shall appoint the generals and field-officers, and all other officers in the army or navy of this State; and the president may appoint, during pleasure, until otherwise directed by the legislature, all necessary civil officers not hereinbefore mentioned.

ART. 17. There shall be an appeal from the supreme court of Delaware, in matters of law and equity, to a court of seven persons, to consist of the president for the time being, who shall preside therein, and six others, to be appointed, three by the legislative council, and three by the house of assembly, who shall continue in office during good behavior, and be commissioned by the president, under the great seal; which court shall be styled the "*court of appeals*," and have all the authority and powers heretofore given by law in the last resort to the King in council, under the old government. The secretary shall be the clerk of this court; and vacancies therein occasioned by death or incapacity, shall be supplied by new elections, in manner aforesaid.

ART. 18. The justices of the supreme court and courts of common pleas, the members of the privy council, the secretary, the trustees of the loan office, and clerks of the court of common pleas, during their continuance in office, and all persons concerned in any army or navy contracts, shall be ineligible to either house of assembly; and any member of either house accepting of any other of the offices hereinbefore mentioned (excepting the office of a justice of the peace) shall have his seat thereby vacated, and a new election shall be ordered.

ART. 19. The legislative council and assembly shall have the power of making the great seal of this State, which shall be kept by the president, or, in his absence, by the vice-president, to be used by them as occasion may require. It shall be called "*The Great Seal of the Delaware State*," and shall be affixed to all laws and commissions.

ART. 20. Commissions shall run in the name of "The Delaware State," and bear test by the president. Writs shall run in the same manner, and bear test in the name of the chief-justice, or justice first named in the commissions for the several courts, and be sealed with the public seals of such courts. Indictments shall conclude, "*Against the peace and dignity of the State.*"

ART. 21. In case of vacancy of the offices above directed to be filled by the president and general assembly, the president and privy council may appoint others in their stead until there shall be a new election.

ART. 22. Every person who shall be chosen a member of either house, or appointed to any office or place of trust, before taking his seat, or entering upon the execution of his office, shall take the following oath, or affirmation, if conscientiously scrupulous of taking an oath, to wit:

"I, A B, will bear true allegiance to the Delaware State, submit to its constitution and laws, and do no act wittingly whereby the freedom thereof may be prejudiced."

And also make and subscribe the following declaration, to wit:

"I, A B, do profess faith in God the Father, and in Jesus Christ His only Son, and in the Holy Ghost, one God, blessed for evermore; and I do acknowledge the holy scripture of the Old and New Testament to be given by divine inspiration."

And all officers shall also take an oath of office.

ART. 23. The president, when he is out of office, and within eighteen months after, and all others offending against the State, either by maladministration, corruption, or other means, by which the safety of the Commonwealth may be endangered, within eighteen months after the offence committed, shall be impeachable by the house of assembly before the legislative council; such impeachment to be prosecuted by the attorney-general, or such other person or persons as the house of assembly may appoint, according to the laws of the land. If found guilty, he or they shall be either forever disabled to hold any office under government, or removed from office *pro tempore*, or subjected to such pains and penalties as the laws shall direct. And all officers shall be removed on conviction of misbehavior at common law, or on impeachment, or upon the address of the general assembly.

ART. 24. All acts of assembly in force in this State on the 15th day of May last (and not hereby altered, or contrary to the resolutions of Congress or of the late house of assembly of this State) shall so continue, until altered or repealed by the legislature of this State, unless where they are temporary, in which case they shall expire at the times respectively limited for their duration.

ART. 25. The common law of England, as well as so much of the statute law as has been heretofore adopted in practice in this State, shall remain in force, unless they shall be altered by a future law of the legislature; such parts only excepted as are repugnant to the rights and privileges contained in this constitution, and the declaration of rights, &c., agreed to by this convention.

ART. 26. No person hereafter imported into this State from Africa ought to be held in slavery under any pretence whatever; and no negro, Indian, or mulatto slave ought to be brought into this State, for sale, from any part of the world.

ART. 27. The first election for the general assembly of this State shall be held on the 21st day of October next, at the court-houses in the several counties, in the manner heretofore used in the election of the assembly, except as to the choice of inspectors and assessors, where assessors have not been chosen on the 16th day of September, instant, which shall be made on the morning of the day of election, by the electors, inhabitants of the respective hundreds in each county. At which time the sheriffs and coroners, for the said counties respectively, are to be elected; and the present sheriffs of the counties of Newcastle and Kent may be rechosen to that office until the 1st day of October, A.D. 1779; and the present sheriff for the county of Sussex may be rechosen to that office until the 1st day of October, A.D. 1778, provided the freemen think proper to reëlect them at every general election: and the present sheriffs and coroners, respectively, shall continue to exercise their offices as heretofore, until the sheriffs and coroners, to be elected on the said 21st day of October, shall be commissioned and sworn into office. The members of the legislative council and assembly shall meet, for transacting the business of the State, on the 28th day of October next, and continue in office until the 1st day of October, which will be in the year 1777; on which day, and on the 1st day of October in each year forever after, the legislative council, assembly, sheriffs, and coroners shall be chosen by ballot, in manner directed by the several laws of this State, for regulating elections of members of assembly and sheriffs and coroners; and the general assembly shall meet on the 20th day of the same month for the transacting the business of the State; and if any of the said 1st and 20th days of October should be Sunday, then, and in such case, the elections shall be held, and the general assembly meet, the next day following.

ART. 28. To prevent any violence or force being used at the said elections, no person shall come armed to any of them, and no muster of the militia shall be made on that day; nor shall any battalion or company give in their votes immediately succeeding each other, if any other voter, who offers to vote, objects thereto; nor shall any battalion or company, in the pay of the continent, or of this or any other State, be suffered to remain at the time and place of holding the said elections, nor within one mile of the said places respectively, for twenty-four hours before the opening said elections, nor within twenty-four hours after the same are closed, so as in any manner to impede

the freely and conveniently carying on the said election: *Provided always*, That every elector may, in a peaceable and orderly manner, give in his vote on the said day of election.

ART. 29. There shall be no establishment of any one religious sect in this State in preference to another; and no clergyman or preacher of the gospel, of any denomination, shall be capable of holding any civil office in this State, or of being a member of either of the branches of the legislature, while they continue in the exercise of the pastorial function.

ART. 30. No article of the declaration of rights and fundamental rules of this State, agreed to by this convention, nor the first, second, fifth, (except that part thereof that relates to the right of suffrage,) twenty-sixth, and twenty-ninth articles of this constitution, ought ever to be violated on any pretence whatever. No other part of this constitution shall be altered, changed, or diminished without the consent of five parts in seven of the assembly, and seven members of the legislative council.

GEORGE READ, *President*.
Attest:
JAMES BOOTH, *Secretary*.
Friday, September 10, 1776.

Reference: Francis Newton Thorpe (ed.), *The Federal and State Constitutions, Colonial Charters, and Other Organic Laws of the States*, Vol. III (Washington: GPO, 1909).

CONSTITUTION OF DELAWARE, 1776

GEORGE by the Grace of God of Great Britain, France and Ireland King Defender of the Faith &c

To whom these presents

shall come Greeting—

WHEREAS our loving Subjects John French Robert Gordon Samuel Lowman Richard Grafton David French Thomas Janiver Rowland Fitz-Gerald &c with many other Inhabitants in our Town of New Castle appertaining to our Government of the Counties of New Castle Kent and Sussex upon Delaware in North America did by their Humble Petition presented unto Sr. William Keith Barronet by our Royal Approbation & appointment Governour of the said Counties on behalfe of themselves the freeholders & Inhabitants of the said Town Sett forth that the said Town of New Castle is the most ancient Settlement on the Bay and River of Delaware that it has been long Distinguished as a port where a Collector of the Customs has been from time to time appointed and constantly resided and Lastly that it is the Seat of Government in the said Counties where the General Assembly is usually conveened all which give the Petitioners hopes that their Supplication and request tho' not to be Granted of right but Grace may nevertheless prove Successful and therefore Humbly pray for our Royal Grant by Letters Patents and the Great Seal of the Government of our said Counties to Incorporate the Free-holders and Inhabitants of the said Town of New Castle into a Body Corporate & Politick with perpetual Succession by what name our sd Governour shall think fitt As Also to Grant such Immunities and privileges as may be thought requisite for the well ordering and ruleing thereof And We being Graciously inclined to promote Trade and Industry with rule and good order amongst our Loving Subjects by granting their reasonable request in that behalf—THEREFORE KNOW YE That We of our Special Grace certain knowledge and meer Motion Have Given Granted Constituted Appointed Ratified & Confirmed— And Do by these presents Give Grant Constitute Appoint Ratify and Confirm unto the said John French Robert Gordon Samuel Lowman Richard Grafton David French Thomas Janvier Rowland Fitz-Gerald and the rest of the Free-holders and Inhabitants of the said Town of New Castle to them and their Successors forever within the Limits Boundaries & Precincts thereof as they are herein after mentioned and described (To Wit). All that Tract of Land—BEGINNING at the Town of New Castle and running up the River Delaware side to the mouth of Christiana Creek and from thence up the said Creek to the Bridge and from the said Christiana Bridge by a straight line to the mouth of Red Lyon Creek where it falls into Delaware River at Hamburgh Island and from thence up the said River—Delaware to the said Town of New Castle the place of beginning To be from henceforth called—known and distinguished by the name of the City of New Castle

and the Libertys and precincts thereof and that they the said John French &c and all other the Freeholders and now Inhabitants our natural born Subjects that follow any manual Trade Mistery or Occupation within the said Town & Liberties and their Successors freeholders and freemen or that shall be hereafter made so by Virtue of these presents shall from henceforth be One Body Corporate & Politick in Fact and in name To be from henceforth called known and distinguished by the Name of the City of New Castle and the Liberties and precincts thereof as aforesaid And for the better ordering ruling and Governing the said City and precincts by encreasing Trade and Industry And by depressing Idleness Vice and Immorality We have of our Special Grace certain knowledge and meer Motion Given Granted released Confirmed Constituted Appointed & Ordained And by these presents Do for Us our Heirs and Successors Give Grant ratify Confirm Constitute Appoint and Ordain That there shall from thenceforth be in the said City a Mayor Recorder Six Aldermen a Town Clerk Six Assistants a Chamberlain or Treasurer a Serjeant at Mace Two Constables & Two Overseers of the Poor to be Assigned Nominated and Appointed as is herein after directed and mentioned Which Mayor Recorder Aldermen and Commonality and their Successors now are and at all times hereafter Shall be One Body Corporate and Politick Which We Do by these presents for Us & Our Successors Create Constitute Make and Ordain And That they the said Body Corporate and politick have a perpetual Succession in Deed Fact and name to be known and distinguished in all Deed Grants Bargains Sales Evidences Writings Minuments or otherwise howsoever by the Name of the Mayor Recorder Aldermen & Commonality of the City of New Castle And That the said Mayor Recorder Aldermen and Commonality by the name aforesaid Shall be persons able and in Law Capable to have get Acquire and to receive and possess Lands Tenements Hereditaments Jurisdictions and Franchises as well without as within the said City & precincts to them and their Successors in fee Simple for term of Life Lives or Years or otherwise And also Goods

Chattels and other things—of what Nature and Quality soever Also to Grant Bargain Sell Lett or Assign such Lands Tenements Hereditaments Goods and Chattles and Do all other things by the Name aforesaid So that the Yearly Income of such Lands Tenements and Hereditaments So to be acquired and purchased by the said Body Corporate and Politick Do not exceed the Sum of One thousand pounds lawfull Money of our Kingdom of Great Brittain And We Do by these presents for Us and our Successors Give Grant Ratify & Confirm unto the Said Body politick and Corporate That they shall be persons able and in Law Capable by the Name aforesaid to Sue and be Sued Implead and be Impleaded Appear & be Appeared unto Defend and be Defended in all and Singular Suits Actions Controversies Complaints Demands Causes and matters whatsoever in any of the Courts of Judicature of Law and Equity within the Government of Our said Counties of New Castle Kent and Sussex upon Delaware And also That the Mayor Recorder Aldermen and Commonality of the said City of New Castle and their Successors Shall and may forever hereafter have One common Seal engraved with a hand grasping an Anchor over which shall be put these words— NEC TOLLITUR UNDIS—to serve for the Sealing of all and Singular the Affairs and business touching concerning and relateing to the said Corporation MOREOVER KNOW YE That We have assigned named Ordained Constituted and Appointed And Do by these presents for us and our Successors Assign Name Ordain constitute and Appoint Our well beloved John French Esqr to be present Mayor of the said City and Clerk of the Market thereof hereby Giving & Granting unto him the said John French present Mayor and Clerk of the Market and unto the Succeeding Mayors—Clerks of the Market power and Authority to Do Execute & perform whatsoever relates and appertains to the said Offices— and therein to remain and continue till an other fitt person be Assigned, Nominated Appointed and Sworn into the said office as is herein aftermentioned and directed And We Have Assigned Named Constituted Ordained and Appointed

And by these presents Assign Name Constitute and Appoint Our well beloved David French Esqr to be Recorder of the said City to Do and perform all and Singular the Matters and things which unto the said office of Recorder doth appertain and belong to enjoy and continue in the same untill an other fitt person be Assigned Appointed and Sworn into the said Office And We have Assigned named Ordained Constituted and appointed And Do by these presents Assign Name Ordain Constitute and Appoint Our well beloved Samuel Lowman Robert Gordon Thomas Janvier Richard Grafton Anthony Houston and John Welch Esqrs Citizens of the said City to be the present Aldermen of the said City to remain and continue to Execute the Offices of Aldermen untill other fitt persons be Elected and Sworn into the said Offices of Aldermen as is herein after mentioned and directed And We have assigned Ordained Constituted and Appointed And Do by these presents Assign Ordain Constitute & Appoint the present prothonotary of the Court of common pleas for the County of New Castle to be Town Clerk of the said City to continue to Execute and perform by himself or a Sufficient Deputy for whom he shall be answerable all things which unto the said Office of Town Clerk doth belong and Appertain until another fitt person be Assigned Nominated Constituted Ordained and Appointed in his Stead And We have Assigned Nominated Ordained Constituted and Appointed And by these presents Do Assign Nominate Constitute Ordain and Appoint James Sykes, John Finney, Wessell Alrichs, David Miller John Vangezel & Richard Bermingham Citizens of the sd City to be the present Assistants of the same to continue to Execute and perform the Offices of Assistants untill other fitt persons shall be Elected and Sworn into the said offices— And We have Assigned Named Constituted Ordained & Appointed And Do by these presents Assign Name Constitute Ordain and Appoint Our well beloved Robert Gordon Esqr to be Chamberlain or Treasurer untill another fitt person be elected and Sworn into the same And We Have Assigned Named Constituted Ordained and Appointed And Do by these presents Assign

Name Constitute Ordain & Appoint That the Sheriffs & Corroners of the County of New Castle from Year to Year respectively shall also be the Sherifs & Coroners within the said City & Liberties and precincts thereof And We have Assigned Named Constituted Ordained and Appointed And Do by these presents Assign Name Constitute Ordain & Appoint John Russell to be Serjeant or Marshall at Mace of the sd City to continue to Execute and perform the sd Office of Sergeant at Mace untill an other fitt person be assigned Appointed and Sworn into the sd Office And We Will And Do for Us and our Successors by these presents Give & Grant unto the said Mayor and Commonality of the said City of New Castle to their Successors from henceforth That the present and Succeeding Mayors of the said City Shall and may have a Mace born before him and them And We have Assigned Named Constituted Ordained & Appointed And Do by these Presents Assign Name Constitute Ordain & Appoint John Rees and Nicholas Meers to be present Over-seers of the poor of the said City untill other fitt persons be Elected and chosen into the said Offices And We have assigned Nominated Constituted Ordained and Appointed And Do by these presents Assign Nominate Constitute Ordain and Appoint James Lloyd and John Kent to be the present Constables of the said City to continue to execute and perform their respective offices untill other fitt persons be Elected and Sworn into the same And We have Given Granted Released & Confirmed And We Do by these presents for Us and Our Successors— Give Grant ratify and Confirm unto the Mayor and Commonality of the said City of New Castle and to their Successors from henceforth That the Mayor Recorder Aldermen and Assistants of the said City shall be called the Common Council of the sd City of New Castle and Liberties or precincts thereof And the Mayor Recorder Aldermen & Assistants aforesaid or the Major part of them of which the Mayor to be One with two at least of the Aldermen shall and may have full power & Authority from time to time to hold the there as occasion shall be make Laws Ordinances Constitutions in Writing and Common

Council within the Courthouse or City Hall of the said City and the same to Alter Diminish and reform from time to time as to them shall seem necessary and convenient for the well Ordering ruling and Governing of the said City and precincts thereof and of the several Tradesmen Victuallers and Artificers and all other the Inhabitants within the Limits of the said City & Liberties or precincts thereof PROVIDED ALWAYS That such Law Constitutions or Ordinances to be hereafter made within the sd City as aforesaid be not repugnant to our prerogative or to that of our Successors or to the Laws of our Kingdom of Great Brittian or to the Laws of the Government of our said Counties anything in these presents to ye contrary in any wise notwithstanding And all such Laws Constitutions & Ordinances—so as aforesaid to be made by the Common Council for the better Ordering and Disposing of the affairs relating to the Corporation aforesaid shall only be binding upon the Inhabitants within the said City and Precincts for the Space of Six Months and unless they be allowed of and Approved by the Governour or Commander in chief of the said Counties for the time being unto whom they shall be transmitted for Confirmation within Six Weeks after they are made & Ordained by the Common Council aforesaid And that such of the Laws Constitutions and Ordinances as aforesaid as shall be approved by our said Governour or Commander in chief shall remain and continue in force untill they are altered or repealed by the Common Council of the City aforesaid And We have Given & Granted And Do by these presents for Us and our Successors Give and Grant power and Authority unto the Common Council of the said City for the time being that they shall or may Make Limit or Ordain Impose or tax reasonable fines and amerciaments against all persons Offending against such Laws Constitutions and Ordinances or either of them to be made and established as aforesaid and all & every such fines Impositions & Amerciaments shall & may take demand require and levy by Warrant under the common seal of the said City for the use and benefit of the Mayor and Commonality of the sd City and their

Successors by distress and sale of the offenders Goods and Chattles if found within the said City or precincts rendering such offender or offenders the over-plus And We Have Given & Granted And Do by these presents for Us & Our Successors Give and Grant unto our said Governour or Commander in chief OF OUR SAID COUNTIES and to the succeeding Governours or Commanders in chief of the same for the time being Annually on the first Tuesday of the Month of May from henceforth by Notification under his or their hands to the Aldermen and Assistants Elect of the said City the Assigning Nominating and Appointing a fit person being a freeholder of the said City who either then did bear or some time before had born the Office of an Alderman within the same to be Mayor and Clerk of the Market for the year ensuing which person so Assigned Nominated and Appointed shall within ten days next after such his Appointment before the Governour or Commander in Chief of the said Counties for ye time being or before such persons as shall be by him the said Governour or Commander in Chief impowered to administer the same take his Corporal Oath for the faithful discharge of the said Offices of Mayor and Clerk of the Market of the said City which person shall remain & continue to execute and perform the said Offices of Mayor & Clerk of the Market untill another fitt person shall be appointed and Sworn as aforesaid into the said Offices And We have Willed Given and Granted And Do by these presents for Us & Our Successors Will Give and Grant that the Recorder & Town Clerk of the sd City of New Castle shall be persons of good Capacity and such as are Inhabitants of the said City who shall respectively hold and enjoy the said Office by respective Commissions from Us & from Our Successors under the Great Seal of the said Counties by Virtue whereof they shall hold and possess the said Offices respectively untill other fitt persons be Assigned Appointed and Sworn into the same in manner aforesaid And We have Given Granted ratified and Confirmed and by these presents Do for Us and Our Successors Give Grant ratify and Confirm unto the present Mayor Recorder Aldermen and

Assistants above named to the respective Successors in the said Offices Annually on the said first tuseday of the month of May power & Authority to Assemble and meet together at the Court House or City Hall of the sd City of New Castle and then and there by the plurality of votes of the persons aforesaid then and there present to elect and choose Six men of good Capacity out of the principal Freeholders to be Aldermen of the said City for the Year ensuing And We have Given and Granted And Do by these presents for Us & Our Successors Give and Grant unto all the Freeholders and Freemen of the said City & precincts full power and Authority to Assemble and meet together on the said first tuseday of the Month of May Annually in the said Court House or City Hall of New Castle immediately after the Election of persons for Aldermen as aforesaid and then and there to Elect and choose by plurality of Votes six persons of good Capacity Freeholders or Inhabitants of the said City to be Assistants for the Year Ensuing Also then and there to Elect and choose one fitt person being a Freeholder or Inhabitant of the said City to be Chamberlain or Treasurer for the Year ensuing Also then and there as aforesaid to Elect and choose Two fit persons Inhabitants of the said City or precincts to be Overseers of ye poor within the same for the Year ensuing Also then and there as aforesaid to Elect and choose two fitt persons Inhabitants of the said City or precincts to be Constables for the said Year Ensuing all which persons whatsoever Elected and chosen at the times and places and in manner aforesaid shall each of them respectively be and appear on the first Tuseday of the Month of June at the Court House or City Hall of New Castle aforesaid by ten of the Clock in the forenoon then and there before the Mayor or Recorder of the said City each & every of them so elected & chosen shall take their Corporal Oath for the Faithfull Discharge of that Office into which they were so elected & chosen respectively and shall therein remain & continue untill other fitt persons shall be Elected and Sworn into the same in manner aforesaid And We Do for us and our Successors by these presents Give and Grant unto the present and Succeeding Mayors of the said City That he the said Mayor for the time being by and with the Advice of the Recorder and Aldermen or the Majority of them shall from time to time have the Nomination and Appointment of a Marshall or Serjeant at Mace being an Inhabitant of the said City which Nomination and Appointment shall be granted to the said Marshall or Serjeant at Mace from the Mayor under the Seal of the sd City and he shall take his Corporal Oath before the Mayor or Recorder faithfully to Execute the said Office untill another fitt person shall be Appointed & Sworn in his Stead And We Will and Appoint by these presents for us and our Successors That upon Neglect or refusal of Any of the Overseers of the Poor or Constables so Elected and chosen as aforesaid to take their respective Oaths for the faithfull discharge of their respective Offices at the time & place afore sd every such person so neglecting or refusing shall forfeit the Sum of Five Pounds Current Money to be levied and employed as Amerciaments and fines above mentioned—And on any Vacancy which shall happen in the last mentioned Offices there shall be other persons Elected and chosen into the same by Common Council of the said City to serve until the next annual Election and the persons last Chosen shall be Subject to the like Fines and penalties on any Neglect or refusal as those immediately before them were and others shall again be Elected and chosen into the said Offices in manner aforesaid And We have Given Granted Appointed ratified & Confirmed And Do by these presents for Us and our Successors Give Grant Appoint ratify and Confirm unto the said John French Esqr present Mayor David French Esqr Recorder And Samuel Lowman Robert Gordon Thomas Janvier Richard Graffton Anthony Houston and John Welch Esqrs present Aldermen of the City of New Castle and the Succeeding Mayors Recorders and Aldermen of the same shall be keepers of the peace of Us and our Successors & Justice to hear and to determine Causes within the sd City and Liberties and precincts thereof and that they or any three of them whereof the Mayor or Recorder to be one shall and may forever hereafter have the power and

Authority by Virtue of these presents to hear and determine all manner of petty Larceny's riots routs extortions or other Trespasses & Offences whatsoever within the said City or Precincts and Liberties thereof from time to time arising or happening or which may arise & happen or that doth in any way belong to the Offices of Justices of the Peace and the correction & punishment of Offences aforesaid and every of them according to Law to do execute and perform and all other things as fully and amply as to the Commission of the Peace Assigned and to be Assigned for the keeping of the Peace in any of the said Counties doth or may belong And We Do by these presents Assign Nominate and Appoint the Prothonotary of the Court of Common Pleas for the County of New Castle present Town Clerk and his Successors in the Office of Town Clerk to be Clerk of the Peace to be holden before the Mayor Recorder and Aldermen of the said City of New Castle and precincts and Liberties thereof And We Do by these presents for us and our Successors Command require & Strictly Charge That the Sherif and Coroner of the County and City of New Castle for the time being Town Clerk of the Peace and pleas Marshall or Serjeant at Mace Constables and every of the Subordinate Officers for the time being within the sd City and precincts jointly & severally as cause shall require that they attend upon the Mayor Recorder and Aldermen of the said City for the time being according to the Duty of their respective Offices and places & the precepts Warrants and process of them and every of them to execute and perform as appertaineth and belongeth to be executed and performed And We Do by these presents for us and our Successors Give and Grant unto the Mayor Recorder and Aldermen of the said City and to their Successors as Justices of the Peace from time to time by Virtue of their or any of their Warrants all & every person or persons for High Treason or Suspicion thereof Malefactors for fellonies or for other Crimes Misdemeanors and breaches of the peace of us & our Successors that shall be apprehended within the sd City or Liberties & precincts thereof That they the sd Mayor Recorder and Aldermen or any of them as Justices aforesaid shall and may send and commit or cause to be sent and committed to the common Goal in said City there to remain and be kept in safe custody by the Keeper or keepers of the sd Goal for ye time being or his or their Deputy's until such offender or offenders shall be from thence delivered by course of Law And We Do by these presents for us and our Successors Strictly require & charge and Command the Keeper or Keepers of the said Goal in the sd City for the time being and his or their Deputies to receive and to take into safe Custody and to keep all & Singular such person or persons so apprehended or to be apprehended sent and committed by Warrant of the said Justices or either of them as aforesaid untill he or they so sent & committed to the said Gaol shall be from thence delivered by due Course of Law And We Do by these presents for us & our Successors Give Grant ratify and Confirm unto the present Mayor Recorder and Aldermen of the sd City and to their Successors or to any three of them whereof the Mayor or Recorder to be One that they shall and may have hold and keep within the sd City for the Town and precincts thereof on every first tuseday of the Month One Court of Common Pleas for all Actions of Debt Trespass on the case detinue Ejectment or other personal Actions which Mayor Recorder and Aldermen or any three of them whereof ye Mayor or Recorder to be one shall hear and determine such pleas and Actions and Judgements give and Executions thereupon Award and in General shall Do and perform every thing relating thereunto which unto Justice according to Law doth appertain or belong as fully and amply as any of the inferiour Courts of pleas can or ought to do in such like case—within any of our said Counties for ye better Ordering of the Citizens of the said City and Liberties Our Will is And We Do by these presents for Us and our Successors Create Appoint and Ordain That all our Natural born Subjects Free holders or Inhabitants within the said City of New Castle and Liberties thereof that follow any Trade Mistery or Occupation and every of them shall from henceforth be and are hereby Created and made free Citizens of the same And We Do by these presents for Us and

our Successors Give and Grant to the Mayor Recorder and Aldermen of the said City or any three of them whereof the Mayor to be one That they shall and may from time to time by an Instrument of freedom under ye common Seal make and Ordain such persons as they shall think fitt free Citizens of the said City and Liberties No Person nor persons whatsoever other than such as are hereby Constituted and made free Citizens of the sd City of New Castle or that has been Admitted thereunto in manner aforesaid shall presume to Use or Occupy any Trade Art or Mistery within the said City and precincts thereof except during the time of publick fairs only, and in case any person or persons who are not made free Citizens by Virtue of these presents or that shall not be admitted thereunto in manner aforesaid shall at any time or times hereafter Use or exercise any Trade Mistery or manual occupation or shall Sell or Expose to sale any manner of Goods Wares or Merchandises whatsoever by retail within the said City or precincts thereof no fair being then held in the same And shall persist to do so after Warning to him or them given by Order of the Mayor of the said City of New Castle for the time being at the place where such person or persons shall Use such Trade Mistery or Manual Occupation or shall sell or Expose to sale such Goods Wares or Merchandises as aforesaid by retail then and in such case it shall and may be Lawfull for the Mayor of the sd City for the time being to cause such Shop or Vendue to be Shutt up and also to impose a reasonable fine on the party offending not exceeding Five Pounds for each offense And the same fine or fines to Levy and take by Warrant under ye common seal of the sd City by distress and Sale of the offenders Goods and Chattles rendering ye overplus if any to the Owners all which fines so Levied and recovered shall be to and for ye only Use and behoof of the Mayor and Commonality of the said City of New Castle for the time being and their Successors forever without rendering or being accountable for the same to us or our Successors And We Will That all persons hereafter to be made free of the sd City as aforesaid Shall and do pay for the Use of the Mayor and Commonality of the said City of New Castle & their Successors at their Admission to be Citizens or free men such Sum or Sums as shall hereafter be Settled and Agreed upon by the common Council of the said City not exceeding the Sum of Five Pounds for each persons freedom And We Do by these presents for us and our Successors Give Grant ratify and confirm unto the Mayor Aldermen & Commonality of the City of New Castle and to their Successors for ever hereafter to hold and keep two Market Days weekly throughout the year yearly and every year, to wit, on every Wednesday and saturday of every week excepting when they shall happen on such holy days as are appointed by publick Authority to be kept holy and the said Weekly Market shall be held and kept in the said City at the Market place near the Court house or City Hall and in no other place of sd City Whatsoever And We do by these presents for us and our Successors Give Grant Ratify and Confirm unto the Mayor & Commonality of said City of New Castle power and Authority to provide and keep just and true Standarts of Weights and Measures agreeable to those appointed & used in that part of our Kingdom of Great Brittain called England Hereby Strictly charging and Commanding the Clerk of the Market for the time being to make due inspection within the said City That no Goods Wares Merchandises Liquors or other things of what kind or Nature soever be sold within the said City and precincts but by weight and Measure agreeable to the afore sd Standarts under such reasonable fines and forfeitures to be imposed levied and applied as other fines and forfeitures before mentioned and as shall hereafter be Agreed upon by the common Council of the sd City not exceeding five pounds for each offense And We Do for us and our Successors by these presents Give Grant Ratify and Confirm unto the sd Corporation and City of New Castle and Liberties and precincts thereof that they shall be from henceforth represented in the General Assembly of our said Counties by two Members to be by the Majority of ye Freeholders & Freemen of the said City and precincts annually chosen to Sitt & Vote in the House of the representatives of the Freemen of the said Counties And We have Given and

Granted And Do by these presents for Us and Successors Give and Grant to all the Freeholders and Freemen of the sd City and precincts full Power and Authority to Assemble and meet together on the Second day of the Month of October annually in the said Court House or City Hall of New Castle and then and there to Elect and choose by plurality of Votes two good and Sufficient Men of their Number to represent the sd City in the General Assembly of our said Counties as aforesaid which Election of the representatives yearly of the said City shall be certified by a return of ye names of ye persons so Elected as aforesaid under ye hands of the Mayor or Recorder and the Common Seal of the said City And Lastly We have and do by these presents for us and our Successors Give Grant Ratify and Confirm unto the sd Mayor & Commonality them or any of them as if the said Powers Authority Liberties Immunities privileges & Franchises whatsoever were herein or hereby more fully and better expressed according to the true intent & meaning of these presents And that no Officer or Officers of us or of any of our Successors should molest or disturb the sd Mayor or Commonality of the said City in the quiet enjoyment of the privileges Granted or intended to be granted as aforesaid To Have and to Hold all and Singular the privileges Advantages Immunities Franchises and all other the premises herein and hereby Given & Granted or herein or hereby that are intended or meant to be given & granted unto the said John French Esqr Mayor David French Esqr Recorder Samuel Lowman Robert Gordon Thomas Janvier Richard Grafton Anthony Houston and John Welch Esqrs Aldermen, James Sykes John Finny Wessel Alrichs David Miller John Vangezel & Richard Bermingham Assistants and their Heirs to and for the Sole and only proper Use and benefit and behoof of the Mayor Recorder Aldermen and Commonality of the said City of New Castle and Liberties and precincts thereof and their Successors forever Yielding Rendering and Paying therefore Yearly and & every Year hereafter unto Us Our Heirs and Successors at the Court House in the said City of New Castle on the Twenty eighth day of May One Beaver Skin if the same be Legally Demanded.

IN TESTIMONY whereof We have Caused these our Letters to be made Pattents and the Great Seal of the Government of our sd Counties to be hereunto affixed Witness our Trusty and well beloved SIR WILLIAM KEITH Barronet by our Royal Approbation and Appointment Governour of our said Counties of New Castle Kent and Sussex upon Delaware and Province of Pennsylvania at New Castle this Twenty eighth day of May in the Tenth Year of our Reign and in the Year of our Lord One Thousand Seven Hundred and twenty four

W. KEITH.
L.S.

References: Delaware History, 1848–1849, Vol. III, 26–36. Also, John Thomas Schaff, *History of Delaware, 1609–1888*, Vol. II (Philadelphia: L.J. Richards and Co., 1888), 862–863.

27

Georgia

The last of the original 13 English colonies that eventually formed the United States was Georgia, chartered in 1733. Chartered as a proprietary trusteeship colony, Georgia is forever linked to the reformer James Oglethorpe, who wanted a governance system under the control of small freeholders. But the growing coastal trade system and inland agricultural wealth soon ended the dream of a paradise of small, independent farmers. Georgia became a crown colony in 1752 and a successful slaveholding economy. Its legislature, which had often fought with the proprietor trustees for power, soon squabbled with the royal governor.

After becoming a crown colony in 1752, Georgia's legislature began to create its own statutes regarding governance rights. In 1754 it established a local court system and nominally accepted the royal governor as an appointing agent. But the legislature used its control over the governor's salary to acquire a voice in the selection of judges. Also, with the view that local governance made a successful legislature, in 1759 it established procedures for appointing constables, many of whom later entered the legislature. In 1761, the assembly passed a statute setting up the election process for its membership. Similar to so many other colonies, the assembly understood the importance of controlling elections by controlling the time, place, who could vote, and who could hold office. The delegates also acknowledged that their reforms were designed to counter the powers of the royal governor.

CHARTER OF THE COLONY, JUNE 9, 1733

GEORGE THE SECOND:

By the grace of God, of Great Britain, France, and Ireland, King, Defender of the Faith, &c. To all to whom these presents shall come, greeting: Whereas we are credibly informed, that many of our poor subjects are, through misfortune and want of employment, reduced to great necessity, insomuch as by their labour they are not able to provide a maintenance for themselves and families; and if they had means to defray their charges of passage, and other expenses incident to new settlements, they would be glad to settle in any of our provinces in America, where, by cultivating the lands at present waste and desolate, they might not only gain a comfortable subsistence for themselves and families, but also strengthen our colonies and increase the trade, navigation, and wealth of these our realms. And whereas our provinces in North America have been frequently ravaged by Indian enemies; more especially that of South Carolina, which in the late war, by the neighbouring savages, was laid waste by fire and sword, and great numbers of the English inhabitants miserably massacred; and our loving subjects who now inhabit there, by reason of the smallness of their numbers, will, in case of a new war, be exposed to the like calamities; inasmuch as their whole southern frontier continueth unsettled, and lieth open to the said savages; and whereas we think it highly becoming our crown and royal dignity to protect all our loving subjects, be they never so distant from us; to extend our fatherly compassion even to the meanest and most infatuate of our people, and to relieve the wants of our above mentioned poor subjects; and that it will be highly conducive for accomplishing those ends, that a regular colony of the said poor people be settled and established in the southern territories of Carolina; and whereas we have been well assured, that if we would be graciously pleased to erect and settle a corporation, for the receiving, managing and disposing of the contributions of our loving subjects, divers persons would be induced to contribute to the purposes aforesaid. *Know ye therefore,* that we have, for the consideration aforesaid, and for the better and more orderly carrying on the said good purposes, of our special grace, certain knowledge and mere motion, willed, ordained, constituted and appointed, and by these presents, for us, our heirs and successors, do will, ordain, constitute, declare and grant, that our right trusty and well beloved John Lord Viscount Percival, of our Kingdom of Ireland, our trusty and well beloved Edward Digby, George Carpenter, James Oglethorpe, George Heathcote, Thomas Tower, Robert Moor, Robert Hucks, Roger Holland, William Sloper, Francis Eyles, John Laroche, James Vernon, William Belitha, Esqrs., A. M., John Burton, B. D., Richard Bundy, A. M., Arthur Bedford, A. M., Samuel Smith, A. M., Adam Anderson, and Thomas Coram, gentlemen, and such other persons as shall be elected in the manner herein after mentioned, and their successors to be elected in the manner herein after directed, be, and shall be one body politic and corporate, in deed and in name, by the name of *The Trustees*

for establishing the Colony of Georgia in America; and them and their successors by the same name, we do, by these presents, for us, our heirs and successors, really and fully make, ordain, constitute and declare, to be one body politic in deed and in name forever; and that by the same name, they and their successors shall and may have perpetual succession; and that they and their successors, by that name, shall and may forever hereafter be persons able and capable in the law, to purchase, have, take, receive and enjoy, to them and their successors, any manors, messuages, lands, tenements, rents, advowsons, liberties, privileges, jurisdictions, franchises, and other hereditaments whatsoever, lying and being in Great Britain, or any part thereof, of whatsoever nature, kind or quality, or value they be, in fee and in perpetuity; not exceeding the yearly value of one thousand pounds, beyond reprises; also estates for lives and for years; and all other manner of goods, chattels and things whatsoever they be; for the better settling and supporting, and maintaining the said colony, and other uses aforesaid; and to give, grant, let and demise the said manors, messuages, lands, tenements, hereditaments, goods, chattels and things whatsoever aforesaid, by lease or leases, for term of years, in possession at the time of granting thereof, and not in reversion, not exceeding the term of thirty-one years from the time of granting thereof; on which in case no fine be taken, shall be reserved the full; and in case a fine be taken, shall be reserved at least a moiety of the value that the same shall reasonably and bona fide be worth at the time of such demise; and that they and their successors, by the name aforesaid, shall and may forever hereafter be persons able, capable in the law, to purchase, have, take, receive and enjoy, to them and their successors, any lands, territories, possessions, tenements, jurisdictions, franchises and hereditaments whatsoever, lying and being in America, of what quantity, quality or value whatsoever they be, for the better settling and supporting, and maintaining the said colony; and that by the name aforesaid they shall and may be able to sue and be sued, plead and be impleaded, answer and be answered unto, defend and be defended in all courts and places what soever, and before whatsoever judges, justices and other officers, of us, our heirs, and successors, in all and singular actions, plaints, pleas, matters, suits and demands, of what kind, nature or quality soever they be; and to act and do all other matters and things in as ample manner and form as any other our liege subjects of this realm of Great Britain; and that they and their successors forever hereafter, shall and may have a common seal to serve, for the causes and businesses of them and their successors; and that it shall and may be lawful for them and their successors, to change, break, alter and make new the said seal, from time to time, and at their pleasure, as they shall think best. And we do further grant, for us, our heirs and successors, that the said corporation and the common council of the said corporation herein after by us appointed, may from time to time, and at all times, meet about their affairs when and where they please, and transact and carry on the business of the said corporation. And for the better execution of the purposes aforesaid, we do, by these presents, for us, our heirs and successors, give and grant to the said corporation and their successors, that they and their successors forever may, upon the third Thursday in the month of March yearly, meet at some convenient place to be appointed by the said corporation, or major part of them who shall be present at any meeting of the said corporation, to be had for the appointing of the said place; and that they or two-thirds of such of them that shall be present at such yearly meetings, and at no other meeting of the said corporation, between the hours of ten in the morning and four in the afternoon of the same day, choose and elect such person or persons to be members of the said corporation, as they shall think beneficial to the good designs of the said corporation. And our further will and pleasure is, that if it shall happen that any person herein after by us appointed, as the common council of the said corporation, or any persons to be elected or admitted members of the said common council in the manner hereafter directed, shall die, or shall by writing under his and their hands respectively resign his or their office or offices of common council man or common council men; the said

corporation, or the major part of such of them as shall be present, shall and may at such meeting, on the said third Thursday in March yearly, in manner as aforesaid, next after such death or resignation, and at no other meeting of the said corporation, into the room or place of such person or persons so dead or so resigning, elect and choose one or more such person or persons, being members of the said corporation, as to them shall seem meet; and our will is, that all and every the person or persons which shall from time to time hereafter be elected common council men of the said corporation as aforesaid, do and shall, before he or they act as common council men of the said corporation, take an oath for the faithful and due execution of their office; which oath the president of the said corporation for the time being, is hereby authorized and required to administer to such person or persons elected as aforesaid. And our will and pleasure is, that the first president of the said corporation is and shall be our trusty and well-beloved, the said Lord John Viscount Percival; and that the said president shall, within thirty days after the passing this charter, cause a summons to be issued to the several members of the said corporation herein particularly named, to meet at such time and place as he shall appoint, to consult about and transact the businesses of said corporation. And our will and pleasure is, and we, by these presents, for us, our heirs and successors, grant, ordain, and direct, that the common council of this corporation shall consist of fifteen in number; and we do, by these presents, nominate, constitute and appoint our right trusty and well-beloved John Lord Viscount Percival, our trusty and beloved Edward Digby, George Carpenter, James Oglethorpe, George Heathcote, Thomas Laroche, James Vernon, William Beletha, Esqrs., and Stephen Hales, Master of Arts, to be the common council of the said corporation, to continue in the said office during their good behaviour. And whereas it is our royal intention, that the members of the said corporation shall be increased by election, as soon as conveniently may be, to a greater number than is hereby nominated; Our further will and pleasure is, and we do hereby, for us, our heirs and successors, ordain and direct, that from the time of such increase of the members of the said corporation, the number of the common council shall be increased to twenty-four; and that the same assembly at which such additional members of the said corporation shall be chosen, there shall likewise be elected, in the manner herein before directed for the election of common council men, nine persons to be the said common council men, and to make up the number twenty-four. And our further will and pleasure is, that our trusty and well-beloved Edward Digby, Esq., shall be the first chairman of the common council of the said corporation; and that the said Lord Viscount Percival shall be and continue president of the said corporation; and that the said Edward Digby shall be and continue chairman of the common council of the said corporation, respectively, until the meeting which shall be had next and immediately after the first meeting of the said corporation, or of the common council of the said corporation respectively, and no longer: at which said second meeting, and every other subsequent and future meeting of the said corporation, or of the common council of the said corporation respectively, in order to preserve an indifferent rotation of the several offices of president of the corporation, and of chairman of the common council of the said corporation, we do direct and ordain, that all and every the person and persons members of the said common council for the time being, and no other, being present at such meetings, shall severally and respectively in their turns, preside at the meetings which shall from time to time be held of the said corporation, or of the common council of the said corporation respectively. And in case any doubt or question shall at any time arise touching or concerning the right of any member of the said common council to preside, at any meeting of the said corporation, or at the common council of the said corporation, the same shall respectively be determined by the major part of the said corporation, or of the common council of the said corporation respectively, who shall be present at such meeting. Provided always, that no member of the said common council having served in the offices of president of the said corporation, or of chairman

of the common council of the said corporation, shall be capable of being or of serving as president or chairman at any meeting of the said corporation, or common council of the said corporation, next and immediately ensuing that in which he so served as president of the said corporation, or chairman of the said common council of the said corporation respectively; unless it shall so happen, that at any such meeting of the said corporation there shall not be any other member of the said common council present. And our will and pleasure is, that at all and every of the meetings of the said corporation, or of the common council of the said corporation, the president or chairman for the time being, shall have a voice, and shall vote and shall act as a member of the said corporation, or of the common council of the said corporation, at such meeting; and in case of any equality of votes, the said president or chairman, for the time being, shall have a casting vote. And our further will and pleasure is, that no president of the said corporation, or chairman of the common council of the said corporation, or member of the said common council or corporation, by us by these presents appointed, or hereafter from time to time to be elected and appointed in manner aforesaid, shall have, take or receive, directly or indirectly, any salary, fee, perquisite, benefit or profit whatsoever, for or by reason of his or their serving the said corporation, or common council of the said corporation, or president, chairman, or common council man, or as being a member of the said corporation. And our will and pleasure is, that the said herein before appointed president, chairman or common council men, before he and they act respectively as such, shall severally take an oath for the faithful and due execution of their trust, to be administered to the president by the Chief Baron of our Court of Exchequer, for the time being, and by the president of the said corporation to the rest of the common council, who are hereby authorized severally and respectively to administer the same. And our will and pleasure is, that all and every person and persons shall have, in his or their own name or names, or in the name or names of any person or persons in trust for him or them, or for his or their benefit, any office, place or employment of profit, under the said corporation, shall be incapable of being elected a member of the said corporation; and if any member of the said corporation, during such time as he shall continue a member thereof, shall in his own name, or in the name of any person or persons in trust for him, or for his benefit, have, hold, exercise, accept, possess or enjoy any office, place or employment of profit under the said corporation, or under the common council of the said corporation, such member shall from the time of his having, holding, exercising, accepting, possessing and enjoying such office, place and employment of profit, cease to be a member of the said corporation. And we do, for us, our heirs and successors, grant unto the said corporation, that they and their successors, or the major part of such of them as shall be present at any meeting of the said corporation, convened and assembled for that purpose by a convenient notice thereof, shall have power from time to time and at all times hereafter, to authorize and appoint such persons as they shall think fit, to take subscriptions, and to gather and collect such moneys as shall be by any person or persons contributed for the purpose aforesaid, and shall and may revoke and make void such authorities and appointments as often as they shall see cause so to do. And we do hereby, for us, our heirs and successors, ordain and direct, that the said corporation every year lay an account in writing before the chancellor or speaker, or commissioners for the custody of the great seal of Great Britain, of us, our heirs and successors, the Chief Justice of the Court of King's Bench, the Master of Rolls, the Chief Justice of the Court of Common Pleas, and the Chief Baron of the Exchequer, of us, our heirs and successors, for the time being, or any two of them, of all moneys and effects by them received or expended for carrying on the good purposes aforesaid. And we do hereby, for us, our heirs and successors, give and grant unto the said corporation and their successors, full power and authority to constitute, ordain and make such and so many by-laws, constitutions, orders and ordinances, as to them or the greater part of them,

at their general meeting for that purpose, shall seem necessary and convenient for the well ordering and governing of the said corporation, and the said by-laws, constitutions, orders and ordinances, or any of them, to alter and annul as they or the major part of them, then present shall see requisite; and in and by such by-laws, rules, orders and ordinances, to set, impose and inflict reasonable pains and penalties upon any offender or offenders who shall transgress, break or violate the said by-laws, constitutions, orders and ordinances, so made as aforesaid, and to mitigate the same as they or the major part of them then present shall think convenient; which said pains and penalties shall and may be levied, sued for, taken, retained and recovered by the said corporation and their successors, by their officers and servants from time to time to be appointed for that purpose, by action of debt, or by any other lawful ways or means, to the use and behoof of the said corporation and their successors; all and singular which by-laws, constitutions, orders and ordinances, so as aforesaid to be made, we will shall be duly observed and kept, under the pains and penalties therein to be contained, so always, as the said by-laws, constitutions, orders and ordinances, pains and penalties, from time to time to be made and imposed, be reasonable, and not contrary or repugnant to the laws or statutes of this our realm; and that such by-laws, constitutions and ordinances, pains and penalties, from time to time to be made and imposed; and any repeal or alteration thereof, or any of them, be likewise agreed to, be established and confirmed by the said general meeting of the said corporation, to be held and kept next after the same shall be respectively made. And whereas the said corporation intend to settle a colony, and to make an habitation and plantation in that part of our province of South Carolina, in America, herein after described; know ye, that we, greatly desiring the happy success of the said corporation, for their further encouragement in accomplishing so excellent a work, have, of our 'foresaid grace, certain knowledge, and mere motion, given and granted, and by these presents, for us, our heirs and successors, do give and grant to the said corporation and their successors, under the reservation, limitation and declaration hereafter expressed, seven undivided parts, the whole in eight equal parts to be divided, of all those lands, countries and territories situate, lying and being in that part of South Carolina, in America, which lies from the most northern part of a stream or river there, commonly called the Savannah, all along the sea coast to the southward, unto the most southern stream of a certain other great water or river called the Alatamaha, and westerly from the heads of the said rivers respectively, in direct lines to the South Seas; and all that share, circuit and precinct of land within the said boundaries, with the islands on the sea lying opposite to the eastern coast of the said lands, within twenty leagues of the same, which are not inhabited already, or settled by any authority derived from the crown of Great Britain, together with all the soils, grounds, havens, ports, gulfs and bays, mines, as well royal mines of gold and silver as other minerals, precious stones, quarries, woods, rivers, waters, fishings, as well royal fishings of whale and sturgeon as other fishings, pearls, commodities, jurisdictions, royalties, franchises, privileges, and pre-eminences within the said frontiers and precincts thereof, and thereunto in any sort belonging or appertaining, and which we by our letter patents may or can grant; and in as ample manner and sort as we may, or any of our royal progenitors have hitherto granted to any company, body, politic or corporate, or to any adventurer or adventurers, undertaker or undertakers, of any discoveries, plantations or traffic, of, in, or unto any foreign parts whatsoever, and in as legal and ample manner as if the same were herein particularly mentioned and expressed: To have, hold, possess and enjoy the said seven undivided parts, the whole into eight equal parts to be divided as aforesaid, of all and singular the lands, countries and territories, with all and singular other the premises herein before by these presents granted or mentioned, or intended to be granted to them the said corporation and their successors, for ever, for the better support of the said colony; to be holden of us, our heirs and successors, as of our honour of Hampton

court, in our county of Middlesex, in free and common soccage, and not in capite; yielding and paying therefor to us, our heirs and successors, yearly for ever, the sum of four shillings for every hundred acres of the said lands which the said corporation shall grant, demise, plant, or settle; the said payment not to commence or to be made until ten years after such grant, demise, planting or settling, and to be answered and paid to us, our heirs and successors, in such manner, and in such species of money or notes as shall be current in payment by proclamation, from time to time in our said province of South Carolina; all which lands, countries, territories and premises hereby granted, or mentioned and intended to be granted, we do, by these presents, make, erect and create, one independent and separate province, by the name of Georgia, by which name, we will, the same henceforth be called; and that all and every person or persons who shall at any time hereafter inhabit or reside within our said province, shall be and hereby are declared to be free, and shall not be subject to or be bound to obey any laws, statutes, or constitutions which have been heretofore made, ordered, and enacted, or which hereafter shall be made, ordered or enacted by, for, or as the laws, orders, statutes, or constitutions of our said province of South Carolina (save and except only the commander in chief of the militia of our said province of Georgia, to our governor for the time being, of South Carolina, in manner hereafter declared) but shall be subject to and bound to obey such laws, orders, statutes and constitutions as shall from time to time be made, ordered, and enacted, for the better government of the said province of Georgia, in the manner herein after declared. And we do hereby, for us, our heirs and successors, ordain, will and establish, that for and during the term of twenty-one years, to commence from the date of these our letters patent, the said corporation assembled for that purpose, shall and may form and prepare laws, statutes and ordinances, fit and necessary for and concerning the government of the said colony, and not repugnant to the laws and statutes of England, and the same shall and may present, under their common seal, to us, our heirs and successors, in our or their privy council, for our or their approbation or disallowance; and the said laws, statutes and ordinances, being approved of by us, our heirs and successors, in our or their privy council, shall from thenceforth be in full force and virtue within our said province of Georgia. And forasmuch as the good and prosperous success of the said colony cannot but chiefly depend, next under the blessing of God and the support of our royal authority, upon the provident and good direction of the whole enterprise; and that it will be too great a burthen upon all the members of the said corporation, to be convened so often as may be requisite to hold meetings for the settling, supporting, ordering and maintaining the said colony: therefore we do will, ordain, and establish that the said common council for the time being, of the said corporation, being assembled for that purpose, or the major part of them, shall from time to time and at all times hereafter, have full power and authority to dispose of, expend, and apply all the moneys and effects belonging to the said corporation, in such manner and ways, and by such expences as they shall think best to conduce to the carrying on and effecting the good purposes herein mentioned and intended; and also, shall have full power, in the name and on the account of the said corporation, and with and under their common seal, to enter under any covenants or contracts for carrying on and effecting the purpose aforesaid. And our further will and pleasure is, that the said common council for the time being, or the major part of such common council which shall be present and assembled for that purpose, from time to time, and at all times hereafter, shall and may nominate, constitute and appoint a treasurer or treasurers, secretary or secretaries, and such other officers, ministers and servants of the said corporation, as to them or the major part of them as shall be present shall seem proper or requisite for the good management of their affairs; and at their will and pleasure to displace, remove, and put out such treasurer or treasurers, secretary or secretaries, and all such other officers, ministers and servants, as often as they shall think fit to do so, and others in the room, office, place or station of him

or them so displaced, removed or put out, to nominate, constitute and appoint; and shall and may determine and appoint such reasonable salaries, perquisites and other rewards for their labour, or service of such officers, servants and persons, as to the said common council shall seem meet; and all such officers, servants and persons shall, before the acting their respective offices, take an oath, to be to them administered by the chairman for the time being of the said common council of the said corporation, who is hereby authorized to administer the same, for the faithful and due execution of their respective offices and places. And our will and pleasure is, that all such person and persons who shall from time to time be chosen or appointed treasurer or treasurers, secretary or secretaries of the said corporation, in manner herein after directed, shall, during such times as they shall serve in the said offices respectively, be incapable of being a member of the said corporation. And we do further, of our special grace, certain knowledge and mere motion, for us, our heirs and successors, grant, by these presents, to the said corporation and their successors, that it shall be lawful for them and their officers or agents, at all times hereafter, to transport and convey out of our realm of Great Britain, or any other of our dominions, into the said province of Georgia, to be there settled, so many of our loving subjects, or any foreigners that are willing to become our subjects and live under our allegiance in the said colony, as shall be willing to go to inhabit or reside there, with sufficient shipping, armor, weapons, powder, shot ordnance, munition, victuals, merchandise and wares, as are esteemed by the wild people, clothing, implements, furniture, cattle, horses, mares, and all other things necessary for the said colony, and for the use and defence, and trade with the people there, and in passing and returning to and from the same. Also we do, for ourselves and successors, declare, by these presents, that all and every the persons which shall happen to be born within the said province, and every of their children and posterity, shall have and enjoy all liberties, franchises and immunities of free denizens and natural born subjects, within any of our dominions, to all intents and purposes, as if abiding and born within this our kingdom of Great Britain, or any other dominion. And for the greater ease and encouragement of our loving subjects, and such others as shall come to inhabit in our said colony, we do, by these presents, for us, our heirs and successors, grant, establish and ordain, that forever, hereafter, there shall be a liberty of conscience allowed in the worship of God, to all persons inhabiting, or which shall inhabit or be resident within our said province, and that all such persons, except papists, shall have a free exercise of religion; so they be contented with the quiet and peaceable enjoyment of the same, not giving offence or scandal to the government. And our further will and pleasure is, and we do hereby, for us, our heirs and successors, declare and grant, that it shall and may be lawful for the said common council, or the major part of them, assembled for that purpose, in the name of the corporation, and under the common seal, to distribute, convey, assign, and set over such particular portions of land, tenements and hereditaments by these presents granted to the said corporation, unto such of our loving subjects naturally born or denizens, or others, that shall be willing to become our subjects, and live under our allegiance in the said colony, upon such terms, and for such estates, and upon such rents, reservations and conditions as the same may be lawfully granted, and as to the said common council, or the major part of them so present, shall seem fit and proper. Provided always, that no grants shall be made of any part of the said lands unto any person being a member of the said corporation, or to any other person in trust for the benefit of any member of the said corporation; and that no person having any estate or interest in law or equity in any part of the said lands, shall be capable of being a member of the said corporation, during the continuance of such estate or interest. Provided also, that no greater quantity of lands be granted, either entirely or in parcels, to or for the use or in trust for any one person than five hundred acres; and that all grants made contrary to the true intent and meaning hereof, shall be absolutely null and void. And we do hereby grant and ordain, that such person or persons for the time being, as shall be thereunto appointed by the said corporation, shall and may at all times, and from time to time hereafter, have full power and authority to administer and give the oaths appointed by an act of parliament made in the first year of the reign of our late royal father, to be taken instead of the oaths of allegiance and supremacy; and also the oath of abjuration, to all and every person and persons which shall at any time be inhabiting or residing within our said colony; and in like cases to administer the solemn affirmation to any of the persons commonly called Quakers, in such manner as by the laws of our realm of Great Britain the same may be administered. And we do, of our further grace, certain knowledge and mere motion, grant, establish and ordain, for us, our heirs and successors, that the said corporation and their successors, shall have full power and authority for and during the term of twenty-one years, to commence from the date of these our letters patent, to erect and constitute judicatories and courts of record, or other courts, to be held in the name of us, our heirs and successors, for the hearing and determining of all manner of crimes, offences, pleas, processes, plaints, actions, matters, causes, and things whatsoever, arising or happening within the said province of Georgia or between persons of Georgia; whether the same be criminal or civil, and whether the said crimes be capital or not capital, and whether the said pleas be real, personal or mixed; and for awarding and making out executions thereupon; to which courts and judicatories, we do hereby, for us, our heirs and successors, give and grant full power and authority, from time to time, to administer oaths for the discovery of truth, in any matter in controversy or depending before them, or the solemn affirmation to any of the persons commonly called Quakers, in such manner as by the laws of our realm of Great Britain the same may be administered. And our further will and pleasure is, that the said corporation and their successors, do from time to time and at all times hereafter, register or cause to be registered all such leases, grants, plantings, conveyances, settlements, and improvements whatsoever, as shall at any time hereafter be made by or in the name of the said corporation, of any lands, tenements or hereditaments within the said province, and shall yearly send and transmit, or cause to be sent or transmitted, authentic accounts of such leases, grants, conveyances, settlements and improvements respectively, unto the auditor of the plantations for the time being, or his deputy, and also to our surveyor for the time being of our said province of South Carolina, to whom we do hereby grant full power and authority from time to time, as often as need shall require, to inspect and survey such of the said lands and premises as shall be demised, granted and settled as aforesaid, which said survey and inspection we do hereby declare to be intended to ascertain the quit-rents, which shall from time to time become due to us, our heirs and successors, according to the reservations herein before mentioned, and for no other purposes whatsoever; hereby, for us, our heirs and successors; strictly enjoining and commanding, that neither our or their surveyor, or any person whatsoever, under the pretext and colour of making the said survey or inspection, shall take, demand or receive any gratuity, fee or reward, of or from any person or persons inhabiting in the said colony, or from the said corporation or common council of the same, on the pain of forfeiture of the said office or offices, and incurring our highest displeasure. Provided always, and our further will and pleasure is, that all leases, grants and conveyances to be made by or in the name of the said corporation of any lands within the said province, or a memorial containing the substance and effect thereof, shall be registered with the auditor of the said plantations, of us, our heirs and successors, within the space of one year, to be computed from the date thereof, otherwise the same shall be void. And our further will and pleasure is, that the rents, issues, and all other profits which shall at any time hereafter come to the said corporation, or the major part of them which shall be present at any meeting for that purpose assembled, shall think will most improve and enlarge the said colony, and best answer the good purposes herein before mentioned, and for defraying all other charges about the same. And our will and pleasure is, that the said corporation and their successors, shall from time to time give in to one of the principal secretaries of state and to the commissioners of trade and plantations, accounts of the progresses of the said colony. And our will and pleasure is, that no act done at any meeting of the said common council of the said corporation, shall be effectual and valid, unless eight members at least of the said common council, including the member who shall serve as chairman at the said meeting, be present, and the major part of them consenting thereunto. And our will and pleasure is, that the common council of the said corporation for the time being, or the major part of them who shall be present, being assembled for that purpose, shall from time to time, for and during and unto the full end and expiration of twenty-one years, to commence from the date of these our letters patent, have full power and authority to nominate, make, constitute, commission, ordain and appoint, by such name or names, style or styles, as to them shall seem meet and fitting, all and singular such governors, judges, magistrates, ministers and officers, civil and military, both by sea and land, within the said districts, as shall by them be thought fit and needful to be made or used for the said government of the said colony; save always and except such officers only as shall by us, our heirs and successors, be from time to time constituted and appointed, for the managing, collecting and receiving such revenues as shall from time to time arise within the said province of Georgia, and become due to us, our heirs and successors. Provided always, and it is our will and pleasure, that every governor of the said province of Georgia, to be appointed by the common council of the said corporation, before he shall enter upon or execute the said office of Governor, shall be approved by us, our heirs or successors, and shall take such oaths and shall qualify himself in such manner in all respects, as any governor or commander in chief of any of our colonies or plantations in America, are by law required to do; and shall give good and sufficient security for observing the several acts of Parliament relating to trade and navigation, and to observe and obey all instructions that shall be sent to him by us, our heirs and successors, or any acting under our or their authority, pursuant to the said acts, or any of them. And we do, by these presents, for us, our heirs and successors, will, grant and ordain, that the said corporation and their successors, shall have full power for and during and until the full end and term of twenty-one years, to commence from the date of these our letters patent, by any commander or other officer or officers by them for that purpose from time to time appointed, to train, instruct, exercise and govern a militia for the special defence and safety of our said colony, to assemble in martial array the inhabitants of the said colony, and to lead and conduct them, and with them to encounter, expulse, repel, resist and pursue, by force of arms, as well by sea as by land, within or without the limits of our said colony; and also to kill, slay and destroy, and conquer by all fitting ways, enterprises and means whatsoever, all and every such person or persons as shall at any time hereafter, in any hostile manner, attempt or enterprise the destruction, invasion, detriment or annoyance of our said colony; and to use and exercise the martial law in time of actual war and invasion or rebellion, in such cases where by law the same may be used or exercised; and also from time to time to erect forts and fortify any place or places within our said colony, and the same to furnish with all necessary ammunition, provisions, and stores of war, for offence and defence, and to commit from time to time the custody or government of the same to such person or persons as to them shall seem meet; and the said forts and fortifications to demolish at their pleasure; and to take and surprise, by all ways and means, all and every such person or persons, with their ships, arms, ammunition and other goods, as shall in an hostile manner invade

or attempt the invading, conquering or annoying of our said colony. And our will and pleasure is, and we do hereby for us, our heirs and successors, declare and grant, that the governor and commander in chief of the province of South Carolina, of us, our heirs and successors, for the time being, shall at all times hereafter have the chief command of the militia of our said province, hereby erected and established; and that such militia shall observe and obey all orders and directions that shall from time to time be given or sent them by the said governor or commander in chief, anything in these presents before contained to the contrary hereof in any wise notwithstanding. And, of our more special grace, certain knowledge and mere motion, we have given and granted, and by these presents, for us, our heirs and successors, do give and grant unto the said corporation and their successors, full power and authority to import and export their goods at and from any port or ports that shall be appointed by us, our heirs and successors, within the said province of Georgia for that purpose, without being obliged to touch at any other port in South Carolina. And we do, by these presents, for us, our heirs and successors, will and declare, that from and after the determination of the said term of one and twenty years, such form of government and method of making laws, statutes and ordinances, for the better governing and ordering the said province of Georgia, and the inhabitants thereof, shall be established and observed within the same, as we, our heirs and successors, shall hereafter ordain and appoint, and shall be agreeable to law; and that from and after the determination of the said term of one and twenty years, the governor of our said province of Georgia, and all officers, civil and military, within the same, shall from time to time be nominated and constituted and appointed by us, our heirs and successors. And lastly, we do hereby, for us, our heirs and successors, grant unto the said corporation and their successors, that these our letters patent, or the enrollments or exemplification thereof, shall be in and by all things, good, firm, valid, sufficient and effectual in the Law, according to the true intent and meaning thereof, and shall be taken, construed and adjudged in all courts and elsewhere, in the most favourable and beneficial sense and for the best advantage of the said corporation and their successors, any omission, imperfection, defect, matter or cause or thing whatsoever to the contrary in any wise notwithstanding. In witness we have caused these our letters to be made patent. Witness ourself at Westminster, the ninth day of June, in the fifth year of our reign.

By writ of privy seal.
COCKS.

Reference: Allen D. Candler (comp.), *The Colonial Records of the State of Georgia*, Vol. I (Atlanta: Franklin Printing and Publishing Co., 1904).

ESTABLISHMENT OF COURTS, DECEMBER 12, 1754

At a Council held in the Council Chamber at Savannah on Thursday the twelfth day of December 1754.

Present
His Excellency John Reynolds, Esquire
The Honorable Patrick Graham
James Habersham
Alexander Kellet Esquires
Noble Jones
Francis Harris

The minutes of the preceeding board were read and approved.

Then was read again Mr. Attorney-General's report of the method of erecting courts of judicature within this province, and the same being read was ordered to be entered in this day's minutes, and is as follows.

Georgia ss The report of the Attorney-General on the business to him referred by his Excellency the Governor and Council relative to the appointing of courts of judicature.

In pursuance of the directions to me given by his Excellency the Governor and Council, I have perused and considered the several articles of his Majesty's instructions and other the papers laid before me which relate to the constituting and erecting of courts of justice and judicature within this province of Georgia and in obedience and conformity thereto I do humbly conceive that, for the speedy administration of justice, the punishing of offences, and for the settling and determining all matters of right and property between the inhabitants of the said province, there be erected and constituted a general court to be held before two or more persons for this purpose, to be appointed as judges thereof by commission from his Excellency; that such general court have jurisdiction and cognizance of all actions, real, personal, and mixed exceeding the value of forth shillings and also have cognizance of all criminal matters, with the like power and authority as used and exercised by the respective courts of Kings Bench, Common Pleas and Exchequer in England, and to be held every three months, viz., the second Tuesday in January, the second Tuesday in April, the second Tuesday in July, and the second Tuesday in October; that liberty of appeal be allowed from the judgment of sentence of the said court to his Excellency the Governor and Council, for which purpose a writ to issue as usual, returnable before the Governor and Council who are to proceed to hear and determine such appeal; wherein such of the Council as shall be at that time judges of the court from when such appeal shall be made shall not be admitted to vote upon such appeal, but they may, nevertheless, be present at the hearing thereof to give the reasons of the judgment given by them in the causes wherein such appeals shall be made; provided, nevertheless, that the sum or value appealed for exceed the sum of three hundred pounds sterling and that security be first given by the appellant to answer such charges as shall be awarded in cases the first sentence be affirmed; and if either party shall not rest satisfied with the judgment of the governor and council that they may then appeal to his Majesty in council, provided the value so appealed for exceed £500 sterling and that such appeal be made within fourteen days after sentence and good security given by the appellant to prosecute the same and answer the condemnation, as also to pay such costs and damages as shall be awarded in case the sentence of the Governor and Council be confirmed; provided, nevertheless, where the matter in question relates to the taking or demanding any duty payable to his Majesty or to any fee of office or annual rent or other such like matter or thing where the rights in future may be bound, in all such cases an appeal to be allowed though the immediate sum or value appealed for be of less value, that where appeals shall be admitted execution to be suspended until final determination of such appeals unless good and sufficient security be given by the appellee to make ample restitution in case, upon the determination of such appeal, the decree of judgment of the said court be reversed and restitution ordered to the appellant; appeals also to be admitted in all cases of fines imposed for misdemeanors, provided the fines so imposed amount to or exceed the value of two hundred pounds sterling, the appellant giving security as before.

That for the regular establishing such general court there be appointed these officers, viz., a clerk of the crown and peace for the business of criminal prosecutions, a clerk of the court, or papers, for making out process entering declarations, etc., and a cryer. That for settling the method of practice in the said court a summary thereof be drawn up with fit rules and orders as occasion shall require; that the fees to be taken by the respective officers be settled and regulated.

That there be a court of chancery for hearing and determining all matters of equity, to be held before his Excellency the Governor as chancellor. The officers necessary will be a master, register, and examiner; this court to sit after each general court if business require.

And I do further apprehend that, agreeable to his Majesty's said instructions, for the preventing long imprisonments for matters criminal there be two courts of oyer and terminer held yearly, the one the second Tuesday in December, the other the second Tuesday in June, where all criminals which may happen to be committed after the respective general courts are to be tried. For which purpose the governor to issue a commission to two members of the council, or judges of the general court, that all prisoners in cases of treason or felony have liberty to petition in open courts for their trials. That they be indicted at the first court of oyer and terminer, unless it appear upon oath that the witnesses against them could not be produced, and that they be tried at the second court or discharged.

That for breaches of the act of trade and for determining controversies concerning salvage, mariner's wages, and other maritime affairs there be held a court of admiralty before his Excellency as Vice Admiral or before whomsoever he shall depute or surrogate for this purpose when occasion shall require. To which court will belong an advocate, a register, and a marshal to be appointed by the Governor and from hence liberty of appeal be allowed to the High Court of Admiralty of Great Britain.

That for punishing slaves committing capital crimes a commission of oyer and terminer be issued by the Governor, when necessary, directed to the justices of the district or division where the offense shall be committed to try the offender on proof of the fact by witnesses, without any jury, and, upon conviction, the commissioners to award execution and set a value upon the slave which is afterwards to be paid to the owner by the general assembly as an encouragement to the people to discover the villanies of their slaves. That for the recovery of small debts and for the ease and convenience of the inhabitants of the province residing at too great a distance from Savannah there be inferior courts hereafter established as shall be thought requisite and necessary for this purpose. All which I humbly submit to the judgment of his Excellency and their honors.

William Clifton

The Board having maturely considered the above report came to the following resolutions.

Resolved, that the respective courts of justice mentioned in the aforesaid report be constituted, as occasion may require, conformable to the said report.

That a court of record be immediately constituted by the name and style of the General Court, to be held yearly at Savannah within this province on the second Tuesday in January, the second Tuesday in April, the second Tuesday in July, and the second Tuesday in October.

That the said General Court have jurisdiction and cognizance of all actions real, personal, and mixed exceeding the value of forty shillings sterling, except where the title to a freehold comes in question, and also have cognizance of all criminal matters, with the like power and authority as used and exercised by the respective courts of King's Bench, Common Pleas and Exchequer in England.

That his Excellency the Governor will grant a commission to Noble Jones and Jonathan Bryan, Esquires, to be judges to hold the said court, which commission is ordered to be entered in this day's minutes and is as follows.

Georgia.

George the Second, by the Grace of God, of Great Britain, France, and Ireland, King, Defender of the Faith, and so forth.

To all to whom these our present letters shall come, greeting.

Know you that we, tendering the state and condition of our province of Georgia and being willing and desirous that justice be duly and regularly administered therein, have thought fit to erect and constitute, and by these presents do erect and constitute, a court of record by the name and [. . .] style of the General Court, to be held yearly at Savannah within our said province on the second Tuesday in January, the second Tuesday in April, the second Tuesday in July, and the second Tuesday in October before our trusty and well-beloved Noble Jones and Jonathan Bryan, Esquires, or one of them, whom we hereby appoint our justices thereof during our pleasure and others our justices appointed for the time being. And we do hereby give and grant unto the said Noble Jones and Jonathan Bryan, and each of them, and all others our justices of the said General Court for the time being full power, jurisdiction, and authority to inquire by the oaths of good and lawful men of the province aforesaid, and

by other ways and means by which the truth of the matter may be better known and inquired into, of all treasons, felonies, and other crimes and criminal offenses whatsoever done or committed within our said province by any persons whatsoever, and the same to hear and determine according to the laws and customs of our said province, saving to us and our successors all fines, forfeitures, and amercements and all other things to us on account thereof belonging and appertaining. And further we give and grant to the said Noble Jones and Jonathan Bryan, and each others our justices of our said General Court for the time being, full power, jurisdiction, and authority to hold pleas in all and all manner of causes, suits, and actions whatsoever, as well criminal as civil, real, personal, and mixed, arising, happening, or being within our said province where the sum or thing demanded shall exceed the value of forty shillings sterling, except only where the title to any freehold shall come in question, and to proceed in such pleas, suits, and actions by such ways, means, and process as may, with the greatest safety, dispatch, and justice, bring the same to a final determination, and also to hear and determine all such pleas, suits, and actions, and judgment thereupon to give and execution thereof to award and issue and this as fully and amply as can or may be done by our courts of King's Bench, Common Pleas, and Exchequer in England, doing therein what of right and justice ought to be done. In testimony whereof, we have caused these our letters to be made patent, and the seal of our said province to be affixed thereto. Witness our trusty and well-beloved John Reynolds, Esquire, our Captain-General and Governor-in-Chief, in and over our said province of Georgia, the twelfth day of December in the twenty-eighth year of our reign.

J. Reynolds
By his Excellency's Command
James Habersham,
Secretary

Reference: Journal of the Minutes of the Governor and Council of Georgia in W. Keith Kavenagh (ed.), Foundations of Colonial America, Vol. III (New York: Chelsea House, 1973), 2058–2062.

ACT ESTABLISHING METHOD OF APPOINTING CONSTABLES, MARCH 27, 1759

Forasmuch as the method of appointing constables and the qualifications of persons to serve in that office, as well as the duties required from the said constables, has not been hitherto established by any laws of this province, and divers obstructions in the administration of justice have been thereby occasioned; for remedy whereof, we humbly pray your most sacred Majesty that it may be enacted. And be it enacted by his Excellency Henry Ellis, Esquire, Captain-General and Governor-in-Chief of the province of Georgia, by and with the advice and consent of the honorable Council and Commons House of Assemby of the said province in General Assembly met, and by the authority of the same, that from and after the twenty-ninth day of March, one thousand seven hundred and fifty-nine, the justices of every district shall, on some day in Easter week, meet at the place where the court of request is usually by them held, or at any other convenient place, and having given notice to the officiating constables then and there to appear and attend the said justices, shall cause the names of the persons of their district hereinafter declared by this act liable to serve the office of constable to be singly written on divers pieces of paper and each rolled up by itself; and the said pieces of paper, so written and rolled up, shall be put in a hat or box and, being well shaken

together, the said justices shall cause to be drawn out of the said box or hat, by one of the said constables, so many of the aforesaid pieces of paper as there shall be constables wanted for that district; and the persons whose names shall be found written upon the several papers so drawn, as aforesaid, shall, and it is hereby declared, lawfully appointed to serve in the office of constable for the immediate ensuing year, and the said justices shall immediately cause the several persons so said fine on the goods and chattels of the offender or offenders, and to be paid into the hands of the church wardens for the use aforesaid.

Council Chamber, 27th March, 1759

By Order of the Commons House of Assembly,
David Montaigut,
Speaker
By Order of the Upper House,
Pat. Houston,
President
Assented to: Henry Ellis.

Reference: W.S. Jenkins and L.A. Hamrick (eds.), *Microfilm Collection of Early State Records,* Georgia (B.2 Reel 1a, 1735–1772) in W. Keith Kavenagh (ed.), *Foundations of Colonial America,* Vol. III (New York: Chelsea House, 1973), 2062–2063.

ACT TO ASCERTAIN MANNER OF ELECTING ASSEMBLY MEMBERS, JUNE 9, 1761

Whereas the manner and form of choosing members of the Commons House of Assembly to represent the inhabitants of this province and the qualifications of electors and those elected members of the Commons House of Assembly has never yet been appointed, fixed, and determined by any law of this province. We, therefore, pray your most sacred Majesty that it may be enacted.

And be it enacted by his Honor James Wright, Esquire, Lieutenant-Governor and Commander-in-Chief of this his Majesty's province of Georgia, by and with the advice and consent of the honorable Council and the Commons House of Assembly of the said province in General Assembly met, and by the authority of the same, that from and after the passing of this act all writs for the election of members of the Commons House of Assembly shall be issued out by the Governor or Commander-in-Chief for the time being with the consent of the Council and shall bear test forty days before the day appointed for the meeting of the said members and shall be directed to the provost marshal in the said writs to cause such elections to be made and to return the names of the persons elected to be members of the Commons House of Assembly. And the provost marshal is hereby empowered and required to execute such writ to him directed and, for the faithful and due performance of which according to the true intent and meaning of this act, the provost marshal shall cause public notice in writing to be affixed at one or more noted place or places in such parish, district, town, or village for which the election of a member or members by him is to be taken, at least ten days before the day of election, of the time and place where such election is by him to be taken.

II. And be it further enacted, by the authority aforesaid, that every free white man, and no other, who has attained to the age of twenty-one years and has been resident in the province six months and is legally possessed in his own right of fifty acres of land in the said parish, district, or village for which the member or members is or are to be elected to represent in the General Assembly, shall be deemed a person qualified for electing a representative or representatives to serve as member or members of the Commons House of Assembly for the parish, district, town, or village wherein he is possessed of the above qualification.

III. And for preventing frauds, as much as may be, in all elections, it is hereby enacted, by the authority aforesaid, that the returning officer shall come to the place at the time appointed by the public notice given and shall enter the names of every person presented or presenting himself as candidate, in a book or roll, leaving a fair column under each candidate's name for the names of the voters, and when a voter comes and votes the returning officer shall repeat distinctly the person or persons' names for whom the vote is given before he writes the voter's name in the fair column under the name of such candidate or candidates as shall be voted for by that person, and that no voter shall alter his voice after it be entered or vote twice at one and the same election, and that the candidate or candidates who, after the poll is closed and the votes summed up, shall be found, upon scrutiny made if demanded, to have the majority of votes shall be deemed and declared to be a member or members of the succeeding Commons House of Assembly.

IV. And be it enacted, by the authority aforesaid, that the time for taking votes at any election shall be between the hours of nine of the clock in the forenoon and six in the afternoon, and that at adjourning the poll, at convenient hours during the time of an election, the returning officer shall first sum up the votes given for each candidate and declare the same to the candidates present, and also declare the same when he has opened the poll at the ensuing meeting, and that the said election shall not continue longer than two days unless a scrutiny is demanded. Provided, nevertheless, that the returning officer is hereby empowered and required to close the poll when he or they have waited two hours after the last vote has been given, or at any time by and with the consent and desire of all the candidates then present.

V. And be it enacted, by the authority aforesaid, that every person who shall be elected and returned, as is before directed by this act, to serve as a member in the Commons House of Assembly of this province shall be qualified in the following manner, viz., that he shall be a free-born subject of Great Britain or of the dominions thereunto belonging, or a foreign person naturalized, professing the christian religion and no other, and that has arrived at the age of twenty-one years, and has been a resident in this province for twelve months before the date of the said writ, and being legally possessed in his own right in this province of a tract of land containing at least five hundred acres.

VI. And be it enacted, by the authority aforesaid, that if any member or members chosen or hereafter to be chosen to serve in this or any other Commons House of Assembly shall refuse to serve, or any member or members should die or depart this province, or shall be expelled the House, so that his or their seat or seats become vacant, then and in such case the House shall, by address to the Governor or Commander-in-Chief for the time being signify the same and desire that a new writ or writs may issue to elect a member or members to fill up the vacancy or vacancies in that House, and, in consequence of such address, a new writ or writs shall be issued to choose in that parish, district, town, or village such other member or members to serve in the place or places of such member or members whose seat or seats are become vacant, and every person so chosen and returned, as aforesaid, shall attend the Commons House of Assembly and shall be reputed, deemed, and judged a member thereof.

VII. And be it enacted, by the authority aforesaid, that if any returning officer, as aforesaid, shall admit of or take the vote of any person refusing, at the request of one of the candidates or any two persons qualified to vote, to take the following oath, "I, A. B., do swear that I am legally possessed in my own right of a freehold estate of fifty acres of land in the township or district of, and that such estate is legally or bona fide in my own right and not made over or granted to me purposely or fraudulently to entitle me to vote at this election," or at the request of any candidate or any two freeholders shall refuse to administer the following oath to any candidate who is hereby obliged to take this oath if so required, "I, A. B., do swear that I am in my own right truly and legally possessed of five hundred acres of land within this province and that the said right is truly and bona fide within myself and not fraudulently made over or granted to me for the purpose of qualifying me to be a representative in General Assembly," or if the provost marshal shall make any fraudulent or shall influence or endeavor to influence or persuade any voter not to vote as he first designed, shall forfeit for each and every such offense the sum of fifty pounds sterling to be to his Majesty for defraying the expense of the sitting of the General Assembly and to be sued

for and recovered in the general court of this province by bill, plaint, or information.

VIII. And be it enacted, by the authority aforesaid, that the provost marshal, or any person properly authorized by him to manage an election, as aforesaid, shall not return himself as a member to serve in General Assembly; and if the provost marshal refuses or neglects, on a summons from the Commons House of Assembly, to attend that House to inform them to the best of his knowledge of any matter or dispute that did arise or may have arisen about the election of the member or members by him returned to serve in Assembly, or refusing to show the poll taken, shall forfeit for every such offense fifty pounds sterling, to be applied and recovered as is herein before directed.

IX. And be it further enacted, by the authority aforesaid, that if any person or persons whatsoever shall, on any day appointed for the election of a member or members to serve in the Commons House of Assembly, as aforesaid, presume to violate the freedom of the said election by any arrest, menaces, or threats, or attempts to overawe, affright, or force any person qualified to vote, against his inclination or conscience, or otherwise by bribery obtain any vote, or who shall, after the election is over, menace, despitefully use, or abuse any person because he has not voted as he or they would have had him; every such person so offending, upon due and sufficient proof made of such his violence or abuse, menacing, or threatening, before any two justices of the peace, shall be bound over to the next general sessions of the peace, himself in twenty pounds sterling money and two sureties, each in ten pounds like money, and to be of good behavior and abide the sentence of the said court where, if the offender or offenders are convicted and found guilty of such offense or offenses, as aforesaid, then he or they shall each of them forfeit a sum not exceeding twenty pounds sterling money and be committed to gaol without bail or mainprize till the same be paid. Which fine so imposed shall be paid as before directed.

X. And be it further enacted, by the authority aforesaid, that no civil officer whatsoever shall execute any writ or other civil process whatsoever upon the body of any person qualified to vote for members of the Commons House of Assembly, as before in this act directed, either in his journey to or in his return from the place of such election, providing he shall not be more than forty-eight hours upon his journey either going to, returning from, or during his stay there upon that account, or within forty-eight hours after the scrutiny for such election is finished; under the penalty of a sum not exceeding twenty pounds sterling money, to be recovered of and from the officer that shall arrest or serve any process, as aforesaid, after such manner and form, and to be disposed of as herein before is directed. And all such writs or warrants executed on the body of any person either going to or being at, within the time limited by this clause, or returning from the place where such election is appointed to be managed, he being qualified to give in his vote thereat, are hereby declared void and null.

XI. And be it enacted, by the authority aforesaid, that this act or any part thereof shall not extend to debar the Commons House of Assembly of the right to judge and determine, agreeable to the directions of this act, the qualifications of any member of members of that House, or to take away from the General Assembly, or any part thereof, any power or privilege whatever that any General Assembly, or part thereof, heretofore of right had, might, could, or ought to have had in the said province, anything herein contained to the contrary in anywise notwithstanding. Provided, always, that this act or any part thereof shall not be construed to take away the power and prerogative given the Governor or Commander-in-Chief for the time being from the Crown to adjourn, prorogue, or dissolve any General Assembly of this province when and as often as he shall think fit and expedient so to do, or to take away any other power or prerogatives whatever had from the Crown.

By Order of the Commons House of Assembly
Grey Elliott,
Speaker
By Order of the Upper House
James Habersham,
In the Council Chamber, the 9th day of June, 1761.
Assented to: James Wright

Reference: W.S. Jenkins and L.A. Hamrick (eds.), *Microfilm Collection of Early State Records*, Georgia (B.2 Reel 1a, 1735–1772) in W. Keith Kavenagh (ed.), *Foundations of Colonial America*, Vol. III (New York: Chelsea House, 1973), 2066–2069.

Part V

Essays on Governance and Defense of Colonial Government

Part V is divided into two chapters. Chapter 28 gives the reader a general overview of governance in the colonies during the eighteenth century. Chapter 29 includes commentaries from leading public figures in the colonies on those politically complicated and often excitable years that led up to the American Revolution. Chapter 28 includes writings on colonial governance from a royal agent and a historian who wanted to explain, primarily to England, the status of governance developments in the colonies proliferated during the late colonial period.

During the crisis over authority between 1763 and 1776, colonial leaders were most concerned with describing and defending their governance systems. As England became more restrictive of colonial governance and political rights, a number of colonial leaders spoke out and wrote of their grievances. Seven works by leading revolutionary participants, out of hundreds produced, have been selected for Chapter 29. These documents provide insight into what those leaders thought of their system of governance as well as why they resisted British aggression. Colonial governance values, at first cautiously approached in those publications, became the central arguments for separation from British domination.

28

Overviews of Colonial Governance

The author of *An Essay upon the Government of the English Plantations* (1701), written in Virginia, the wealthiest and most valuable of British colonies, is unknown. Louis B. Wright, a close observer of eighteenth-century Virginia governance, believes that the first William Byrd wrote *An Essay*. Certainly Byrd provided notes for Robert Beverley's masterful *History and Present State of Virginia* (1705), and Beverley quoted from *An Essay* in his history. William Byrd (1652–1704) was born in London to a middleclass tradesman. In 1670 he moved to Virginia to join a cousin, a large and successful tobacco planter, and soon rose into that colony's governing hierarchy. Byrd built a home in upcountry Westover, the future site of his son's great mansion of the same name. In 1676 he sided with Nathaniel Bacon's rebels against what he called a tyrannical governor, Sir William Berkeley. Byrd escaped prosecution when Bacon's rebellion failed, and he later became a member of the House of Burgesses. Byrd soon joined Governor Francis Nicholson's Council and in 1703 became its president. Before he died, Byrd broke with Nicholson, and declared himself a staunch defender of the rights of the Burgesses.

An *Essay* combines remarks on trade and commerce with detailed analysis of the system of governance. It makes a major contribution to how governance had developed in the colonies to the start of the eighteenth century. (In the text presented in this volume, I have deleted the preface and the long chapter on economic interests and the personal lives of the colonists.) The author links growing business success with the necessity for an orderly system of governance, a key factor in governance development. *An Essay* begins its political discussion with commentary on how the colonies had recovered from the ordeal of 1689, in which they fought against the movement for colonial consolidation, yet states that most of the colonies were supportive of crown's authority over them. But the author vociferously pointed out that the King should not have more power in the colonies than he had in England. The author also calls for the rights of colonial legislatures to make their own laws for self-governance, and to create their own court systems. The author notes that if the King knew how poorly his royal governors performed he would support stronger colonial legislators. In fact, *An Essay* turns into a book of grievances and recommendations on how to reform England's governing relations with the colonies.

After reconfirming the value of the legislature to colonial governance order, attacking again the governors, and suggesting that England knows too little about the shape of colonial governance, the author makes an argument for colony-wide governance. He recommends the formation of a general assembly uniting all of the colonies. Of course, the author says, the very size of the colonies makes this a difficult task. He then suggests creating five separate governing districts. Then, government of all the colonies should be annexed to the crown and all remaining proprietary colonies should be disbanded. Indeed, colonists debated the advantages and disadvantages of colony-wide unity up to the American Revolution.

The second comprehensive study, *An Essay on the Government of the Colonies* (1752), is by the Scotland-born Archibald Kennedy (1685–1763), who came to New York as an army officer around 1720. As an ally of Governor Robert Hunter, Kennedy became famous for setting up barriers to Indian invasion. By 1722 Kennedy held the collectorship of the port of New York, a lucrative post, and in 1727 he joined the Governor's Council (the New York upper house of the legislature). Kennedy also became a successful land speculator. In 1740 he received a commission to settle the boundary dispute between Rhode Island and Massachusetts. He became well known as a political author and he wrote important essays on frontier defenses and the need for colonies to cooperate in mutual defense. Kennedy is most famous for *Serious Considerations on the Present State of Affairs of the Northern Colonies* (1754) and the pamphlet included in this volume, *An Essay on the Government of the Colonies* (1752).

In the *Essay*, Kennedy advocated self-sufficiency for the colonies. He wanted to see even more financial success and better trade links with England. But, despite his praise for the colonies, his experiences in colonial governance made Kennedy a critic of the quality of leadership and he wanted to reform election laws to attract better leaders to colonial government. He also was suspicious about Parliamentary power and believed that the King was in the best position to protect the common law rights of the colonists. Kennedy found merit in how the colonies structured their branches of governance and he argued that the lower houses of the legislatures, the branch closest to the people, should have equal authority with the governors and councils. Yet, Kennedy warned the legislatures that they must pay an adequate salary to their governors and not use their taxing privileges to control the executive offices. Kennedy well understood governance tensions within the colonies and in his *Essay* projected their continuation.

ANONYMOUS, *AN ESSAY UPON THE GOVERNMENT OF THE ENGLISH PLANTATIONS,* 1701

AS OF late many Controversies have arisen in the *English* Nation; so 'tis observable, that the two great Topicks of Trade and Plantations have had their Parts in the Dispute; and indeed it must be confess'd, that (considering the present Circumstances of the World) they are of the greatest importance to all Nations, but more especially the *English*.

Almost all that hath been hitherto written concerning the Plantations hath had a more peculiar Relation to their Trade, and accordingly the several Advocates either for their Freedom, or binding them to a more strict Dependance upon the Crown of *England,* have framed their Arguments so as they thought might best answer those Purposes; from whence it may be very naturally inferr'd, that some By Ends of their own have had a great Influence over many of them, and that private Interest was the great *Diana* for which they contested.

The Design of these Papers

The Design of these Papers is not to treat of the Trade, but the Government of the Plantations; not how to make them great, and rich, by an open free Traffick, but happy, by a Just and Equal

Government; that they may enjoy their Obscurity, and the poor way of living which Nature is pleased to afford them out of the Earth, in Peace; and be protected in the Possession thereof, by their lawful Mother *England*.

I am sensible the *English* Plantations may be rendred very serviceable and beneficial to their Mother Kingdom, and I do not in the least doubt she will make the best Advantage of them she can; 'tis what others would do if they were in her place; and therefore I shall not complain of any Hardships in Trade, neither shall it be mentioned but as it comes in the way, in pursuit of the main Design I have laid down.

The Countries under the *English* Government on the Continent of *America* are healthy and fertile, and very well situate both for Pleasure and Profit, especially *Virginia* and *Maryland*, which, as they are the best and most advantagious to the Crown of *England*; so likewise is the Air and Climate of them most agreeable to the *English* Constitutions of Body, the Land richest, the Rivers most commodious, and naturally the whole Countries far excelling any part of the Continent either on the North or South of them.

The chiefest Thing wanting to make the Inhabitants of these Plantations happy, is a good Constitution of Government; and it seems strange, that so little care hath been heretofore taken of that, since it could not be any Prejudice, but of great Advantage even to *England* it self, as perhaps may appear by what shall be offered hereafter.

'Tis true, many Propositions have been made for regulating the Governments of particular Plantations, several of which are now extant; but being mostly calculated by Persons who seem to be biassed by Interest, Prejudice, Revenge, Ambition, or other private Ends I dare not rely on them: Some there are which I shall make bold to use some Parts of, as I find them for my Purpose.

Objections against this Discourse

But before I proceed further, it is necessary to answer some Objections that may be made against my self, and the Work I am going about.

It hath been alledged by some that the Plantations are prejudicial to *England*; but this is already so well answered by Sir *J. Child* in his New Discourse of Trade,[1] from Page 178, to Page 216, by the Author of the *Essay upon Ways and Means*, in his Discourses on the Publick Revenues and the Trade of *England*, Part II. p. 193, to 209, and several other Writings which have been Published, that I cannot think it needful to say any thing more about it.

The Objections I shall take notice of, are these following:

1. It may be objected, that I being an Inhabitant of the Plantations, may probably be too much biassed to their Interest, and therefore am not to be relied on.

2. That the Plantation Governments are already setled well enough; and it may be dangerous to make any great Alterations in them.

3. That it is necessary the King should be more Absolute in the Plantations than he is in *England*: And consequently,

4. That the setling a free Constitution of Government in the Plantations will be prejudicial to the King's Service.

Answer to those Objections

In answer to all which, I beg leave to offer the following Considerations.

1. That, let the Author be what he will, the most material Thing to be respected, is the good or evil Tendency of the Work. If his Majesty's Service seems chiefly aimed at, and no private Interest mixed with it, then I hope that Objection is removed: And for my self, I can with a great deal of Truth and Sincerity affirm, that I have not the least Thought or Design of any thing but his Majesty's Interest and Service, and therein of the Good of all his Subjects in general; but whether the Means I shall propose, may be any wise conducive to those Ends, is humbly submitted to those who have the Honour to be intrusted with the Charge of those Affairs.

The Plantation Governments never well setled

2. If the Governments of the Plantations are already well setled, there needs not any Alteration,

(that, I think, every good Man will grant:) But if upon inquiry, it appears, that none of them have ever been well setled; that the present Method of managing them is inconvenient and prejudicial; and that much better Ways may be found: If, I say, these things can be shewn, why should they not be received: If, being considered, they are not approved, they may be rejected, no Alteration will be made, nor any harm done; but rather Good: For my Attempt may set some better Hand to work on the same Subject; and being instructed by others Observations on my Errors, may be more capable to make Amendments: But this, I think, may be safely said, that if any Alterations in the Government of the Plantations are necessary, they may be much more easily done now they are in their Infancy, than hereafter when they grow more populous, and the Evils have taken deeper Root, and are more interwoven with the Laws and Constitutions of the several Colonies.

The King ought not to have a more absolute Power in the Plantations than in England

3. It may perhaps be said that it is necessary the King should have a more absolute Power in the Plantations than he hath in *England*. I know this hath been said, and pretended to be asserted by Argument; and to make it more passable, it hath been framed into a sort of a *Syllogism*, thus: All such *Kingdoms, Principalities, Dominions,* &c. *as are dependent on the Crown of* England, *and are not a Part of the Empire of the King of* England, *are subject to such Laws as the King is pleased to impose on them; But the* English *Plantations in* America *are dependent on the Crown of* England, *and are not part of the Empire of the King of* England: Ergo, *they are subject to such Laws as the King shall please to impose.* Now it is observable, that the main Stress of this Matter depends upon the Distinction between the *Crown of* England, and the *Empire of the King of* England: And if there is no such Distinction (as possibly there may not) the whole falls to Ground: But if there be such a Distinction, then the clear Tendency of the Argument, is to lay the Plantations intirely at the King's Feet, for him to do what he pleases with them; and the Parliament are not at all concerned in the

Business, only upon sufferance. This I take to be the clear Consequence of the Argument, which no King ever yet pretended to; and for which the Lords and Commons of *England* are very much obliged to the Inventer.

But tho' the King's Right and Prerogative are pretended in the Argument, there were other Reasons for inventing it; and that will appear, if it be remembered that it was first made use of upon the following Occasion. In former times a certain Gentleman was made Governour of one of the *English* Plantations, and had a large Commission for his Office, which he put in Execution after such a manner, that the People were not able to forbear shewing the highest Resentments of such Usage; and at last had recourse to Arms.

And hereupon to vindicate the Governour's Proceedings, it was thought necessary to start this Argument of the King's absolute Power in the Plantations, thereby to lay the Odium of an ill Governour's wicked Actions upon the King.

By the ancient known Laws of the Land the King's Power is sufficient to make himself a great Prince, and his Subjects a happy People; and those very Men that raise these strange Arguments for Absolute Power do not aim at the King's Service in it: But they know, that if they make the King Absolute, his Lieutenant will be so of course; and that is their chief Design.

Thus the King's Power is pretended to be made great, whilst in reality his Interest is destroyed, and so is the Interest of *England* too: for these are the true Reasons that many People who are poor and miserable at home, will not come to the Plantations because they know they shall be ill used.

From what is said, I think it appears very plain, that it is not for the Interest or Service either of the King or Kingdom of *England*, that the Plantations should be under an unlimited Government: the true Interest of *England*, is to have the Plantations cherished, and the poor People encouraged to come hither, every Man here being of great Value to *England*, and most of those that come, are not able to do much good at home.

Whatever Power the King hath in the Plantations must be executed by his Lieutenants: and if it should so happen that the King be mistaken in the Man, and send one who would aim more at his own Interest than the King's Service; and by Extortion, Bribery, and other the like Practices (too often complained of in some Places) should so distract the People, that they make Commotions or Insurrections against him: The King cannot possibly know this till it is too late; and then he will be obliged to inflict the severest Punishments upon some of the most considerable Offenders, to the Ruin of them and their Families, who otherwise might have done his Majesty good Service.

Neither is this all; for by such Commotions the Product of one Year at least will be lost in that Colony where they happen, which will be a greater Prejudice to *England* than the best Governour will ever be able to make amends for; the Loss of the Tobacco made in one Year in *Virginia*, considering the Customs and the Merchants Damage, by their shipping and Stock being unimployed, will amount to at least 500000£. prejudice to the King and Kingdom of *England*.

I know it will be said, that all this proceeds either from groundless Jealousies of I know not what Dangers to happen, no one knows when; or else, that I am very much prejudiced against some of the present Governours of the Plantations; to which I answer: That it is not to be supposed such things should happen every Day; but since they have been heretofore, it is probable, they may be again, and the Consequence being so very dangerous, the more Reason there is to endeavour the Prevention of them: And for the other Imputation, I can with a great deal of Truth say, that I have the Honour of being known but to two of the King's Governours, and for both of them, I have the most profound Respect and Regard imaginable; nor can I believe that either of them will find fault with me for endeavouring to prevent those male-Administrations in others, of which they will never be guilty themselves.

A free Constitution of Government in the Plantations not prejudicial to the King's Service

4. The other Objection to this Work is, That the setling a free Constitution of Government in the Plantations may be prejudicial to the King's Service. To this I answer, That by a free Constitution of Government, I mean, that the Inhabitants of the Plantations may enjoy their Liberties and Estates, and have Justice equally and impartially administered unto them; and that it should not be in the power of any Governour to prevent this. Now by enjoying Liberty, I understand, the Liberty of their Persons being free from Arbitrary, illegal Imprisonments; not that they should have great Liberties of Trade, or any other Liberties or Priviledges, that may be thought prejudicial to the King or Kingdom of *England*; for my Design is not to complain of our Subjection, or any thing of that Nature; but to shew as well as I can, what may be done for the Interest and Service both of *England* and the Plantations.

It is no Advantage to the King, that his Governours should have it in their Power to gripe and squeeze the People in the Plantations, nor is it ever done, for any other Reason, than their own private Gain. I have often heard Complaints made, that the Governours and their Officers and Creatures, have been guilty of ill things to raise Estates for themselves, or to gratify their own Revenge, or some other Passion; but I never heard, that any of the Plantations were oppressed to raise Money for the King's Service, and indeed I think it is past Dispute, that the King's and Plantations Interest is the same, and that those who pretend, the King hath, or ought to have an unlimited Power in the Plantations, are a sort of People, whose Designs make their Interests run counter to that both of the King and Plantations.

Thus having briefly answered those Objections which perhaps may be made to what I shall offer: I proceed to the main Design, which is to shew several things, which I must beg leave to say, I conceive are amiss, and to propose some Methods for redressing those Grievances.

The Heads of the following Discourse

The Particulars which I shall treat of may properly enough be ranked under these several

Heads, *viz. Religion, Laws, Trade, People, Relation of one Plantation to another, Governours, King.*

Grievances relating to Religion

The present Inconveniencies relating to Religion, in short are these. 1. That there is not a good free Liberty of Conscience established; but generally whatever Religion or Sect happens to be most numerous, they have the Power over all the rest; thus the Independants in *New-England,* and the Quakers in *Pensylvania,* abuse all Mankind that come among them, and are not of their Persuasion; and in *New-York* it is as bad, or rather worse; for there the contending Parties are pritty near equal; from whence it follows, that (sometimes one, and sometimes the other prevailing,) those who happen to have the best Interest and most favour in the Government, exert their utmost Skill and Industry to ruin the others.

In our Government of *Virginia* we are, or pretend most of us to be of the Church of *England;* some few Roman Catholicks amongst us, some Quakers, who at present seem to be greatly increasing; and about two or three Meetings of Dissenters, and those in the out-parts of the Countrey, where at present are no Church of *England* Ministers, nor can any be put well there, no sufficient Provision being made for their Maintenance; all the Ministers Salaries are paid in Tobacco, which in those places is of so small value, that they cannot well subsist upon the Salary allowed by Law.

But notwithstanding the Church of *England* is so generally established here, yet there is scarce any sort of Church Government established amongst us; the Laws indeed do direct building of Churches, and have ascertain'd what Salaries shall be paid to the Clergy, but it is not well determined who are Patrons of the Parishes, what Right of presentation they have, in what Cases the King, or the Bishop may present *jure devoluto,* and many other Defects of that Nature there are, as yet unprovided for; here also I may add, that there is no established Court for the Punishment of Scandalous Ministers, nor any Care taken to prevent Dilapidations, neither are

there any Courts where Incestuous Marriages, and other Causes of the like nature are properly triable.

In some places no care at all is taken, either of the Religion or Morality of the Inhabitants, as particularly, *North-Carolina,* and in this almost all the Proprieties and Charter-Governments are to blame.

I shall not take upon me to offer much towards remedying these Grievances of Religion, because I think it is an improper Subject for me; but it is to be wish'd, that some Care were taken to instruct the People well in Morality, that is, what all Perswasions either do, or pretend to desire.

Grievances on Account of their Laws

The Inconveniences the Plantations labour under, on Account of their Laws, are very many.

It is a great Unhappiness, that no one can tell what is Law, and what is not, in the Plantations; some hold that the Law of *England* is chiefly to be respected, and where that is deficient, the Laws of the several Colonies are to take place; others are of Opinion, that the Laws of the Colonies are to take first place, and that the Law of *England* is of force only where they are silent; others there are, who contend for the Laws of the Colonies, in Conjunction with those that were in force in *England* at the first Settlement of the Colony, and lay down that as the measure of our Obedience, alleging, that we are not bound to observe any late Acts of Parliament made in *England,* except such only where the Reason of the Law is the same here, that it is in *England;* but this leaving too great a Latitude to the Judge; some others hold that no late Acts of the Parliament of *England* do bind the Plantations, but those only, wherein the Plantations are particularly named. Thus are we left in the dark, in one of the most considerable Points of our Rights; and the Case being so doubtful, we are too often obliged to depend upon the Crooked Cord of a Judge's Discretion, in Matters of the greatest Moment and Value.

Of late Years great Doubts have been raised, how far the Legislative Authority is in the

Assemblies of the several Colonies; whether they have Power to make certain Acts or Ordinances in the nature of by-Laws only; or, whether they can make Acts of Attainder, Naturalization, for setling or disposing of Titles to Lands within their own Jurisdiction, and other things of the like Nature; and where Necessity requires, make such Acts as best suit the Circumstances and Constitution of the Country, even tho' in some Particulars, they plainly differ from the Laws of *England*.

And as there have been Doubts made concerning the Enacting of Laws with us, so likewise there have been great Controversies concerning the Repeal of Laws made here: The Assemblies have held, that when any Law made by them, and not assented to by the King in *England* is repealed by them; such Repeal doth intirely annul and abrogate, and even (as it were) annihilate the former Law, as if it never had been made, and that it cannot by any means be revived, but by the same Power that at first enacted it, which was the Assembly; but the Governours have held, that tho' the King hath not assented to the first, yet he hath the Liberty of refusing his Assent to the repealing Law, and by Proclamation may repeal that, and then the other is revived of course: This Dispute, and others of the like Nature, ran very high in the late Reigns.

It is also to be observed as a great Defect, that no one of these Colonies on the Continent, have any tolerable Body of Laws; all of them have some sort of Laws or other; but there is not any such thing amongst them all, as a regular Constitution of Government, and good Laws for Directions of the several Officers, and other Persons therein, with suitable Penalties to enforce Obedience to them.

This seems to have been a Fault in the Beginning; for then it was put into bad Hands, and hath been little mended since: One notorious Instance may be given in *Virginia*. This Colony was at first given for the Encouragement of it to a Company of Adventurers, who by Charter from King *James* the first, were constituted a Corporation, and they set up a sort of Government here, the Chief Magistrates whereof were called

Governours and Council; and they (I suppose) as the chief Members of the Corporation, constituted the highest Court of Judicature; afterwards this Countrey was taken into the King's Hands, and the same Constitution of Governor and Council remained; and they to this Day continue to be the highest Court of Judicature in the Countrey; tho' we have no Law to establish them as such, neither have they ever had any Commission for that purpose, and till *April* 1699, were never sworn to do Justice, but being made Counsellors, they took their Places as Judges of Course.

From hence it may be observ'd, that no great Stress is to be laid on any Argument against Alterations in the Plantations, barely because Changes may be dangerous, for (it seems) a Regular Settlement hath never yet been made, and therefore 'tis time to be done now.

Courts of Judicature

After what has been said concerning the Defects in the Legislative Authority, and the Laws of the Plantations; It is not to be thought strange, that the Establishment of the Courts of Judicature is defective also, that being the Superstructure and the other the Foundation. . . .

Grievances with Relation to the Governours

6. The next concerning Governours is a tender Point, and must be touched with clean Hands; and when I profess that I do not design to expose any particular Person now in Office, I hope Liberty may be allowed me, to remark some Grievances that the Plantations have, and may have Cause to complain of, if they knew where.

And herein I shall but lightly mention some things, part of which at least, perhaps it may be necessary to reform hereafter, not accusing any Person for what is past.

Some Governours either through Weakness or Prejudice, have contributed very much to raise Factions in the Colonies under their Command, by making use of, and encouraging some one particular Sort or Sett of Men, and rejecting all others, and these Favourites being oftentimes of mean

Education and base Spirits, cannot bear their good Fortunes, but thinking absolute Command only is their Province, either for private Interest, or to gratifie their Ambition, Revenge, or some other Passion, they hardly ever fail to run all Things into Confusion; and of these Actions by Favourites, Instances are not wanting.

The King's Governours in the Plantations either have, or pretend to have very large Powers within their Provinces, which together with the Trusts reposed in them, of disposing of all Places of Honour and Profit, and of being chief Judges in the Supream Courts of Judicature, (as they are in many Places, if not all) render them so absolute, that it is almost impossible to lay any sort of Restraint upon them.

On the other side, in some of the Proprieties, the Hands of the Government are so feeble, that they cannot protect themselves against the Insolencies of the Common People, which makes them very subject to Anarchy and Confusion.

The chief End of many Governours coming to the Plantations, having been to get Estates for themselves, very unwarrantable Methods have sometimes been made use of to compass those Ends, as by engrossing several Offices into their own Hands, selling them or letting them out at a yearly Rent of such a part of the Profits, and also by Extortion and Presents, (or Bribery) these things have been heretofore, and in ill Times may be done again.

And here I must beg Leave to say, that I am of Opinion, the Court of *England* hath hitherto gone upon wrong Principles, in appointing Governours of the Plantations; for those Places have been generally given as the last Rewards for past Services, and they expecting nothing after that, were almost necessitated, then to make Provision for their whole Lives, whereby they were in a manner forced upon such Methods (whether good or evil) as would compass those Ends.

Another very considerable difficulty the Plantations lie under from their Governours, is, that there is no way left to represent their evil Treatment to the King; for nothing of that Nature can be done without Money, no Money can be had without an Assembly, and the Governour

always hath a Negative in their Proceedings, and not only so, but if he fears any thing of that Nature, he can let alone calling one, or (being called) can dissolve them at pleasure.

King unacquainted with the true State of the Plantations

7. But the last and greatest Unhappiness the Plantations labour under, is, that the King and Court of *England* are altogether Strangers to the true State of Affairs in *America,* for that is the true Cause why their Grievances have not been long since redress'd.

The present Establishment of the Lords Commissioners for Trade and Plantations is very necessary and expedient for that Purpose, and perhaps may be rendred much more so, but they being Strangers to the Affairs in these Parts, are too often obliged to depend on the Relation of others who pretend to be better acquainted. Misrepresentations in those Cases may be very dangerous, and cannot well be prevented, there not being as yet any Method setled for them to gain certain Information of the true State of the Plantations.

Remedies for the aforementioned Grievances

Hitherto I have taken notice of some of the most material Inconveniencies attending these Plantations: Now I must beg Leave to offer such Remedies to Consideration as with Submission I conceive may prevent the like Grievances for the future.

To propose Schemes of Government, I know, hath always been esteemed a difficult Task, and the more, because the Proposer is look'd upon as obliged to answer all Objections that shall be made against them, and it is not impossible to raise many Objections against the best Government in the World, tho' perhaps it would be difficult to make any real Amendments.

I do not pretend to assert, that what I offer is of necessity to be approved, and that better cannot be done; I shall only presume to offer some few Generals to consideration; if they are well accepted, I have my Reward, if not, many

Men of much greater Abilities than I am, have lost their Labours in such Cases, and therefore I shall be contented.

And as I began to lay open the Inconveniencies and Grievances of the Plantations, in order as they came under the General Heads set down in the beginning, so I shall likewise endeavour to propose the Remedies in the same Method; and,

Remedies for the Grievances of Religion

1. For Religion; I have already said, I take it to be improper for me to offer much upon that Subject, and therefore, I shall only presume to mention two things, which I take to be of necessity, for the Maintenance and Support of the Civil Government.

Liberty of Conscience

1. That sufficient Provision be made for all People, to enjoy the same Liberty of Conscience in the Plantations, that is indulged to them in *England*, upon the same Terms, and not otherwise; and as Dissenters should be sure of this Liberty, so likewise good Care should be taken that they may not abuse it; particularly, it is necessary to make such a Settlement, that no one may find it his Interest to leave the Church of *England*; as now in Virginia every Housholder is obliged by Law to provide himself with Arms and Ammunition, and to go to Musters of the *Militia*; if they fail, they are to pay such a Fine: But the Law for imposing it being somewhat defective, and therefore the Fines not duly levied, many People (who have no great Sense of any Religion,) turn Quakers, chiefly to save the Expence and Trouble of providing Arms and Ammunition, and of going to Musters, and also by professing themselves Quakers, they are eased of being Constables, Church-wardens, and all such troublesome Offices, which other People are obliged to execute.

Against Immorality

2. Tho' perhaps it may not be convenient to force all People to be of one Religion, yet it may be requisite to oblige every one to profess and practise some sort of Religion or other: to this end I humbly propose, that severe Laws be made against Blasphemy, Prophaneness, Cursing, Swearing, Sabbath-breaking, &c. with suitable Penalties to enforce the Observation thereof, and that all possible Diligence be used by the Governours, and other principal Officers of the Plantations to put those Laws in Effectual Execution within their respective Provinces.

Remedies for the Grievances relating to the Laws

2. For remedying of the Grievances mentioned under the Head of Laws, I humbly propose,

1. That some Rule be established, to know what Laws the Plantations are to be subject to, and particularly, how far the late Acts of Parliament do affect them, where they are not expressly mentioned.

Legislature

2. That it be agreed how far the Legislature is in their Assemblies; whether they have Power of Naturalization, Attainders of Treason, Illegitimating of Heirs, cutting off Intails, settling Titles to Lands, and other things of that nature; and whether they may make Laws disagreable to the Laws of *England*, in such Cases, where the Circumstances of the Places are vastly different, as concerning Plantations, Waste, the Church, &c.

Courts of Judicature

3. That a good Constitution of Courts of Judicature be established in the several Plantations, as shall be most agreeable to their respective Forms of Government, and other Circumstances.

That the Judges of the Supream Courts in every Province hold their Offices *quam diu se bene gesserint*, and that Provision be made to ascertain what shall be adjudged Misbehaviour in them, or at least, that care be taken, that it be not absolutely in the Governour's Breast, to displace any

Judge at pleasure, without shewing his Reasons for the same, together with the Judge's Answer thereto.

That the last Resort of Justice may not be to the Chief Governours and Council here, and thence to the King and Council in *England,* as is now practised in most places; but that from the Judges commissionated as aforesaid, an Appeal directly to *England* may be allowed to such People as think themselves injured, in any Sum exceeding the Value of five hundred Pounds *Sterl.*

Lands to be confirmed by the King

4. That in the King's Colonies, his Majesty would be graciously pleased to confirm all Lands to the several Possessors, (where any privat Persons Interest is not concerned) as was done by King *Charles* the second in his Charter to *Virginia,* of which also Care should be taken, that it be not infringed, as heretofore it hath been.

Tenants of the Proprietors to be secured in their Lands

And that by some Law for that purpose, good and wholsom Provisions be made, for the setling and adjusting the Inhabitants Titles to those Lands they hold of Proprietors, that those People may not be continually obliged to a servile Dependance upon their Landlords, and thereby be sometimes necessitated either to behave themselves disrespectively and disobediently to the Governour, acting by the King's Authority there, or to be in danger of losing their Lands, being forced to pay extravagant Fines for Confirmation of their Titles, or of being some other way liable to suffer under the Proprietors, or their Agents Displeasure.

I am very far from desiring, that the Right of the Proprietors in their Lands should be injured, therefore (for Explanation) I add further, that I do not propose, that the Proprietors shall be compelled to part with their Land at any set Price; in that let them make such reasonable Terms as they can; but whatever the Terms are, let the Inhabitants be secured by good Laws from any Tricks or Designs, which may be put upon them

thereafter, for that will certainly cause Disorders and Mutinies, which are publick Inconveniencies and by no means to be tolerated for any private Man's Advantage; or if the People find themselves so far in the Proprietors Power, that they are of Necessity obliged to submit to him, then all that Interest will most surely be employed in prejudice of the King's Government there; and of this an Instance may be given, but it is an Invidious Task to tell Men of their Faults, and therefore I shall not mention them. . . .

Remedy of Grievances that one Plantation is to another

5. To redress the Grievances that one Plantation may suffer by another, some Things have been already proposed under the Head of Trade; as particularly, the Setling an equal Liberty of Trade, and the same Standard of Coin throughout all the *English* Plantations on the Continent; the Reasonableness of which, I suppose, is already so clearly evinced, that I think it needless to say any thing more to it here.

For a further Redress to these Grievances, it is humbly proposed, That by some General Law, to be binding to all the Colonies on the Continent, a certain Method be established, 1. To decide all Controversies between Colony and Colony. 2. To bring Persons to condign Punishment, who commit Offences against the Laws of one Colony, and then fly into another, or who living in one Colony, go into another, and commit Offences, and then return to their own Habitation. 3. To compel Fugitive Debtors to pay their just Debts, and runaway Servants and Slaves, to be returned to their Masters living in other Colonies. 4. To adjust all Disputes concerning Trade or Commerce in the several Colonies, and all other Matters whatsoever relating to the general Benefit of them all.

General Assembly of all the Provinces proposed by the Author of the Essay on Ways and Means

And here I must beg leave to take notice of a Scheme, for the General good Government of these Northern Plantations, set down in the aforementioned Discourses of the Publick Revenues, &c. Part 2d. Page 259. which Scheme with some little Alteration (the Government of the Colonies being rightly constituted) will perhaps prove the most effectual Remedy for all Grievances of this Nature, that can be proposed; but under the present Management, or whilst so many Colonies are governed by Proprietors, perhaps nothing can be proposed more prejudicial to the Interest of *England*.

The first Contriver of that Scheme was a Person not well acquainted with the State of every particular Colony here, and therefore no wonder if he hath committed an Error, in proposing an equal number of Deputies for the several Provinces, when they are so vastly different, for numbers of People, extent of Territory, and of the Value of them in their Trade, especially that to *Europe*.

Therefore with submission I conceive, that those Deputies would be more equally proportion'd in manner following, *viz. Virginia* four, *Mary-Land* three, *New-York* two, *Boston* three, *Connecticut* two, *Rhode Island* two, *Pensylvania* one, the two *Carolina*'s one, each of the two *Jersey*'s one.

And as angry as the Gentleman seems to be with *Virginia*, I think he cannot find fault with allowing one Deputy more for that, than for any of the rest, because it hath the most Inhabitants, is the eldest and most profitable of all the *English* Plantations in *America*; and if at such a Convention, we should pretend to take place of all our Neighbours, perhaps they may not give any good Reason to the contrary.

It is there proposed that these Deputies may always meet at *New-York*, and that the Chief Governour there for the time being, shall preside as High Commissioner amongst them; this was well designed no doubt by the Proposer: But under favour I presume it would be much more convenient and useful too, if they met by turns, sometimes in one Province, and sometimes in another; and the chief Governour in the Province where they meet, being commissionated by his Majesty, may preside as Commissioner in manner aforementioned.

The Court of the *Amphictiones*, in Imitation of which this is proposed, did not always meet in one place, but sometimes at *Pylae*, and sometimes at *Delphi*, and without question there were a great many Reasons for their so doing; but in this Case I conceive there are more.

1. It is necessary that those Deputies should be well acquainted with the true State of the whole Continent, which at present they know little of, and no way more proper to instruct them in it, than by holding these Conventions, sometimes at one place, and sometimes at another; which in time would make the most considerable Persons of every Province, become personally acquainted; for the better sort of People would look upon it as a piece of Gentile Education, to let their Sons go in Company of the Deputies of the Province to these Conventions.

2. It seems a little unreasonable, that the Province of *New-York*, and consequently the Governour thereof for the time being, should be so much advanced in Dignity above the rest of the Colonies and their Governours; some of the other are more considerable, the Governments more valuable, are more immediately depending upon the King, and by far the more profitable to *England*.

3. It is unequal that *New York* should have such an Opportunity of drawing so much Money to it every Year from all the other Colonies.

To obviate these and many other Objections of this nature which may be made, it is humbly proposed, That the whole Continent be divided into five Circuits or Divisions, thus, 1. *Virginia*. 2. *Mary-Land*. 3. *Pensylvania*, and the two *Jersey*'s. 4. *New-York*. 5. *Boston, Connecticut*, and *Rhode Island*; in each of which Division, let it be held by turns one after another, in a certain Order.

Remedy of the Grievances from the Governours

4. The next general Head is as much as may be to remedy the Grievances that may happen to the Plantations by their Governours.

Under the Head of Laws it is already proposed, That the last Resort of Justice in any Province, may not be to the chief Governour there; the Reason is plain, to wit, it is very dangerous to establish any Judicature, which cannot be called to Account for male-administrations; and that the Governours of the Plantations are so, is already made appear in the Grievances before complained of under this Head.

The Government of all the Plantations to be annexed to the Crown

For the better Regulation and Management of these Plantations, it is humbly proposed, That the Government of them all may be annexed to the Crown by Act of Parliament, for without that, it will be impossible to keep them upon an equal Foot; but some Tricks or other will be plaid by the Charter Governments, let their Pretentions be never so fair. Without question *New-England* Men pretend, that they would not entertain Pyrates upon any account in the World, and yet it is observable, that tho' they have long used those Parts, none of them have been taken till of late, since the Government of the Earl of *Bellamont*, who may properly be called the first Governour of the *English* Interest in that Province.

I am not ignorant that many Persons whose Interests are concerned, will look upon this as a very unjust Proposition, and object the great Injustice of such an Action, as very much tending to the Destruction of Property, and the like; to all which I shall make but little Answer, and that in this manner.

That in the beginning, *Virginia* was planted by a Company, who had a Charter for their so doing; and afterwards (the good of the whole so requiring) not only the Government, but the very Property of the Land was taken into the King's Hands, and so remains at this Day.

The Government of *Mary-Land*, is now in the King's Hands, and yet the Lord *Baltimore* enjoys his Property in the Land as he did heretofore, and not only so, but all other Revenues that were setled on him by the Assembly of that Province.

The Government of *New-England*, is now in the King's Hands; and if the Publick Welfare required it, why should not the Proprieties of *Pensylvania*, the *Jersey's* and the *Carolina's* be likewise governed in the same manner?

2. The Propriety of the Soil may remain to the Proprietor, as heretofore, and need not be prejudiced by the King's appointing Governours in those Parts: And if this be not satisfactory, but they still pretend to have the Governments intirely in their own Hands, I beg leave to admonish them to consult with their Counsellors at Law, how far the King hath Power to grant the Supream Government of the Plantations, to any Person or Persons, and their Heirs, without the assent of the Parliament.

I shall say no more to this Point at present; tho it may very reasonably be urged, that in times of Danger, *England* must be at the Charge to defend them all, which cannot well be done without taking the Government.

That it is necessary for all the Colonies to be united under one Head, for their common Defence; and that it will be much more so, if the *French*, or any other Nation, possess themselves of the River *Messachippe*, and the Lakes to the West-ward.

That in case of a War with *Spain*, nothing could tend more to the Advantage of *England*, than having all these Colonies under the Crown, to give such Assistance as should be necessary towards any Design upon the *West-Indies*, which would never be done by the Proprieties, unless they saw some extraordinary private Advantage by it.

I say, all these Considerations may reasonably be urged, but Time permits me not to examine them at present.

Representations in England of the State of the Plantations

A true Representation in *England* of the State of Affairs in the Colonies, would very much conduce to the keeping of the Governours in good order, or at least from notorious Transgressions, for fear of being complained of at Home; therefore with Submission, I shall by and by propose such Methods, as seem most feasable to procure such Representations to be made.

Against Governours engrossing Offices, Bribery, &c.

It hath already been complained of, as a Grievance, that sometimes Governours do engross into their own Hands several Offices, and others they let out for such a part of the yearly Profits: And for the prevention of the like Practices, and of all sorts of Bribery, Extortion, and other Misdemeanours, for the future, perhaps no Method will prove more effectual than by laying severe Injunctions upon the King's Governours, that they do not presume to keep any Place vacant, more than such a space of Time as shall be thought requisite, and that they do not take any manner of Present or Gratuity for the bestowing of any Office, that they do not upon any Pretence whatsoever take any manner of Gift, Reward, or Perquisite; that they be not any ways concerned in Trade.

Encouragements to Governours to behave themselves well

And that none of the Governours may pretend a necessity of minding something besides their Offices, to get their Living by, their Salaries may be so much enlarged, as will make them sufficient for their Maintenance, and to spare.

For a farther Encouragement to them to behave themselves well in their Governments, it seems reasonable to contrive it in such manner for the Future, that such good Behavior may recommend them to farther Rewards at Home, (and not that these Governments be given as formerly, for Rewards of past Services, and so the Governours be obliged to make the best of it they can, because they expect nothing to come after.) To this end it may perhaps be found convenient, to provide that hereafter all Governours behaving themselves well in the Plantations, and having been there above three years, shall obtain the King's leave to resign, without any Mismanagements laid to their Charge, may have a yearly Pension allowed them, (after their return Home) of a fourth part of the value of the Established Salary in the Governments they left, which Pensions should be duly paid, till some other Preferments were

bestowed on them, to the value thereof: And if after all these Encouragements, any Governour dare offend, let him fall without Mercy.

The King and Court of England unacquainted with the State of the Plantations

7. The last and greatest Grievance I mentioned, is, that the King and Court of *England* are very much unacquainted with the true State of Affairs in the *American* Plantations, for the Redress whereof it is humbly proposed.

Remedy for this Grievance

1. That every Colony have an Agent constantly residing in *England*, to give an account from time to time, as he shall be thereto required, of all the Affairs and Transactions of the Plantation he is authorized by; and lest this Agent be corrupted and wrought upon, to give wrong Informations, as a check upon him,

2. Let one Person be commissioned from *England*, to travel through all the Plantations, to make enquiry into, and give a true Representation of the State of their Affairs; and these two Persons being Checks one upon the other, would both of them be obliged to speak the Truth.

That this last Proposition may be the better understood; I beg leave to set it down somewhat more particularly.

1. Let one Person, thereunto commissionated by his Majesty, travel through all the Colonies on the Continent.

And the better to enable him to do Service, let him have Power to sit in the Councils of every Colony where he cames: Let him have free access to all Records, Council-Books, Publick Accounts, and all other Books and Papers relating to the Government, or any Office of Trust or Profit. Let him have Authority to inquire into, and examine the State of all the Colonies where he comes; and for his better Guidance and Direction herein, a Scheme of material and pertinent Queries may be drawn up and given him; as particularly to enquire 1. Concerning the Legislature in the Plantations, In whom it is invested, What Powers they have, What their Priviledges, Methods of Proceedings, And how often they are conven'd.

2. Concerning the Civil Government: What the Governours Power? What the Councils? How many of them there are? How they are made? What Offices they hold, and what Value those Offices are of? &c.

3. Concerning the public Offices of the Government; How many there are? Of what Value? In whose Gift? How executed? What Estates they have in them?

4. Concerning the *Militia*; What numbers of them? How armed? How commanded? In how long time they may be ready for service?

5. Concerning the *Indians*; How many Nations are tributary to the Crown of *England*? What their Number and Strength? Where scituate? What *Indian* Enemies most dangerous? What Trade with them may be most profitable? What the best Method of Defence against them?

6. Concerning Courts of Justice; How many there are? Where held? Who Judges? What their Jurisdiction? What Commissions they have? How Justice is administred? How long Causes are generally depending?

7. Concerning the Revenue; What particular Branches there are? How Collected? What the Charge of Collection? Who keeps the Public Money in Bank? How much every particular Branch brings in, and to what Uses applied? What Money in Bank? Or, what Debts, and how contracted?

8. Concerning Religion; What Religion most numerous? What established by Law? What number of the Church of *England*? What Provision made for the Clergy? What Ecclesiastick Authority?

9. Concerning Works of Piety and Charity; What Foundations for Learning? What Maintenance for Poor? By whom founded? By what Authority? How endowed? How the Primitive Institutions are observed?

10. Concerning Trade; What the Product of the Countrey for Exportation? Whither carried? What usually imported, and from whence? What Ports? What Towns? What their Privileges? How governed? What Manufactures? Whither carried? What number of Ships and Vessels? What Trade they are imployed in? How the Trade is managed? Whether by Money or Barter?

11. Concerning Money; How plenty Money is? What Coin most current? At what Value? What the Exchange of remitting Money to *England*?

12. Concerning Grievances; What the greatest Grievances? What the Cause of them? How they may be redressed?

I might add many more Queries, as concerning the number of People, the Value of Lands, the Scituation of Places, the Conveniencies of Offence or Defence, the King's Rents, the Proprietors Interest, the Wealth of the Inhabitants, &c. But I purposely omit them for Brevity sake, the Particulars before mentioned, being sufficient to make the Method clearly apprehended.

These Queries (together with such other as shall be thought necessary,) being proposed in the Plantations to the Governours, Councils, General Assemblies, Courts of Judicature, Lawyers, Clerks, Clergymen, Magistrates, Merchants, &c. their Answers will give a great Light into the true State of Affairs in these Parts; and also such a Persons own Observations might be of great Use, if carefully made.

And that no one may be fearful to answer the Truth to the aforementioned Queries, let both Queries and Answers be kept secret, till they are laid before the Commissioners of Trade in *England*, and if they find any thing material, let them send Orders for a more particular Inquiry, and let Care be taken, that no Man suffer for speaking the Truth in these Cases.

The main Thing in this Proposition to be consider'd, is, whether the Advantage of it will be greater than the Charge, for such Inquiries cannot be made without some Charge, tho' that need not be much; if a very great Man be employed in such a Service, then indeed the Cost will be great also; but if one that is not above the Business, who will be active and industrious, be employed, a Salary of five hundred Pounds a Year (with an Allowance of ten Shillings a Day, whilst he is travelling from Place to Place) will be sufficient; if he behave himself well, he will be thereby recommended to further Favour at his Return home; if otherwise, that is more than he deserves.

And perhaps it may not be convenient to let any one enjoy this Office above five years, and so as one returns, another may be sent.

Now if this Commissioner be obliged to give the best Account he can, of the State of those Colonies through which he travels, if the several Governours be directed to represent the State of their respective Provinces, if the Convention of the whole Continent aforementioned, remonstrate the Affairs of them all, and if the Agents of every Colony residing in *England,* be required from time to time, to give a true and impartial Relation of the Constitution and Transactions of their respective Colonies; I say, if all these Persons be obliged to give their several Representations of the State of these Colonies, it is reasonable to believe, they will be necessitated both to enquire after, and to represent the Truth, lest they contradict one another.

By these means it is probable, the King and Court of *England* may be made thoroughly sensible of the true State of Affairs in this remote Part of the World, which it is presum'd, will be the first and greatest Step towards remedying any former Mismanagements.

Reference: Anonymous, *An Essay upon the Government of the English Plantations* (London: Printed for Richard Parker at the *Unicorn,* under the Piazza of the Royal Exchange, 1701).

ARCHIBALD KENNEDY, *AN ESSAY ON THE GOVERNMENT OF THE COLONIES,* 1752

. . .

Seventhly, Of grasping after Dominion, more than belonged to him.

This appears from a Letter to the same Gentleman, dated *May* 10th, 1673.

How this Affair ended, I have not been able to learn from any Part of their History. Most People, however, know what Amendments in their Constitution, from Time to Time, have been made, and for what Reasons: The last was thought severe; but the Alternate was given them, either to take it upon those Conditions, or they were to have no Charter.

Numerous Instances of the Encroachments and Abuse of Power in our Colony Assemblies might be given, which I shall wave; what the Event will be, is hard to determine: The many Complaints, however, that have gone, and daily going Home, upon this Subject, have created Impressions with his Majesty, his Ministers, and the Parliament, not at all in our Favour. Our Neighbour Colony is, at present, in the Hands of the Potter; in what Shape they may turn off the Wheel we shall soon know. My Intention in this, upon the Whole, is no more, than to convince, if possible, our Assembly that they are in the Wrong, and do make a bad Use of their Power; in which if they persevere, it will infallibly bring our Constitution and Privileges into Danger. This, at least, is my Way of thinking. As this is a Subject of no small Importance to me and mine, as well as, I conceive, to us all, I hope a little Warmth (should it so happen) will be pardoned.

Previous to this it may be necessary, as few of our Assembly-men have had the Advantage of a Liberal Education, or the Opportunity of Books to inform themselves of the Nature of Government (*especially that of our own,*) to present them with a short Sketch of it, which I accidentally met with; and is as follows:

'The Design of Civil Government is to secure the Persons and Properties, and Peace of Mankind, from the Invasions and Injuries of their Neighbours: Whereas, if there were no such Thing as Government amongst Men, the stronger would often make Inroads upon the Peace and Possessions, the Liberties and the Lives of those that were weaker; and universal Confusion and Disorder, Mischiefs and Murthers, and ten

Thousand Miseries would over-spread the Face of the Earth.

'In order to this general Good, *viz.* the Preservation of the Persons of Men, with their Peace and Possessions; Mankind have been led by the Principles of Reason and Self-Preservation, to join themselves into distinct Civil Societies; wherein, as by a Compact, expressed or implied, every single Person is concerned in the Welfare and Safety of all the rest; and all engage their Assistance to desend any of the Rest, when their Peace or Possessions are invaded; so that by this Means, every single Member of the Society has the Wisdom and Strength of the Whole engaged for his Security and Defence: To attain this End most happily, different Societies have chosen different Forms of Government, as they thought most conducive to obtain it.

'The most regular Mixture seems to be that wherein the chosen Representatives of the People have their distinct Share of Government. The Nobles, or great Men, have their Share; and a single Person, or the King, has his Share in this Authority; and all agreed upon by the whole Community. This is called a mixed Monarchy; and herein these three Estates of the Kingdom, are supported by mutual Assistance, and mutual Limitations; not only to secure the common Peace, the Liberty of the Nation from Enemies, but to guard it also from any dangerous Inroads that might be made upon it, by any of these three Powers themselves.

Such is the Happiness of *Great-Britain*, under the King, Lords, and Commons.

'Here let it be noted, That whosoever has the Power of making Laws, whether the King, Nobles, or the People, or all these together, yet still the particular Execution of these Laws, must be committed to many particular Magistrates or Officers; and they are usually fixed in a Subordination to one another; each of them fulfiling their several Posts, throughout the Nation, in order to secure the general Peace.

'In all Forms of Government there is, as before hinted, a Compact or Agreement between the Governors and the Governed, expressed or implied, *viz.* that the Governors shall make it

their Care and Business to protect the People in their Lives, Liberties and Properties, by restraining or punishing those who injure, attack, or assault them; and that the Governed submit to be punished, if any of them are found guilty of those Practices; and also that they oblige themselves to pay such Homage, Honours and Taxes; and yield such Assistance to the Governors, with their natural Powers, and their Money or Possessions, as may best obtain the great Ends of Government, and the common Safety of the whole Society.

'For this Purpose, therefore, each Person, by his Compact, willingly abridges himself of some Part of his original Liberty or Property, for the common Service of the Society of which he is a Member: And he engages himself, with his Powers and Capacity to defend and preserve the Peace, and ·Order and Government of the Society, so long as he and his Fellow-Subjects are protected by it, in the Enjoyment of all their natural Rights and Liberties. The very Reason of Man, and the Nature of Things, shew us the Necessity of such Agreements.

'From this View of Things it appears, that tho' no particular Form of Government, besides the antient *Jewish*, could claim divine Right, yet all Government is from God, as he is the Author of Reason and Nature, and the God of Order and Justice: And every particular Government which is agreed upon by Men, so far as it retains the original Design of Government, and faithfully preserves the Peace and Liberties of Mankind, ought to be submitted to, and supported by the Authority of God, our Creator, who, by the Light of Reason, hath led Mankind into Civil Government, in order to their mutual Help and Preservation, and Peace.

'In this Sense it is, that the two great Apostle, *Peter* and *Paul*, vindicate Civil Governors, and demand Subjection to them, from Christians. Rom. xiii. 1, *&c. Let every Soul be subject to the higher Powers; for there is no Power but of God. The Powers that be, are ordained of God: Whosoever, therefore, resisteth the Power, resisteth the Ordinance of God; and they that resist, shall receive to themselves Damnation,* (i. e. *are condemn'd;*) *for Rulers are not a Terror to the good Works, but to the evil.* 1 Pet. ii. 13.

Submit yourselves to every Ordinance of Man for the Lord's Sake; whether it be to the King, as supreme, or to Governors, as to them who are sent by him, for the Punishment of evil Deers, and we Praise of them that do well. What St. *Paul* faith, is, *ordained of God, i. e.* in general; as Civil Government, or Civil Powers. St. *Peter* calls it *the Ordinance of Man, i. e.* in particular; as to the several Forms of this Government, which Men agree upon or appoint: And, indeed, God has left to Men to agree upon and appoint the particular Forms: And so far as any of them pursue and attain this End, they must be submitted to, and supported as an Ordinance both of God and Man.'

What Connection there is between this System, and the Constitution of *Great-Britain*, let those acquainted with it, judge:—A Constitution envied and admired by every State and Power on Earth; and which Nothing has been able to injure, or ever will be able to injure, but those intestine Encroachments and Divisions amorgst themselves; and while the Ballance of that Power, lodged with the three Branches, is kept in a due Poise, will last as long as Time lasts. Of this glorious System we are but a very faint Resemblance; if any at all, it is the most disagreeable Part of it, that, *viz.* of ercroaching upon the two upper Branches of the Legislature; in this we have shewn a good Deal of Dexterity. But more of this hereafter.

We are no more than a little Corporation, in the same Manner as a Mayor, Aldermen, and Common-Council are impowered, by his Majesty's Letters Patent, to form Rules and Orders for the Government of a City, in its several Wards and Districts; even so; tho' in somewhat a higher Degree, and more extensive Sphere; but all to the same Purpose is a Governor, Council and Assembly, to govern a Colony, in its several Counties and Precincts, by the same Power: Every Law or Rule made, that is not peculiarly adapted to their respective Communities, has no Meaning; and every Law made, that in any Shape clashes or interferes with the Laws of *Great-Britain*, are, *ipso Facto* void. By this I understand, that the Liberties and Properties of *British* Subjects abroad, established and cemented by the Treasure and Blood of

our Ancestors, Time out of Mind, is not left to the Caprice and Humour of a Colony Assembly.— O *Fortunati!* I would not, therefore, advise our worthy Assembly, or their Leaders, to prosane those sacred Terms, either to frighten or mistead the Ignorant. Our Liberties and Properties are out of their Reach; they have Nothing to do with them: Every Subject within the King's Dominions, the meanest as well as the greatest, have a Right to the common Law of *England*, and the Great Charter, established and confirmed, as Sir *Edward Coke* tells us, by two and thirty Acts of Parliament, and is only deciaratory of the fundamental Grounds of the common Law, and no more than a Confirmation or Restitution of the Privileges which were previously claimed and due thereby; and all this we were intitled to, before Assemblies had a Being, and which our Posterity will enjoy when they are no more. I would, therefore, advise those Gentlemen, for the Future, to drop those parliamentary Airs and Stile, about Liberty and Property, and keep within their Sphere, and make the best Use they can of his Majesty's Instructions and Commission, because it would be High-Treason to fit and act without it. This is our Charter; and we may, if weplease, be extreamly happy in the Privileges we enjoy from it; that alone, of having it in our Power to tax ourselves, is invaluable; of this, I doubt, we shall never be truly sensible, till, by some Misconduct of our own, we come to lose it. If we abuse, or make a wicked Use of his Majesty's Favours, we are, of them, but Tenants at Will; we only hold them curing Pleasure, and good Behaviour. In most Corporations, where there appears an Abuse of Power or Neglect of Duty, a *Quo Warranto* is necessary to set Things to rights; in our Case it is not wanted, tho', (as that great Lawyer Lord Chief Justice *Hale*, has remarked, in Relation to the Island *Jersey*) we are Parcel of the Dominions of the Crown of *England*; we are no Part, nor ever were, of the Realm of *England*, but a Peculiar of the Crown; and by a natural and necessary Consequence, exempted from parliamentary Aids. Thus you see our Dependency and the Reason of it, is altogether upon his Majesty's Grace and Favour. If we don't approve of our present System of Government, let us pray for a better: In the mean Time, let us not contemptuously treat those Favours the Crown has been pleased already to confer upon us. That this is the Case, is but too obvious.

The Constitution, or Frame of Government the Crown has been pleased to favour us with, is by a Governor and Council of his own Appointment; and to which, by his Directions, are added the Representatives of the People; of which his Majesty's Commission and Instructions are the Basis. This is an Emblem, or faint Representation of the *British* Constitution; and will, with equal Propriety, answer all the good Purposes intended, if we have but Sagacity enough to make a proper Use of it. Here are three Branches in the Legislature, whose Powers are sufficiently distinguished and pointed out to them; and while the Ballance is duly kept up, that is, while each of the Branches keep candidly and strictly within its own Sphere of Action, without encroaching, infringing, or maliciously endeavouring, for any particular Ends, to vilify or lessen the Powers of any other of the Branches, we may conclude ourselves in a happy Way; on the Contrary, if we see any one of the Branches, assuming to itself any Part of that Power, originally lodged, and intended by his Majesty to be lodged with the other Branches, and scrambling vehemently, out of all Measure and Character, for more Power than ever was intended it, you may conclude, that every Step taken for that Purpose, is a Nail in our Coffin, and tends to an Alteration, if not a Dissolution of the Constitution. That each, in their Turns, have attempted this, is beyond Dispute. Those Attempts from a Governor, can only be by Fits and Starts, out of Pique or Prejudice to Particulars; they cannot long subsist: He may be guilty of some few Acts of Oppression; but considering he has not only the other two Branches of the Legislature to check him, but even his own Commission and Instructions, nay, even the whole Body of the Laws of *England,* and one particularly adapted to the Purpose, which makes him accountable in *Westminster-Hall,* for any Mis-conduct here. There Mr. *Lowther* was called to an Account for Acts of Oppression,

and was like to have payed severely for it, had he not screened himself by the Act of Grace. He was allowed, upon a regular Complaint, to come home to defend himself; at the Conclusion thereof, he was committed by the Council-Board, till he entred into a Recognizance with Sureties in £. 20,000; and was also ordered to be prosecuted by the Attorney-General. From hence I would infer, that no Governor, from any Acts of his *qua* Governor, can indanger our Constitution. From a Council we have not much to apprehend, even if they were to join any one of the other Branches, provided the third keeps it's Ground. The Council are in the Nature of Moderators between the Extreams, without whose Concurrence they have no Power to act: Should they, however, neglect their Duty, or abuse the Powers they are intrusted with, they are accountable to his Majesty, and a Suspension soon puts an End to their Being.

From an Assembly, if we value our Constitution, we have every Thing to dread; they have the press on their Side, which greatly preponderates in the Ballance, and will be doing (I with I could say fairly) what every other monied Person does; that is, turn it to their own particular Advantage; and in this Kind of Traffick our Assemblies have, of late Years, shown great Dexterity, even so far as greatly to lessen that Dignity and Power, so essential to Government, lodged with their Superiors, the Governor, and Council; and to add to our Misfortune, there is no Remedy, at present, in Being, to cure this Mischief, but either a great Alteration, or a total Dissolution or the Constitution; dissolving an Assembly is none, but the most effectual Method to continue the Mischief: This we may learn, in some from an Advertisement of their own, or from some of their Friends, of the 17th of *February*, in the *Gazette*, in these Words, 'Notwithstanding the utmost Efforts of the Court Party had been exerted, yet our two late Members carried the Elections by a very great Majority; and thus, I am persuaded, it will be, should we have an Election every Month in the Year, for we are determined not to be worried out; and we know our Interest too well, to be deceived either by Paper or Parchment.' I cannot conceive what this Advertisement refers to, unless it be to the King's Commission, which, if I mistake not, is on Parchment, as the Instructions are on Paper.

Thus it is evident, a Dissolution is no Cure for the Abuse of Power in an Assembly: And this brings to my Mind an Observation of a noted Author, on this Point, *viz.* 'That when the Ballance of Power is duly fixed in a State, Nothing is more dangerous or unwise, than to give Way to the first Steps of popular Encroachments; which is usually done, either in Hopes of procuring Ease and Quiet from some vexatious Clamour, or else made Merchandize, and merely bought and sold. This is the breaking into a Constitution to serve a present Expedient, or supply a present Exigency; the Remedy of an Empirick, to stisle the present Pain, but with certain Prospect of sudden and terrible Returns. When a Child grows easy and content by being humour'd; and when a Lover becomes satisfied by small Compliances, without further Pursuits; then expect to find popular Assemblies content with small Concessions. If there could one single Example be brought, from the whole Compass of History, of any one popular Assembly, who, after beginning to contend for Power, ever sat down quietly with a certain Share; or if one Instance could be produced, of a popular Assembly, that ever knew, or proposed, or declared what Share of Power was their Due; then might there be some Hopes, that it were a Matter to be adjusted by Reasonings, by Conferences, or Debates: But since all this is manifestly otherwise, I see no Course to be taken, in a settled State, but a steady, constant Resolution, in those to whom the Rest of the Ballance of Power is intrusted, never to give Way so far, to popular Clamours, as to make the least Breach in the Constitution, through which a Million of Abuses and Encroachments, will certainly, in Time, force their Way.

'Health, in the natural Body, consists in the just Proportion of those Salts, Sulphurs, and other Principles which compose our Fluids: If any of them becomes predominant, or too much weakened, Sickness ensues: And in order to restore an equal Ballance, we are frequently obliged to have Recourse to a Remedy, which, to a Man in Health, would prove a slow Poison.

'Most of the Revolutions of Government, in *Greece* and *Rome,* began from the Abuse of Power in those selected for the Preservation of the People; which generally ended in the Tyranny of a single Person. This shews the People are their own Dupes.

'The *Romans* chose Legislators to pick up the best Laws wherever they were to be found, and to digest them into Order; and during the Exercise of their Office, suspended the Consular Power: But they soon affected kingly State, destroyed the Nobles, and oppressed the People.

'The *Ephori* in *Sparta* usurped the absolute Authority, and were as cruel Tyrants as any in their Ages.

'The *Athemans* chose four Hundred Men for the Administration of Affairs, who became a Body of Tyrants: They murdered, in cold Blood, great Numbers of the best Men, without any Provocation, for the mere Lust of Cruelty.

'In *Carthage* the Ballance of Power got so far on the Side of the People, as to bring their Government to a *Dominatio Plebis;* as was that of *Rome,* at last, which ended in the Tyranny of the *Cæsars.* Thus it may appear, Tyranny is not confined to Numbers.'

Now, if I may be allowed to compare small Things with great; if it evidently appears, that those great and free and independent States, lost their Liberties from an over Ballance of Power, usurped by their popular Assemblies; and if I can shew, that our little, diminutive, dependent States are following that Example, as fast as ever they can; and that the same Causes eternally produce the same Effects; I hope I shall be intitled to the Thanks of some of my thoughtless, unwary Country-men; and tho' it may not affect us in so fatal a Manner, our Liberty being, (as before mentioned) otherwise secured; yet it must infallibly indanger our Constitution: We are but yet, as it were, in the Hands of the Potter; in a probationary State of Good-Behaviour; if we totter upon three Legs, he can add or diminish, or turn us off in what-ever Shape he pleases; and who dare say, *What doest thou?*

If any impartial Thinker, or indeed that can think at all, would give himself the Trouble seriously to reflect, and compare our present Situation and Constitution, with any other upon the Face of the Earth, I am confident he would determine in our Favour. We have, from the Infancy of Times here, been nursed up and indulged, at an infinite Expence to the Crown, and People of *England:* Even at this Day, they are at the Expence of £.10,000 Sterling, yearly; and have been at no less, for any Thing I know, every Year ever since we had a Being, for our Preservation. We are exempted from all parliamentary Aids; we have never added any Thing to the Revenue of *Great-Britain,* as some of our Neighbour Colonies have done, of immense Sums: Our Plan of Government is from that of *Old-England;* the most complete System known; to which, if any Additions can possibly be made, we have it in our Power to make them: We have it in our Power to tax ourselves, as Conveniency sutes; which bears no Proportion to those Taxes paid by a like Number of our Fellow-Subjects, in *Great-Britain.* Can mortal Men expect, then, to be happier? or any reasonable Man or set of Men, with for, or endeavour at a Change?

Let us now see what grateful Returns we have made, on our Parts, for those Favours.

A general Retrospection into the Proceedings of our Assembly, is a Task I have neither Inclination nor Leisure to undertake; and shall, therefore, leave it to those who may hereafter have the Curiosity to collect the Debates of that House, for the Benefit of the Community; and shall only content myself with giving a short Specimen of their Conduct for—Years past.

The Commission and Instructions directed to his Excellency the Governor, but intended for the Good of the Whole; which, by the Bye, I cannot help thinking, that if they were in every Body's Hands, as a Family-Piece or House Bible, and not cooped up like the *Sibylline Oracles,* to which Recourse was only had upon extraordinary Emergency, it might be of mighty Use; the People would become acquainted and in Love with their Constitution! they would there see, through the Whole, the benevolent Intentions of our most gracious Sovereign the King, and our Mother-Country: Whereas, at present, they are represented, by some of our Dealers in Politicks, as big with that Monster, *Prerogative,* a Thing which some of our weak Members are taught to dread as much as ever Children were that of *Raw-Head and Bloody-Bones.*

Thus by wicked Instruments, for wicked Purposes, are weak Minds imposed upon; for whose Sake I shall endeavour to explain the Word, which, I doubt, is but ill understood, even by those the Perverters of it: If I am mistaken, I shall readily stand corrected.

There is, in every Family, a Sort of Government without any fixed Rules; and indeed it is impossible, even in a little Family, to form Rules for every Circumstance; and therefore it is better conceived than expressed; but perfectly understood by every Individual belonging to the Family. The Study of the Father or Master, is for the Good of the Whole; all Appeals are to him; he has a Power, from the Reason and Nature of Things, to check the Insolent, or Indolent, and to encourage the Industrious: In short, the whole Affairs of the Family are immediately under the Care or Direction of the Father or Master; and this is a natural Prerogative, known and acknowledged by every Man living, who has ever had a Family, or been any Ways concerned in a Family, in all Ages and in all Places. His Majesty, as he is our political Father, his political Prerogative, from the like Circumstances and Reasons, is equally necessary. And this political Authority has been allowed the supreme Director, in all States, in all Ages, and in all Places; and without it, there would be a Failure of Justice.

In the Commission and Instructions, as I was observing, there are some Powers in the Crown, which it cannot divest itself of, that, *viz.* of the Militia, Guards, and Garrisons; and tho' his Majesty has given particular Directions for the Regulation of the Militia here, (a Part so essential to every State and Government) yet our late worthy Assembly thought fit to drop it altogether; for which, as they have given us no Reasons, they must give us Leave to guess; and I think there can be but two, that, *viz.* of lessening the Power of the Captain General; or that the Road to those Commissions, is not generally through the Assembly-House.

It is plain the Intention of the Crown, in our Constitution, was to bring it up, as near as possible, to that of the original Plan. All Monies raised by Parliament, are issued by Warrant from the Lords of the Treasury. His Majesty has been pleased to direct, that all Monies raised in the Colonies, shall be issued by Warrant under the Hand of the Governor in Council. What due Regard has been paid to this Instruction, is notorious, and the Reason plain; because, otherwise, the Assembly would, in a great Measure, lose those Applications for Gratification of Services done, or pretended to be done, by their Friends and Dependents; of which they take upon themselves to be the sole Judges, in Derogation of the Power lodged with the other Branches of the Legislature, and Violation of his Majesty's Commands.

This will appear in a clearer Light, from the Proceeding of our late Assembly, and the Council's Address to his Excellency, upon that Point; to which I beg Leave to refer. But, as I have met with an Address in the Proceedings of a neighbouring Colony, upon the same Subject, done with great Spirit and Accuracy, I shall make no other Apology for inserting so much of it, as relates to the Subject; and is as follows:

'—And now we are come to that Part of this Controversy, which we are no less surprized than confounded should ever be made One, since, as the Gentlemen Money Bill, is, with them, sacred and not to be touched with profane Hands; and with this Proviso too, *viz.* 'That if any of them die or are removed, so much of the aforesaid Allowances to be paid, as shall be at that Time due; and no more.' If an Officer, then, dies or is removed, the Governor, it is true, may put another in his Place; but he can have no Salary or Allowance, till the Assembly phase; and that Allowance is just as they please to like the Person. It is not a new Thing with some of our

Assemblies, to add or substract a Figure in the Salary of of the Officers, according to the Nature of the Application; and even to drop an useful Office, upon Occasion, if they disapprove of the Officer; witness the Weigh-Master General's Office. This, I think, is an Encroachment with a Witness, as it creates a Dependence of all the Officers of the Government, upon an Assembly; which, of Course, quite inverts the very Order and Nature of Government.

In *Great-Britain*, to defray the necessary Services of the Government, Estimates are laid before the House of Commons, of which they, if they please, may judge of the Necessity, as well as of the *Quantum*; the Funds, however, are raised; but the Application is left to his Majesty. If there are any Misapplications, it is with the Commons to enquire; and Nothing is more dreaded, than a parliamentary Scrutiny.

The Disposition of Officers, is an inherent Right of the Crown; and is, indeed, a Part of that Power lodged in that Branch of the Legislature, in order to keep up the Ballance; and without it, it would lose of its Weight. It is his Majesty's Intentions, that we should follow the same Method; but, those Intentions our Assemblies have treated according to their usual Complaisance.

The proper Appointments of the Civil List, for his Majesty's Support, is for Life; which, from long Experience, is found most conducive to the Benefit of the Community.

It is his Majesty's Royal Will and Pleasure, that there be paid to his Governor and Captain General, £. 1200 Sterling, yearly, out of his Revenue arising in his said Province; and it is his express Will and Pleasure, that all Laws made for the Supply and Support of Government, be indefinite, and without Limitation, as to Point of Time: As the Commission is, the Meaning I think is plain, that it should last, at least, as long as the Commission; and in this Sense, most of those Colonies immediately under his Majesty's Direction, have taken it; and accordingly, as I am informed, observe it, and enjoy Peace and the Favour of the Crown, while *New-York* and *New-Jersey* are, at present, famous all over his Majesty's Dominions, for worrying one another, and Contempt of Royal Orders and Instructions: But instead of this, our Assembly tell him he may take £. 1200, if he pleases, but it shall be at 40 *per* C. Discount; and even that, but from Year to Year; it is this or Nothing; there is no Alternate. This, however, is paying no great Compliment to his Majesty's express Royal Will and Pleasure, and but poor Returns of Gratitude for *Ten Thousand Pounds* Sterling, laid out upon us yearly, by his Majesty. That of a yearly Support is but of a late Standing; it was not so from the Beginning. From this Period, however, we may date the Commencement of all our Confusions. Five Years was the common Method; and I believe I may challenge the most sanguine Party-Man, to point out any dreadful Consequences that attended it. This, I say, was the Method, this ought to be the Method, and this will be the Method, however terrible, at present, it may appear; and if we do not follow it, it will be done to our Hands; or we shall have no Peace in our *Israel* and the King no Government.

Can any Thing be more absurd, than to imagine a Governor, sent abroad to govern a People, and to be supported according to the Dignity of his Office, and under certain Restrictions and Instructions, essential to that Government; but to obtain that Support, every Instruction must be given up, one after another, or have no Support? which is just throwing the Governor into their Hands: This has been the Practice for many Years, and his Majesty and his Ministers know it too; what the Event will be, Time only can discover. Some Remedy must be found, or the People will at last govern.

A Governor is no sooner appointed, than the first Question is, Into whose Hands shall I throw myself? the Answer is ready, Into whose but such as can best manage the Assembly. Hence Prime Ministers and Courtiers are established; and, of Course, Anti-courtiers: Hence Parties are formed; and thus the Peace of the Publick is destroyed, honest Neighbours set together by the Ears, and all Good-fellowship excluded the Society; Elections are carried on with great Animosity, and at a vast Expence, as if our Alls were at Stake: And what is all this for? Is the publick Good really the

Point in View? or is it to shew how dexterously the one Side can manage the Assembly for him, and the other against him? Let us be told what mighty Advantage the Publick has reaped from that repeated Round of Squabbles we have been pestred with, with no other View than to distress a worthy Gentleman.

Thus, I think, the Reasonableness, and even the Necessity of supporting a Governor, according to his Majesty's Royal Will and Pleasure, that is independently of any Body but himself, is evident, as it will destroy all those Sources of Contention.

In *Virginia*, the *Two Shillings* Sterling, upon every Hogshead of Tobacco exported, makes the Support easy to the People, who are at this Time, and like to continue in all Duty and Obedience. It is the same in the *Leeward-Islands*, from the *Four* and an *Half per* C. and we hear of no *Fraca's* amongst them.

A gentle Tax upon Lands here, would answer all these Purposes, relieve the Merchant, and encourage Trade, at this Time in a languishing Condition.

If a Man of Worth and Honour falls to our Share, (which indeed, as Matters stand at present, we can hardly expect) he will, if supported according to his Dignity, naturally incline to do us all the good Offices in his Power, if we ourselves don't take Pains to prevent him; and he, the Council, and General Assembly, will have that Time, hitherto spent in trifling Squabbles, to think of securing us from abroad, and encouraging Trade and Industry at home.

The Manner of our supporting our Judges, is equally ridiculous and absurd. It is agreed on all Hands, that those Offices ought to be held for Life, independent both of Crown and People, and under no Bias; but our Assembly are determined to keep them too, under their Thumbs; and tell them, we will allow so much for this Year, but if you do not behave as we think you should do, we will give you less next Year, and perhaps Nothing at all. This would have little Weight with a Man of Fortune and Integrity, in that Office; but might prove too powerful a Temptation to such as have Nothing else to depend upon. As the Commissions, therefore, for good Reasons, are for Life; so ought, for the same Reasons, the Salaries to be.

I have been informed, that in *New-England*, there was a long Debate in the House, whether the Governor's Salary should be paid at the Beginning or at the End of the Year, that they might be the better able to judge of his Good-Behaviour; and, if I am not mistaken, it was carried for the latter.

Reference: Archibald Kennedy, *An Essay on the Government of the Colonies* (New York: J. Parker, 1752).

29

Defenses of Colonial Governance

After the end of the French and Indian War (1763), Britain became increasingly concerned with what it called the legislative arrogance of the colonies. Parliament expected
the ungrateful colonies, which had gained safe frontiers as a result of the defeat of France,
to pay for the colonial wars. As a result, during the next decade Britain passed a series of
laws designed to control the activities of the colonial legislatures. These laws, repugnant to
the colonial civil leaders, were resisted by a steady flow of spoken and published defenses of
legislative prerogatives. The central concern of the writers in Chapter 29 is to support the
long established colonial precedence of self-governance. Seven colonial leaders who wrote
on theories of governance, out of countless numbers, have been selected because of the
cogency of their arguments in defense of their governing systems. These seven efforts reveal
much about colonial governance values as they cautiously make the case that only through
independence can the colonies be freed from oppressive British controls. Their arguments
will be taken up in the chronological order in which the authors wrote them.

First is *A Vindication of the British Colonies* (1765) by James Otis (1725–1783), son of a
leading Massachusetts legislator and brother of the historian, Mercy Otis Warren. James
Otis graduated from Harvard College, practiced law, became a justice of the peace, served
on the admiralty court, and in 1761 gained election to the Massachusetts General Court.
He became the bitter opponent of governor Thomas Hutchinson. In 1762 Otis wrote
A Vindication of the Conduct of the House of Representatives and in 1764 wrote *The Rights of
British Colonist Asserted and Proved*. In the *Rights*, Otis spoke out against British taxing pow-
ers. Although his later career was marred by erratic behavior, if not madness, Otis certainly
was one of the earliest colonial leaders to recognize the need for an independent legislature.

In his brilliantly argued *Vindication*, Otis crafted a major statement about colonial legislative rights. He asked how a Parliament so far away could maintain that it represented the
colonial people. Because colonists neither voted for nor were represented in Parliament,
Otis claimed Parliament had no right to legislate for the colonies. The colonies had for
years legislated for themselves, he claimed, and their long established self-governance had
become a part of their political way of life. Having gone to the brink of calling for independence, Otis backed away and declared his loyalty to England, and especially the Crown.

Richard Bland, a brilliant and witty orator and keen student of the theory of governance, essentially agreed with Otis. Born in Williamsburg, Virginia, Bland (1710–1776)
was educated at the local College of William and Mary, owned a plantation and practiced
law, and became an expert on constitutional law. He rose through the governing ranks in
Virginia, first as a justice of the peace and later as a militia colonel, and eventually took

his seat in the House of Burgesses where he served for a number of years. In his first major essay, *The Colonel Dismounted* (1764), Bland joined with other Virginians in defense of the legislative rights of duly elected officials and in favor of Virginians making their own laws.

In the speech included here, later printed as a pamphlet, *An Inquiry into the Rights of the British Colonies* (1765), Bland talked brilliantly of the rights of colonial governments. He repeated his view of legislative autonomy and announced that what applied to Virginia also was the right of each of the other 13 American colonies. In addition, Bland called for a divided system of authority in which the legislatures had equal rights with the executives to govern the colonies. In pamphlet form, the *Inquiry* was circulated throughout the colonies and was said to have influenced Thomas Jefferson's views. Later, as a delegate to the First and Second Continental congresses, the once cautious Virginia solon accepted independence as the only way to protect the colonial governmental process.

Thomas Jefferson (1743–1826), a younger colleague and protégé of Bland, needs little introduction. This brilliant writer and poor orator, graduate of the College of William and Mary, and lawyer, rose rapidly in Virginia's House of Burgesses, having first been elected to that body in his twenties. Known for his knowledge of the history of governance throughout the Western world, young Jefferson exploded onto the political scene as an early advocate of independence. Jefferson's *A Summary View of the Rights of British America* (1774), foretelling the contents of the later *Declaration of Independence*, argued for legislative rights in opposition to Parliament's attempts to limit those rights. In *A Summary View*, Jefferson called on delegates to the Continental Congress to issue a united complaint against encroachment on the rights of legislative government. He concluded by calling on the Crown to join the colonies in resisting the untoward and illegal aggression of Parliament against colonial governance.

More cautious than Jefferson, but equally worried, John Dickinson (1732–1808), was born in Talbot County, Maryland, to wealthy landowners and was raised in Delaware. He studied law in England and in 1757 moved to Philadelphia where he rose to the heights of the legal profession. Dickinson had served in the Delaware assembly, and later the Pennsylvania assembly, where he became a leading opponent of the executive branch of government. He wrote of his fears of an arbitrary Parliament's control of colonial government. Dickinson achieved some fame with his 1765 "Declaration of Rights and Grievances" against the British Stamp Act. In 1767, with the folksy *Letters from a Farmer in Pennsylvania*, Dickinson became famous throughout the colonies as a defender of legislative prerogatives, although he claimed to be moderate in his views on how to protect the colonies. He did, however, point out that English control of taxing power threatened colonial liberties.

Against parliamentary encroachment on those legislative rights, in 1774 Dickinson helped to organize the Pennsylvania Committee of Correspondence to communicate with and share grievances with other colonial governments. In 1774 he also called for election of a Continental Congress, and in January 1775, wrote a *Declaration of the Causes and Necessity to Take Up Arms*. Included in this chapter is Dickinson's 1774 *Essay on the Constitutional Power of Great Britain*, a pamphlet seldom read today and a clear statement of a conservative moved to call for mutual defense of colonial governance rights. In that pamphlet, Dickinson discussed in detail the rights of colonial governance and declared that England had usurped them. He concluded that more than one hundred years of self-government had given colonials some voice in determining their own political destiny. Yet, Dickinson was one of only a handful of delegates to Congress who voted against the *Declaration of Independence*. Still, he was forced to become a reluctant revolutionary.

The next document in this chapter is a 1775 call for elections to the Continental Congress by South Carolina's Henry Laurens (1724–1792). Born in Charleston of humble means, Laurens rose to become one of the city's leading merchants and a great planter. He served in the militia, entered the South Carolina Assembly, and refused to join the Governor's Council. In 1775 Laurens became leader of the first South Carolina Provincial Congress and president of the Council of Safety. He later drafted South Carolina's first state constitution, and served for years in the Continental Congress. In this June 1775 address to the South Carolina's Provincial Congress, Laurens called for force of arms to protect what he hoped would become his new country. Laurens stated that he opposed any attack on American rights and freedoms. But he also wanted tolerance toward those who believed that their government and liberties had not yet been threatened. Laurens concluded that he joined the association that would free Americans.

James Wilson (1742–1798), born and educated in Scotland, moved to Philadelphia in 1765 where he taught college and read law under John Dickinson. In 1774 he became a member of the Pennsylvania Committee of Correspondence. In 1768 Wilson wrote *Considerations on the Nature and Extent of Legislative Authority of the British Parliament*, a tract he updated and circulated throughout the colonies in early 1775. In that 1775 document he wrote about two principles of governance that he claimed well reflected the values of the emerging American people. The first was that governance power came from all of the people, not just a few as in Britain. Second, he declared that Parliament had no authority over the colonies. Although a radical democrat, Wilson was a cautious revolutionary. Nevertheless, in that pamphlet and in a January 1776 speech at the Pennsylvania convention, Wilson described why self-governance was worth protecting and what he hoped to create in the new nation. He accepted election to the Continental Congress and reluctantly voted for the *Declaration of Independence*. Wilson later stated that independence had been forced on the colonies and he wondered what kind of government the new American nation proposed to adopt.

Another major leader who requires little introduction is John Adams (1735–1826), lawyer, scholar, and public servant from Massachusetts. A Harvard College graduate, Adams became one of the most brilliant political theoretical minds of the late colonial and Revolutionary period. His *Thoughts on Government* (1776) is included here, not so much because it is a ringing cry for independence but more for what it says about the kind of governance that developed in the colonies throughout the eighteenth century. In *Thoughts*, Adams wrote of his suspicions of all government, favored a strong legislature to keep internal order, wanted a free judicial system, and called for the governor to be given limited, carefully spelled-out powers. In *Thoughts*, Adams displayed his near encyclopedic knowledge of the history of governance, including Massachusetts's own governing experience. That work became the model for the Massachusetts's state constitution of 1780 (see Volume III, Part VII), and certainly a blueprint for the first and second American federal constitutions. Thus, Adams fittingly has the last word on what many colonial and revolutionary leaders believed was the governing system they were defending against British encroachment.

JAMES OTIS, *A VINDICATION OF THE BRITISH COLONIES*, 1765

IT HAD been long expected that some American pen would be drawn in support of those measures which to all thinking men must appear to be very extraordinary. Those who are above party can peruse the speculations of a Whig or a Tory, a Quaker or a Jacobite, with the same composure of mind.

Those who confine themselves within the bounds of moderation and decency are so far respectable. All who grow outrageous are disgustful. The "head of a *tribunitian veto*" with a mob at his heels and a grand *Asiatic* monarch with a shoal of sycophants clinging about him, like the little wretches in the well-known print of Hobbe's Leviathan, may be objects of equal diversion, derision, and contempt. Mankind ever were, are, and will be, divisible into the great and small vulgar. Both will have their respective heads. The laws of nature are uniform and invariable. The same causes will produce the same effects from generation to generation. He that would be a great captain must for a season exult in the honor of being a little one.

Bred on the mountains had *proud* Julius been,
He'd *shone* a *sturdy* wrestler on the green.

The Halifax gentleman having discovered that Governor H—pk—ns is "totally unacquainted with style and diction," and yet "eagerly fond to pass upon the world for a man of letters," great perfection might be reasonably expected in the composition of the friendly epistle. Instead of this are found inaccuracies in abundance, declamation and false logic without end; *verse* is retailed in the shape of *prose*, solecisms are attempted to be passed off for good grammar, and the most indelicate fustian for the fine taste. The whole performance is truly *Filmerian*. The picture is very well charged with shade and thick darkness, intermixed with here and there a ray of light, now and then a flash, and once in a while is heard a little rumbling thunder from a few distant broken clouds.

Some future bard may sing the present times,
And HE be made the hero of the song.

These two lines are crowded together in one short sentence in a prosaic form.

The gentleman has given us a portrait of the English nation. It contains but a dozen lines, and expresses or plainly implies the following wonderful group of ideas, viz., "A high pitch of glory and power, envy and admiration of surrounding slaves, holding fast the balance of Europe, a rival in arts and arms of every period, ancient and modern, impatience, jealousy, pride and folly, prodigality, particularly in laying wagers to the value of kingdoms, and a quick sensibility and consciousness of dignity, which renders plain simple truth intolerable." As the English nation expired about sixty years since in the union of the two kingdoms, 'tis needless to inquire whether this be a just character of that once brave and generous, free and loyal people; but if this should be intended for a filial compliment to Great Britain, 'tis a very indifferent one. In the late war America joined in the stakes: the bet was not for the safety of the colonies alone; it was for the salvation of Great Britain as well as the plantations, i.e., for the whole community. Cornwall raises and pays one company of dragoons, Devonshire another. Is Cornwall more obliged to Devonshire than Devonshire is to Cornwall? They are both obliged by the strongest ties of duty and loyalty to the gracious prince who protects and defends both; to each other they owe but love and good will.

I cannot think Mr. H—k—s or any other of the writers who have the misfortune to fall under the sore displeasure of the Halifax gentleman ever really intended to encourage so groundless a claim as an independent, uncontrollable provincial legislative. Most of them 'tis well known expressly disavow such a claim. It is certain that the Parliament of Great Britain hath a just, clear, equitable, and constitutional right, power, and authority to bind the colonies by all acts wherein they are named. Every lawyer, nay, every tyro, knows this. No less certain is it that the Parliament of Great Britain has a just and equitable right, power, and authority to *impose taxes on the colonies, internal and external, on lands as well as on trade*. This is involved in the idea of a supreme legislative or sovereign power of a state. It will, however, by no means from thence follow that 'tis always expedient and in all circumstances equitable for the supreme and sovereign legislative to tax the colonies, much less that 'tis reasonable this right should be practiced upon without allowing the colonies an actual representation. An equal representation of the whole state is, at least in theory, of the essence of a perfect parliament or supreme legislative.

There is not the least color of a contradiction between the passages from the *Rights of the Colonies* cited pages 6 and 7. It must indeed be confessed and lamented that the last citation involves a sophism unworthy the pen from whence it fell. But the critic with all his sagacity has not pointed where the fallacy lies. He has reduced His Honor's argument to the form of a syllogism, which is conclusive. "The people of Great Britain have not any sort of power over the Americans; the House of Commons have no greater authority than the people of Great Britain who are their constituents; *ergo,* the House of Commons have not any sort of power over the Americans." This I take to be literally true. Yet by the following reduction the fallacy of His Honor's argument will appear: "The common people of Great Britain have no sovereign absolute authority over their fellow subjects in America"; the House of Commons alone have no greater authority than the common people of Great Britain; *ergo,* the British Parliament, the King's Majesty, Lords, and Commons, have no sovereign absolute authority over the subjects in the colonies. Who does not see the fallacy of this conclusion? The inquiry was not of the sole and separate power and authority of the House of Commons, but of the authority of that august and transcendent body the Parliament, which is composed of the three branches of the grand legislature of the nation considered as united. But all this shows that the last citation at most is but an implicit, and is far from an "express denial of the authority of Parliament," and should by that candor that is inseparable from a liberal mind have been imputed to mere inadvertency.

We come now to the *rationale* of the epistle. "I have endeavored," says the gentleman, "to investigate the *true, natural relation,* if I *may so speak,* between the colonies and their mother state, *abstracted* from *compact* or *positive institution.*" What a parade is here? What "a solemnity" does "he give to his performance"? "If I may so speak." Who would not think the world was about to be favored with some extraordinary discovery too mighty for the powers and precision of language?

Let us attend the course of the bubble. "But here," adds he, "I can find nothing satisfactory. Yet till this *relation* is clearly defined upon *rational* and *natural principles* our *reasoning* upon the *measures* of the colonies' obedience will be *desultory* and inconclusive. Every connection or relation in life has its reciprocal duties; we know the relation between a parent and a child, husband and wife, master and servant, and from thence are able to deduce their respective obligations. But we have no notices of any *such* precise natural relation between a *mother state* and its colonies, and therefore cannot reason with so much certainty upon

the *power* of the one or the *duties* of the other." If, as the gentleman tells us, he could not find anything satisfactory, he could only guess what reasoning would follow; and I leave it to his readers to determine whether he has not proved that he guessed very rightly. He has placed the relation of master and servant among what he calls natural relations. In a state of nature, where all are equal, I believe the gentleman would be as much puzzled to find his master or servant as others now may be to find his equal. 'Tis a little strange he should attempt to reason on a subject of which he confesses he could find no "satisfactory notices." But he seems determined to flounder on through thick and thin, be his reasonings "desultory" or conclusive.

"The ancients," says he, "have *transmitted* (for handed down; 'tis a wonder it had not been *transported*) to us nothing that is applicable to the state of the modern colonies, because the *relation* between these ('and their mother state' should have been added) is formed by *political compact.*" *Brave!* "And the *condition* of each variant in their original and from each other." Better and better still! If *condition* means the present state, and I think it can mean nothing else, what a delectable piece of jargon does the close of this period make. It amounts to this: "The present state of each modern colony is variant in its original, and from each other." Be this as it may, if the *relation* of modern colonies to their mother states is founded on *political compact,* how came the gentleman to beat his brains to find out "their *natural relation abstracted from compact or positive institution*"? To what purpose he has done this he tells us when he confesses he can find nothing "*satisfactory*" about it. Are not *natural* and merely *political or civil relations* different things? Is it not a little jargonical and inconsistent in one breath to talk of "investigating the *true, natural, clearly defined* relation of the colonies to their mother state, abstracted from compact or positive institution," and in the next to affirm that so far as relates to modern colonies this relation depends or "is founded on political compact"? Was there a natural relation between ancient states and their colonies and none between the modern states and their colonies? Is not a "political compact" the same thing with a "positive institution"? Is this "freeing a subject from embarrassment"? Well might the gentleman "shun the walk of metaphysics." I wish he had not so much avoided that of logic. He everywhere seems to consider *power* and *duty* as correlates. Surely he should be the last man to charge his adversary with "vague and diffuse talk of" those leveling notions, "rights and privileges." He bewilders himself for half a poor creeping page more, abruptly sings a *requiem* to his sweet soul, composes the surges of his "philosophically inquisitive mind" fatigued with its late flight after natural and political relations, and very gravely contents himself with considering the "colonies' rights upon the footing of their charters." This foothold, by a new and bold figure in rhetoric, he calls "the only plain avenues that lead to the truth of this matter."

. . . facilis descensus Averni.

The gentleman is at a loss to "conceive how it comes to pass that the colonies now claim *any other or greater* rights than are expressly granted to them" by charter. Is the gentleman a British-born subject and a lawyer, and ignorant that charters from the crown have usually been given for enlarging the liberties and privileges of the grantees, not for limiting them, much less for curtailing those essential rights which all His Majesty's subjects are entitled to by the laws of God and nature as well as by the common law and by the constitution of their country?

The distinction between personal and political rights is a new invention, and, as applied, has perplexed the author of it. He everywhere confounds the terms rights, liberties, and privileges, which in legal as well as vulgar acceptation denote very different ideas. This is a common mistake with those who cannot see any difference between power and right, between a blind, slavish submission and a loyal, generous, and rational obedience to the supreme authority of a state.

The rights of men are *natural* or *civil*. Both these are divisible into *absolute* and *relative*. The natural absolute personal rights of individuals are

so far from being opposed to political or civil rights that they are the very basis of all municipal laws of any great value. "The absolute rights of individuals regarded by the municipal laws compose what is called *political* or *civil liberty*." "The absolute liberties of Englishmen, as frequently declared in Parliament, are principally three: the right of *personal* security, personal *liberty*, and private property." "Besides these three *primary rights*, there are others which are *secondary* and *subordinate* (to preserve the former from unlawful attacks): (1) The constitution or power of Parliament; (2) The limitation of the King's prerogative (and to vindicate them when actually violated); (3) The regular administration of justice; (4) The right of petitioning for redress of grievances; (5) The right of having and using arms for self-defense." See Mr. Blackstone's accurate and elegant analysis of the laws of England. The gentleman seems to have taken this and some other of his distinctions from that excellent treatise very ill understood. The analysis had given this general view of the *objects* of the laws of England: I. Rights of persons; II. Rights of things; III. Private wrongs; IV. Public wrongs. Rights of persons are divided into these: (1) of natural persons; (2) of bodies politic or corporate, i.e., artificial persons or subordinate societies. The rights of these are by the Letter Writer strangely confounded with the political and civil rights of natural persons. And because corporate rights so far as they depend upon charter are matters of the mere favor and grace of the donor or founder, he thence infers that "the colonies have no rights independent of their charters," and that "they can claim no greater than those give them." This is a contradiction to what he admitted in the preceding page, viz., that "by the common law every colonist hath a right to his life, liberty, and property." And he was so vulgar as to call these the "subject's birthright." But what is this birthright worth if it depends merely upon a colony charter that, as he says rightly enough, may be taken away by the Parliament? I wish the gentleman would answer these questions. Would he think an estate worth much that might be taken from him at the pleasure of another? Are charters from the crown usually given for enlarging the liberties and privileges of the grantees in consideration of some special merit and services done the state, or would he have his readers consider them like the ordinances of a French monarch, for limiting and curtailing those rights which all Britons and all British subjects are entitled to by the laws of God and nature, as well as by the common law and the constitution of their country so admirably built on the principles of the former? By which of these laws in contradistinction to the other are the rights of life, liberty, and estate, personal?

The gentleman's positions and principles that "the several New England charters ascertain, define, and limit the respective *rights* and privileges of each colony," and that "the colonies have no rights independent of their charter," and that "they can claim no greater than those give them," if true, would afford a curious train of consequences. Life, liberty, and property are by the law of nature as well as by the common law secured to the happy inhabitants of South Britain, and constitute their *primary* civil or political rights. But in the colonies these and all other rights, according to our author, depend upon charter. Therefore those of the colonies who have no charter have no right to life, liberty, or property. And in those colonies who have charters, these invaluable blessings depend on the mere good will, grace, and pleasure of the supreme power, and all their charters and of course all their rights, even to life, liberty, and property, may be taken away at pleasure. Thus every charter in England may be taken away, for they are but voluntary and gracious grants of the crown of certain limited, local, political privileges superadded to those of the common law. But would it be expedient to strike such a blow without the most urgent necessity? "In all states there is (and must be) an absolute supreme power, to which the right of *legislation* belongs: and which by the singular constitution of these kingdoms is vested in the King, Lords, and Commons." Now Magna Carta is but a law of their making, and they may alter it at pleasure; but does it thence follow that it would be expedient to repeal every statute from William the Conqueror to this time? But by the gentleman's

principles this may be done wantonly and without any reason at all. Further, by his logic the Parliament may make the monarchy absolute or reduce it to a republic, both which would be contrary to the trust reposed in them by the constitution, which is to preserve, not destroy it; and to this all are sworn, from the King's Majesty in his coronation oath to the meanest subject in the oath of allegiance. Into such absurd and treasonable doctrines must the gentleman run in order to be consistent. Nay, all the vagaries of Filmer, Mainwaring, and Sibthorpe, and of the whole tribe of King Adam's subjects will follow. As 1. That Adam was the first monarch of this earth. No prince has a title to his crown but he who can prove himself to be the eldest heir male of the body of Adam. That all other princes are usurpers and tyrants. That according to Filmer, God hath given to every father over his children, and much more to every prince over his subjects, a power "absolute, arbitrary and unlimited, and unlimitable over the lives, liberties, and estates of such children and subjects; so that he may take or alienate their estates, sell, castrate, or use their persons as he pleases, they being all his slaves, and the father or prince, lord proprietor of everything, and his unbounded will their law." This is the substance of one of Mr. Locke's inferences from these words of Filmer, "God hath given to the father a right or liberty to alien his power over his children to any other; whence we find the sale and gift of children to have been much in use in the beginning of the world when men had their servants for a possession and inheritance as well as other goods (and chattels), whereupon we find the power of *castrating* and making eunuchs (for singing songs like "Lillibullero," etc.) much in use in old times." *Obs.* 155. "Law is nothing else but the will of him that hath the power of the *supreme* father." Horrid blasphemy! The Lord omnipotent reigneth, but to whom hath he committed his supreme power and authority? The pope claims to be but lord lieutenant of Heaven, and before Sir Robert none but the devil ever had vanity or folly enough to contend for the whole power of the supreme father. According to Filmer and his followers, among which the Halifax gentleman is a close imitator, "they that shed innocent blood, even the blood of their sons and their daughters whom they sacrificed unto the idols of Canaan," did no more than they had a right to do. Upon such principles Pharoah was a pious, virtuous prince. And the drowning the infants in the Nile was as justifiable a piece of preventive policy as seizing the ships of the French without a declaration of war. The Philistine rulers too acted very commendably in depriving the Hebrews of the use of iron, it being very certain that any [of] the most polite people without the free use of this invaluable metal would in one century return to the savage state of the Indians. "If the example of what hath been done," says Mr. Locke, "be the rule of what ought to be, history would have furnished our author with instances of this absolute fatherly power in its height and perfection, and he might have showed us in Peru people that begot children on purpose to fatten and eat them." Mr. Locke has recited a story of this kind, so horrid that I would for the honor of the human species think it incredible and but the mere flight of imagination in *Garcilaso de Vega;* like Swift's proposal to the people of Ireland, to fatten their children for sale in Leadenhall market, as almost the only branch of commerce that would give no offense to the good people of England. See the story cited by Mr. Locke in his treatise on government, chaps. II and VI. The Filmerians often preach the principles of anarchy in one breath and those of despotism in another. The gentleman says, "The individuals of the colonists participate of every blessing the English constitution can give them. As corporations created by the crown they are confined within the primitive views of their institution. Whether therefore their *indulgence* is *liberal* or *scanty* can be no cause of complaint; for when they accepted of their charters they *tacitly* submitted to the terms and conditions of them." This is admirable! To be sure a liberal indulgence could be no cause of complaint. I have heard of a scanty allowance, and it often happens in a transportation across the Atlantic; but what is a *scanty indulgence?* I am in doubt under what species of Hellenism to rank it. Is it Doric or Ionic? Attic I am sure it is not. But

at present I am content it should pass as very good English for a poor pittance of bread, water, stinking beef, and coarse clothes instead of the roast beef of Old Engand praised and sung by such authors as delight in compositions like "Lillibullero." Has a servant no reason to complain that his allowance is scanty, that he is half naked and more than half starved, while his less faithful and less loyal fellow servant is well-fed, plump, gay, and clothed in purple and scarlet and fine linen, faring sumptuously every day upon the spoils of his neighbor? But admitting the former has no right to complain or utter a single sigh, the forced effect of "submissive fear and mingled rage," I cannot for the heart of me conceive how he "participates of every blessing" of his fellow servant; unless the gentleman will contend that half a loaf is equal to a whole one, and that *Martyn* and *Jack* were really a couple of scoundrels for denying that the crusts Lord Peter would have palmed upon them were very good Banstead-down mutton. That "the colonists do not hold their rights as a privilege granted them nor enjoy them as a grace and favor bestowed, but possess them as an inherent indefeasible right," as Mr. H—k—s very justly asserts, is a self-evident proposition to everyone in the least versed in the laws of nature and nations, or but moderately skilled in the common law, except the learned gentleman of Halifax. Even the King's writs are divided into those which the subject hath a right to *ex debito justitiae* and those which depend upon mere grace and favor. These may be denied, the others cannot. The essential rights of British colonists stand on the same basis with those of their fellow subjects of the same rank in any of the three kingdoms.

What the gentleman adds, viz., "that this postulatum of Mr. H—pk—s cannot be true with regard to political rights," by which he evidently means the peculiar privileges of subordinate powers granted by charter, is (asking his pardon) mere impertinence, and in a gentleman of his sense could arise only from a certain set of prejudices having so far blinded him as to make him confound the ideas of corporate subordinate privileges with essential, natural, and civil rights, as is above most abundantly demonstrated, and clearly appears from his own words: "The force of an act of Parliament over the colonies is *predicated* upon the common law, the origin and basis of all those inherent *rights* and *privileges* which constitute the boast and felicity of a Briton." I wish he had said the justly boasted felicity of a Briton, because in that case I should not have suspected him of a Filmerian sneer in this place, which jealousy his dogmas elsewhere will justify. The inherent, indefeasible rights of the subject, so much derided and despised in other parts of the performance, are here admitted, in jest or in earnest, I care not which. The origin of those rights is in the law of nature and its author. This law is the grand basis of the common law and of all other municipal laws that are worth a rush. True it is that every act of Parliament which names the colonies or describes them as by the words "plantations or dominions" binds them. But this is not so strictly and properly speaking by the common law as by the law of nature and by the constitution of a parliament or sovereign and supreme legislative in a state. 'Tis as true that when the colonies are not named or described by an act of Parliament, they are not bound by it.

What is the reason of all this? . . . Surely the bare naming of the colonies hath no magical charm or force in it. That the colonies should be bound by acts of Parliament wherein they are named is an exception from a general rule or maxim. What is that rule or maxim? It is that the colonies being separate dominions and at a distance from the realm, or mother state, and in fact unrepresented in Parliament shall be governed by laws of their own making; and unless named in acts of Parliament shall not be bound by them. . . . Yet as a mark of, and to preserve their dependency on, and subordination to, the mother state, and to prevent *imperium in imperio*, the greatest of all political solecisms, the mother state justly asserts the right and authority to bind her colonies where she really thinks the good of the whole requires it; and of this she remains the supreme judge, from whose final determination there is no appeal. The mother state hath also an undoubted right to unite a colony to itself and

wholly to abrogate and annihilate all colony or subordinate legislation and administration if such alteration shall appear for the best interest of the whole community. But should this be done needlessly and wantonly and without allowing the colonies a representation, the exercise of the power that would otherwise be just and equitable would cease to be distinguished by those amiable qualities. Should a mother state even think it reasonable to impose internal as well as external taxes on six millions of subjects in their remote dominions without allowing them one voice, it would be matter of wonder and astonishment; but it could not be said that the supreme legislative had exceeded the bounds of their power and authority, nor would this render a petition undutiful and seditious. Those six millions must on such an event, unless blind, see themselves reduced to the mortifying condition of mere ciphers and blanks in society. Should all this ever happen to the British colonies, which God forbid, might it not be truly and safely affirmed that the representation in the House of Commons would be very unequal? The right of a supreme power in a state to tax its colonies is a thing that is clear and evident; and yet the mode of exercising that right may be questionable in point of reason and equity. It may be thought to be unequal and contrary to sound policy to exercise the right, clear as it is, without allowing a representation to the colonies. And though a representation would avail the colonies very little in this generation, yet to posterity it might be an invaluable blessing. It may also in future ages be very beneficial to Great Britain. Is it to be believed that when a continent of 3000 miles in length shall have more inhabitants than there are at this day in Great Britain, France, and Ireland, perhaps in all Europe, they will be quite content with the bare name of British subjects, and to the end of time supinely acquiesce in laws made, as it may happen, against their interest by an assembly 3000 miles beyond sea, and where, should they agree in the sentiments with the Halifax gentleman, it may be thought that an admission of an American member would "sully and defile the purity of the whole body"? One hundred years will give this continent more inhabitants than there are in the three kingdoms.

Many great and good men have complained of the inequality of the representation in Great Britain. This inequality can never be a reason for making it more so; which, however, is the method of reasoning adopted by the Halifax gentleman. At his rate, it would be just that half the counties and boroughs in Great Britain which now return members should be curtailed of their right. If so, why not half the remainder, and so on till the House of Commons will be reduced to a single member, and when he was split, one branch of the legislature would be annihilated. By a like process the House of Lords, the second branch of the legislature, might be destroyed. This would be a shorter cut to absolute and unlimited monarchy than ever Filmer was fortunate enough to invent. This brings us to the consideration of the maxim that "no Englishman can be taxed but by his own consent, in person or by his representative. This dry maxim, taken in a literal sense and little understood *like* the song of "Lillibullero" has made all the mischief in the colonies," says the gentleman. I cannot conceive how this or any other dry maxim, or the song of "Lillibullero" like it, well or ill understood, can make any mischief in the colonies. What notable harm has the song of "Lillibullero" wrought in the colonies, or what like it has this "dry maxim" effected? "It is," says the gentleman, "the opinion of the House of Commons and *may* be considered as a law of Parliament that they are the representatives of every British subject wheresoever he be." *Festina lente domine!* This may be true in one sense. The supreme legislative indeed represents the whole society or community, as well the dominions as the realm; and this is the true reason why the dominions are justly bound by such acts of Parliament as name them. This is implied in the idea of a supreme sovereign power; and if the Parliament had not such authority the colonies would be independent, which none but rebels, fools, or madmen will contend for. God forbid these colonies should ever prove undutiful to their mother country! Whenever such a day shall come it will be the beginning of a terrible scene.

Were these colonies left to themselves tomorrow, America would be a mere shambles of blood and confusion before little petty states could be settled. How many millions must perish in building up great empires? How many more must be ruined by their fall? Let any man reflect on the revolutions of government, ancient and modern, and he will think himself happy in being born here in the infancy of these settlements, and from his soul deprecate their once entertaining any sentiments but those of loyalty, patience, meekness, and forbearance under any hardships that in the course of time they may be subjected to. These, as far as may be consistent with the character of men and Christians, must be submitted to. If it is the opinion of the present honorable House of Commons that they in *fact represent* the colonies, it is more than I know. Should this be their opinion, the gentleman may if he pleases "consider it as a law of Parliament." But I should rather choose to consider it only as the very respectable opinion of one branch of the supreme legislative. The opinion of the House of Lords and then above all the sanction of the King's Majesty must be superadded, and the concurrence of both is absolutely necessary to make any opinion of the House of Commons an act or law of *Parliament.* 'Tis humbly conceived that it was not as representatives in *fact* of the colonies that the House of Commons granted His Majesty an external tax on the colonies in the instance of the late act. Nor, if before this time an act for granting internal taxes on the colonies should be passed, could I conceive that the House of Commons are our representatives in fact. As one branch of the supreme legislative, they have an undoubted right to originate any bills that, by naming them, shall bind the colonies when passed into an act, let it be for levying internal or external taxes, or for any other regulation that may appear needful. But I cannot find it affirmed or declared in one act of Parliament, history, or journal of Parliamentary proceedings, nor in one English law book, that a British House of Commons are in *fact* the representatives of all the plebeian subjects, without as well as within the *realm.* Lord Coke indeed says that "the House of Commons represent all the commons of *England,* electors and nonelectors"; but he nowhere asserts that the House of Commons in *fact* represent the provincials of Ireland and other dominions out of the *realm*. He says, however, the people of Ireland are not represented in the English Parliament, and assigns that as the very reason why, in general, acts of Parliament are confined to the realm. Though from the necessity of the thing, in several cases, by naming them the provinces are bound. In the *Fourth Institute*, speaking of the truly high and most honorable court on earth, and never more so than in the present state of the British Parliament and nation, his lordship says, "This court consisteth of the King's Majesty, sitting there as in his royal political capacity and of the three estates of the *realm*, viz., of the lords spiritual, archbishops and bishops, being in number 24, who sit there by succession in respect of their counties, or baronies parcel of their bishoprics, which they hold also in their politic capacity; and every one of these, when any Parliament is to be holden, ought, *ex debito justitiae*, to have a [writ of] summons. The lords temporal, dukes, marquises, earls, viscounts, and barons, who sit there by reason of their dignities which they hold by descent or creation, in number at this time 106, and likewise every one of these being of full age, ought to have a writ of summons *ex debito justitiae*. The third estate is the *commons* of the *realm*, whereof there be knights of shires or counties, citizens of cities, and burgesses of burghs. All which are respectively elected by the shires or counties, cities, and burghs by force of the King's writ *ex debito justitiae*, and none of them ought to be omitted; and *these represent all the commons of the whole realm, and trusted for them, and are in number at this time* 493." 4 *Inst*. 1.

Here is not one word of the House of Commons representing or being trusted by or for the provincials of Ireland or the colonists in America. And though in page 4 of the same *Institute* he says, "*in many cases multitudes are bound by acts of Parliament which are not parties to the election of knights, citizens, and burgesses, as all they that have no freehold or have freehold in ancient demesne, and all women, having freehold or no freehold, and men within the age of twenty-one years etc.*"—this

"etc." may be supplied with female infants, lunatics, idiots, and bedlamites in general. Yet this will not prove that these nonelectors are in *fact* represented and in *fact* trust the representatives in the House of Commons. In estimation of law they are justly deemed as represented. They have all fathers, brothers, friends, or neighbors in the House of Commons, and many *ladies* have husbands there. Few of the members have any of these endearing ties to America. We are as to any personal knowledge they have of us as perfect strangers to most of them as the savages in *California*. But according to our Letter Writer we are not only in *law* but in *deed* represented in the House of Commons. How does he support this? Why, he has dreamt that some one House of Commons in some former reign once thought they were *in fact* our representatives. That "the opinion of a House of Commons is a law of Parliament," therefore " 'tis determined by act of Parliament that we are and shall believe we are in *fact* represented in the House of Commons." Here's more logic. Suppose some future House of Commons should be of opinion that they were the true and proper representatives of all the common people upon the globe; would that make them so and oblige all mankind to believe and submit to it? Would a fiction of the common law of England satisfy the innumerable multitudes on the face of the whole earth that they were in *fact* represented and consenting to all such taxes and tributes as might be demanded of them? Will any man's calling himself my agent, representative, or trustee make him so in fact? At this rate a House of Commons in one of the colonies have but to conceive an opinion that they represent all the common people of Great Britain, and according to our author they would in *fact* represent them and have a right to tax them. 'Tis strange the gentleman can see no difference between a literal sense of a fundamental principle or "dry maxim" as he calls it, and no sense at all. Does it follow because it is "impracticable that each individual should be in *fact* represented" that therefore there should be no representation at all, or a very unequal one? Because the little insignificant isles of Jersey, Guernsey, and Man have never obtained a representation, is it reasonable that the whole kingdom of Ireland and the plantations should be forever excluded from returning members to the British Parliament, even should the Parliament impose external and internal taxes on them and take from them every subordinate power of local legislation? If this would be equal and rational why might not Wales have been excluded from returning members, why may they not be excluded now, and Devonshire and Cornwall, and every other county and borough share the same fate? Matter of fact is one thing, matter of right another. The people of a state may in *fact* be very unequally represented; but few men would, like our author, in effect contend that it were best they should not be represented at all. Has the gentleman forgot the maxim "that equity is equality." 'Tis hoped he will not consider this as a leveling principle, as it has been more than once called. How astonishing is it that the instances of the unequal representation in Great Britain, to which he might have added those of "ten Cornish barns and an ale house," should be brought as an argument to prove that "the right of being represented in Parliament" is "an *utopian privilege,*" a "phantom," a "cloud in the shape of Juno"? This is far from a fine compliment to the honorable House of Commons, of which as one of the branches of the supreme legislative and of the privilege of sitting with them it would have been more decent to have made a different choice of expressions. To atone for this indelicacy, the next moment the pendulum vibrates as far the other way.

In page 13, the Parliament is represented as so pure and perfect that "*the beauty and symmetry of this body would be destroyed and its purity defiled by the unnatural mixture of representatives from* every part of the British dominions. Parthians, Medes, Elamites, and the dwellers of Mesopotamia, etc., *would not in such a case speak the same language.* What a heterogeneous council would this form? What a monster in government would it be?" Let me add, was ever insolence equal to this? Are the inhabitants of British America all a parcel of transported thieves, robbers, and rebels, or descended from such? Are the colonists blasted

lepers, whose company would infect the whole House of Commons? There are some in the colonies who value themselves on their descent. We have the names of *Tudor* and of *Stuart,* of *Howard, Seymour,* and of *Russell,* who boast an unsullied descent from our ancient princes and nobles, or at least claim the honor of being of the same blood. Can none of these be returned as members without breeding a plague in the House? If this writer is a European, his insults upon the British colonies are quite unpardonable; if he be a native he is an ungrateful parricide. Is he a venal hireling of a party, his employers on either side the Atlantic should discard him as a mere Sir Martyn Marplot? Depend upon it, one such letter as his, if known to breathe the sentiments of the great, would tend more to disgust the colonies against the conduct of their superiors than a hundred thousand such pamphlets as the author scolds at Parliaments are not only "as ancient as our Saxon ancestors" but as old as the commonwealths of Israel, Greece, and Rome; nay as old as the first compact for changing a simple democracy into any other form of government. "Attendance in Parliament" is not, therefore, as the gentleman conceives, a "duty arising from a tenure of lands or the feudal system" but from the nature of man, of society, and of all original, just, social, and civil compacts for forming a state. "So that the privilege of sitting in it," i.e., in a parliament or grand council of a nation, is not "territorial" in the sense of the Letter Writer, nor in its nature "confined to Great Britain." What is there, what can there be that should naturally and necessarily confine the privilege of returning members to the inhabitants of Great Britain more than to those of London and Westminster?

The gentleman says "the Parliament may levy internal taxes as well as regulate trade, there is no essential difference." By regulating trade I suppose he means, according to the common sophism, taxing trade. Even in this sense 'tis admitted the Parliament have the same right to levy internal taxes on the colonies as to regulate trade, and that the right of levying both is undoubtedly in the Parliament. Yet 'tis humbly conceived and hoped that before the authority is fully exerted in either case it will be thought to be but reasonable and equitable that the dominions should be in *fact* represented. Else it will follow that the provincials in Europe, Asia, Africa, and America ought to all generations to content themselves with having no more share, weight, or influence, even in the provincial government of their respective countries, than the Hottentots have in that of China, or the Ethiopians in that of Great Britain.

I should be glad to know how the gentleman came by his assurance that "a stamp duty is confessedly the most reasonable and equitable that can be devised." Some few may be of this opinion, and there never was a new invented tax or excise but its favorers and partisans would highly extol as the most just and equitable device imaginable. This is a trite game "at ways and means." But bold assertions will not pass for clear proofs with "philosophically inquisitive minds." If "the shaft is sped" and the aim so good, I wonder the gentleman should even faintly pretend to "desire not to see a stamp duty established among us," or "wish to prevent the blow." Were I convinced, as he is, that it is reasonable and best that the colonies should be taxed by Parliament without being allowed a representation, and that it is become not only necessary to levy internal taxes on them but that the art of man could not devise so equitable and reasonable a tax as a stamp duty, I should heartily pray for its establishment.

The gentleman nowhere discovers his temper more plainly than in his comparison of Greece and Rome in their conduct towards their colonies. 'Tis well known the Grecians were kind, humane, just, and generous towards theirs. 'Tis as notorious that the Romans were severe, cruel, brutal, and barbarous towards theirs. I have ever pleased myself in thinking that Great Britain since the Revolution might be justly compared to Greece in its care and protection of its colonies. I also imagined that the French and Spaniards followed the Roman example. But our Letter Writer tells quite a different story. He compliments the nation and comforts the colonies by declaring that these "exactly resemble those of Rome. The *Roman coloniae*," says he, "did not enjoy all the rights of

Roman citizens. They only *used* the Roman laws and religion and served in their legions, but had no right of suffrage or bearing honors." "In these respects," adds he, "our English colonies exactly resemble them. We enjoy the English laws and religion but not the right of suffrage or of bearing honors in Great Britain."

Is this enjoying the rights, liberties, and privileges of British-born subjects within the realm to all intents, constructions, and purposes? I find all this confirmed to the colonists, not only by the common law and by their charters, but by act of Parliament. Where does the gentleman find it decreed that the British "*coloniae* have no right of bearing honors in Great Britain"? Has not the King's Majesty, the fountain of honor, an undoubted right by his prerogative to confer any rank he may be graciously pleased to bestow on his American subjects, as well as on those in Great Britain? Cannot the word of a King as easily make even a Halifaxian Letter Writer or his Rhode Island friend a knight of the garter or thistle as if either of them had been dropped and drawn their first breath in one of the three kingdoms?

The gentleman may in his anger wish for the laws of "Draco to be enforced on America," and in his fierce anger, for the "iron rod of a Spanish inquisitor." These may be sudden gusts of passion, without malice prepense, that only hurt his cause, and which his employers will not thank him for. But hard, very hard must his heart be who could employ all his stock of learning in a deliberate attempt to reduce the rights of the colonists to the narrow bound of a bare permission to "use the English laws and religion without a suffrage in things sacred or civil and without a right to bear honors in Great Britain," "except that of being shot at for six pence a day in her armies at home as well as abroad." What is the English religion? Pray wherein does it differ from that of Scotland, Ireland, and the plantations? If it differs, and the colonies are obliged to *use* the religion of the metropolis on her embracing paganism, so must the colonies. Since the Revolution all dissenters, both at home and abroad, papists only excepted, have enjoyed a free and generous toleration.

Would the gentleman deprive all Protestant dissenters of this invaluable blessing? If he is an American by birth, what does he deserve of his country for attempting to realize to this and to all future generations the dreary prospect of confinement to the use of the laws and religion of a region 3000 miles beyond sea, in framing which laws and in forming the modes of which religion they shall have no voice nor suffrage, nor shall they have any preferment in church or state, though they shall be taxed without their consent to the support of both?

> . . . *aes triplex*
> *Circa pectus erat.*

The gentleman hath been at great pains in order to represent the merchants of America as a parcel of infamous smugglers. He says, "smuggling had well nigh become established in some of the colonies." 'Tis notoriously known who have been the great abettors and patrons of smugglers and who have shared the greatest part of the profits. All the riot at Ephesus proceeded from certain collectors of the revenues of Diana of the Ephesians; the shrine makers and silversmiths were but their tools. The craft was in danger, but if it had been only that of Demetrius and his journeymen we might not have heard of that day's uproar. 'Tis a very unjust aspersion to charge the American merchants in general with a design to elude and evade the acts of trade. I cannot so well tell how matters have been managed at Halifax or Rhode Island; but in some other colonies only a few favorites have been indulged in the lucrative crime of smuggling, which, after an eminent writer, the gentleman calls a crime "against the law of nature"; 'tis a wonder it had not been recorded from some old commentator *crimen lesae Majestatis, high treason.* The like indulgence, as far as I can learn, has in Rhode Island been confined also to a few choice friends. The article of molasses is everywhere to be excepted. It was known at home that the importation of this was universally tolerated, paying about one tenth of the duties imposed by the old act. The connivance became very general.

I have perused Mr. H—k—s' book over and over but cannot find the least reflection on Dr. Spry; nor do I think any was intended. The Doctor perhaps may thank the gentleman for bringing his name into question, but I doubt, notwithstanding the gentleman's assertions to the contrary, whether the Doctor's "appointments place him above any kind of influence." I believe he is under the influence of honor and conscience, a clear head, and a good heart, all which the gentleman seems too much a stranger to. And should the Doctor also be under that influence which flows from a general aversion and contempt of flattery and falsehood, he must conceive an opinion of his Halifax neighbor that will be very mortifying to one who hopes to make his court to the great, and to the Doctor among the rest, by abusing the colonies. The Doctor hath been in America some months, but I have not heard of one cause that has been tried before him. This is a tolerable proof either that smuggling was not so common a thing as the Letter Writer asserts, or that those who used to be concerned in it are reformed. I think it proves both.

In the 21st and last page but one of the *Letter,* the gentleman bethought himself, and having in a manner finished his epistle, makes an apology for not following Mr. H—k—s "with somewhat more of method." His excuse is that Mr. H—k—s hath not "divided his argument with precision." He then formally proceeds to a curious and, as he doubtless thought, precise division of the argument. "The dispute," says he, "between Great Britain and the colonies consists of two parts. First, the jurisdiction of Parliament; and secondly, the exercise of that jurisdiction. His honor has blended these together, and nowhere marked the division between them. The first I have principally remarked upon." I know of no dispute between Great Britain and her colonies. Who is so hardy as to dispute the jurisdiction of the Parliament? But were there a thousand disputes between Great Britain and the colonies, if the colonists in general were as the Letter Writer represents them, "a simple, credulous, and hitherto loyal people," in danger of "having their minds embittered and their affections alienated from Great Britain by a few pamphlets," and if "from the pride of some and ignorance of others the cry against mother country had spread from colony to colony; and it were to be feared that prejudices and resentments were kindled among them which it will be difficult ever thoroughly to sooth or extinguish," all which insinuations are however very injurious—what would this prove against *The Rights of Colonies Examined* or any other of the pamphlets that have been lately published in America? . . . These, so far as I can find, are all the pamphlets that have been published in America upon the proposed new regulations of the colonies. From the knowledge I have of the sentiments of the "head of the *tribunitian veto*," as the gentleman is pleased to describe him, I take upon me to declare that I have heard him in the most public manner declare his submission to the authority of Parliament; and that from his soul he detests and abhors the thought of making a question of their jurisdiction.

The following passages from *The Rights of the British Colonies Asserted and Proved* may serve to show how careful a hand the Halifax gentleman is at a matter of fact.

"I also lay it down as one of the first principles from whence I intend to deduce the civil rights of the British colonies that all of them are subject to and dependent on Great Britain, and that therefore as over subordinate governments the Parliament of Great Britain has an undoubted power and lawful authority to make acts for the general good that, by naming them, shall and ought to be equally binding as upon the subjects of Great Britain within the realm." "When the Parliament shall think fit to allow the colonists a representation in the House of Commons, the equity of their taxing the colonies will be as clear as their power is at present of doing it without, if they please." "No such claim (i.e., of an independent legislative) was ever thought of by the colonists. They are all better men and better subjects; and many of them too well versed in the laws of nature and nations and the law and constitution of Great Britain to think they have a right to more than a *provincial subordinate legislative*. All power is of GOD. Next and only subordinate to Him in the present state of the well-formed,

beautiful[ly] constructed British monarchy, standing where I hope it ever will stand, for the pillars are fixed in judgment, righteousness, and truth, is the King and Parliament." "From all which it seems plain that the reason why Ireland and the plantations are not bound unless named by an act of Parliament is because they are *not represented* in the British Parliament. Yet in special cases the British Parliament has an undoubted right, as well as power, to bind both by their acts. But whether this can be extended to an indefinite taxation of both is the great question. I conceive the spirit of the British constitution must make an exception of all taxes until it is thought fit to unite a dominion to the realm. Such taxation must be considered either as uniting the dominions to the realm or disfranchising them. If they are united they will be entitled to a representation as well as Wales; if they are so taxed without a union or representation, they are so far disfranchised." "The sum of my argument is: that civil government is of God; that the administrators of it were originally the whole people; that they might have devolved it on whom they pleased; that this devolution is fiduciary, for the good of the whole; that by the British constitution this devolution is on the King, Lords, and Commons, the supreme, sacred, and uncontrollable legislative power, not only in the realm but through the dominions; that by the abdication, the original compact was broken to pieces; that by the Revolution it was renewed and more firmly established, and the rights and liberties of the subject in all parts of the dominions more fully explained and confirmed; that in consequence of this establishment and the act of succession and union, His Majesty GEORGE III is rightful King and sovereign, and, with his Parliament, the supreme legislative of Great Britain, France, and Ireland, and the dominions thereto belonging; that this constitution is the most free one and by far the best now existing on earth; that by this constitution every man in the dominions is a free man; that no part of His Majesty's dominions can be taxed without their consent; that every part has a right to be represented in the supreme or some subordinate legislature; that the refusal of this would seem to be a contradiction in practice to the theory of the constitution; that the colonies are subordinate dominions and are now in such a state as to make it best for the good of the whole that they should not only be continued in the enjoyment of subordinate legislation but be also represented in some proportion to their number and estates in the grand legislature of the nation; that this would firmly unite all parts of the British empire in the greatest peace and prosperity, and render it invulnerable and perpetual." *Rights of the British Colonies Asserted and Proved,* pp. 32, 48, 59, 61, 64. Can the gentleman read these passages and say they imply any question of the power and authority of Parliament? Will he not blush when he reflects that he hath indiscriminately asserted that these pamphlets "have a tendency to embitter the minds of a simple, credulous, and hitherto loyal people, and to alienate their affections from Great Britain, their best friend and alma mater"? Can terms expressive of greater loyalty or submission to the jurisdiction and authority of Parliament be conceived than many that are to

be found in those pamphlets? Yet the gentleman has the effrontery to talk of the "frequent abuse poured forth in pamphlets against the mother country," and laments that before his, "not one filial pen in America had been drawn in her vindication." How grand we look! Are not his dragoons enough, but he must fight with his pen too? I believe he must be a man of parlous courage; and yet he is modest withal. He says he has "no ambition of appearing in print," though he is the only loyal subject His Majesty hath in his American dominions and master of the only filial pen worth a button. If this be true, well might he call his countrymen a parcel of scoundrels, rebels, smugglers, and traitors. I shall take leave of my gentleman by desiring him to reflect in his cooler hours and well consider what would soon be his fate if the Americans should treat him as he most richly deserves.

Reference: James Otis, *A Vindication of the British Colonies* (Boston: J. Alman, 1769).

RICHARD BLAND, AN INQUIRY INTO THE RIGHTS OF THE BRITISH COLONIES, 1766

Sir,

I take the Liberty to address you, as the Author of "The Regulations lately made concerning the Colonies, and the Taxes imposed upon them considered." It is not to the Man, whoever you are, that I address myself; but it is to the Author of a Pamphlet which, according to the Light I view it in, endeavours to fix Shackles upon the *American* Colonies: Shackles which, however nicely polished, can by no Means sit easy upon Men who have just Sentiments of their own Rights and Liberties.

You have indeed brought this Trouble upon yourself, for you say that

many Steps have been lately taken by the Ministry to cement and perfect the necessary Connexion between the Colonies and the Mother Kingdom, which every Man who is sincerely interested in what is interesting to his

Country will anxiously consider the Propriety of, will inquire into the Information, and canvas the Principles upon which they have been adopted; and will be ready to applaud what has been well done, condemn what has been done amiss, and suggest any Emendations, Improvements, or Additions, which may be within his Knowledge, and occur to his Reflexion.

Encouraged therefore by so candid an Invitation, I have undertaken to examine, with an honest Plainness and Freedom, whether the Ministry, by imposing Taxes upon the Colonies by Authority of Parliament, have pursued a wise and salutary Plan of Government, or whether they have exerted pernicious and destructive Acts of Power.

I pretend not to concern myself with the Regulations lately made to encourage Population in the new Acquisitions: Time can only determine whether the Reasons upon which they have been founded are agreeable to the Maxims of Trade and sound Policy, or not. However, I will venture to observe that if the most powerful inducement towards peopling those Acquisitions is to arise from the Expectation of a Constitution to be established in them similar to the other Royal Governments in *America*, it must be a strong Circumstance, in my Opinion, against their being settled by *Englishmen*, or even by *Foreigners*, who do not live under the most despotick Government; since, upon your Principles of Colony Government, such a Constitution will not be worth their Acceptance.

The Question is whether the Colonies are represented in the *British* Parliament or not? You affirm it to be an indubitable Fact that they are represented, and from thence you infer a Right in the Parliament to impose Taxes of every Kind upon them. You do not insist upon the *Power*, but upon the *Right* of Parliament to impose Taxes upon the Colonies. This is certainly a very proper Distinction, as *Right* and *Power* have very different Meanings, and convey very different Ideas: For had you told us that the Parliament of *Great Britain* have *Power*, by the Fleets and Armies of the Kingdom, to impose Taxes and to raise Contributions upon the Colonies, I should not have presumed to dispute the Point with you; but as you insist upon the *Right* only, I must beg Leave to differ from you in Opinion, and shall give my Reasons for it.

But I must first recapitulate your Arguments in Support of this Right in the Parliament. You say

the Inhabitants of the Colonies do not indeed choose Members of Parliament, neither are nine Tenths of the People of *Britain* Electors; for the Right of Election is annexed to certain Species of Property; to peculiar Franchises, and to Inhabitancy in some particular Places. But these Descriptions comprehend only a very small Part of the Lands, the Property and People of *Britain*; all Copy-Hold, all Lease-Hold Estates under the Crown, under the Church, or under private Persons, though for

Terms ever so long; all landed Property in short that is not Freehold, and all monied Property whatsoever, are excluded. The Possessors of these have no Votes in the Election of Members of Parliament; Women and Persons under Age, be their Property ever so large, and all of it Freehold, have none: The Merchants of *London*, a numerous and respectable Body of Men, whose Opulence exceeds all that *America* can collect; the Proprietors of that vast Accumulation of Wealth, the Publick Funds; the Inhabitants of *Leeds*, of *Halifax*, of *Birmingham*, and of *Manchester*, Towns that are each of them larger than the largest in the Plantations; many of lesser Note, that are incorporated; and that great Corporation the *East India* Company, whose Rights over the Countries they possess fall very little short of Sovereignty, and whose Trade and whose Fleets are sufficient to constitute them a maritime Power, are all in the same Circumstances: And yet are they not represented in Parliament? Is their vast Property subject to Taxation without their Consent? Are they all arbitrarily bound by Laws to which they have not agreed? The Colonies are exactly in the same Situation; all *British* Subjects are really in the same; none are actually, all are virtually, represented in Parliament: For every Member of Parliament sits in the House not as a Representative of his own Constituents, but as one of that august Assembly by which all the Commons of *Great Britain* are represented.

This is the Sum of what you advance, in all the Pomp of Parliamentary Declamation, to prove that the Colonies are represented in Parliament, and therefore subject to their Taxation; but notwithstanding this Way of reasoning, I cannot comprehend how Men who are excluded from voting at the Election of Members of Parliament can be represented in that Assembly, or how those who are elected do not sit in the House as Representatives of their Constituents. These Assertions appear to me not only paradoxical, but contrary to the fundamental Principles of the *English* Constitution.

To illustrate this important Disquisition, I conceive we must recur to the civil Constitution of *England*, and from thence deduce and ascertain the Rights and Privileges of the People at the first Establishment of the Government, and discover the Alterations that have been made in them from Time to Time; and it is from the Laws of the Kingdom, founded upon the Principles of the Law of Nature, that we are to show the Obligation every Member of the State is under to pay Obedience to its Institutions. From these Principles I shall endeavour to prove that the Inhabitants of *Britain*, who have no Vote in the Election of Members of Parliament, are not represented in that Assembly, and yet that they owe Obedience to the Laws of Parliament; which, as to them, are constitutional, and not arbitrary. As to the Colonies, I shall consider them afterwards.

Now it is a Fact, as certain as History can make it, that the present civil Constitution of *England* derives its Original from those *Saxons* who, coming over to the Assistance of the *Britons* in the Time of their King *Vortigern*, made themselves Masters of the Kingdom, and established a Form of Government in it similar to that they had been accustomed to live under in their native Country; as similar, at least, as the Difference of their Situation and Circumstances would permit. This Government, like that from whence they came, was founded upon Principles of the most perfect Liberty: The conquered Lands were divided among the Individuals in Proportion to the Rank they held in the Nation; and every Freeman, that is, every Freeholder, was a Member of their Wittinagemot, or Parliament. The other Part of the Nation, or the Non-Proprietors of Land, were of little Estimation. They, as in *Germany*, were either Slaves, mere Hewers of Wood and Drawers of Water, or Freedmen; who, being of foreign Extraction, had been manumitted by their Masters, and were excluded from the high Privilege of having a Share in the Administration of the Commonwealth, unless they became Proprietors of Land (which they might obtain by Purchase or Donation) and in that Case they had a Right to sit with the Freemen, in the Parliament or sovereign Legislature of the State.

How long this Right of being personally present in the Parliament continued, or when the Custom of sending Representatives to this great Council of the Nation, was first introduced, cannot be determined with Precision; but let the Custom of Representation be introduced when it will, it is certain that every Freeman, or, which was the same Thing in the Eye of the Constitution, every Freeholder, had a Right to vote at the Election of Members of Parliament, and therefore might be said, with great Propriety, to be present in that Assembly, either in his own Person or by Representation. This Right of Election in the Freeholders is evident from the Statute 1st *Hen.* 5. Ch. 1st, which limits the Right of Election to those Freeholders only who are resident in the Counties the Day of the Date of the Writ of Election; but yet every resident Freeholder indiscriminately, let his Freehold be ever so small, had a Right to vote at the Election of Knights for his Country, so that they were actually represented: And this Right of Election continued until it was taken away by the Statute 8th *Hen.* 6. Ch. 7. from those Freeholders who had not a clear Freehold Estate of forty Shillings by the Year at the least.

Now this Statute was deprivative of the Right of those Freeholders who came within the Description of it; but of what did it deprive them, if they were represented notwithstanding their Right of Election was taken from them? The mere Act of voting was nothing, of no Value, if they were represented as constitutionally without it as with it: But when by the fundamental Principles of the Constitution they were to be considered as Members of the Legislature, and as such had a Right to be present in Person, or to send their Procurators or Attornies, and by them to give their Suffrage in the supreme Council of the Nation, this Statute deprived them of an essential Right; a Right without which, by the ancient Constitution of the State, all other Liberties were but a Species of Bondage.

As these Freeholders then were deprived of their Rights to substitute Delegates to Parliament, they could not be represented, but were placed in the same Condition with the Non-Proprietors of Land, who were excluded by the original Constitution from having any Share in the Legislature, but who, notwithstanding such Exclusion, are bound to pay Obedience to the Laws of Parliament, even if they should consist of nine Tenths of the People of *Britain;* but then the Obligation of these Laws does not arise from their being virtually represented in Parliament, but from a quite different Reason.

Men in a State of Nature are absolutely free and independent of one another as to sovereign Jurisdiction, but when they enter into a Society, and by their own Consent become Members of it, they must submit to the Laws of the Society according to which they agree to be governed; for it is evident, by the very Act of Association, that each Member subjects himself to the Authority of that Body in whom, by common Consent, the legislative Power of the State is placed: But though they must submit to the Laws, so long as they remain Members of the Society, yet they retain so much of their natural Freedom as to have a Right to retire from the Society, to renounce the Benefits of it, to enter into another Society, and to settle in another Country; for their Engagements to the Society, and their Submission to the publick Authority of the State, do not oblige them to continue in it longer than they find it will conduce to their Happiness, which they have a natural Right to promote. This natural Right remains with every Man, and he cannot justly be deprived of it by any civil Authority. Every Person therefore who is denied his Share in the Legislature of the State to which he had an original Right, and every Person who from his particular Circumstances is excluded from this great Privilege, and refuses to exercise his natural Right of quitting the Country, but remains in it, and continues to exercise the Rights of a Citizen in all other Respects, must be subject to the Laws which by these Acts he *implicitly,* or to use your own Phrase, *virtually* consents to: For Men may subject themselves to Laws, by consenting to them *implicitly;* that is, by conforming to them, by adhering to the Society, and accepting the Benefits of its Constitution, as well, as *explicitly* and directly, in their own Persons, or by their Representatives substituted in their Room.

Thus, if a Man whose Property does not entitle him to be an Elector of Members of Parliament and therefore cannot be represented, or have any Share in the Legislature

inherits or takes any Thing by the Laws of the Country to which he has no indubitable Right in Nature, or which, if he has a Right to it, he cannot tell how to get or keep without the Aid of the Laws and the Advantage of Society, then, when he takes this Inheritance, or whatever it is, *with* it he takes and owns the Laws that gave it him. And since the Security he has from the Laws of the Country, in Respect of his Person and Rights, is *Equivalent* for his Submission to them, he cannot accept *that* Security without being obliged, in Equity, to pay *this* Submission: Nay his very continuing in the Country shows that he either likes the Constitution, or likes it better, notwithstanding the Alteration made in it to his Disadvantage, than any other; or at least he thinks it better, in his Circumstances, to conform to it, than to seek any other; that is, he is content to be comprehended in it.

From hence it is evident that the Obligation of the Laws of Parliament upon the People of *Britain* who have no Right to be Electors does not arise from their being *virtually* represented, but from a quite different Principle; a Principle of the Law of Nature, true, certain, and universal, applicable to every Sort of Government, and not contrary to the common Understanding of Mankind.

If you say what is a real Fact, that nine Tenths of the People of *Britain* are deprived of the high Privilege of being Electors, it shows a great Defect in the present Constitution, which has departed so much from its original Purity; but never can prove that those People are even *virtually* represented in Parliament. And here give me leave to observe that it would be a Work worthy of the best patriotick Spirits in the Nation to effectuate an Alteration in this putrid Part of the Constitution; and, by restoring it to its pristine Perfection, prevent any "Order of Rank of the Subjects from imposing upon or binding the rest without their Consent." But, I fear, the Gangrene has taken too deep Hold to be eradicated in these Days of Venality.

But if those People of *Britain* who are excluded from being Electors are not represented in Parliament, the Conclusion is much stronger against the People of the Colonies being represented; who are considered by the *British* Government itself, in every Instance of Parliamentary Legislation, as a distinct People. It has been determined by the Lords of the Privy Council that "Acts of Parliament made in *England* without naming the foreign Plantations will not bind them." Now what can be the Reason of this Determination, but that the Lords of Privy Council are of Opinion the Colonies are a distinct People from the Inhabitants of *Britain*, and are not represented in Parliament. If, as you contend, the Colonies are *exactly in the same Situation* with the Subjects in *Britain*, the Laws will in every Instance be equally binding upon them, as upon those Subjects, unless you can discover two Species of *virtual* Representation; the one to respect the Subjects in *Britain*, and always existing in Time of Parliament; the other to respect the Colonies, a mere Non-Entity, if I may be allowed the Term, and never existing but when the Parliament thinks proper to produce it into Being by any particular Act in which the Colonies happen to be named. But I must examine the Case of the Colonies more distinctly.

It is in vain to search into the civil Constitution of *England* for Directions in fixing the proper Connexion between the Colonies and the Mother Kingdom; I mean what their reciprocal Duties to each other are, and what Obedience is due from the Children to the general Parent. The planting Colonies from *Britain* is but of recent Date, and nothing relative to such Plantation can be collected from the ancient Laws of the Kingdom; neither can we receive any better Information by extending our Inquiry into the History of the Colonies established by the several Nations in the more early Ages of the World. All the Colonies (except those of *Georgia* and *Nova Scotia*) formed from the *English* Nation, in *North America*, were planted in a Manner, and under a Dependence, of which there is not an Instance in all the Colonies of the Ancients; and therefore, I conceive, it must afford a good Degree of Surprise to find an *English* Civilian giving it as his Sentiment that the *English* Colonies ought to be governed by the *Roman* Laws, and for no better Reason than because the *Spanish* Colonies, as he says, are governed by those Laws. The *Romans* established their Colonies in the Midst of vanquished Nations, upon Principles which best secured their Conquests; the Privileges granted to them were not always the same; their Policy in the Government of their Colonies and the conquered Nations being always directed by arbitrary Principles to the End they aimed at, the subjecting the whole Earth to their Empire. But the Colonies in *North America*, except those planted within the present Century, were founded by *Englishmen*; who, becoming private Adventurers, established themselves, without any Expense to the Nation, in this uncultivated and almost uninhabited Country; so that their Case is plainly distinguishable from that of the *Roman*, or any other Colonies of the ancient World.

As then we can receive no Light from the Laws of the Kingdom, or from ancient History, to direct us in our Inquiry, we must have Recourse to the Law of Nature, and those Rights of Mankind which flow from it.

I have observed before that when Subjects are deprived of their civil Rights, or are dissatisfied with the Place they hold in the Community, they have a natural Right to quit the Society of which they are Members, and to retire into another Country. Now when Men exercise this Right, and withdraw themselves from their Country, they recover their natural Freedom and Independence: The Jurisdiction and Sovereignty of the State they have quitted ceases; and if they unite, and by common Consent take Possession of a new Country, and form themselves into a political Society, they become a sovereign State, independent of the State from which they separated. If then the Subjects of *England* have a natural Right to relinquish their Country, and by retiring from it, and associating together, to form a new political Society and independent State, they must have a Right, by Compact with the Sovereign of the Nation, to remove into a new Country, and to form a civil Establishment upon the Terms of the Compact. In such a Case, the Terms of the Compact must be obligatory and binding upon the Parties; they must be the Magna Charta, the fundamental Principles of Government, to this new Society; and every Infringement of them must be wrong, and may be opposed. It will be necessary then to examine whether any such Compact was entered into between the Sovereign and those *English* Subjects who established themselves in *America*.

You have told us that "before the first and great Act of Navigation the Inhabitants of *North America* were but a few unhappy Fugitives, who had wandered thither to enjoy their civil and religious Liberties, which they were deprived of at Home." If this was true, it is evident, from what has been said upon the Law of Nature, that they have a Right to a civil independent Establishment of their own, and that *Great Britain* has no *Right* to interfere in it. But you have been guilty of a gross Anachronism in your Chronology, and a great Errour in your Account of the first Settlement of the Colonies in *North America*; for it is a notorious Fact that they were not settled by Fugitives from their native Country, but by Men who came over voluntarily, at their own Expense, and under Charters from the Crown, obtained for that Purpose, long before the first and great Act of Navigation.

The first of these Charters was granted to Sir *Walter Raleigh* by Queen *Elizabeth* under her great Seal, and was confirmed by the Parliament of *England* in the Year 1584. By this Charter the whole Country to be possessed by Sir *Walter Raleigh* was granted to him, his Heirs and Assigns, in perpetual Sovereignty, in as extensive a Manner as the Crown could grant, or had ever granted before to any Person or Persons, with full Power of Legislation, and to establish a civil Government in it as near as conveniently might be agreeable to the Form of the *English* Government and Policy thereof. The Country was to be united to the Realm of *England* in perfect LEAGUE AND AMITY, was to be within the Allegiance of the Crown of *England*, and to be held by Homage, and the Payment of one Fifth of

all Gold and Silver Ore, which was reserved for all Services, Duties, and Demands.

Sir *Walter Raleigh*, under this Charter, took Possession of *North America*, upon that Part of the Continent which gave him a Right to the Tract of Country which lies between the twenty fifth Degree of Latitude and the Gulf of *St. Lawrence*; but a Variety of Accidents happening in the Course of his Exertions to establish a Colony, and perhaps being overborn by the Expense of so great a Work, he made an Assignment to divers Gentlemen and Merchants of *London*, in the 31st Year of the Queen's Reign, for continuing his Plantation in *America*. These Assignees were not more successful in their Attempts than the Proprietor himself had been; but being animated with the Expectation of mighty Advantages from the Accomplishment of their Undertaking, they, with others, who associated with them, obtained new Charters from King *James* the First, in whom all Sir *Walter Raleigh*'s Rights became vested upon his Attainder; containing the same extensive Jurisdictions, Royalties, Privileges, Franchises, and Pre-eminences, and the same Powers to establish a civil Government in the Colony, as had been granted to Sir *W. Raleigh*, with an express Clause of Exemption for ever from all Taxes or Impositions upon their Import and Export Trade.

Under these Charters the Proprietors effectually prosecuted, and happily succeeded, in planting a Colony upon that Part of the Continent which is now called *Virginia*. This Colony, after struggling through immense Difficulties, without receiving the least Assistance from the *English* Government, attained to such a Degree of Perfection that in the Year 1621 a General Assembly, or legislative Authority, was established in the Governour, Council, and House of Burgesses, who were elected by the Freeholders as their Representatives; and they have continued from that Time to exercise the Power of Legislation over the Colony.

But on the 15th of *July*, 1624, King *James* dissolved the Company by Proclamation, and took the Colony under his immediate Dependence; which occasioned much Confusion, and created mighty Apprehensions in the Colony lest they should be deprived of the Rights and Privileges granted them by the Company, according to the Powers contained in their Charters.

To put an End to this Confusion, and to conciliate the Colony to the new System of Government the Crown intended to establish among them, K. *Charles* the First, upon the Demise of his Father, by Proclamation the 13th of *May*, 1625, declared

that *Virginia* should be immediately dependent upon the Crown; that the Affairs of the Colony should be vested in a Council, consisting of a few Persons of Understanding and Quality, to be subordinate and attendant to the Privy Council in *England*; that he was resolved to establish another Council in *Virginia*, to be subordinate to the Council in *England* for the Colony; and that he would maintain the necessary Officers, Ministers, Forces, Ammunition, and Fortifications thereof, at his own Charge.

But this Proclamation had an Effect quite different from what was intended; instead of allaying, it increased the Confusion of the Colony; they now thought their regular Constitution was to be destroyed, and a Perrogative Government established over them; or, as they express themselves in their Remonstrance, that "their Rights and Privileges were to be assaulted." This general Disquietude and Dissatisfaction continued until they received a Letter from the Lords of the Privy Council, dated *July* the 22d, 1634, containing the Royal Assurance and Confirmation that "all their Estates, Trade, Freedom, and Privileges, should be enjoyed by them in as extensive a Manner as they enjoyed them before the recalling the Company's Patent;" whereupon they became reconciled, and began again to exert themselves in the Improvement of the Colony.

Being now in full Possession of the Rights and Privileges of *Englishmen*, which they esteemed more than their Lives, their Affection for the Royal Government grew almost to Enthusiasm; for upon an Attempt to restore the Company's

Charter by Authority of Parliament, the General Assembly, upon the 1st of *April*, 1642, drew up a Declaration or Protestation, in the Form of an Act, by which they declared

they never would submit to the Government of any Company or Proprietor, or to so unnatural a Distance as a Company or other Person to interpose between the Crown and the Subjects; that they were born under Monarchy, and would never degenerate from the Condition of their Births by being subject to any other Government; and every Person who should attempt to reduce them under any other Government was declared an Enemy to the Country, and his Estate was to be forfeited.

This Act, being presented to the King, at his Court at *York*, *July* 5th, 1644 drew from him a most gracious Answer, under his Royal Signet, in which he gave them the fullest Assurances that they should be always immediately dependent upon the Crown, and that the Form of Government should never be changed. But after the King's Death they gave a more eminent Instance of their Attachment to Royal Government, in their Opposition to the Parliament, and forcing the Parliament Commissioners, who were sent over with a Squadron of Ships of War to take Possession of the Country, into Articles of Surrender, before they would submit to their Obedience. As these Articles reflect no small Honour upon this Infant Colony, and as they are not commonly known, I will give an Abstract of such of them as relate to the present Subject.

1. The Plantation of *Virginia*, and all the Inhabitants thereof, shall be and remain in due Subjection to the Commonwealth of *England*, not as a conquered Country, but as a Country submitting by their own voluntary Act, and shall enjoy such Freedoms and Privileges as belong to the free People of England[.]
2. The General Assembly as formerly shall convene, and transact the Affairs of the Colony.
3. The People of *Virginia* shall have a free Trade, as the People of *England*, to all Places, and with all Nations.

4. *Virginia* shall be free from all Taxes, Customs, and Impositions whatsoever; and none shall be imposed on them without Consent of the General Assembly; and that neither Forts nor Castles be erected, or Garrisons maintained, without their Consent.

Upon this Surrender of the Colony to the Parliament, Sir *W. Berkeley,* the Royal Governour, was removed, and three other Governours were successively elected by the House of Burgesses; but in *January* 1659 Sir *William Berkeley* was replaced at the Head of the Government by the People, who unanimously renounced their Obedience to the Parliament, and restored the Royal Authority by proclaiming *Charles* the 2d. King of *England, Scotland, France, Ireland,* and *Virginia;* so that he was King in *Virginia* some Time before he had any certain Assurance of being restored to his Throne in *England.*

From this Detail of the Charters, and other Acts of the Crown, under which the first Colony in *North America* was established, it is evident that "the Colonists were not a few unhappy Fugitives who had wandered into a distant Part of the World to enjoy their civil and religious Liberties, which they were deprived of at home," but had a regular Government long before the first Act of Navigation, and were respected as a distinct State, independent, as to their *internal* Government, of the original Kingdom, but united with her, as to their *external* Polity, in the closest and most intimate League and Amity, under the same Allegiance, and enjoying the Benefits of a reciprocal Intercourse.

But allow me to make a Reflection or two upon the preceding Account of the first Settlement of an *English* Colony in *North America.*

America was no Part of the Kingdom of *England;* it was possessed by a savage People, scattered through the Country, who were not subject to the *English* Dominion, nor owed Obedience to its Laws. This independent Country was settled by *Englishmen* at their own Expense, under particular Stipulations with the Crown: These Stipulations then must be the sacred Band of Union between *England* and her Colonies, and

cannot be infringed without Injustice. But you Object that "no Power can abridge the Authority of Parliament, which has never exempted any from the Submission they owe to it; and no other Power can grant such an Exemption."

I will not dispute the Authority of the Parliament, which is without Doubt supreme within the Body of the Kingdom, and cannot be abridged by any other Power; but may not the King have Prerogatives which he has a Right to exercise without the Consent of Parliament? If he has, perhaps that of granting License to his Subjects to remove into a *new* Country, and to settle therein upon particular Conditions, may be one. If he has no such Prerogative, I cannot discover how the Royal Engagements can be made good, that "the Freedom and other Benefits of the *British* Constitution" shall be secured to those People who shall settle in a new Country under such Engagements; the Freedom, and other Benefits of the *British* Constitution, cannot be secured to a People without they are exempted from being taxed by any Authority but that of their Representatives, chosen by themselves. This is an essential Part of *British* Freedom; but if the King cannot grant such an Exemption, in Right of his Prerogative, the Royal Promises cannot be fulfilled; and all Charters which have been granted by our former Kings, for this Purpose, must be Deceptions upon the Subjects who accepted them, which to say would be a high Reflection upon the Honour of the Crown. But there was a Time when some Parts of *England* itself were exempt from the Laws of Parliament: The Inhabitants of the County Palatine of *Chester* were not subject to such Laws *ab antiquo* ["from ancient days"], because they did not send Representatives to Parliament, but had their own *Commune Concilium* ["corporate council"]; by whose Authority, with the Consent of their Earl, their Laws were made. If this Exemption was not derived originally from the Crown, it must have arisen from that great Principle in the *British* Constitution by which the Freemen in the Nation are not subject to any Laws but such as are made by Representatives elected by themselves to Parliament; so that, in either Case, it is an Instance extremely applicable to the Colonies, who contend for no other Right but that of directing their internal Government by Laws made with their own Consent, which has been preserved to them by repeated Acts and Declarations of the Crown.

The Constitution of the Colonies, being established upon the Principles of *British* Liberty, has never been infringed by the immediate Act of the Crown; but the Powers of Government, agreeably to this Constitution, have been constantly declared in the King's Commissions to their Governours, which, as often as they pass the Great Seal, are *new* Declarations and Confirmations of the Rights of the Colonies. Even in the Reign of *Charles* the Second, a Time by no Means favourable to Liberty, these Rights of the Colonies were maintained inviolate; for when it was thought necessary to establish a permanent Revenue for the Support of Government in *Virginia*, the King did not apply to the *English* Parliament, but to the General Assembly, and sent over an Act, under the Great Seal of *England*, by which it was enacted "by the King's Most Excellent Majesty, by and with the Consent of the General Assembly," that two Shillings per Hogshead upon all Tobacco exported, one Shilling and Threepence per Tun upon Shipping, and Sixpence per Poll for every Person imported, not being actually a Mariner in Pay, were to be paid for ever as a Revenue for the Support of the Government in the Colony.

I have taken Notice of this Act, not only because it shows the proper Fountain from whence all Supplies to be raised in the Colonies ought to flow, but also as it affords an Instance that Royalty itself did not disdain formerly to be named as a Part of the Legislature of the Colony; though now, to serve a Purpose destructive of their Rights, and to introduce Principles of Despotism unknown to a free Constitution, the Legislature of the Colonies are degraded even below the Corporation of a petty Borough in *England*.

It must be admitted that after the Restoration the Colonies lost that Liberty of Commerce with foreign Nations they had enjoyed before that Time.

As it became a fundamental Law of the other States of *Europe* to prohibit all foreign Trade with their Colonies, *England* demanded such an exclusive Trade with her Colonies. This was effected by the Act of 25th *Charles* 2d, and some other subsequent Acts; which not only circumscribed the Trade of the Colonies with foreign Nations within very narrow Limits, but imposed Duties upon several Articles of their own Manufactory exported from one Colony to another. These Acts, which imposed severer Restrictions upon the Trade of the Colonies than were imposed upon the Trade of *England*, deprived the Colonies, so far as these Restrictions extended, of the Privileges of *English* Subjects, and constituted an unnatural Difference between Men under the same Allegiance, born equally free, and entitled to the same civil Rights. In this Light did the People of *Virginia* view the Act of 25th *Charles* 2d, when they sent Agents to the *English* Court to represent against "Taxes and Impositions being laid on the Colony by any Authority but that of their General Assembly." The Right of imposing *internal* Duties upon their Trade by Authority of Parliament was then disputed, though you say it was never called into Question; and the Agents sent from *Virginia* upon this Occasion obtained a Declaration from *Charles* 2d the 19th of *April* 1676, under his Privy Seal, that Impositions or "Taxes ought not be laid upon the Inhabitants and Proprietors of the Colony but by the common Consent of the General Assembly, except such Impositions as the Parliament should lay on the Commodities imported into *England* from the Colony:" And he ordered a Charter to be made out, and to pass the Great Seal, for securing this Right, among others, to the Colony.

But whether the Act of 25th *Charles* 2d, or any of the other Acts, have been complained of as Infringements of the Rights of the Colonies or not, is immaterial; for if a Man of superiour Strength takes my Coat from me, that cannot give him a Right to my Cloak, nor am I obliged to submit to be deprived of all my Estate because I may have given up some Part of it without Complaint. Besides, I have proved irrefragably that the Colonies are not represented in Parliament, and consequently, upon your own Position, that no new Law can bind them that is made without the Concurrence of their Representatives; and if so, then every Act of Parliament that imposes *internal* Taxes upon the Colonies is an Act of *Power*, and not of *Right*. I must speak freely, I am considering a Question which affects the *Rights* of above two Millions of as loyal Subjects as belong to the *British* Crown, and must use Terms adequate to the Importance of it; I say that *Power* abstracted from *Right* cannot give a just Title to Dominion. If a Man invades my Property, he becomes an Aggressor, and puts himself into a State of War with me: I have a Right to oppose this Invader; If I have not Strength to repel him, I must submit, but he acquires no Right to my Estate which he has usurped. Whenever I recover Strength I may renew my Claim, and attempt to regain my Possession; if I am never strong enough, my Son, or his Son, may, when able, recover the natural Right of his Ancestor which has been unjustly taken from him.

I hope I shall not be charged with Insolence, in delivering the Sentiments of an honest Mind with Freedom: I am speaking of the *Rights* of a People; *Rights* imply *Equality* in the Instances to which they belong, and must be treated without Respect to the Dignity of the Persons concerned in them. If "the *British* Empire in *Europe* and in *America* is the same *Power*," if the "Subjects in both are the same People, and all equally participate in the Adversity and Prosperity of the Whole," what Distinctions can the Difference of their Situations make, and why is this Distinction made between them? Why is the Trade of the Colonies more circumscribed than the Trade of *Britain*? And why are Impositions laid upon the one which are not laid upon the other? If the Parliament "have a *Right* to impose Taxes of *every Kind* upon the Colonies," they ought in Justice, as the same People, to have the same Sources to raise them from: Their Commerce ought to be equally free with the Commerce of *Britain*, otherwise it will be loading them with Burthens at the same Time that they are deprived of Strength to sustain them; it will be forcing them to make Bricks without Straw. I acknowledge the Parliament is the

sovereign legislative Power of the *British* Nation, and that by a full Exertion of their Power they can deprive the Colonists of the Freedom and other Benefits of the *British* Constitution which have been secured to them by our Kings; they can abrogate all their civil Rights and Liberties; but by what *Right* is it that the Parliament can exercise such a Power over the Colonists, who have as natural a Right to the Liberties and Privileges of *Englishmen* as if they were actually resident within the Kingdom? The Colonies are subordinate to the Authority of Parliament; subordinate I mean in Degree, but not absolutely so: For if by a Vote of the *British* Senate the Colonists were to be delivered up to the Rule of a *French* or *Turkish* Tyranny, they may refuse Obedience to such a Vote, and may oppose the Execution of it by Force. Great is the Power of Parliament, but, great as it is, it cannot, constitutionally, deprive the People of their *natural* Rights; nor, in Virtue of the same Principle, can it deprive them of their *civil* Rights, which are founded in Compact, without their own Consent. There is, I confess, a considerable Difference between these two Cases as to the Right of Resistance: In the first, if the Colonists should be dismembered from the Nation by Act of Parliament, and abandoned to another Power, they have a natural Right to defend their Liberties by open Force, and may lawfully resist; and, if they are able, repel the Power to whose Authority they are abandoned. But in the other, if they are deprived of their civil Rights, if great and manifest Oppressions are imposed upon them by the State on which they are dependent, their Remedy is to lay their Complaints at the Foot of the Throne, and to suffer patiently rather than disturb the publick Peace, which nothing but a Denial of Justice can excuse them in breaking. But if this Justice should be denied, if the most humble and dutiful Representations should be rejected, nay not even deigned to be received, what is to be done? To such a Question *Thucydides* would make the *Corinthians* reply, that if "a decent and condescending Behaviour is shown on the Part of the Colonies, it would be base in the Mother State to press too far on such Moderation:" And he would make the *Corcyreans* answer, that "every Colony, whilst used in a proper Manner, ought to pay Honour and Regard to its Mother State; but, when treated with Injury and Violence, is become an Alien. They were not sent out to be the Slaves, but to be the Equals of those that remain behind."

But, according to your Scheme, the Colonies are to be prohibited from uniting in a Representation of their general Grievances to the common Sovereign. This Moment "the British Empire in Europe and in America is the same Power; its Subjects in both are the same People; each is equally important to the other, and mutual Benefits, mutual Necessities, cement their Connexion." The next Moment "the Colonies are unconnected with each other, different in their Manners, opposite in their Principles, and clash in their Interests and in their Views, from Rivalry in Trade, and the Jealousy of Neighbourhood. This happy Division, which was effected by Accident, is to be continued throughout by Design; and all Bond of Union between them" is excluded from your vast System. Divide et impera ["Divide and rule"] is your Maxim in Colony Administration, lest "an Alliance should be formed dangerous to the Mother Country." Ungenerous Insinuation! detestable Thought! abhorrent to every Native of the Colonies! who, by an Uniformity of Conduct, have ever demonstrated the deepest Loyalty to their King, as the Father of his People, and an unshaken Attachment to the Interest of Great Britain. But you must entertain a most despicable Opinion of the Understandings of the Colonists to imagine that they will allow Divisions to be fomented between them about inconsiderable Things, when the closest Union becomes necessary to maintain in a constitutional Way their dearest Interests.

Another Writer, fond of his new System of placing Great Britain as the Centre of Attraction to the Colonies, says that

they must be guarded against having or forming any Principle of Coherence with each other above that whereby they cohere in the Centre; having no other Principle of Intercommunication between each other than that by which they are in joint Communication with Great Britain, as the common Centre of all. At the same Time that they are each, in their respective Parts and Subordinations, so framed as to be acted by this first Mover, they should always remain incapable of any Coherence, or of so conspiring amongst themselves as to create any other equal Force which might recoil back on this first Mover; nor is it more necessary to preserve the several Governments subordinate within their respective Orbs than it is essential to the Preservation of the Empire to keep them disconnected and independent of each other. [Thomas Pownall, The Administration of the Colonies (1766)]

But how is this "Principle of Coherence," as this elegant Writer calls it, between the Colonies, to be prevented? The Colonies upon the Continent of North America lie united to each other in one Tract of Country, and are equally concerned to maintain their common Liberty. If he will attend then to the Laws of Attraction in natural as well as political Philosophy, he will find that Bodies in Contact, and cemented by mutual Interests, cohere more strongly than those which are at a Distance, and have no common Interests to preserve. But this natural Law is to be destroyed; and the Colonies, whose real Interests are the same, and therefore ought to be united in the closest Communication, are to be disjoined, and all intercommunication between them prevented. But how is this System of Administration to be established? Is it to be done by a military Force, quartered upon private Families? Is it to be done by extending the Jurisdiction of Courts of Admiralty, and thereby depriving the Colonists of legal Trials in the Courts of common Law? Or is it to be done by harassing the Colonists, and giving overbearing Taxgatherers an Opportunity of ruining Men, perhaps better Subjects than themselves, by dragging them from one Colony to another, before Prerogative Judges, exercising a despotick Sway in Inquisitorial Courts? Oppression has produced very great and unexpected Events: The Helvetick Confederacy, the States of the United Netherlands, are Instances in the Annals of *Europe* of the glorious Actions a petty People, in Comparison, can perform when united in the Cause of Liberty. May the Colonies ever remain under a constitutional Subordination to *Great Britain!* It is their Interest to live under such a Subordination; and it is their Duty, by an Exertion of all their Strength and Abilities, when called upon by their common Sovereign, to advance the Grandeur and the Glory of the Nation. May the interests of *Great Britain* and her Colonies be ever united so as that whilst they are retained in a legal and just Dependence no unnatural or unlimited Rule may be exercised over them; but that they may enjoy the Freedom, and other Benefits of the *British* Constitution, to the latest Page in History!

I flatter myself, by what has been said, your Position of a *virtual* Representation is sufficiently refuted; and that there is really no such Representation known in the *British* Constitution, and consequently that the Colonies are not subject to an *internal* Taxation by Authority of Parliament.

I could extend this Inquiry to a much greater Length, by examining into the Policy of the late Acts of Parliament, which impose heavy and severe Taxes, Duties, and Prohibitions, upon the Colonies; I could point out some very disagreeable Consequences, respecting the Trade and Manufactures of *Britain*, which must necessarily result from these Acts; I could prove that the Revenues arising from the Trade of the Colonies,

and the Advantage of their Exports to *Great Britain* in the Balance of her Trade with foreign Nations, exceed infinitely all the Expense she has been at, all the Expense she can be at, in their Protection; and perhaps I could show that the Bounties given upon some Articles exported from the Colonies were not intended, primarily, as Instances of Attention to their Interest, but arose as well from the Consideration of the disadvantageous Dependence of *Great Britain* upon other Nations for the principal Articles of her naval Stores, as from her losing Trade for those Articles; I could demonstrate that these Bounties are by no Means adequate to her Savings in such foreign Trade, if the Articles upon which they are given can be procured from the Colonies in Quantities sufficient to answer her Consumption; and that the Excess of these Savings is so much clear Profit to the Nation, upon the Supposition that these Bounties are drawn from it; but, as they will remain in it, and be laid out in its Manufactures and Exports, that the whole Sum which used to be paid to Foreigners for the Purchase of these Articles will be saved to the Nation. I say I could extend my Inquiry, by examining these several Matters; but as the Subject is delicate, and would carry me to a great Length, I shall leave them to the Reader's own Reflection.

Reference: Richard Bland, *An Inquiry into the Rights of the British Colonies* (Williamsburg: Alexander Purdie and Co., 1766).

THOMAS JEFFERSON, *A SUMMARY VIEW OF THE RIGHTS OF BRITISH AMERICA,* 1774

RESOLVED, That it be an instruction to the said deputies, when assembled in General Congress, with the deputies from the other states of British America, to propose to the said Congress, that an humble and dutiful address be presented to his Majesty, begging leave to lay before him, as Chief Magistrate of the British empire, the united complaints of his Majesty's subjects in America; complaints which are excited by many unwarrantable encroachments and usurpations, attempted

to be made by the legislature of one part of the empire, upon the rights which God, and the laws, have given equally and independently to all. To represent to his Majesty that these, his States, have often individually made humble application to his imperial Throne, to obtain, through its intervention, some redress of their injured rights; to none of which, was ever even an answer condescended. Humbly to hope that this, their joint address, penned in the language of truth, and divested of those expressions of servility, which would persuade his Majesty that we are asking favors, and not rights, shall obtain from his Majesty a more respectful acceptance; and this his Majesty will think we have reason to expect, when he reflects that he is no more than the chief officer of the people, appointed by the laws, and circumscribed with definite powers, to assist in working the great machine of government, erected for their use, and, consequently, subject to their superintendence; and, in order that these, our rights, as well as the invasions of them, may be laid more fully before his Majesty, to take a view of them, from the origin and first settlement of these countries.

To remind him that our ancestors, before their emigration to America, were the free inhabitants of the British dominions in Europe, and possessed a right, which nature has given to all men, of departing from the country in which chance, not choice, has placed them, of going in quest of new habitations, and of there establishing new societies, under such laws and regulations as, to them, shall seem most likely to promote public happiness. That their Saxon ancestors had, under this universal law, in like manner, left their native wilds and woods in the North of Europe, had possessed themselves of the Island of Britain, then less charged with inhabitants, and had established there that system of laws which has so long been the glory and protection of that country. Nor was ever any claim of superiority or dependence asserted over them, by that mother country from which they had migrated: and were such a claim made, it is believed his Majesty's subjects in Great Britain have too firm a feeling of the rights derived to them from their ancestors, to bow down the sovereignty of their state before such visionary pretensions. And it is thought that no circumstance has occurred to distinguish, materially, the British from the Saxon emigration. America was conquered, and her settlements made and firmly established, at the expense of individuals, and not of the British public. Their own blood was spilt in acquiring lands for their settlement, their own fortunes expended in making that settlement effectual. For themselves they fought, for themselves they conquered, and for themselves alone

they have right to hold. No shilling was ever issued from the public treasures of his Majesty, or his ancestors, for their assistance, till of very late times, after the colonies had become established on a firm and permanent footing. That then, indeed, having become valuable to Great Britain for her commercial purposes, his Parliament was pleased to lend them assistance against an enemy who would fain have drawn to herself the benefits of their commerce, to the great aggrandisement of herself, and danger of Great Britain. Such assistance, and in such circumstances, they had often before given to Portugal and other allied states, with whom they carry on a commercial intercourse. Yet these states never supposed that by calling in her aid, they thereby submitted themselves to her sovereignty. Had such terms been proposed, they would have rejected them with disdain, and trusted for better, to the moderation of their enemies, or to a vigorous exertion of their own force. We do not, however, mean to underrate those aids, which, to us, were doubtless valuable, on whatever principles granted: but we would shew that they cannot give a title to that authority which the British Parliament would arrogate over us; and that may amply be repaid by our giving to the inhabitants of Great Britain such exclusive privileges in trade as may be advantageous to them, and, at the same time, not too restrictive to ourselves. That settlement having been thus effected in the wilds of America, the emigrants thought proper to adopt that system of laws, under which they had hitherto lived in the mother country, and to continue their union with her, by submitting themselves to the same common sovereign, who was thereby made the central link, connecting the several parts of the empire thus newly multiplied.

But that not long were they permitted, however far they thought themselves removed from the hand of oppression, to hold undisturbed the rights thus acquired at the hazard of their lives and loss of their fortunes. A family of Princes was then on the British throne, whose treasonable crimes against their people, brought on them, afterwards, the exertion of those sacred and sovereign rights of punishment, reserved in the hands of the people for cases of extreme necessity, and judged by the constitution unsafe to be delegated to any other judicature. While every day brought forth some new and unjustifiable exertion of power over their subjects on that side of the water, it was not to be expected that those here, much less able at that time to oppose the designs of despotism, should be exempted from injury. Accordingly, this country which had been acquired by the lives, the labors, and fortunes of individual adventurers, was by these Princes, several times, parted out and distributed among the favorites and followers of their fortunes; and, by an assumed right of the Crown alone, were erected into distinct and independent governments; a measure, which it is believed, his Majesty's prudence and understanding would prevent him from imitating at this day; as no exercise of such power, of dividing and dismembering a country, has ever occurred in his Majesty's realm of England, though now of very ancient standing; nor could it be justified or acquiesced under there, or in any part of his Majesty's empire.

That the exercise of a free trade with all parts of the world, possessed by the American colonists, as of natural right, and which no law of their own had taken away or abridged, was next the object of unjust encroachment. Some of the colonies having thought proper to continue the administration of their government in the name and under the authority of his Majesty, King Charles the first, whom, notwithstanding his late deposition by the Commonwealth of England, they continued in the sovereignty of their State, the Parliament, for the Commonwealth, took the same in high offence, and assumed upon themselves the power of prohibiting their trade with all other parts of the world, except the Island of Great Britain. This arbitrary act, however, they soon recalled, and by solemn treaty entered into on the 12th day of March, 1651, between the said Commonwealth, by their Commissioners, and the colony of Virginia by their House of Burgesses, it was expressly stipulated by the eighth article of the said treaty, that they should have 'free trade as the people of England do enjoy to all places and with all nations, according to the laws of that Commonwealth.' But that, upon the restoration

of his Majesty, King Charles the second, their rights of free commerce fell once more a victim to arbitrary power; and by several acts of his reign, as well as of some of his successors, the trade of the colonies was laid under such restrictions, as show what hopes they might form from the justice of a British Parliament, were its uncontrolled power admitted over these States. History has informed us, that bodies of men as well as of individuals, are susceptible of the spirit of tyranny. A view of these acts of Parliament for regulation, as it has been affectedly called, of the American trade, if all other evidences were removed out of the case, would undeniably evince the truth of this observation. Besides the duties they impose on our articles of export and import, they prohibit our going to any markets Northward of Cape Finisterra, in the kingdom of Spain, for the sale of commodities which Great Britain will not take from us, and for the purchase of others, with which she cannot supply us; and that, for no other than the arbitrary purpose of purchasing for themselves, by a sacrifice of our rights and interests, certain privileges in their commerce with an allied state, who, in confidence, that their exclusive trade with America will be continued, while the principles and power of the British Parliament be the same, have indulged themselves in every exorbitance which their avarice could dictate or our necessity extort: have raised their commodities called for in America, to the double and treble of what they sold for, before such exclusive privileges were given them, and of what better commodities of the same kind would cost us elsewhere; and, at the same time, give us much less for what we carry thither, than might be had at more convenient ports. That these acts prohibit us from carrying, in quest of other purchasers, the surplus of our tobaccos, remaining after the consumption of Great Britain is supplied: so that we must leave them with the British merchant, for whatever he will please to allow us, to be by him re-shipped to foreign markets, where he will reap the benefits of making sale of them for full value. That, to heighten still the idea of Parliamentary justice, and to show with what moderation they are like to exercise power, where themselves are to feel no part of its weight, we take leave to mention to his Majesty, certain other acts of the British Parliament, by which they would prohibit us from manufacturing, for our own use, the articles we raise on our own lands, with our own labor. By an act passed in the fifth year of the reign of his late Majesty, King George the second, an American subject is forbidden to make a hat for himself, of the fur which he has taken, perhaps, on his own soil; an instance of despotism, to which no parallel can be produced in the most arbitrary ages of British history. By one other act, passed in the twenty-third year of the same reign, the iron which we make, we are forbidden to manufacture; and, heavy as that article is, and necessary in every branch of husbandry, besides commission and insurance, we are to pay freight for it to Great Britain, and freight for it back again, for the purpose of supporting, not men, but machines, in the island of Great Britain. In the same spirit of equal and impartial legislation, is to be viewed the act of Parliament, passed in the fifth year of the same reign, by which American lands are made subject to the demands of British creditors, while their own lands were still continued unanswerable for their debts; from which, one of these conclusions must necessarily follow, either that justice is not the same thing in America as in Britain, or else, that the British Parliament pay less regard to it here than there. But, that we do not point out to his Majesty the injustice of these acts, with intent to rest on that principle the cause of their nullity; but to show that experience confirms the propriety of those political principles, which exempt us from the jurisdiction of the British Parliament. The true ground on which we declare these acts void, is, that the British Parliament has no right to exercise authority over us.

That these exercises of usurped power have not been confined to instances alone, in which themselves were interested; but they have also intermeddled with the regulation of the internal affairs of the colonies. The act of the 9th of Anne for establishing a post office in America, seems to have had little connection with British convenience, except that of accommodating his

Majesty's ministers and favorites with the sale of a lucrative and easy office.

That thus have we hastened through the reigns which preceded his Majesty's, during which the violation of our rights were less alarming, because repeated at more distant intervals, than that rapid and bold succession of injuries, which is likely to distinguish the present from all other periods of American story. Scarcely have our minds been able to emerge from the astonishment into which one stroke of Parliamentary thunder has involved us, before another more heavy and more alarming is fallen on us. Single acts of tyranny may be ascribed to the accidental opinion of a day; but a series of oppressions, begun at a distinguished period, and pursued unalterably through every change of ministers, too plainly prove a deliberate, systematical plan of reducing us to slavery.

That the act, passed in the 4th year of his majesty's reign, entitled "An act for granting certain duties in the British colonies and plantations in America, &c."

One other act, passed in the 5th year of his reign, entitled "An act for granting and applying certain stamp duties and other duties in the British colonies and plantations in America, &c."

One other act, passed in the 6th year of his reign, entitled "An act for the better securing the dependency of his majesty's dominions in America upon the crown and parliament of Great Britain;" and one other act, passed in the 7th year of his reign, entitled "An act for granting duties on paper, tea, &c." form that connected chain of parliamentary usurpation, which has already been the subject of frequent applications to his majesty, and the houses of lords and commons of Great Britain; and no answers having yet been condescended to any of these, we shall not trouble his majesty with a repetition of the matters they contained.

But that one other act, passed in the same 7th year of the reign, having been a peculiar attempt, must ever require peculiar mention; it is entitled "An act for suspending the legislature of New York."

One free and independent legislature, hereby takes upon itself to suspend the powers of another, free and independent as itself. Thus exhibiting a phenomenon unknown in nature, the creator, and creature of its own power. Not only the principles of common sense, but the common feelings of human nature must be surrendered up, before his Majesty's subjects here, can be persuaded to believe, that they hold their political existence at the will of a British Parliament. Shall these governments be dissolved, their property annihilated, and their people reduced to a state of nature, at the imperious breath of a body of men whom they never saw, in whom they never confided, and over whom they have no powers of punishment or removal, let their crimes against the American public be ever so great? Can any one reason be assigned, why one hundred and sixty thousand electors in the island of Great Britain, should give law to four millions in the States of America, every individual of whom is equal to every individual of them in virtue, in understanding, and in bodily strength? Were this to be admitted, instead of being a free people, as we have hitherto supposed, and mean to continue ourselves, we should suddenly be found the slaves, not of one, but of one hundred and sixty thousand tyrants; distinguished, too, from all others, by this singular circumstance, that they are removed from the reach of fear, the only restraining motive which may hold the hand of a tyrant.

That, by 'an act to discontinue in such manner, and for such time as are therein mentioned, the landing and discharging, lading or shipping of goods, wares and merchandize, at the town and within the harbor of Boston, in the province of Massachusetts bay, in North America,' which was passed at the last session of the British Parliament, a large and populous town, whose trade was their sole subsistence, was deprived of that trade, and involved in utter ruin. Let us for a while, suppose the question of right suspended, in order to examine this act on principles of justice. An act of Parliament had been passed, imposing duties on teas, to be paid in America, against which act the Americans had protested, as inauthoritative. The East India Company, who till that time, had never sent a pound of tea to America on their own account, step forth on that occasion, the

asserters of Parliamentary right, and send hither many ship loads of that obnoxious commodity. The masters of their several vessels, however, on their arrival in America, wisely attended to admonition, and returned with their cargoes. In the province of New-England alone, the remonstrances of the people were disregarded, and a compliance, after being many days waited for, was flatly refused. Whether in this, the master of the vessel was governed by his obstinacy, or his instructions, let those who know, say. There are extraordinary situations which require extraordinary interposition. An exasperated people, who feel that they possess power, are not easily restrained within limits strictly regular. A number of them assembled in the town of Boston, threw the tea into the ocean, and dispersed without doing any other act of violence. If in this they did wrong, they were known, and were amenable to the laws of the land; against which, it could not be objected, that they had ever, in any instance, been obstructed or diverted from the regular course, in favor of popular offenders. They should, therefore, not have been distrusted on this occasion. But that ill-fated colony had formerly been bold in their enmities against the House of Stuart, and were now devoted to ruin, by that unseen hand which governs the momentous affairs of this great empire. On the partial representations of a few worthless ministerial dependants, whose constant office it has been to keep that government embroiled, and who, by their treacheries, hope to obtain the dignity of British knighthood, without calling for a party accused, without asking a proof, without attempting a distinction between the guilty and the innocent, the whole of that ancient and wealthy town, is in a moment reduced from opulence to beggary. Men who had spent their lives in extending the British commerce, who had invested, in that place, the wealth their honest endeavors had merited, found themselves and their families, thrown at once on the world, for subsistence by its charities. Not the hundredth part of the inhabitants of that town, had been concerned in the act complained of; many of them were in Great Britain, and in other parts beyond the sea; yet all were involved in one indiscriminate ruin, by a new executive power, unheard of till then, that of a British Parliament. A property of the value of many millions of money, was sacrificed to revenge, not repay, the loss of a few thousands. This is administering justice with a heavy hand indeed! And when is this tempest to be arrested in its course? Two wharves are to be opened again when his Majesty shall think proper: the residue, which lined the extensive shores of the bay of Boston, are forever interdicted the exercise of commerce. This little exception seems to have been thrown in for no other purpose, than that of setting a precedent for investing his Majesty with legislative powers. If the pulse of his people shall beat calmly under this experiment, another and another will be tried, till the measure of despotism be filled up. It would be an insult on common sense, to pretend that this exception was made, in order to restore its commerce to that great town. The trade, which cannot be received at two wharves alone, must of necessity be transferred to some other place; to which it will soon be followed by that of the two wharves. Considered in this light, it would be an insolent and cruel mockery at the annihilation of the town of Boston. By the act for the suppression of riots and tumults in the town of Boston, passed also in the last session of Parliament, a murder committed there, is, if the Governor pleases, to be tried in the court of King's bench, in the island of Great Britain, by a jury of Middlesex. The witnesses, too, on receipt of such a sum as the Governor shall think it reasonable for them to expend, are to enter into recognizance to appear at the trial. This is, in other words, taxing them to the amount of their recognizance; and that amount may be whatever a Governor pleases. For who does his Majesty think can be prevailed on to cross the Atlantic for the sole purpose of bearing evidence to a fact? His expenses are to be borne, indeed, as they shall be estimated by a Governor; but who are to feed the wife and children whom he leaves behind, and who have had no other subsistence but his daily labor? Those epidemical disorders, too, so terrible in a foreign climate, is the cure of them to be estimated among the articles of expense, and their

danger to be warded off by the Almighty power of a Parliament? And the wretched criminal, if he happen to have offended on the American side, stripped of his privilege of trial by peers of his vicinage, removed from the place where alone full evidence could be obtained, without money, without counsel, without friends, without exculpatory proof, is tried before Judges predetermined to condemn. The cowards who would suffer a countryman to be torn from the bowels of their society, in order to be thus offered a sacrifice to Parliamentary tyranny, would merit that everlasting infamy now fixed on the authors of the act! A clause, for a similar purpose, had been introduced into an act passed in the twelfth year of his Majesty's reign, entitled, 'an act for the better securing and preserving his Majesty's Dock-yards, Magazines, Ships, Ammunition and Stores;' against which, as meriting the same censures, the several colonies have already protested.

That these are the acts of power, assumed by a body of men foreign to our constitutions, and unacknowledged by our laws; against which we do, on behalf of the inhabitants of British America, enter this, our solemn and determined protest. And we do earnestly intreat his Majesty, as yet the only mediatory power between the several States of the British empire, to recommend to his Parliament of Great Britain, the total revocation of these acts, which, however nugatory they may be, may yet prove the cause of further discontents and jealousies among us.

That we next proceed to consider the conduct of his Majesty, as holding the Executive powers of the laws of these States, and mark out his deviations from the line of duty. By the Constitution of Great Britain, as well as of the several American States, his Majesty possesses the power of refusing to pass into a law, any bill which has already passed the other two branches of the legislature. His Majesty, however, and his ancestors, conscious of the impropriety of opposing their single opinion to the united wisdom of two Houses of Parliament, while their proceedings were unbiassed by interested principles, for several ages past, have modestly declined the exercise of this power, in that part of his empire called Great

Britain. But, by change of circumstances, other principles than those of justice simply, have obtained an influence on their determinations. The addition of new States to the British empire has produced an addition of new, and, sometimes, opposite interests. It is now, therefore, the great office of his Majesty to resume the exercise of his negative power, and to prevent the passage of laws by any one legislature of the empire, which might bear injuriously on the rights and interests of another. Yet this will not excuse the wanton exercise of this power, which we have seen his Majesty practice on the laws of the American legislature. For the most trifling reasons, and, sometimes for no conceivable reason at all, his Majesty has rejected laws of the most salutary tendency. The abolition of domestic slavery is the great object of desire in those colonies, where it was, unhappily, introduced in their infant state. But previous to the enfranchisement of the slaves we have, it is necessary to exclude all further importations from Africa. Yet our repeated attempts to effect this, by prohibitions, and by imposing duties which might amount to a prohibition, having been hitherto defeated by his Majesty's negative: thus preferring the immediate advantages of a few British corsairs, to the lasting interests of the American States, and to the rights of human nature, deeply wounded by this infamous practice. Nay, the single interposition of an interested individual against a law was scarcely ever known to fail of success, though, in the opposite scale, were placed the interests of a whole country. That this is so shameful an abuse of a power, trusted with his Majesty for other purposes, as if, not reformed, would call for some legal restrictions.

With equal inattention to the necessities of his people here, has his Majesty permitted our laws to lie neglected, in England, for years, neither confirming them by his assent, nor annulling them by his negative: so, that such of them as have no suspending clause, we hold on the most precarious of all tenures, his Majesty's will; and such of them as suspend themselves till his Majesty's assent be obtained, we have feared might be called into existence at some future and distant period, when time and change of circumstances shall have rendered them destructive to his people here. And, to render this grievance still more oppressive, his Majesty, by his instructions, has laid his Governors under such restrictions, that they can pass no law, of any moment, unless it have such suspending clause: so that, however immediate may be the call for legislative interposition, the law cannot be executed, till it has twice crossed the Atlantic, by which time the evil may have spent its whole force.

But in what terms reconcilable to Majesty, and at the same time to truth, shall we speak of a late instruction to his Majesty's Governor of the colony of Virginia, by which he is forbidden to assent to any law for the division of a county, unless the new county will consent to have no representative in Assembly? That colony has as yet affixed no boundary to the Westward. Their Western counties, therefore, are of an indefinite extent. Some of them are actually seated many hundred miles from their Eastern limits. Is it possible, then, that his Majesty can have bestowed a single thought on the situation of those people, who, in order to obtain justice for injuries, however great or small, must, by the laws of that colony, attend their county court at such a distance, with all their witnesses, monthly, till their litigation be determined? Or does his Majesty seriously wish, and publish it to the world, that his subjects should give up the glorious right of representation, with all the benefits derived from that, and submit themselves the absolute slaves of his sovereign will? Or is it rather meant to confine the legislative body to their present numbers, that they may be the cheaper bargain, whenever they shall become worth a purchase?

One of the articles of impeachment against Tresilian, and the other Judges of Westminster Hall, in the reign of Richard the Second, for which they suffered death, as traitors to their country, was, that they had advised the King, that he might dissolve his Parliament at any time; and succeeding kings have adopted the opinion of these unjust Judges. Since the establishment, however, of the British constitution, at the glorious Revolution, on its free and ancient principles, neither his Majesty, nor his ancestors, have exercised such a power of dissolution in the island of Great Britain; and when his Majesty was petitioned, by the united voice of his people there, to dissolve the present Parliament, who had become obnoxious to them, his Ministers were heard to declare, in open Parliament, that his Majesty possessed no such power by the constitution. But how different their language, and his practice, here! To declare, as their duty required, the known rights of their country, to oppose the usurpation of every foreign judicature, to disregard the imperious mandates of a Minister or Governor, have been the avowed causes of dissolving Houses of Representatives in America. But if such powers be really vested in his Majesty, can he suppose they are there placed to awe the members from such purposes as these? When the representative body have lost the confidence of their constituents, when they have notoriously made sale of their most valuable rights, when they have assumed to themselves powers which the people never put into their hands, then, indeed, their continuing in office becomes dangerous to the State, and calls for an exercise of the power of dissolution. Such being the cause for which the representative body should, and should not, be dissolved, will it not appear strange, to an unbiassed observer, that that of Great Britain was not dissolved, while those of the colonies have repeatedly incurred that sentence?

But your Majesty, or your Governors, have carried this power beyond every limit known or provided for by the laws. After dissolving one House of Representatives, they have refused to call another, so that, for a great length of time, the legislature provided by the laws, has been out of existence. From the nature of things, every society must, at all times, possess within itself the sovereign powers of legislation. The feelings of human nature revolt against the supposition of a State so situated, as that it may not, in any emergency, provide against dangers which, perhaps, threaten immediate ruin. While those bodies are in existence to whom the people have delegated the powers of legislation, they alone possess, and may exercise, those powers. But when they are dissolved, by the lopping off one or more of their

branches, the power reverts to the people, who may use it to unlimited extent, either assembling together in person, sending deputies, or in any other way they may think proper. We forbear to trace consequences further; the dangers are conspicuous with which this practice is replete.

That we shall, at this time also, take notice of an error in the nature of our land holdings, which crept in at a very early period of our settlement. The introduction of the Feudal tenures into the kingdom of England, though ancient, is well enough understood to set this matter in a proper light. In the earlier ages of the Saxon settlement, feudal holdings were certainly altogether unknown, and very few, if any, had been introduced at the time of the Norman conquest. Our Saxon ancestors held their lands, as they did their personal property, in absolute dominion, disincumbered with any superior, answering nearly to the nature of those possessions which the Feudalist term Allodial. William the Norman, first introduced that system generally. The lands which had belonged to those who fell in the battle of Hastings, and in the subsequent insurrections of his reign, formed a considerable proportion of the lands of the whole kingdom. These he granted out, subject to feudal duties, as did he also those of a great number of his new subjects, who, by persuasions or threats, were induced to surrender them for that purpose. But still, much was left in the hands of his Saxon subjects, held of no superior, and not subject to feudal conditions. These, therefore, by express laws, enacted to render uniform the system of military defence, were made liable to the same military duties as if they had been feuds; and the Norman lawyers soon found means to saddle them, also, with the other feudal burthens. But still they had not been surrendered to the King, they were not derived from his grant, and therefore they were not holden of him. A general principle was introduced, that "all lands in England were held either mediately or immediately of the Crown;" but this was borrowed from those holdings which were truly feudal, and only applied to others for the purposes of illustration. Feudal holdings were, therefore, but exceptions out of the Saxon laws of possession, under which all lands were held in absolute right. These, therefore, still form the basis or ground-work of the Common law, to prevail wheresoever the exceptions have not taken place. America was not conquered by William the Norman, nor its lands surrendered to him or any of his successors. Possessions there are, undoubtedly, of the Allodial nature. Our ancestors, however, who migrated hither, were laborers, not lawyers. The fictitious principle, that all lands belong originally to the King, they were early persuaded to believe real, and accordingly took grants of their own lands from the Crown. And while the Crown continued to grant for small sums and on reasonable rents, there was no inducement to arrest the error, and lay it open to public view. But his Majesty has lately taken on him to advance the terms of purchase and of holding, to the double of what they were; by which means, the acquisition of lands being rendered difficult, the population of our country is likely to be checked. It is time, therefore, for us to lay this matter before his Majesty, and to declare, that he has no right to grant lands of himself. From the nature and purpose of civil institutions, all the lands within the limits, which any particular party has circumscribed around itself, are assumed by that society, and subject to their allotment; this may be done by themselves assembled collectively, or by their legislature, to whom they may have delegated sovereign authority; and, if they are allotted in neither of these ways, each individual of the society, may appropriate to himself such lands as he finds vacant, and occupancy will give him title.

That, in order to enforce the arbitrary measures before complained of, his Majesty has, from time to time, sent among us large bodies of armed forces, not made up of the people here, nor raised by the authority of our laws. Did his Majesty possess such a right as this, it might swallow up all our other rights, whenever he should think proper. But his Majesty has no right to land a single armed man on our shores; and those whom he sends here are liable to our laws, for the suppression and punishment of riots, routs, and unlawful assemblies, or are hostile bodies invading us in defiance of law. When, in the course of

the late war, it became expedient that a body of Hanoverian troops should be brought over for the defence of Great Britain, his Majesty's grandfather, our late sovereign, did not pretend to introduce them under any authority he possessed. Such a measure would have given just alarm to his subjects of Great Britain, whose liberties would not be safe if armed men of another country, and of another spirit, might be brought into the realm at any time, without the consent of their legislature. He, therefore, applied to Parliament, who passed an act for that purpose, limiting the number to be brought in, and the time they were to continue. In like manner is his Majesty restrained in every part of the empire. He possesses indeed the executive power of the laws in every State; but they are the laws of the particular State, which he is to administer within that State, and not those of any one within the limits of another. Every State must judge for itself, the number of armed men which they may safely trust among them, of whom they are to consist, and under what restrictions they are to be laid. To render these proceedings still more criminal against our laws, instead of subjecting the military to the civil power, his majesty has expressly made the civil subordinate to the military. But can his Majesty thus put down all law under his feet? Can he erect a power superior to that which erected himself? He has done it indeed by force; but let him remember that force cannot give right.

That these are our grievances, which we have thus laid before his Majesty, with that freedom of language and sentiment which becomes a free people claiming their rights as derived from the laws of nature, and not as the gift of their Chief Magistrate. Let those flatter, who fear: it is not an American art. To give praise where it is not due might be well from the venal, but would ill beseem those who are asserting the rights of human nature. They know, and will, therefore, say, that Kings are the servants, not the proprietors of the people. Open your breast, Sire, to liberal and expanded thought. Let not the name of George the Third, be a blot on the page of history. You are surrounded by British counsellors, but remember that they are parties. You have no ministers for American affairs, because you have none taken from among us, nor amenable to the laws on which they are to give you advice. It behooves you, therefore, to think and to act for yourself and your people. The great principles of right and wrong are legible to every reader; to pursue them, requires not the aid of many counsellors. The whole art of government consists in the art of being honest. Only aim to do your duty, and mankind will give you credit where you fail. No longer persevere in sacrificing the rights of one part of the empire to the inordinate desires of another; but deal out to all, equal and impartial right. Let no act be passed by any one legislature, which may infringe on the rights and liberties of another. This is the important post in which fortune has placed you, holding the balance of a great, if a well-poised empire. This, Sire, is the advice of your great American council, on the observance of which may perhaps depend your felicity and future fame, and the preservation of that harmony which alone can continue, both to Great Britain and America, the reciprocal advantages of their connection. It is neither our wish nor our interest to separate from her. We are willing, on our part, to sacrifice everything which reason can ask, to the restoration of that tranquillity for which all must wish. On their part, let

them be ready to establish union on a generous plan. Let them name their terms, but let them be just. Accept of every commercial preference it is in our power to give, for such things as we can raise for their use, or they make for ours. But let them not think to exclude us from going to other markets to dispose of those commodities which they cannot use, nor to supply those wants which they cannot supply. Still less, let it be proposed, that our properties, within our own territories, shall be taxed or regulated by any power on earth, but our own. The God who gave us life, gave us liberty at the same time: the hand of force may destroy, but cannot disjoin them. This, Sire, is our last, our determined resolution. And that you will be pleased to interpose, with that efficacy which your earnest endeavors may insure, to procure redress of these our great grievances, to quiet the minds of your subjects in British America against any apprehensions of future encroachment, to establish fraternal love and harmony through the whole empire, and that that may continue to the latest ages of time, is the fervent prayer of all British America.

Reference: Adrienne Koch and William Peden (eds.), *The Life and Selected Writings of Thomas Jefferson* (New York: Random House, 1944).

JOHN DICKINSON, *ESSAY ON THE CONSTITUTIONAL POWER OF GREAT BRITAIN,* 1774

The authority of parliament has within these few years been a question much agitated; and great difficulty, we understand, has occurred, in tracing the line between the rights of the mother country and those of the colonies. The modern doctrine of the former is indeed truly remarkable; for though it points out, what *are not* our rights, yet we can never learn from it, what *are* our rights. As for example—*Great-Britain* claims a right to take away nine-tenths of our estates—have we a *right* to the remaining tenth? No.—To say we have, is a "traiterous" position, denying her supreme legislature. So far from *having property,*

according to these late found novels, *we are ourselves a property.*

We pretend not to any considerable share of learning; but, thanks be to divine Goodness, common sense, experience, and some acquaintance with the constitution, teach us a few salutary truths on this important subject.

Whatever difficulty may occur in tracing the line, yet we contend, that by the laws of God, and by the laws of the constitution, a line there must be, beyond which her authority cannot extend. For all these laws are "grounded on reason, full of justice, and true equity," mild, and calculated to promote the freedom and welfare of men. These objects never can be attained by abolishing every restriction, on the part of the *governors*, and extinguishing every right, on the part of the *governed*.

SUPPOSE it be allowed, that the line is not *expressly drawn*, is it thence to be concluded, there is no *implied* line? No English lawyer, we presume, will venture to make the bold assertion. "The king may reject what bills, may make what treaties, may coin what money, may create what peers, and may pardon what offences, *he pleases*." But is his prerogative respecting these branches of it, unlimited? By no means. The words following those next above quoted from the "commentaries on the laws of *England*," are—unless where the constitution hath *expressly*, or *by evident consequence*, laid down some *exception* or BOUNDARY; *declaring*, that thus far the prerogative shall go, and no farther." There are "some boundaries" then, besides the "express exceptions;" and according to the strong expression here used, "the constitution *declares* there are." What "evident consequence" forms those "boundaries?"

THE happiness of the people is the end, and, if the term is allowable, we would call it the body of the constitution. Freedom is the spirit or soul. As the soul, speaking of nature, has a right to prevent or relieve, if it can, any mischief to the body of the individual, and to keep it in the best health; so the soul, speaking of the constitution, has a right to prevent, or relieve, any mischief to the body of the society, and to keep that in the best health. The "evident consequence" mentioned, must mean a tendency to injure this health, that is, to diminish the happiness of the people—or it must mean nothing. If therefore the constitution "DECLARES *by evident consequence*," that a tendency to diminish the happiness of the people, is a proof, that power exceeds a "boundary," beyond which it ought not to "go;" the matter is brought to this single point, whether taking our money from us without our consent, depriving us of trial by jury, changing constitutions of government, and abolishing the privilege of the writ of *habeas corpus*, by seizing and carrying us to *England*, have not a greater tendency to diminish our happiness,

than any enormities a king can commit under pretence of prerogative, can have to diminish the happiness of the subjects in *England*. To come to a decision upon this point, no long time need be required. To make this comparison, is stating the claim of parliament in the most favourable light: for it puts the *assumed* power of parliament, to do, "IN ALL CASES WHATSOEVER," *what they please*, upon the same footing with the *acknowledged* power of the king, "to make what peers—pardon what offences, &c. *he pleases*." But in *this* light, that power is not intitled to be viewed. Such is the wisdom of the *English* constitution, that it "declares" the king may transgress a "boundary laid down by evident consequence," even by using *the power* with which he is *expressly* vested by the constitution, in doing *those very acts* which he is *expressly* trusted by the constitution to do—as by creating too many or improper persons, peers; or by pardoning too many or too great offences, &c. But has the constitution of ENGLAND *expressly* "declared," that the parliament of *Great-Britain* may take away the money of *English* colonists without their consent, and deprive them of trial by jury, &c? It cannot be pretended. True it is, that it has been solemnly declared by *parliament*, that *parliament has* such a power. But that declaration leaves the point just as it was before: for if parliament had not the power before, the declaration could not give it. Indeed if parliament is really "omnipotent," that power is just and constitutional.

We further observe, that the constitution has not expressly drawn the line beyond which, if a king, shall "go," resistance becomes *lawful*. The learned author of those commentaries, that notwithstanding some human frailties, do him so much honour, has thought proper, when treating of this subject, to point out the "*precedent*" of the revolution, as fixing the line. We would not venture any reflection on so great a man. It may not become us. Nor can we be provoked by his expressions concerning colonists; because they perhaps contain his real, though hasty sentiments. Surely, it was not his intention to condemn those excellent men, who casting every tender consideration behind them, nobly presented themselves against the tyranny of the unfortunate and misguided *Charles's* reign; those men, whom the house of commons, even after the restoration, would not suffer to be censured.

WE are sensible of the objection that may be made, as to drawing a line between rights on each side, and the case of a plain violation of rights.—We think it not material. Circumstances have *actually* produced, and may again produce this question.—What conduct of a prince renders resistance lawful? *James* the second and his father violated *express rights of their subjects*, by doing what *their own express rights* gave them no title to do, as by raising money, and levying troops, without consent of parliament. It is not even *settled*, what violation of those will justify resistance. But may not some future prince, confining himself to the exercise of *his own express rights*, such as have been mentioned, act in a manner, that will be a transgression of a "boundary" laid down by "evident consequence," the "constitution *declaring* he should go no further?" May not this exercise of these *his express rights*, be so far extended, as to introduce *universal confusion* and a *subversion of the ends of government?* The whole may be oppressive, and yet any single instance legal. The cases may be improbable; but we have seen and now feel events once as little expected. Is it not *possible*, that one of these cases *may* happen;—if it *does*, has the constitution *expressly* drawn, a line, beyond which resistance becomes lawful? It has not. But it may be said, a king *cannot arm* against his subjects—he *cannot raise money*, without consent of parliament. This is the constitutional check upon him. If he should, it would be a violation of *their express rights*. If *their purses* are shut, *his power* shrinks. True. Unhappy colonists! Our money may be taken from us—and standing armies established over us, without our consent— every *expressly* declared constitutional check dissolved, and the modes of opposition for relief so contracted, as to leave us only the miserable alternative of supplication or violence. And these, it seems, are the liberties of *Americans*.—Because the constitution has not "*expressly declared*" the line between the rights of the mother country and *those* of her colonists, *therefore*, the latter have *no*

rights.—A logic, equally edifying to the heads and hearts of men of sense and humanity.

WE assert, a line there must be, and shall now proceed with great deference to the judgment of others, to trace that line, according to the ideas we entertain: and it is with satisfaction we can say, that the records, statutes, law-books, and most approved writers of our mother country, those "dead but most faithful counsellors" (as sir *Edward Coke* calls them) "who cannot be daunted by fear, nor muzzled by affection, reward, or hope of preferment, and therefore may safely be believed," confirm the principles we maintain.

LIBERTY, life, or property, can, with no consistency of words or ideas, be termed a *right* of the *possessors*, while *others* have a *right* of taking them away *at pleasure*. The most distinguished authors, that have written on government, declare it to be "instituted *for the benefit of the people*; and that it never will have this tendency, where "it is *unlimited*." Even conquest itself is held not to destroy all the rights of the conquered. Such is the merciful reverence judged by the best and wisest men to be due to human nature, and frequently observed even by conquerors themselves.

PROTECTION and obedience are reciprocal duties.

IN fine, a power of government, in its nature tending to the misery of the people, as a power that is *unlimited*, or in other words, a power *in which the people have no share*, is proved to be, by reason and the experience of all ages and countries, cannot be a *rightful* or *legal* power. For, as an excellent bishop of the church of *England* argues, "the *ends of government* cannot be answered by a total dissolution of all happiness at present, and of all hopes for the future."

THE just inference therefore from these premises, would be an exclusion of *any* power of parliament over these colonies, rather than the admission of an *unbounded* power.

WE well know, that the colonists are charged by many persons in *Great-Britain*, with attempting to obtain such an exclusion and a total independence on her. As well we know the accusation to be utterly false. We are become criminal in the sight of such persons, by refusing to be guilty of the highest crime against ourselves and our posterity. *Nolumus leges Angliæ mutari*. This is the rebellion with which we are stigmatized.—[We have committed the like offence, that was objected by the polite aud humane *Fimbria*, against a *rude* senator of his time. We have "*disrespectfully* refused to receive the *whole* weapon into our body." We could not do it, *and live*. But *that* must be acknowledged to be a poor excuse, equally inconsistent with good breeding and the supreme legislature of *Great-Britain*.]

FOR these ten years past we have been incessantly attacked. Hard is our fate, when, to escape the character of rebels, we must be degraded into that of slaves: as if there was no medium, between the two extremes of anarchy and despotism, where innocence and freedom could find repose and safety.

Why should we be exhibited to mankind, as a people adjudged by parliament unworthy of freedom? The thought alone is insupportable. Even those unhappy persons, who have had the misfortune of being born under the yoke of bondage, imposed by the cruel laws, if they may be called laws, of the land, where they received their birth, no sooner breathe the air of *England*, though they touch her shore only by accident, than they instantly become freemen. Strange contradiction. The *same* kingdom at the *same* time, the *asylum* and the *bane* of liberty.

To return to the charge against us, we can safely appeal to that Being, from whom no thought can be concealed, that our warmest wish and utmost ambition is, that we and our posterity may ever remain subordinate to, and dependent upon our parent state.—This submission our reason approves, our affection dictates, our duty commands, and our interest inforces.

IF this submission indeed implies a dissolution of our constitution, and a renunciation of our liberty, we should be unworthy of our relation to her, if we should not frankly declare, that we regard it with horror; and every true *Englishman* will applaud this just distinction and candid declaration. [Our defence necessarily touches chords in unison with the fibres of his honest heart. They must vibrate in sympathetic tones. If we,

his kindred, should be base enough to promise the humiliating subjection, he could not believe us. We should suffer all the infamy of the engagement, without finding the benefit expected from being thought as contemptible as we should undertake to be.]

BUT this submission implies not such insupportable evils: and our amazement is inexpressible, when we consider the gradual increase of these colonies, from their slender beginnings in the last century to their late flourishing condition, and how prodigiously, since their settlement, our parent state has advanced in wealth, force and influence, till she is become the first power on the sea, and the envy of the world—that these our better days should not strike conviction into every mind, that the freedom and happiness of the colonists are not inconsistent with her authority and prosperity.

THE experience of more than one hundred years will surely be deemed, by wise men, to have some weight in the scale of evidence to support our opinion. We might justly ask of her, why we are not permitted to go on, as we have been used to do since our existence, conferring mutual benefits, thereby strengthening each other, more and more discovering the reciprocal advantages of our connection, and daily cultivating affections, encouraged by those advantages? . . .

THE legislative authority claimed by parliament over these colonies consists of two heads—first, a general power of internal legislation; and secondly, a power of regulating our trade; both, she contends are unlimited. Under the first, may be included among other powers, those of forbidding us to worship our Creator in the manner we think most acceptable to him—imposing taxes on us—collecting them by their own officers—inforcing the collection by admiralty courts or courts martial—abolishing trials by jury—establishing a standing army among us in time of peace, without consent of our assemblies—paying them with our money—seizing our young men for recruits—changing constitutions of government—stopping the press—declaring any action, even a meeting of the smallest number, to consider of peaceable modes to obtain redress of grievances high treason—taking colonists to *Great-Britain* to be tried—exempting "murderers" of colonists from punishment, by carrying them to *England*, to answer indictments found in the colonies— shutting up our ports—prohibiting us from slitting iron to build our houses,—making hats to cover our heads, or clothing to cover the rest of our bodies, &c. . . .

A DEPENDENCE on the crown and PARLIAMENT of *Great-Britain*, is a novelty—a dreadful novelty.—It may be compared to the engine invented by the *Greeks* for the destruction of *Troy*. It is full of armed enemies, and the walls of the constitution must be thrown down, before it can be introduced among us.

WHEN it is considered that the king, as king of *England*, has a power in *making* laws—the power of *executing* them—of *finally* determining on *appeals*—of calling upon us for *supplies* in times of war, or any emergency—that every branch of the *prerogative* binds us, as the subjects are bound thereby in *England*—and that all our intercourse with *foreigners* is regulated by parliament.—Colonists may "surely" be acknowledged to speak with truth, and precision, in answer to the "elegantly" exprest question—"what king *it* is," &c. by saying that "his most gracious majesty *George* the third," *is* the king of *England*, and therefore, "*the king*," they—profess themselves to be "*loyal subjects of?*"

WE are aware of the objection, that, "if the king of *England* is therefore king of the colonies, they are subject to the general legislative authority of that kingdom." The premises by no means warrant this conclusion. It is built on a mere supposition, that the colonies are thereby acknowledged to be *within the realm*, and on an incantation expected to be wrought by some magic force in those words. To be subordinately connected with *England*, the colonies *have contracted*. To be subject to the general legislative authority of that kingdom, they *never contracted*. Such a power as may be necessary to *preserve this connection* she has.—The authority of the *sovereign*, and the authority of controuling our intercourse with *foreign nations* form that power. *Such a power* leaves the colonies free. But a general legislative power,

is not a power to preserve that connection, but to distress and enslave them. If the first power cannot subsist, without the last, she has no right even to the first,—the colonies were deceived in their contract—and the power must be unjust and illegal; for God has given to them *a better right* to preserve their liberty, than to her to destroy it. In other words, supposing, king, lords and commons acting in parliament, constitute a *sovereignty* over the colonies, is that sovereignty constitutionally *absolute* or *limited*? That states without freedom, should *by principle* grow out of a free state, is as impossible, as that sparrows, should be produced from the eggs of an eagle. The sovereignty over the colonies, must be *limited*.—*Hesiod* long since said, "half is *better* than the whole;" and the saying never was more justly applicable, than on the present occasion. Had the unhappy *Charles* remembered and regarded it, his private virtues might long have adorned a throne, from which his public measures precipitated him in blood. To argue on this subject from other instances of parliamentary power, is shifting the ground. The connection of the colonies with *England*, is a point of an unprecedented and delicate nature. It can be compared to no other case; and to receive a just determination, it must be considered with reference to its own peculiar circumstances. The common law extends to colonies; yet mr. justice *Blackstone* says "such parts of the law as are neither *necessary* nor *convenient* for them, as the jurisdiction of the spiritual courts, &c. are therefore not in force." If even the COMMON LAW, in force within the realm of *England*, when the colonists quitted it, is thus abridged by the peculiar circumstances of colonies, at least equally just, and constitutional is it, that the *power of making new laws* within the realm of *England*, should be abridged with respect to colonies, by those peculiar circumstances.

THE laws of *England* with respect to prerogative, and in other instances, have accomodated all its movements—unless unnatural obstructions interfere—

"*Spiritus intus alit, totamque infusa perartus*
Mens agitat molem, & magno se corpore miscet."

ANOTHER argument for the extravagant power of internal legislation over us remains.—It has been urged with great warmth against us, that *"precedents"* shew this power is rightfully vested in parliament.

SUBMISSION to unjust sentences proves not a *right* to pass them. Carelessness or regard for the peace and welfare of the community, may cause the submission. Submission may sometimes be a less evil than opposition, and therefore a duty. In such cases it is a submission to the *divine authority,* which forbids us to injure our country; not to the *assumed authority,* on which the unjust sentences were founded. But *when* submission becomes inconsistent with and destructive of the *public good,* the same veneration for and duty to the *divine authority,* commands us to oppose. The all wise Creator of man imprest certain laws on his nature. A desire of happiness, and of society, are two of those laws. They were not intended to destroy, but to support each other. Man has therefore a right to *promote* the *best* union of both, in order to enjoy both in the *highest* degree. Thus, while this right is properly exercised, desires, that seem *selfish,* by a happy combination, produce the welfare of *others.* "This is removing submission from a foundation unable to support it, and injurious to the honour of GOD, and fixing it upon much firmer ground.

No sensible or good man ever suspected mr. *Hooker* of being a *weak* or *factious* person, "yet he plainly enough teacheth, that a society upon experience of universal evil, *have a right* to try by *another* form to answer more effectually the ends of government"—and mr. *Hoadley* asks—"would the *ends of government* be destroyed, should the miserable condition of the people of *France, which hath proceeded from the king's being absolute,* awaken the thoughts of the wisest heads amongst them; and move them all to exert themselves, so as that those ends should be better answered for the time to come?"

WHAT mind can relish the hardy proposition, that because precedents have been introduced by the inattention or timidity of *some,* and the cunning or violence of *others, therefore* the latter have a *right* to make the former miserable—that is, that

precedents that ought never to have been set, yet being set, repeal the eternal laws of natural justice, humanity and equity.

THE argument from precedents begins unluckily for its advocates. The *first* produced against us by the gentleman before mentioned, was an act passed by the *commonwealth* parliament in 1650 to *"punish" Virginia, Barbadoes, Antigua,* and *Burmudas, for their fidelity to Charles the second. So ancient* is the *right* of parliament to *"punish"* colonists *for doing their duty.* But the parliament had before overturned *church* and *throne,* so that there is an older "precedent" set against these.

THAT parliament sat amidst the ruins that surrounded it, fiercer than *Marius* among those of *Carthage.* Brutal power became an irresistible argument of boundless right. What the stile of an *Aristotle* could not prove, the point of a *Cromwell's* sword sufficiently demonstrated. Innocence and justice sighed and submitted—what more could they do? The restoration took place, and a *legal* parliament would not doubt but it had as extensive a right as an *illegal* one. The revolution succeeded, and with it *methods* for blending together the powers of the king and people in a manner before unknown. A new political alembic was fixed on the great principle of resistance, and in it, severe experiments were to be made on every other principle of the constitution. How the *boldness of ministers* and *contempt of the people* have increased since that period, not a man the least acquainted with *English* history can be ignorant. The colonies were in a state of infancy—still in a state of childhood. Not a single statute concerning them is recollected to have been past before the revolution, but such as related to the regulation of trade. "Precedents" were afterwards made, that, when they grew up, the authority of a *master* might succeed that of a *parent.*

PRECEDENTS, it is apprehended, are no otherwise regarded in the *English* laws than as they establish *certainty for the benefit of the people*— according to the maxim—"miserable is the servitude when the laws are *uncertain.*" Precedents militating against the welfare or happiness of a people, are inconsistent with the grand original principle on which they ought to be founded.

Their supposed sanction increases in proportion to the repetitions of injustice. They must be void. In subjects of dispute between man and man, precedents may be of use, though not founded on the best reason. They cause a certainty, and all may govern themselves accordingly. If they take from an individual one day, they may give to him the next. But precedents to overthrow *principles*, to justify the *perpetual* oppression of *all*, and to *impair the power of the constitution*, though a cloud of them appear, have no more force than the volumes of dust that surround a triumphal car. They may obscure it: they cannot stop it. What would the liberties of the people of *England* have been at this time, if precedents could have made laws inconsistent with the constitution? Precedents tending to make men unhappy, can with propriety of character be quoted only by those beings, to whom the misery of men is a delight.

"IF the usage had been immemorial and uniform, and ten thousand instances could have been produced, it would not have been sufficient; because the practice must likewise be agreeable to the *principles of the law*, in order to be good: whereas this is a practice inconsistent with, and in direct opposition to the *first and clearest principles of the law*"—to those *feelings of humanity*, out of which mankind will not *be reasoned*, when power advances with gigantic strides, threatening dissolution to a state—to those *inherent, though latent powers of society*, which no *elimate*, no *time*, no constitution, no *contract*, can ever destroy or diminish."

A PARLIAMENTARY power of *internal legislation* over these colonies, appears therefore to us, equally contradictory to humanity and the constitution, and illegal.

As to the second head, a power of regulating our trade, our opinion is, that it is legally vested in parliament, not as a supreme legislature over these colonies, but as the supreme legislature and full *representative* of the parent state, and the, only judge between her and her children in commercial interests, which the nature of the case, in the progress of their growth admitted. It has been urged, with great vehemence against us, and seems to be thought their *fort* by our adversaries, "that a power of regulation is a power of legislation, and a power of legislation, if constitutional, must be universal and supreme in the utmost sense of the words. It is therefore concluded, that the colonists, by acknowledging the power of regulation, have acknowledged every other power. On this objection we observe, that according to a maxim of law, "it is deceitful and dangerous to deal in general propositions." The freedom and happiness of states depend not on *artful arguments*, but on *a few plain principles*. The plausible appearance of the objection consists in a confused comprehension of several points, intirely distinct in their nature, and leading to consequences directly opposite to each other. There was a time, when *England* had no colonies. Trade was the object she attended to, in encouraging them. A love of freedom was manifestly the chief motive of the adventurers. The connection of colonies with their parent state, may be called a new object of the *English* laws. That her right extinguishes all their rights,—rights essential to freedom, and which they would have enjoyed, by remaining in their parent state, is offensive to reason, humanity, and the constitution of that state. Colonies could not have been planted on *these* terms. What *Englishman*, but an ideot, would have become a colonist on these conditions? to mention no more particulars, "that every shilling he gained, might rightfully be taken from him—trial by jury abolished—the building houses, or making cloths with the materials found or raised in the colonies prohibited—and armed men set over him to govern him in every action?"

HAD these provinces never been settled—had all the inhabitants of them now living, been born in *England*, and resident there, they would now enjoy the rights of *Englishmen*, that is, they would be free *in that kingdom*. We claim *in the colonies* these and no other rights. *There* no other kingdom or state interferes. But their trade, however important it may be, as the affairs of mankind are circumstanced, turns on other principles. All the power of parliament cannot regulate *that* at their pleasure. It must be regulated not by parliament alone, but by treaties and alliances *formed by the king without the consent of the nation*, with other states and kingdoms. *The freedom of a people consists in being governed by laws, in which no alteration can be made, without their consent.* Yet the wholesome force of these laws is *confined* to the limits of their own country. That is, a supreme legislature to a people, which acts *internally* over that people, and inevitably implies *personal* assent, *representation*, or *slavery*. When an universal empire is established, and not till then, can regulations of trade properly be called, acts of supreme legislature. It seems from many authorities, as if almost the whole power of regulating the trade of *England* was originally vested in the crown. One restriction appears to have been, that no duty could be imposed without the consent of parliament. Trade was little regarded by our warlike ancestors. As commerce became of more importance, and duties, and severities were judged necessary additions to its first simple state, parliament more and more interfered. The constitution was always free, but not always exactly in the same manner. "By the feudal law, all *navigable* rivers and *havens* were computed among the regalia, and were subject to the sovereign of the state. And in *England* it hath always been held, that the king is lord of the whole shore, and particularly is guardian of the ports and havens, which are the inlets and gates of the realm; and therefore, so early as the reign of king *John*, we find ships seized by the king's officers, for putting in at a place that was not a legal port. These legal ports were undoubtedly at first assigned by the crown; since to each of them a court of portmote is incident, the jurisdiction of which must flow from the royal authority. The erection of beacons, light-houses, and sea marks is also a branch of the royal prerogative. The powers of establishing public marts, regulating of weights and measures, and the giving authority to, or making current, money, *the medium of commerce*, belong to the crown. By making peace or war, leagues and treaties, the king may open or stop trade as he pleases. The admiralty courts are grounded on the necessity of supporting a jurisdiction so extensive, though opposite to the usual doctrines of the common law. The laws of *Oleron* were made by *Richard* the first, and are still used in those courts." In the "mare clausum," are several regulations made by kings. Time forbids a more exact inquiry into this point: but such it is apprehended, will on inquiry be found to have been the power of the crown, that our argument may gain, but cannot lose. We will proceed on a concession, that the power of regulating trade is vested in parliament. . . .

Reference: John Dickinson, *Essay on the Constitutional Power of Great Britain* (Philadephia: n.p., 1774). Dickinson heavily documented his essay; the reader is referred to the original document fo these notes.

HENRY LAURENS, *TO SOUTH CAROLINA COMMITTEE*, 1775

Gentlemen

After I have explained my self upon two parts of this Association I shall obey your Order & sign it with alacrity_ if I subscribe with mental reservations I shall be criminal in my own view & subject my self to the charge on some future day of hypocrisy & dissimulation_ this Paper Gentlemen, is in its nature & may be in its consequences the most important of any to which my signature has been annexed, I compare it to my last Will & Testament but with these awful distinctions_ the former is signed by my hand & sealed with a bit of common black Wax_ this is to be signed by my hand & may be Sealed with my Blood_ by the former I transmit my Estate to my Children according to my own Will_ by signing I may forfeit my Estate into the hands of my Enemies. An engagement of this magnitude, requires some consideration_ & although I hold my self bound by the Majority of Voices for signing it in its present state I cannot agree with some Gentlemen who have declared their dissent to the insertion of certain words expressive of our "Duty & Loyalty" to the King, nor with those who according to the bare Letter of this Association would persuade us that we ought to hold indiscriminately every Man who shall refuse to sign it Inimical to the liberty of the Colonies_ I have not premeditated a Speech for this occasion, I have thought much of the subject_ my words will flow from the Heart_ I am not anxious to influence any Man_ I have concerted measures with no Man_ what I have to offer will afford no subject for debate, I therefore hope for & humbly claim a patient hearing & a candid interpretation of my sentiments_

The Voice was general_ "Hear the Chair_ go on_ go on" but I clearly perceived by the discomposure of a few countenances_ displeasure was raised in as many hearts.

The first part Gentlemen on which I am desirous of explaining my own thoughts_ is the introduction of our selves, as "Subscribers & Inhabitants of this Colony." in preference to a proposed amendment by adding these words "His Majesty's most dutiful & Loyal subjects"

I attended to your debates, it was my Duty to do so without the interposition of my private opinions_ I remarked that Gentlemen from all parts of the House approved of the Motion for inserting the proposed declaration of Duty & Loyalty to the King_ these were at one time told that such a declaration in the Body of a Contract to bear Arms against the King would be "absurd"_ "contradictory"_ at other times they were quieted by assurances that "the profession of Loyalty was implied & to be understood" that "our Association was only for defence." upon the whole I was convinced that the proposed declaration was pleasing & acceptable to a great number probably to a large Majority of Members, very few I believe would have appeared against it upon a Question_ I was among the former & have reserved my self, to make the declaration explicitly, immediately before I put my Name to this Paper._ Gentlemen_ I have taken & repeatedly taken the Oath of Allegiance to King George the third_ I now profess to be

one of His Majesty's most dutiful & Loyal subjects, willing at all times to do my utmost in defence of His Person Crown & Dignity_ I neither wish his Death nor to remove him from the Throne, the Crown from his Head or the Sceptre from his hand, I pray for his Life, that he may at a long distant Day transmit the Crown & Sceptre to the only true & Legal Hereditary Heir in the Line of the Royal House of Hanover_ by Covenanting in this Paper "to go forth, to bear Arms, & to repel force by force" I mean to act in terms of my Oath of Allegiance_ His Majesty has been misinformed: Ill advised by some of our fellow subjects, who are His Majesty's Enemies & the Enemies of his faithful Americans, against these I am willing & shall be willing to bear Arms & to repel force by force in any Command suitable to my Rank, whenever such shall appear in hostile Acts against my Country_ against every Invader of our Rights & Liberties I shall be ready to make all possible opposition_ I shall do so with the greater chearfulness from a strong hope of being Instrumental in restoring to His Majesty His undoubted Right of Reigning over a vast Empire of Freemen of recovering to him the Possession of the Hearts of Millions of his faithful Subjects of which he has been robbed by the machinations of a few Wicked Men who falsely call themselves his freinds._ these Gentlemen are the genuine sentiments of my Breast, I know the declaration however, will avail me nothing, if we fail of success in our attempts to defend our Rights_ the longest Sword if a Wicked Ministry are to be gratified will measure & establish Right. Declarations by the Conquered will be treated as mere pretences of Loyalty & heard with Contempt; nevertheless I feel some satisfaction at present & may find Consolation upon a future day, it if I should be reduced to a necessity of making explanations from a higher eminence than the Pedestal on which I now stand.

The second part of this Association on which I desire to explain my self before I subscribe, is the *late subjoined declaration* that, "*we will hold all those Persons Inimical to the*

Liberty of the Colonies who shall refuse to sub-scribe," this is a Doctrine Gentlemen which was also, as I will remember, very much disrelished by many of our Members_ to me in its fullest extent & according to an opinion just now delivered by a Gentleman behind the Chair it is abhorrent & detestable

I should be a mean wretch if I subscribed to it through fear with mental reservations; I should be a dishonest Man, a Villain if I did so before I had made this open declaration; that I hold it possible_ I think it probable_ I know it Certain_ that there are Men who are not Inimical_ I wish we had expressed our meaning by an English word, I beleive this is not to be found in any of our vulgar Dictionaries, & some of us in remote parts of the Country may not be Possessed of a Latin Vocabulary_ I say Gentlemen, there are certain Men who are not Enemies to their Country_ who are friends to all America_ who were born among us_ some who have lived to a longer date than by which the Royal Psalm[ist] limits the Life of Man_ they are upwards of threescore Years & ten_ whole Lives have been spent in Acts of benignity & Public service, Acts which prove beyond all Controversy their Love for their Country_ such Men there are who when you present this Paper to them will tell you_ they are true friends to America_ they acknowledge that we are greatly aggrieved & oppressed_ they wish well to our Cause_ are willing to give up their fortunes as security for their good behaviour & in testimony of their sincerity_ but that they cannot, they dare not, for many reasons subscribe to the Association_ I do not recollect one tis true_ but there may be among us some Quakers or Men of Quaker principles on the Lawfulness of going to War & especially Civil War, Men who confide in the goodness of our Cause & the overruling Providence of God_ such Men may refuse to subscribe this Covenant & yet give you the most indubitable proofs of their friendship & good will towards the Colonies._

Other Men there are, who are not less freindly to America than we ourselves_ but who think we have precipitated a Measure which ought to have been delayed at least until we had received some advices from our Continental Congress; from our own Delegates; in whom we have lodged our whole Power & solemnly engaged to be bound by their determinations_ of this Class of refusers, there may be some who are such staunch such vigorous freinds, as will without hesitation declare they are willing to Bleed & Die in defence of the just Rights of the Colonies when the proper time arrives, but that we are premature_ we are too hasty_ Can I then Gentlemen implicitly sign a Paper_ anathematize good Men_ & declare those to be Enemies whom I beleive & know to be our freinds? I cannot be such a Fool_ I dare not be such a Villian._ I hate all Dogmatic & arbitrary dictates over Mens Consciences_ here Gentlemen is a Book_ from which we have just heard Prayers, an Orthodox Book in which I find a Doctrine similar to that which I now object to in our intended Association_ "Which Faith except every one do keep whole & undefiled without doubt he shall Perish Everlastingly" Long was this Athanasian Test, a stumbling block in the cause of Religion in general, a bar to the honour & prosperity of the Church established by Law_ upon that foundation Deists erected their batteries, Luke warm Christians pleaded for their indifference_ how said such Men can a Religion which contains such unmerciful Doctrines be true, or acceptable to Mankind?_ Honest minded Men of narrow & fervorous Zeal for the same religion_ abandoned & detested that Church which maintained such intolerant damnatory tenets, as essential to Salvation.

When I was a Boy before there were any settled principles of Religion in my mind, I have heard my Father & Mother & many other good old People profess that Creed with great warmth of Devotion_ I, at the same time inwardly exclaiming_ this can't be true_ I cannot beleive it_ I would join the bigots to Mother Church. at length the day came when that Church Reprobated her favorite system which stands in her Common Prayer as the stated Test of Orthodox Faith to be made on certain solemn Days_ of which this . . . _ it is no more heard_ our Churches are silent_ and_ (here I was going on to draw a parallel between the Reprobatory Clauses in our Association & the Creed of St. Athanasius, but Mr. Parson Tenant very rudely interrupted me_ "the Chair" said he "is out of order"_ "I think the Chair is out of order"_ I begged his Pardon "I had permission to speak & was as I humbly conceived in very good order"_ he proceeded in attempting to confuse me_ I exclaimed, "I will speak! I will be heard or I will be the first Man who will refuse to sign your Paper! I speak not merely as Your President, I speak as a Member as a Freeman_ if I am not heard as a Man, I will not sign as your President_ the utmost of your resentment will be to take my Life_ take it & deprive me of a very few Years_ I will not hold a Life upon dishonorable terms_ I will not be forced to sign any Paper contrary to the dictates of my Conscience to save my Life_" the universal Voice was "go on Mr. President", "go on"_ "Hear the Chair" "Hear the Chair"

After a moments Pause I concluded_ Gentlemen I meant to say in a few words, that I *could not*, I *dared not* promise to hold any Man an Enemy to the Colonies, if I knew him to be a freind_ merely because he would not at first asking subscribe this Association which I hold in my hand_ I have proved what we all know that many Cases may exist, of refusal to sign this Paper by Men who are firm freinds to our cause_ but perhaps my abhorrence to intolerant doctrines may not be as palatable to some Gentlemen, nor my reasoning allowed to be as applicable to our present Case because I have referred only to my own feelings & to one Instance of arbitrary Rule over the Consciences of Men in Tenets of Religion_ Permit me therefore to produce one Instance of Noble toleration in the Political walk_ an example which greatly influences my mind & which I recommend as worthy our imitation_ I remember to have read an anecdote in Dalrymple's Memoirs & have been reading it this Morning of an Ancestor

of the late Lord Lyttelton_ Sir Charles_ who had been an Officer of distinction under King James 2d_ & had also been active in the Revolution & bringing in the Prince of Orange_ when that Prince was seated on the Throne & declared King of England, he offered Sir Charles a Regiment in Flanders & to make him a Major General_ Sir Charles declined the promotion_ the King desired to know why he refused?_ He answered, "because I am under grat obliga[tions] to my old Master, I hear he will be *there*; if he should be *in the* . . . I dare not trust my self_ I fear I should go over to him"_ the King replied_ "You are a Man of honour, Sir Charles_ you act upon principle; don't disturb the Government & we shall be very good freinds."

this example of tolerance I say is worthy of our imitatio[n] I would not mean to prescribe for other Gentlemen, but I declare the Spirit of persecution is hateful to *me*, it is impossible for *me* to cherish it Men may agree in general & in the grand essential points but no two Men beleive in all points exactly alike_ some Men can swallow the doctrine of Predestination without a gulp who hold that of transubstantiation [absurd] & blasphemous_ I have been led Gentlemen into these particulars by that declaration which I heard from behind the Chair_ "that we should that we ought to, hold every Man without exception who should refuse to sign the Association, an Enemy"_ "hold him an Enemy & forbear all dealings or intercourse with him for Ever."_ Gentlemen 'tis impossible to me to sign upon such terms, I am, as I have repeatedly said, certain that some will refuse to sign who are freinds to our Cause; if I know a Man to be our freind how can I be so base as to stigmatize him by the harsh epithet of Enemy_ but understand me right, I mean no unfavorable salvo for particular purposes No_ I shall in all cases exercise my judgement & make an honest determination_ I think I shall be able to distinguish between mere pretences of Men who have never given any proofs of their freindship & or attachment & those whose Lives have been devoted to the service of our Country. I say I shall make the proper distinction & determine accordingly_ And Now under these necessary explanations of my Duty & Loyalty to my King & Charity for my Neighbours I will cheerfully subscribe this Association with my hand & upon proper occasion be ready to seal it with my Blood_ & then without a shaking hand I signed_

    Henry Laurens.

Reference: David R. Chesmitt (ed.), *The Papers of Henry Laurens*, Vol. 10 (?: G&G Press, 1985).

JAMES WILSON, *SPEECH DELIVERED IN THE CONVENTION OF PENNSYLVANIA,* 1775

WHENCE, Sir, proceeds all the invidious and ill-grounded clamour against the colonists of America? Why are they stigmatized, in Britain, as licentious and ungovernable? Why is their virtuous opposition to the illegal attempts of their governours represented under the falsest colours, and placed in the most ungracious point of view? This opposition, when exhibited in its true light, and when viewed, with unjaundiced eyes, from a proper situation, and at a proper distance, stands confessed the lovely offspring of freedom. It breathes the spirit of its parent. Of this ethereal spirit, the whole conduct, and particularly the late conduct, of the colonists has shown them eminently possessed. It has animated and regulated every part of their proceedings. It has been recognised to be genuine, by all those symptoms and effects, by which it has been distinguished in other ages and other countries. It has been calm and regular: it has not acted without occasion: it has not acted disproportionably to the occasion. As the attempts, open or secret, to undermine or to destroy it, have been repeated or enforced; in a just degree, its vigilance and its vigour have been exerted to defeat or to disappoint them. As its exertions have been sufficient for those purposes hitherto, let us hence draw a joyful prognostick, that they will continue sufficient for those purposes hereafter. It is not yet exhausted; it will still operate irresistibly whenever a necessary occasion shall call forth its strength.

Permit me, sir, by appealing, in a few instances, to the spirit and conduct of the colonists, to evince, that what I have said of them is just. Did they disclose any uneasiness at the proceedings and claims of the British parliament, before those claims and proceedings afforded a reasonable cause for it? Did they even disclose any uneasiness, when a reasonable cause for it was *first* given? Our rights were invaded by their regulations of our internal policy. We submitted to them: we were unwilling to oppose them. The spirit of liberty was slow to act. When those invasions were renewed; when the efficacy and malignancy of them were attempted to be redoubled by the stamp act; when chains were formed for us; and preparations were made for rivetting them on our limbs—what measures did we pursue? The spirit of liberty found it necessary now to act: but she acted with the calmness and decent dignity suited to her character. Were we rash or seditious? Did we discover want of loyalty to our sovereign? Did we betray want of affection to our brethren in Britain? Let our dutiful and reverential petitions to the throne—let our respectful, though firm, remonstrances to the parliament—let our warm and affectionate addresses to our brethren, and (we will still call them) our friends in Great Britain—let all those, transmitted from every part of the continent, testify the truth. By their testimony let our conduct be tried.

As our proceedings during the existence and operation of the stamp act prove fully and incontestably the painful sensations that tortured our breasts from the prospect of disunion with Britain; the peals of joy, which burst forth universally, upon the repeal of that odious statute, loudly proclaim the heartfelt delight produced in us by a reconciliation with her. Unsuspicious, because undesigning, we buried our complaints, and the causes of them, in oblivion, and returned, with eagerness, to our former unreserved confidence. Our connexion with our parent country, and the reciprocal blessings resulting from it to her and to us, were the favourite and pleasing topicks of our publick discourses and our private conversations. Lulled into delightful security, we dreamt of nothing but increasing fondness and friendship, cemented and strengthened by a kind and perpetual communication of good offices. Soon, however, too soon, were we awakened from the soothing dreams! Our enemies renewed their designs against us, not with less malice, but with more art. Under the plausible presence of regulating our trade, and, at the same time, of making provision for the administration of justice, and the support of government, in some of the colonies, they pursued their scheme of depriving us of our property without our consent. As the attempts to distress us, and to degrade us to a rank inferiour to that of freemen, appeared now to be reduced into a regular system, it became proper, on our part, to form a regular system for counteracting them. We ceased to import goods from Great Britain. Was this measure dictated by selfishness or by licentiousness? Did it not injure ourselves, while it injured the British merchants and manufacturers? Was it inconsistent with the peaceful demeanour of subjects to abstain from making purchases, when our freedom and our safety rendered it necessary for us to abstain from them? A regard for our freedom and our safety was our only motive; for no sooner had the parliament, by repealing part of the revenue laws, inspired us with the flattering hopes that they had departed from their intentions of oppressing and of taxing us, than we forsook our plan for defeating those intentions, and began to import as formerly. Far from being peevish or captious, we took no publick notice even of their declaratory law of dominion over us: our candour led us to consider it as a decent expedient of retreating from the actual exercise of that dominion.

But, alas! the root of bitterness still remained. The duty on tea was reserved to furnish occasion to the ministry for a new effort to enslave and to ruin us; and the East India Company were chosen, and consented, to be the detested instruments of ministerial despotism and cruelty. A cargo of their tea arrived at Boston. By a low artifice of the governour, and by the wicked activity of the tools of government, it was rendered impossible to store it up, or to send it back; as was done at other places. A number of persons unknown destroyed it.

Let us here make a concession to our enemies: let us suppose that the transaction deserves all the dark and hideous colours, in which they have painted it: let us even suppose—for our cause admits of an excess of candour—that all their exaggerated accounts of it were confined strictly to the truth: what will follow? Will it follow, that every British colony in America, or even the colony of Massachusetts Bay, or even the town of Boston in that colony, merits the imputation of being factious and seditious? Let the frequent mobs and riots that have happened in Great Britain upon much more trivial occasions shame our calumniators into silence. Will it follow, because the rules of order and regular government were, in that instance, violated by the offenders, that, for this reason, the principles of the constitution, and the maxims of justice, must be violated by their punishment? Will it follow, because those who were guilty could not be known, that, therefore, those who were known not to be guilty must suffer? Will it follow, that even the guilty should be condemned without being heard?—That they should be condemned upon partial testimony, upon the representations of their avowed and embittered enemies? Why were they not tried in courts of justice known to their constitution, and by juries of their neighbourhood? Their courts and their juries were not, in the case of Captain Preston, transported beyond the bounds of justice by their resentment: why, then, should it be presumed, that, in the case of those offenders, they would be prevented from doing justice by their affection? But the colonists, it seems, must be stript of their judicial, as well as of their legislative powers. They must be bound by a legislature, they must be tried by a jurisdiction, not their own. Their constitutions must be changed: their liberties must be abridged: and those, who shall be most infamously active in changing their constitutions and abridging their liberties, must, by an express provision, be exempted from punishment.

I do not exaggerate the matter, sir, when I extend these observations to all the colonists. The parliament meant to extend the effects of their proceedings to all the colonists. The plan, on which their proceedings are formed, extends to them all. From an incident, of no very uncommon or atrocious nature, which happened in one colony, in one town in that colony, and in which only a few of the inhabitants of that town took a part, an occasion has been taken by those, who probably intended it, and who certainly prepared the way for it, to impose upon that colony, and to lay a foundation and a precedent for imposing upon all the rest, a system of statutes, arbitrary, unconstitutional, oppressive, in every view and in every degree subversive of the rights, and inconsistent with even the name of freemen.

Were the colonists so blind as not to discern the consequences of these measures? Were they so supinely inactive as to take no steps for guarding against them? They were not. They ought not to have been so. We saw a breach made in those barriers, which our ancestors, British and American, with so much care, with so much danger, with so much treasure, and with so much blood, had erected, cemented, and established for the security of their liberties and—with filial piety let us mention it—of ours: we saw the attack actually begun upon one part: ought we to have folded our hands in indolence, to have lulled our eyes in slumbers, till the attack was carried on, so as to become irresistible, in every part? Sir, I presume to think not. We were roused; we were alarmed, as we had reason to be. But still our measures have been such as the spirit of liberty and of loyalty directed; not such as a spirit of sedition or of disaffection would pursue. Our counsels have been conducted without rashness and faction: our resolutions have been taken without phrensy or fury.

That the sentiments of every individual concerning that important object, his liberty, might be known and regarded, meetings have been held, and deliberations carried on in every particular district. That the sentiments of all those individuals might gradually and regularly be collected into a single point, and the conduct of each inspired and directed by the result of the whole united, county committees—provincial conventions—a continental congress have been appointed, have met and resolved. By this means, a chain—more inestimable, and, while the necessity for it continues, we hope, more indissoluble than one of gold—a chain of freedom has been formed, of which every individual in these colonies, who is willing to preserve the greatest of human blessings, his liberty, has the pleasure of beholding himself a link.

Are these measures, sir, the brats of disloyalty, of disaffection? There are miscreants among us—wasps that suck poison from the most salubrious flowers—who tell us they are. They tell us that all those assemblies are unlawful, and unauthorized by our constitutions; and that all their deliberations and resolutions are so many transgressions of the duty of subjects. The utmost malice brooding over the utmost baseness, and nothing but such a hated commixture, must have hatched this calumny. Do not those men know—would they have others not to know—that it was impossible for the inhabitants of the same province, and for the legislatures of the different provinces, to communicate their sentiments to one another in the modes appointed for such purposes, by their different constitutions? Do not they know—would they have others not to know—that all this was rendered impossible by those very persons, who now, or whose minions now, urge this objection against us? Do not they know—would they have others not to know—that the different assemblies, who could be dissolved by the governours, were, in consequence of ministerial mandates, dissolved by them, whenever they attempted to turn their attention to the greatest objects, which, as guardians of the liberty of their constituents, could be presented to their view? The arch enemy of the human race torments them only for those actions, to which he has tempted, but to which he has not necessarily obliged them. Those men refine even upon infernal malice: they accuse, they threaten us (superlative impudence!) for taking those very steps, which we were laid under the disagreeable necessity of taking by themselves, or by those in whose hateful service they are enlisted. But let them know, that our counsels, our deliberations, our resolutions, if not authorized by the forms, because that was rendered impossible by our enemies, are nevertheless authorized by that which weighs much more in the scale of reason—by the spirit of our constitutions. Was the convention of the barons at Running Meade, where the tyranny of John was checked, and magna charta was signed, authorized by the forms of the constitution? Was the convention parliament, that recalled Charles the second, and restored the monarchy, authorized by the forms of the constitution? Was the convention of lords and commons, that placed King William on the throne, and secured the monarchy and liberty likewise, authorized by the forms of the constitution? I cannot conceal my emotions of pleasure, when I observe, that the objections of our adversaries cannot be urged against us, but in common with those venerable assemblies, whose proceedings formed such an accession to British liberty and British renown.

The resolutions entered into, and the recommendations given, by the continental congress, have stamped, in the plainest characters, the genuine and enlightened spirit of liberty upon the conduct observed, and the measures pursued, in consequence of them. As the invasions of our rights have become more and more formidable, our opposition to them has increased in firmness and vigour, in a just, and in no more than a just, proportion. We will not import goods from Great Britain or Ireland: in a little time we will suspend our exportations to them: and, if the same illiberal and destructive system of policy be still carried on against us, in a little time more we will not consume their manufactures. In that colony where the attacks have been most open, immediate, and direct, some farther steps have been taken, and those steps have met with the deserved approbation of the other provinces.

Is this scheme of conduct allied to rebellion? Can any symptoms of disloyalty to his majesty, of disinclination to his illustrious family, or of disregard to his authority be traced in it? Those, who would blend, and whose crimes have made it necessary for them to blend, the tyrannick acts of

administration with the lawful measures of government, and to veil every flagitious procedure of the ministry under the venerable mantle of majesty, pretend to discover, and employ their emissaries to publish the pretended discovery of such symptoms. We are not, however, to be imposed upon by such shallow artifices. We know, that we have not violated the laws or the constitution; and that, therefore, we are safe as long as the laws retain their force and the constitution its vigour; and that, whatever our demeanour be, we cannot be safe much longer. But another object demands our attention.

We behold—sir, with the deepest anguish we behold—that our opposition has not been as effectual as it has been constitutional. The hearts of our oppressors have not relented: our complaints have not been heard: our grievances have not been redressed: our rights are still invaded: and have we no cause to dread, that the invasions of them will be enforced in a manner, against which all reason and argument, and all opposition of every peaceful kind, will be vain? Our opposition has hitherto increased with our oppression: shall it, in the most desperate of all contingencies, observe the same proportion?

Let us pause, sir, before we give an answer to this question: the fate of us; the fate of millions now alive; the fate of millions yet unborn depends upon the answer. Let it be the result of calmness and of intrepidity: let it be dictated by the principles of loyalty, and the principles of liberty. Let it be such, as never, in the worst events, to give us reason to reproach ourselves, or others reason to reproach us for having done too much or too little.

Perhaps the following resolution may be found not altogether unbefitting our present situation. With the greatest deference I submit it to the mature consideration of this assembly.

"That the act of the British parliament for altering the charter and constitution of the colony of Massachusetts Bay, and those 'for the impartial administration of justice' in that colony, for shutting the port of Boston, and for quartering soldiers on the inhabitants of the colonies, are unconstitutional and void; and can confer no authority upon those who act under colour of them. That the crown cannot, by its prerogative, alter the charter or constitution of that colony: that all attempts to alter the said charter or constitution, unless by the authority of the legislature of that colony, are manifest violations of the rights of that colony, and illegal: that all force employed to carry such unjust and illegal attempts into execution is force without authority: that it is the right of British subjects to resist such force: that this right is founded both upon the letter and the spirit of the British constitution."

To prove, at this time, that those acts are unconstitutional and void is, I apprehend, altogether unnecessary. The doctrine has been proved fully, on other occasions, and has received the concurring assent of British America. It rests upon plain and indubitable truths. We do not send members to the British parliament: we have parliaments (it is immaterial what name they go by) of our own.

That a void act can confer no authority upon those, who proceed under colour of it, is a selfevident proposition.

Before I proceed to the other clauses, I think it useful to recur to some of the fundamental maxims of the British constitution; upon which, as upon a rock, our wise ancestors erected that stable fabrick, against which the gates of hell have not hitherto prevailed. Those maxims I shall apply fairly, and, I flatter myself, satisfactorily to evince every particular contained in the resolution.

The government of Britain, sir, was never an arbitrary government: our ancestors were never inconsiderate enough to trust those rights, which God and nature had given them, unreservedly into the hands of their princes. However difficult it may be, in other states, to prove an original contract subsisting in any other manner, and on any other conditions, than are naturally and necessarily implied in the very idea of the first institution of a state; it is the easiest thing imaginable, since the revolution of 1688, to prove it in our constitution, and to ascertain some of the material articles, of which it consists. It has been often appealed to: it has been often broken, at least on one part: it has been often renewed: it

has been often confirmed: it still subsists in its full force: "it binds the king as much as the meanest subject."a The measures of his power, and the limits, beyond which he cannot extend it, are circumscribed and regulated by the same authority, and with the same precision, as the measures of the subject's obedience, and the limits, beyond which he is under no obligation to practise it, are fixed and ascertained. Liberty is, by the constitution, of equal stability, of equal antiquity, and of equal authority with prerogative. The duties of the king and those of the subject are plainly reciprocal: they can be violated on neither side, unless they be performed on the other.b The law is the common standard, by which the excesses of prerogative as well as the excesses of liberty are to be regulated and reformed.

Of this great compact between the king and his people, one essential article to be performed on his part is—that, in those cases where provision is expressly made and limitations set by the laws, his government shall be conducted according to those provisions, and restrained according to those limitations—that, in those cases, which are not expressly provided for by the laws, it shall be conducted by the best rules of discretion, agreeably to the general spirit of the laws, and subserviently to their ultimate end—the interest and happiness of his subjects—that, in no case, it shall be conducted contrary to the express, or to the implied principles of the constitution.

These general maxims, which we may justly consider as fundamentals of our government, will, by a plain and obvious application of them to the parts of the resolution remaining to be proved, demonstrate them to be strictly agreeable to the laws and constitution.

We can be at no loss in resolving, that the king cannot, by his prerogative, alter the charter or constitution of the colony of Massachusetts Bay. Upon what principle could such an exertion of prerogative be justified? On the acts of parliament? They are already proved to be void. On the discretionary power which the king has of acting where the laws are silent? That power must be subservient to the interest and happiness of those, concerning whom it operates. But I go farther.

Instead of being supported by law, or the principles of prerogative, such an alteration is totally and absolutely repugnant to both. It is contrary to express law. The charter and constitution we speak of are confirmed by the only legislative power capable of confirming them: and no other power, but that which can ratify, can destroy. If it is contrary to express law, the consequence is necessary, that it is contrary to the principles of prerogative: for prerogative can operate only when the law is silent.

In no view can this alteration be justified, or so much as excused. It cannot be justified or excused by the acts of parliament; because the authority of parliament does not extend to it: it cannot be justified or excused by the operation of prerogative; because this is none of the cases, in which prerogative can operate: it cannot be justified or excused by the legislative authority of the colony: because that authority never has been, and, I presume, never will be given for any such purpose.

If I have proceeded hitherto, as I am persuaded I have, upon safe and sure ground, I can, with great confidence, advance a step farther, and say, that all attempts to alter the charter or constitution of that colony, unless by the authority of its own legislature, are violations of its rights, and illegal.

If those attempts are illegal, must not all force, employed to carry them into execution, be force employed against law, and without authority? The conclusion is unavoidable.

Have not British subjects, then, a right to resist such force—force acting without authority—force employed contrary to law—force employed to destroy the very existence of law and of liberty? They have, sir, and this right is secured to them both by the letter and the spirit of the British constitution, by which the measures and the conditions of their obedience are appointed. The British liberties, sir, and the means and the right of defending them, are not the grants of princes; and of what our princes never granted they surely can never deprive us.

I beg leave, here, to mention and to obviate some plausible but ill founded objections, that have been, and will be, held forth by our adversaries, against the principles of the resolution now before us. It will be observed, that those employed for bringing about the proposed alteration in the charter and constitution of the colony of Massachusetts Bay act by virtue of a commission for that purpose from his majesty: that all resistance of forces commissioned by his majesty, is resistance of his majesty's authority and government, contrary to the duty of allegiance, and treasonable. These objections will be displayed in their most specious colours: every artifice of chicanery and sophistry will be put in practice to establish them: law authorities, perhaps, will be quoted and tortured to prove them. Those principles of our constitution, which were designed to preserve and to secure the liberty of the people, and, for the sake of that, the tranquility of government, will be perverted on this, as they have been on many other occasions, from their true intention; and will be made use of for the contrary purpose of endangering the latter, and destroying the former. The names of the most exalted virtues, on one hand, and of the most atrocious crimes, on the other, will be employed in direct contradiction to the nature of those virtues, and of those crimes: and, in this manner, those who cannot look beyond names, will be deceived; and those, whose aim it is to deceive by names, will have an opportunity of accomplishing it. But, sir, this disguise will not impose upon us. We will look to things as well as to names: and, by doing so, we shall be fully satisfied, that all those objections rest upon mere verbal sophistry, and have not even the remotest alliance with the principles of reason or of law.

In the first place, then, I say, that the persons who allege, that those, employed to alter the charter and constitution of Massachusetts Bay, act by virtue of a commission from his majesty for that purpose, speak improperly, and contrary to the truth of the case. I say, they act by virtue of no such commission: I say, it is impossible they can act by virtue of such a commission. What is called a commission either contains particular directions for the purpose mentioned; or it contains no such particular directions. In neither case can those, who act for that purpose, act by virtue of a commission. In one case, what is called a commission is void; it has no legal existence; it can communicate no authority. In the other case, it extends not to the purpose mentioned. The latter point is too plain to be insisted on—I prove the former.

"Id rex potest," says the law, "quod de jure potest."c The king's power is a power according to law. His commands, if the authority of Lord Chief Justice Haled may be depended upon, are under the directive power of the law; and consequently invalid, if unlawful. Commissions, says my Lord Coke,e are legal; and are like the king's writs; and none are lawful, but such as are allowed by the common law, or warranted by some act of parliament.

Let us examine any commission expressly directing those to whom it is given, to use military force for carrying into execution the alterations proposed to be made in the charter and constitution of Massachusetts Bay, by the foregoing maxims and authorities; and what we have said concerning it will appear obvious and conclusive. It is not warranted by any act of parliament; because, as has been mentioned on this, and has been proved on other occasions, any such act is void. It is not warranted, and I believe it will not be pretended that it is warranted, by the common law. It is not warranted by the royal prerogative; because, as has already been fully shown, it is diametrically opposite to the principles and the ends of prerogative. Upon what foundation, then, can it lean and be supported? Upon none. Like an enchanted castle, it may terrify those, whose eyes are affected by the magick influence of the sorcerers, despotism and slavery: but so soon as the charm is dissolved, and the genuine rays of liberty and of the constitution dart in upon us, the formidable appearance vanishes, and we discover that it was the baseless fabrick of a vision, that never had any real existence.

I have dwelt the longer upon this part of the objections urged against us by our adversaries; because this part is the foundation of all the others. We have now removed it; and they must fall of course. For if the force, acting for the purposes we have mentioned, does not act, and cannot act, by virtue of any commission from his majesty, the consequence is undeniable, that it acts without his majesty's authority; that the resistance of it is no resistance of his majesty's authority; nor incompatible with the duties of allegiance.

And now, sir, let me appeal to the impartial tribunal of reason and truth—let me appeal to every unprejudiced and judicious observer of the laws of Britain, and of the constitution of the British government—let me appeal, I say, whether the principles on which I argue, or the principles on which alone my arguments can be opposed, are those which ought to be adhered to and acted upon—which of them are most consonant to our laws and liberties—which of them have the strongest, and are likely to have the most effectual, tendency to establish and secure the royal power and dignity.

Are we deficient in loyalty to his majesty? Let our conduct convict, for it will fully convict, the insinuation, that we are, of falsehood. Our loyalty has always appeared in the true form of loyalty—in obeying our sovereign according to law:f let those, who would require it in any other form, know, that we call the persons who execute his commands, when contrary to law, disloyal and traitors. Are we enemies to the power of the crown? No, sir: we are its best friends: this friendship prompts us to wish, that the power of the crown may be firmly established on the most solid basis: but we know, that the constitution alone will perpetuate the former, and securely uphold the latter. Are our principles irreverent to majesty? They are quite the reverse: we ascribe to it perfection, almost divine. We say, that the king can do no wrong: we say, that to do wrong is the property, not of power, but of weakness. We feel oppression; and will oppose it; but we know—for our constitution tells us—that oppression can never spring from the throne. We must, therefore, search elsewhere for its source: our infallible guide will direct us to it. Our constitution tells us, that all oppression springs from the ministers of the throne. The attributes of perfection, ascribed to the king, are, neither by the constitution, nor in fact, communicable to his ministers. They may do wrong: they have often done wrong: they have been often punished for doing wrong.

Here we may discern the true cause of all the impudent clamour and unsupported accusations of the ministers and of their minions, that have been raised and made against the conduct of the Americans. Those ministers and minions are sensible, that the opposition is directed, not against his majesty, but against them: because they have abused his majesty's confidence, brought discredit upon his government, and derogated from his justice. They see the publick vengeance collected in dark clouds around them: their consciences tell them, that it should be hurled, like a thunder bolt, at their guilty heads. Appalled with guilt and fear, they skulk behind the throne. Is it disrespectful to drag them into publick view, and make a distinction between them and his majesty, under whose venerable name they daringly attempt to shelter their crimes? Nothing can more effectually contribute to establish his majesty on the throne, and to secure to him the affections of his people, than this distinction. By it we are taught to consider all the blessings of government as flowing from the throne; and to consider every instance of oppression as proceeding, which in truth is oftenest the case, from the ministers.

If, now, it is true, that all force employed for the purposes so often mentioned, is force unwarranted by any act of parliament; unsupported by any principle of the common law; unauthorized by any commission from the crown—that, instead of being employed for the support of the constitution and his majesty's government, it must be employed for the support of oppression and ministerial tyranny—if all this is true—and I flatter myself it appears to be true—can any one hesitate to say, that to resist such force is lawful: and that both the letter and the spirit of the British constitution justify such resistance?

Resistance, both by the letter and the spirit of the British constitution, may be carried farther, when necessity requires it, than I have carried it. Many examples in the English history might be adduced, and many authorities of the greatest weight might be brought, to show, that when the king, forgetting his character and his dignity, has stepped forth, and openly avowed and taken a part in such iniquitous conduct as has been described; in such cases, indeed, the distinction above mentioned, wisely made by the constitution for the security of the crown, could not be applied; because the crown had unconstitutionally rendered the application of it impossible. What has been the consequence? The distinction between him and his ministers has been lost: but they have not been raised to his situation: he has sunk to theirs.

Reference: Robert Green McCloskey (ed.), *The Works of James Wilson,* Vol. II (Cambridge: Billmap Press, 1967), 747–758.

JOHN ADAMS, *THOUGHTS ON GOVERNMENT,* 1776

My dear Sir: If I was equal to the task of forming a plan for the government of a colony, I should be flattered with your request and very happy to comply with it because, as the divine science of politics is the science of social happiness, and the blessings of society depend entirely on the constitutions of government, which are generally institutions that last for many generations, there can be no employment more agreeable to a benevolent mind than a research after the best.

Pope flattered tyrants too much when he said,
    For forms of government let fools contest,
    That which is best administered is best.
                                        [Essay on Man]

Nothing can be more fallacious than this. But poets read history to collect flowers, not fruits; they attend to fanciful images, not the effects of social institutions. Nothing is more certain from the history of nations and nature of man than that some forms of government are better fitted for being well administered than others.

We ought to consider what is the end of government before we determine which is the best form. Upon this point all speculative politicians will agree that the happiness of society is the end of government, as all divines and moral philosophers will agree that the happiness of the individual is the end of man. From this principle it will follow that the form of government which communicates ease, comfort, security, or, in one word, happiness to the greatest number of persons and in the greatest degree is the best.

All sober inquirers after truth, ancient and modern, pagan and Christian, have declared that the happiness of man, as well as his dignity, consists in virtue. Confucius, Zoroaster, Socrates, Mahomet, not to mention authorities really sacred, have agreed in this.

If there is a form of government, then, whose principle and foundation is virtue, will not every sober man acknowledge it better calculated to promote the general happiness than any other form?

Fear is the foundation of most governments; but it is so sordid and brutal a passion and renders men in whose breasts it predominates so stupid and miserable that Americans will not be likely to approve of any political institution which is founded on it.

Honor is truly sacred but holds a lower rank in the scale of moral excellence than virtue. Indeed, the former is but a part of the latter and consequently has not equal pretensions to support a frame of government productive of human happiness.

The foundation of every government is some principle or passion in the minds of the people. The noblest principles and most generous affections in our nature, then, have the fairest chance to support the noblest and most generous models of government.

A man must be indifferent to the sneers of modern Englishmen to mention in their company the names of Sidney, Harrington, Locke, Milton, Nedham, Neville, Burnet, and Hoadly. No small fortitude is necessary to confess that one has read them. The wretched condition of this country, however, for ten or fifteen years past has frequently reminded me of their principles and reasonings. They will convince any candid mind that there is no good government but what is republican. That the only valuable part of the British constitution is so because the very definition of a republic is "an empire of laws, and not of men." That, as a republic is the best of governments, so that particular arrangement of the powers of society or, in other words, that form of government which is best contrived to secure an impartial and exact execution of the laws is the best of republics.

Of republics there is an inexhaustible variety because the possible combinations of the powers of society are capable of innumerable variations.

As good government is an empire of laws, how shall your laws be made? In a large society inhabiting an extensive country, it is impossible that the whole should assemble to make laws. The first necessary step, then, is to depute power from the many to a few of the most wise and good. But by what rules shall you choose your representatives? Agree upon the number and qualifications of persons who shall have the benefit of choosing or annex this privilege to the inhabitants of a certain extent of ground.

The principal difficulty lies, and the greatest care should be employed, in constituting this representative assembly. It should be in miniature an exact portrait of the people at large. It should think, feel, reason, and act like them. That it may be the interest of this assembly to do strict justice at all times, it should be an equal representation, or, in other words, equal interests among the people should have equal interests in it. Great care should be taken to effect this and to prevent unfair, partial, and corrupt elections. Such regulations, however, may be better made in times of greater tranquility than the present; and they will spring up themselves naturally when all the powers of government come to be in the hands of the people's friends. At present, it will be safest to proceed in all established modes to which the people have been familiarized by habit.

A representation of the people in one assembly being obtained, a question arises whether all the powers of government—legislative, executive, and judicial—shall be left in this body? I think a people cannot be long free, nor ever happy, whose government is in one assembly. My reasons for this opinion are as follow:

1. A single assembly is liable to all the vices, follies, and frailties of an individual—subject to fits of humor, starts of passion, flights of enthusiasm, partialities, or prejudice—and consequently productive of hasty results and absurd judgments. And all these errors ought to be corrected and defects supplied by some controlling power.

2. A single assembly is apt to be avaricious and in time will not scruple to exempt itself from burdens which it will lay without compunction on its constituents.

3. A single assembly is apt to grow ambitious and after a time will not hesitate to vote itself perpetual. This was one fault of the Long Parliament,b but more remarkably of Holland, whose assembly first voted themselves from annual to sentennial, then for life, and after a course of years, that all vacancies happening by death or otherwise should be filled by themselves without any application to constituents at all.

4. A representative assembly, although extremely well qualified and absolutely necessary as a branch of the legislative, is unfit to exercise the executive power for want of two essential properties, secrecy and dispatch.

5. A representative assembly is still less qualified for the judicial power because it is too numerous, too slow, and too little skilled in the laws.

6. Because a single assembly, possessed of all the powers of government, would make arbitrary laws for their own interest, execute all laws arbitrarily for their own interest, and adjudge all controversies in their own favor.

But shall the whole power of legislation rest in one assembly? Most of the foregoing reasons apply equally to prove that the legislative power ought to be more complex, to which we may add that if the legislative power is wholly in one assembly and the executive in another or in a single person, these two powers will oppose and encroach upon each other until the contest shall end in war, and the whole power, legislative and executive, be usurped by the strongest.

The judicial power, in such case, could not mediate or hold the balance between the two contending powers because the legislative would undermine it. And this shows the necessity, too, of giving the executive power a negative upon the legislative; otherwise this will be continually encroaching upon that.

To avoid these dangers, let a distinct assembly be constituted as a mediator between the two extreme branches of the legislature, that which represents the people and that which is vested with the executive power.

Let the representative assembly then elect by ballot, from among themselves or their constituents or both, a distinct assembly which, for the sake of perspicuity, we will call a council. It may consist of any number you please, say twenty or thirty, and should have a free and independent exercise of its judgment and consequently a negative voice in the legislature.

These two bodies, thus constituted and made integral parts of the legislature, let them unite and by joint ballot choose a governor, who, after being stripped of most of those badges of domination called prerogatives, should have a free and independent exercise of his judgment and be made also an integral part of the legislature. This, I know, is liable to objections; and, if you please, you may make him only president of the council, as in Connecticut. But as the governor is to be invested with the executive power with consent of council, I think he ought to have a negative upon the legislative. If he is annually elective, as he ought to be, he will always have so much reverence and affection for the people, their representatives and counsellors, that, although you give him an independent exercise of his judgment, he will seldom use it in opposition to the two houses, except in cases the public utility of which would be conspicuous; and some such cases would happen.

In the present exigency of American affairs, when by an act of Parliament we are put out of the royal protection and consequently discharged from our allegiance, and it has become necessary to assume government for our immediate security, the governor, lieutenant-governor, secretary, treasurer, commissary, attorney-general should be chosen by joint ballot of both houses. And these and all other elections, especially of representatives and counsellors, should be annual, there not being in the whole circle of the sciences a maxim more infallible than this, "where annual elections end, there slavery begins."

These great men, in this respect, should be once a year—

Like bubbles on the sea of matter borne,
They rise, they break, and to that sea return.

This will teach them the great political virtues of humility, patience, and moderation, without which every man in power becomes a ravenous beast of prey.

This mode of constituting the great offices of state will answer very well for the present; but if by experiment it should be found inconvenient, the legislature may at its leisure devise other methods of creating them; by elections of the people at large, as in Connecticut; or it may enlarge the term for which they shall be chosen to seven years, or three years, or for life; or make any other alterations which the society shall find productive of its ease, its safety, its freedom, or, in one word, its happiness.

A rotation of all offices, as well as of representatives and counsellors, has many advocates and is contended for with many plausible arguments. It would be attended no doubt with many advantages; and if the society has a sufficient number of suitable characters to supply the great number of vacancies which would be made by such a rotation, I can see no objection to it. These persons may be allowed to serve for three years and then be excluded three years, or for any longer or shorter term.

Any seven or nine of the legislative council may be made a quorum for doing business as a privy council, to advise the governor in the

exercise of the executive branch of power and in all acts of state.

The governor should have the command of the militia and of all your armies. The power of pardons should be with the governor and council.

Judges, justices, and all other officers, civil and military, should be nominated and appointed by the governor with the advice and consent of council, unless you choose to have a government more popular; if you do, all officers, civil and military, may be chosen by joint ballot of both houses; or, in order to preserve the independence and importance of each house, by ballot of one house, concurred in by the other. Sheriffs should be chosen by the freeholders of counties; so should registers of deeds and clerks of counties.

All officers should have commissions under the hand of the governor and seal of the colony.

The dignity and stability of government in all its branches, the morals of the people, and every blessing of society depend so much upon an upright and skillful administration of justice that the judicial power ought to be distinct from both the legislative and executive, and independent upon both, that so it may be a check upon both, as both should be checks upon that. The judges, therefore, should be always men of learning and experience in the laws, of exemplary morals, great patience, calmness, coolness, and attention. Their minds should not be distracted with jarring interests; they should not be dependent upon any man, or body of men. To these ends, they should hold estates for life in their offices; or, in other words, their commissions should be during good behavior and their salaries ascertained and established by law. For misbehavior the grand inquest of the colony, the house of representatives, should impeach them before the governor and council, where they should have time and opportunity to make their defense; but, if convicted, should be removed from their offices and subjected to such other punishment as shall be thought proper.

A militia law requiring all men, or with very few exceptions besides cases of conscience, to be provided with arms and ammunition, to be trained at certain seasons; and requiring counties, towns, or other small districts to be provided with public stocks of ammunition and entrenching utensils and with some settled plans for transporting provisions after the militia, when marched to defend their country against sudden invasions; and requiring certain districts to be provided with field-pieces, companies of matrosses, and perhaps some regiments of light-horse is always a wise institution, and in the present circumstances of our country indispensable.

Laws for the liberal education of youth, especially of the lower class of people, are so extremely wise and useful that to a humane and generous mind no expense for this purpose would be thought extravagant.

The very mention of sumptuary laws will excite a smile. Whether our countrymen have wisdom and virtue enough to submit to them, I know not; but the happiness of the people might be greatly promoted by them, and a revenue saved sufficient to carry on this war forever. Frugality is a great revenue, besides curing us of vanities, levities, and fopperies, which are real antidotes to all great, manly, and warlike virtues.

But must not all commissions run in the name of a king? No. Why may they not as well run thus, "The colony of—to A. B. greeting," and be tested by the governor?

Why may not writs, instead of running in the name of the king, run thus, "The colony of—to the sheriff," etc., and be tested by the chief justice?

Why may not indictments conclude, "against the peace of the colony of—and the dignity of the same?"

A constitution founded on these principles introduces knowledge among the people and inspires them with a conscious dignity becoming freemen; a general emulation takes place which causes good humor, sociability, good manners, and good morals to be general. That elevation of sentiment inspired by such a government makes the common people brave and enterprising. That ambition which is inspired by it makes them sober, industrious, and frugal. You will find among them some elegance, perhaps, but more solidity; a little pleasure, but a great deal of business; some politeness, but more civility. If you compare such a country with the regions of domination, whether monarchical or aristocratical, you will fancy yourself in Arcadia or Elysium.

If the colonies should assume governments separately, they should be left entirely to their own choice of the forms; and if a continental constitution should be formed, it should be a congress containing a fair and adequate representation of the colonies, and its authority should sacredly be confined to these cases, namely: war, trade, disputes between colony and colony, the post office, and the unappropriated lands of the crown, as they used to be called.

These colonies, under such forms of government and in such a union, would be unconquerable by all the monarchies of Europe.

You and I, my dear friend, have been sent into life at a time when the greatest lawgivers of antiquity would have wished to live. How few of the human race have ever enjoyed an opportunity of making an election of government—more than of air, soil, or climate—for themselves or their children! When, before the present epocha, had three millions of people full power and a fair opportunity to form and establish the wisest and happiest government that human wisdom can contrive? I hope you will avail yourself and your country of that extensive learning and indefatigable industry which you possess to assist her in the formation of the happiest governments and the best character of a great people. For myself, I must beg you to keep my name out of sight; for this feeble attempt, if it should be known to be mine, would oblige me to apply to myself those lines of the immortal John Milton in one of his sonnets:

I did but prompt the age to quit their clogs
By the known rules of ancient liberty,
When straight a barbarous noise environs me
Of owls and cuckoos, asses, apes, and dogs.

Reference: Charles Francis Adams (ed.), *The Works of John Adams*, Vol. IV (Boston: Little, Brown, 1850–1856), 193–200.

Part VI

Plans for Unity, Divided Colonies, and United Independence

The third and final part of Volume II has as its central concern unity and division both among the 13 colonies and within each colony as they headed toward independence. Part VI is divided into three chapters. Chapter 30 deals with the issues that arose from the Albany Conference of 1756, which was called by Benjamin Franklin. (Archibald Kennedy, see Part V, Chapter 28, is supposed to have influenced Franklin's desire to see the colonies bring their governments together for mutual defense.) Soon after the Albany Conference ended there was disagreement in the individual northern colonies over whether to and how to combine their governments. This dissent revealed earlier problems of unity, and was a harbinger of later issues that concerned uniting the colonies to achieve independence. (The struggle is reminiscent of the problems over dominion status seen in the last part of Volume I. The struggle continues in all of Volume III.) Chapter 31 addresses the internal divisions among and within the colonies. The documents in this chapter show disharmony among the freemen over authority within a colony. Chapter 32 takes up the colonies' movement to unity as they separately and collectively turned toward independence. That the colonies were wary of one another merely reveals the ways they had developed separate but similar governing systems. That they came together in declaring independence neither overcame their mutual distrust nor boded well for unification under the Confederation Congress (see Part VIII in Volume III).

30

Unity Proposed and Deferred

The Albany Congress of 1754 emerged from the fertile political mind of Benjamin Franklin, who wanted the northern colonies to unite against the French and Native American threats on their borders. Franklin also hoped that a unified and disciplined governing unit could resist the growing presence in the colonies of an oppressive British government, thus the Albany Conference presented a unified plan of governance to the colonies. In the second document of this chapter, Stephen Hopkins of Rhode Island explains his support for the plan. The Assembly of Connecticut at first endorsed the plan, but then in October 1754 a committee of the Assembly rejected it in a report to the full General Assembly. The report claimed that if united in governance with other colonies, Connecticut's legislative prerogatives would be placed in jeopardy. For the same reason, the Massachusetts General Court rejected the Albany Plan of Union. Finally, in April 1755, "Philolethes" responded to Stephen Hopkins's defense of Union. "Philolethes" attacked Hopkins for misunderstanding just how wary Rhode Island legislators were toward any plan that they believed diminished their power. Anyone looking to find hope that the colonies could cooperate in governance would be startled by the venomous attack on Hopkins.

ALBANY PLAN OF UNION, 1754

It is proposed, that humble application be made for an act of Parliament of Great Britain, by virtue of which one general government may be formed in America, including all the said colonies, within and under which government each colony may retain its present constitution, except in the particulars wherein a change may be directed by the said act, as hereafter follows.

President-general and grand council

That the said general government be administered by a President-General, to be appointed and supported by the crown; and a Grand Council, to be chosen by the representatives of the people of the several colonies met in their respective Assemblies.

Election of members

That within—months after the passing of such act, the House of Representatives that happens to be sitting within that time, or that shall be especially for that purpose convened, may and shall choose members for the Grand Council in the following proportion—that is to say:

Massachusetts Bay	7
New Hampshire	2

Connecticut	5
Rhode Island	2
New York	4
New Jersey	3
Pennsylvania	6
Maryland	4
Virginia	7
North Carolina	4
South Carolina	4
	48

Place of First Meeting

—who shall meet for the first time at the city of Philadelphia in Pennsylvania, being called by the President-General as soon as conveniently may be after his appointment.

New Election

That there shall be a new election of the members of the Grand Council every three years; and on the death or resignation of any member, his place should be supplied by a new choice at the next sitting of the Assembly of the colony he represented.

Proportion of Members After the First Three Years

That after the first three years, when the proportion of money arising out of each colony to the general treasury can be known, the number of members to be chosen for each colony shall from time to time, in all ensuing elections, be regulated by that proportion, yet so as that the number to be chosen by any one province be not more than seven, nor less than two.

Meetings of the Grand Council, and Call

That the Grand Council shall meet once in every year, and oftener if occasion require, at such time and place as they shall adjourn to at the last preceding meeting, or as they shall be called to meet by the President-General on any emergency, he having first obtained in writing the consent of seven of the members to such call, and sent due and timely notice to the whole.

Continuance

That the Grand Council have power to choose their speaker and shall neither be dissolved, prorogued, nor continued sitting longer than six weeks at one time, without their own consent or the special command of the crown.

Members' Allowance

That the members of the Grand Council shall be allowed for their service ten shillings sterling per diem during their session and journey to and from the place of meeting; twenty miles to be reckoned a day's journey.

Assent of President-general and His Duty

That the assent of the President-General be requisite to all acts of the Grand Council, and that it be his office and duty to cause them to be carried into execution.

Power Of President-general and Grand Council; Treaties of Peace and War

That the President-General, with the advice of the Grand Council, hold or direct all Indian treaties in which the general interest of the colonies may be concerned; and make peace or declare war with Indian nations.

Indian Trade

That they make such laws as they judge necessary for regulating all Indian trade.

Indian Purchases

That they make all purchases, from Indians for the crown, of lands not now within the bounds of particular colonies, or that shall not be within their bounds when some of them are reduced to more convenient dimensions.

New Settlements

That they make new settlements on such purchases, by granting lands in the King's name, reserving a quit-rent to the crown for the use of the general treasury.

Laws to Govern Them

That they make laws for regulating and governing such new settlements till the crown shall think it fit to form them into particular governments.

Raise Soldiers and Equip Vessels, &c

That they raise and pay soldiers and build forts for the defence of any of the colonies, and equip vessels of force to guard the coasts and protect the trade on the ocean, lakes, or great rivers; but they shall not impress men in any colony without the consent of the legislature.

Power to Make Laws, Lay Duties, &c

That for these purposes they have power to make laws, and lay and levy such general duties, imposts, or taxes as to them shall appear most equal and just (considering the ability and other circumstances of the inhabitants in the several colonies), and such as may be collected with the least inconvenience to the people; rather discouraging luxury than loading industry with unnecessary burthens.

General Treasurer and Particular Treasurer

That they may appoint a General Treasurer and Particular Treasurer in each government, when necessary; and from time to time may order the sums in the treasuries of each government into the general treasury, or draw on them for special payments, as they find most convenient.

Money, How to Issue

Yet no money to issue but by joint orders of the President-General and Grand Council; except where sums have been appropriated to particular purposes, and the President-General is previously empowered by an act to draw such sums.

Accounts

That the general accounts shall be yearly settled and reported to the several Assemblies.

Quorum

That a Quorum of the Grand Council, empowered to act with the President-General, do consist of twenty-five members, among whom there shall be one or more from a majority of the colonies.

Laws to be Transmitted

That the laws made by them for the purposes aforesaid shall not be repugnant, but, as near as may be, agreeable to the laws of England, and shall be transmitted to the King in Council for approbation as soon as may be after their passing; and if not disapproved within three years after presentation, to remain in force.

Death of the President-general

That in case of the death of the President-General, the Speaker of the Grand Council for the time being shall succeed, and be vested with the same powers and authorities, to continue till the King's pleasure be known.

Officers, How Appointed

That all military commission officers, whether for land or sea service, to act under this general constitution, shall be nominated by the President-General; but the approbation of the Grand Council is to be obtained before they receive their commissions. And all civil officers are to be nominated by the Grand Council, and to receive the President-General's approbation before they officiate.

Vacancies, How Supplied

But in case of vacancy by death or removal of any officer, civil or military, under this constitution, the Governor of the province in which such vacancy happens may appoint, till the pleasure of the President-General and Grand Council can be known.

Each Colony May Defend Itself On Emergency, &c. That the particular military as well as civil establishments in each colony remain in their present state, the general constitution notwithstanding; and that on sudden emergencies any colony may defend itself, and lay the accounts of expense thence arising before the President-General and General Council, who may allow and order payment of the same, as far as they judge such accounts just and reasonable.

Reference: Francis Newton Thorpe (ed.), *The Federal and State Constitutions, Colonial Charters, and Other Organic Laws of the States,* Vol. I (Washington: GPO, 1909).

STEPHEN HOPKINS OF RHODE ISLAND DEFENDS THE PLAN, 1754

At a Meeting in the Court-House at Albany, on Wednesday, the 10th of July, 1754, p.m.
Present:
THE HON. JAMES DE LANCEY, ESQ., LIEUTENANT GOVERNOR OF THE PROVINCE OF NEW-YORK:
JOSEPH MURRAY, WILLIAM JOHNSON, JOHN CHAMBERS, AND WILLIAM SMITH, ESQRS., OF THE COUNCIL OF THE SAID PROVINCE OF NEW-YORK.
COMMISSIONERS FOR THE SEVERAL STATES.

"Samuel Wells, John Chandler, Thomas Hutchinson, Oliver Partridge, and John Worthington, Esqrs., for the Massachusetts.

"Theodore Atkinson, Richard Wibird, Meshec Weare, and Henry Sherburne, jun., Esqrs., for New-Hampshire.

"William Pitkin, Roger Wolcot, jun., and Elisha Williams, Esqrs., for Connecticut.

"Stephen Hopkins and Martin Howard, jun., Esqrs., for Rhode-Island.

"Benjamin Tasker, jun., and Abraham Barnes, Esqrs., for Maryland.

"John Penn, Richard Peters, Isaac Norris, and Benjamin Franklin, Esqrs., for Pennsylvania.

"The Consideration of the Plan of an Union was resumed; which Plan is as follows:

"Plan of a proposed Union of the several Colonies of Massachusetts-Bay, New-Hampshire, Connecticut, Rhode-Island, New-York, New-Jersey, Pennsylvania, Maryland, Virginia, North-Carolina, and South Carolina, for their mutual Defence and Security, and for the Extending the British Settlements in North-America.

"That humble Application be made for an Act of the Parliament of Great-Britain, by Virtue of which One General Government may be formed in America, including all the said Colonies; within and under which Government, each Colony may retain its present Constitution, except in the Particulars wherein a Change may be directed by the said Act, as hereafter follows.

"That the said General Government be administered by a President General, to be appointed and supported by the Crown; and a Grand Council, to be chosen by the Representatives of the People of the several Colonies, met in their respective Assemblies.

"That within Months after the Passing of such Act, the House of Representatives in the several Assemblies, that happen to be fitting within that Time, or that shall be especially for that Purpose convened, may and shall chuse Members for the Grand Council, in the following Proportions; that is to say:

Massachusetts-Bay,	7
New-Hampshire,	2
Connecticut,	5
Rhode-Island,	2
New-York,	4
New-Jersey,	3
Pennsylvania,	6
Maryland,	4
Virginia,	7
North-Carolina,	4
South Carolina,	4
	48

"Who shall meet for the first Time at the City of Philadelphia in Pennsylvania, being called by the President General, as soon as conveniently may be, after his Appointment.

"That there shall be a new Election of Members for the Grand Council every three Years; and on the Death or Resignation of any Member, his Place shall be supplyed by a new Choice, at the next Sitting of the Assembly of the Colony he represented.

"That after the first three Years, when the Proportion of Money arising out of each Colony to the General Treasury, can be known, the Number of Members to be chosen for each Colony, shall from time to time, in all ensuing Elections, be regulated by that Proportion (yet so as that the Number to be chosen by any one Province, be not more than seven, nor less than two).

"That the Grand Council shall meet once in every Year, and oftener if Occasion require, at such Time and Place as they shall adjourn to at the last preceding Meeting, or as they shall be called to meet at by the President General on any Emergency; he having first obtained in writing, the Consent of seven of the Members to such Call, and sent due and timely Notice to the whole.

"That the Grand Council have Power to chuse their Speaker, and shall neither be dissolved, prorogued, nor continue sitting longer than six Weeks at one Time, without their own Consent, or the special Command of the Crown.

"That the Members of the Grand Council shall be allowed for their Service, Ten Shillings Sterling per Diem, during their Session and Journey to and from the Place of Meeting, twenty Miles to be reckoned a Day's Journey.

"That the Assent of the President General be requisite to all Acts of the Grand Council; and that it be his Office and Duty to cause them to be carried into Execution.

"That the President General, with the Advice of the Grand Council, hold or direct all Indian Treaties, in which the general Interest or Welfare of the Colonies may be concerned; and to make Peace or declare War with Indian Nations. That they make such Laws as they judge necessary for regulating all Indian Trade. That they make all Purchases from transmitted to the King in

Council, for Approbation, as soon as may be, after their passing; and if not disapproved within three Years after Presentation, to remain in Force.

"That in Case of the Death of the President General, the Speaker of the Grand Council for the Time being, shall succeed, and be vested with the same Power and Authorities, and continue 'till the King's Pleasure be known.

"That all Military Commission Officers, whether for Land or Sea Service, to act under this General Constitution, be nominated by the President General, but the Approbation of the Grand Council is to be obtained, before they receive their Commissions. And all Civil Officers are to be nominated by the Grand Council, and to receive the President General's Approbation, before they officiate. But in Case of Vacancy, by Death or Removal of any Officer, Civil or Military, under this Constitution, the Governor of the Provinces in which such Vacancy happens, may appoint, 'till the Pleasure of the President General and Grand Council can be known.

"That the particular Military as well as Civil Establishments in each Colony, remain in their present State, this General Constitution notwithstanding; and that on sudden Emergencies, any Colony may defend itself, and lay the Accounts of Expence thence arisen, before the President General and Grand Council, who may allow and order Payment of the same, as far as they judge such Accounts just and reasonable.

After Debate on the foregoing Plan:

"RESOLVED, That the Commissioners from the several Governments, be desired to lay the same before their respective Constituents, for their Consideration; and that the Secretary to this Board, transmit a Copy thereof, with this Vote thereon, to the Governor of each of the Colonies, which have not sent their Commissioners to this Congress.

"ORDERED, That all His Majesty's Governments on this Continent, may have Liberty from time to time, to take Copies of the Proceedings of this Congress, or any Parts thereof, paying for the same; and that no other Copies be delivered by the Secretary."

The Board continued in session until the 11th of July, and then His Honour, the Lieutenant-Governor of New-York, and the Commissioners of the several Governments, rose without any further adjournments.

Mr. Hopkins Enters Upon His Personal Defence

Thus having seen Abstracts of the Authorities given the Commissioners who were at Albany, and of those Letters from the Crown, which occasioned such Authorities to be given; together with the State of the British and French Colonies in America, and the proposed Plan of Union, formed in Consequence of the whole: From an impartial View thereof, let every Man judge, Whether it was not the Intent of all the Colonies who sent Commissioners, that they should form some General Scheme or Plan, for the Safety and Defence of the English Colonies, and the Indians in their Alliance? Look into the Commission from Governor Greene; and after full Powers are given to do every Thing relative to the Indians in Alliance with us, What mean these following Words? "And also, what else may be necessary to prohibit the French, and their Allies the Indians, from encroaching on the Lands within the Dominious of His Majesty. And in general, as far as the Abilities of this Government will permit, to act in Conjunction with the said Commissioners, in every Thing necessary for the Good of His Majesty's Subjects in these Parts. And to answer as far as we can, the Designs of His Majesty's Instructions to this Colony, communicated to us by the Earl of Holdernesse." Surely such Words as these, have some Meaning; and if the Commissioners were so unhappy as quite to mistake their Meaning, let those penetrating Wits who think so, shew to the World, how they are to be understood. But if those Authorities were too extensive, let them be blamed who gave such Authorities, and not those who executed them in the most sparing Manner possible. And will any Man believe, such exact Likeness in Substance, should be in the Authorities given by every Government to to their Commissioners, without having any Conference together about it, if the Directions from the Crown had not pointed it out to them in so plain a Manner, that they all understood them alike? And is it not as plain, from the Letters since received from the Secretaries of

State, that they all understood them in the Sense the King intended them?

Altho' all this were allowed, yet some may say, If you had Powers given you to enter into some such General Scheme, you ought not to have consented to one so hurtful and destructive of our Liberties as this is! Whether the Plan formed at Albany, be a good one, or a bad one, I shall not undertake to determin; yet let it be considered, that the Rhode-Island Commissioners were but two of the whole Number, and therefore were far from being able to govern or form Things as they might think best; neither did they ever pretend they could not be mistaken; and Errors of Judgment will always be forgiven by Men of Candor.

And now let us examin what the Commissioners did relating to this Plan, and we shall find, they did no more than form it, and agree to lay it before the General Assemblies of the Colonies from whence they came, for their Consideration. They did not, as is falsly asserted, order it to be sent home. They did not establish it as an Act or Ordinance of the Board of Commissioners, as they all might have done, by the Authorities given them. They did not leave it in the Power of any one to obtain a Copy of it, and send it Home; but strictly forbid their Secretary to give any Copy, except to the Colonies. Nor did they ever agree to any Thing more, than to carry it to their respective Governments, and lay it before their Constituents. And agreeable to the Resolve of the Board of Commissioners, those from Rhode-Island, did lay this Plan, with all other their Proceedings at Albany, before the General Assembly, at their Session in August last, for their Consideration. Was this criminal! Was this betraying their Trust! Or was there any Thing more in this, than their Duty! Even Envy and Ignorance joined together, cannot say there was! And those who have been bold enough to assert, That any Thing more relating to this Plan of Union, was done, suffered to be done, or connived at, by the Commissioners, are hereby publicly called upon, to prove their Assertions, or confess their Falshood.

Once more, let us hold up this so much talked of Plan of Union, and view it in another Light: And here, to do my Adversaries all the Justice they can possibly desire, I will, for Argument-sake, confess it to be as bad as they represent it to be. Viewing it in this Light, it must be found contrary to, and subversive of our happy Constitution, and all those valuable Privileges we enjoy under it. This destructive Plan was laid before the General Assembly, for their Consideration, in the Month of August last: This gave an Opportunity to those Patriots belonging to the Council, who now say so much against this Plan, to have exerted themselves in Defence of our Liberties, so much in Danger, and prevented the Dismal Effects so much feared. Well! What have these Champions for Liberty, done in this Matter? Have they not let it lie before the Assembly between six and seven Months, without taking it once under Consideration? Or, Have they ever rejected it? or so much as once in all this Time, moved to have one Word wrote Home, to prevent its taking Place? Was it bad, as they say 'tis, then certainly 'twas their Duty to have done all in their Power to prevent its taking Effect. All Men must confess, the Plan was either good or bad; if 'twas good, Why do they blame it? if 'twas bad, Why have they done Nothing about it?

Now, let every sober-minded Man determin, Whether these Men can be real Friends to the Colony, who placed in the foremost Offices, and intrusted with its Safety, could let a Thing so dangerous to its Interest, lie unobserved by the General Assembly, near seven Months, 'till perhaps it may be too late to prevent it? And then to serve a private Party Turn, suddenly to roar out, The Colony is in Danger! All who have Eyes, will see thro' such thin Disguises, and be assured, that the Designs of those Men, are only to blast the Reputation of one of the Rhode-Island Commissioners, who at present may seem to stand in their Way, and not to do the Colony any Service; for if that had been the Case, they would have told us these Things sooner.

What could the Commissioners for Rhode-Island have done more? or what could they have done less than they did, relative to this Plan? It was not in their Power to procure a better; and whether it was good or bad, it was equally their Duty to lay it before the Assembly who sent them: They did so, and did no more; and every Member of both Houses of Assembly can bear Witness, I have never used the least Endeavour to induce them to accede to it. If it is bad, as some are pleas'd to represent it, Must not every Man say, They who have suffered it to lie thus long, are the very Men who have betrayed their Trust, and the Interest of the Colony?

Real want of Merit occasions these Men's Endeavour to rise upon the Ruin of their Neighbour's Reputation. But can the Faults of my Neighbour, make me fit for an Office? And can the valuable Privileges of this Colony be safe in those Hands, where every Thing else seems to be neglected, but what will serve their private Purposes? As I am a Candidate for an Office, I sincerely desire all Men may put their Country's Interest in the first Place, and give their Votes only where they think 'tis most safe; and assure themselves, such a Conduct will perfectly please the Colony's, and their Friend,

STEPHEN HOPKINS.

Reference: Rhode Island Historical Tracts, No. 9 (Providence: Sidney & Rider, 1880).

REASONS CONSIDERED BY THE ASSEMBLY OF CONNECTICUT, OCTOBER 2, 1754

Capt. Henry Glover, Mr. Daniel Booth, for New Town.

Mr. Samuel Olmsted, Mr. Stephen Smith, for Ridgfield.

Majr. Elihu Chauncey, Mr. Ezra Baldwin, for Durham.

Majr. Jabez Hamlin, Mr. Seth Wetmore, for Middletown.

Capt. Ephraim Terry, Mr. Joseph Olmsted, for Enfield.

Capt. Jabez Lyon, Col. Thomas Chandler, for Woodstock.

Col. Hezekiah Sabin, Mr. Boaz Sterns, for Killingsley.

Capt. Theophilus Nichols, Capt. Robert Fairchild, for Stratford.

Mr. Stephen Hopkins, Mr. Caleb Hummiston, for
Waterbury.
Mr. Ambrose Wittlesey, Capt. Jed. Chapman, for
Saybrook.
Col. Shubael Conant, Speaker } of the House of
Representatives.
Majr Elihu Chauncey, Clerk

The Commissioners appointed by the
Assembly of the Colony of Connecticut in
May last, in behalf of said Colony, to meet
such Commissioners as should be appointed by
his Majesty's other governments in America at
a general interview at Albany on the 14th day
of June last and joyn with Commissioners of
the other Colonies in concerting proper measures for the general defence and safety of his
Majesty's subjects in said governments and the
Indians in alliance with them against the French
and their Indians, agreeable to the desire of the
Commissioners of the several governments met
as aforesaid, have laid before this Assembly for
consideration the Plan of a proposed Union
of the several Colonies of Massachusets Bay,
New Hampshire, Connecticut, Rhode Island,
New York, New Jersey, Pensilvania, Maryland,
Virginia, North Carolina, and South Carolina,
for their mutual defence and security, and for
extending the British settlements in North
America. Upon deliberate and mature consideration thereof,

Resolved, That it is the opinion of this
Assembly, and it is hereby declared to be the
opinion thereof, that the limits of the proposed
plan of union are of too large extent to be in
any good manner administred, considered, conducted and defended, by one President General
and Council; and that a defensive war managed
by such government having so large a [236] fron-
tier will prove ruinous to it; || that the same in
course of time may be dangerous and hurtful to
his Majesty's interest, and tends to subvert the
liberties and privileges, and to discourage and
lessen the industry of his Majesty's good subjects
inhabiting these Colonies: And therefore, that
no application be made in behalf of this Colony
to the Parliament of Great Britain for an act to

form any such government on the said proposed
plan as therein is expressed; and that reasons be
offered against any such motion.

Resolved by this Assembly, That his Honour the
Governour be desired, and he is hereby desired,
to send to the Agent for this Colony at the Court
of Great Britain the resolution of this Assembly
concerning the Plan of Union proposed by the
Commissioners of the several Colonies, who met
at Albany on the 14th of June last to concert
proper measures for the general defence and safety
of his Majesty's subjects in said governments; and
that he likewise send said agent the Reasons
considered and offered by this Assembly concerning the said plan of a proposed union of the
Colonies of Massachusets Bay, New Hampshire,
Connecticut, Rhode Island, New York, New
Jersey, Pennsylvania, Maryland, Virginia, North
Carolina, and South Carolina, for their mutual
defence, &c.; and also to send the Representation
of the state of the Colonies of North America in
relation to the French; to be used and improved
by the said agent upon any consideration that may
be had on said plan. And that the agent aforesaid
be directed, that in case any of the other Colonies
aforesaid shall make humble application for an
act of the Parliament of Great Britain, by virtue
of which one general government may be formed
in America, including the said Colonies and to be
administred in manner and form as is proposed in
said plan, he move the Parliament to be heard by
learned counsel thereon in behalf of this Colony;
and that the reasons aforementioned, with any
other arguments that appear just and reasonable
in the case, be insisted on and in the most advantageous manner urged, to prevent any such act
being made or passed in the Parliament of Great
Britain.

Resolved by this Assembly, That his Honour the
Governour be desired, and he is hereby desired, to
give attention to all the steps taken by the several
governments on this continent relating to the
plan of the proposed union of the several Colonies
in North America for their mutual defence &c.,
and use means, as he shall judge prudent, to prevent any further proceedings thereon. And in
case any of the Colonies therein mentioned shall

make application to the Parliament for an act to be made and passed in the manner in said plan proposed, that he prepare whatsoever shall be needful to prevent such act. And in case any plan for a union of said Colonies be proposed, in order to be enacted in Parliament, that his Honour the Governor furnish the Agent of this Colony with whatever reasons may be further suggested for an alteration thereof in various parts, that the extent may be lessened by dividing the same into two districts, that the liberties and privileges of the people may be better secured than in said plan is provided; and that he give the reasons shewing the proportions made in said plan are not just and equal, and furnish the Agent with proper evidence, shewing in the best manner the nature of the case admits, what the proportion, especially of this Colony, is with relation to the other Colonies.

Reference: Charles J. Hoadly (ed.), *The Public Records of the Colony of Connecticut, 1751–1757*, Vol. X (Hartford: Case, Lockwood, Brainard Co., 1877), 292–294.

MASSACHUSETTS OPPOSES THE ALBANY PLAN, DECEMBER 14, 1754*

Sabbati 14. Die Decembris, A.D. 1754.

THE House again took under Consideration the Report of the Committee on the Union; and the Plan of Union accompanying of it: And after a large Debate thereon, the Question was put, *Whether the House accept of the General Plan of Union, as Reported by the Commissioners convened at* Albany *in June last?*

It pass'd in the Negative.

Sent up for Concurrence.

The Question was then put, *Whether the House accept of the Partial Plan of Union reported by the last Committee of both Houses, appointed on the Union?* It pass'd in the Negative.

Sent up for Concurrence.

Then the Question was put, *Whether in taking the Sense of the House, with Regard to the proposed Union of the Colonies being general or partial, it shall be determined by Yeas and Nays?*

Resolved in the Affirmative.

On a Motion made and seconded, *Voted,* That any Member of the House may have the Liberty of entering in the Journal of the House, his Reasons for voting for, or against a general Union of the several Colonies.

The Question was then put, *Whether it be the Mind of the House, that there be a General Union of his Majesty's Colonies on this Continent, except those of* Nova-Scotia *and* Georgia?

Resolved in the Affirmative.

*For Connecticut's response to the Albany plan, see p. 365.

Yeas.	Nays.
The Hon. Samuel Welles, Esq;	Hon. James Allen, Esq;
Mr. James Bowdoin,	Mr. Samuel Niles, Jun.
Capt. Joseph Williams,	Mr. Jacob Cushing,
Samuel Miller, Esq;	Mr, Simon Plympton,
Mr. Josiah Quincy,	John Choate, Esq;
Mr. William Bowdoin,	Mr. Benjamin Greenleafe,
Henry Gibbs, Esq;	Joseph Gerrish, Jun. Esq;
Capt. Benjamin Newhall,	Mr. Humphry Hobson,
John Tasker, Esq;	Caleb Cushing, Esq;
Joseph Frye, Esq;	Mr. Isaac Morrill
Robert Hale, Esq;	Capt. Benjamin Milliken,
Mr. William Stevens,	Mr. Elijah Porter,
Mr. Jonathan Foster,	Capt. John Dodge,
Mr. James Russell,	William Brattle, Esq;
Mr. John Hunt,	Mr. Simon Hunt,

Mr. Edward Walker,
Henry Gibbs, Esq;
Capt. John Noyes,

Mr. Elisha Jones,
Mr. Stephen Hall, Jun.
Nathanael Russell, Esq;
Hon. Chambers Russell, Esq;
Josiah Dwight, Esq;
Capt. Israel Ashley,

John Chandler, Jun. Esq;
William Ayres, Esq;

John Murray, Esq;
Timothy Ruggles, Esq;
Thomas Foster, Esq;
Thomas Clap, Esq;
Gamaliel Bradford, Esq;
John Winslow, Esq;
Capt. Nathanael Smith,
David Stockbridge, Esq;

Ebenezer Nichols, Esq;
Mr. Samuel Witt,
William Lawrence, Esq;
Capt, Enoch Kidder,
Mr. Benjamin Hills,

Samuel Livermore, Esq;
Thomas Reed, Esq;
Mr. Joseph Houlton,
William Richardson, Esq;
Mr. John Haywood,

Mr. Phineas Haywood,
Capt. Nathan Tyler,
Mr. Daniel Greenwood,
Capt. Josiah Edson,
Mr. Israel Turner,
Mr. Isaac Bonny,

Mr. Jacob Porter,
Mr. Israel Tisdale,

Mr, John Bradbury,

Mr. Elisha Barrow,
James Otis, Esq;

Capt. Aaron Kinsley,
Capt. Nathanael Sole,
Mr. Benjamin Day,
Mr. John Winslow,
Jedediah Prebble, Esq;

Nathanael Sparhawk, Esq;
Capt. Ichabod Goodwin,
John Storer, Esq;

Ordered, That Mr. *James Bowdoin,* Col. *Otis,* Col. *Choate,* Col. *Brattle,* Col. *Hale,* Mr. *Tasker,* and Judge *Russell,* with such as the honourable Board shall join, be a Committee to consider of and report a general Plan of *Union* of the several Colonies on this Continent, except those of *Nova-Scotia,* and *Georgia.*

Sent up for Concurrence.

Ordered, That Col. *Otis* go up to the honourable Board, and enquire whether they have pass'd on the Excise-Bill; and if not, to desire it may be sent down.

Who returned he had delivered the Message.

John Chandler, Esq; brought down the said Bill accordingly.

And after making sundry Amendments therein, the said Bill was sent up again.

Sent up for Concurrence.

Reference: Journals of the House of Representatives of Massachusetts, 1754–1755 (Boston: Massachusetts Historical Society, 1956).

A SHORT REPLY TO STEPHEN HOPKINS BY PHILOLETHES, APRIL 10, 1755

LET the Reader in the first Place, observe, the above named Gentleman introduces his pompous Piece, with Abstracts of the Authorities given by the several Governments to their Commissioners, and of several Letters from the Secretaries of State, together with a Representation of the State of the English and French Colonies in North-America; and then proceeds to his sophistical Arguments, to clear himself from Imputation of Guilt, with Respect to his Conduct at Albany, and false Charges against the Heads of the Legislature; and

concludes with his ungentleman-like Reflections upon all who shall animadvert.

In the first Place, the Public may be assured, that the above named Gentleman has grossly abused them, by printing only particular Paragraphs of the Commissions given by the several Governors to the Commissioners, in order to deceive his Readers, neglecting whatever Words or Sentences did not answer his Purpose. To demonstrate the Gentleman's Fallacy, I shall only mention one Paragraph in the Commission given by Horatio

Sharpe, Esq., Governor of Maryland, to the Commissioners of that Province, which is as follows: "But you are to understand, that you are not impowered to stipulate or engage, that this Province will advance any Sum of Money, or Number of Men, towards erecting Forts, or garrisoning them, or to such Purposes; but you shall only well observe, what Proposals are made by the other Commissioners, and endeavour to learn how far the Execution of what they may propose, can be necessary or useful, and consider well the Reasonableness of any such Propositions, and to make Return, &c." This is what the above-named Gentleman has not printed; and if any Gentleman will give himself the Trouble to examin the original Commissions in the Secretary's Office, he will find, that such Parts as are not for his Purpose, he has omitted; and yet this Gentleman has the Front to assert in his 13th pag. referring to the Plan formed at Albany, That "they did not establish it as an Act or Ordinance of the Board of Commissioners, as they all might have done, by the Authorities given them;" which last Sentence is false in fact.

SECONDLY: His printing Paragraphs of the Letters from the Ministers of State to the several Governments, is to insinuate to his Readers, that His Majesty and the Ministers of State had ordered them, or at least expected that such a Plan should be established, which is contrary to Magna Charta. I am perswaded, the British Parliament were surprised that the Governments should petition for a Confirmation of a Plan, which, the Instant it was established, would revoke all His Majesty's Governors Commissions in North-America, and destroy every Charter, by erecting a Power above Law, over the several Legislatures. [NOTE.—Some of the Letters from the Ministry, were dated Octob. 26, which was after the Plan got Home, and was the Foundation of said Letters.]

THIRDLY: As to the Representation of the State of the English and French Colonies in North-America, we are all sensible, that if the French are suffered to do what they please, they will soon increase their Numbers, and put themselves into such a Position, as to annoy and disturb the English Colonies; and the only Union of the Inhabitants of the several Governments, is

true Protestant Principles, which leads them forth to fight for their King and Country freely, without Force or Compulsion, and therefore we want no arbitrary supream sovereign Court of Jurisdiction over a free People, to lay Taxes, Imposts, and Duties upon our Land, Trade, and Merchandize; but are ready, when our most gracious Sovereign commands, to oppose the common Enemy, and not desist, till there are any to trouble us or our Posterity. But what good End will be answered, for the Governments to be obliged to conform to this Plan of Union? Why this; a Number of mercenary Gentlemen will heap to themselves Riches out of the public Stock; and those Gentlemen who have purchased all the Lands to the Rivers and Lakes, when the Colonies have built a Row of Forts, and are at the Expence of keeping a standing Army in them, which may cost the smallest Colony Ten Thousand Pounds Sterling per Annum, will enhance their Estates to ten Times their present Value, and build them convenient Houses for the Fur Trade, at the several Government's Expence.

FOURTHLY: We are now come to the Plan of Union; in which the Names of those who compos'd this august Congress, are first inserted, and then the several Governments: And here observe, they say, "That humble Application be made for an Act of Parliament of Great-Britain, by Virtue of which, One General Government may be formed in America, &c." Now, How was this Application to be made? It is not said, That humble Application be made by the several Governments, if they acceded to said Plan; nor was the President of said Congress at Albany, ordered (by any Thing that appears) to wait any fix'd Time, to receive the Assent or Dissent of the several Governments; nor have the Governments been informed by that Congress that they ever designed to wait their Consent to said Plan; And how improbable is it, that they ever designed to wait for the Governments Resolve, when neither Time, Place, nor Person was pointed out to receive the Governments Answer; Notwithstanding, the Plan is at Home, and by our Agent's Letter, before the Parliament for Confirmation.

FIFTHLY: In his sophistical Arguments to clear himself from the Imputation of Guilt, with

Respect to his Conduct at Albany, in the 12th pag. he makes an artful Flourish, by saying, "Thus having seen Abstracts of the Authorities given the Commissioners, and those Letters which occasioned such Authorities; the State of the British and French Colonies, the Plan formed in Consequence thereof: Now let every Man judge, &c." All which did not impower him to introduce an Authority over our Legislature, so as to destroy our Charter, as said Plan virtually doth. I shall pass to pag. 13, where the Gentleman saith, "Whether the Plan formed at Albany, be a good one or a bad one, I shall not undertake to determin"; but forgets himself in pag. 14, and says, "All Men must confess the Plan was either good or bad." What Authority has this Gentleman above all others, that every Man must confess the Plan was either good or bad? No doubt to conceal his own Sentiments; should he declare it a good Plan, he might be apprehensive of incuring the Displeasure of the People in general: if a bad one, he must sacrifice his Honor and Reputation with those Gentlemen, who with him, approved of said Plan at Albany. He goes on, and says, "What could the Commissioners for Rhode-Island have done more? or what could they have done less than they did, relative to this Plan? It was not in their Power to procure a better; and whether it was good or bad, it was equally their Duty to lay it before the Assembly, &c." What Authority, or what Right had this Gentleman to bring any Plan from Albany? If he could not bring a good one, he might have done less, and brought none, by rejecting it. We have bad Schemes enough in the Colony of Rhode-Island, without bringing more into it. "Let it be considered (says he) the Rhode-Island Commissioners were but two of the whole Number," which consisted of Twenty-seven. Now, upon a Supposition, that the Plan is established at Home, then Rhode-Island is to have Two out of Forty-eight; and if Forty six of the Grand Council should consent to lay Ten Thousand Pounds Sterling per Annum, upon our Colony, being but Two, it is not in their Power to prevent it. But I desire to know, Whether it was not in the Power of our sagacious Commissioners to protest against said Plan, or [as] those worthy Patriots to their.

Government, the Commissioners of Connecticut did? It was far from a good Plea, for consenting to said Plan, because but Two in Number; if but One, he might have left it, and acquainted the other Commissioners, That his Government did [not] authorize him to dispose of the Government, and bring a Deed of Conveyance for them to sign.

SIXTHLY: This penetrating, judicious Gentleman, proceeds to his false Charges against the Heads of the Legislature, and concludes with Reflections, which every candid Person must treat with Contempt, in pag. 14. "This destructive Plan (he says) was laid before the General Assembly, in the Month of August last: This gave an Opportunity to those Patriots belonging to the Council, who now say so much against this Plan, to have exerted themselves, &c. Well! What have these Champions for Liberty done in this Matter? Have they not let it lie before the Assembly between six and seven Months, without taking it once under Consideration? Or, Have they ever rejected it? or so much as once in all this Time, moved to have one Word wrote Home, to prevent it; and then to serve a private Party Turn, suddenly to roar out, The Colony is in Danger! &c." What Education the afore-named Gentleman had in his Minority, I know not; but this I know, it is far beneath the Character of a well-bred Gentleman to assert Falshoods against the Heads of a Government, and make no Distinction between them and the lowest Peasants. That this Gentleman has falsly accused the Governor and Council, the Records will make appear; and the Lower House can witness against him. I shall therefore observe the Measures taken by the Governor and Council, from time to time, relating to this Plan. In August last, this cunning Gentleman presented to the General Assembly, a Number of Sheets in Folio, in which were contained a Variety of Matters, and the Plan of Union artfully tack'd to the rest, which being read in the Lower House, the Report was received, and in Consequence, all their Doings, &c. No doubt, some Advocates, of Mr. Hopkins's, discovered the Absurdity of said Plan, which they conceal'd, to prevent any Reflections on his Character: However, the Vote of the Lower House was sent to the Governor and

Council, who perceived the Fraud, of the Plan's being included with their other Proceedings, and acquainted the Lower House. That they concur'd with their Vote, reserving a further Consideration upon the Plan of Union. The Lower House confessed the Reserve just. Many important Affairs lying before the Assembly, at their Session in October following, prevented the Council from proceeding to a further Consideration of the Plan of Union; and had no Suspicion of its being sent Home, without the Privity of the other Colonies; however, in December, Governor Greene receiv'd a Letter from the Agent, dated Octob. 9, 1754, with the following Words contain'd therein: "The Parliament is like to meet for Dispatch of Business, in about six Weeks Time, when I am apt to think, some Application will be made to them, respecting the Union of the several Governments in North-America, Proposals for that Purpose being lately come to hand, as they were agreed on by the Congress at Albany, &c." This Information surprised the Governor, who in February Session, presented to the Council the said Letter, and being resolved to have something done, laid the Letter before the Lower House, to induce them to pass a Vote for a Letter to be sent Home, in order to prevent establishing the said Plan: But a Gentleman, zealously attach'd to Mr. Hopkins, made Application to one of the Council, being that they would not reject the Plan, which would be a Dishonor to the Commissioners. Any Gentleman may discover the Reason why some of the Lower House made use of every Artifice to prevent the Plan from being deliberated on, and no Vote obtain'd from the Lower House in February Session, concerning the same. The Governor and Council being dissatisfied therewith, in March following (when the Assembly met) sent to the Lower House, the following Resolve in writing, viz.:

"To the House of Deputies"

"GENTLEMEN:

"WHEREAS the Plan proposed at the Congress at Albany last Summer, in order to an Union of His Majesty's Northern Colonies, for

their common Defence, was not acceded to, when presented unto the General Assembly in August, but by them reserved for a further Consideration. And now this House having duly examined and considered said Plan, do find the same to be a Scheme, which if carried into Execution, will virtually deprive this Government, at least, of some of its most valuable Privileges, if not effectually overturn and destroy our present happy Constitution; Wherefore, it is strongly recommended to you, Gentlemen, That an authentic Copy of all the Proceedings at Albany, be made out, and sent forthwith to our Agent in Great-Britain, with Instructions, That he exert himself to the utmost, in order to prevent the said Plan of Union, or any Thing contain'd therein, to the Purport or Effect thereof, being carried or passed into an Act of the Parliament of Great-Britain.

Voted and past per Order,
THOMAS WARD, Secy."

Every Gentleman may now judge, Whether the Governor and Council have not once moved, in six or seven Months, concerning the said Plan? and, Whether they merited such indecent Language as this Gentleman has taken the Freedom to treat them with. In his 14th pag. there is a gross Reflection on the Governor and Council, which ought not to be pass'd over in Silence, where he says, "Can the valuable Privileges of this Colony, be safe in those Hands, where every Thing else seems to be neglected, but what will serve their private Purposes, &c." I shall here put this Gentleman in mind of the many Neglects he has been guilty of, which the Records of the Colony will evince. Was he not appointed one of a Committee near three Years past, to prepare the Case of the Northern Boundary Line, and present the same to the Governor, which he has neglected to this Day, tho' repeatedly called upon by the Governor, and those concerned? Did not this Gentleman undertake to form a Letter near two Years past, to send to our Agent, in order to recover our Privileges in making Paper Money, and amused the People, that he would even go Home himself, if the Letter had not the proper effect? all which he has neglected. Let him also remember, how he engaged in May last, to settle the Colony's Accounts with Mr. Brenton (which has occasioned so much Uneasiness in the Government) promising, That he would devote himself to the same; and tho' he has frequently been urg'd by the Assembly to finish it, has not yet found Time. How he undertook to answer the Earl of Holdernesse's and Sir Thomas Robinson's Letters, and a Letter from this Government for Canon, &c. &c., all which he has neglected, tho' our Liberties, Properties, and whatever we esteem valuable, depended upon the Performance of them. And the Inhabitants of this Colony must be sensible, that this Gentleman is over fond of having all Matters of Consequence committed to his Management; and has his Admirers in the Assembly, who (contrary to Decency and good Manners) nominate1 this Man of Wisdom, in Opposition to every other Man, tho' he gives himself little concern about any Thing, except in agreeing to the Plan of Union, expecting, at least, to be a Member of the Grand Council.

I shall now conclude, with observing to the Inhabitants of this Colony, wherein this Gentleman has endeavour'd to impose on them. 1. By omiting Paragraphs in the several Commissions, which might frustrate his Designs. 2. His inserting Paragraphs of the Letters from our Prime Ministers, to insinuate, that they had them at Albany to form the Plan by, when those Paragraphs in Sir Thomas Robinson's Letter of Octob. 26, was wrote when the Plan got Home. 3. His publishing the State of the English and French Colonies, to justify the forming said Plan, yet does not acknowledge, whether he approves or disapproves thereof; altho' in his Defence, he ingenuously confesses, that he was concerned in the Forming of it. 4. His asserting the Plan was laid before the Assembly between six and seven Months, without the least Notice being taken of it by the Council. 5. His Vindication of his Conduct at Albany, proves him guilty of what he dare not own nor deny. 6. His indecent Reflections against the Governor and Council, should excite every Man in the Colony to resent, and treat with the Contempt it deserves.

All which is submitted, by

PHILOLETHES.
RHODE-ISLAND, APRIL 10, 1755.

Reference: Rhode Island Historical Tracts, No. 9 (Providence: Sidney & Rider, 1880).

31

Internal Division

Chapter 31 concerns the internal divisions within the colonies over governance authority. North Carolina is one important example among others because its citizens disagreed most strongly over that authority. (Similarily, Pennsylvania and New York had geographical squabbles among its citizens and their leaders.) The June 1765 Address to the People of Greenville County, North Carolina claims corruption and political oppression by leaders in the county. The Regulators of North Carolina advertised that the western part of the colony was underrepresented in the legislature. Others wrote of excessive taxes that were unfairly assessed. Everywhere in the colony, it seemed, government authority was under challenge. Finally for North Carolina, the Regulator and future Revolutionary radical Herman Husband explained why the colony was so divided. For considerations of space, only one final document has been selected to show the internal divisions within the colonies on the eve of the Revolution. On June 14, 1776, just days before independence was declared, the mechanics of New York City accused their revolutionary leaders of underrepresenting the city in delegates selected for the Continental Congress.

ADDRESS TO PEOPLE OF GRANVILLE COUNTY, NORTH CAROLINA, JUNE 6, 1765

Well, Gentlemen, it is not our mode, or form of Government, nor yet the body of our laws, that we are quarrelling with, but with the malpractices of the Officers of our County Court, and the abuses which we suffer by those empowered to manage our public affairs. . . . It is well known, that there is a law which provides that a lawyer shall take no more than 15/ for this fee in the County Court. Well Gentlemen, which of you have had your business done for 15/? Do not the Lawyers exact 30s for every cause, and 3, 4, or 5 pounds for every cause that is attended with the least difficulty? Yes: they do Gentlemen, and laugh at our stupidity and tame submission to these damned extravagancies. And besides the double fees, which they exact from you, do they not lengthen

out your lawsuits, by artifices and delays, so long as they perceive you have any money to grease their fists with? And numberless other develish devices to rob you of your livings in a manner diametrically opposite to the policy of our State, and the intention of our Legislature. . . .

Need I mention one instance to set forth the misery which we groan under? Does not daily experience shew us the gaping jaws of ruin, open, and ready to devour us? Are not your lands executed your negroes, horses, cattle, hogs, corn, beds, and household furniture? Are not these things, I say, taken and sold for one tenth of their value? Not to satisfy the just debts which you have contracted; but to satisfy the cursed exorbitant demands of the Clerks, Lawyers and Sheriffs. . . . It is reasonable

Gentlemen, that these Officers should be allowed such fees, as may give them a genteel maintenance, but then is it reasonable that they should rob the County to support themselves in such damned extravagancies, and laugh at us for being such simpletons as to suffer it? . . .

It is not a persons labour, nor yet his effects that will do, but if he has but one horse to plow with, one bed to lie on, or one cow to give a little milk for his children, they must all go to raise money which is not to be had. And lastly if his personal estate (sold at one tenth of its value) will not do, then his lands (which perhaps has cost him many years toil and labour) must go the same way to satisfy these cursed hungry caterpillars, that are eating and will eat out the bowels of our Commonwealth, if they be not pulled down from their nests in a very short time, and what need I say, Gentlemen, to urge the necessity there is for a reformation. If these things were absolutely according to law, it

would be enough to make us turn rebels, and throw off all submission to such tyrannical laws. . . . But, as these practices are diametrically opposite to the law, it is our absolute duty, as well as our Interests, to put a stop to them, before they quite ruin our County. Or, Are [we] become the willing slaves of these lawless Officers, and hug our chains of bondage and remain contented under these accumulated calamities. . . ? Here I am this day with my life in my hand, to see my fellow subjects animated with a spirit of liberty and freedom, and to see them lay a foundation for the recovery thereof, and the clearing our County from arbitrary tyranny.

Reference: William K. Boyd (ed.), *Some Eighteenth-Century Tracts Concerning North Carolina* (Raleigh: Edwards and Broughton Company, 1927), 186–92, in Lindley S. Butler and Alan W. Watson (eds.), *The North Carolina Experience* (Chapel Hill: University of North Carolina Press, 1984).

NORTH CAROLINA REGULATORS' ADVERTISEMENT, AUGUST 6, 1766

Whereas that great good may come of this great designed Evil the Stamp Law while the sons of Liberty withstood the Lords in Parliament in behalf of true Liberty let not Officers under them carry on unjust Oppression in our own Province in order thereunto as there is many Evils of that nature complained of in this County of Orange in private amongst the Inhabitants therefore let us remove them (or if there is no cause) let us remove the Jealousies out of our minds.

Honest rulers in power will be glad to see us examine this matter freely there is certainly more honest men among us than rogues & yet rogues is harbored among us sometimes almost publickly, every honest man is willing to give part of his substance to support rulers and laws to save the other part from rogues and it is his duty as well

as right to see and examine whether such rulers abuse such trust, otherwise that part so given may do more hurt than good, even if all were rogues in that case we could not subsist but would be obliged to frame laws to make ourselves honest and the same reasoning holds good against the notion of a Mason Club; this tho' it must be desired by all or the greatest number of men, yet when grievances of such public nature are not redressed the reason is everybody's business is no Bodys.

Reference: William L. Saunders (ed.), *The Colonial Records of North Carolina*, Vol. VII (Raleigh: State of North Carolina, 1886–90), 249–50, in Lindley S. Butler and Alan W. Watson (eds.), *The North Carolina Experience* (Chapel Hill: University of North Carolina Press, 1984).

PETITION OF CITIZENS OF ROWAN AND ORANGE COUNTIES, OCTOBER 4, 1768

To the Worshipful House of Representatives of North Carolina:

Your Poor Petitioners having been Continually Squez'd and oppressed by our Publick Officers both with Regard to their fees as also in the Laying on of Taxes as well as in Collecting together with Iniquitious Appropriations, and Wrong Applications of the same, & being Grieved thus to have our substance torn from us, and no ends nor Bounds were Like to be Set to such Illegal practices we applied to our public officers to give us some satisfaction on the several Heads which they Repeatedly denied, us. . . . We humbly supplicate your Worships to take under your serious Consideration, we labour under Extreem hardships about our Levies Money is very scarce hardly any to be had would we Purchase it at ten times its value & we exceeding Poor & lie at a great distance from Trade which renders it almost Impossible to gain sustenance by our utmost Endeavours, Gods Sake Gentlemen in an affairs of such Importance; on your Breath depends the Ruin or Prosperity of poor Families, and so to Gentlemen Rowling in affluence, a few shillings per man, may seem triffling yet to Poor People who must have their Bed and Bedclothes yea their Wives Petticoats taken and sold to Defray. . . . We Humbly begg of your Worships, to take it into your serious Considerations the sums to Erect a Publick Edifice it is a Pitiful Consideration to us poor Wretches to think where or how we shall Raise our Parts, of the sd. sums Designed for that Purpose; Good God Gentlemen what will become of us when these Demands come against us Paper Money we have none & gold or silver we can Purchase none of the Contingencies of Government Must be Paid, and which we are

Willing to Pay, tho if we sell our Beds from under us and in this Time of Distress it is as much as we can support our selves under. . . . We Humbly Begg you would Consider the Laws as they now stand, Recovery of small Debts your own good sence will point out to you the hardships we Labour under by attending Courts of Justice at great Distances for small Triffles, or be forced to part with our small substance wrong. You can not but observe how Ruinous the Law as it now stands must be to the Poor but as an Honest good judge or Majestrate better even with a bad Cause than a Corapt one will do with the Best fram'd Laws on Earth we humble Begg you would be pleas'd to Use your Influence with our Worthy, Virtuous, Governor, to discontinue from time to Time such Officers as would be found to be ye Bane of Society and Put in the Common Wealth, at the same time to Encourage the Poor, and Despis'd to stand for them This would Cause Joy and Gladness to Spring from every Heart, this would cause Labour and Industry to prevail over Murmuring Discontent, this would Raise your poor Petitioners from an indigent Heartless to a flourishing Opulent and Hoping People otherwise Charge and disatisfaction and Melancholy must Prevail over such as Remain and Numbers, must Defect the Province and seek elsewhere an Asylum from Tyranny and Oppression.

Reference: Legislative Papers, North Carolina Archives, Raleigh, in Lindley S. Butler and Alan W. Watson (eds.), *The North Carolina Experience* (Chapel Hill: University of North Carolina Press, 1984).

IMPARTIAL RELATION OF THE FIRST RISE AND CAUSE, 1770

In Orange County the first Disturbance is generally ascribed to have arisen; but *Granville and Halifax* Counties were deeply engaged in the same Quarrel many Years before *Orange:* So that it may be necessary to give a few Paragraphs out of some of their Papers, to shew, that it was the same Grievance and Oppression that incensed all the Counties, without corresponding with each other.—For though *Granville* County had been at War, as it were, some Years before the Disturbance in *Orange,* yet we never heard of it till it broke out in *Orange.*

The Paragraphs in the *Granville* Paper runs as follow,

"A serious Address to the Inhabitants of *Granville* County, containing a brief Narrative of our deplorable Situation by the Wrongs we suffer,—
"And some necessary Hints, with respect to a Reformation.
"Save my Country, Heavens, shall be my last.— Pope.

Then, after treating on the Nature of Law in general, and of our Constitution, in Praise of it, he proceeds thus.—

"Well, Gentlemen, it is not our Form or Mode of Government, nor yet the Body of our Laws that we are quarreling with, but with the Malpractices of the Officers of our County Court, and the Abuses that we suffer by those that are impowered to manage our publick Affairs: This is the Grievance, Gentlemen, that demands our serious Attention.—And I shall,

"Thirdly, Shew the notorious and intolerable Abuses that has crept into the Practice of the Law, in this County, and I doubt not but into other Counties also; though that does not concern us. In the first Place, there is a Law that provides that a Lawyer shall take no more than Fifteen Shillings for their Fee in the County Court.— Well, Gentlemen, which of you has had your Business done for Fifteen Shillings? They exact Thirty for every Cause: And Three—Four—and Five Pounds for every Cause attended with the least Difficulty, and laugh at us for our Stupidity and same Submission to these D—m—d, &c."

"A poor Man is supposed to have given his Judgment Bond for Five Pounds; and this Bond is by his Creditor thrown into Court.—The Clerk of the County has to enter it on the Docket, and issue Execution, the Work of one long Minute, for which the poor Man has to pay him the trifling Sum of Forty-one Shillings and Five-pence.—The Clerk, in Consideration he is a poor Man, takes it out in Work, at Eighteen-pence a Day.—The poor Man works some more than Twenty-seven Days to pay for this one Minute's Writing.

"Well, the poor Man reflects thus,—At this Rate, when shall I get to Labour for my Family? I have a Wife and Parcel of small Children suffering at Home, and here I have lost a whole Month, and I don't know for what; for my Merchant is as far from being paid yet as ever.—However, I will go Home now, and try and do what I can.—Stay, Neighbour, you have not half done yet,—there is a D—d Lawyer's Mouth to stop yet;—for you impowered him to confess that you owed this Five Pounds, and you have Thirty Shillings to pay him for that, or go and work nineteen Days

more; and then you must work as long to pay the Sheriff for his Trouble; and then you may go home and see your Horses and Cows sold, and all your personal Estate, for one Tenth Part of the Value, to pay off your Merchant. And lastly, if the Debt is so great, that all your personal Estate will not do to raise the Money, which is not to be had,—then goes your Lands the same way to satisfy these cursed hungry Caterpillars, that will eat out the very Bowels of our Common-wealth, if they are not pulled down from their Nests in a very short time.—And what Need, I say, to urge a Reformation.—If these Things were absolutely according to Law, it were enough to make us throw off all Submission to such tyrannical Laws; for were such Things tolerated, it would rob us of the Means of Living; and it would be better to die in Defence of our Privileges than to perish for want of the Means of Subsistance.—But as these Practices are contrary to Law, it is our Duty to put a Stop to them before they quite ruin our County, or that we become willing Slaves to these lawless Wretches, and hug our Chains of Bondage, and remain contented under these accumulated Calamities.

"Oh, Gentlemen, I hope better Things of you.—I believe there are few of you but has felt the Weight of those Iron Fists.—And I hope there are none of you but will lend a Hand towards bringing about this necessary Work; and in order to bring it about effectually, we must proceed with Circumspection; not fearful, but careful.

"1st. Let us be careful to keep sober,—nor do nothing rashly,—but act with Deliberation.

"2dly. Let us do nothing against the known established Laws of our Land, that we appear not as a Faction, endeavoring to subvert the Laws, and overturn the System of our Government;— But let us take Care to appear what really we are, Free Subjects by Birth, endeavoring to recover our lost native Rights, of reducing the Malpractices of the Officers of our Court down to the Standard of our Law."

This Paper was large, and deserved to have been printed at Length, but my Ability would not aford it.—It was dated, "*Nutbush, Granville* County, the 6th of *June*, Anno Dom. 1765."

And tho' it was the adjacent County to *Orange*, yet the first that ever we heard of it was in 1767, at our *August* Court, after we had tried to plead our own Cause at the Bar against Extortion.—Then some Persons who lived adjoining *Granville* Line told us they feared that Matter would ruin some of us, for that just such a Case had been undertook in *Granville* County some years ago, and that they were at Law about it to that Day. And by what I have since learned, the Method they proceeded in was by Petitioning the Legislative Body against the Mal-Practices of the Officers mentioned in the Paragraphs cited.—And thereupon the Officers sued the Subscribers for a Lible; indicted the Author of the Paper, and imprisoned him: Which Law-Suits have remained to this Day.

There were other Counties, such as *Brumswick, Cumberland,* and some more, had wholly Declined paying Taxes as early as 1766, if not before, as nearly as I could collect Acounts;—but the Government made no noise about all this till *Orange* could no longer be kept quiet,—who never had knowledge of the Dissatisfaction of these Counties; so that the Thing did not spread by Industry of any in propagating or Communicating the Grievances, but the same Cause naturally produced the same Effect.

But now I shall drop other Counties and begin with *Orange*, having, as I said before, as perfect a knowledge of the whole Proceedings as any one Man in the Province.

Sometime in the latter Part of Summer, in the Year 1766, at an Inferior Court in the County of *Orange*, a Paper was presented and read to the Representatives and Magistrates of the County, as follows, viz.

No. I.

"WHEREAS that great Good may come of this Great designed Evil, the Stamp Law, while the Sons of Liberty withstand the Lords in Parliament, in Behalf of true Liberty, Let not Officers under them carry on unjust Oppression in our own Province; in order thereto, as there is many Evils of that Nature complained of in this County of *Orange* in private amongst the Inhabitants, Therefore, let us remove them;—[10] or if there is no cause, let us remove the Jealousies out of our Minds.—Honest Rulers in Power will be glad to see us examine this Matter freely—And certainly there is more honest Men among us than Rogues; yet Rogues is harboured among us sometimes almost publickly.

"Every honest Man is willing to give Part of his Substance to support Rulers, and Laws, to save the other Part from Rogues; and it is his Duty, as well as Right, to see and examine whether such Rulers abuse such trust;—Otherwise that Part so given may do more Hurt than Good.

"Even if we were all Rogues, in that Case we could not subsist; but would be obliged to frame Laws to make ourselves honest.—And the same Reasoning holds good against the Notion of a Mason Club.

"Thus, though it (meaning Justice) must be desired by all, or the greatest Number of Men, yet when Grievances of such publick Nature are not redressed, the Reason is, every Body's Business is no Body's.—Therefore, the following Proposal is offered to the Publick, *to wit,* Let each Neighbourhood throughout the County meet together, and appoint one or more Men to attend a general Meeting on the *Monday* before next *November* Court, at a suitable Place, where there is no Liquor, (at *Maddock's* Mill, if no Objection;) at which meeting, let it be judiciously enquired into, Whether the Freemen of this County labour under any Abuses of Power or not; and let the same be notified in Writing, if any is found, and the Matter freely conversed upon, and Proper Measures used for Amendment.

"This Method will certainly cause the wicked Men in Power to tremble; and there is no Damage can attend such a Meeting, nor nothing hinder it but a cowardly dastardly Spirit: Which if it does at this Time, while Liberty prevails, we must mutter and grumble under any Abuses of Power until such a noble Spirit prevails in our Posterity; For, take this as a Maxim, that while Men are Men, though you should see all those Sons of Liberty (Who has just now Redeemed us, from tyranny) set in Offices, and Vested with Power, they would soon corrupt again and oppress, if they were not called upon to give an Account of their Stewardship."

This Paper being publickly read at Court, in Audience of our Chiefs, Mr. *Loyd*, one of our Assembly-men, declared his Approbation of it, and the Rest Acknowledged it was reasonable.— And *Loyd*, altered the Day of Meeting to the 10th of *October*; and we being thus encouraged, Several Neighbourhoods held Meetings, and conjunctively Drew up the following Paper.

"AT a Meeting of the Neighbourhood of *Deep-River*, the 20th of *August*, 1766.—Unanimously agreed to appoint *W.— C—.* and *W—M—*to attend at a general Meeting on the 10th of *October* at *Maddock's* Mill, where they are judiciously to examine, whether the Freemen in this County labour under any Abuses of Power, and in particular to examine into the publick Tax, and inform themselves of Every Particular thereof, by what Laws and for what Uses it is laid, in order to Remove some Jealousies out of our Minds.

"And the Representatives, Vestry-men, and other Officers, are Requested to give the Members of the said Meeting what Information and Satisfaction they can.—So far as they value the Good- will of every honest Freeholder, and the executing Publick Offices, pleasant and delightsome."

In Pursuance hereof, about twelve Men met, but none of the Officers appeared (though they had frequently gave out Word beforehand, that they would be there—Late in the Day Mr. *James Watson* came alone, and brought Word from Colonel *Faning*, the other Representative, that he had always intended fully to meet us, till a Day or two ago he observed in one of our Papers the Word judiciously, which signified, he said, by a Court of Authority:—And had some other Objections, such as the Mill being no suitably Place. And concluding, that, in short (says he) Colonel *Fanning* Looks on it as an Insurrection, &c. &c.

One reason why we have so few men who concern themselves properly in maintaining our rights, is a very capital error that prevails among most dissenting sects, that this is a business that belongs to the world.

Christians is the light of the world—this is a most certain truth; and when the state is deprived of the light of so many christians as is among dissenters, her light becomes almost quite darkness.

For there is a certain proportion of christians in all ages who ought to be the light of the world, and to govern the churches. The government of their particular churches, set up among one another, is only helps to the government over the whole; and is no ways different in its nature. So that if it is necessary to choose christians to sit in synods, presbyteries, associations or yearly meetings, so it is necessary to have such in assemblies.

I shall now proceed to the 3d head, to consider of a method to remove these burdens.

When the time of an election coms on, and those men of the world, who rule by wealth, and whose business it is to corrupt their fellow subjects, and cheat them by flattery and corruption; out of their liberty come to ask your votes,—do you despise their offers, and say to them, Your money perish with you.

Can it be supposed that such men will take care of your interest who begin with debauching your morals, and ruining your souls by drunkenness?— Will that man have the least regard for your civil interest and property who first attempts to ruin your virtue?—What opinion must they have of such people, who, for a few days riot and [91] gluttony will sell their liberties, but that they are asses, that want to be watered?

While men are thus slaves to their lusts, they will never be free. Men that do so easily sell their souls will not value their country.—Where there is no virtue, there can be no liberty;—it is all licentiousness. What Issachars are such People who gives their votes for a man who neither fears God nor loves mankind! who, by the very method that he pursues to obtain his election, deserves to forfeit the favour and esteem of all lovers of virtue and honesty. Whom can they blame for their oppression but themselves; their own hands do make the fetters by which they are bound. Those who lay out so much money upon an election, has it in their view to make you pay for it in the round. Secondly, Forever despise that man who has betray'd the liberty of his constituents; this will lay a restraint upon the venal disposition of such as Incline to sell their country for Preferment. It would be a check to hinder them from going into the schemes of a Governor.—Never send those who depend on favour for a living, or on the perplexity of the laws, nor any who have ever discovered a want of good principles.

North-Carolinians, if you remain under these burdens, it must be your own faults;—you will stand recorded for asses to all generations if you do not assert your privileges before it is too late to recover them.

It is not disloyalty, nor injurious, to give Instructions to the candidates you choose, and take their solemn promise and obligation, that they will follow those instructions. This is far more noble than rioting a few days in drunkenness. Assemblymen are your servants, and it is but reasonable they be made accountable to you for their conduct.

Mark any clerk, lawyer or Scotch merchant, or any sect of men, who are connected with certain companies, callings and combinations, whose interests jar with the interest of the publick good.—And when they come to solicit you with invitations to entertainments, &c. shun them as you would the pestilence.—Send a man who is the choice of the country, and not one who sets up himself, and is the choice of a party; whose interest clashes with the good of the publick. Send a christian, or a man whom, you think in your consciences is a real honest good man;—for this is the christian, let his belief, as to creeds and opinions be what it will.

Beware of being corrupted by flattery, for such men study the art of managing those springs of action within us, and will easily make us slaves by our own consent.—There is more passions than one that these men work upon; there is drunkenness, love of honour, flattery of great men, love of interest, preferment, or some worldly advantage.—They, by taking hold of these springs within us, insensibly lead us into bondage.

When any man, who has much of this world, so that his interest weighs down a great number of his poor neighbours, and employs that interest contrary to the principles of virtue and honesty, any person of the least discernment may see he is a curse to the nation.

When men's votes is solicited, or over-awed by some superiors, the election is not free.—Men in power and of large fortunes threaten us out of our liberty, by the weight of their interest.

North-Carolinians, Are you sensible what you are doing, when, for some small favour, or sordid gratification, you sell your votes to such as want to inslave your country?—you are publishing to all the world, that you are asses.—You are despised already by the sister colonies.—You are hurting your trade; for men of public [93] generous spirits, who have fortunes to promote trade, are discouraged from coming among you.

You are also encouraging your own assemblymen to inslave you; for when they, who are elected, see that those who had a right to elect them had no concern for their true interest, but that they were elected by chance, or power of their own, or some great man's interest, such men will be the more ready to vote in the assembly with as much indifference about the interest of their constituents as they had in voting them in.

You may always suspect every one who overawes or wants to corrupt you; the same person will load you with burdens. You may easily find out who was tools to the governor, and who concurred in past assemblies to lay burdens on us, the edifice, paying the troops, the associates salaries, &c. Send not one of them ever any more; let them stand as beacons; set a mark on them, that ages to come may hold their memories in obhorrence.

May not Carolina cry and utter her voice, and say, That she will have her publick accounts settled; that she will have her lawyers and officers subject to the laws.—That she will pay no taxes but what are agreeable to law.—That she will pay no officer nor lawyer any more fees than the law allows.—That she will hold conferences to consult her representatives, and give them instructions; and make it a condition of their election, that they assert their privileges in the assembly, and cry aloud for appeal of all oppressive laws.

Finally, My brethren, whenever it is in your power, take care to have the house of assembly filled with good honest and faithful men; and encourage and instruct them on all occasions: And be sure to let your elections be no expense to them.

Reference: William K. Boyd (ed.), *Some Eighteenth-Century Tracts Concerning North Carolina* (Raleigh: Edwards and Broughton Company, 1927), 254–259, 322–324.

ADDRESS OF THE MECHANICS OF NEW YORK, JUNE 14, 1776

Elected Delegates: With due confidence in the declaration which you lately made to the Chairman of our General Committee that you are, at all times, ready and willing to attend to every request of your "constituents or any part of them"; we, the Mechanicks in Union, though a very inconsiderable part of your constituents, beg leave to represent that one of the clauses in your Resolve respecting the establishment of a new form of Government is erroneously construed, and for that reason may serve the most dangerous purposes; for it is well known how indefatigable the emissaries of the British Government are in the pursuit of every scheme which is likely to bring disgrace upon our ruler, and ruin upon us all. At the same time we cheerfully acknowledge that the genuine spirit of liberty which animates the other parts of that Resolve, did not permit us to interpret it in any other sense than that which is the most obvious, and likewise the most favourable to the natural rights of man.

We could not, we never can, believe you intended that the future delegates or yourselves should be vested with the power of framing a new Constitution for this Colony, and that its inhabitants at large should not exercise the right which God has given them, in common with all men, to judge whether it be consistent with their interest to accept or reject a Constitution framed for that State of which they are members. This is the birthright of every man, to whatever state he may belong. There he is, or ought to be,

by inalienable right, a co-legislator with all the other members of that community. Conscious of our own want of abilities, we are, alas! but too sensible that every individual is not qualified for assisting in the framing of a Constitution. But that share of common sense which the Almighty has bountifully distributed amongst mankind in general, is sufficient to quicken every one's feeling, and enable him to judge rightly what degree of safety and what advantages he is likely to enjoy, or be deprived of, under any Constitution proposed to him.

For this reason, should a preposterous confidence in the abilities and integrity of our future Delegates delude us into measures which might imply a renunciation of our inalienable right to ratify our laws, we believe that your wisdom, your patriotism, your own interest, nay, your ambition itself, would urge you to exert all the powers of persuasion you possess, and try every method which, in your opinion, would deter us from perpetrating that impious and frantick act of self-destruction; for as it would precipitate us into a state of absolute slavery, the lawful power which till now you have received from your constituents to be exercised over a free people, would be annihilated by that unnatural act. It might probably accelerate our political death; but it must immediately cause your own.

Reference: Peter Force, *American Archives,* 4th Ser., Vol. VI (Washington: GPO, 1835), 895.

32

Toward Independence and Unity

This third and final chapter of Part VI takes the colonists into united independence. (A perceptive eye will notice continued dissension over colony-wide unity in these documents.) In the first document, the separate colonial and revolutionary legislatures send delegates to the Continental Congress. A most stirring, if unique, document in support of unity is the famous Suffolk Resolve from Massachusetts in September 1774, which set out its grievances against oppressive British actions and declared that all colonies should come together in mutual defense.

As momentum gathered for independence, the delegates to the Continental Congress began to write about national grievances. On October 12, 1774, a Congressional committee made up of Virginia's Richard Henry Lee and New York's William Livingston, composed a memorial of grievances. In May 1775, a committee from Mecklenburg County, North Carolina, declared that the county joined other colonies in uniting their governments to withstand British oppression. But the North Carolina delegates in the Continental Congress wrote that, although all the colonies had united, some took on more responsibility than others. They cautioned that all of the colonies must stand together to protect their governing systems.

By November 1775, Congress had begun to respond to inquiries by some colonies about forming revolutionary governments. To the provincial convention of New Hampshire the Congress recommended the formation of a government separate from Britain. Then, in November 1775, the Continental Congress called on all colonies to "adopt such a government as shall, in the opinion of the representatives of the people, best conduce to the happiness and safety of their constituents in particular, and America in general."

In December 1775, worry over forming the new state governments came from the frightened citizenry of Portsmouth, New Hampshire, because they feared other new states would not defend them from British aggression. But, said those citizens, if Congress forms a new national government, they will go along. Indeed, Congress had moved on. On May 15, 1776, the Congress took up a committee report that accused the King of supporting Parliamentary aggression against the colonial and newly formed legislative governments. The people of the colonies rejected the governance authority of the King of England. Lastly, a Declaration of Independence on July 4, 1776 described the British threat to the colonial governments and cut all ties with that country. Thomas Jefferson's stirring words declared the United States a separate republic. That Declaration summed up the form of governance and the freedom-loving values of the people that had been created throughout the course of many years. Above all, the Declaration said that colonial leaders knew, or the people had taught them, that governance derived "their just powers from the consent of the governed."

That most essential part of our governing principles and practice would be tested (see Volume III), and perhaps continues to be tested today.

COLONIES SEND DELEGATES TO THE CONTINENTAL CONGRESS, JUNE–SEPTEMBER 1774

For the Province of New Hampshire:

At a meeting of the deputies appointed by the several towns in this province, held at Exeter, in the county of Rockingham, 21st July, 1774, for the election of delegates, on behalf of this province, to join the General Congress proposed. Present, 85 members.

The Honble. John Wentworth, Esqr., in the chair.

Voted, That Major John Sullivan, and Colo. Nathaniel Folsom, Esqrs., be appointed and impowered as delegates, on the part of this province, to attend and assist in the General Congress of delegates from the other Colonies, at such time and place as may be appointed, to devise, consult, and adopt measures, as may have the most likely tendency to extricate the Colonies from their present difficulties; to secure and perpetuate their rights, liberties, and privileges, and to restore that peace, harmony, & mutual confidence which once happily subsisted between the parent country and her Colonies.

Attested:
J. WENTWORTH, *Chairman.*

For the Province of Massachusetts-Bay:

In the House of Representatives, June 17th, 1774.

This house having duly considered, and being deeply affected with the unhappy differences which have long subsisted and are encreasing between Great Britain and the American Colonies, do resolve, that a meeting of Committees from the several Colonies on this Continent is highly expedient and necessary, to consult upon the present state of the Colonies, and the miseries to which they are and must be reduced by the operation of certain acts of Parliament respecting America,

and to deliberate and determine upon wise and proper measures, to be by them recommended to all the Colonies, for the recovery and establishment of their just rights & liberties, civil & religious, and the restoration of union & harmony between Great Britain and the Colonies, most ardently desired by all good men. Therefore, Resolved, That the Honble. James Bowdoin, esqr., the Honble. Thomas Cushing, esqr., Mr. Samuel Adams, John Adams, & Robert Treat Paine, esqrs., be, and they are hereby appointed a Committee on the part of this province, for the purpose aforesaid, any three of whom to be a quorum, to meet such committees or delegates from the other Colonies as have been or may be appointed, either by their respective houses of Burgesses, or representatives, or by convention, or by the committees of correspondence appointed by the respective houses of Assembly, in the city of Philadelphia, or any other place that shall be judged most suitable by the Committee, on the first day of September next; & that the Speaker of the House be directed, in a letter to the speakers of the house of Burgesses or representatives in the several Colonies, to inform them of the substance of these Resolves.

Attested:
SAMUEL ADAMS, *Clerk.*

For Rhode Island:

By the Honble. Joseph Wanton, esqr., governor, captain-general, and commander in chief of and over the English Colony of Rhode-Island and Providence plantations, in New England in America.

To the Honourable Stephen Hopkins, esqr., and the Honourable Samuel Ward, esqr., greeting:

Whereas the General Assembly of the Colony aforesaid have nominated and appointed you, the said Stephen Hopkins & Samuel Ward, to represent the people of this Colony in general congress of representatives from this and the other Colonies, at such time and place as should be agreed upon by the major part of the committees appointed, or to be appointed by the colonies in general:

I do therefore hereby authorize, impower, and commissionate you, the said Stephen Hopkins & Samuel Ward, to repair to the city of Philadelphia, it being the place agreed upon by the major part of the colonies; and there, in behalf of this Colony, to meet and join with the commissioners or delegates from the other colonies, in consulting upon proper measures to obtain a repeal of the several acts of the British parliament, for levying taxes upon his Majesty's subjects in America, without their consent, and particularly an act lately passed for blocking up the port of Boston, and upon proper measures to establish the rights and liberties of the Colonies, upon a just and solid foundation, agreable to the instructions given you by the general Assembly.

[L. S.] GIVEN under my hand and the seal of the said colony, this tenth day of August, in the year of our Lord 1774, and the 14th of the reign of his most sacred Majesty George the third, by the grace of God, king of Great Britain, & so forth.

Signed
J. WANTON.
By his honour's command,
HENRY WARD, *Secy.*

For Connecticut:

In the House of Representatives of the Colony of Connecticut,
June 3d, 1774.

Whereas a congress of commissioners from the several British colonies in America, is proposed by some of our neighbouring colonies, and thought necessary; and whereas it may be found expedient that such Congress should be convened before the next Session of this Assembly:

Resolved, by this house, that the committee of correspondence be, and they are hereby empowered, on application to them made, or from time to time, as may be found necessary, to appoint a suitable number to attend such congres, or convention of commissioners, or committees of the several Colonies in British America, and

the persons thus to be chosen shall be, and they are hereby directed, in behalf of this Colony, to attend such Congress; to consult and advise on proper measures for advancing the best good of the Colonies, and such conferences, from time to time, to report to this house.

True Extract & Copy from the Journal of the house.

Attest
WILLIAM WILLIAMS, *Clerk.*

Colony of Connecticut, ss.

NEW LONDON, *July 13th, 1774.*
At a meeting of the Committee of Correspondence for this Colony:

The honourable EBENEZER SILLIMAN, Esqr. in the chair:

The honble. Eliphalet Dyer, the honble. William Samuel Johnston, Erastus Wolcott, Silas Deane, and Richard Law, Esqrs. were nominated pursuant to the act of the honourable House of Representatives of the said Colony, at their session in May last, either three of which are hereby authorised and empowered, in behalf of this Colony, to attend the general Congress of the colonies proposed to be held at Philadelphia, on the first day of September next, or at such other time & place as shall be agreed on by the Colonies, to consult and advise with the Commissioners or Committees of the several English Colonies in America, on proper measures for advancing the best good of the Colonies.

(Signed:)
Ebenezer Silliman, William Williams, Benjamin Payne, Erastus Wolcott, Joseph Trumbull, Samuel H. Parsons, Nathan. Wales, jun. Silas Deane.

Colony of Connecticut, ss.

HARTFORD, *August* [ ], *1774.*
At a Meeting of the Committee of Correspondence for this colony:
Erastus Wolcott, Chairman.

The honourable William Samuel Johnston1, Erastus Wolcott, and Richard Law, Esqrs. nominated by this committee at their meeting at

New-London, on the 13th of July last, as persons proper to attend the general congress, to be held at Philadelphia, on the 1st. of September next, as by said appointment, being unable, by reason of previous engagements and the state of their health, to attend said Congress, on behalf of this colony; the honble. Roger Sherman, & Joseph Trumbull, Esqrs. were nominated in the place of the aforesaid gentlemen, as persons proper to attend said Congress, in behalf of this Colony, either of which are empowered, with the honble. Eliphalet Dyer, and Silas Deane, Esqr. for that purpose.

(Signed)
William Williams, Benjamin Payne, Joseph Trumbull, Nathl. Wales, Jun, Sam. H. Parsons, Samuel Bishop.

For New York:

By duly certifyed polls, taken by proper persons, in seven wards, it appears that James Duane, John Jay, Philip Livingston, Isaac Low, & John Alsop, Esqrs. were elected as Delegates for the City & County of New York, to attend the Congress at Philadelphia, the first day of September next; and at a meeting of the Committees of several districts in the County of West-Chester, the same gentlemen were appointed to represent that County. Also by a Letter from Jacob Lansing, Junr., chairman, in behalf of the Committee for Albany, it appears, that that City & County had adopted the same for their delegates. By another letter,1 it appears, that the Committees from the several districts in the County of Duchess, had likewise adopted the same as delegates to represent that County in Congress, & that Committees of other towns approve of them as their delegates.

By a writing duly attested, it appears, the County of Suffolk, in the Colony of New York, have appointed Colo. William Floyd, to represent them at the Congress.

For New Jersey:

To James Kinsey, William Livingston, John D'hart, Stephen Crane, & Richard Smith, Esqrs. each and every of you:

The Committees, appointed by the several Counties of the Colony of New Jersey, to nominate Deputies, to represent the same in the general congress of deputies from the other Colonies in America, convened at the City of New Brunswick, have nominated and appointed, and do hereby nominate and appoint you, and each of you, deputies, to represent the Colony of New Jersey in the said general congress.

In testimony whereof, the Chairmen of the several Committees here met, have hereunto set their hands, this twenty third day of July, in the fourteenth year of the reign of our Sovereign Lord George the third, and in the year of our Lord 1774.

(Signed)
William P. Smith [Essex County], Jacob Ford [Morris County], John Moores [Middlesex County], Robert Johnson, Robert Field, Robert Friend Price, Peter Zabriskie [Bergen County], Samuel Tucker [Hunterdon County], Edward Taylor [Monmouth County], Hendrick Fisher, Archibald Stewart, Thomas Anderson, Abra Brown, Mark Thompson.

For Pennsylvania:

Extract from votes of the assembly.
FRIDAY, *July 22d. 1774, a. m.*
The Committee of the whole house, taking into their most serious consideration, the unfortunate differences which have long subsisted between Great-Britain and the American Colonies, and been greatly increased by the operation and effects of divers late acts of the British Parliament:

Resolved, N.C.D. That there is an absolute necessity that a Congress of Deputies from the several Colonies, be held as soon as conveniently may be, to consult together upon the present unhappy State of the Colonies, and to form and adopt a plan for the purposes of obtaining redress of American grievances, ascertaining American rights upon the most solid and constitutional principles, and for establishing that Union & harmony between Great-Britain and the Colonies, which is indispensably necessary to the welfare and happiness of both.

Eodem Die, P.M.

The house resumed the consideration of the resolve from the Committee of the whole house, and, after some debate thereon, adopting and confirming the same,

Resolved, N.C.D. That the honble. Joseph Galloway, speaker; Samuel Rhoads, Thomas Mifflin, Chas Humphreys, John Morton, George Ross, & Edward Biddle, Esqrs, be and they are hereby appointed a Committee, on the part of this Province, for the purposes aforesaid, and that they, or any four of them, do meet such Committees or Delegates from the other Colonies, as have been or may be appointed, either by their respective houses of representatives, or by convention, or by the provincial or Colony Committees, at such time and place, as shall be generally agreed on by such Committees.

For the Three Counties Newcastle, Kent, & Sussex, on Delaware:

August 1, 1774, A.M.

The Representatives of the freemen of the Government of the Counties of Newcastle, Kent, & Sussex, on Delaware, met at Newcastle, in pursuance of circular letters from the Speaker of the house, who was requested to write and forward the same to the several Members of Assembly, by the Committees of correspondence for the several Counties aforesaid, chosen and appointed for that among other purposes, by the freeholders and freemen of the said Counties respectively: And having chosen a Chairman, and read the resolves of the three respective Counties, and sundry letters from the Committees of correspondence along the Continent, they unanimously entered into the following resolution, viz:

We, the representatives aforesaid, by virtue of the power delegated to us, as aforesaid, taking into our most serious consideration the several acts of the British parliament, for restraining manufactures in his Majesty's colonies and plantations in North-America,—for taking away the property of the Colonists without their participation or consent,—for the introduction of the arbitrary powers of excise into the Customs here,—for the making all revenue excises liable without Jury, and under the decision of a single dependant Judge,—for the trial, in England, of persons accused of capital crimes, committed in the Colonies,—for the shutting up the port of Boston,—for new-modelling the government of the Massachusetts-Bay, and the operation of the same on the property, liberty, and lives of the Colonists; and also considering, that the most eligible mode of determining upon the premises, and of endeavouring to procure relief and redress of our grievances, would have been by us assembled in a Legislative capacity, but that as the house had adjourned to the thirtieth day of September next, and it is not to be expected, that his Honour the Governor would call us, by writs of summons, on this occasion, having refused to do the like in his other Province of Pennsylvania; the next most proper method, of answering the expectations and desires of our Constituents, and of contributing our aid to the general cause of America, is to appoint commissioners or deputies in behalf of the people of this government, to meet and act with those appointed by the other provinces, in general Congress; and we do, therefore, unanimously nominate and appoint Cæsar Rodney, Thomas M'Kean, and George Read, Esqrs. or any two of them, deputies, on the part and behalf of this government, in a general continental congress, proposed to be held at the city of Philadelphia, on the first Monday in September next, or at any other time or place that may be generally agreed on, then and there, to consult and advise with the deputies from the other colonies, and to determine upon all such prudent and lawful measures, as may be judged most expedient for the Colonies immediately and unitedly to adopt, in order to obtain relief for an oppressed people, and the redress of our general grievances.

Signed by order of the convention,
CÆSAR RODNEY, *Chairman.*

For Maryland:

At a Meeting of the Committees appointed by the several Counties of the province of Maryland, at the City of Annapolis, the 22d day of June, 1774, and continued by adjournment, from day to day, till the 25th of the same month:

Matthew Tilghman, Esqr. in the Chair:
John Ducket, Clerk:

Resolved, That Matthew Tilghman, Thomas Johnson, Junr., Robert Goldsborough, William Paca, and Samuel Chase, Esqrs. or any two or more of them, be deputies for this province, to attend a General Congress of deputies from the Colonies, at such time and place as may be agreed on, to effect one general plan of conduct, operating on the commercial connexion of the colonies with the mother country, for the relief of Boston, and preservation of American liberty.

For Virginia:

Monday the 1st of August, in the year of our Lord, 1774.

At a general meeting of Delegates from the different Counties in this Colony, convened in the city of Williamsburgh, to take under their consideration the present critical and alarming situation of the Continent of North-America:

The Honourable Peyton Randolph in the Chair:

It was unanimously resolved; that it is the opinion of this meeting, that it will be highly conducive to the security and happiness of the British Empire, that a general congress of deputies from all the Colonies, assemble as quickly as the nature of their situations will admit, to consider of the most proper and effectual manner of so operating on the commercial connexion of the colonies with the Mother Country, as to procure redress for the much injured province of Massachusetts-Bay, to secure British America from the ravage and ruin of arbitrary taxes, and speedily as possible to procure the return of that harmony and Union, so beneficial to the whole Empire, and so ardently desired by all British America.

Friday, August 5th, 1774.

The Meeting proceeded to the choice of Delegates, to represent this Colony in general Congress, when the honble. Peyton Randolph, Richard Henry Lee, George Washington, Patrick Henry, Richard Bland, Benjamin Harrison, & Edmund Pendleton, Esqrs. were appointed for that purpose.

For South-Carolina

In the commons, house of Assembly, Tuesday, the 2d day of August, 1774.

Colonel Powell acquainted the house, that during the recess of this house, viz: on the 6th, 7th & 8th days of July last at a general meeting of the inhabitants of this colony, they having under consideration the acts of parliament lately passed with regard to the port of Boston and Colony of Massachusetts-Bay as well as other American grievances, had nominated and appointed the honble. Henry Middleton, John Rutledge, Thomas Lynch, Christopher Gadsden,& Edward Rutledge, Esqrs. deputies on the part and behalf of this Colony, to meet the deputies of the other Colonies of North America, in general Congress, the first Monday in September next at Philadelphia, or at any other time and place that may be generally agreed on, there to consider the acts lately passed, and bills depending in parliament with regard to the port of Boston and Colony of Massachusetts-Bay, which acts & bills in the precedent and consequences affect the whole Continent of America—also the grievances under which America labours, by reason of the several acts of parliament that impose taxes or duties for raising a revenue, and lay unnecessary restraints and burdens on Trade; and of the statutes, parliamentary acts, and royal instructions, which make an invidious distinction between his majesty's subjects in Great-Britain and America, with full power and authority to concert, agree to, and effectually prosecute such legal measures, as in the opinion of the said deputies, and of the deputies so to be assembled, shall be most likely to obtain a repeal of the said acts, and a redress of those grievances: and thereupon moved that this house do resolve to recognize, ratify, and confirm said appointment of the deputies for the purposes aforesaid.

Resolved, N.C.D. That this house do recognize, ratify, and confirm the appointment of the said deputies for the purposes mentioned in the said motion.

Attested,
THOMAS FARR, Junr. *Clerk.*

A motion was made and seconded that a Committee be appointed to draw up some rules of conduct to be observed by the Congress in debating and determining questions that come under consideration, But after some debate another motion was made and seconded that the farther consideration of this question be deferred untill tomorrow, which was carried by a large majority. Whereupon a motion was made to adjourn, and the vote (?) being put, agreed that the Congress be adjourned to meet at this place tomorrow morning 10 o Clock.

Tuesday, September 6, 1774

At 10 o'clock a. m.
The Congress met according to adjournment.
Present: The same members as yesterday, and moreover, from the colony of Virginia, Richard

Henry Lee, Esqr., from counties of Newcastle, Kent and Sussex on Delaware, Thomas McKean, Esqr.

The Congress, resuming the consideration of appointing a Committee to draw up rules of conduct to be observed in debating and determining the questions, that come under consideration, after a good deal of debate the motion was diverted to facts

1. Shall a Committee be appointed to draw up rules for the proceedings of this Congress. Carried in the Negative.

2. Shall a Committee be appointed to fix the mode of voting by allowing to each province one or more votes, so as to establish an equitable representation according to the respective importance of each Colony. Carried in the negative.

Upon motion the Question was put and

Resolved, That in determining questions in this Congress, each Colony or Province shall have one Vote.—The Congress not being possess'd of, or at present able to procure proper materials for ascertaining the importance of each Colony.

Reference: Worthington Chauncey Ford (ed.), *Journal of the Continental Congress, 1774–1789,* Vol. I (Washington: GPO, 1904).

SUFFOLK RESOLVES, MASSACHUSETTS, SEPTEMBER 9, 1774

At a meeting of the delegates of every town & district in the county of Suffolk, on tuesday the 6th of Septr., at the house of Mr. Richard Woodward, of Deadham, & by adjournment, at the house of Mr. [Daniel] Vose, of Milton, on Friday the 9th instant, Joseph Palmer, esq. being chosen moderator, and William Thompson, esq. clerk, a committee was chosen to bring in a report to the convention, and the following being several times read, and put paragraph by paragraph, was unanimously voted, viz.

Whereas the power but not the justice, the vengeance but not the wisdom of Great-Britain, which of old persecuted, scourged, and exiled our fugitive parents from their native shores, now

pursues us, their guiltless children, with unrelenting severity: And whereas, this, then savage and uncultivated desart, was purchased by the toil and treasure, or acquired by the blood and valor of those our venerable progenitors; to us they bequeathed the dearbought inheritance, to our care and protection they consigned it, and the most sacred obligations are upon us to transmit the glorious purchase, unfettered by power, unclogged with shackles, to our innocent and beloved offspring. On the fortitude, on the wisdom and on the exertions of this important day, is suspended the fate of this new world, and of unborn millions. If a boundless extent of continent, swarming with millions, will tamely submit to live, move and have their being at the arbitrary will of a licentious minister, they basely yield to voluntary slavery, and future generations shall load their memories with incessant execrations.—On the other hand, if we arrest the hand which would ransack our pockets, if we disarm the parricide which points the dagger to our bosoms, if we nobly defeat that fatal edict which proclaims a power to frame laws for us in all cases whatsoever, thereby entailing the endless and numberless curses of slavery upon us, our heirs and their heirs forever; if we successfully resist that unparalleled usurpation of unconstitutional power, whereby our capital is robbed of the means of life; whereby the streets of Boston are thronged with military executioners; whereby our coasts are lined and harbours crouded with ships of war; whereby the charter of the colony, that sacred barrier against the encroachments of tyranny, is mutilated and, in effect, annihilated; whereby a murderous law is framed to shelter villains from the hands of justice; whereby the unalienable and inestimable inheritance, which we derived from nature, the constitution of Britain, and the privileges warranted to us in the charter of the province, is totally wrecked, annulled, and vacated, posterity will acknowledge that virtue which preserved them free and happy; and while we enjoy the rewards and blessings of the faithful, the torrent of panegyrists will roll our reputations to that latest period, when the streams of time shall be absorbed in the abyss of eternity.—Therefore, we have resolved, and do *resolve,*

1. That whereas his majesty, George the Third, is the rightful successor to the throne of Great-Britain, and justly entitled to the allegiance of the British realm, and agreeable to compact, of the English colonies in America—therefore, we, the heirs and successors of the first planters of this colony, do cheerfully acknowledge the said George the Third to be our rightful sovereign, and that said covenant is the tenure and claim on which are founded our allegiance and submission.

2. That it is an indispensable duty which we owe to God, our country, ourselves and posterity, by all lawful ways and means in our power to maintain, defend and preserve those civil and religious rights and liberties, for which many of our fathers fought, bled and died, and to hand them down entire to future generations.

3. That the late acts of the British parliament for blocking up the harbour of Boston, for altering the established form of government in this colony, and for screening the most flagitious violators of the laws of the province from a legal trial, are gross infractions of those rights to which we are justly entitled by the laws of nature, the British constitution, and the charter of the province.

4. That no obedience is due from this province to either or any part of the acts above-mentioned, but that they be rejected as the attempts of a wicked administration to enslave America.

5. That so long as the justices of our superior court of judicature, court of assize, &c. and inferior court of common pleas in this county are appointed, or hold their places, by any other tenure than that which the charter and the laws of the province direct, they must be considered as under undue influence, and are therefore unconstitutional officers, and, as such, no regard ought to be paid to them by the people of this county.

6. That if the justices of the superior court of judicature, assize, &c. justices of the court of common pleas, or of the general sessions of the peace, shall sit and act during their present disqualified state, this county will support, and bear harmless, all sheriffs and their deputies, constables, jurors and other officers who shall refuse to carry into execution the orders of said courts; and, as far as possible, to prevent the many inconveniencies which must be occasioned by a suspension of the courts of justice, we do most earnestly recommend it to all creditors, that they shew all reasonable and even generous forbearance to their debtors; and to all debtors, to pay their just debts with all possible speed, and if any disputes relative to debts or trespasses shall arise, which cannot be settled by the parties, we recommend it to them to submit all such causes to arbitration; and it is our opinion that the contending parties or either of them, who shall refuse so to do, ought to be considered as co-operating with the enemies of this country.

7. That it be recommended to the collectors of taxes, constables and all other officers, who have public monies in their hands, to retain the same, and not to make any payment thereof to the provincial county treasurer until the civil government of the province is placed upon a constitutional foundation, or until it shall otherwise be ordered by the proposed provincial Congress.

8. That the persons who have accepted seats at the council board, by virtue of a mandamus from the King, in conformity to the late act of the British parliament, entitled, an act for the regulating the government of the Massachusetts-Bay, have acted in direct violation of the duty they owe to their country, and have thereby given great and just offence to this people; therefore, resolved, that this county do recommend it to all persons, who have so highly offended by accepting said departments, and have not already publicly resigned their seats at the council board, to make public resignations of their places at said board, on or before the 20th day of this instant, September; and that all persons refusing so to do, shall, from and after said day, be considered by this county as obstinate and incorrigible enemies to this country.

9. That the fortifications begun and now carrying on upon Boston Neck, are justly alarming to this county, and gives us reason to apprehend some hostile intention against that town, more especially as the commander in chief has, in a very extraordinary manner, removed the powder from the magazine at Charlestown, and has also forbidden the keeper of the magazine at Boston, to deliver out to the owners, the powder, which they had lodged in said magazine.

10. That the late act of parliament for establishing the Roman Catholic religion and the French laws in that extensive country, now called Canada, is dangerous in an extreme degree to the Protestant religion and to the civil rights and liberties of all America; and, therefore, as men and Protestant Christians, we are indispensably obliged to take all proper measures for our security.

11. That whereas our enemies have flattered themselves that they shall make an easy prey of this numerous, brave and hardy people, from an apprehension that they are unacquainted with military discipline; we, therefore, for the honour, defence and security of this county and province, advise, as it has been recommended to take away all commissions from the officers of the militia, that those who now hold commissions, or such other persons, be elected in each town as officers in the militia, as shall be judged of sufficient capacity for that purpose, and who have evidenced themselves the inflexible friends to the rights of the people; and that the inhabitants of those towns and districts, who are qualified, do use their utmost diligence to acquaint themselves with the art of war as soon as possible, and do, for that purpose, appear under arms at least once every week.

12. That during the present hostile appearances on the part of Great-Britain, notwithstanding the many insults and oppressions which we most sensibly resent, yet, nevertheless, from our affection to his majesty, which we have at all times evidenced, we are determined to act merely upon the defensive, so long as such conduct may be vindicated by reason and the principles of self-preservation, but no longer.

13. That, as we understand it has been in contemplation to apprehend sundry persons of this county, who have rendered themselves conspicuous in contending for the violated rights and liberties of their countrymen; we do recommend, should such an audacious measure be put in practice, to seize and keep in safe custody, every servant of the present tyrannical and unconstitutional government throughout the county and province, until the persons so apprehended be liberated from the hands of our adversaries, and restored safe and uninjured to their respective friends and families.

14. That until our rights are fully restored to us, we will, to the utmost of our power, and we recommend the same to the other counties, to withhold all commercial intercourse with Great-Britain, Ireland, and the West-Indies, and abstain from the consumption of British merchandise and manufactures, and especially of East-India teas and piece goods, with such additions, alterations, and exceptions only, as the General Congress of the colonies may agree to.

15. That under our present circumstances, it is incumbent on us to encourage arts and manufactures amongst us, by all means in our power, and that be and are hereby appointed a committee, to consider of the best ways and means to promote and establish the same, and to report to this convention as soon as may be.

16. That the exigencies of our public affairs, demand that a provincial Congress be called to consult such measures as may be adopted, and vigorously executed by the whole people; and we do recommend it to the several towns in this county, to chuse members for such a provincial Congress, to be holden at Concord, on the second Tuesday of October, next ensuing.

17. That this county, confiding in the wisdom and integrity of the continental Congress, now sitting at Philadelphia, pay all due respect and submission to such measures as may be recommended by them to the colonies, for the restoration and establishment of our just rights, civil and religious, and for renewing that harmony and union between Great-Britain and the colonies, so earnestly wished for by all good men.

18. That whereas the universal uneasiness which prevails among all orders of men, arising from the wicked and oppressive measures of the present administration, may influence some unthinking persons to commit outrage upon private property; we would heartily recommend to all persons of this community, not to engage in any routs, riots, or licentious attacks upon the properties of any person whatsoever, as being subversive of all order and government; but, by a steady, manly, uniform, and persevering opposition, to convince our enemies, that in a contest so important, in a cause so solemn,

our conduct shall be such as to merit the approbation of the wise, and the admiration of the brave and free of every age and of every country.

19. That should our enemies, by any sudden manœuvres, render it necessary to ask the aid and assistance of our brethren in the country, some one of the committee of correspondence, or a select man of such town, or the town adjoining, where such hostilities shall commence, or shall be expected to commence, shall despatch couriers with written messages to the select men, or committees of correspondence, of the several towns in the vicinity, with a written account of such matter, who shall despatch others to committees more remote, until proper and sufficient assistance be obtained, and that the expense of said couriers be defrayed by the county, until it shall be otherwise ordered by the provincial Congress.1

At a meeting of delegates from the several towns and districts in the county of Suffolk, held at Milton, on Friday, the 9th day of September, 1774—*Voted,*

That Dr. Joseph Warren, of Boston, &c.2 be a committee to wait on his excellency the governor, to inform him, that this county are alarmed at the fortifications making on Boston Neck, and to remonstrate against the same, and the repeated insults offered by the soldiery, to persons passing and repassing into that town, and to confer with him upon those subjects.

Attest,
WILLIAM THOMPSON, *Clerk*.

Reference: Worthington Chauncey Ford (ed.), *Journal of the Continental Congress, 1774–1789*, Vol. I (Washington: GPO, 1904).

RESOLUTION AND DECLARATION OF RIGHTS IN CONTINENTAL CONGRESS, OCTOBER 1774

October 4, 1774

Resolved unanimously, That a memorial be prepared to the people of British America, stating to them the necessity of a firm, united, and invariable observation of the measures recommended by the Congress, as they tender the invaluable

rights and liberties derived to them from the laws and constitution of their country.

Also an address to the people of Great Britain.

Mr. [Richard Henry] Lee, Mr. [William] Livingston, and Mr. [John] Jay are appointed a committee to prepare a draught of the memorial & address.

October 12, 1774

The Congress met according to adjournment.

The committee appointed to prepare a plan for carrying into effect, the non-importation, non-consumption, and non-exportation agreement, brought in a report, which was read:

Ordered, That the same do lie on the table, for the perusal of the members:

The Congress then resumed the consideration of the rights and grievances of these colonies, and after deliberating on the subject this & the following day, adjourned till Friday.

October 14, 1774

The Congress met according to adjournment, & resuming the consideration of the subject under debate—came into the following Resolutions:

Whereas, since the close of the last war, the British parliament, claiming a power of right to bind the people of America, by statute in all cases whatsoever, hath in some acts expressly imposed taxes on them, and in others, under various pretences, but in fact for the purpose of raising a revenue, hath imposed rates and duties payable in these colonies, established a board of commissioners, with unconstitutional powers, and extended the jurisdiction of courts of Admiralty, not only for collecting the said duties, but for the trial of causes merely arising within the body of a county.

And whereas, in consequence of other statutes, judges, who before held only estates at will in their offices, have been made dependant on the Crown alone for their salaries, and standing armies kept in times of peace:

And it has lately been resolved in Parliament, that by force of a statute, made in the thirty-fifth year of the reign of king Henry the eighth, colonists may be transported to England, and tried there upon accusations for treasons, and misprisions, or concealments of treasons committed in the colonies; and by a late statute, such trial have been directed in cases therein mentioned.

And whereas, in the last session of parliament, three statutes were made; "one, intituled "An act to discontinue, in such manner and for such time as therein mentioned, the landing and discharging, lading, or shipping of goods, wares & merchandise, at the town, and within the harbour of Boston, in the province of Massachusetts-bay, in North-America;" another, intituled "An act for the better regulating the government the province of the Massachusetts-bay in New-England;" and another, intituled "An act for the impartial administration of justice, in the cases of persons questioned for any act done by them in the execution of the law, or for the suppression of riots and tumults, in the province of the Massachusetts-bay, in New-England." And another statute was then made, "for making more effectual provision for the government of the province of Quebec, &c." All which statutes are impolitic, unjust, and cruel, as well as unconstitutional, and most dangerous and destructive of American rights.

And whereas, Assemblies have been frequently dissolved, contrary to the rights of the people, when they attempted to deliberate on grievances; and their dutiful, humble, loyal, & reasonable petitions to the crown for redress, have been repeatedly treated with contempt, by his majesty's ministers of state:

The good people of the several Colonies of New-hampshire, Massachusetts-bay, Rhode-island and Providence plantations, Connecticut, New-York, New-Jersey, Pennsylvania, Newcastle, Kent and Sussex on Delaware, Maryland, Virginia, North Carolina, and South Carolina, justly alarmed at these arbitrary proceedings of parliament and administration, have severally elected, constituted, and appointed deputies to meet and sit in general congress, in the city of Philadelphia, in order to obtain such establishment, as that their religion, laws, and liberties may not be subverted:

Whereupon the deputies so appointed being now assembled, in a full and free representation of these Colonies, taking into their most serious consideration, the best means of attaining the ends aforesaid, do, in the first place, as Englishmen, their ancestors in like cases have usually done, for asserting and vindicating their rights and liberties, declare,

That the inhabitants of the English Colonies in North America, by the immutable laws of nature, the principles of the English constitution, and the several charters or compacts, have the following Rights:

Resolved, N.C.D. 1. That they are entitled to life, liberty, & property, and they have never ceded to any sovereign power whatever, a right to dispose of either without their consent.

Resolved, N.C.D. 2. That our ancestors, who first settled these colonies, were at the time of their emigration from the mother country, entitled to all the rights, liberties, and immunities of free and natural-born subjects, within the realm of England.

Resolved, N.C.D. 3. That by such emigration they by no means forfeited, surrendered, or lost any of those rights, but that they were, and their descendants now are, entitled to the exercise and enjoyment of all such of them, as their local and other circumstances enable them to exercise and enjoy.

Resolved, 4. That the foundation of English liberty, and of all free government, is a right in the people to participate in their legislative council: and as the English colonists are not represented, and from their local and other circumstances, cannot properly be represented in the British parliament, they are entitled to a free and exclusive power of legislation in their several provincial legislatures, where their right of representation can alone be preserved, in all cases of taxation and internal polity, subject only to the negative of their sovereign, in such manner as has been heretofore used and accustomed. But, from the necessity of the case, and a regard to the mutual interest of both countries, we cheerfully consent to the operation of such acts of the British parliament, as are bona fide, restrained to the regulation of our external commerce, for the purpose of securing the commercial advantages of the whole empire to the mother country, and the commercial benefits of its respective members; excluding every idea of taxation, internal or external, for raising a revenue on the subjects in America, without their consent.

Resolved, N.C.D. 5. That the respective colonies are entitled to the common law of England, and more especially to the great and inestimable privilege of being tried by their peers of the vicinage, according to the course of that law.

Resolved, 6. That they are entitled to the benefit of such of the English statutes as existed at the time of their colonization; and which they have, by experience, respectively found to be applicable to their several local and other circumstances.

Resolved, N.C.D. 7. That these, his majesty's colonies, are likewise entitled to all the immunities and privileges granted & confirmed to them by royal charters, or secured by their several codes of provincial laws.

Resolved, N.C.D. 8. That they have a right peaceably to assemble, consider of their grievances, and petition the King; and that all prosecutions, prohibitory proclamations, and commitments for the same, are illegal.

Resolved, N.C.D. 9. That the keeping a Standing army in these colonies, in times of peace, without the consent of the legislature of that colony, in which such army is kept, is against law.

Resolved, N.C.D. 10. It is indispensably necessary to good government, and rendered essential by the English constitution, that the constituent branches of the legislature be independent of each other; that, therefore, the exercise of legislative power in several colonies, by a council appointed, during pleasure, by the crown, is unconstitutional, dangerous, and destructive to the freedom of American legislation.

All and each of which the aforesaid deputies, in behalf of themselves and their constituents, do claim, demand, and insist on, as their indubitable rights and liberties; which cannot be legally taken from them, altered or abridged by any power whatever, without their own consent, by their representatives in their several provincial legislatures.

In the course of our inquiry, we find many infringements and violations of the foregoing rights, which, from an ardent desire, that harmony and mutual intercourse of affection and interest may be restored, we pass over for the present, and proceed to state such acts and measures as have been adopted since the last war, which demonstrate a system formed to enslave America.

Resolved, N.C.D. That the following acts of Parliament are infringements and violations of the rights of the colonists; and that the repeal of them is essentially necessary in order to restore harmony between Great-Britain and the American colonies, viz:

The several acts of 4 Geo. 3. ch. 15, & ch. 34.—5 Geo. 3. ch. 25.—6 Geo. 3. ch. 52.—7 Geo. 3. ch. 41, & ch. 46.—8 Geo. 3. ch. 22, which impose duties for the purpose of raising a revenue in America, extend the powers of the admiralty courts beyond their ancient limits, deprive the American subject of trial by jury, authorize the judges' certificate to indemnify the prosecutor from damages, that he might otherwise be liable to, requiring oppressive security from a claimant of ships and goods seized, before he shall be allowed to defend his property, and are subversive of American rights.

Also the 12 Geo. 3. ch. 24, entitled "An act for the better securing his Majesty's dock-yards, magazines, ships, ammunition, and stores," which declares a new offence in America, and deprives the American subject of a constitutional trial by a jury of the vicinage, by authorizing the trial of any person, charged with the committing any offence described in the said act, out of the realm, to be indicted and tried for the same in any shire or county within the realm.

Also the three acts passed in the last session of parliament, for stopping the port and blocking up the harbour of Boston, for altering the charter & government of the Massachusetts-bay, and that which is entituled "An act for the better administration of Justice," &c.

Also the act passed in the same session for establishing the Roman Catholick Religion in the province of Quebec, abolishing the equitable system of English laws, and erecting a tyranny there, to the great danger, from so total a dissimilarity of Religion, law, and government of the neighbouring British colonies, by the assistance of whose blood and treasure the said country was conquered from France.

Also the act passed in the same session for the better providing suitable quarters for officers and soldiers in his Majesty's services North-America.

Also, that the keeping a standing army in several of these colonies, in time of peace, without the consent of the legislature of that colony in which such army is kept, is against law.

To these grievous acts and measures, Americans cannot submit, but in hopes that their fellow subjects in Great-Britain will, on a revision of them, restore us to that state in which both countries found happiness and prosperity, we have for the present only resolved to pursue the following peaceable measures:

1st. To enter into a non-importation, non-consumption, and non-exportation agreement or association

2. To prepare an address to the people of Great-Britain, and a memorial to the inhabitants of British America, &

3. To prepare a loyal address to his Majesty; agreeable to Resolutions already entered into.

Reference: Worthington Chauncey Ford (ed.), *Journal of the Continental Congress, 1774–1789*, Vol. I (Washington: GPO, 1904).

MECKLENBURG RESOLVES, NORTH CAROLINA, MAY 31, 1775

This day the Committee of this county met and passed the following resolves:

Whereas by an address presented to his majesty by both Houses of Parliament in February last, the American colonies are declared to be in a state of actual rebellion, we conceive that all laws and commissions confirmed by or derived from the authority of the King and Parliament are annulled and vacated and the former civil constitution of these colonies for the present wholly suspended. To provide in some degree for the exigencies of this county, in the present alarming period, we deem it proper and necessary to pass the following resolves, viz:

1. That all commissions civil and military heretofore granted by the Crown to be exercised in these colonies are null and void and the constitution of each particular colony wholly suspended.

2. That the Provincial Congress of each Province under the direction of the great Continental Congress is invested with all legislative and executive powers within their respective Provinces and that no other legislative or executive power does or can exist at this time in any of these colonies.

3. As all former laws are now suspended in this Province and the Congress have not yet provided others we judge it necessary for the better preservation of good order, to form certain rules and regulations for the internal government of this county until laws shall be provided for us by the Congress.

4. That the inhabitants of this county do meet on a certain day appointed by the committee and having formed themselves into nine companies (to wit) eight in the county and one in the town of Charlotte do choose a Colonel and other military officers who shall hold and exercise their several powers by virtue of this choice and independent of the Crown of Great Britain and former constitution of this Province.

5. That for the better preservation of the peace and administration of justice each of those companies do choose from their own body two discreet freeholders who shall be empowered each by himself and singly to decide and determine all matters of controversy arising within said company under the sum of twenty shillings and jointly and together all controversies under the sum of forty shillings, that so as their decisions may admit of appeal to the convention of the selectmen of the county and also that any one of these men shall have power to examine and commit to confinement persons accused of petit larceny.

6. That those two selectmen thus chosen do jointly and together choose from the body of their particular body two persons properly qualified to act as constables who may assist them in the execution of their office.

7. That upon the complaint of any persons to either of these selectmen he do issue his warrant directed to the constable commanding him to bring the aggressor before him or them to answer said complaint.

8. That these eighteen selectmen thus appointed do meet every third Thursday in January, April, July and October, at the Court House in Charlotte, to hear and determine all matters of controversy for sums exceeding forty shillings, also appeals, and in cases of felony to commit the person or persons convicted thereof to close confinement until the Provincial Congress shall provide and establish laws and modes of proceedings in all such cases.

9. That these eighteen selectmen thus convened do choose a clerk to record the transactions of said convention and that said clerk upon the application of any person or persons aggrieved do issue his warrant to one of the constables of the company to which the offender belongs, directing said constable to summon and warn said offender to appear before the convention at their next sitting to answer the aforesaid complaint.

10. That any person making complaint upon oath to the clerk or any member of the convention that he has reason to suspect that any person or persons indebted to him in a sum above forty shillings intends clandestinely to withdraw from the county without paying such debt the clerk or such member shall issue his warrant to the constable commanding him to take such person into safe custody until the next sitting of the convention.

11. That when a debtor for a sum above forty shillings shall abscond and leave the county the warrant granted as aforesaid shall extend to any goods or chattels of said debtor as may be found and such goods or chattels be seized and held in custody by the constable for the space of thirty days, in which time if the debtor fail to return and discharge the debt the constable shall return the warrant to one of the selectmen of the company where the goods are found, who shall issue orders to the constable to sell such part of said goods as

shall amount to the sum due, that when the debt exceeds forty shillings the return shall be made to the convention who shall issue orders for sale.

12. That all receivers and collectors of quit rents, public and county taxes, do pay the same into the hands of the chairman of this committee to be by them disbursed as the public exigencies may require, and that such receivers and collectors proceed no further in their office until they be approved of by and have given to this committee good and sufficient security for a faithful return of such monies when collected.

13. That the committee be accountable to the county for the application of all monies received from such public officers.

14. That all the officers hold their commissions during the pleasure of their several constituents.

15. That this committee will sustain all damages that ever hereafter may accrue to all or any of these officers thus appointed and thus acting on account of their obedience and conformity of these resolves.

16. That whatever person hereafter shall receive a commission from the Crown or attempt to exercise any such commission heretofore received shall be deemed an enemy to his country and upon information being made to the captain of the company in which he resides, the said company shall cause him to be apprehended and conveyed before the two selectmen of the said company, who upon proof of the fact, shall commit him the said offender to safe custody until the next sitting of the committee, who shall deal with him as prudence may direct.

17. That any person refusing to yield obedience to the above resolves shall be considered equally criminal and liable to the same punishment as the offenders above last mentioned.

18. That these resolves be in full force and virtue until instructions from the Provincial Congress regulating the jurisprudence of the Province shall provide otherwise or the legislative body of Great Britain resign its unjust and arbitrary pretensions with respect to America.

19. That the eight Militia companies in this county provide themselves with proper arms and accoutrements and hold themselves in readiness to execute the commands and directions of the General Congress of this Province and of this Committee.

20. That the committee appoint Colonel Thomas Polk and Dr. Joseph Kennedy to purchase three hundred pounds of powder, six hundred pounds of lead and one thousand flints for the use of the militia of this county and deposit the same in such place as the committee hereafter may direct.

Signed by order of the Committee.
EPHRAIM BREVARD,
Clerk of Committee.

Reference: William L. Saunders (ed.), *The Colonial Records of North Carolina*, Vol. IX (Raleigh: Josephus Daniels, 1890).

ADDRESS OF NORTH CAROLINA DELEGATES TO CONTINENTAL CONGRESS, JUNE 19, 1775

GENTLEMEN,

When the liberties of a People are invaded, and Men in authority are laboring to raise a Structure of Arbitrary Power upon the Ruins of a free Constitution; when the first Minister of Britain exerts every Influence that private address or public violence can give him to shake the Barriers of personal Security and private Property it is natural for us Inhabitants of America deeply interested in the events of his Designs to be anxious for our approaching Fate and to look up to the Sources which God and the Constitution furnish to ward off or alleviate the impending Calamity.

Thus circumstanced the Inhabitants of the United American Colonies by their Representatives met in Congress at Philadelphia in September last devised a plan of commercial Opposition as a peaceful Expedient to bring about a Reconciliation with the parent State upon Terms constitutional and honorable to us both. A most humble and dutiful Petition to the Throne accompanied it. The first of these has not had sufficient time to work the Effect proposed by it. The latter however flattered with a gracious reception upon the first Introduction to the Throne was afterwards buried in a Mass of useless Papers upon the Table of the House of Commons and shared the common Fate of American Remonstrances and Petitions—to be rejected and forgot.

To the woeful Catalogue of Oppressions recited in the Proceedings of the late Congress are now superadded Bills passed in Parliament for prohibiting the Fishery of the New England Colonies and restraining the Trade of other Colonies to Great Britain Ireland and the British West Indies. The Minister still continues to pour Troops into the Town of Boston. Some have lately arrived and many more are hourly expected, thus reducing that once flourishing City to a Garrison dealing out from thence his Instruments of Tyranny and oppression to overawe and enslave the other Colonies. His Designs have hitherto proved unsuccessful. Heaven seems to have assumed the protection of the injured insulted Colonists and signally to have appeared in their Favour: when in the last Battle at Lexington six hundred raw, undisciplined Provincials defeated eighteen Hundred regular Troops and pursued them into their Camp.

No engagements are sufficiently sacred to secure the performance of them when the Fears or Expectations of the General make it convenient for him to dispense with them. After the most solemn Compacts to the contrary the Inhabitants of the Town of Boston are doomed to suffer the most abject distress from the want of the common necessaries of Life confined within the Walls of the City and not permitted to seek a Refuge amongst their neighbors in the Country. These are the miseries which they suffer for their brave Defence of the common cause of British America. They were destined as a first victim to ministerial Tyranny. But Fellow Subjects think not that his Schemes are to end here. No, if success should strengthen his hands the Inhabitants

of the Southern Colonies would soon feel the Weight of his Vengeance.

The Provinces of New Hampshire, Rhode Island and Connecticut in Imitation of their Massachusetts Brethren, have enlisted Bodies of Troops preparing for the last Extremity and determined to live free or not at all. New York has to the disgrace of those who would represent her as inimical to the Liberties of America boldly stood forth determined to brave every Extremity rather than submit to the Edicts of a Minister or desert the protection of their constitutional Rights and Privileges; New Jersey, Pennsylvania and the Provinces to the Southward have taken an honorable share in the line of Defence armed and equipped to avert the Calamity, dreading a civil War as the most awful scourge of Heaven and to plunge their swords in the breasts of their Fellow Subjects as the greatest of all human Calamities and the most painful Exertions of human Fortitude, but determined at all Events to suffer the Excess of human Misery rather than be brought to the feet of an insulting Minister.

North Carolina alone remains an inactive Spectator of this general defensive Armament. Supine and careless, she seems to forget even the Duty she owes to her own local Circumstances and Situation. Have you not Fellow Citizens a dangerous Enemy in your own Bosom and after Measures which the Minister has condescended to in Order to carry into Execution his darling Schemes do you think he would hesitate to raise the hand of the servant against the master? Doctor Johnston a pensioned Tool of the Ministry in a Pamphlet intituled "Taxation no Tyranny," speaks the Intentions of Administration in a language too plain to leave anything to doubt. The Slaves should be set free, an "Act which the Lovers of Liberty must surely commend, if they are furnished with arms for defence and utensils for Husbandry and settled in some simple form of Government within the Country they may be more honest and grateful than their Masters," are the words of this prostituted Court Favourite.

Have we not been informed that the Canadians are to be embodied and the Indians bribed to ravage the Frontiers of the Eastern Colonies? Has not General Carlton already given a specimen of his power by forming a Canadian Regiment of Men inimical to our Liberty and Religion? Can you think that your Province is the singular object of ministerial favour and that in the common crush it will stand secure? Be assured it will not. The Bait the Minister has thrown out to you is a delusive one, it leads to Destruction. Have you not by various public Acts declared your resolution not to be bound to ministerial Shackles, but that you will live in a free Constitution or perish in the Ruins of it? Do you imagine that after this you are his Favourites? You are not. Do you ask why then you are exempted from the Penalties of the Bill restraining Trade? The Reason is obvious—Britain cannot keep up its Naval Force without you; you supply the very sinews of her strength. Restrain your Naval Stores and all the Powers of Europe can scarcely supply her; restrain them and you strengthen the hands of America in the glorious contention for her liberty. Through you the Minister wishes to disunite the whole Colonial Link; we know your virtue too well to dread his success; you have the Example of New York to animate you, she spurns the proffered Boon and views the exemption of that Province from the Restraining Bill as the Smiles of a Minister who looks graciously in her face while he stabs her to the heart.

It becomes the duty of us in whom you have deposited the most sacred trusts to warn you of your danger and of the most effectual means to ward it off. It is the Right of every English Subject to be prepared with Weapons for his defence. We conjure you by the Ties of Religion Virtue and Love of your Country to follow the Example of your sister Colonies and to form yourselves into a Militia. The Election of the officers and the Arrangement of the men must depend upon yourselves. Study the Art of Military with the utmost attention, view it as the Science upon which your future security depends.

Carefully preserve the small quantity of gunpowder which you have amongst you; it will be the last Resource when every other means of Safety fail you—Great Britain has cut you off from further supplies. We enjoin you as you tender the safety of yourselves and Fellow Colonists as you would wish to live and die free that you would reserve what Ammunition you have as a sacred Deposit. He in part betrays his Country who sports it away, perhaps in every Charge he fires he gives with it the means of preserving the life of a fellow being.

We cannot conclude without urging again to you the Necessity of arming and instructing yourselves to be in readiness to defend yourselves against any violence that may be exerted against your Persons and Properties. In one word fellow subjects the Crisis of America is not at a great distance. If she falls Britain must go Hand in Hand with her to Destruction. Everything depends upon your present Exertion and prudent perseverence, be in a state of Readiness to repell every stroke that though you must wound and endanger her, strengthen the hands of civil Government by resisting every Act of lawless power, stem Tyranny in its commencement, oppose every effort of an Arbitrary Minister and by checking his licentiousness preserve the liberty of the Constitution and the honor of your sovereign, look to the reigning Monarch of Britain as your rightful and lawful sovereign, dare every danger and difficulty in support of his person crown and dignity and consider every man as a Traitor to his King who infringing the Rights of his American Subjects attempts to invade those glorious Revolution principles which placed him on the Throne and must preserve him there.

We are Gentlemen

Your most obedient and very humble servants

WILLIAM HOOPER
JOSEPH HEWES
RICHARD CASWELL.

Reference: William L. Saunders (ed.), *The Colonial Records of North Carolina*, Vol. X (Raleigh: Josephus Daniels, 1890).

CONGRESS ADVISES NEW HAMPSHIRE TO CALL PROVINCIAL CONVENTION TO ESTABLISH A GOVERNMENT, NOVEMBER 3, 1775

The Congress, taking into consideration the report of the Com[mitt]ee on the New Hampshire Instructions,

Resolved, That it be recommended to the provincial Convention of New Hampshire, to call a full and free representation of the people, and that the representatives, if they think it necessary, establish such a form of government, as, in their judgment, will best produce the happiness of the people, and most effectually secure peace and good order in the province, during the continuance of the present dispute between G[reat] Britain and the colonies.

Reference: Worthington Chauncey Ford (ed.), *Journal of the Continental Congress, 1774–1789,* Vol. III (Washington: GPO, 1905).

CONGRESS ADVISES SOUTH CAROLINA, NOVEMBER 4, 1775

Resolved, That if the Convention, or, in their recess, the council of safety of South Carolina, shall think it expedient for the security of that colony, to seize or destroy, and shall seize or destroy, any ship or vessel of war, this Congress will approve of such proceeding.

Resolved, That the town of Charleston ought to be defended against any attempts that may be made to take possession thereof by the enemies of America, and that the convention or council of safety of the colony of South Carolina, ought to pursue such measures, as to them shall seem most efficacious for that purpose, and that they proceed immediately to erect such fortifications and batteries in or near Charleston, as will best conduce to promote its security, the expence to be paid by the said Colony.

Resolved, That if the Convention of South Carolina shall find it necessary to establish a form of government in that colony, it be recommended to that Convention to call a full and free representation of the people, and that the said representatives, if they think it necessary, shall establish such a form of government as in their judgment will best produce the happiness of the people, and most effectually secure peace and good order in the colony, during the continuance of the present dispute between Great Britain and the colonies.

Reference: Worthington Chauncey Ford (ed.), *Journal of the Continental Congress, 1774–1789,* Vol. III (Washington: GPO, 1905).

INSTRUCTIONS TO REPRESENTATIVES OF PORTSMOUTH, NEW HAMPSHIRE, DECEMBER 25, 1775

To the Honourable Congress of the Colony of New Hampshire, now convened at Exeter for the preservation of the Lives, Liberties & Properties of the Inhabitants of said Colony.

The Memorials & Remonstrance of the Inhabitants of the Town of Portsmouth in Town meeting assembled, humbly shews:

That the great rise of Goods has given much uneasiness not only to the Inhabitants of this Town, (already being much distressed by being the Frontier & the total Loss of its Trade) but also to those of the Colony in general:

Altho' the Honorable Continental Congress have recommended that the Committees of the several Towns should regulate this matter, yet inasmuch as we have been informed, that Goods, altho' high here, are higher at Newbury & Salem & higher still at Cambridge, wee are of opinion that it is too extensive as well as too delicate an affair to be in the power of any Town Committee to rectify. Wee therefore look up to the superiour Wisdom of the Congress intreating that they will take up the Matter on a general plan and afford such reliefe as the nature of the case requires. And your Memorialists will ever pray &c.

JOHN PENHALLOW, Town Clerk.
Portsmouth, Decr 25th, 1775.
Portsmouth, N.H., December 25, 1775.

Last Monday, at a publick town meeting, the following gentlemen were chosen Delegates to represent this town in Provincial Congress now convened at Exeter; and, by a Committee appointed to draw up Instructions for them, they were the next day unanimously voted by the Town.

To Samuel Cutts and Samuel Sherburne, Esqrs., and Captain Pierce Long.

GENTLEMEN: As the approaching session of the Congress will be attended with the consideration of matters of more importance than ever came before any body of men in this Colony, your constituents desire your strict attention to these their instructions, supposing your motives in accepting our choice of you to be those, alone, of promoting the public good. The precept sent to this town for the choice of Delegates, mentions our taking up a form of government in this Colony. This we conceive to be a measure to be entered on with the greatest caution, calmness and deliberation. We are of opinion that the present times are too unsettled to admit of perfecting a form, stable and permanent; and that to attempt it now would injure us, by furnishing our enemies in Great Britain with arguments to persuade the good people there that we are aiming at independency, which we totally disavow. We should therefore prefer the government of the Congress, till God, in his providence, shall afford us quieter times.

If, however, the Congress shall think proper to establish a new form of government, we enjoin you that no private pique or prejudice may seclude from the appointment to any place of honor or profit men of approved honour and integrity; whether members likely to be appointed to such places, who you have every reason to think sought an election, that you do everything in your power to prevent their appointment.

The courts of justice in this Colony, you are sensible, have long slept. We earnestly require you that you use your influence in the Congress that the law may have its course, not only for the punishment of offenders but to enforce the payment of just debts, under such regulations as the Congress, in their wisdom, shall think proper. As the dastardly and inhuman behaviour of the persons hitherto intrusted by the British Ministry to execute their designs against America, convince us that they will take all advantages of the weakness of any part, while they artfully avoid all such as are in a situation to make a resistance we desire you will pay proper attention to the further fortifying and guarding the port of Piscataqua, now the frontier of the Colony; and that in general, you spare no pains to have every part of this Colony in a state of defence. At the same time, however, that we give you this instruction, we recommend it to you that, if a plan of accommodation be proposed, the completion of which will terminate in an honourable settlement of the present disputes, you give your assent thereto; and we the more readily advise this, because we are by no means of opinion that the present measures are countenanced by the British nation in general (ever remarked for their true valour and love of freedom, and who when they are fully acquainted with the dispute, will undoubtedly approve the conduct of their sons, so like that of their ancestors at the Revolution) but rather that they are the schemes of a set of men lost to every sentiment of true honour, and sunk into a state of dissipation and luxury, which they are endeavouring to support by subjugating the most loyal subjects their master could boast of.

As we are firmly persuaded the measures we are taking for the preservation of our freedom are highly justifiable in the sight of God and man, we are determined to hazard our lives and fortunes in the prosecution of them, convinced that our brethren in every part of the colony are actuated by the same motives, and will readily pay their proportion of the publick expense: You will, therefore, be careful to see that the proportion be equitably adjusted with respect to this town, which has already greatly suffered by the loss of its trade, almost its only support, and of the revival of which there is at present no prospect.

We particularty recommend that you strictly guard against every measure that may have a tendency to cause disunion; and that, at all times, you keep sight of this recommendation, as a disagreement among ourselves is what our enemies are earnestly wishing for, and, consequently, what we should be more particularly careful to see them disappointed in. You will use your endeavours that any Committees of Safety which may be appointed by the Colony Congress, may be directed, in their recess, to sit in this town, which, in all probability, will be the seat of action, and may want the readiest assistance; and that the said Committee be kept under short adjournments. We entertain the highest and most grateful sense

of the merit and bravery of such of our brethren as, at this time, are called forth to "jeopard their lives in the high places of the field," and hope this Colony will be behind hand in none, to see that they are properly rewarded, taking due care, at the same time, to keep up the very just and necessary line of distinction between the civil and military powers.

You will, from time to time, inform the Town Committee of Safety of such matters of importance as are proposed to be transacted in Congress, and take their advice and instruction thereon, or that of our constituents in town meeting assembled, if the said Committee shall think proper.

Reference: Nathaniel Bouton (ed.), *New Hampshire Provincial Town and State Papers,* Vol. II (21 vols.; Concord: George E. Jenks, 1867–1943).

CONGRESS OFFERS PLAN TO ADOPT NATIONAL GOVERNMENT, MAY 10, 1776

Resolved, That it be recommended to the respective assemblies and conventions of the United Colonies, where no government sufficient to the exigencies of their affairs have been hitherto established, to adopt such government as shall, in the opinion of the representatives of the

people, best conduce to the happiness and safety of their constituents in particular, and America in general.

Reference: Worthington Chauncey Ford (ed.), *Journal of the Continental Congress, 1774–1789,* Vol. IV (Washington: GPO, 1906).

CONGRESS APPROVES PREAMBLE BY JOHN ADAMS, MAY 15, 1776

The Congress took into consideration the draught of the preamble brought in by the committee, which was agreed to as follows:

Whereas his Britannic Majesty, in conjunction with the lords and commons of Great Britain, has, by a late act of Parliament, excluded the inhabitants of these United Colonies from the protection of his crown; And whereas, no answer, whatever, to the humble petitions of the colonies for redress of grievances and reconciliation with Great Britain, has been or is likely to be given; but, the whole force of that kingdom,

aided by foreign mercenaries, is to be exerted for the destruction of the good people of these colonies; And whereas, it appears absolutely irreconcileable to reason and good Conscience, for the people of these colonies now to take the oaths and affirmations necessary for the support of any government under the crown of Great Britain, and it is necessary that the exercise of every kind of authority under the said crown should be totally suppressed, and all the powers of government exerted, under the authority of the people of the colonies, for the preservation of internal peace, virtue, and good order, as well as for the defence of their lives, liberties, and properties, against the hostile invasions and cruel depredations of their enemies; therefore, resolved, &c.

Ordered, That the said preamble, with the resolution passed the 10th instant, be published.

Reference: Worthington Chauncey Ford (ed.), *Journal of the Continental Congress, 1774–1789,* Vol. IV (Washington: GPO, 1906).

DECLARATION OF INDEPENDENCE, JULY 4, 1776

IN CONGRESS, JULY 4, 1776

The unanimous Declaration of the thirteen united States of America

WHEN in the Course of human events, it becomes necessary for one people to dissolve the political bands which have connected them with another, and to assume among the Powers of the earth, the separate and equal station to which the Laws of Nature and of Nature's God entitle them, a decent respect to the opinions of mankind requires that they should declare the causes which impel them to the separation.

We hold these truths to be self-evident, that all men are created equal, that they are endowed by their Creator with certain unalienable Rights, that among these are Life, Liberty and the pursuit of Happiness. That to secure these rights, Governments are instituted among Men, deriving their just powers from the consent of the governed, That whenever any Form of Government becomes destructive of these ends, it is the Right of the People to alter or to abolish it, and to institute new Government, laying its foundation on such principles and organizing its powers in such form, as to them shall seem most likely to effect their Safety and Happiness. Prudence, indeed, will dictate that Governments long established should not be changed for light and transient causes; and accordingly all experience hath shown, that mankind are more disposed to suffer, while evils are sufferable, than to right themselves by abolishing the forms to which they are accustomed. But when a long train of abuses and usurpations, pursuing invariably the same Object evinces a design to reduce them under absolute Despotism, it is their right, it is their duty, to throw off such Government, and to provide new Guards for their future security.—Such has been

the patient sufferance of these Colonies; and such is now the necessity which constrains them to alter their former Systems of Government. The history of the present King of Great Britain is a history of repeated injuries and usurpations, all having in direct object the establishment of an absolute Tyranny over these States. To prove this, let Facts be submitted to a candid world.

He has refused his Assent to Laws, the most wholesome and necessary for the public good.

He has forbidden his Governors to pass Laws of immediate and pressing importance, unless suspended in their operation till his Assent should be obtained; and when so suspended, he has utterly neglected to attend to them.

He has refused to pass other Laws for the accommodation of large districts of people, unless those people would relinquish the right of Representation in the Legislature, a right inestimable to them and formidable to tyrants only.

He has called together legislative bodies at places unusual, uncomfortable, and distant from the depository of their Public Records, for the sole purpose of fatiguing them into compliance with his measures.

He has dissolved Representative Houses repeatedly, for opposing with manly firmness his invasions on the rights of the people.

He has refused for a long time, after such dissolutions, to cause others to be elected; whereby the Legislative Powers, incapable of Annihilation, have returned to the People at large for their exercise; the State remaining in the mean time exposed to all the dangers of invasion from without, and convulsions within.

He has endeavoured to prevent the population of these States; for that purpose obstructing the

Laws for Naturalization of Foreigners; refusing to
pass others to encourage their migration hither,
and raising the conditions of new Appropriations
of Lands.

He has obstructed the Administration of
Justice, by refusing his Assent to Laws for establishing Judiciary Powers.

He has made Judges dependent on his Will
alone, for the tenure of their offices, and the
amount and payment of their salaries.

He has erected a multitude of New Offices,
and sent hither swarms of Officers to harrass our
People, and eat out their substance.

He has kept among us, in times of peace,
Standing Armies without the Consent of our legislature.

He has affected to render the Military independent of and superior to the Civil Power.

He has combined with others to subject us
to a jurisdiction foreign to our constitution, and
unacknowledged by our laws; giving his Assent to
their Acts of pretended Legislation:

For quartering large bodies of armed troops
among us:

For protecting them, by a mock Trial, from
Punishment for any Murders which they should
commit on the Inhabitants of these States:

For cutting off our Trade with all parts of the
world:

For imposing Taxes on us without our
Consent:

For depriving us in many cases, of the benefits
of Trial by Jury:

For transporting us beyond Seas to be tried for
pretended offences:

For abolishing the free System of English Laws
in a neighbouring Province, establishing therein
an Arbitrary government, and enlarging its
Boundaries so as to render it at once an example
and fit instrument for introducing the same absolute rule into these Colonies:

For taking away our Charters, abolishing our
most valuable Laws, and altering fundamentally
the Forms of our Governments:

For suspending our own Legislatures, and
declaring themselves invested with Power to legislate for us in all cases whatsoever.

He has abdicated Government here, by declaring us out of his Protection and waging War
against us.

He has plundered our seas, ravaged our Coasts,
burnt our towns, and destroyed the Lives of our
people.

He is at this time transporting large Armies
of foreign Mercenaries to compleat the works
of death, desolation and tyranny, already begun
with circumstances of Cruelty & perfidy scarcely
paralleled in the most barbarous ages, and totally
unworthy the Head of a civilized nation.

He has constrained our fellow Citizens taken
Captive on the high Seas to bear Arms against
their Country, to become the executioners of
their friends and Brethren, or to fall themselves
by their Hands.

He has excited domestic insurrections amongst
us, and has endeavoured to bring on the inhabitants of our frontiers, the merciless Indian Savages,
whose known rule of warfare, is an undistinguished
destruction of all ages, sexes and conditions.

In every stage of these Oppressions We have
Petitioned for Redress in the most humble terms:
Our repeated Petitions have been answered only
by repeated injury. A Prince, whose character
is thus marked by every act which may define a
Tyrant, is unfit to be the ruler of a free People.

Nor have We been wanting in attention to our
British brethren. We have warned them from time
to time of attempts by their legislature to extend
an unwarrantable jurisdiction over us. We have
reminded them of the circumstances of our emigration and settlement here. We have appealed to
their native justice and magnanimity, and we have
conjured them by the ties of our common kindred
to disavow these usurpations, which, would inevitably interrupt our connections and correspondence. They too have been deaf to the voice of
justice and of consanguinity. We must, therefore,
acquiesce in the necessity, which denounces our
Separation, and hold them, as we hold the rest of
mankind, Enemies in War, in Peace Friends.

We, therefore, the Representatives of the
united States of America, in General Congress,
Assembled, appealing to the Supreme Judge of
the world for the rectitude of our intentions,

do, in the Name, and by Authority of the good People of these Colonies, solemnly publish and declare, That these United Colonies are, and of Right ought to be Free and Independent States; that they are Absolved from all Allegiance to the British Crown, and that all political connection between them and the State of Great Britain, is and ought to be totally dissolved; and that as Free and Independent States, they have full Power to levy War, conclude Peace, contract Alliances, establish Commerce, and to do all other Acts and Things which Independent States may of right do. And for the support of this Declaration, with a firm reliance on the Protection of Divine Providence, we mutually pledge to each other our Lives, our Fortunes and our sacred Honor.

JOHN HANCOCK.

New Hampshire

JOSIAH BARTLETT, WM. WHIPPLE,

MATTHEW THORNTON.

Massachusetts Bay

SAML. ADAMS, JOHN ADAMS,

ROBT. TREAT PAINE, ELBRIDGE GERRY.

Rhode Island

STEP. HOPKINS,

WILLIAM ELLERY.

Connecticut

ROGER SHERMAN, SAM'EL HUNTINGTON,

WM. WILLIAMS, OLIVER WOLCOTT.

New York

WM. FLOYD, PHIL. LIVINGSTON,

FRANS. LEWIS, LEWIS MORRIS.

New Jersey

RICHD. STOCKTON, JNO. WITHER-SPOON, FRAS. HOPKINSON,

JOHN HART, ABRA. CLARK.

Pennsylvania

ROBT. MORRIS,

BENJAMIN RUSH, BENJA. FRANKLIN,

JAS. SMITH,

GEO. TAYLOR,

JOHN MORTON, GEO. CLYMER,

JAMES WILSON, GEO. ROSS.

Delaware

CÆsar RODNEY, GEO. READ,

THO. M'KEAN.

Maryland

SAMUEL CHASE, WM. PACA, THOS., STONE,

CHARLES CARROLL of Carrollton.

Virginia

GEORGE WYTHE, RICHARD HENRY LEE, TH JEFFERSON, BENJA. HARRISON,

THOS. NELSON, jr., FRANCIS LIGHTFOOT LEE, CARTER BRANTON.

North Carolina

WM. HOOPER, JOSEPH HEWES,

JOHN PENN.

South Carolina

EDWARD RUTLEDGE,

THOS. HEYWARD, Junr.,

THOMAS LYNCH, Junr.,

ARTHUR MIDDLETON.

Georgia

BUTTON
GWINNETT,

LYMAN HALL,

GEO. WALTON.

Reference: Francis Newton Thorpe (ed.), *The Federal and State Constitutions, Colonial Charters, and Other Organic Laws of the States*, Vol. I (Washington: GPO, 1909).